THE
SALEM WITCH
TRIALS

THE
SALEM WITCH
TRIALS

A DAY-BY-DAY

CHRONICLE OF A COMMUNITY

UNDER SIEGE

MARILYNNE K. ROACH

Cooper Square Press

First Cooper Square Press edition 2002

This Cooper Square Press hardcover edition of *The Salem Witch Trials* is an original publication. It is published by arrangement with the author.

Published by Cooper Square Press
A Member of the Rowman & Littlefield Publishing Group
200 Park Avenue South, Suite 1109
New York, New York 10003-1503
www.coopersquarepress.com

Distributed by National Book Network

Library of Congress Cataloging-in-Publication Data

Roach, Marilynne K.
   The Salem witch trials : a day-to-day chronicle of a community under siege / Marilynne K. Roach.–1st Cooper Square Press ed.
      p. cm.
Includes bibliographical references and index.
ISBN 0-8154-1221-5 (cloth : alk. paper)
   1. Witchcraft—Massachusetts—Salem—History—17th century. 2. Salem (Mass.)—Social conditions. 3. Trials (Witchcraft)—Massachusetts—Salem. I. Title.

BF1575 .R63 2002
133.4'3'097445—dc21   2002004682

⊚™ The paper used in this publication meets the minimum requirements of American National Standard for Information Sciences—Permanence of Paper for Printed Library Materials, ANSI/NISO Z39.48-1992.
Manufactured in the United States of America.

CONTENTS

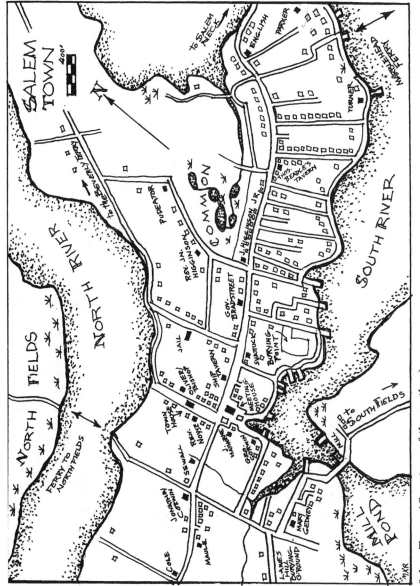

Salem Town. (*Courtesy of the author.*)

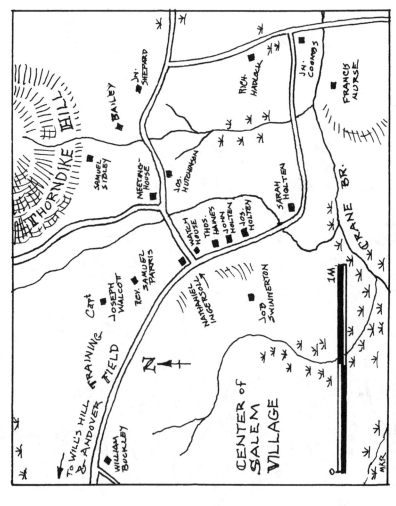

Center of Salem Village. (*Courtesy of the author.*)

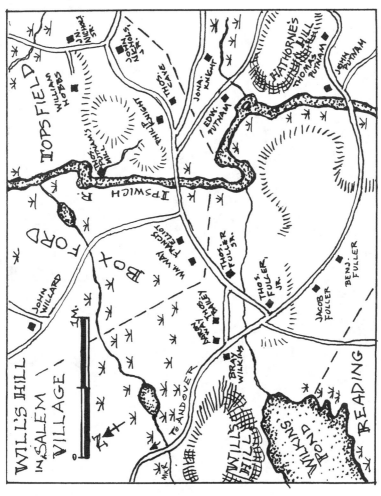

Will's Hill. (*Courtesy of the author.*)

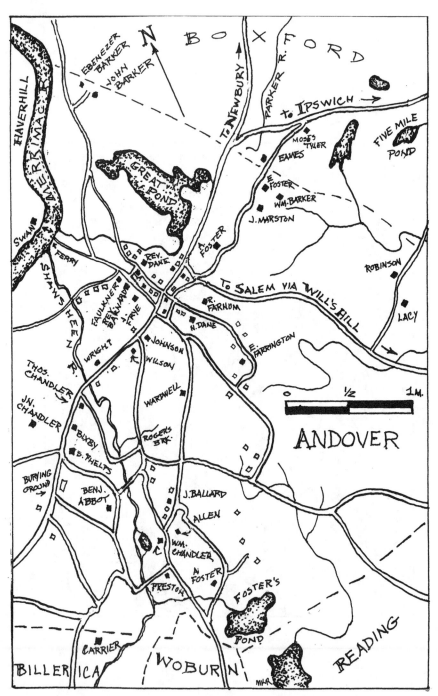

Andover. Suspect Ann Foster's location, in the family homestead with her son Abraham, is variously placed in the north part of Andover, south by Foster's Pond, or near Roger's Brook. Son Andrew, Jr. lived elsewhere. (*Courtesy of the author.*)

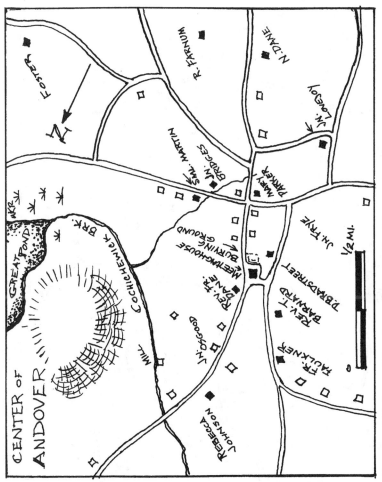

Center of Andover. (*Courtesy of the author.*)

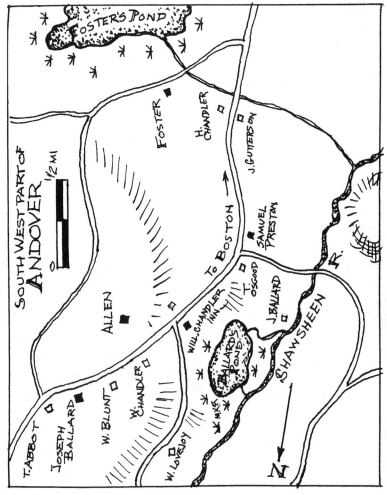

Southwest Andover. (*Courtesy of the author.*)

PROLOGUE

On the eve of 1692, the causes and catalysts that would ignite the Salem witchcraft trials lay scattered among hundreds of lives on two continents, smoldering unsuspected in the shadows of the human heart, could be discerned only by the omniscient eye of Providence—or the Devil's restless attention.

The Prince of Air and Darkness might look upon New England and spy the flickering, unspoken thoughts of those living in the settlements. When the last cold sunset of the year 1691 reflected from such western windows as had glass, and darkness flowed in from the ocean, the wintry land below might appear peaceful.

But down there in Salem Village the fleecy backs of Tom Putnam's flock surged into the sheepfold under the watchful gaze of their owner, who had yet to notice his daughter's suicidal fear. Down there, Rebecca Nurse sat in her own home with her extended and supportive family, while Sarah Good, a few fields away, plodded on cold feet toward temporary lodging, a useless husband, and children she could hardly care for.

Upcountry, among the more prosperous farms of Andover, widowed Rebecca Johnson swept out the meeting house and wondered if her kidnapped relatives were dead or alive. A few miles away the discontented farmer Samuel Wardwell checked his haystacks and brooded over ambitions he never seemed able to accomplish.

Downriver from the Village at Salem's port, where some folk tossed and burned with smallpox, the wealthy, Jersey-born Philippe L'Anglois fumed in his counting house over the nervous legislature's recent attempt to regulate French settlers in coastal towns. His wife, Mary, meanwhile, who had her own head for business, closed up her dry goods shop in the corner of their fine new house and went to supervise her kitchen and the large family of children, most of whom she, as lawful wife, had borne. Across the common the aged Rev. John Higginson sighed over his books and worried about his sea-going sons who had disappeared off Arabia, his daughter deserted by her husband, and the several years of back pay that his congregation owed him. Closer to the center of town Rev. Nicholas Noyes studied the prophetic parts of Scripture, endlessly fascinated.

Southward, where Boston's wharves bristled into the harbor, drunken songs rose from sailors' taverns as other businesses closed. Robert Calef turned the key on his textile shop and headed down the snowy street to gossip in his favorite coffee house. Other merchants, like Samuel Sewall, a part-time judge, shut their ledgers and repaired to their families. Old John Alden, for all his estate, brooded on how best to pay the ransom for his son and colleagues held hostage by the French in Acadia. More anonymously, the orphaned hired girl Mercy Short, who now ladled stew in her employer's kitchen, had herself endured a Canadian captivity that haunted her still.

In his North End study, lamp light revealed the young minister Cotton Mather, who continued to write—and to blow his nose, still in the grip of a winter-long cold. All the responsibilities of a large congregation rested on him in the absence of his colleague and father, Increase Mather, currently in England to negotiate with the King for the restoration of a charter for Massachusetts. Also in London, seeking advancement, was Maine-born Boston trader William Phips, half pirate (his enemies said), half politician.

Northeast from Massachusetts Bay, Rev. George Burroughs of Wells, Maine, having escaped prior wrangles in Salem Village, sat in his parsonage—which also served as the local garrison—with his children and a third apprehensive wife and felt, perhaps, as did others on the coast, secure from frontier attack as long as the snow lay deep enough. For France and England continued to spar over territory, and their respective colonies were mired in King William's War. Upcountry, unknown to the English settlers, Canadian soldiers advanced on snowshoes—French woodsmen and their Algonquin allies—armed by Quebec with attack orders from the Sun King at Versailles. The forest also sheltered scattered Algonquin families in hungry winter camps. Harried from their planting and fishing grounds, some took hostages and sold them to the French for money and supplies, or traded them to the English for their own captured kin.

But none of this would be news to a Devil who could look upon them all—farmers, fishermen, and housewives; the loving and the loveless homes; the neighborly and the quarrelsome; the comfortable and the wretched. With his slightest nudge they would prove with deadly certainty to have more in common than they thought.

INTRODUCTION

Part I: A New Approach

Mr. Burroughs, I will not write in your book though you do kill me!

—Mercy Lewis

This volume offers a key to the mystery of the Salem witch trials, one of American history's favorite stereotypes of intolerance and superstition, a tragedy with popular associations of magical evil and Halloween jokes. This day-by-day narrative of events in their proper sequence unfolds the causes and effects of what really happened. The extensive notes provide a key for those who wish to verify sources and to investigate further. For although these trials are often treated as a symbol and a byword, they were *real* events involving *real* people—not history's scapegoats and whipping-boys.

Rather than argue a single theory to explain the tragedy, this book tells what happened to the people who lived through the events. It presents the story as a whole and tells it from scratch using original sources whenever possible. It does not hope to include everything, for some facts vanished unrecorded. It does augment contemporary accounts of the trials and their related problems with records of the courts and legislature; by wills, deeds, and letters; by almanacs and artifacts; by tide tables and the shape of the land itself. Some sources contradict, but often one obscurity explains another.

Because this is a *story*, spelling and punctuation are standardized to maintain narrative flow. Dates appear as they were recorded in the Old Style (when the year began on March 25 and was eleven days behind) used before England's 1752 adoption of the Gregorian Calendar, but begin the year in January as contemporary almanacs did. Three asterisks indicate approximate dates in the narrative.

Europe's Inner Demons, Norman Cohn's study of European witch hunts, firmly states that no testimony that includes fantastic elements may be taken in any way to indicate actual events. This book more closely follows Sherlock Holmes's advice to exclude the impossible and assume the rest—no matter how improbable— is real. Some of the afflicted faked their symptoms (though whether consciously or unconsciously is an open question), and a few other witnesses were reputed liars. But unless otherwise indicated, material here presents what people *believed* happened on the occasions described.[1]

Mercy Lewis, for example, said that when she saw the apparition of Rev. George Burroughs on the evening of May 7, 1692, he threatened and tortured her because she refused to declare her allegiance to him by signing her name in his book, a volume she had never seen in his study when she used to work for him. Thomas and Edward Putnam deposed that they had been present when this happened, had heard her side of the conversation, and had feared Mercy's limbs would be disjointed as she shouted: "Mr. Burroughs, I will not write in your book though you do kill me!" From this testimony I do not deduce that Reverend Burroughs did any such thing. But neither do I assume that Mercy and the Putnams invented the testimony. I accept that Mercy experienced violent seizures on May 7, 1692, that the Putnam brothers saw only the writhing girl but no specters, and that Mercy thought she saw Burroughs. I also surmise that she had worked for him earlier and that he owned a number of books.[2]

Because the "confessions" were coerced from the suspects, any details that they include are as likely to refer to the magistrates' leading questions as to any actual events—although some seem to repeat current gossip. I do not think the accused were witches (although a few may have acted as cunningfolk even while they considered themselves Christian). The pin-riddled dolls reputedly found in Bridget Bishop's house were not necessarily hers. Many in the general population engaged in fortune-telling and countermagic. Considering human nature, someone must have at least tried to perform malevolent magic, but there is no proof of it.

Nor is there evidence of Witchcraft the religion as it is practiced today. In 1692 the accused described witchcraft with as much loathing as the courts. Only Abigail Hobbs spoke before the trials of her allegiance to the Devil (though she later denied it), and modern Witches don't acknowledge a Devil. (To avoid confusion, "Witch" capitalized within a sentence refers to the religion, while "witch" refers to every other meaning.)

Part II: The Visible and Invisible Worlds

It were hard to some witches to take away life either of man or beast—yet when they once begin it, then it is easy to them.

—John Godfrey

Except for the obvious fact that, as with witchcraft suspects elsewhere, New England's accused were mostly women, the Salem cases are not easily explained. Two of the men executed in 1692 were suspected wife-beaters. Some of the accused women were viragos, others visible saints. A few were noticeably eccentric, but so were some of the afflicted. Some practiced folk magic, yet so did some of the accusers. The whole was briaried in confusion.

The witch scare flared up in New England where British settlements clustered along the coast and up the major rivers. Beyond lay a largely unknown continent that could astonish the English with a moose or a merman, a place with more passenger pigeons in it than people, and more unseen spirits, the people knew, than pigeons. Even the most secular and cynical knew that they did not fully grasp or even imagine the extent of this world's wonders. The majority accepted that it was all under the watchful eye and hand of Providence —God's active presence—with order and purpose in every part.[3]

The orthodox Puritan churches had come to New England to conduct their lives in the way they felt God required, undisturbed by kings, bishops, or enthusiasts of other sects. The orthodox view shared much that was common to the rest of the world's religions (the reality of spirit), to Christianity (original sin), to Protestantism (souls answerable to God directly), to Calvinism (the inability of some to ever attain salvation), and to English Puritanism in general (a covenant between themselves and God). They took their conscious part in the long stream of history that they saw flowing from Eden to a Final Judgment, when all designs and purposes would be clear at last.[4]

Until then, they knew, Hell begrudged their attempt at a God-fearing society and rejoiced more at the corruption of one New England lamb than the easy conquest of a London rake. While the state of one's soul was vitally important, the earthly work needed to keep body and soul together between harvests was long and hard, and not all took religion constantly to heart. Even the most pious were capable of happiness common to other, less devout mortals. They enjoyed their victuals, liked a good scarlet cloak if they could afford it, got carried away at harvest frolics, and indulged in roughhouse after musters when whole neighborhoods turned out to picnic. They played musical instruments—though not during religious services—and sang. Farmers' sons danced competitive jigs against each other, and even ministers bowled at nine-pins in the garden.[5]

Whether they thought much about it or not, the people, like the scientist Sir Isaac Newton, knew that the visible, physical world about them was balanced by the invisible world of spirit where the soul would dwell after the body's death. Angels traversed both worlds and swarmed about outnumbered humanity as thickly as mosquitoes. The good sought to protect and advise, the evil to terrify and corrupt. For although created sinless, they, like humanity, had the free-will to choose wrong, and some of them had embraced evil.[6]

Too proud to tend younger, more highly favored humanity, those angels let resentment fester until some plotted even against God. They failed, and God cast them from Heaven to languish chained in darkness. This imprisonment was, as Increase Mather reminded his Boston congregation, metaphorical. It signified the misery of their loss, a spiritual exile from God, which, however, they were too stubborn to regret or repent of.[7]

Even in their fallen state, rebel angels—more properly called devils—retained many powers, including knowledge of the future. They whispered evil ideas to unwitting victims' minds, or appeared before them in any deceitful guise—a fly, a hog, a shining angel, or a longtime friend. One devil disguised itself as a noted minister and gave progressively bad advice to a certain man in England until the listener tried to touch its arm and found no tangible substance.[8]

The rebel leader was identified as Lucifer ("Bringer-of-Light"), now called Satan ("Adversary"). Although some spoke as if Satan were nearly a counterpoint to God, the Puritans generally regarded him as a general to an eager army. "When we speak of the Devil," said Cotton Mather, "'tis a name of multitude; it means not one individual Devil . . . but it means a kind, which a multitude belongs unto."[9]

Mortals knew no wickedness was too great for spirits devoid of mercy or self-restraint. But while a devil's abilities were obviously far greater than mankind's, they were also obviously far less than the power of God. The thorniest problem lay in the knowledge that, while devils delighted to plague people, God was ultimately in charge. Therefore God, in effect, "allowed" devils to inflict these trials. God, after all, permitted some mortals to savage the innocent.[10]

Why, people wondered, were some endowed with grace, a vital spiritual quality as arbitrary and absolute as perfect pitch, while others were predestined to damnation? Why did one three-year-old Holyoke twin drown in a well and the other live to be president of Harvard? Certainly God had plenty of reason to punish erring humanity, but the cause and effect of suffering were not always clear. "Shall we receive good at the hands of God," Job had asked, "and shall we not receive evil?" (meaning evil as an unhappy punishment rather than a moral wrong).[11]

Since God's Providence worked through nature, even natural woes could be a warning to the incautious, a punishment to the sinful, or a test to the godly. Because the actions of individuals affected not only their own lives but the lives of their families and the community, everyone shared the consequences of wrong acts. The recommended response to ill-fortune was to search one's fallible soul for defect or complacency and amend the fault, whether as an individual or, if necessary, as a community.[12]

The reasons for such manifestations of Providence could be obscure, unfathomable, and the frequent subject of debate. Puritan and non-Puritan alike noticed their neighbors' misfortunes—a lame horse or a dead child—and wondered if this were God's punishment. With good and evil so obviously present in the world, to question the Devil's reality was to doubt God's. Few doubted.[13]

Since there was a Devil, it followed that some wicked or foolish mortals would pay allegiance to him in return for *maleficium* (the power to work evil magic). Some cultures assumed *maleficium* was a naturally deadly quality like venom, counteracted only by the witch's death. Despite a persistently similar folklore, it was theologically inconsistent in the Christian West to think mortals made magic. Only disincarnate angels could produce such effects and only evil angels would. Therefore, contemporary scholars argued, devils performed the magic for the witches, who either consciously collaborated or were deluded into thinking they did it themselves.[14]

Most notions about witchcraft came from folklore and pre-dated the religious, legal, and scientific explanations the seventeenth century used to make sense of what everyone "knew" happened. Witches (they knew) were basically envious, resented their neighbors' successes, and enjoyed their misfortunes. Consequently, witches pilfered supplies at a distance or spoiled them from spite. They maimed, maddened, or killed livestock. They hurt or killed people by sudden disaster or slow illness.[15]

Witches worked their harm in person under an excuse of neighborliness. They traveled invisibly by casting a spell of confusion to prevent others from seeing them, or stepped from their own unconscious bodies to travel in spirit only. They might fly, using an ordinary stick as a steed, steal the neighbor's horse, or harness the neighbor himself with a magic bridle to reach their meetings.* They were shape-shifters who changed their forms in the same way that they managed invisibility, but they also had familiar spirits—imps—in animal guise and it was often difficult to distinguish a witch from her familiar.[16]

Witches could also cast charms from a distance. They burnt a wisp of roof straw to set a house afire, or toyed with a basin of water to sink ships. They tied knots in cords to bind all manner of bodily functions, stabbed cloth or wax images, or worked on actual pieces of their victims—hair or nail pairings—because the scraps still contained the target's vital spirits. Even a witch's glance was thought to transmit spectral poison due to the ancient, world-wide notion of the evil-eye.[17]

People might become witches by a deliberate compact with the Devil or they could slide into witchcraft by using folk methods like countermagic and fortune

---

*No broom riding was reported in the Salem witch trials.

telling. Since these "little sorceries" were magic, they attracted devils like flies to carrion. Devils also made trouble without invitation. Their harassed targets might, Cotton Mather speculated, cooperate just to be left in peace—a bad decision, he thought, but not as culpable as premeditated allegiance.[18]

Witches were considered to be anti-Christian—against all good really—rather than simply non-Christian. The only real pagans were the unconverted native tribes. The settlers—Puritan and non-Puritan alike—spoke of them as worshipping the Devil, but tended to assume, with cultural bias, that these people didn't know any better and had been deceived into thinking that lying devils were gods. Although *pow-wows* (shamans) were called witches, none was formally accused.[19]

Any mortal *might* be a witch—men, women, and children from four to eighty were arrested—but nearly all suspects were women. Most female defendants were middle-aged or older, usually past childbearing, but with few or no children in a culture that valued large families. Their risk of conviction increased with their age and worsened in widowhood or desertion. Although most were acquitted, they were often still half-suspected and put under expensive bonds for good behavior.[20]

Except for a few loners, men were usually suspected in association with their wives during the more virulent panics. Braggarts who claimed magical powers denied those claims in court, where they were fined and punished for lying, their denials—unlike the women's—believed. Children, except for a few teenage daughters assumed to be their mothers' apprentices, were suspected only during the few larger outbreaks. At such times people feared not just a particular suspect, but the possibility of an organized conspiracy.[21]

Surviving records indicate that more than 120 individuals (88 women and 32 men) were suspected of witchcraft in New England between 1638 and 1691, excluding those who turned out to be only Quakers. Some suspects were in court repeatedly, and others not at all. Some 121 trials involved 85 women and 36 men. Of these, 38 cases were slander suits brought *against* an accuser (by 27 women and 11 men). Spotty records for the 83 actual witch trials resulted in 11 to 17 executions, one or two of them of men, plus 3 guilty verdicts reversed (2 women and 1 man).

Most cases occurred in Connecticut and Massachusetts, where the majority of the English population lived. The rate of accusation in Essex County, Massachusetts (whose county seat is Salem), was the same as in Essex County of old England (where most of the families hailed from). But sparsely settled Hampshire County in the Connecticut River Valley had more accusations per head than anywhere else in Massachusetts. The majority of Massachusetts's people clustered in Suffolk and Middlesex Counties and produced only one-third of the known cases, but all of the pre-1692 executions. That all capital cases were tried at Boston may have affected the fates of local suspects, since the Boston magistrates would have been more aware of established local suspicions, but not all the original records have survived.[22]

By the seventeenth century, Western witch-lore included powers formerly applied to nature spirits (like spectral butter theft) or any menstruating woman (a glance that tarnished mirrors or dried up mother's milk), plus the even then outdated medieval view of woman's nature (grasping and destructive).[23]

Western religion has usually been blamed for this situation, but while its forms have tended toward male authority and metaphor, the matter is more complicated than that. The pagan Mesopotamian world, where Judaism began, worshipped the goddess Ishtar at the same time it feared ferocious, bird-like spirit-women who attacked sleeping children. The Roman author Apuleius, himself a practicing magician sarcastic toward Christianity, included foolish women working their *maleficium* as well as an exalted description of the goddess Isis in his first-century novel *Metamorphosis*. Pagan Rome, which accepted most foreign cults, still condemned sorcerers to be burnt or torn apart by wild animals. Literature's stereotyped witch, like Canidia in Horace's *Satires*, was well established before the Judeo-Christian tradition took effect.[24]

But why accusers thought themselves at risk from specific suspects is not always clear in the surviving documents. Even the most copious notes did not include every meaningful glance or words left unsaid, much less the clashing personalities that could give whole new meaning to otherwise innocuous events.

A reputation for witchcraft was no small burden for a suspect. The more humble might wonder what personal faults opened the way for such a misapprehension. Snappish exasperation at the charge, however, could seem to confirm the suspicion. To uneasy neighbors, a suspect's constant demands for charity eroded neighborliness in a world where people had to share much of the necessary work. If the constant small favors were refused or delayed, she might give them a tongue lashing as if they were selfish children. The neighbors' resentment, shouted in anger or left to smolder, made the next mishap seem like the suspect's punishment on them and a verification of their fears.[25]

It was also possible, though risky, to cultivate a witch-reputation in order to intimidate others. The often suspected, but never convicted Andover herdsman John Godfrey described the situation in 1659. "If witches were not kindly entertained," Godfrey told a neighbor meaningfully,

the Devil will appear unto them and ask them if they were grieved or vexed with anybody, and ask them what he should do for them. And if they [the neighbors] would not give them beer or victuals, they [the witches] might let all the beer run out of the cellar, and if they looked steadfastly upon any creature it would die. And it were hard to some witches to take away life either of man or beast—yet when they once begin it, then it is easy to them.[26]

A witch's nature was turbulent, and women, then as later, needed to do far less than men to seem so. Yet no one accused Goodwife Elizabeth Fanning of witchcraft when she came before the same court as Rachel Clenton (who was accused) in March 1692. Charged earlier for violence against her husband and neighbors, Fanning was charged with the theft of a hog and with attempting to strangle another woman in a drunken rage. Once when she asked a neighbor for a day's work with his team, he growled that he would give her *two* day's work if she would just stay away from him. Whereupon she "clapped her tail at him" and shouted that he should kiss it. Although less flamboyant encounters than this were associated with witchcraft suspects, apparently none of Goody Fanning's malice seemed like *maleficium* to her neighbors. Yet Rebecca Nurse and other respectable matrons were suspected and even convicted.[27]

Not all misfortune seemed to be *maleficium*, nor were all witch suspects widely suspected or formally accused. Usually the community as a whole had to share the distrust before anything was done about it on either a spiritual or a legal level.

Ministers, faced with nervous parishioners, advised prayer and a turning to God, since a godly life, though it offered no immunity, strengthened one against misfortune. They advised supposed victims to consider what needed amendment in their own lives, and cautioned against folk charms that were no more than magic themselves. Ministers generally recommended caution, and often concealed the names of suspects to protect them. Only one minister fits the stereotype of a lying (rather than mistaken) accuser—Mr. Thorpe of York, Maine (probably the unqualified John Thorpe), who accused his landlady Elizabeth Baily after she evicted him for chronic drunkenness.[28]

Magistrates hesitated to accept all the testimony set before them. On the one hand, they saw the certainty of fearful neighbors who, having to live with the situation, risked the court fees losers incurred and risked a face-to-face encounter with a person whom they thought commanded magical powers. Yet, magistrates also knew how gossiping suspicion got out of hand, so they consulted the standard British works on the subject by Richard Bernard, John Perkins, and John Gaule.[29]

All of these books warned against the court's acceptance of folk methods to uncover witchcraft, and drew careful distinctions between matters of presumption—reasons to examine a problem—and matters of conviction. Conclusive proof for witchcraft, as for other crimes, was a voluntary confession plus other evidence of the act, or proper evidence by two credible witnesses. Confession without supporting evidence, wrote Gaule, could be the suspect's delusion, while apparent evidence without a confession could be coincidence. The two witnesses had to have observed the same event, not merely two similar events one apiece. But since magic, like poison, left so few material clues, courts could give more weight to circumstantial evidence.[30]

Based on British precedent and Biblical tradition, the 1641 Massachusetts Body of Liberties included witchcraft among its capital crimes (as did English law): "If any man or woman be a witch, (that is hath or consulteth with a familiar spirit,) they shall be put to death." That the witch worked harm was understood, and this was the version in force up to and during 1692 when the Province's laws were re-written and the penalty reduced as a result of that summer's trials. (The law does not specify *maleficium* but was apparently interpreted as if it did. British law drew a distinction between fatal and non-fatal magic but had, since James I's 1604 law, made both capital.)[31]

The courts accepted that magic *could* happen, even if it did not in every suspected case, because it was accepted by the culture. Massachusetts magistrates treated the idea of *maleficium* seriously, but expected legal solutions, not mob actions. Including the slander suits, these accounted for 90 percent of British North America's witchcraft cases. That *maleficium* could cause suffering and death seemed as obvious as the suffering and death caused by firearms. But proof was difficult and most suspicions only stewed in gossip and speculation. Those who thought themselves victims of witchcraft—men and women about equally—suffered according to cultural expectations.[32]

Men testified mainly to sick and dead livestock, bad luck, and nightmares taken for waking experiences. Some reported attacks by spectral animals and a few probably had physical ailments aggravated by worry. Grown women, whose work brought them closer to female suspects, reported domestic losses from recalcitrant butter to children's illnesses. For the most part, they feared for their own "bewitched" children, but some felt jabbed and choked themselves, and a few suffered the convulsions more often reported by younger unmarried women.[33]

Seizures were the rarest and most extreme symptom of bewitchment short of death, the hardest for later generations to take seriously. (Convulsions were more frequent in 1692, but even then only a tenth of the witnesses were so afflicted.) The afflicted accusers included all ages and sexes, but most were single females in their late teens and twenties. They were of an age to marry and to find a settled place in life but outnumbered the available young men. Some lived in intact families, but others were refugees from the war in Maine that had killed and scattered their kin. They worked as hired help in other women's kitchens for room and board and just over half of a hired man's pay.[34]

In the early stages, once the problem seemed more than ordinary illness, the afflicted woman or her family tried to imagine a likely enemy. Questions like "What ails you?" became "*Who* ails you?" She recalled half-forgotten gossip and heard names whispered or spoken aloud by concerned family members. Eventually, she convinced herself that a specific person was the cause, but unless others agreed, the identification never seemed real enough, or at least did not stand up in court. If she were believed, the terror continued and grew, its furious clamor not quite enough to mask the prideful thrill of power that being the center of attention brought. Even so, at least seven of the approximately sixty men, women, and children afflicted in 1692 died without recovering.[35]

All of the "bewitched" symptoms of 1692 have been observed since without malefic associations. The human body is still susceptible to nonphysical influences that can sicken (with a fear of nonexistent toxins), kill (with stress that sends the heart into fibrillation), or cure (with placebos). Stress can also overwhelm a body by genuine, even painful symptoms with no physical cause: blindness, deafness, paralysis, and—rare now in the West—convulsions. This hysteria, also called conversion disorder or somatization, is not to be confused with the usual sarcastic use of the term to dismiss a sufferer's sincerity.[36]

Twentieth-century office and factory workers, bored by repetitive yet exacting tasks, feel the nausea of air pollution or the prickling of insect infestation—when neither is, in fact, present. Malaysian factory workers have spied traditional blue devils under their microscopes, while American school children have become, one after the other, bilious, breathless, and dizzy enough to require medical help.[37]

Hysterical symptoms are as mentally contagious three centuries later as they were in the seventeenth century among those who identify strongly enough with each other's situation. Hyperventilation alone can produce many of the bewitched effects: cramped throat, suffocation, fainting, and even seizures. Either of these maladies—hysteria and hyperventilation—can be caused by anxiety or fear. Once that fear produces real pain, this seems to confirm the sufferer's original apprehension, which in turn intensifies the pains.[38]

Many in 1692 believed the descriptions of invisible witch attacks, but cooler heads knew devils could counterfeit the effect to deceive a victim. Others thought the whole thing faked and took evidence of exaggeration or falsehood as proof that all the episodes were false and all the afflicted were liars. Robert Calef later dismissed the afflicted as "vile varlets" known before and since for their "whoredoms, incest, etc."; but what little is known about them suggests they were no worse, proportionally, than the rest of the population.[39]

"They are in their fits tempted to be witches," Deodat Lawson observed. Some had tried fortune-telling, but again, probably no more than the rest of the population, and not as the organized circle later tradition assumed. Little sorceries were thoroughly ingrained in British folk culture, and much of science was still associated with natural magic. Astrologers claimed a scientific basis for their craft. Alchemists hoped for spiritual enlightenment as much as for gold. John Winthrop Jr.—long-time governor of Connecticut, son of a Massachusetts governor and father of witchcraft judge Wait-Still Winthrop—studied alchemy for years.[40]

The closest New England *may* have had to magic professionals were the cunning folk, village specialists who revealed unknown and future events, offered healing, or identified evil witches. They were sometimes called "good witches" or "healing witches," but considered their results due to natural magic, the work of holy angels, or a gift from God. Such practitioners—though not the ministers—considered this consistent with Christianity. Some English cunning folk refused all payment, others made a lucrative living, and some lapsed into *maleficium* when they used their magic to threaten. A few were rogues like the man who "discovered" lost horses his partner had first stolen. If there were any in New England, they did not call themselves cunning folk, though others did. They probably felt better able than most to combat other people's *maleficium*.[41]

Although ministers periodically warned against magical involvement, people still conjured with common household objects—a sieve and shears, a Bible and a key, sprouting peas, an egg, or hot nails—to ask the whereabouts of a lost thimble or determine a sweetheart's fidelity.[42]

If they feared a neighbor's *maleficium*, they repelled the evil with a dose of good magic and nailed an iron horseshoe at the threshold, surrounded their house with sprigs of fresh laurel, fed their ailing cows red ochre pigment mixed with the animal's own milk, or hung hole stones over the stable rick to keep spirits from getting at the horses by night. If this didn't work, they might try to turn the evil back on the witch by burning, boiling, or otherwise hurting a piece of the bewitched—a lock of a sick child's hair, a slice of dead sow's ear. To wound the witch, people shot at supposed familiars, or thrust red hot pokers into churns of milk that refused to yield butter. Or they confronted the suspected witch directly to "scratch" her and draw blood to deactivate the magic.[43]

For the most part, communities held uneasy truces with resident suspects against whom they could prove nothing definite. They suspected more individuals than they ever took to court, where magistrates were usually reluctant to convict and where the accused might well sue them for slander. Thus, nervous neighbors made do with countermagic and ignored their minister's warnings that this spiritual vigilantism amounted to inviting the Devil to get rid of a devil.[44]

Part III: Woes from Without and Animosity Within—1661–1691

Such uncharitable expressions . . . will let out peace and order and let in confusion and every evil work.

—Salem Village Arbitration Committee

The Salem witchcraft trials erupted during an eight-year war while Massachusetts steered an unauthorized government with a nearly empty treasury through the hazards of French imperialism, Algonquin resentment, and English suspicion. As the rapid spread of witch accusations showed, the whole region was susceptible to panic in 1692. Because the scare began in Salem Village, local troubles provided the catalyst. Problems of self-government in an area with vexingly ambiguous boundaries tangled with political, economic, and church issues.

Salem Village, also called Salem Farms, was not a town in itself but a rural district of Salem, Massachusetts. The original territory had circled the harbor from Marblehead to Manchester, but much of this area had been divided into four other towns.[45]

Most of Salem's inhabitants were traders or craftsmen, and most of them lived on the peninsula between the North and South Rivers. The congregation here was populous enough in 1692 to have two ministers. Seventy-six-year-old Rev. John Higginson had served the town since 1660. He was "eminent for learning, humility, [and] charity," according to an English visitor. "He uses soft words, but hard arguments, and labors more to show the truth of his cause, than his spleen." But he could be firm if necessary. As his younger collegue, Nicholas Noyes, wrote of Higginson:

"Reproofs like lightning from him flew;
But consolations dropped like dew."[46]

Rev. Noyes was known for such verses, along with his learning and delightful conversation. (However, *none* of this would be evident during the witch trials. More likely his life-long fascination with prophecies—especially the book of Revelations—deepened his concerns at the apparent spiritual threat to his congregation.)[47]

Besides their meeting house at the crossroads by the Ship Tavern, the residents had a town house up the rise in the center of the street with a Latin grammar school on the ground floor and space above for town meetings and the occasional county court. Every day but the Sabbath, mallets in the shipyards below clattered, the workers building craft to ply coastal and international waters for the rising local merchants. As the century passed it seemed to many farmers that the more control Salem's merchants had over local politics, the less concern they showed for country neighbors.[48]

Salem Village lay northwest of the harbor, approachable by boat up the fingering estuaries or along the road that ran west from town past the Quaker meeting house, then north along the ledges of bedrock that would later be called Gallows Hill. One branch of the road turned toward Boston, the other divided again further north, angling toward Andover and Ipswich. Various craftsmen lived on the Ipswich road among the farms in the easterly Ryal Side section. A few more clustered along the route to Andover where Nathaniel Ingersoll kept a tavern in the area that became a Village center, once a meeting house was built at its easterly crossroad.[49]

The "farms" themselves comprised several large inland grants divided, over three generations, by sale, lease, or inheritance. The richer land lay east and south toward town—like John Proctor's rented farm, and acreage owned by the Nurse and Porter families. The Putnams managed well enough—though not quite as well—on their hillier upland holdings westward. The Wilkins family lived even more remotely over the Ipswich River at Will's Hill. Others—single men or whole families—had neither house nor land, but labored in other men's fields as hired help. Refugees from the war Eastward—down east in Maine, then part of Massachusetts—had moved in during the century's last quarter, although not as many as crowded Salem town and Boston.[50]

The Villagers dated their existence as a distinct—though not independent—community from the hard-won General Court order of **October 8, 1672**, that allowed them to organize their own parish rather than make the long journey to town for religious services. They inscribed the order at the head of a new Village record book with a description of their territory in Salem's northwest corner. Conflicting surveys overlapped Village boundaries with those of Andover, Topsfield, and Wenham. Consequently, two sets of tax collectors hounded some households while others found that different towns had granted the same land to two parties. Women as well as men came to blows in the resulting disputes, but town and province authorities were maddeningly slow to resolve the conflict.[51]

The government was, in fact, preoccupied. When King Charles II regained his crown in **April 1661** at the demise of England's Puritan Commonwealth, he revoked all charters—for cities, companies, universities, and colonies—then renewed them on proof of loyalty. But Massachusetts acted more independently than most colonies, and its original charter was for a business company, not a proper province under a royally appointed governor. Massachusetts, for the time being, sent agents to plead their cause before the King and endured inspection by various Crown-appointed agents. England officially canceled Massachusetts' government in **June 1684**, though word did not reach Boston until **July 1685**.[52]

The Village, meanwhile, found its first ministerial candidate in twenty-three-year-old John Bayley of Newbury. The inhabitants voted to pay him £40 "for the present year" in **November 1672** and determined, a month later, to build a meeting house. Next spring, the Village men, under the eye of a professional carpenter, raised a thirty-four- by twenty-eight-foot frame on an acre donated by Joseph Hutchinson at the Village center's easterly crossroad. The plain, barn-like structure was based on the traditional court and market houses of East Anglia, rather than anything ecclesiastical, as it was intended for both civil and religious gatherings. They installed shutters to exclude weather and wandering animals, and furnished it with a second-hand pulpit and deacon's bench donated by the Salem church.[53]

Although the Villagers now enjoyed sermons in their own neighborhood, they were not yet a church. Seventeenth-century Congregational churches contained within the general congregation a core of full members who, having experienced a spiritual conversion indicating a state of grace, were eligible for the sacraments of baptism and communion, and—if free white males of legal age—a vote in church matters. The rest of the flock, though not technically members, shared the same general beliefs.[54]

In **November 1673** the Village offered Bayley another year at £40, increased that winter on his request by £7 for firewood. They also voted to build, on land donated by Nathaniel Putnam, a ministry house—a parsonage—of one twenty-eight-foot by twenty-foot room up and one down plus an eleven-foot end lean-to. Putnam, with several friends and relatives, also deeded Bayley over forty assorted acres as a private bonus. However, fourteen inhabitants neglected to pay the ministerial rates, and the Village had to sue them.[55]

Some Villagers had moved to have Bayley ordained their permanent minister and to gather their church separate from the parent Salem organization. But by **winter 1678–1679**, this had caused "some uncomfortable divisions and contentions," as Bayley put it. Most, however, supported him, like twenty-six-year-old Thomas Putnam Jr., married to Bayley's sixteen-year-old sister-in-law Ann Carr.[56]

But Nathaniel Putnam, regretting his earlier largesse, declared Bayley unqualified. When Bayley repeated his wish to stay in the community that he considered home—he had just transferred membership from the Newbury to the Salem church—the opposition claimed that Bayley neglected even his own family prayers and asked the Salem church to help find a new minister.[57]

When the name-calling grew to a slander suit, Rev. John Higginson investigated for the Salem church. He found only a few opposed to Bayley and thought the majority should rule, but the brotherly love that he hoped for did not prevail. Bayley accepted the Village's offer of £55 for another year with freedom to leave at the end. Both sides continued to petition the General Court until the upper house ordered that Bayley be accepted and ordained as the majority wanted. But the lower house declined to meddle with church policy and insisted Bayley remain only the contracted year. Then the Village could hire him or another. Both houses ordered the Village pay Bayley £60 for his time.[58]

To clarify the tangle, a Village committee asked the legislature just *who* could vote for a minister, only to be told the law was as for other towns. Twenty-four Bayley supporters had to explain yet again that they were neither a town nor a church. Until then, they asked that all law-abiding free-holders have a say about the minister as the original order had allowed. The legislature agreed, but added that Salem—both town and church—must approve the choice. Although general taxes supported most New England churches as a municipal necessity (as England supported Anglican churches), they were separate from the civil government by their own lights. The legislature had a duty to protect their existence but was not to interfere with doctrine.[59]

When, after the charter's loss, Anglican England established a property requirement for votes in addition to eligibility by church membership, Massachusetts reluctantly consented. The male inhabitants of a place voted on local matters (including a minister's pay), whether church members or not. Church members (if men) decided all other church questions (like who would be the minister), although women members and nonmembers also made themselves heard indirectly. Salem Village did not yet have a formally gathered church; in the interim all Village men could vote on church matters.[60]

After his ministerial stint Bayley stayed in the Village as a private inhabitant and slowly collected back pay. Joseph Hutchinson and Nathaniel Putnam, for all their earlier charges of incompetence, conveyed Bayley the lands about his house "as a testimony of our good affection." Bayley also acquired the parsonage at some point, for when he moved to his next congregation in Killingworth, Connecticut—for £70 plus a land grant—he rented out the Village house and land. By 1692 he had left the ministry entirely and was a physician in Roxbury, Massachusetts.[61]

The next candidate, twenty-eight-year-old George Burroughs, was a short, dark, frequently impatient man much stronger than he looked. His grandfather and namesake had been an eminent minister in England, and his father Nathaniel a merchant in Maryland and Massachusetts. He graduated from Harvard College in 1670, a year after Bayley, and joined the Roxbury Church. Although he owned inherited lands in Maryland and England, Burroughs served at frontier posts most of his life. He preached at Falmouth (now Portland, Maine) in Casco Bay from 1674 to 1676, when Indian forces burnt the town. Burroughs helped evacuate the women and children to Cushing's Island, where they lived on fish, berries and spring water until Massachusetts sent bread.[62]

Burroughs was in Salisbury, Massachusetts, with other refugees when Salem Village approached him in **November 1680** with an offer of £93-6-8* a year for three years, then £60 a year thereafter plus wood. (That same year Elizabeth Morse of nearby Newbury was tried, convicted, and condemned to death for witchcraft; a year later she would be informally reprieved.) He agreed on condition "that in case any difference should arise in time to come, that we engage on both sides to submit to council for a peaceable issue."[63]

Burroughs, his wife Hannah, and their children boarded with John Putnam Sr. Hannah seemed a "very good and dutiful wife to him," Putnam thought, although Burroughs was "very sharp" toward her and tried to involve Putnam in their disputes. Fortunately, the inhabitants voted to build a new ministry house on land purchased from Nathaniel Ingersoll, Joseph Holten Sr., and Joseph Hutchinson.[64]

This forty-two- by twenty-foot house sat well back from the Andover road, facing south to catch the winter sun. It had four main rooms, four hearths, two to a floor, plus garret space and a stone-walled cellar under the parlor (sitting room and master bedroom), with steps rising into the hall (the main room). Mrs. Burroughs died soon after moving in, probably from childbirth, and, as his £60 annual

---

* English money of the time consisted of pounds (£), shillings (s), and pence (d); 12 pence = 1 shilling, 20 shillings = £1. 2/6 or 2s 6d = 2 shillings and 6 pence.

salary was delayed, her husband borrowed money for her funeral from John Putnam.[65]

A **December 1681** meeting voted to specify that the Village owned the new parsonage and its lands, which were intended only for the use of the resident minister. The record did not say if the decision was due to general practicality or to a specific dispute, for there were factions still. Jeremiah Watts and others wanted to make the Village a separate town but knew they could not until local quarrels ceased. They held fruitless meetings to air and settle their grievances until Burroughs refused to call any more. Whereupon Watts berated Burroughs in a letter that accused all ministers of not leading their flocks to Christian agreement, but aiming instead "to bring all to pulpit preaching, and there they may deliver what they please and none must object. And this we must pay largely for." After he compared ministers with Satan he found himself sued for slander. The court admonished him and dismissed his charges against the churches.[66]

But Salem Village was not the only community to suffer salary disputes with its minister. Andover, a more prosperous town just north west of Salem Village, had its own problems at the same time. After serving as minister and schoolmaster for thirty-three years, sixty-five-year-old Francis Dane informed the town in **March 1681** that although he was willing to continue teaching, due to "bodily infirmity" he felt no longer capable of "carrying on the public worship of God" (at least not alone). He was taken aback, however, when the town canceled his entire salary and replaced him with twenty-two-year-old Thomas Barnard, a recent Harvard graduate. His family was small now that his children were grown, the town informed Dane, and he already had sufficient "accommodations of land and meadow" to "comfortably subsist without being a burden to them." Dane, who had continued to deliver public prayers and an occasional sermon, refused to accept this decision. After the selectmen petitioned the General Court for help, a committee of legislators and local ministers met in Andover to mediate. They heard the town claim destitution, but noted that Dane's "wonted maintenance" (now not paid at all) "was not large."[67]

In **March 1682**, the committee advised Andover to pay Dane £30 a year (or more if he needed it) and advised Dane to forget "all former disgusts as befits a minister of the gospel" and to carry on as much of the work as he was able to do (so the town would not begrudge his salary). They also recommended broadening the tax base, for in Andover only "the least number of the inhabitants" (presumably full church members) contributed to the ministers' salary. The committee thought that all who benefited from public services should "according to his ability, be assessed to pay his due proportion." Andover split the salary, paying Barnard £50 a year, the use of a parsonage, and "all his firewood" and paying Dane £30 as long as he could "carry on a part of the work." Once Dane retired for good, Barnard would receive all £80.

Even with the threat of frontier war, Burroughs returned, with other refugees, to Casco Bay in **March 1683**. After four Sabbaths without him, the Village petitioned the county court, which ordered both parties to meet to settle the matter. Negotiations began with a unanimous agreement to follow the court's advice and a private agreement between Burroughs and his old landlord that Putnam could subtract the £7-1-10 owed from Mrs. Burroughs's funeral from the £33-6-8 the Village still owed their minister.[68]

But four days later, when Burroughs presented his paperwork to the Village, Putnam made the embarrassed county marshal arrest the minister for debt. Nathaniel Ingersoll and five others posted the £14 bond to keep Burroughs from being jailed and then collected depositions in his favor. However, Putnam dropped the suit, possibly because the Village soon voted to pay Burroughs £15. The remainder was slow coming, but Burroughs returned to Maine with his children and a second wife.

In **August 1683**, after making do with lay sermons from Salem's schoolmaster and a variety of candidates, the Village invited Deodat Lawson to serve for a trial period. Lawson, a melancholy man, was the son of an English Puritan minister whose fortunes had declined after the restoration of Charles II and a mother whose dying wish was for her newborn to enter God's service.* After his father scrimped to provide six years of college, young Lawson emigrated to New England and preached on Martha's Vineyard. When the Village approached him, he was a member of Boston's Second Church, unhappily laboring at secular pursuits to support his wife Jane and their two children.[69]

The Village offered Lawson £60 a year in **January 1684**, but no wood, then added thirty cords in **April** while reducing his salary to £40. By **September 1684**, when a committee asked if Lawson favored a permanent settlement, the salary was again £60 and no wood. While he considered, the people plastered the Meeting house interior, installed galleries and a few glass-paned casements, and hung a sounding board over the pulpit. By **March 1686** there was talk of giving Lawson the parsonage.[70]

Meanwhile, Edward Randolph, the most persistent of the British agents, recommended that the King be more firm with Massachusetts for refusing to part with their old charter. Rev. Increase Mather told a Boston town meeting that it was foolish to deliberately throw away liberties when no one knew what the Crown intended.[71]

A son, brother, and father of ministers, Mather had preached in England, Ireland, and the Isle of Jersey during the Puritan Commonwealth before returning home to accept a call from Boston's Second Church. Now his eldest son Cotton

---

* The Latin *deodat* means God given. A *deodand* is a gift to God (via charity) of a thing that has inadvertently caused the death of its owner.

was his cominister, and Increase was not only rector of Harvard but fast becoming a spokesman for local liberties. Randolph called him "the bellows of sedition," intercepted his overseas mail, and circulated treasonous forgeries under Mather's initials.[72]

England forbade Massachusetts to govern by its charter in **October 1684** (while Lawson considered the Village's offer), leaving the province in political limbo for two years while King James, brother and successor to Charles II, was embroiled in suppressing the Monmouth Rebellion. During that time some Massachusetts towns saved money by not sending representatives to a legislature that wasn't supposed to exist.[73]

England finally named a temporary president and council to act as sole authority over Massachusetts Bay, New Hampshire, Maine, and Narraganset combined. Randolph was appointed secretary and registrar, but the rest were local merchants. President Joseph Dudley—one of the few New Englanders on good terms with Randolph and an Anglican by choice—was the worldly youngest son of the early Puritan Governor Thomas Dudley. But this provisional government was soon absorbed into the Dominion of New England, which stretched from Maine to West Jersey. In **December 1686**, while Salem Village pressed Lawson to stay, the Royal Governor arrived in Boston with several shiploads of red-coats and a man-of-war. Sir Edmund Andros, veteran of the Monmouth Rebellion and former governor of New York, was to rule with forty-two councilors of his own selection—Randolph and Dudley among them. They could only advise, however, and Andros frequently ignored them.[74]

No one could vote, except on purely local matters at a single annual town meeting. Nor could anyone, not even towns, own land except the Crown, which might lease back usage rights for a stiff fee. What people *could* do was pay the long-neglected shipping taxes and numerous other legal fees at whatever price quoted by his tax collectors—who pocketed the difference.[75]

The friction caused by Andros's efforts to establish an Anglican church—in a place whose founders had traveled so far to escape the bishops' authority—made many Congregationalists fear for their religion. Even Andros's own men speculated that soon Anglicanism would be required (as it was in Virginia). For a time after the Restoration, Catholics and Nonconformists—as Anglicans called all other British Protestants—were jailed and fined in England. They were still forbidden to teach, attend university, or hold most public offices, and only Anglican marriages were legal there.[76]

In the Village meanwhile, Mrs. Lawson hoped to stay, but her husband was yet unsure. When the Village asked for a vote of the inhabitants, four strongly objected: Joseph Hutchinson, Job Swinnerton, Joseph Porter, and Daniel Andrews. The Village wanted unanimity for their call and, when, in **February 1687**, the four proved immovable, put the question before a board of Salem laymen—

Bartholomew Gedney, John Hathorne, and William Brown—and the two Salem ministers—John Higginson and Nicholas Noyes.[77]

The arbiters hoped the Villagers' "uncharitable expressions and uncomely reflections" were due more to "weakness than willfulness" and not "the effects of settled prejudice and resolved animosity." For such attitudes "have a tendency to make such a gap, as we fear, if not timely prevented will let out peace and order and let in confusion and every evil work." They did not think the objections of Lawson's opponents severe enough to disqualify him, but noticed the move to ordain him "hath not been so inoffensively managed as might have been." They recommended a year's cooling off, reminded the Village of its contract with Lawson, and asked them *not* to ask for more advice in the future if they ignored it now.[78]

The Village voted to take the advice "in general": to pay Lawson for as long as he stayed but not to build a kitchen lean-to on the parsonage. Some time in the **winter of 1687**, Lawson took a temporary post as chaplain (for £5-11-6) with an expedition ordered by Andros. (Sir Edmund may have had a dim view of Nonconformists, but he did allow chaplains for them.)[79]

Andros's redcoats were intended not just to keep the locals in check, but to protect the frontiers against increased French and Indian threats. The Abenaki, Penobscot, and other Eastward tribes had the more personal reasons to fight, due to continued encroachment by English settlers on their fishing rights and crop lands. King Louis XIV of France used this situation to further his own imperial plans. France already largely financed the government and defense of her colonies, whereas England mostly left hers to fend for themselves. But as both New France and New England would be involved when the parent nations fought in Europe, Louis wanted the native tribes for *his* allies.[80]

Andros's redcoats and sailors might have been a welcome help, but proved a drunken lot who shouted bawdry at the local women, fought the constables, and kept folk awake all hours with their brawls. Militiamen impressed to serve with the regulars Eastward in the teeth of winter found that British officers flogged them or tied them neck and heels if they didn't toady fast enough, shortened sick men's rations, and killed anyone who couldn't keep up—just as Indian raiding parties did to their weaker captives.[81]

Andros's civil and military style was, in fact, standard, but some worried that he favored the Indians and really meant to aid French Canada. King James was, after all, on good terms with his cousin King Louis at whose court James had spent most of his exiled youth. And France had, moreover, recently outlawed Protestantism.[82]

Deodat Lawson returned from Maine to collect his back pay from the Village, but he had no wish to remain after his wife and daughter died unexpectedly. Some gossips saw this as a divine judgment on a shepherd who abandoned his flock to traipse Eastward. Lawson, stung by the criticism, moved to Boston. He accepted a post at Boston's First Church and soon remarried.[83]

The Village tussled all the while over Topsfield's boundary, over the ownership of Joseph Hutchinson's donated meeting-house acre—the fuss came to a head just before Hutchinson opposed Lawson's ordination—and over the Village Record Book. A committee studied it all during Lawson's stay, "to have inspection into the defects thereof to see what should not be there, and to see what should be there that is not there," until it was a tangle of crossings-out and additions. Now it seemed best to transcribe the whole, as the Salem mediators had advised— provided the Villagers retained the original, repealed past decisions *only* at meetings warned for the purpose, and recorded *all* results in the presence of the same meeting. The Village had already decided to enter and cross-check all votes, but never actually did so. Now they chose a committee* from both sides of the ordination issue to view the records and decide what "grievous" or "unprofitable" entries to omit. The inhabitants disagreed with the committee's recommendations on only one, unrecorded, issue, and agreed to void several unspecified votes from Bayley's and Burroughs's days. Thomas Putnam transcribed the rest by **April 1687** when the Village approved the work and paid him forty shillings.[84]

When a copy of King James's Declaration of Indulgence arrived at Boston in **August 1687**, worried Puritans were relieved to hear that all penal laws against Nonconformists (and Catholics) were now revoked. The local churches chose Increase Mather to deliver their thanks to the King personally and, although they did not say so explicitly, to present their case against the Dominion government. After a winter dodging Randolph's trumped-up charges, Mather left in disguise one March night past the spy at his door and hid among the marshes until he boarded a ship to England.[85]

The Village's next ministerial candidate, Samuel Parris, arrived from Boston before **June 1688**. He had grown up in London, where his family endured the Restoration, the Great Fire, and the Great Plague (when their Boston kin thought them all dead). Young Samuel and his father Thomas, a hatter and merchant, moved to Barbados, but Thomas sent the boy north to Harvard College. However, on his father's death in 1673, Samuel had to leave without a degree to settle the estate in Barbados. He inherited the island property—most of it tied up in an eighty-two-year lease—while his elder brother in England, Rev. John Parris, inherited the English and Irish properties. Two middle brothers were already dead, so there was only Samuel to carry on the family business.[86]

After a few years as merchant and middleman in Bridgetown, he returned to Boston in 1680 and married Elizabeth Eldredge, a fellow member of the First Church and five years his senior. Their first child, Thomas, was born the next year, followed by Elizabeth Jr.—Betty—the year after. Operating from his Boston wharf and warehouse, Parris enjoyed a moderate prosperity (counter to what his oppo-

---

*Joseph Porter, Daniel Andrews, Captain Jonathan Putnam, Thomas Putnam, and Jonathan Walcott.

nents would later say) but decided to risk it to become a minister. He still had rental property to fall back on.[87]

He finished his studies somehow, for none of the local synods *or* eventual enemies ever questioned his academic qualifications. Ministers were expected to base their statements on a thorough knowledge of Scripture and other ancient texts in the original tongues: Latin, Greek, and Hebrew.[88]

Parris preached temporarily in Stow, a town chronically between pastors. His daughter Susannah was born not long before Increase Mather sailed for England. The family was in Salem Village by **June 1688**, when the four Goodwin children were bewitched in Boston. (Mary Glover was arrested for that. She was an elderly Catholic Irishwoman, suspected at least partly from fear of her French coreligionists. Andros's court tried her with a jury of Andros's men [at a time when Puritans were being excluded from juries], Judge Joseph Dudley presiding, and a board of physicians to test her sanity. She was found guilty and hanged in **November 1688**. Cotton Mather and his wife took the eldest afflicted girl into their home after this to help her beleaguered family and to observe the case at close hand.)[89]

Besides his immediate family, Parris's Village household included his niece Abigail Williams and three slaves: two "Spanish Indian" adults, John and Tituba Indian, and a "Negro lad," who died the following March at age fifteen. Parris may have brought them from Barbados or he may have purchased them in Boston. (The enslaved population of Massachusetts at this time consisted of about 200 Africans and a smaller number of Indians. A few free African families also lived in the Boston area.)[90]

After only a half year's trial period, various committees formally invited Parris to settle as Village minister. The Village even voted in his favor one Sabbath, but Parris would not be rushed. He mulled the offer all that winter and spring while attending the spiritual needs of Samuel Wilkins, a sinner who found religion late and died seeing Christ and Satan fight for his soul above the bed. Meanwhile the Province's political situation steadily worsened. The summer the Parris family moved to Salem Village in 1688, New England learned of the birth of the King's son, who would be raised Catholic like his parents and who, being male, replaced his Protestant half-sisters in the line of succession. Andros was in New York at the time but ordered a thousand men to march Eastward that winter—just after Goody Glover was hanged—to build forts at Pemaquid and Pejebscot (now Brunswick). He put the country on alert and shuttled back and forth all winter between Maine and Boston. Rumors circulated of royal plans to counter local resistance with Indian attacks, or to surrender them to Catholic Canada, or to demolish Boston with the bombs supposedly buried beneath it.[91]

In fact, King James had received Increase Mather and his requests with all courtesy and promised New England "a *Magna Charter* for liberty of conscience." However, the English anti-Catholic pressures against James only grew after the new heir's birth. One faction hoped to replace him with his eldest daughter Mary, married to her cousin William, Prince of Orange (in the Netherlands), who, besides being Protestant, had an army at his disposal. William invaded England, and after a short resistance in Ireland, James returned to exile in France. Increase Mather had to begin his negotiations all over again.[92]

When the proclamation of William's ascendance arrived in Boston, Andros arrested the messenger for importing such a "traitorous and treasonous libel." He ordered an alert against Dutch attack and ordered the arrest of Cotton Mather, who had followed his father in the opposition movement. Before this could happen, Boston revolted on **April 18, 1689**, capturing the redcoat garrison and man-of-war. An indignant Andros was obliged to surrender. Two former councilors, William Stoughton and Wait-Still Winthrop, joined the provisional government under former governor Simon Bradstreet, but less popular men like Edward Randolph and Joseph Dudley were jailed with Andros. Cotton Mather read a "Declaration of Gentlemen and Merchants" from the Town House balcony to calm the excited crowd and to avoid reprisals against Andros and his men.[93]

The Eastward militia disarmed their redcoat officers and sent them under guard to Boston, while most of the regulars simply wandered off after the council ordered the militia home. Immediately, Indian forces attacked Maine and New Hampshire. Massachusetts returned militia Eastward for a summer of fierce skirmishes around Casco Bay. (The militiamen brought back stories of the heavy loads that Rev. George Burroughs could lift for so small a man when he helped them unload supplies at Falmouth.)[94]

Eleven days after Andros's surrender, in **April 1689**, another Salem Village committee* asked Parris to settle and offered £60 a year. They wanted a speedy answer, but Parris knew how his predecessors' woes had increased once ordination loomed. Ideally, a minister was expected to serve for life, and a candidate had to balance the hope that he could rightly serve the spiritual needs of a specific community and still provide for his own family's present and future needs. Most of rural salaries were in "country pay," which could be cloth, a calf's head, a swarm of bees, a day's ploughing, a beached whale, or sheep dung as well as the usual vegetables, meat, and butter.[95]

Parris listed his own terms:

1. The percentage of money to produce (they offered one-third money) could increase if and when the Village had more coinage available.
2. Provisions for his own household would be credited at the committee's quoted values, even if their market value fluctuated up or down.†

---

*Nathaniel Ingersoll, Edward Putnam, Daniel Rea, and Thomas Fuller Jr.

†The value of produce was: wheat 4s a bushel; Indian corn 2s a bushel; barley, rye and malt 3s a bushel; pork 1d a pound; beef 1½d a pound; butter 2d a pound.

3. The £60 would come from inhabitants living within the Village bounds.
4. He wanted prior notice of what people intended to pay him with—unless they could spare only one choice—in case he had no use for it.
5. "Firewood to be given in yearly, freely."
6. The Village would choose two men to oversee all this.
7. Sabbath contributions in folded papers were to be credited toward the donor's share of Parris's salary.
8. The salary might be increased if God sent prosperity or decreased by abatement in hard times.[96]

They balked at items five and seven. Since the Village had no common woodland for his fuel, they offered an additional £6 a year—a third in money—to buy thirty cords himself. (They had earlier provided Burroughs with wood, and Lawson too for a few months.) Parris hoped one Villager would sell him the whole £6 worth, but no one offered. They did agree to sell him wood at four shillings a cord throughout his stay—whatever the market price—so he agreed to the extra £6 for a year.[97]

It was already the custom that donors of wrapped contributions in the collection box sign them in order to be credited, as in Lawson's time. Now, "after much agitation," according to Parris, they decided that strangers—non-residents who attended regularly but who could not be rated—might write whether the contribution was intended for the minister or for general church funds.[98]

This appeared to settle the matter, but neither this **April 29, 1689**, meeting, nor others on **May 17** and **May 21** were ever recorded in the Village Book—only alluded to in later court cases. Parris did not attend the next recorded meeting on **June 18, 1689**, when the Village decided his quarterly salary would begin **July 1, 1689**. The inhabitants noted that they would collect the agreed-on £66—one third in money, the rest in goods and merchantable produce at the quoted prices. For his part, Parris would keep the ministry house in repair during his residence, but they would mend the ministry pasture fences.[99]

In **October 1689**, "a general meeting of the inhabitants" voted, with "one man only dissenting," to give the ministry house, barn, and two acres to Parris outright. The Villagers had become used to reversing earlier decisions. As usual, the meeting's record omitted the exact number of inhabitants present, the names of those who proposed the gift, or the name of the nay-sayer. A parsonage usually remained public property, but it was not unusual for a congregation to present their minister with a house after many years of service or as a bonus at the beginning. Parris, being the first actually ordained, therefore intended to stay the rest of his life in the Village. He built a lean-to off the back of the house that he thought he owned, and purchased other lots around the two acres.[100]

The Salem Village Church gathered officially on the chill afternoon of Tuesday, **November 19, 1689**, to witness the ordination of Samuel Parris as their minister.

Salem's pastor Nicholas Noyes presided. He began by asking the invited elders and the Village brethren if any objected to the candidate doctrinally or morally. No one did, and the brethren—full church members—raised their hands in consent. Then Noyes, with Rev. Samuel Philips of Rowley and Rev. John Hale of Beverly, placed their hands on Parris's head in blessing while Noyes charged him to shepherd his flock faithfully, to devote himself to study and exhortation, and to be an example to them all. Then Philips, representing the rest, offered Parris the right hand of fellowship to seal the deed.[101]

Although Parris's ordination sermon referred to several touchy matters (and to others that would be), it contained nothing unfamiliar or unorthodox. Based on the text "And the Lord said unto Joshua, this day have I rolled away the reproach of Egypt from off you," the sermon concerned sacraments, which he could now distribute. Like the wandering Israelites, said Parris, the Village had lacked access to its sacraments, which it might have enjoyed sooner had they cooperated. Admittedly, some restless souls had stirred "spiritual disquietness" for this worthy cause, but it did not become their opponents to claim, with "a profane pagan-like spirit," that they were no better off than before. The word of God through sermons moved souls to feel grace, of which the now available sacraments were the outward sign and expression. "And remember," he added to the core of full members, "it is not the bare privation, but the contempt of sacraments . . . [which] is damnable and destructive. Therefore you cannot hereafter live without partaking of the ordinances, but you will of necessity heighten your sins by such neglects and omissions."[102]

Then he summarized his and his congregation's respective duties. For his part, said Parris, he was not to lord it over them but to be a servant of the Lord God who required he be not just an example, but "to make differences between the clean and unclean, so as to labor to change and purge the one, and confirm and strengthen the other. . . . And what I do this way, without partial respect to persons, you must not, you cannot, you ought not to be angry: for so I am commanded."

In return, the congregation owed him the respect, love, and obedience due his office, but only "so far as I watch your souls," he said, and referred to Hebrews 13:17, which emphasized the accountability of spiritual leadership as well as its joys. He reminded them of his contract by paraphrasing the Cambridge Platform, an earlier ministerial conference that had tried to define some consistency among the many independent churches: "You are to communicate to me

---

*Because Parris's salary became controversial, and because his comments influenced later interpretations of the matter, here is the Platform's phrasing: "The Scripture alleged requiring this maintenance as a bounden duty, and due debt, and not as a matter of alms and free gift, therefore people are not at liberty to do or not to do, what and when they please in this matter, . . . but ought of duty to minister of their 'carnal things' to make them that labor among them in a word or doctrine, as well as they ought to pay any other workmen their wages."

of your carnal good things, . . . and that not as a piece of alms or charity, but of justice and duty."*

For all this he desired their prayers and their cooperation: "You are to endeavour by all lawful means to make my heavy work, as much as in you lies, light and cheerful. . . . And not by unchristian-like behaviour to myself, or one another, or other Churches of God," or to any whether members of a church or not, "to add to my burden and to make my life among you grievous and my labor among you [spiritually] unprofitable."

Then, in the increasingly cold November dusk, Parris ended his sermon by asking all present to "pray for a sufficiency of grace, that both you and I may give up a good account" to God of their association. The members of the new church formally embodied as the men signed their names after Parris's under their covenant, which he had written in his clear hand at the start of a new church record book. The women members, by custom, did not, and Parris inscribed their names in a second column.[103]

The next inhabitants meeting a few weeks later directed Constable Edward Bishop to collect unpaid ministerial rates from thirty-eight delinquents, "by distress" if necessary as the law allowed. This may have been belated opposition to the ordination, but Topsfield and other towns had similar problems during the upsets of the Andros regime.[104]

While the Village dealt with these matters, King Louis returned the formidable Louis de Baude, Count Frontenac as governor of Canada with specific orders to attack English settlements. The Count was to send a land force south down the lakes to join warships in New York Harbor, then deport the settlers. As wind and winter delayed the ships, Frontenac substituted three small war parties of *coureurs de bois* (woodsmen) and Abenaki on snowshoes directed against New York, New Hampshire, and Maine. Shortly after Massachusetts shipped Andros, Randolph, and Dudley back to England—"civilly," as the King ordered—the first war party struck Schenectady in **February 1690**, killed about sixty inhabitants, and marched eighty or ninety off to Canada.[105]

Salem Village was close to the frontier, but the winter's worst upset was Ezekiel Cheever's suspected horse theft, when, in his rush for a midwife, the farmer borrowed neighbor Joseph Putnam's horse. It took three such meetings before Cheever would apologize, which was all that was required, and Parris cautioned them all against festering grudges.[106]

The second snowshoe force burnt Salmon Falls, New Hampshire, in **March 1690** and killed about thirty people before taking forty-four captives to Quebec. Consequently, Sir William Phips volunteered money and his leadership for an expedition against Port Royal, a town that armed Indians and sheltered privateers. Despite his title, Sir William had grown up on the coast of Maine. He rose in the world only after he became a shipwright in Boston, married a rich widow, and learned to read at age twenty-one. He formed grand schemes to raise sunken treasure in the Caribbean and failed. Then, solely on a promise of shares *if* the next attempt succeeded, he found a near piratical crew to serve unpaid *and* persuaded King Charles II to loan him a government ship. The King required that Phips give free passage to Edward Randolph and the order canceling the charter, so their arrival in Massachusetts was not welcome.[107]

This expedition also failed, but a third—privately backed by English investors—succeeded wildly. Phips's share alone was £16,000 and a Knighthood of the Golden Fleece from King James. Phips bought himself a government post in the Dominion of Massachusetts, but when he returned to Boston, Andros had already filled the position and did not hide his low opinion of the self-made adventurer. Back in England, Phips joined Increase Mather and other American agents just before King James was deposed. Consequently, Phips missed Andros's overthrow but arrived a year later as the Boston militia renewed old plans to attack Port Royal.[108]

Phips sailed for Acadia in **April 1690** with 280 sailors and over 400 militia in seven vessels. Observing the courtesy of war, he demanded that Port Royal surrender, for doing so guaranteed the noncombatants' safety (though it did not prevent looting). Due to the number of attackers and the fort's dilapidation, Governor Meneval consented. There weren't enough militia to garrison the place, so Phips accepted the people's oath not to make trouble, and the fleet returned with the town's leaders and fifty-nine soldiers to trade for English hostages.[109]

Then they heard how a third war party from Canada had joined the second, banded with other local Indian leaders, and besieged Fort Loyal at Falmouth on Casco Bay. After five days and four nights, the garrison surrendered on the French leader's promise that the women, children, and wounded men could proceed safely to the next fort. Nevertheless, most were slaughtered as soon as they tried to leave. The survivors watched the town burn before they were marched away from their unburied dead toward Quebec as English ships appeared, too late, in the harbor. Without waiting for orders, four nearby garrisons evacuated twenty miles south to Saco, then twenty more miles to Wells. Refugees fled to Boston and Salem.[110]

Acting Governor Simon Bradstreet begged England for arms, ammunition, and ships. The Maine settlements, wrote Deputy Governor Thomas Danforth, "are utterly ruinated and depopulated." Moreover, the colony owed over £20,000 to the troops that Andros had levied, yet "people are now so very poor, that many profess they have not corn for their families, and those to whom wages are due, cry, that if they have them not, they and their families must starve."[111]

While all this shadowed the region, the Salem Village church decided to observe the Lord's Supper every six weeks, instead of the usual four, and to set conservative requirements for new membership (which Parris would try to broaden in the next few years). Several joined by transfer, like Sarah Bishop from the Topsfield church, or by a confession of faith and the recommendation of other members, like Martha Corey. (The third wife of Giles Corey, Martha had lived many years of her first marriage apart from her husband as the single mother of her mulatto son Ben. Now that she felt grace, she liked to style herself a "Gospel woman.")[112]

At New York's invitation, an **April 1690** conference of combined colonies planned to attack Canada. New York and Connecticut militias would march up the lakes with Mohawk, Oneida, and Mohegan allies against Montreal, while Massachusetts and the rest attacked Quebec by sea. Delayed by waiting for nonexistent English help, Phips's fleet of thirty-two vessels and 2,200 militiamen sailed in **August 1690** for the St. Lawrence, where, just when an outbreak of smallpox erupted on board, the wind turned. The pilot-less fleet took three weeks to sail the three-day distance to Quebec. This gave the city time to evacuate the countryside and arm itself, and time for wild rumors to circulate that the heretics wore necklaces strung with the severed ears of Jesuits. And because New York's forces had been immobilized by smallpox and dysentery, it allowed Frontenac to move most of his troops from Montreal to Quebec.[113]

For the next few days an English landing party unsuccessfully tried to outflank the city in an icy rain, while the fleet discovered the difficulty of firing cannonballs over Quebec's heights while French artillery riddled their ships from above. With supplies low on both sides, the French and English exchanged a few hostages, and the fleet left the jubilant city. They sailed into thick fog, thicker snow, and winter storms that scattered vessels as far as the West Indies. From **November 1690** through **March 1691**, survivors limped home to Boston bringing dysentery and fever with them.[114]

The possible meaning of Heaven's painful providences had already been discussed during the fleet's absence. The Boston area Congregational ministers gathered periodically in the college at Cambridge to talk shop and to discuss policy. In **October 1690,** Samuel Parris and Ezekiel Cheever attended one of the first meetings as representatives of the Village church that had proposed the topic for discussion: "What shall be done towards the reformation of the miscarriages for which New England now suffers by the heavy judgments of God?"[115]

The next Village inhabitants' meeting considered "some propositions that Mr. Parris hath made to the people" (but did not list them) and voted to pay him £60 for the year, "Mr. Parris having relinquished the £6 voted . . . for firewood." (He more likely relinquished the sum in return for the wood itself, since he had agreed to the extra £6 for only a year.)[116]

Meanwhile, Massachusetts owed the near-mutinous militia over £40,000. With towns like Salem petitioning for relief in tending the sick and wounded, the legislature levied a tax to cover the expense, spread it over two years, and paid the soldiers in paper bills of credit. To show good faith, Phips exchanged a goodly sum of hard money for these bills. (Few trusted them and they shortly fell in value to sixteen shillings in the pound.) Phips then sailed to England in the teeth of **winter 1691** for help against Canada. Elisha Cooke and Thomas Oakes had preceded him, sent to expedite Increase Mather's charter negotiations. They brought General Court commissions that finally named Mather and his contact Sir Henry Ashurst as official agents, but they were also determined to get the old charter reconfirmed. This, Mather now knew, was impossible. The King and his men were preoccupied, moreover, with the new administration, Irish rebellion, and French threats to the Netherlands. Cooke and Oakes opposed compromise, and the four found it hardly possible to work together. Still, they feigned unanimity to face Andros and his men before the Lords of Trade, and surprised them by entering only two of the 124 complaints: taxes and the arrest of the messenger with King William's proclamation. They did so to protect New England's own dubious actions from scrutiny. As oppressive as Andros's rule was, his methods were entirely legal and customary. The plan worked, although it was hard to accept that Andros would not be punished but rather made governor of Virginia. (He was nearly named governor of Massachusetts!) Joseph Dudley became chief justice and chief of the council for New York.[117]

Salem Village began the new year arguing about the land under the parsonage. A **January 1691** inhabitants' meeting chose a committee—Joseph Hutchinson Sr., Joseph Porter, Daniel Andrews, Francis Nurse, and Thomas Putnam—"to get a full and legal assurance of the land which belongs to our ministry house which the inhabitants have purchased" from Joseph Holten Sr. and Nathaniel Ingersoll. They did not record any results at the subsequent meetings, however. That the land and its buildings had been given to Parris the year before was not noted, but the same gathering also set the rate for Parris's next year's salary at the full £66.[118]

In addition, the Village decided to petition the government for the right to tax nonresidents who attended their church, since Salem Village had had years of trouble getting rates from Beverly and Topsfield people. Then, because of the worsening frontier situation, the Village built a small watchhouse on a knoll opposite Ingersoll's. Stocked with firewood and candles, it could shelter guards or serve as a lock-up.[119]

The Village church installed two deacons, Edward Putnam and Nathaniel Ingersoll, in **December 1690** and **June 1691**, respectively. They had long performed their duties informally, tending to the material needs of church and meetinghouse. The brethren had voted for them unanimously in **December 1690**, but Ingersoll accepted the office only after months of soul searching.[120]

Thomas Putnam's twenty-seven-year-old wife Ann joined the church in **June 1691**, a month after the death of her widowed mother Elizabeth Carr. Nine years before, when Ann's father George Carr died, Thomas and other sons-in-law accused the widow and her sons of withholding the daughters' inheritance. As was more and more usual, the Carr sons inherited land and shipping but the daughters received only small sums of money. When the widow's estate was probated later that June, Mrs. Ann Putnam's inheritance amounted to a mere shilling.[121]

New York's revolutionary government surrendered that same spring to newly arrived Governor Henry Slaughter after a long defiant siege. The leaders, Jacob Leisler and Jacob Milborne, were tried for treason before Justice Joseph Dudley, found guilty, condemned to death, hanged, drawn, and quartered, and their estates were confiscated from the heirs. When news reached Boston, where Milborne's brother William was a Baptist minister and where no one knew what England might inflict on local rebels, Major Andrew Belcher declared that Massachusetts should have hanged Dudley when they had the chance.[122]

Winter's cease-fire Eastward ended **May 1, 1691**, but a promised exchange of prisoners at Wells—where George Burroughs was now minister—came to nothing. No Indians showed up until **June 9, 1691.** Minutes after Captain James Converse received reinforcements from Essex County, the influential Penobscot chief Agamagus (called Moxus) led a force of two hundred warriors against the garrison. Wells survived, but the raiders had better luck against Berwick, Exeter, and York. Troops at Pejebscot just barely held out, compelling the attackers to waste ammunition that would otherwise have been used against the Isles of Shoals.[123]

In the midst of this crisis, Benjamin Nurse of Salem Village was called to active duty in **June 1691**. At twenty-six, he was the youngest of Francis and Rebecca Nurse's eight children. Benjamin and his wife Tamsin, then with child, lived and worked with his parents at the Nurse homestead. Francis hired John Hadlock, who had finished his own service only six months earlier, to take Benjamin's place at two shillings, six pence a week (plus his military pay) and the loan of a gun. Although perfectly legal, it would not have escaped the notice of refugee neighbors—like the Sheldons, twice driven from Scarborough, or Thomas Putnam's hired girl Mercy Lewis, orphaned and displaced by the attacks on Casco Bay.[124]

Although Acadia's Port Royal was still allied to New England since its surrender, Massachusetts could not afford to garrison the place. If France reclaimed it, the town would not only be a supply depot for raiders and a port for privateers but would also cut off English access to the fur trade. When Joseph Robineau de Villebon, the new Commander of Acadia, reclaimed Port Royal in **October 1691** (where he captured a ship full of New England merchants) and offered support to the Indians from his base on the Saint John River, Canadian attack seemed imminent. George Burroughs and his townsmen in Wells twice petitioned Massachusetts for help. They had survived the **June 1691** siege, they wrote, but were able to harvest only a six-month supply of corn due to continued attacks. Most of the cattle had been killed or stolen while the town hid in the garrisons. One youth was captured before their eyes when he ventured out for firewood. They needed food, arms, and men.[125]

Raiding parties also killed a family in Dunstable, Massachusetts, in **September 1691** and then attacked Berwick in Maine and Sandy Beach in New Hampshire. A month later, they re-entered Massachusetts and killed families along the Merri-mack River and in Rowley, not far from Salem Village.[126]

While all this went on, Elisha Cooke and Thomas Oakes ignored Increase Mather and petitioned the King directly for the old charter. England still considered Mather the senior agent, but alarmed him with a charter draft that not only allowed the Crown-appointed governor to choose all magistrates but to veto any of his Assembly's acts. If all freemen were allowed to vote, the Lords Chief Justices explained to Mather, "the King's governor would be made a governor of clouts" (of rags). Mather lost his composure and answered he would *die* rather than accept that. His consent was not necessary, said the Lords coolly, for "the agents of New-England were not plenipotentiaries from a sovereign state." Even if they did not agree with the King's decision, they must "take what would follow." The possibilities included a revived Dominion or rule by an absentee London-based corporation. Cooke and Oakes rejected Mather's warning that any attempt to use the old charter would only result in another order forbidding it, which, Mather said, "no man of estate or brain" would do.[127]

The King insisted that a military man head the province, but agreed to fill the post with someone acceptable to the inhabitants. He let Increase Mather propose candidates for governor and for magistrates. (Subsequent governors, however, would be royal appointees.) Mather named Sir William Phips governor, William Stoughton deputy governor, Isaac Addington secretary, and nearly thirty others as councillors. All had held office before, although some, like Stoughton, were not reelected because of prior service under Andros. Mather did *not* include former magistrates Thomas Oakes and Elisha Cooke. King William signed this new charter in **October 1691** and sealed it at last with the great seal.[128]

But months would pass before New England learned of this. Meanwhile, only frontier attack seemed certain. Witchcraft suspicions flared up in Massachusetts when Mary Randall went before the Hampshire County Court in Springfield, **September 29, 1691**. Although suspicious, the magistrates released her on a £10 bond for good behavior put up by her father.* Martha Sparks of Chelmsford in Middlesex County was arrested and questioned **October 27, 1691**. The magistrates sent her to the Boston jail until a new government could deal with the case. As her husband Henry was with the militia Eastward, her young children were left with her parents, even though the grandmother was bedridden. (The reason for her accusation is lost, but Goody Sparks's own kin had thought she acted insanely thirteen years earlier when she beat her mother bloody.)[129]

---

*The record calls her Mary Randolph and Mary Randall, daughter of William Randall but gives no location. Later sources say Northampton or Westfield.

With life so precarious, people everywhere fell behind in taxes. Salem Village, however, not only delayed but disputed the minister's rates, including his seemingly settled fuel allowance. Parris's wood supply was nearly gone by **October 8, 1691,** when the Village hosted the weekly Thursday Lecture—an extra optional sermon that local churches took in rotation. He would have had no fuel at all, Parris reminded the people afterward, had not Mr. Corwin brought some from Salem. But the next inhabitants' meeting elected five unsympathetic men to the rates committee: Joseph Porter, Joseph Hutchinson, Daniel Andrews, Joseph Putnam, and Francis Nurse. They voted, despite the contract, *not* to collect Parris's salary that year.[130]

Winter closed in with day after day of strong northerly gales. "Brethren," Parris addressed a church meeting in his cold home on **November 2, 1691**, "I have not much to trouble you with now"; but they all knew the committee that the last Village meeting had chosen, and perhaps knew what those men intended better than he did. "But, you see, I have hardly any wood to burn. I need say no more, but leave the matter to your serious and godly consideration."[131]

The seventeen brethren present voted to have Captain John Putnam and the two Deacons ask the Village rates committee, on the church's behalf, to set and collect the minister's rates. But when they did, the rates committee claimed they could not begin to consider any business without a written request from the church and pastor. The three reported this new requirement to Parris and the others on **November 10, 1691**, but only three other members showed up for the depressing news: Thomas Putnam, Thomas Wilkins, and Peter Prescott. The weather, meanwhile, underscored Parris's request as violent storm of wind and rain drenched the region on **November 8, 1691**, followed by snow and bitter wind on **November 12**.[132]

Parris called another church meeting for Wednesday, **November 18, 1691**, the first clear day after twenty-four hours of snow and hail on a northeast wind. He commented on the poor turnout at the last few church meetings and insisted he did not call them unnecessarily. Then, after discussion, those present voted unanimously to sue the delinquent rates committee and composed a complaint on the spot. Three members signed on behalf of the whole church—Nathaniel and Thomas Putnam and Thomas Wilkins—and again they chose Captain John Putnam and the two deacons to present it. Parris, meanwhile, twice reminded them he "had scarce wood enough to burn till tomorrow."[133]

The following Sunday, **November 22, 1691**, was the next scheduled communion service at the Village. Parris began a series of sacrament sermons on the text of Psalm 110:1. "The Lord said unto my Lord, 'Sit thou at my right hand, until I make thine enemies thy footstool.'" The verse was taken to be God's statement to Christ, a promise of "consolation of the faithful." Christ, our mediator, for all His suffering, is exalted and victorious at last, for God's kingdom prevails, with "not one sheep lost, not one obstinate enemy but conquered." (But "because of the coldness and shortness of the season," Parris ended the afternoon sermon sooner than otherwise.)[134]

The rates committee warned a meeting for ten o'clock, **December 1, 1691,** specifically to discuss the **June 18, 1689,** meeting that had set Parris's yearly salary, the **October 10, 1689,** meeting that gave Parris the ministry house and land, and whether either was a legal meeting properly warned. Then, acting as if his contract were void, they decided to pay Parris "by voluntary contributions or by subscription." They itemized the program in the Record Book, but never recorded what actually happened.[135]

The meeting may have been the occasion remembered years later by three of the rates committee—Joseph Porter, Daniel Andrews, and Joseph Putnam—when several men who had not voted for Parris in the first place asked for a clarification of "those things that concerned Mr. Parris" and a reading of the "entry, that some call a salary." This sparked considerable heat and ended (as they recalled it) with Parris announcing he had never heard *that* before and that "they were knaves and cheaters that entered it," so any supposed agreements between him and the people were ended. Parris's opponents doubtless disagreed with his supporters about ownership of the parsonage and whether his salary included wood, but the record remained blank for the rest of the year. Since Parris had been ordained, neither he nor the church could easily break off their association.[136]

December began with rain and snow. Smallpox lingered in Salem where the selectmen twice abated widow Schafflin twenty-eight shillings of her county rate, "her man being gone and sickness in her family." Captain Jonathan Putnam went to Boston as a representative to the General Court, which—having outfitted the sloop *Mary* to guard the coast—now prohibited any French from living in frontier towns or seaports without permission from Acting Governor Simon Bradstreet and the Council. (Salem's Protestant French inhabitants both resented being lumped with King Louis's agents and ignored the order.) Boston shops kept the Puritan custom of not observing Christmas. In such a time of uncertainty, Cotton Mather noticed, "storms of discontent" among the people disrupted everyday life.[137]

John Hadlock visited the Village on leave from Eastward to collect twenty shillings of pay from Francis Nurse on **December 18, 1691**. Nurse's friends also helped: Jonathan Walcott wrote an agreement for Daniel Andrews to pay Hadlock on Walcott's account "according to the bargain that you made with me to ease Goodman Nurse." Hadlock returned to Maine, Benjamin Nurse stayed home with his wife and infant daughter, and the local refugees had the opportunity to wonder why—with the country in a constant danger of invasion—some men had to face the enemy over and over so that others never had to leave home once.[138]

Parris reflected on the broken contract in his cold parsonage while his wife, children, and slaves moved about their daily tasks. In this apprehensive time, his daughter and his niece may have yielded to the temptation of scrying their futures. Betty and Abigail were too young to have specific sweethearts in mind, but at least two local girls did make a "Venus glass"* that winter to reveal their future husbands, and any girl's own future depended on her husband's trade. Whoever they were, they dropped an egg white into a beer glass of water and watched the patterns that it formed. One of them saw the cloud of albumin form a coffin's hard angles, to proclaim her a bride of death.[139]

---

*Chadwick Hansen suggests the albumin acted as a gazing crystal. Seventeenth-century antiquarian John Aubrey said the egg was exposed to the sun in Leo (August). A version of this surviving among Wampanoag girls at Gay Head also required the white's exposure to the sun. In these cases the egg white might suggest forms as it decayed.

PART I

1692

1

JANUARY 1692

> *Serve me.*
>
> —Satan

January 1, 1692 • Friday
Salem Village

Tides ran high at half-past five in Massachusetts Bay, pushing the creeks backward toward Salem Village in the dark, for the mid-winter days were briefer than the space of a single tide. Because the moon waned its crescent in the damp sign of Scorpio, almanac-makers predicted rain or snow.[1]

But a fine line divided predicting how events might logically proceed and divining the unknowable future. Whatever was happening in Salem Village was still hidden, the secret of a few girls. (By later tradition, a sizable group of them habitually gathered in the parsonage kitchen, where the Caribbean slave woman Tituba taught them magic. But surviving contemporary accounts never mention this. The only proven conjurations were projects from the settlers' own British folk tradition.)[2]

While Betty and Abigail perhaps unnerved themselves with their little sorceries, Samuel Parris's salary again came due, and again went unpaid.[3]

January 3, 1692 • Sunday
Salem Village

A great snow fell this Sabbath, sacrament day in the Village as in most other churches. It shrouded Boston, where Samuel Sewall made note of it, and Salem Village, where the more remote households might be snowbound. Rev. Samuel Parris waded through it from his cold parsonage to the colder Meeting House for the morning and the afternoon services and continued his sermon series on the text of Psalm 110:1: "The Lord said unto my Lord, 'Sit thou at my right hand, until I make thine enemies thy footstool.'"

Christ sits at God's right hand and intercedes for sinful humanity, said Parris, "yea, all mankind, the whole race of apostate Adam" for "even the very Elect, are by nature dead in sin and trespasses." Sometimes, however, it seems as if "Christ hath placed His church in this world, as in a sea, and suffereth many storms and tempests to threaten its shipwreck," Parris continued as the snow raged outside, "whilst in the meantime He Himself seems to be fast asleep." But this was to humble sinners and to make the Church more watchful, to frighten them back to good behavior like "young children over bold with fire or water" whose desperate parents hold them over the danger so the parental bluff might teach them the risk.

Parris's sermons usually had little to do with Hell, but on this Sabbath he repeated the truism of the Devil's hostility toward the Church. "It is the main drift of the Devil to pull it all down," but Christ would defend His church against its three great foes: the "inward enemies" of a Christian's own sins, outward persecutions, and the power of death. Satan would not prevail even though aided by "wicked and reprobate men (the assistants of Satan to afflict the Church)." But because the unheated meeting house was so cold, Parris did not enlarge further on the theme, and the meeting ended.[4]

London

Meanwhile, across the Atlantic in London, Increase Mather's four-year effort to restore Massachusetts's charter concluded at Whitehall. While word of the outcome headed west across the ocean, he and newly appointed Governor Sir William Phips each kissed King William's hand in thanks.[5]

January 6, 1692 • Wednesday
Boston

A Quarterly Court sat for Suffolk County in Boston to consider a number of continuing cases. Most involved disputed merchandise, including a shipload of tobacco confiscated by the Royal Customs Inspector Jahleel Brenton.[6]

January 8, 1692 • Friday
Salem Village

Almanacs predicted cold, but instead a January thaw brought a week of sun and rain that dissolved roads as well as snow.[7]

The men of Salem Village gathered in their meeting house at two o'clock and voted for a committee to present their independence petition to Salem's town meeting, the same matter for which they were also petitioning the General Court. They chose Nathaniel Putnam, John Putnam Sr., Francis Nurse, Joseph Hutchinson Sr., Joseph Porter, and Thomas Flint. If Salem wouldn't grant their request outright, these men were instructed, they were to ask for freedom from all charges relating only to Salem town in exchange for Salem Village maintaining its own roads and its own poor.[8]

January 11, 1692 • Monday
Salem Town

The Village petition committee picked their way through the mud to Salem's town meeting and again presented their plea for separation. While they represented a sizable part of the Village, they were not empowered—in the opinion of Salem town—to act on its behalf, so the matter was again postponed.[9]

January 12, 1692 • Tuesday
Salem Town

By now the false spring had so liquefied the roads that it seemed more like March than January.[10]

Nevertheless, some snow remained in Salem Town around the middle of the month when Alice Parker's neighbors found her lying on "the dirt and snow," seemingly dead. One of the women assured the men that Goodwife Parker had had fits of unconsciousness before, but the men were skittish about touching her, and it was a time before one dared to sling her over his shoulder. Despite the commotion she showed no signs of waking, even when the man lost hold and dropped her on the stony ground. At last they got her home and to bed, but while they undressed her, she suddenly sat up and laughed. If it did not occur to anyone then, it must have crossed their minds later that witches were supposedly able to shed their bodies like cast-off coats while their spirits went abroad to work invisible mischief. (That was the folk-belief. Ministers said body and soul separated only at the finality of death.)[11]

January 14, 1692 • Thursday
Boston

Almanacs predicted cold, windy weather to clear the sky and to make travel easier, perhaps, for those attending Lecture. Acting Governor Simon Bradstreet and the General Court had already proclaimed this Lecture Day a public fast—a day to contemplate society's shortcomings and to pray for help to correct them. Cotton Mather addressed his Boston listeners on the need for spiritual awakening. "A sinful sleep is indeed, a deadly sleep; it is a stupefying, and a venomous bed of nightshade whereupon men lie when they sleep in sin." It was his, and others,' long-held opinion that New England churches were in danger of complacent stagnation. The people needed a reformation where individuals would reexamine and reevaluate their lives, and congregations would rededicate themselves to their rightful purposes.[12]

January 15, 1692 • Friday
Salem Village

Rev. Samuel Parris purchased a triangular two-acre orchard off the meeting house road from John Shepard, a Village man who had moved to Rowley after his first wife's death. Parris considered the plot from its white oak tree to its heap of boundary stones, found it worth the £10 investment, and signed the deed.[13]

At home, meanwhile, his niece Abigail was not yet noticeably ill. All seemed as before, but from Tituba's later "confession" it would appear that dramatic and astonishing events had occurred beneath the routine of ordinary life.

As Tituba dropped off to sleep, she saw a tall, darkly clad, white-haired man standing by her. He planned to kill the children, he announced, and she, Tituba, would help him or he would kill her, too. He was a god, he confided, and looked pleased when Tituba appeared to believe this. She must believe in him, he insisted, flourishing a document. If she served him faithfully for six years (only six years like a bond servant's term, not the perpetual servitude of slavery), he would give her many fine things, but if she declined, he would treat her as he meant to treat the girls.[14]

January 16–19, 1692 • Saturday–Tuesday
Salem Village

The spirit came again to offer bribes in the form of creatures like small bright birds—green and white and yellow. But Tituba defied him. He was no god, she declared. This was a matter for her master. But when she headed for the stairs and Parris's study, the man-devil stopped her roughly. She was to serve *him* now, he repeated, and promised to return on Wednesday.[15]

Outside, the weather remained windy while sleet and snow hid the young moon. Indoors, the adult Parrises at last noticed Betty and Abigail's worsening symptoms. They found the girls crouched under chairs and stools and twisted in puzzling postures. The two girls gestured oddly and gabbled phrases neither they nor anyone else could understand. Abigail complained of pains in her head. (Since Thomas and baby Susanna were never mentioned in any of the accounts, presumably they were not affected.)[16]

January 20, 1692 • Wednesday
Salem Village

While Rev. and Mrs. Parris were in the parlor with Betty and Abigail, Tituba stood in the other room—the hall—well within earshot of the girls' cries.

Suddenly (as her later testimony detailed) four women appeared in one corner of the hall while the man-devil just as suddenly materialized behind Tituba. He gripped her firmly. "Go," he commanded, "and do hurt to them, and pinch them." The six moved across the entry to the parlor, where the Parrises neither looked up nor noticed that anyone else was there, for the Devil had enchanted them.

Tituba refused to harm the children, so the witches swarmed around her, hauled her across the room, and forced her hands to pinch Betty and then Abigail. The women vanished after this victory, but the man-devil wasn't finished. Rev. Parris, he said, would pray now as usual. And, as usual, he would read a Biblical passage and, to see if she understood, would ask Tituba to tell him about it. But she would *not* remember, the man-devil emphasized, not *any* of it. He promised to return on Friday and to show her his book. Only six years of service, he repeated. That was all he required.[17]

In the visible world it was St. Agnes Eve, a date between winter and spring in European latitudes, and a traditional time for fortune-telling. In New England, where neither saints' days nor divination was encouraged, the customs were, nevertheless, part of the culture. Some of the more curious or anxious people may have tried them, young girls mostly, wanting to divine their future husbands. Girls back in Northumberland used hard-boiled eggs, the yolks removed and replaced by salt. A girl ate one, shell and all, with the proper rhymes and motions, hoping to dream of her future husband so that she would recognize him in real life. (The charm was not unlike the egg-and-glass project that had frightened at least two Village girls into fits.)[18]

At some time this winter, widow Rebecca Johnson of Andover and her daughter turned a sieve to learn if the widow's absent brother-in-law, Moses Haggat, were alive or dead. "By Saint Peter and Saint Paul," they recited, using a charm that their minister's maid had told them, "if Haggat be dead, let this sieve turn round." And the sieve jerked round. (But it lied, for Haggat lived.)[19]

January 22, 1692 • Friday
Salem Village

The man-devil arrived early Friday morning to tell Tituba that she must sign his book with her blood. He handed her a pin tied to a stick so she could prick her finger, but before he could slip the book from his pocket, Mrs. Parris called for Tituba from the other room—and he vanished.[20]

January 23, 1692 • Saturday
Salem Village

Salem Village wasn't finished with its petition to the town by any means. Joseph Putnam wrote an official order for a Village meeting to be held the following Lecture Day and had the notice tacked to the message post outside the Meeting House.[21]

***
Salem Village

As the moon waxed full, apparitions continued to plague Tituba (as she later testified). A hog or a great black dog would suddenly leap from the shadows and command, "Serve me," before assuming the shape of a man. Sometimes he had a little yellow bird with him, or a pair of cats—one red, the other black—the size of a small dog. The witches also returned to torment her, and while the two from Boston were yet unknown to her, she recognized the others now as Sarah Good and Sarah Osborn, both of Salem Village. "Serve me," the Devil repeated, "serve me," until Tituba signed his book with her own blood in a crescent mark.* She saw nine other marks on the page, some red, some yellowish. Two of them, the Devil said, were Good's and Osborn's.[22]

---

*Tituba's mark is printed in SWP 755, as "A:C." Because several words in the sentence are capitalized, this seems to mean she signed with "a 'C'."

January 24, 1692 • Sunday
Boston

In Boston the Sabbath weather was temperate enough for Governor Bradstreet to attend the afternoon service at South Meeting House, the first time, as Samuel Sewall noted, that the old man had ventured to meeting all January.[23]

January 25, 1692 • Monday
York, Maine

Nevertheless, snow was falling thickly on the coast of Maine that Monday morning when Shubael Dummer, the minister of York, stepped from his door. He swung into his horse's saddle and was shot dead. The neighbors, hearing gunfire, realized they were under attack by a band of French and Abenaki and ran for the blockhouses. About fifty English died in the first rush—even French accounts said women and children were killed—and about seventy to a hundred were taken prisoner. Keeping out of range of the blockhouses, the attackers burnt the other buildings, slaughtered horses and cattle, and swept all outlying farms within five miles. Remembering Dummer's past reluctance to return certain captives, the invaders stripped and mutilated his corpse.

Before they marched off their hostages, they sent back the youngest children and the oldest women—a mercy proffered in return for the Indian women and children spared in an earlier English attack. Dummer's widow was among those freed, yet afterward she shuttled back and forth to the raiders' camp so often, begging for the release of her son, that they took her with the rest of the hostages.

Captain John Flood's militia arrived from Portsmouth, New Hampshire, in time to pursue the party only a short way before losing them. The survivors could do little but contemplate the ashes of ruined York and the hacked body of its late minister. Many had advised Dummer to leave such a dangerous frontier area—the congregation could hardly pay him—yet he had stayed.[24]

January 26, 1692 • Tuesday
Boston

Assistants William Stoughton and Samuel Sewall, among others, presided over Suffolk County's Quarterly Court at Boston, and John Goodwin—father of the once-bewitched children—served on one of the trial juries. Most of the cases involved property and debts. Rev. Peter Thatcher of Milton petitioned for possession of his late father's Boston house and land from his widowed stepmother Margaret Thatcher who, as everyone knew, was already wealthy thanks to inheritances from her father and first husband. The jury found for the petitioner, but the stepmother appealed. Anthony Checkley, who had represented the absent Captain John Alden in earlier court cases, sued him for £5 back pay. The jury found for Alden this time, but the court dismissed Alden's own suit against Mark Emerson for defamation of character. The former hostage had told all and sundry how, during his two-and-a-half-year captivity in Maine, he had often seen old Alden sell the Indians powder and shot.[25]

In the midst of all the legal bustle, Boston heard the sobering news of York. It was sad enough for Assistant Samuel Sewall, a distant cousin of Rev. Dummer, but the news would terrify those like the Boston serving maid Mercy Short who had lived through just such an attack on Salmon Falls and had been taken captive to Quebec.[26]

Yet, amid this disaster came the happier news that their own Sir William Phips was now Captain General and Governor in Chief of the Province of Massachusetts Bay in New England (New England being everything between New York and Newfoundland). What joy Lady Mary Phips felt at this elevation was offset by her recollection of the horoscope in one of her husband's trunks. Years before he made his mark in the world—he had explained to her after she first discovered the document—when he was in London, an old neighborhood astrologer (whom he hardly knew) presented him with a prediction of notable events in his life. Lady Phips had marveled at the predictions: his finding a great treasure (as he had) and being entrusted overseas by his king (as he was), to be followed by adversity and the nearly ruinous reproaches of enemies whom he would, however, outlast for a thirteen-year rule and a peaceful retirement.

With the king granting Phips the governorship, those predictions seemed too exact to be safe, too much a coincidence to be within human knowledge. Lady Phips could no longer bear to have the horoscope in her house, so she burned it.[27]

January 27, 1692 • Wednesday
Wells, Maine

One young man, captured at York, escaped to Wells with a tale of attackers shooting and hacking victims among the flames. George Burroughs, minister of Wells and once of Salem Village, had himself barely escaped more than one raid in Maine. With the county seat at York burned, moreover, all public record of his various deeds and land grants was destroyed. But today's appearance of two Indians with a flag of truce was more pressing than his own personal concerns. The English, the messengers said, might ransom the captives at Sagadahoc in a fortnight, three weeks at most. Burroughs immediately sent this news south to the Massachusetts governor and council.[28]

January 28, 1692 • Thursday
Salem Village

Almanacs predicted wet weather, wind, and cold. The Salem area Lecture was held in the Village meeting house, and afterward the Village men stayed behind for their meeting. They reconfirmed the earlier committee and its demands to Salem town, and clarified that if they were allowed to care for their own poor and for their own roads, they would still pay all county rates along with Salem. The Village men decided to meet March 1 to discuss the results of these negotiations.[29]

January 29, 1692 • Friday
Salem

In the Northfields area of Salem, halfway between the Village and the town, eighty-year-old George Jacobs Sr. dictated his will, for he could neither read nor write. He bequeathed the homestead to his wife Mary for her lifetime, to their son George after her, and then to George's son, also named George. But if either son or grandson died early, it would pass to Jacobs's daughter Ann and her husband John Andrews. Grandchildren would get the moveables, with George Jr.'s daughter Margaret receiving certain household goods from the gun room plus one milk cow. But in spite of age and rheumatism, old Jacobs was very much alive. He was still vigorously in charge. Even though the imperious old man had to stump about with the help of two walking sticks, he could still balance on one and strike the maid servant Sarah Churchill with the other (or so special testimony said).[30]

January 31, 1692 • Sunday
Maine

Almanacs predicted raw weather as the moon waned into its last quarter. Eastward, in the wintry wilderness this Sabbath, the York hostages watched as one of their Indian captors, dressed in the late Rev. Dummer's clothes, parodied a sermon. (Dummer's widow died soon after, her death hastened, the other captives thought, by sorrow).[31]

2

FEBRUARY 1692

*They ... enquired dilligently into the sufferings
of the afflicted ... and feared the hand of Satan
was in them.*

—Rev. John Hale

February 1, 1692 • Monday
Salem Town

The Salem selectmen met to decide, among other matters, the seating order for
the town's meeting house—a touchy problem decided by worldly rank rather
than by church membership. They designated two of the "hindermost" seats on
the men's side for conversion into pews for three prominent citizens (at their
own expense). One, the merchant Philip English, preferred Anglican worship,
but, as one of the "better sort," he rated a pew. Because this was a meeting of
the selectmen only, rather than the town, the Salem Village question remained
unresolved.[1]

February 2, 1692 • Tuesday
Boston

The widowed Mrs. Margaret Thatcher was back when the Suffolk County Court reconvened, this time to charge Bridget Denmark with stealing £5 worth of goods from her: two cups, two cambric handkerchiefs, gloves, and a stone ring. The young woman, a Maine refugee, had been tried in September for drowning a man in the mud and water off a Boston dock one April night. The clerk's record did not preserve a reason for the lethal altercation, but the jury found her guilty only of accidental manslaughter. The magistrates fined her £20 and ordered her back to prison until she paid it, along with court fees and a summer's worth of room and board at the jail. Since she was free to steal in December, perhaps Mrs. Thatcher had bought Bridget's time by paying her bills, which amounted to several years of a hired girl's pay.[2]

Early February
Salem Village

In Salem Village life went on around the ailing girls. Sarah Good—not her apparition—visited the parsonage. Although her own family had known better days, she was now a near vagrant; her present husband was of so little help that she was often reduced to begging. She made givers uneasy, as if they insulted her by offering the charity, yet she seldom hid her disgust if the gift were too little. On this particular occasion, when Rev. Samuel Parris gave something to her child, Sarah went off muttering under her breath. He could not hear exactly what she said, but oddly, his girls were worse after this encounter.[3]

Sarah's father, John Soulart, a well-to-do innkeeper of Wenham referred to in town records as "the Frenchman," had been found dead, "accessory to his own death by drowning himself," when she was eighteen. Her mother remarried, and the children had years of legal difficulty extracting their inheritances from the stepfather's control. Sarah was offered three acres of meadow, less than her fair share, but she still hadn't received it ten years later in 1682 when she and her siblings sued. By then, she had married Daniel Poole, who ran up a tailor bill of £7-18-2—a suit for himself plus two petticoats for his wife—and then promptly died. Funeral expenses included 7 shillings for the coffin, 3 shillings for the grave, and 3 shillings 6 pence for rum. Sarah had to sell everything—a horse, two cows, and all the moveables. By February 1683, she was married to William Good, at which point her stepfather parted with the meadow. He entrusted it not to Sarah, but, as was customary, to her husband. Then the first husband's creditor sued the Goods, who thereby lost part of Sarah's meadow. They sold the rest before summer's end, with Sarah giving up her dower rights to it by "free consent," as the legal term put it.[4]

Apparently William Good found little employment at his trade of weaving or even as a laborer. By 1689, when their daughter Dorcas was about a year old, they had no home of their own. Samuel and Mary Abbey took them in and then turned them out "for quietness sake" due to Sarah's turbulent temper. With smallpox in the area she had no end of trouble trying to find lodging. Even her kinsman Zachariah Herrick refused her shelter. Suspecting she might nest in his barn anyway and accidentally fire the hay with her pipe, he sent his son and grandson to make sure she left the property. (Other relatives were either unwilling or unable to help. For example, by 1691 Sarah's sister Bethia Herrick had been deserted by her husband John, who took her money and left her and their two children at the mercy of Wenham's poor fund. Bethia's sister, Abigail Larkum, took her in, but that didn't work because her brother-in-law Mordecai kept trying to find ways to get his hands on her.)[5]

The Goods found somewhere to stay just south of the Village, but Sarah resorted to begging for her children's sake: four-year-old Dorcas and another girl born in December 1691. Sarah no longer attended meeting, "for want of clothes," as she would say. The two petticoats that helped get her into debt were now ten years old.[6]

February 7, 1692 • Sunday
Boston

The congregation of Boston's North Meeting House, where Cotton Mather presided, contributed over £62 this sacrament Sabbath to help ransom the York captives.[7]

February 8, 1692 • Monday
Boston

As soon as a copy of the new charter arrived, the criticism began. A strong faction wanted the old Charter restored and nothing else. Others were relieved that the militias—their only defense—were not outlawed or that Maine was not amputated from Massachusetts. The new charter reconfirmed land titles and insured liberty of religion, excluding Roman Catholics, as the Crown insisted, but including Quakers and other radical Protestants.[8]

Phips being a New England man helped, although some could not forgive his humble origins. Others feared that future royal appointees would be less sympathetic and grumbled that the new governor was only a "shoeing-horn" for tyranny to come. However, the legislature still retained more power than other similar political bodies in America or Ireland. Eager to promote his father's long labors, Cotton Mather composed several "Political Fables" to circulate in manuscript. He distilled the political arguments after the manner of Aesop, with the actors portrayed as birds, animals, and classical deities. Increase Mather, for one, appeared as an eagle and as the messenger god Mercury.[9]

February 12, 1692 • Friday
Boston

Cotton Mather observed his twenty-ninth birthday by meditating on his life and by beginning a new journal volume. He hoped for a reformation in the churches and for an easing of membership requirements in his own congregation. He had lately written an introduction for a soon-to-be-published sermon on the Last Judgment by Rev. Samuel Lee, who had recently died while captive in a French prison. Like Sir Isaac Newton, Mather speculated that this final divine reckoning might happen soon. (The year 1697 seemed a likely time. Although it was presumptuous to assume one could ever know such a thing, the cryptic book of Revelation listed calamities that would precede the Final Judgment, including the Devil's last great assault, and eventual defeat.) Awakening the churches and preparing the congregations would be all the more important if it did occur, even if not in his lifetime, but the question would be the same faced at one's own death: if you had to account for your life to God *right now*, what would you say?

On a more mundane level, Cotton Mather worried about his precarious health, for he was subject to a reoccurring fever which had been aggravated by serving the large congregation single-handedly in his father's absence. (Increase, meanwhile, worried his son would damage his health from overwork.) "But," Cotton wrote optimistically, "who can tell what *miraculous* things, I may see, before this year be out!"[10]

February 13, 1692 • Saturday
Boston

Cotton Mather wrote to Major John Richards, an influential member of North Church known to resist innovations. "It is time for churches to do some remarkable thing, in the matter of returning unto God," Mather wrote, then asked for approval of a special service for members to renew their commitment to the Covenant. Richards, however, apparently showed no enthusiasm. It would not be the only advice from Mather that he would ignore this year.[11]

February 14, 1692 • Sunday
Salem Village

Almanacs predicted cold rain or snow this Sabbath, a sacrament day in Salem Village, and Parris continued his sermon series on the text: "The Lord said unto my Lord, 'Sit thou at my right hand, until I make thine enemies thy footstool.'"

"It is a woful piece of corruption in an evil time, when the wicked prosper, and the godly party meet with vexations," said Parris (perhaps thinking of the stubborn rates committee). "To cry down divine Providence, as if God had forsaken the earth, and there were no profit in His service, . . . this is an error that in the times of the Churches' adversity the godly themselves are apt to slide into." But such adversity "teacheth us to war a good warfare, to subdue all our spiritual enemies, if we would reign with Christ in His Kingdom." It was Parris's task, as minister, to separate "the precious and the vile" among the applicants for a truly holy church, "to encourage and comfort" those who acted according to God's laws, and "to refute and reject" the others.

Although only those who had reason to believe they were elect should take Communion, the overconscientious must not make excessive dismay or unnecessary self-doubt a stumbling block, said Parris:

> Although . . . the intercession of Christ be made in the Heavens, yet the fruits of it are enjoyed in the Earth even as the body of the Sun placed in the Heavens . . . influenceth us and the earth with its warming beams. Therefor if we would know whither Christ intercedes for us, there is no need to ascend up into Heaven, but to descend into our own hearts, and examine whither we have the benefit of it. We need not climb up into the clouds to see whither the sun shines or no. . . . The Church may meet with storms, but it will never sink. For Christ sits not idle in the Heavens, but takes the most faithful care of his little ship [the Church] bound for the port of Heaven.[12]

February 15, 1692 • Monday
Salem Village

Hannah Putnam, wife of John Putnam the weaver, gave birth to an apparently healthy daughter. As it was customary for neighboring women to help each other at such times, her kinswoman and near neighbor Mrs. Ann Putnam likely visited to help Hannah through the travail of her first birth.[13]

February 16, 1692 • Tuesday
Salem Village

Physician William Griggs Sr. purchased a homestead below Leach's Hill in the Ryal Side section of the Village from farmer Jacob Barney for £71. The plot was wedged into a crossroads except for a two-acre rectangle at the very corner reserved for a future school house. Griggs had earlier lived in Boston, Roxbury, and Rumney Marsh, but now resided in the Village and paid its rates (for at least the past two years). His children were grown, but a son lived in nearby Beverly, and Griggs's niece Elizabeth Hubbard lived with her aunt and uncle.[14]

February 19, 1692 • Friday
Boston

Major Elisha Hutchinson, commander of Boston's regiment, set out in a high wind on a borrowed horse to take command Eastward. Major General Wait Winthrop, William Stoughton, Isaac Addington, and Samuel Sewall (who owned the horse) accompanied him as far as the ferry at the north tip of Boston and watched Hutchinson cross the choppy river's mouth.[15]

Eastward

Alden had already sailed to Sagadahoc with the collected ransom and had redeemed many of the recent captives, but the remaining inhabitants of York were close to abandoning their town. As this reaction was just what King Louis wanted, Massachusetts leaders sent Captains James Converse and Enoch Greenleaf with their men to urge that York stand fast. Hutchinson was ordered to establish a system of communications in the region to prevent, if possible, any more surprise attacks.[16]

February 23, 1692 • Tuesday
London, England

Overseas, Increase Mather and his brother Samuel, a minister in England, visited a certain London gentlewoman who had lately seen her dead son's ghost. Her son, they learned, "had been a very civil young man, but more airy in his temper than was pleasing to his serious Mother." A fortnight after his death, she said, he had appeared to her and said, "Mother, you are solicitous about my spiritual welfare. Trouble your self no more, for I am happy." Then he vanished.

Souls of the dead, the Mathers could have told her, did not usually stroll about visiting relatives before heading for Heaven or Hell. Although the encouraging incident sounded real, the ministers knew such apparitions could well be evil spirits in disguise sent to prey on people's grief. Constant contact between the Visible and Invisible World, as Increase later wrote, "would breed confusion."[17]

Across the cold waters of the Atlantic in New England rain began to fall, just as the almanacs predicted, a week-long soaker driven by an east wind.[18]

February 24, 1692 • Wednesday
Salem Village

For two months the Parris household had applied one home remedy after another to ease Betty and Abigail's bizarre ailments. Books recommended parsnip seeds or asafetida in wine, a draft of soot or blood with heartshorn, spirits of castor with oil of amber. The more exotic prescribed an elixir of dewdrops refined into dust. Nothing the Parrises tried worked. The girls did not improve, but continued to flinch, crouch, and gabble. Abigail's head still hurt, and they both felt dull aches, sharp twinges, and smothering fear. Sometimes the panic was so intense their bodies collapsed as if boneless, or contorted stiffly in seizures while they struggled and gasped, unable to speak.[19]

The Parrises sought the advice of doctor after doctor until one physician—traditionally assumed to have been William Griggs—diagnosed the girls as "under an evil hand." The neighbors, too, concluded Betty and Abigail were bewitched. For the time being, Mr. and Mrs. Parris applied prayer rather than law. But they certainly knew of the Goodwin children, bewitched only a few years before in Boston. The old woman those children accused had not only admitted her guilt but had demonstrated her magical techniques before the court. Yet in Groton the Knapp girl, after accusing a neighbor, proved to be possessed by a lying demon. There was no doubt of that after the demon spoke through the girl's mouth in a stranger's voice to a room full of people.[20]

February 25, 1692 • Thursday
Salem Village

Mr. and Mrs. Parris left home to attend Thursday Lecture in one of the neighboring towns. This gave Parris an opportunity to speak with other area ministers about his girls' condition and to invite them to observe the situation. The outing also allowed John and Tituba, free from Parris's vigilant eye, to prepare a witch-cake while the master and mistress were out. The cake—Tituba's only proven attempt at magic—was intended to be an antidote to *maleficia*—to oppose witchcraft. Acting on instructions from neighbor Mary Sibley, Tituba mixed rye meal with a dash of the sick girls' urine, patted the mess into a small loaf, and baked it in hot ashes. She and John fed it to the dog—presumably the family dog—and awaited results.[21]

Betty and Abigail may have watched this project, well aware of what it was expected to do. If someone sent evil to pain them, part of that person was in the evil that afflicted them, the sufferers. By tormenting the tormented substance—in this case their urine, now safely away from their bodies—it was hoped to injure the essence of the evil-doer still lurking within it. Baking the cake and letting the dog devour it was an attempt to hurt the responsible witch, who might then reveal herself.[22]

But such charms were risky, as Parris and the other ministers had warned, and this one only opened the girls' eyes to the Invisible World. If the cause of their discomforts had seemed abstract before, it was now clear that others expected this countermagic to reveal a specific culprit. Ever since Dr. Griggs's diagnosis, it was no longer a matter of *what* ailed them, but *who*. When Mr. and Mrs. Parris returned home from Lecture, they knew nothing of the experiment but found the girls worse off than ever. Now Betty and Abigail reported seeing the forms of actual people who pinched and hit them, the cause of the girls' pain now clearly manifested to them.[23]

That same day two other girls were afflicted: Ann Putnam, daughter of Thomas and Ann Putnam, and Elizabeth Hubbard, niece of Dr. Griggs. Each lived more than a mile in opposite directions from the parsonage. However, Betty's brother and sister, though living in the same household, were not affected.[24]

February 26, 1692 • Friday
Salem Village

As Betty and Abigail's symptoms flared, the two blamed Tituba for their pain, which had intensified since the woman had made the witch-cake charm. Betty's parents demanded to know the identity of the invisible tormentors, but this only rattled the girls further. They had already overheard whispered speculations from neighbors and from members of their own alarmed household. So now, when the adults suggested names, the girls confirmed some of them as those of their tormentors—names of people none of the adults seemed to respect, people the adults thought likely to wish harm, people it was safe to name.[25]

The girls reported Tituba's form pursuing them about the room when no one else could see it. Even stranger, they knew the real Tituba's whereabouts and what she did when she was well out of their sight. Horrified, Mr. and Mrs. Parris watched as the girls' necks, arms, and backs contorted in ways that seemed not only beyond their own abilities, but beyond the power of epilepsy. At times something seemed to strangle them as they gasped for breath. They were, indeed, as badly afflicted as the Goodwin children.[26]

When several Salem gentlemen and neighboring ministers, as invited, visited the Parris home and observed the girls' suffering firsthand, they—like the physician—concluded that the problems were likely preternatural.* They "feared the hand of Satan was in them," as Rev. Hale of Beverly observed. But they also knew Satan did not always use witches for his dirty work. Rather than

---

*Hale doesn't date this meeting which occurred between Feb. 25 and 29—after the witch-cake and before the arrests. The visitors, not named, likely included Rev. John Hale of Beverly, Rev. Nicholas Noyes, and Capt. Stephen Sewall of Salem.

suggest witch-finding techniques or legal recourse, they advised Parris to pray and to "sit still and wait upon the Providence of God to see what time might discover." They also questioned Tituba, who admitted making the witch-cake, but denied being a witch. The woman who had owned her previously in Barbados, Tituba told them, had been a witch and had taught her methods for discovering and preventing magical harm. But Tituba herself was *not* a witch. She did not mention Goody Sibley.[27]

February 27, 1692 • Saturday
Salem Village

The problem was spreading beyond the Parris household. An unknown apparition had tormented Ann Putnam Jr. since Thursday. Today, between pinches and attempts to make Ann sign a certain book, the specter announced itself as Sarah Good.[28]

After walking clear across the Village from her Uncle Griggs's house on an errand to the family, Elizabeth Hubbard was also bedeviled. On her way home, face into the biting northeast wind, she was certain a wolf stalked her. There were wolves still, though bounties had made them rare. Elizabeth thought Sarah Good had either ordered this creature to pursue and to terrorize her or else had transformed herself into a wolf for the chase. Elizabeth also reported being harassed by the spirit of Sarah Osborn. Goody Osborn, nearly bedridden, lived in the northern part of the Village on her first husband's farm with her considerably younger second husband, who had begun as her bondservant. They seem to have had a son and a daughter, but the sons of her first marriage ought to have inherited the farm when they came of age. Despite their father's will, they somehow never had. Beyond this whispered scandal there were rumors hinting that Sarah's second husband beat her.[29]

February 28, 1692 • Sunday
Salem Village

The wind and rain intensified all through the night and howled over New England throughout the Sabbath. The weather kept old Governor Bradstreet from attending Meeting in Boston, and flooded rivers already full of the melted excess from up-country snows. Westward, the Connecticut River washed away buildings and bridges. Its torrents rampaged over twenty-six feet above normal, drowning cattle and croplands.[30]

In Salem Village, Elizabeth Hubbard's troubles continued, caused, she thought, by Sarah Good. The other girls were no better. It likely occurred to someone, amid the alarming reality of humanly uncontrollable storms and floods, that Satan could control tempests and that witches could whistle up storms.[31]

February 29, 1692 • Monday
Salem Town

All four girls were in such a frightening condition over Sabbath that something clearly had to be done. Ann's father, Thomas Putnam, along with his brother Edward, Joseph Hutchinson, and Thomas Preston (a son-in-law of Francis and Rebecca Nurse) traveled the wet, treacherous roads to Salem town. Once there, they swore out official complaints before magistrates John Hathorne and Jonathan Corwin to charge Sarah Good, Tituba Indian, and Sarah Osborn with "suspicion of witchcraft," whereby there had been "much mischief done Elizabeth Parris, Abigail Williams, Ann Putnam and Elizabeth Hubbard . . . sundry times within this two months and lately also done, at Salem Village contrary to the peace of our Sovereign Lord and Lady William & Mary, King & Queen of England etc." As only one of these four complaints had any of the afflicted in his own household, their accusations represented a neighborhood action against a common danger.[32]

The magistrates issued arrest warrants for Tituba and Sarah Osborn to Constable Joseph Herrick of Ryal Side, and one for Sarah Good to Constable George Locker in charge of the Strong Water Brook area. The constables were to take the three women to Ingersoll's ordinary in Salem Village by ten o'clock the following day for questioning. Besides being a lieutenant in the militia and a deacon in the church, Nathaniel Ingersoll ran a licensed ordinary in his house—a tavern that served meals as well as drinks. As there were few public buildings in rural areas, such places were often used for government purposes. The watch house, moreover, stood just across the road and could be used as a lock-up.[33]

Salem Village

Tituba, still unconfined, spent the day going about her usual duties at the parsonage. But the Devil and his four witches (as she later testified) pestered her while she scrubbed the lean-to chamber. They ordered her to hurt the children again and then come to Boston for further business—or suffer the consequences. Tituba rebelled, declaring that she would not take *their* orders, but would fear God instead. The specters were unimpressed, for Tituba's earlier voluntary compliance bound her to them.

Specters flocked around her at prayer time: the man-devil; Goody Good with a cat at her side and a bird on her hand; the two as-yet-unknown women; and a swarm of familiars. Little yellow birds flew above the family's praying heads, while a yellow dog crouched in the shadows. Red and black cats pawed Tituba rudely mewing, "Serve us." A bird with a woman's head fluttered into sight and turned into Sarah Osborn.

Mr. and Mrs. Parris witnessed none of this otherworldly uproar, but Abigail and Betty saw it all, now that their frightened eyes and impressionable minds were open to the Invisible World.

Tituba tried her best to concentrate on Parris's prayers, but the witches distracted her until she heard nothing but what *they* wanted her to hear. Sarah Good offered her one of the yellow birds.* Tituba thought the pretty creature might help to cheer the children, but then she noticed how it pecked nourishment from a bloody spot between the witch's fingers. Horrified, Tituba refused the "gift."

Tituba's spectral conflict continued as Parris petitioned Heaven, unaware how brutally the man-devil and his witches bullied Tituba, and blind to the imps that crowded his hall. One creature watched from the hearth. It was long-nosed, winged, two-legged, three feet high, and hairy all over. The man-devil tried bribery. Would Tituba like this imp for a familiar? She would not. Would she like the cats? If she pinched the cats, the girls would feel the pain. Tituba refused again and the cats clawed her, trying to suckle. When she pushed them away, they nearly knocked her into the fire. Intimidated and terrified, she pinched them after all and the girls felt pain.

As soon as prayers ended, the impatient witches hauled Tituba to the girls and forced her to pinch them directly, then rushed her from the house into the cold night. Before she knew it, she was perched on a pole in front of Goodwives Good and Osborn. They were all flying through the air, unable to see where they headed.

Soon they landed at Thomas Putnam's house and hurried inside, where neighbors were holding a prayer meeting for Putnam's tormented daughter Ann. Good and Osborn produced a knife and ordered Tituba to kill the girl. Ann herself saw all this and later confirmed it. Her family and neighbors could not perceive the unfolding crisis, but they could see Ann's terrified reactions. Tituba again refused the order, wrestling for control of the knife while the witches threatened to slit Tituba's throat or cut off her head. The blade hovered near Ann's neck, but Tituba continued to struggle and at last the witches fell back. They set off for Boston by themselves, while the man-devil returned Tituba to the parsonage.[34]

In a more mundane interpretation of the events and evidence, Tituba—already pressed by extra chores that accompanied illness in a household—spent part of the day scrubbing the lean-to chamber. Having endured for years the constricted life of a slave, she was now accused of deliberate and injurious witchcraft by some

---

*Yellow was the Devil's color. The spectral yellow birds were perhaps based on stories of yellowhammers, European buntings (*Emberiza citrinella*) not native to New England. Their alarm cry sounds like distant speech or rattling pebbles, their eggs are marked with scribbles associated with magical writing, and they were reputed to drink the Devil's blood each May Day.

of the very children she tended and cared for. She lived under the suspicious eyes of neighbors who believed the accusation, and under the authority of owners who were rapidly reaching the same conclusion. (Months later, after the trials and imprisonment, Tituba would say that Parris beat her to make her confess and to name her sister witches, and that all her confession stories were due to this physical intimidation.)[35]

During the evening Betty and Abigail reported sighting the human-headed bird that had earlier turned into Sarah Osborn. In her own home surrounded by neighbors and family, young Ann Putnam cried out that Tituba and Sarah Osborn were trying to cut off her head with a knife in revenge for refusing to kill herself.[36]

3

MARCH 1692

We must not believe all that these distracted children say.

—Martha Corey

March 1, 1692 • Tuesday
Salem Village

By Tuesday morning when Constable Locker wrote his report, all three suspects were in custody at Ingersoll's ordinary. While Goodwife Hannah Ingersoll examined the three for images, witch marks, and the like (without finding any), Sarah Osborn protested that she was more likely to be a *victim* of witchcraft than a witch, and Tituba nervously held one arm as if trying to hide something. William Good came by later to tell Goody Ingersoll about an odd wart below his wife's right shoulder. He had never noticed it before last night, he said, and wanted to be sure Goody Ingersoll saw it.[1]

After a week of fierce storms, the weather finally cleared, and the wind shifted to the northeast. Many coastal roads were still flooded and impassable, but nothing prevented people from flocking to Salem Village once news of the arrests spread. Even old Giles Corey came to gape, although his wife Martha thought it a pack of nonsense. During their argument she pulled the saddle from his horse, but Giles went anyway. By the time magistrates John Hathorne and Jonathan Corwin rode up from Salem town, there was such a crowd that proceedings were moved from Ingersoll's to the nearby meeting house.[2]

In the ordinary course of things Hathorne and Corwin would have been in Boston representing Salem at the Court of Assistants, but until the new Charter could be put into effect, such higher government matters were suspended. They were in the Village only as local magistrates to handle the preliminary stages of a legal action. (Both men were well-to-do merchants who, like their fathers before them, served many years of public office. Posterity would remember them mainly for their actions during the witch scare.) Today they came prepared to take notes and appointed Ezekiel Cheever to do likewise, for as son and namesake of the Boston schoolmaster, he probably knew shorthand. Selectman Joseph Putnam, Thomas's younger half-brother, also prepared to record the highlights of this unusual event.[3]

Sarah Good, Sarah Osborn, and Tituba were all present in the meeting house for opening remarks and opening prayers, but each was interrogated separately with only one of the accused in the building at a time. (Good said, "You brought in two more," but Hathorne noted that Osborn was not present at Good's exam so suspects were questioned with one in the building at a time. The other two were probably guarded back at Ingersoll's or in the watch house.) The magistrates questioned Sarah Good first, with Hathorne doing nearly all the talking. The four afflicted girls—Betty Parris, Abigail Williams, Ann Putnam, and Elizabeth Hubbard—appeared discomforted from the start. All had experienced seizures that morning before court.[4]

"Sarah Good," asked Hathorne, "what evil spirit have you familiarity with?"[5]

"None."

"Have you made no contract with the Devil?"

"No."

"Why do you hurt these children?"

"I do not hurt them," she said. "I scorn it."

"Who do you employ then to do it?"

"I employ nobody."

"What creature do you employ then?"

"No creature, but I am falsely accused." And as for that visit to Rev. Parris's home, Sarah insisted, "I did not mutter, but I thanked him for what he gave my child." Yet if her muffled remarks had not been a curse against the household, it might have been a conversation with familiars, for Betty and Abigail were hurt shortly after this encounter.

Hathorne ordered the four girls to look at the suspect and make sure of their identification of her as one of their tormentors. All were certain she was, and said she had hurt them for the past two months as well as that very morning. Sarah Good denied being anywhere near their homes at those times. At her denial the girls became, as the magistrates noted, "all dreadfully tortured and tormented." Although they stood some distance from the defendant, the girls said her spirit lunged from her body at them.

"Sarah Good," said Hathorne, "do you not see now what you have done? Why do you not tell us the truth? Why do you thus torment these poor children?"

"I do not torment them."

"Who do you employ then?"

"I employ nobody. I scorn it."

"How came they thus tormented?"

"What do I know? You bring others here and now you charge me with it."

"Why, who was it?"

The girls cried out. Sarah Good watched them writhe for a moment. "I do not know," she said, "but it was some you brought into the meeting house with you."

"We brought you into the meeting house."

"But you brought in two more."

"Who was it then that tormented the children?"

"It was Osborn."

Hearing this, the girls recovered, only to say that Osborn *and* Good were hurting them.

No, she did not attend Meeting but, Sarah Good explained, that was for lack of clothes. The questioning returned to what she was in the habit of muttering when she left people.

"If I must tell, I will tell," she began.

"Do tell us then."

"If I must tell, I will tell. It is the commandments. I may say my commandments I hope," she added sarcastically.

"What commandment is it?"

"If I must tell, I will tell. It is a psalm."

"What psalm?"

After a long pause Sarah mumbled part of a psalm.

"Who do you serve?" Hathorne asked bluntly.

"I serve God."

"What god do you serve?" he countered, for everyone present knew that witches acknowledged Satan as their deity.

"The God that made heaven and earth," she said. She seemed, Cheever noted, oddly unwilling to pronounce the word "God" and retorted "in a very wicked, spiteful manner . . . with base and abusive words and many lies."

Someone—unidentified by the record—recalled that her own husband once said he was afraid she was either a witch or would soon become one. Hathorne asked William Good if he had actually seen her do anything suspicious. No, Will admitted, it was not like that, just her general bad carriage toward him. "And indeed," he added, "I may say with tears, that she is an enemy to all good."

The court was ready to agree with this punning opinion and held Sarah Good for trial.

Sarah Osborn, known to be in poor health, had long been housebound before the constable hurried her away for questioning. The afflicted girls identified her in court and seemed visibly hurt immediately thereafter, even though Osborn was kept a good distance from them.[6]

"What evil spirit have you familiarity with?" Hathorne asked the defendant.

"None." She had never seen the Devil in all her life, she continued in response to the barrage of questions. Nor did she hurt the children or employ any spirit to do so.

"What familiarity have you with Sarah Good?" asked Hathorne, for their specters were often seen together.

"None. I have not seen her these two years."

"Where did you see her then?"

"One day, agoing to town."

"What communications had you with her?"

"I had none," Osborn replied. "Only, 'How do you do,' or so. I did not know her by name."

"What did you call her then?"

She floundered for words and at last said she had called her Sarah. (The impoverished Goods were only William and Sarah to neighbors like Goodman and Goodwife Osborn who, however, knew enough to address the prominent magistrate and his privileged wife as Mister and Mistress Hathorne.)

"Sarah Good saith that it was you that hurt the children," Hathorne challenged.

"I do not know that the Devil goes about in my likeness to do any hurt," she protested. (Osborn was the first, but not the last, to question the reliability of spectral evidence.)

Hathorne ordered that the girls stand to identify her. All four insisted she was one of their tormentors; even her clothing was the same as what the specter wore.

Three people (Cheever did not record who) testified that Sarah Osborn had declared she was more likely to be a victim of witchcraft. When Hathorne questioned her about her remark, she replied that once, frightened in her sleep, she saw—or dreamed she saw—a form like an Indian, all black. It pinched her neck and pulled her by the back of the head toward the house door.

"Did you never see anything else?"

She said no, but others in the meeting house reminded the court about a lying spirit episode.

"What lying spirit is this?" Hathorne asked, knowing that the Devil was called the "Prince of Lies." "Hath the Devil ever deceived you, and been false to you?"

"I do not know the Devil. I never did see him."

"What lying spirit was it then?"

"It was a voice that I thought I heard."

"What did it propound to you?"

"That I should go no more to Meeting, but I said I would, and did go next Sabbath day."

"Were you never tempted further?"

"No."

"Why did you yield thus far to the Devil as never to go to Meeting since?"

"Alas! I have been sick and not able to go." This was an acceptable excuse, if true. She had, in fact, been ill the past year and two months as her husband and others now testified.

Yet there was enough strangeness here for Sarah Osborn to be held for further trial.

Court recessed for the noon meal. The magistrates, marshal, and two constables dined up the road at Ingersoll's on cider, cakes and other victuals while the prisoners mulled the morning's events.[7]

When Constable Joseph Herrick led Tituba into the meeting house that afternoon, the girls writhed and cried as they had when confronted by Sarah Good and Sarah Osborn.[8]

"Tituba," said Hathorne, "what evil spirit have you familiarity with?"

"None."

"Why do you hurt these poor children? What harm have they done unto you?"

"They do no harm to me. I no hurt them at all."

"Why have you done it?" he persisted.

"I have done nothing. I can't tell when the Devil works."

"What? Doth the Devil tell you he hurts them?"

"No, he tells me nothing."

"Do you never see something appear in some shape?"

"No. Never see anything."

"What familiarity have you with the Devil, or what is it you converse withall? Tell the truth," Hathorne badgered. "Who is it that hurts them?"

"The Devil, for aught I know."

"What appearance or how doth he appear when he hurts them? With what shape or what is he like that hurts them?"

"Like a man, I think. Yesterday, I being in the lean-to chamber, I saw a thing like a man that told me: serve him. And I told him no, I would not do such a thing."

Once Tituba ceased to insist on her innocence and ignorance of these matters the court found her answers more acceptable. The tortured girls stilled and listened as she confirmed their fears and accusations. But Tituba found no rest, for answering the questions did not end them.

"Who have you seen?"

"Four women sometimes hurt the children."

"Who were they?"

"Goody Osborn and Sarah Good," plus two unknown women who came up from Boston with a tall man. They hurt the children and threatened to hurt her also if she would not help them. "At first I did agree with them, but afterward I told them, 'I do so no more.'" When Hathorne asked why she hadn't refused earlier, she said, "Why, they tell me I had done so before, and therefore I must go on."

What sort of apparition, Hathorne continued, first persuaded her? "One like a man just as I was going to sleep came to me. This was when the children was first hurt. He said he would kill the children and . . . if I would not serve him he would do so to me." The court asked about other specters, so she told them the spirits appeared "sometimes like a hog, sometimes like a great black dog."

"But what did they say unto you?"

"The black dog said, 'Serve me.' But I said, 'I am afraid.' He said if I did not, he would do worse to me."

"What did you say to it?"

" 'I will serve you no longer.' Then he said he would hurt me. And then he looks like a man and threatens to hurt me."

"What other creatures have you seen?"

Question followed answer as she described the yellow bird, one of the "pretty things" the man offered as bribes, and the aggressive cats "one red, another black as big as a little dog."

"What made you hold your arm when you were searched?" asked Hathorne. "What had you there?" Familiar spirits like those cats often drank nourishment from a witch's wounds or suckled their milk like an infant.

"I had nothing."

"Do not these cats suck you?"

"No, never yet. I would not let them, but they had almost thrust me into the fire."

"How do you hurt those that you pinch? Do you get these cats or other things to do it for you? Tell us, how is it done?"

"The man sends the cats to me and bids me pinch them."

"Did you not pinch Elizabeth Hubbard this morning?"

"I think I went over to Mr. Griggs's and have pinched her this day in the morning. The man brought Mr. Griggs's maid to me and made me pinch her." (A "pinch" was anything from a tweak to the tortures of the rack.)[9]

"Did you ever go with these women?"

"They are very strong and pull me and make me go with them." She had been to Mr. Griggs's only once; maybe the witches sent a spirit disguised to look like her. "They tell me they will hurt me. Last night they tell me I must kill somebody with the knife."

"Who were they that told you so?"

"Sarah Good and Osborn, and they would have had me kill Thomas Putnam's child last night."

Lieutenant Fuller and others verified that Ann Putnam had been tormented at that time. She not only reported those very specters present, but said that they threatened to decapitate her. Ann Putnam added that she *felt* the knife when the witches ordered her to cut her own throat; then they threatened that Tituba would do it if she would not.

"Why did you not tell your master?" Hathorne asked Tituba.

"I was afraid. They said they would cut off my head if I told."

"Who tells you so?" asked Hathorne.

"The man, Good, and Osborn's wife." Sarah Good had appeared the evening before with that bloodthirsty bird of hers and wouldn't let Tituba hear her master's prayers.

"Did you not hurt Mr. Currin's child?" Hathorne asked, but Tituba denied it—Good and Osborn had done that. (Cheever's spelling presumably referred to Mr. Corwin, the magistrate. His only surviving son, George, already lamed at age six by a near fatal kick from a horse, was now just under nine, about the age when he almost drowned. The records say no more about this.)[10]

"Did you never practice witchcraft in your own country?"

"No. Never before now."

"Did you see them do it now?" he asked, meaning: Could she see the specters?

"Yes, today, but that was in the morning."

"But did you see them do it now while you are examining?"

"No, I did not see them, but I saw them hurt at other times." Perhaps they sent familiars, she speculated, for Good had a cat as well as the bird.

"What hath Osborn got to go with her?"

"Something. I don't know what it is. I can't name it. I don't know how it looks. She hath two of them." Prodded by endless questions, she described the imps that had warmed themselves before Parris's hearth the night before, the human-headed bird—Abigail Williams testified that she too had seen this creature—and the hairy thing. But Sarah Good, said Tituba, was responsible for the wolf that chased Elizabeth Hubbard.

"What clothes doth the man appear unto you in?" asked Hathorne.

"Black clothes sometimes, sometimes serge coat [a skirt or petticoat] of other color. A tall man with white hair, I think."

"What apparel does the woman wear?"

"I don't know what color."

"What kind of clothes hath she?" he persisted.

"A black silk hood with a white silk hood under it, with top knots. Which woman I know not, but have seen her in Boston when I lived there."

"What clothes the little woman?"

"A serge coat with a white cap, as I think."

At this point the girls' seizures resumed so the magistrate asked, "Do you see who it is that torments these children now?"

"Yes, it is Goody Good. She hurts them in her own shape," said Tituba. Elizabeth Hubbard contorted alarmingly as the other girls agreed.

"And who is it that hurts them now?" he asked.

"I am blind now," cried Tituba. "I cannot see."

"And after that," Corwin wrote, she "was once or twice taken dumb herself." She was, moreover, as afflicted as the girls. Good and Osborn hurt her, Tituba said at last, and this the magistrates believed.

All three suspects were held for future trials. Sarah Osborn and Tituba were taken to Salem jail, while Sarah Good was assigned to the other Essex County jail at Ipswich. She was, for the time being, confined with her infant under guard at the house of her kinsman, Constable Joseph Herrick, off the Ipswich road. Her four-year-old daughter Dorcas was left in the uncertain care of William Good.[11]

After the court cleared the meeting house, Salem Village's general inhabitants' meeting, already warned for one o'clock, convened belatedly. Turning to more mundane matters, a majority of Village men rejected Salem town's offer to free them from maintaining town roads in return for supporting all their own poor. Consequently, they determined to petition the General Court for complete separation. They chose Captain John Putnam and his son Jonathan to handle that matter and appointed Daniel Andrews to tell Salem town that they refused its latest offer.[12]

Walking home in the dark after the meeting, William Allen and John Hughes heard an odd repetitive noise ahead. Frightened, they pressed on and saw an unidentifiable beast crouched on the ground. They stepped closer. The shape flew apart and become three women who fled so quickly they seemed to vanish. Nevertheless, Allen and Hughes were sure they had glimpsed Good, Osborn, and Tituba.[13]

That same evening, when Elizabeth Hubbard once again felt sharp jabs and wrenching pinches, she reported the shape of a vengeful Sarah Good. Samuel Sibley (whose wife had suggested the witch-cake) was among the sympathetic neighbors gathered in her uncle's house.

"There stands Sarah Good upon the table by you," Elizabeth cried to Sibley, "with all her naked breast, and bare footed, bare legged. Oh, nasty slut. If I had something, I would kill her." Sibley gripped his walking staff and struck the air where the girl pointed. "You have hit her right across the back," said Elizabeth. "You have almost killed her."[14]

Not far away at Constable Herrick's farm, Sarah Good's three guards checked on their prisoner and found her gone, leaving shoes and stockings behind. None of the men wanted to wake the Constable and tell him.[15]

Sarah Good presumably saw a chance to slip away, and took it so quickly—in order to take it at all—that she had no time to collect her shoes and stockings. But, desperate as she was, she found nowhere to flee. Barefoot in a Massachusetts March, hampered by the infant in her arms, Sarah reappeared some time in the night, to the guards' great relief. When told of the escape, Herrick and his wife checked the prisoner and found her arm bloody from wrist to elbow. It had not been so the night before, and seemed all the more sinister when they heard the news of Elizabeth Hubbard's vision.[16]

March 2, 1692 • Wednesday
Ipswich

It was noon before the guard Samuel Braybrook took Good and her baby to Ipswich jail, with Sarah riding a sideways pillion seat behind his saddle. Two routes skirted Wenham Pond to Ipswich, and one passed Sarah's childhood home with all her memories of a more prosperous time, ended by her father's suicide. The ten-mile trip took about three hours, during which Sarah thrice slid from the horse and tried to escape. Three times Braybrook had to catch her and to wrestle her back up on the pillion. She flung herself about, insulting the magistrates. She would not confess to witchcraft, she declared, unless they could prove it. And there was no danger of *that* because the only evidence against her was from a mere Indian (Tituba). Yet, as Braybrook reported (without explaining how), she also tried to kill herself.[17]

Salem Town

Meanwhile, Hathorne and Corwin further questioned Sarah Osborn and Tituba in Salem prison. Osborn still denied the charges, but Tituba added to her confession and told how the spirits had forced her to hurt Betty and Abigail. She described the pin and stick that she was to draw her blood with for the purpose of signing the Devil's book, the nine signature marks already written in it, and how the Devil had threatened decapitation if she confessed in court.[18]

Her talking seemed to anger some invisible being, for as the magistrates watched, Tituba became afflicted again. Once she recovered, she said Good and Osborn were 'tormenting her from spite. So the magistrates had a woman search Tituba, and thus discovered—as Rev. John Hale would describe them—"the marks of the Devil's wounding of her," marks not mentioned when Goody Ingersoll had searched her before the questioning.* The magistrates believed Tituba regretted her association with the Devil and now suffered for her brave confession. The consistency of her story—with itself over days of questioning, and with the statements of others—also impressed them.[19]

Salem Village

William Allen and John Hughes, who had encountered the unknown beast the evening before, continued to see apparitions. A great white dog trailed Hughes home in the dark from Goodman Sibley's at eight o'clock. Later, in a closed room no animal could enter, he saw a light at the foot of his bed, and when he sat up, a big gray cat in the middle of it.[20]

On the same night Allen, in his own bed in his own chamber, saw Sarah Good with an unusual light about her. He managed to kick her when she sat on his foot, whereupon both she and the light vanished.[21]

March 3, 1692 • Thursday
Salem Village

With three suspects under lock and key, the afflicted girls calmed somewhat, but did not immediately recover. Specters of an unknown woman and of Sarah Good's daughter, Dorcas, continued to plague Ann Putnam Jr. Although only four or five years old, Dorcas held the Devil's book and thrust it at Ann to make her sign it. This furious little apparition bit and pinched and choked as viciously as any adult witch.[22]

Salem Town

Meanwhile, various magistrates examined Tituba, Osborn, and Good (presumably all in Salem jail) and each held to her original story. Tituba, however, added that when Deodat Lawson's wife and child had died in Salem Village, that too had been witchcraft.[23]

March 4, 1692 • Friday
Boston

When the Suffolk County Court reconvened in Boston, it straightaway adjourned for another two weeks. The most pressing problems were in Essex County.[24]

---

*Calef later said these wounds were from Parris's beating her to make her confess and accuse, but Goody Ingersoll did not note them before the examination at which Tituba "confessed."

March 5, 1692 • Saturday
Salem Town

The magistrates again transferred Sarah Good from Ipswich to Salem jail, where they questioned her and Tituba. Neither changed her story. The magistrates believed Tituba partly because her answers were so consistent (and invading a parsonage would be such a coup for the Devil). Perhaps most decisive of all, Sarah Good's contradictions and evasions sounded as if she were trying to hide something.[25]

March 6, 1692 • Sunday
Salem

Ann Putnam Jr., still beset, thought she recognized the new tormenting specter as Elizabeth Proctor, third wife of John Proctor. Goody Proctor was a granddaughter of the Lynn healer Goody Burt, who had been tried for—and acquitted of—witchcraft over thirty years earlier. John Proctor was originally from Ipswich, where he still owned considerable inherited land. He lived on a large rented farm in Salem just south of the Village boundary, so he was not part of Village politics or taxed to pay Village rates. He had held a license to sell liquor from his house to travelers since 1666, a task that fell largely to his wives, daughters, and servants. The family was charged in 1678 for allegedly accepting items in pawn for drink and for selling cider to a supposedly drunken Indian. Zerubabel Endicott, "gentleman," had testified, "I observed always good order in the house," and thought ill-will fueled the accusations. But Proctor's eldest son, Benjamin, then eighteen, testified that his father came home at an "unseasonable time" with a wooden bottle of rum and drank to drunkenness. The Proctors' maid Mary Warren, one of the refugees from the frontier war, would soon refer to frequent quarrels between her master and mistress. Elizabeth Hubbard had been to the Proctors' house only the week before, the day Sarah Good's wolf had chased her home.[26]

March 7, 1692 • Monday
London, England

Overseas, Increase Mather and his youngest son Samuel, who had spent the last few years in English schools, left London with Governor Phips for the long trip home.[27]

Cambridge

Back in New England, meanwhile, the eldest Mather son, Cotton, moderated a meeting of the local Congregational ministers at the Harvard College library in

Cambridge.* At Cotton Mather's suggestion, they discussed "the reformation of our provoking evils" as individuals and as churches, "and the recovery of practical religion in our hearts and lives." The recent "most heavy and wasting judgments of heaven upon our distressed land" only emphasized the seriousness of the situation. The ministers unanimously recommended that each congregation take stock of all amiss within it and seek divine help to resolve the problems.[28]

Boston

The judgments included not only the scorched-earth raids by the French and their Indian allies, but also the possible presence of witches. Since witchcraft was a hanging offense, and since all capital cases were ordinarily tried in Boston before the highest court, the three suspects were transferred to Boston jail. The trip from Salem Town's jail took most of a day, southward through Lynn past winter-bleached salt marshes to a ferry where the Mystic and Charles Rivers met the harbor. Beyond lay the peninsula of Boston, so populous it held three Congregational churches, plus Episcopal, Baptist, Huguenot, and Quaker congregations. The wooden town clustered east and north of a steep three-pronged hill topped by an alarm beacon. Some newer buildings were brick, but the prison near the marketplace was stone, unlike the wooden Essex County jails. Here the prison keeper John Arnold took charge of Sarah Good, Sarah Osborn, and Tituba and began to chalk up their bills for room and board.[29†]

The basic fee was two shillings, sixpence a week—about as much as a woman could hope to earn in a week—plus processing fees and fees for shackles. Boston's jail seemed to be an open common room bordered by smaller rooms where some of the prisoners were locked at night (and from which some escaped by removing the window bars). Like the smaller Essex County jails, it was set inside a fenced yard that less dangerous prisoners could exercise in. Wealthy prisoners could even rent a room in the prison keeper's house and attend religious meetings under guard. It is not clear if any of the rooms were underground, although there may have been windowless inner rooms. References to "dungeons" may be metaphorical, synonymous with "close confinement" or "close prison," a term an earlier prisoner used when confined full-time to a room with an exterior window. Even then the jails, intended to hold prisoners only temporarily, were hot in summer and cold in winter, infested with lice, and stank at all times of dung and tobacco. Prisons, as one visiting Englishman said a few years before, were "suburbs of Hell."[30]

---

*This is dated March 6 (Sabbath), but meetings were the first Monday of a month.

†Dates on jail bills usually match mittimus dates even when there wasn't enough time to transport the prisoner on the same day.

March 8, 1692 • Tuesday
Salem Town

Salem's town meeting convened, with Major Bartholomew Gedney serving as moderator, to elect town officers. They chose seven selectmen, including the merchants Philip English and Captain John Higginson Jr. (son of Salem's elder minister), along with Israel Porter and Daniel Andrews of Salem Village. The seven new constables included Sergeant John Putnam Jr. and Jonathan Putnam, both of Salem Village (and both cousins of Thomas Putnam). Then the new selectmen considered a loan for repairs to Salem town's meeting house.[31]

March 9, 1692 • Wednesday
Salem Village

Spring began, according to the Almanacs, as the sun passed into Aries, although the weather, in typical New England fashion, was expected to be cold and blustery.[32]

Vengeful specters still harassed the afflicted girls. Tituba's spirit, because of her confession, was no longer among them, but the shapes of Goodwives Good and Osborn roamed at will. Only two days after their Boston imprisonment began, John Arnold spent fourteen shillings on chains for Good and Osborn—and added the sum to their accounts.[33]

A set of chains, probably fetters on their ankles, could weigh eight pounds. At one point the Boston jail had an inventory of leglocks, handlocks, neck irons, and "bilboes great and small" (iron rods with sliding shackles). Although the three probably had to share the same confined space, Tituba may well have felt some satisfaction at knowing Parris would be billed for her fees and at seeing free-born whites who scorned her in shackles themselves.[34]

March 11, 1692 • Friday
Salem Village

Samuel Parris, meanwhile, had kept two or three private fasts at home, as had the families of the other afflicted girls. (A day's abstinence sharpened the prayer's concentration.) Later, the Village congregation would hold a public fast and several days of public humiliation—an occasion to consider what community shortcomings made them so vulnerable. Neighboring churches did likewise, perhaps in response to the Boston ministers' general suggestions. Today, though, Samuel Parris welcomed John Hale and other local pastors to pray and fast in the privacy of his home.[35]

Betty and Abigail were present, both well-educated, well-behaved girls (as even the most severe contemporary critic of the trials would admit). They were quiet during the sermons and prayers, but acted and spoke oddly when each prayer ended. Abigail convulsed now and again, her limbs twisting rigidly before she could relax them.[36]

Around this time, and perhaps at the encouragement of his fellows, Parris sent his daughter Betty away from the tensions of Salem Village. (She would spend the rest of the year in Salem town at the home of merchant Stephen Sewall, a distant relative. Betty's torments would not immediately stop and she was still numbered among the afflicted in late March, but her name did not appear on any further warrants.*)[37]

March 12, 1692 • Saturday
Salem Village

Ann Putnam Jr. continued to be badly tortured by a specter whom she identified as Martha Corey, a fully communing member of the Village church. By ten o'clock Saturday morning, Ann's uncle, Edward Putnam, and neighbor Ezekiel Cheever, both deacons, decided to inform Goody Corey of this. It was only decent that her fellow church members look into the matter first. But since it was possible that one assumed to be a member of God's elect might be in reality an agent of the Devil, the two men decided to see if the physical Martha Corey was wearing the same clothes as the spectral one.[38]

Martha, Giles Corey's third wife (younger than her husband but not a young woman), seldom hesitated to voice her opinions. She had joined the church in April 1690 and referred to herself as a Gospel Woman ever since. Before that, she had been married to Henry Rich of Salem town and had a son Thomas by him. While married to her first husband Henry, she had also borne a mulatto son, Ben, around 1677 and spent the next decade boarding in Salem with that son, who was now fifteen and old enough to be apprenticed. Surviving records do not explain this episode, but the circumstances had not prevented her joining the Village church, where she presented a son Thomas for baptism. (As the records indicated this was a child, he was probably another Thomas, Giles's son.†)[39]

The deacons set out mid-afternoon and stopped first at Thomas Putnam's house to ask young Ann about the apparition's clothes. But she could not see the Invisible World that day. Ann felt the tormenting specter and heard it say that her sight would not return until evening when the specter would "pay her off" for daring to

---

*When Lawson visited Parris March 19 he saw Abigail, but didn't mention Betty whom he met in Salem the 25th.

†"Thomas, son of sister Kory," was baptized May 4, 1690. Thomas Rich was older than his fifteen-year-old half-brother Ben, so he was too old to be this Thomas. Those over twelve were expected to make the decision to be baptized themselves. It was unusual, but not unheard of for half-siblings to share a name.

identify it. With this information in mind, the men set out for the Corey farm, where they found Martha alone in the house.

"I know what you are come for," she said with a smile as soon as they entered. "You are come to talk with me about being a witch, but I am none. I cannot help people's talking of me."

Edward Putnam replied that they came because one of the afflicted had named her.

"But does she tell you what clothes I have on?" she asked. The men said nothing, so she repeated, "But does she tell you what clothes I have on?"

They thought her oddly eager, but explained that Ann said the specter had blinded her until evening to prevent such a comparison. Yet, Goody Corey, far from being unnerved, merely shrugged it off with a smile. When the deacons added that the complaint was a reflection against the rest of the church as well, Martha showed no concern for that but only for the talk against herself. She had no sympathy for the three arrested suspects and said the Devil probably needed little effort to make witches of such "idle slothful persons" who "minded nothing that was good." But she herself had professed Christ and rejoiced to hear the Word of God.

Putnam and Cheever reminded her that outward profession was never a guarantee of actual election, for witches had crept into other congregations before this outbreak. Martha lectured the men at length on how the Devil had come among them in a great rage, and God had forsaken the earth. (Her opinion had evidently changed since her verdict of nonsense back on March 1 when she had tussled with her husband over the saddle.)[40]

The two deacons returned by way of Thomas Putnam's, where Ann, as foretold, had been well all afternoon. But once they left for their own homes, the spectral Martha Corey, back as promised, badly tormented her.

***

Salem

Martha Corey's specter was the first to afflict Mary Warren, the twenty-year-old servant to John and Elizabeth Proctor. (With a shortage of young men, it was no longer unusual for women of her age and generation to be unmarried. However, if she didn't find a husband she faced years of domestic service and no home of her own.) Sitting in a daze, Mary reached toward what at first appeared to be the form of Goody Corey. But when she pulled the insubstantial form to her lap, it looked like her master whom she had not noticed before.

"It is nobody," said the real Proctor from across the room, "but it is my shadow that you see." Yet, she could not see him there, only the specter sitting on her lap. "I see there is no heed to any of your talkings," he said, "for you are all possessed with the Devil, for it is nothing but my shape."[41] (The real Goody Corey apparently confronted Mary Warren at Proctor's house around this time, but Mary's later account of it would be mostly hazy hindsight.)[42]

Proctor applied his own cure: he kept her busy at the spinning wheel and threatened to beat her if she had any more fits. And it seemed to work, for she remained well until he had to be away for a day and Mary, without his authoritative presence, relapsed into fits and torments.[43]

March 13, 1692 • Sunday
Salem Village

Prowling specters again interrupted Salem Village's Sabbath. Middle-aged Bethshua Pope went terrifyingly, though temporarily, blind. Although this happened in the Village meeting house, Mrs. Pope was a member by birth and by marriage of two prosperous Quaker families. Neighbors of the Coreys, she and her husband Joseph and their surviving children shared the Pope farm with his widowed mother Gertrude.[44]

At home, young Ann Putnam identified another of her spectral tormentors. Staring into the Invisible World, Ann discerned the apparition of a pale woman seated in her grandmother's chair. She did not know the specter's name, but described its intangible form to the others in the room. She thought she remembered where the woman sat in the meeting house. This information, however uncertain and vague, inspired her mother, Ann Sr., and the maid Mercy Lewis to suggest names in the hope of jogging the girl's memory. She at last agreed to one of them: Rebecca Nurse, a member of the Salem town church who usually attended the nearer Village Meetings.[45]

March 14, 1692 • Monday
Andover

Sabbaths in Andover, a more peaceful and prosperous community than Salem Village, were also plagued of late by restless and disobedient young people—though not by specters—during, after, and between services. Once today's town meeting elected town officers, the new selectmen ordered that the tithing man and constables prevent such interruptions in the future.[46]

Salem Village

In Salem Village, invisible forces caused Abigail Williams to twist and convulse. She said they were the specters of Martha Corey and Elizabeth Proctor.[47]

But the Putnams perhaps doubted the accuracy of young Ann's visions, at least when it came to church members, for Thomas Putnam invited Martha Corey to meet his daughter face to face. No sooner did Martha set foot in the house, however, than Ann crumpled, her feet, head, and hands horribly contorted as she choked and writhed before the eyes of her parents and uncle Edward. She wailed to Goody Corey that *she* was the cause, and immediately her tongue thrust out and her teeth bit down as if in punishment. Once she could speak, she said to Martha, "There is a yellow bird a sucking between your fore finger and middle finger. I see it."

Martha Corey rubbed her hand where Ann pointed, but then the girl could no longer see the bird and collapsed when she tried to approach. It was Goody Corey's spirit who had covered Mrs. Pope's eyes last Sabbath at Meeting, Ann explained. She imitated the specter's gesture only to find her own hands fastened over her eyes; no matter how hard she or any helpful bystander pulled, it was to no avail. When her hands finally came free, Ann saw into the Invisible World, where a man, skewered on a spit, roasted in her parents' hearth. "Goody Corey," she cried, "you be a turning of it."

The maid, Mercy Lewis (a refugee from the wars in Maine where everyone had heard of Indians burning captives to death), snatched a stick and struck at the spot where Ann indicated. The terrifying vision disappeared from Ann's sight, but only temporarily. The roasting man blinked back into Ann's view and Mercy swung again.

"Do not if you love yourself," Ann warned, but it was too late. Mercy shrieked as Goody Corey's specter (according to Ann) struck the maid with an iron rod. Now both girls felt torturous pain and begged Martha Corey to leave.

Mercy discerned shadowy, unidentifiable forms of women in the room. "I won't, I won't," she shouted. "They would have me to write." She fell, violently twisting and convulsing. As could be expected, this ended Goody Corey's visit, but now Mercy was afflicted with fits so severe that two or three men were needed to restrain her.

Late that evening at nearly eleven o'clock, while she rested in a chair facing the hearth, the chair—with Mercy in it—began inching toward the fire. Two men grabbed the chair to stop its forward motion but it only dragged them along too. Edward Putnam positioned himself between the hearth and the girl's feet, and lifted. Thus, among the three of them, they were only just able to keep her from being cast into the fire feet foremost.[48]

***

Salem

During this week Martha Corey's husband Giles found one of his oxen unable to rise, dragging "his hinder parts as if he had been hipshot," though the beast had just walked from the woods moments before. Later, the ox simply stood up as if nothing were wrong. Then his cat was "strangely taken on the sudden" as if dying, and Martha recommended knocking the animal on the head. Giles refused and the cat recovered as mysteriously as the ox. Martha commonly went to bed later than her husband, who—well aware of the gossip—watched her kneel, wordlessly, at the hearth as if praying.[49]

Giles himself had been in and out of trouble for years. He had stolen various items (including dry goods from Justice Corwin's father) and had possibly beaten a half-witted handyman to death. He was generally "a very quarrelsome and contentious bad neighbor," as Robert Moulton phrased it. Twelve bushels of apples were stolen from Moulton after one clash with Corey, and his saw-mill stopped working after another. Moulton apparently suspected ordinary sabotage, but in 1679 Mary Gloyd claimed invisible horses had chased her from Corey's milk yard. That was back when John Proctor accused Corey of setting the Proctor house on fire. The two sued each other until it was proven that Corey had not left his bed all that night, and one of Proctor's sons confessed to carelessness with a lamp. Despite all this, Giles was admitted to communion with the Salem town church in 1691 at age eighty, which meant he was able to convince the congregation that he had experienced God's saving grace.[50]

March 15, 1692 • Tuesday
Salem Village

While almanacs predicted typically dour March weather, Elizabeth Hubbard reported seeing the specter of Martha Corey, and Abigail Williams identified Rebecca Nurse among her tormentors. (The afflicted were highly suggestible—to each other's motions and to other people's theories, gossip, and fears—but how much contact there was among them outside the courtroom is not clear. Some unidentified "afflicted persons" were at Ingersoll's at other times, and some afflicted witnesses stayed overnight in the Village after a suspect was questioned. The younger girls were probably kept home, and it seems unlikely the grown women would have socialized with the hired girls.) The real Rebecca Nurse, elderly and unwell—possibly pale from illness like her alleged specter—kept close to her hearth these days.[51]

***

Ipswich

Elsewhere, as news of the witchcraft cases spread, folk wondered about suspicious characters in their own towns. About nine o'clock one night in Ipswich, where Sarah Good had spent three nights in jail, James Fuller Jr. told Goodman Perry how his sister Mary Fuller and Margery Thorn had both been "taken" by fits. At this point, Rachel Clenton entered the house. She was an impoverished local woman in much the same situation as Sarah Good, except Rachel had no children and no husband either since the divorce, only an unproven reputation for witch-craft. When Fuller asked her why she came, she snapped that it was to hear what lies he told about her, and sat down, uninvited.

But when Fuller's nephew rushed in shouting that his sister Betty was dead, Rachel ran out. Fuller dashed after but saw no sign of her even in the bright moonlight. Fuller's niece proved to be in a "dead" faint, but it took three or four hours for her to regain consciousness. When at last she could speak, she told her family how she had spotted something in a corner of the stoop so terrifying that she had turned and run, but not fast enough, for the thing had followed and knocked her down.*[52]

March 17, 1692 • Thursday
Boston

Boston prison keeper John Arnold petitioned the Suffolk County Court for £10 overdue him on his 1690 salary, which was granted—on paper at least.[53]

March 18, 1692 • Friday
Salem Village

Mrs. Ann Putnam Sr. had tended to her seizure-racked daughter for the past month and now had to deal with the maid's fits also. Ann Sr. still had to cook three meals a day and care for the five other children and her husband. Moreover, she had re-alized she was once again with child. By mid-afternoon she had to lie down, but instead of resting, she viewed the Invisible World, and for the next two hours fought off the specter of Rebecca Nurse.[54]

So now even grown women fell prey. Besides Mrs. Putnam the afflicted adults included the somewhat older Mrs. Bethshua Pope who had suffered hysterical blindness on March 13 and who was also in the early stages of yet another preg-nancy; Sarah Bibber who worked as hired help with her husband; and "an ancient woman named Goodall" (probably widow Margaret Goodale, stepmother of the man Giles Corey beat to death).[55]

March 19, 1692 • Saturday
Salem Village

Again and again the specters of Martha Corey and Rebecca Nurse attacked Mrs. Ann Putnam to punish her for refusing to join them. Only God's help, Mrs. Putnam was sure, let her survive this day at all.[56]

---

*Nearly a year later, Mary Fuller said that this happened March 23 or 24, while James Fuller said it happened March 15. James recalled a moonlit night. The moon was full March 22, and in its first quarter March 15.

Goody Corey's specter was so busy and pernicious that Edward Putnam and Henry Kenney made official complaints against her before John Hathorne and Jonathan Corwin in Salem for afflicting Ann Putnam Sr., Ann Putnam Jr., Kenney's kinswoman* Mercy Lewis, Abigail Williams, and Elizabeth Hubbard. The magistrates ordered Essex County Sheriff George Herrick to bring the suspect to Ingersoll's for examination on Monday at noon.[57]

Meanwhile, Rev. Deodat Lawson of Boston (once of Salem Village) had learned from Village friends about Tituba's statement that his first wife and child had died of evil magic.† Discussing this matter with "some concerned in the court," it was mutually decided that Lawson should be present to hear for himself. He traveled to Salem Village on the 19th. No sooner had he settled at Ingersoll's than Captain Jonathan Walcott's daughter Mary arrived to speak with him. After she delivered the message but still lingered by the door, she suddenly exclaimed she had been bitten on the wrist. Lawson and Ingersoll examined her wrist by candle light—it was late and the almanac had predicted a cloudy day—and saw what looked like upper and lower teeth-marks.[58]

Sabbath began at sundown, about quarter to seven, but as visiting the sick was an act of kindness and the parsonage no distance away, Lawson paid a call on Rev. Samuel Parris "in the beginning of the evening." During his visit Parris's niece Abigail Williams had a spell of running back and forth in the room. She stretched her arms high overhead, flapped them as if flying, and called, "Whish, whish, whish!" as she ran. Abruptly, she stopped short and stared into the empty air at the specter of Goody Nurse. "Do you not see her? Why there she stands!" But no one else but Abigail could see her or the book that the specter pushed at her. "I won't, I won't, I won't take it!" she shouted. "I do not know what book it is. I am sure it is none of God's book. It is the Devil's book for aught I know." She charged into the fireplace, threw burning sticks into the room, and ran against the hearth back as if, Lawson thought, she meant to run up the chimney. It was not the first time, the Parrises told Lawson, once things calmed.[59]

Across the Village the Coreys sat by their own fire. Giles was at least half-inclined to believe the rumors about his wife. For one thing, they had already quarreled about how he prayed. It was for him to offer family prayers, but Martha chimed right in to criticize his phrasing. Giles had already declared in public that he knew things about his wife that would fix her business. Now she suggested they go to bed, but Giles said that he would pray first. Yet when he tried, he was unable to even open his mouth, much less put two words together. "My wife did perceive it and came towards me and said she was coming to me," Corey would testify. "After this, in a little space" he was able to pray again.[60]

---

*Probably Henry Kenney Sr. made the complaint. Henry Kenney Jr. was married to Priscilla, Mercy Lewis's sister.

†Cause of the deaths was reported by a confessor and only Tituba had confessed so far.

March 20, 1692 • Sunday
Salem Village

Reverend Deodat Lawson was the guest preacher in Salem Village this Sabbath. He delivered the opening prayer amid the confusion of "several sore fits," for many of the afflicted *and* Martha Corey were present.* The congregation sang a psalm in better order, but when Lawson was about to read his sermon's introductory text, Abigail Williams interrupted. "Now stand up," she ordered, "and name your text." After he read it, Abigail observed, "It is a long text." No sooner had he begun the sermon (unfortunately neither text nor sermon has survived) than Mrs. Pope snapped, "Now there is enough of that." But Lawson managed to deliver it with only a few muffled comments. People sitting near the afflicted hushed most of their remarks, and they were able to cure each other's strangled tortures by a touch of the hand. Abigail pointed out Martha Corey's spirit, slyly leaving her body on the bench as if all were normal, perched on a beam above the congregation with her yellow bird. She saw the bird fly boldly to the pulpit and land on Lawson's hat, where it hung on a peg, but neighbors squelched her additional comments. There was more chattering during the afternoon service, and the day remained tense while the real Martha Corey, displaying considerable fortitude, brazened it out in the face of her neighbors' suspicions.[61]

Before she left for home, Goody Corey let it be known that *she* could clear up the matter of her accusation. *She* could open the eyes of the ministers and magistrates to the truth because neither mischievous girls nor the Devil himself could stand victoriously before a Gospel Woman like herself. It would be unpardonable, she said, for a Gospel Woman to do such things.[62]

But the specter in her shape tormented Abigail Williams and Elizabeth Hubbard. Rebecca Nurse's shape also persecuted Abigail, but did not touch the Hubbard or Walcott girls who could, however, see it. Mrs. Putnam also suffered now and again, but as it was the Sabbath, she at least felt greater ease between fits than on other days. Leafing through Scripture seemed to help.[63]

March 21, 1692 • Monday
Salem Village

Constable Joseph Herrick, under orders from Marshal George Herrick,[†] had Martha Corey in custody at Ingersoll's by Monday morning. Whenever the Constable had arrived at the Corey house—on Sunday evening as soon as Sabbath ended or first

---

*According to Lawson they were Mrs. Pope, Goody Bibber, Abigail Williams, Mary Walcott, Mercy Lewis, and Elizabeth Hubbard.

†Joseph Herrick was born in Salem while George moved to Salem around 1686.

thing Monday—Martha had a pot of ointment by her. While any prudent house-wife could brew a number of useful salves, witches, as everyone knew, could mix a greater and more pernicious variety. When she was questioned about it, Giles spoke up to say that she had made it according to instructions from Major Bartholomew Gedney, a respectable Salem merchant, physician, and town official.[64]

Planting season or not, a second witchcraft examination (when the first had proved so exciting) was too much for most folk to miss. Once again the proceed-ings moved to the meeting house, which had already been packed with spectators before noon (when John Hathorne and Jonathan Corwin arrived, taken away from their business concerns by these unusual events). By now ten people were af-flicted (out of a population of 525 to 550) and most of them were likely present (except for Betty Parris and the "ancient" Goody Goodale). The magistrates ap-pointed Samuel Parris to take notes, and Rev. Nicholas Noyes opened with a top-ical prayer that Deodat Lawson thought moving. The afflicted fell writhing, and Hathorne demanded that the defendant explain herself.[65]

"Pray give me leave to go to prayer," said Martha Corey. The court tried to ig-nore this, but she persisted in her request. Her boldness amazed the audience, for women—except for scolds and such radicals as proselytizing Quakers—did not make public statements. Even when women joined a church a man read aloud their statements of faith.

"We do not send for you to go to prayer," Hathorne replied, "but tell me why you hurt these."

"I am an innocent person. I never had to do with witchcraft since I was born. I am a Gospel Woman."

"Do not you see these complain of you?" he asked, indicating the afflicted.

"The Lord open the eyes of the magistrates and ministers," Martha said, getting in her prayer anyway. "The Lord show His power to discover the guilty."

She continued to deny any guilt and insisted that a Gospel Woman like herself could not possibly be involved with witchcraft. But her apparent foreknowledge of Ezekiel Cheever and Edward Putnam's intention to check her attire now loomed against her. Cheever interrupted the proceedings to snap that she oughtn't begin with a lie. She knew, Martha answered, because the men said that her clothes had been mentioned. "You speak falsely," said Cheever, for young Ann was "blinded" that day. Well, Martha amended, her husband had said the children identified specters by their clothes. But Giles denied this.[66]

Hathorne impatiently reminded her that she was under oath. "How come you to the knowledge?"

"I did but ask."

"You dare thus to lie in all this assembly? You are now before authority. I ex-pect the truth. You promised it. Speak now and tell who told you what clothes."

"Nobody."

He kept on and on with the same question until she said, in effect, that she had guessed the reason. "But you said you knew so," he reminded her. The afflicted became even more agitated, and shouted that the Devil was whispering in Goody Corey's ear.

"What did he say to you?" asked Hathorne.

"We must not believe all that these distracted children say," Martha protested.

But Hathorne ignored this. "Cannot you tell what that man whispered?"

"I saw nobody."

"But did not you hear?"

"No."

The afflicted could hear, and could also see the trussed and impaled apparition of someone roasting over a spectral fire next to the defendant. They themselves felt bit, jabbed, and strangled—and cried out that Corey did it.

Hathorne repetitiously urged her to confess and not to continue in so obvious a lie. "If you would expect mercy of God," he emphasized, "you must look for it in God's way, by confession." (But this would help only Martha's soul, which was beyond the court's jurisdiction.)

It was indeed wrong to lie, she said, and added, "We must not believe distracted persons."

Hathorne was in no mood to have Goody Corey advise him, and returned the questioning to another sore point. "Did you not say our eyes were blinded; you would open them?"

"Yes, to accuse the innocent," she explained. That was blindness indeed.

Henry Crosby, her stepson-in-law, testified how she had earlier said that neither the girls nor the Devil could stand before *her* and that *she* would open the eyes of the ministers and magistrates to the truth. But since the afflicted were literally unable to keep on their feet in her presence, Martha's expression had a sinister ring to the assembled. "They cannot stand before others," she protested.

But the questions continued relentlessly. "What did you mean by that—the Devil could not stand before you?" She denied saying this but three or four people testified that she had—"sober witnesses," Parris noted, not the afflicted.

"What can I do?" cried Martha. "Many rise up against me."

"Why, confess," said Hathorne.

"So I would, if I were guilty."

"Here are sober persons. What do you say to them? You are a Gospel Woman," he added sarcastically. "Will you lie?"

"Next Sabbath is sacrament day," shouted Abigail Williams, "but she shall not come there."

"I do not care," Martha snapped.

"You charge these children with distraction. It is a note of distraction when persons vary in a minute, but these fix upon you. This is not the manner of distraction."

"When all are against me, what can I help it?"

"Now tell me the truth, will you? Why did you say that the magistrates' and ministers' eyes were blinded, you would open them?"

She laughed and denied it despite the earlier testimony. Her answers became more confused. Nevertheless she still insisted on her innocence, and said she never harmed the girls in person, in specter, or by proxy with familiars. She denied the existence of the yellow bird familiar and again insisted she was a Gospel Woman. Ah, the afflicted cried, she was a Gospel Witch!

Ann Putnam Jr. added that when neighbors came to pray for her, she saw the shapes of Goody Corey and maybe Goody Nurse also praying—but to the Devil. Martha again protested that the girls were distracted, and Hathorne and Noyes both pointed out that everyone else there believed the girls bewitched.

The magistrates suggested that perhaps she had promised *not* to confess. Her reluctance for Giles to attend the first examinations and their tussle over the saddle now seemed as if she were trying to protect someone. A voice called out from the audience that she didn't want the witches to be discovered. When Goody Corey laughed again, it was taken as a cruel mockery of the afflicted.

"Do not you believe there are witches in the country?"

"I do not know that there is any."

"Do not you know that Tituba confessed it?"

"I did not hear her speak."

"I find you will own nothing without several witnesses," said the magistrate, "and yet you will deny for all."

He ordered her to stop biting her lip, for the afflicted were now suggestible to her every move, Elizabeth Hubbard and Mercy Lewis especially. "What harm is there in it?" she asked. But if she clenched her hands, her alleged victims felt it—and showed the bruises. If she slumped forward against the seat that served as a bar, they felt pain from that, too. Mrs. Bethshua Pope felt as if her bowels were being torn and threw her muff at Martha Corey to make her stop. But the soft muff fell short of its mark, so Mrs. Pope pulled off her shoe and lobbed it against the defendant's head. By now, if Martha merely shifted her feet, the afflicted stamped thunderously like helpless puppets.[67]

"I believe it is apparent she practeseth witchcraft in the congregation," observed Rev. Noyes. "There is no need of images."

The afflicted said Goody Corey had covenanted with the Devil for ten years of service and only four remained. They saw the yellow bird suckle at her fingers and witnessed the Devil whispering into her ear. They insisted that she brought them a book and pestered them to sign it.

"What book?" she huffed. "Where should I have a book? I showed them none, nor have none, nor brought none."

But the afflicted heard a drum beating assembly and knew the local witches were mustering right outside the meeting house.

A neighbor Needham testified how another stepson-in-law, John Parker, had thought Goody Corey a witch long before.

"Who is your god?" asked Hathorne bluntly, knowing as well as anyone that witches worshipped Satan.

"The God that made me," she countered.

Hathorne continued with this line of questioning, but her answers were such that they could be taken either way. When she did say "Jehovah" and "God Almighty," Hathorne asked, "Doth *he* tell you?" (for the Devil was a known liar). Her responses to common catechism questions—which a self-styled Gospel Woman ought to have known cold—were somewhat odd, Lawson thought, yet proved nothing.

More influential were the pinches and twinges that the afflicted felt whenever Martha Corey moved her hands. The court ordered that the defendant's hands be held, and immediately the alleged torment ceased.

"Do not you see these children and women are rational and sober as their neighbors when your hands are fastened?" Hathorne inquired. As he spoke, the afflicted convulsed again and, sure enough, Goody Corey was squeezing her fingers, even though her hands were being held.

"She hath bit her lip," the marshal reported, and the afflicted erupted again.

The magistrate ignored her denials. "Why did you say, if you were a witch you should have no pardon?"

"Because I am a Gospel Woman!"* Martha Corey protested.

But the magistrates had heard and seen enough and consigned her to Salem jail, which at least prevented her specter from badgering the afflicted for the rest of the day. Although Mrs. Ann Putnam suffered fewer seizures today, she felt as if her strength were nearly gone, and elsewhere little Dorcas Good's irate specter went for Mary Walcott's throat.[68]

The magistrates, Marshal George Herrick, and their horses restored themselves at Ingersoll's for a total bill of four shillings sixpence, and returned to Salem with their prisoner.[69]

March 22, 1692 • Tuesday
Salem Village

As soon as daylight appeared this day of the full moon, the Rebecca Nurse specter, clad as if for bed in shift† and nightcap, lit into Mrs. Ann Putnam, threatening hor-

---

*The original has a blank where "Gospel" is assumed to go.

†A woman's long loose shift served as an undergarment by day and as a nightgown by night.

rors if she refused to sign the apparition's little red book. Mrs. Putnam quoted scripture to fortify her resistance. Neither God nor Jesus Christ, sneered the apparition, could save her soul, which she, Nurse, would rip from Mrs. Putnam's body. The battle raged two hours before the specter retreated.[70]

Salem Town

The almanacs predicted wet snow or rain for the Village representatives to plod through to attend Salem's general town meeting. Salem, without cutting the Village loose entirely as petitioned, reiterated the Villagers' exemption from supporting the town's ministers, since the Village already supported its own (Rev. Parris may have found irony in this) as long as it continued to pay for other expenses common with Salem. Since the Villagers complained about helping pay to repair the town's meeting house, they were released from this obligation in exchange for assuming all costs of Village road repairs.[71]

***

Salem Village

Some time around this date another committee visited a second church member whose specter was allegedly tormenting folk—Rebecca Nurse, a Salem town church member who usually attended the nearer Village Meetings. Israel and Elizabeth Porter "being desired to go," as they later worded it, visited the home of Francis and Rebecca Nurse to speak with her. Also present were Daniel Andrews (Porter's brother-in-law) and Peter Cloyse (Rebecca's brother-in-law). The proper way to deal with scandalous rumors against a member was for the offended party to speak with the suspect party (as had been attempted with Ann Putnam Jr. and Martha Corey). If that didn't work, the offended party was to try again with two witnesses. Despite the witnesses, and despite the fact that Elizabeth was John Hathorne's sister, the Porters seem to have come more as friends of the suspect.[72]

Seventy years old and hard of hearing, Rebecca Nurse had been frail for years and ill for nearly a week. Despite her illness, she told her visitors, she had experienced a good deal of spiritual comfort during her convalescence. Then, without prompting, she mentioned the terrible afflictions in the Village, especially those in Rev. Parris's house. She prayed for the girls, but did not visit them, she explained, because she too had once been subject to fits. Since her son-in-law, Thomas Preston, had been among those who swore out the first complaint against Tituba, Osborn, and Good, she would have been well informed of the troubles. However, she was still unaware of rumors that had her recuperating from wounds received when the afflicted and others had struck her specter. Rebecca Nurse was certain that many of those now denounced were as innocent as herself.[73]

The Porters mentioned that some did accuse her.

She sat there amazed, the Porters noticed, quite unlike Martha Corey, who had seemed to know all ahead of time. "Well," Goody Nurse finally said, "as to this thing, I am as innocent as the child unborn; but surely, what sin hath God found out in me unrepented of, that he should lay such an affliction upon me in my old age?"

March 23, 1692 • Wednesday
Salem Village

While the real Rebecca Nurse prayed for her suffering neighbors, specters in her and Goody Corey's guise plagued Mrs. Ann Putnam. When Deodat Lawson visited the Putnam home, he found her resting on the bed recovering from a seizure under the care of family and friends. Both she and her husband asked that he pray with them—although, she said, the specters threatened to prevent him as they had prevented her earlier.[74]

Nevertheless, Lawson prayed without interruption. It was only afterward that Thomas Putnam noticed his wife seemed to be asleep. He found that she was also stiff as a plank when he tried to sit her on his lap. But once she finally relaxed enough to sit, she jerked into motion. Eyes tightly shut, she flailed her arms and legs and argued with the spectral Rebecca Nurse.

"Goodwife Nurse, be gone! Be gone! Be gone! Are you not ashamed?" How could a woman who professed to be elect afflict her so? "What hurt did I ever do you in my life?" Nurse had only two years to live before the Devil collected her soul, "for this your name is blotted out of God's book, and it shall never be put in God's book again!" Mrs. Putnam continued to argue, using symbolism from Revelation to declare that her own soul was "clothed with the white robes of Christ's righteousness" and out of the specter's reach.

Lawson jotted notes while the quarrel continued about a scriptural passage that Mrs. Putnam was prevented from naming, which the specter said didn't exist. "I am sure you cannot stand before that text," Mrs. Putnam answered, but her mouth wrenched to one side and her body strained as she tried to say it. "I will tell, I will tell," she gasped. "It is, it is, it is!" Her struggle increased until she blurted, "It is the third chapter of the Revelations!"

Lawson had mixed feelings about reading the passage since it was almost being used as a charm against the specter—as Cunning Folk might do it. However, he decided to try this once and before he reached the end, Mrs. Putnam's eyes opened. She relaxed as he read the part that referred to the specter's spiritual state. "'I know your works. You have the name of being alive and you are dead.'"

The other Putnams told Lawson of various passages in which she had found relief before, such as, "Comfort, comfort my people, say your God." Some she took as reassurance of her own election, while verses of opposite meaning she applied to Goody Nurse's damnation. (Mrs. Putnam still mourned the deaths of some of her and her sisters' children—infant mortality was sadly common—while all eight of Rebecca's children had survived to raise families of their own, which was unusual. But what real life disputes the two women actually had are not recorded.)[75]

Elsewhere, the forms of Rebecca Nurse and Martha Corey tormented Abigail Williams, while Elizabeth Hubbard only glimpsed Nurse's specter but was not harmed by it.[76]

Salem Town

Consequently, Edward and Jonathan Putnam appeared in Salem before the magistrates John Hathorne and Jonathan Corwin to enter complaints against Rebecca Nurse for tormenting Mrs. Ann Putnam Sr., Ann Putnam Jr., Abigail Williams, "and others" and against Dorcas Good, Sarah's four-year-old daughter. The magistrates issued arrest warrants to Marshal George Herrick ordering that he have the two at Ingersoll's by eight o'clock the next morning.[77]

At Sea

Meanwhile, escorted by a sloop and a brigantine to guard against privateers, Captains John Alden and James Converse sailed from Boston for Saint John, Canada. They carried ransom money and French soldiers taken at Port Royal to trade for Colonel Edward Tyng, Alden's son, and the other captives. However, not all of the French soldiers were being returned, for some (probably Protestant) had married and settled in New England. (But the French demanded them all, so Tyng and young Alden would not be released, but instead sent to Quebec.)[78]

March 24, 1692 • Thursday
Salem Village

The afflicted continued to be tormented and Mrs. Ann Putnam convulsed even before court convened. Marshal George Herrick brought Rebecca Nurse to Ingersoll's by eight o'clock and ordered Samuel Braybrook to fetch Dorcas Good. Rev. Deodat Lawson saw her at Ingersoll's, where she seemed an ordinary little girl, as "hale and well as other children."[79]

Lawson was among the onlookers packing the meeting house when the marshal led Rebecca Nurse in to stand before John Hathorne and Jonathan Corwin. Rev. John Hale spoke the opening prayer, and Rev. Samuel Parris prepared to take notes of the proceedings. The afflicted were agitated from the start. Although Goody Nurse insisted on her innocence, she lacked Martha Corey's abrasive cockiness and Hathorne seemed a little more inclined to believe her.[80]

"Goody Nurse," Hathorne said, indicating the afflicted, "here are two—Ann Putnam the child and Abigail Williams—complain of your hurting them. What do you say to it?"

"I can say before my Eternal Father I am innocent, and God will clear my innocency."

"Here is never a one in the assembly but desires it, but if you be guilty pray God discover you."

Henry Kenney, a Village farmer and kinsman of Mercy Lewis, testified of an encounter with the defendant that had left him twice subject to "an amazed condition." Mrs. Putnam's symptoms, however, were far more severe and serious.[81]

"Here are not only these," said Hathorne, indicating the girls, "but here is the wife of Mr. Thomas Putnam who accuseth you by credible information, and that both of tempting her to iniquity and of greatly hurting her."

"I am innocent and clear," said Goody Nurse, "and have not been able to get out of doors these eight or nine days."

Edward Putnam read a deposition, probably about what he had seen of the afflicted's fits. "Is this true, Goody Nurse?" asked the magistrate.

"I never afflicted no child, never in my life."

"You see these accuse you. Is it true?"

"No."

"Are you an innocent person relating to this witchcraft?"

Before Goody Nurse could answer, Mrs. Putnam began shouting at her, accusing her of aiding the Devil. "Did you not bring the black man with you? Did you not bid me tempt God and die? How oft have you eat and drunk your own damnation?" (by taking communion under false pretenses).[82]

"What do you say to them?" Hathorne asked.

"Oh Lord, help me," Rebecca Nurse implored, spreading her hands as she spoke. The afflicted flinched and moaned as their pains matched the motion of her hands.

"Do you not see what a solemn condition these are in?" asked the magistrate. "When your hands are loose, the persons are afflicted."

Two of the older girls, Mary Walcott and Elizabeth Hubbard, cried that Nurse's specter was hurting them—it never had before—and Mary raised her arm to show the crescent of a fresh bite.

"Here are two grown persons now accuse you," said Hathorne. "What say you?"

"The Lord knows I have not hurt them," she protested. "I am an innocent person."

Lawson had to leave at this point, probably to prepare for his afternoon lecture. By now the afflicted not only felt buffeted and pinched, but could see the Devil whisper in Nurse's ear amid a swarm of familiars. The victims' convulsions were so extreme that many wept to see it.

"It is very awful to all to see these agonies," said Hathorne, "and you an old professor [of religion] thus charged with contracting with the Devil by the effects of it, and yet to see you stand with dry eyes, when there are so many wet."

"You do not know my heart."

"You would do well, if you are guilty, to confess and give glory to God."

"I am as clear as the child unborn."

"What uncertainty there may be in apparitions I know not," he said with some understatement, "yet this with me strikes hard upon you: that you are at this very present charged with familiar spirits. This is your bodily person they speak to. They say now they see these familiar spirits come to your bodily person. Now what do you say to that?"

"I have none, Sir."

"If you have, confess and give glory to God. I pray God clear you if you be innocent, and if you be guilty, discover you. And therefore give me an upright answer: have you any familiarity with these spirits?"

"No. I have none but with God alone."

"How came you sick, for there is an odd discourse of that in the mouths of many."

"I am sick at my stomach."

"Have you no wounds?" he asked, referring to the blows aimed at her specter.

"I have none but old age."

The afflicted set up a din at the reappearance of the whispering Devil and his flock of birds. The accusers flinched at Goody Nurse's every move: they felt pinched when she moved her hands; their spines bent backward to the breaking point if she but leaned against a support. The court inquired as to what she thought of all this apparent cause and effect, and she replied, "It is all false. I am clear."

"Possibly you may apprehend you are no witch, but have you not been led astray by temptations that way?"

"I have not."

"What a sad thing it is," he commented, referring to Martha Corey and the present defendant, "that a church member here, and now another at Salem, should be thus accused and charged."

"A sad thing sure enough!" shouted Mrs. Pope, convulsing.

Several others followed and, as far as the magistrates and witnesses could tell, Rebecca Nurse's spirit seemed to rage among the afflicted and then, from their reactions, dash outside to gallop on horseback around the meeting house riding behind the Devil. The afflicted screeched so stridently at one point that they startled Deodat Lawson who was walking some distance away. Inside the building each onlooker feared the surrounding folk would convulse next, and in the commotion Parris was unable to hear and note all the testimony. Mrs. Putnam, nearly paralyzed, could stir neither hand nor foot. The situation seemed so critical that the court allowed her husband Thomas to carry her outside. Once through the doors, the spell broke.[83]

"Tell us," said the court when the racket subsided, "have you not had invisible appearances more than what is common in nature?"

"I have none, nor never had in my life."

"Do you think these suffer voluntarily or involuntarily?" the magistrate asked, for some (Proctor, for example) doubted the genuineness of the "fits."

"I cannot tell."

"That is strange. Everyone can judge," he said (although Martha Corey's guesses had not impressed him).

"I must be silent."

"They accuse you of hurting them, and if you think it is not unwillingly but by design, you must look upon them as murderers," he explained, for witchcraft was a hanging crime.

"I cannot tell what to think of it."

He harped on the question which she did not quite catch, being unable to hear it, but the afflicted said she was listening to the Devil instead.

"Well then, give an answer now," Hathorne snapped. "Do you think these suffer against their wills or not?"

"I do not think these suffer against their wills."

"Why did you never visit these afflicted persons?"

"Because I was afraid I should have fits, too."

He watched the afflicted batter about at her slightest movement. "Is it not an unaccountable case that when you are examined these persons are afflicted?"

"I have got nobody to look to but God!" she exclaimed, and as she gestured the afflicted writhed worse than ever.

"Do you believe these afflicted persons are bewitched?" he asked over the discord.

"I do think they are."

"When this witchcraft came upon the stage, there was no suspicion of Tituba. She professed much love to that child Betty Parris, but it was her apparition did the mischief, and why should not you also be guilty, for your apparition doth hurt also?"

"Would you have me belie myself?" Goody Nurse cocked her head, perhaps to hear better, and Elizabeth Hubbard's neck wrenched sideways.

"Set up Goody Nurse's head!" Abigail Williams cried. "The maid's neck will be broke!" So somebody forcibly braced the old woman's head, and the girl's neck relaxed.

The court ordered Samuel Parris to read a paper of notes that he had taken during one of Mrs. Putnam's seizures. "What do you think of this?" the magistrate asked the defendant.

"I cannot help it," Goody Nurse protested. "The Devil may appear in my shape."

But the magistrates had heard enough. They held Rebecca Nurse simply for the torments that she had seemingly caused during the examination itself, and ordered her to Salem jail.[84]

They examined little Dorcas Good next. By now, the afflicted were so suggestible that they felt gripping torments if the child merely looked at them. Although an officer held Dorcas's head still, all the afflicted in her line of vision flinched and winced. Many complained that she bit them and as proof displayed small bite marks on their skin—smaller, by implication, than their own teeth could make. The magistrates ordered Dorcas Good to Salem prison (the prison keeper's house, apparently).[85]

This Thursday was Salem Village's regular turn to host the weekly Lecture and nearly everyone present for the morning's examinations—people from all the surrounding area—remained to hear it. Deodat Lawson, the invited speaker, chose the topical text Zechariah 3:2, "And the Lord said unto Satan, 'The Lord rebuke thee, O Satan: . . . is not this a brand plucked out of the fire?'" It was a passage where Satan, about to accuse a man, was himself shunted aside and the man's sins forgiven.[86]

Lawson reminded his listeners how Satan's constant malice opposed anyone and anything that might comfort humanity here or save them hereafter. Being a spirit, Satan could strike not only the body—to induce natural illness or violent tortures—but could also strike the mind by "raising mists of darkness and ignorance in the understanding" and by "false representations to the eyes"—or at the soul—by luring it to corruption. This Satan might do directly by suggestions to the victim's mind, or indirectly through mortal converts—the witches—who let the Devil "use their bodies and minds, shapes and representations to affright and afflict others at his pleasure."

Surely the defection of church members—the presumed elect—was part of a plot to divide the churches internally and to overthrow God's people in New England. However, Lawson emphasized, no one had yet been *proven* guilty of this crime, and such an accusation would "be a matter of deep humiliation to such as are innocent." He fervently hoped no one was guilty of witchcraft, and advised his listeners to look to their own improvement rather than to suppose that their own lives never encouraged the Devil.

While neighbors speculated (or decided) who else among them might be a witch, and while the subdued afflicted wondered who sent their pains, Lawson

warned that their "inveterate anger and ill-will makes way for the Devil." Therefore, he urged them, "Give no place to the Devil by rash censuring of others without sufficient grounds, or false accusing any willingly."

But the audience paid more attention to Lawson's statement that witches *allowed* Satan to use their specters more than they recalled his warning against Satan's "false representations." The magistrates heard Lawson advise that they prosecute evil-doers and protect the innocent, but did not take to heart his admonition
to use "all regular ways and means that are according to the rule of God to discover" witches (legal methods, not torture or folk-tests). Goody Sibley heard him
warn against the risks of countermagic, itself a form of witchcraft, even if intended
to help the afflicted. He discouraged the burning of hair or boiling of urine to hurt
a witch or scratching a suspect to weaken her power. The girls who had tried
fortune telling listened with varying attention as he condemned the use of sieve
and shears, Bible and key, or egg white in a glass. Householders heard the old
warnings against horseshoes on the threshold and holed stones above the hay
rick, but more than this Lawson would not say, lest the foolishly desperate copy
the methods.

Instead, he recommended prayer and trust in God. Devils, according to the afflicted, mustered like militia in Salem Village, so Lawson used a common military
metaphor for prayer when he urged the people to "put on the whole armor of
God" as protection against the Devil's wiles, and to "ARM! ARM! ARM!" The armor
represented truth, righteousness, peace, salvation, and the word of God, so to arm,
he explained, meant to "PRAY! PRAY! PRAY!" Lawson's war-like phrasing—
especially in a time of imminent frontier attack—seemed to make a greater impression on his audience than his precautions. "Let us admit no parley, give no
quarter, let none of Satan's forces or furies [which would include witches] be more
vigilant to hurt us than we are to resist and repress them." In the long run, however, Lawson concluded, they would all do well to remember that Satan could *not*
win—Christ had already overcome him. "All Satan's strugglings now, are but those
of a conquered enemy."[87]

But despite the arrests and Lawson's cautions, the afflicted were badly agitated
this evening. Nor did old Giles Corey know what to think of his arrested wife
Martha. At some time during the day, he had related the suspicious goings-on at
home to Rev. Noyes, who made notes of the events.[88]

March 25, 1692 • Friday
Salem Village

Crossing Cow House River on his way to Salem Village, John Proctor encountered
Samuel Sibley at Walter Philip's tavern and asked how the folks at the Village were.
Very bad last night, Sibley answered, including Proctor's maid Mary Warren, who

had remained overnight after court. He was going there now to fetch the jade,* Proctor said rudely, and he would rather have given up forty pence than let her go in the first place. Sibley was surprised since Mary was, after all, a witness.

If those girls were allowed to continue, warned Proctor, "we should all be devils and witches quickly. They should rather be had to the whipping post." So now he meant to "fetch his jade home and thresh the Devil out of her." As for the rest, "Hang them!" he fumed, "hang them!" When Mary's fits started, he told Sibley, he kept her busy at the spinning wheel and threatened to thresh her if she tried *that* again. It worked, too, until he had to be away for a day, "and then she must have her fits again forsooth."[89]

Around two in the afternoon, the spectral Rebecca Nurse began to lash Ann Putnam Jr. with a chain—six strokes within a half-hour. Her uncle Edward, among others, saw on her flesh, besides bite marks, the impressions of chain links.[90]

Salem Town

Away from the Village at Stephen Sewall's house in Salem town, Betty Parris had such terrible seizures that her hosts feared she would die. When she recovered enough to describe the apparition, Betty told Mrs. Sewall how the dark shape of a menacing man terrorized her. He also promised her anything that she wanted, and a trip to a golden city besides, *if* she obeyed him. Mrs. Sewall explained that this was the Devil, who "was a liar from the beginning," and urged the girl to tell him so if he came back. And so she must have, for Betty did recover.[91]

(When Rev. John Hale prayed with a certain afflicted girl—perhaps Betty, though perhaps another—she admitted she had tried fortune telling by egg and glass. "After her confession of it, and manifestation of repentance for it, and our prayers to God for her," Hale would write, "she was speedily released from those bonds of Satan." Such little sorceries as these were dangerously close to witchcraft. They were not the capital crime itself, Hale added, only "because such persons act ignorantly, not considering they hereby go to the Devil." But some suspected as much for, as Lawson noticed, the afflicted "are in their fits tempted to be witches.")[92]

Salem Village

Others had likewise gone to the Devil in ignorance and then had second thoughts after Lawson's lecture. Somehow, Samuel Parris learned of Mary Sibley's part in concocting the countermagic witch-cake, and lectured her at length in his study "about her grand error" of using "diabolical means." As ill as his girls had been before, it was the cake charm that let all Hell break loose.

---

*A jade is a worn-out horse, a term, when applied to a woman, comparable to "bitch."

It was customary for such slips by communing members to be confessed and apologized for to the rest of the church. Parris composed a paper describing the event, its effects, and her repentance. He read it to her, and Goody Sibley, "with tears," agreed with it.[93]

March 26, 1692 • Saturday
Salem Village

The spectral Elizabeth Proctor, and Martha Corey, who materialized much more clearly now, continued to attack Mercy Lewis.[94]

Salem Town

Deodat Lawson was in Salem town, where Stephen Sewall told him about Betty Parris's encounter with the Devil. Then Lawson and senior Salem minister John Higginson accompanied magistrates John Hathorne and Jonathan Corwin when they questioned Dorcas Good at the home of prisonkeeper William Dounton. Dorcas said she had a little snake that suckled on her hand. Where? the men asked, pointing to possible spots. Not *there*, she said, but *here*. They saw a deep red spot the size of a flea bite on her lowest forefinger joint. Did the black man give her the snake? asked the magistrates. Oh no, the child corrected. Her mother did.[95]

March 27, 1692 • Sunday
Salem Village

Anglicans in Boston celebrated Easter, which Nonconformists did not observe. It also happened to be a sacrament Sabbath by the Village church's schedule, so Samuel Parris delivered a topical sermon "occasioned" (as he noted in his manuscript) "by dreadful witchcraft broke out here a few weeks past" (in his own household, no less; by now some Villagers must have wondered why the Devil felt so at home there). Two of the "vehemently suspected" witches recently examined and committed "by civil authority" were a "member of this church, and another of Salem." Puritans observed few ceremonies but they greatly valued the sacrament of communion, which now seemed to have been invaded by Satan's followers. However, this was not the first time. For his sermon's text, Parris quoted Christ's remark about the traitorous Judas Iscariot among the disciples: "'Have I not chosen you twelve,'" Parris read, "'and one of you is a Devil?'"[96]

Immediately a woman stood up and stalked from the meeting house with a great slam of the door. It was Sarah Cloyse, the startled congregation realized, one of Rebecca Nurse's sisters. Her family had had much ado, they later learned, to persuade her to attend Meeting at all, even though she was a communing member. (The afflicted would later testify that Goody Cloyse curtsied to the Devil outside at the gate and set her hand to his book showing where *her* allegiance lay.) What her communing husband did was nowhere mentioned.[97]

"By Devil," said Parris, after he could continue, "is ordinarily meant any wicked angel or spirit. Sometimes it is put for the prince or head of the evil spirits, or fallen angels. Sometimes it is used for vile and wicked persons, the worst of such, who for their villainy and impiety do most resemble devils and wicked spirits."

Like Judas Iscariot in the text, such people were not devils by nature, but devils "for likeness and operation." Christ's church, Parris reminded them, "consists of good and bad, as a garden that has weeds as well as flowers," not only true saints but hypocrites who give lip service to Christ "but prefer farms and merchandise above Him and above His ordinances," sinners given up to "that lust of covetousness, which is made so light of, and which so sadly prevails in these perilous times."

None were worse than good people corrupted, those capable of good who instead chose evil. "Hypocrites are the sons and heirs of the Devil, the free-holders of Hell, whereas other sinners are but tenants." Nevertheless, there were still good people in the church. "Pray we also that not one true saint may suffer as a devil either in name or body. The Devil would represent the best saints as devils if he could" (as tormenting specters for example) "but," Parris dismissed the idea, "it is not easy to imagine that his power is of such extent."

Speaking to the full members waiting for communion, he warned, "We are either saints or devils," and the horrifying hypocrisy of "devils" taking communion could only subject them to Satan's power and "the hottest of God's wrath." Therefore, "if there be any such among us, forbear to come this day to the Lord's Table."

Parris also urged the congregation "to be deeply humbled" that even suspected witches could be found in New England's churches; to be much in prayer over the matter; and to ponder the weaknesses that could make any of the congregation devils: drunkenness, pride, envy, slanders, lies, and murder. Being a church member would not ensure salvation. "This you and I may be," said Parris, "and yet devils for all that."

(Unfortunately, his sermon notes do not indicate how much he may have enlarged on these other sins, or on the miracles of Christ that preceded the incident in the text. The congregation apparently paid more attention to his remarks about devils among them. The afflicted folk paid particular attention to a passage about the disciples' confusion over the idea of communion—when they mistook a literal consumption of Christ's flesh and blood in the bread and wine—for its actual, spiritual meaning.)[98]

When the communing members (excepting Goody Cloyse) remained for the Lord's Supper, Parris read aloud the paper that he had discussed with Mary Sibley. He asked that the voting members (the men) raise their hands to indicate they accepted the apology for "her rashness." The vote was unanimous.[99]

March 28, 1692 • Monday
Salem Village

John Tarbell, one of Rebecca Nurse's sons-in-law, visited Thomas Putnam's house to ask if the girls there had named Rebecca Nurse before any of the other afflicted had. Just *who* had begun the accusations? Young Ann said that when she was still the only one in the house tormented, she saw the shape of a pale-faced woman in her grandmother's seat, but had not known her name. Who, Tarbell insisted, actually *named* Goody Nurse? Mercy Lewis said it was Mrs. Putnam, but Mrs. Putnam was certain she had heard it from Mercy.

"Thus they turned it upon one another," Tarbell later recalled, "saying, 'It was you,' and 'It was you that told her.'"[100]

William Rayment of nearby Beverly and Daniel Eliot (Sarah Cloyse's stepson-in-law) made similar inquiries of some of the afflicted at Ingersoll's. The girls (not named in the men's later account) were free of their fits for the time being and perhaps, like others, giddy with relief. Rayment mentioned a rumor that the court would examine Elizabeth Proctor the following day, and Goody Ingersoll said she did not believe it.

"There is Goody Proctor," cried one of the girls, gesturing toward the empty air.

"Old witch," said another, "I'll have her hang."

Goody Ingersoll reproved them sharply. Rayment saw no apparition and told the girl that he thought she lied. "They seemed to make a jest of it," he thought. According to Eliot, the girl told him, "She did it for sport. They must have some sport."[101]

March 29, 1692 • Tuesday
Salem Village

The spectral Elizabeth Proctor tormented Abigail Williams at her uncle's house and tormented Mercy Lewis at Thomas Putnam's. When Samuel Barton and John Houghton arrived to help the family tend the afflicted, Thomas Putnam and his wife told them that Mercy Lewis had named Elizabeth Proctor in a fit. Mercy interrupted to say she had cried only, "There she is." If she named anyone, the girl said, she did so while out of her head.[102]

Ipswich

In Ipswich a regularly scheduled Essex County Court convened, presided over by magistrates Samuel Appleton, Robert Pike, John Hathorne, and Jonathan Corwin. (Nathaniel Saltonstall was absent due to a fall that morning.) The court took depositions concerning the charge that Sarah Good's brother-in-law, Mordecai Larkin of Wenham, had raped his hired girl. He denied it, but plenty of other women, in-

cluding two more of Sarah's sisters, testified against him. The bawdy and belligerent Elizabeth Fanning also appeared before the bench for having butchered a
neighbor's hog and for having beaten a neighbor woman with her bare hands. But
most of the cases were ordinary: trespass, debt, the theft of Walter Philips's mare,
and a rash of card playing in the watch house when the men should have been on
duty. The court appointed new constables including Joseph Fuller—father of the
girl struck by the spectral Rachel Clenton—whose first order was to arrest Rachel
and to warn witnesses of her hearing scheduled for the next day. He arrested
Rachel that very morning and left her in the custody of blacksmith Samuel
Ordway.[103]

Born Rachel Haffield, she had once exercised more worldly influence than
usual for a single woman by managing her widowed mother's considerable estate.
The widow was fined for perjury after affirming in court, and then denying, that
Rachel had struck her. In 1665, at the late age of thirty-six, Rachel married
Lawrence Clenton, a twenty-five-year old bondservant, after first using her personal inheritance to buy his remaining time. Clenton and his former master, Robert
Cross, seemed poised to take charge of widow Haffield's property. In response to
the perceived threat to his own possible claim, Rachel's brother-in-law, Thomas
White, quickly acquired a court order declaring the old woman "*non compos men-
tis*" to place her *and* her property under his control. He then sued Lawrence's former master Cross for the money that Rachel had paid him, claiming it was not hers
to give. For a time it seemed as if Rachel and her husband would both be sold for
debt. Without the alluring prospect of her property, Lawrence soon lost all interest in his wife. For the next sixteen years she lived in poverty and neglect, repeatedly petitioning the authorities for a divorce. Lawrence, meanwhile, took up with
one woman after another and was found guilty of both fornication and attempted
rape. The courts occasionally ordered him to provide for his wife, but he seldom
complied with these repeated decrees or with other court orders to provide child
support for his various bastards. After he finally left for Rhode Island to marry one
of his women (bigamously), Massachusetts finally granted a divorce in 1681.
Rachel did not accept her changed fortunes meekly. Unjustly disinherited, she was
reduced to begging and did so with angry forwardness, throwing stones and
curses if refused. By 1687 folk wondered if she might be a witch.[104]

Dartmouth, England

Over the sea in Dartmouth, England, unaware of the turmoil at home, Rev. Increase Mather, his son Samuel, Governor Phips with the Charter, and his clerk Benjamin Jackson boarded the frigate *Nonsuch*, Captain Richard Short commanding,
and all set sail for New England. Short's right hand troubled him from a recent
wound—a sliver of steel was still lodged in it—but he gave his cabin to Phips and

his entourage. (During the voyage Short would pursue some distant craft to capture as prizes only to lose the wind. The following day they seized the French-owned *Katherine*, full of sugar, cotton, and cocoa, and learned the other two vessels had not been merchantmen at all, but French men-of-war. There would, furthermore, be some question whether Phips or Short was entitled to this prize. Phips as Admiral clearly outranked Captain Short; yet Short, a Royal Navy man, had trouble accepting the self-made Phips as his superior. He also thought Phips could have shown more gratitude for the courtesies of room and board. Short would have preferred that Phips's clerk Jackson not always have his head together with the ship's malcontent purser, Mathew Cary. On the other hand, according to Cary and others, Short was often drunk and abusive, ashore and at sea, and therefore careless as well as cruel, even to his officers.)[105]

March 30, 1692 • Wednesday
Ipswich

If all went as planned, Rachel Clenton appeared before the magistrates in Ipswich at eight o'clock in the morning. (Unfortunately, no examination notes have survived.) One of the summoned witnesses, Mary Thorn—who had been taken by fits at an earlier date—was too ill to appear. The court eventually collected depositions from neighbors that ranged from Betty Fuller's unconsciousness, through Rachel's frequent displays of uncivil and ungrateful behavior, to her possible theft of beer and milk by spectral means. Thomas Burnham said he twice stood watch at night to see who stole his milk and twice saw what looked like Rachel Clenton milking a certain cow, later found dead. The first time she vanished. The second time she turned into a gray cat and escaped over the top of his house, claws scratching on the wooden shingles. (Rachel was, however, nowhere near as turbulent and bellicose as Goody Fanning, who had not been accused of witchcraft.)[106]

(The warrant for Rachel's arrest clearly stated the examination was to be held on March 30, which, presumably, it was. Goody Clenton's bill at the Ipswich jail, however, began on April 11, so perhaps she was held in Salem at first. At some unstated time—her specter must have been active—blacksmith Thomas Manning chained her. As he charged only one shilling six pence to mend and install the fetters instead of the usual five shillings, they seem to have been secondhand.)[107]

March 31, 1692 • Thursday
Salem Town

Salem town hosted the week's Lecture and made it a public fast that included prayers for the afflicted and a consideration of the disrupted community's spiritual state. This was probably the lecture when old George Jacobs made a disturbance—perhaps doubting that the afflicted *were* afflicted.[108]

Salem Village

In Salem Village, the spectral Rebecca Nurse tormented Abigail Williams while about forty other witches invaded her uncle's parsonage to hold a Devil's Supper. These hellish communicants, in defiance of Parris's sermon, parodied the Lord's Supper with bread red as raw meat and a red drink that could not be proper wine, all served by female deacons Sarah Good and Sarah Cloyse.[109]

"Oh Goodwife Cloyse!" exclaimed Abigail. "I did not think to see you here! Is this a time to receive the sacrament? You ran away on the Lord's Day, and scorned to receive it in the meeting house, and is this a time to receive it? I wonder at you!"

The afflicted had several times seen such gatherings that mocked Congregational communion, thanksgivings, and fasts. Since March 31 was a fast day in Salem, the witches would not have likewise abstained. But on one of their own fast days, according to one of the afflicted girls, they ordered their victim not to eat and, whenever she tried to defy them, choked her.[110]

4

APRIL 1692

Oh! You are a grievous liar!

—Sarah Cloyse

April 1, 1692 • Friday
Salem Village

Mercy Lewis, the Putnam's maid, resisted the spectral witches' meaty sacrament. "I will not eat, I will not drink, it is blood." She turned her head away. "That is not the Bread of Life. That is not the Water of Life. Christ gives the Bread of Life. I will have none of it." She spat at her tormentors.

Then a shining figure appeared and the specters flinched from his commanding presence. As she watched, Mercy lost awareness of the room and the people around her. Instead she saw a gloriously bright place lit by neither sun nor candles. She heard voices sing of Christ and about the Book of Life—the opposite of the Devil's book.

"Thou worthy art to take the book,
    its seals to open, too."

For he ransomed us, the unseen choir sang, "From every tribe, and tongue, and folk" to join the Kingdom of God.

Now she saw the singers, a multitude in glittering white robes, who began Psalm 110, the text of Parris's January sermons:

> "The Lord did say unto my Lord,
>   sit thou at my right hand,
>   'Til I thine enemies make a stool
>   whereon thy feet may stand."

"How long shall I stay here?" asked Mercy. She could not bear to leave. "Let me be along with you."

> "Praise ye the Lord, sing to the Lord!
>   a new melodious song . . ."

The multitude sang the 149th Psalm describing how God's people would triumph over "the heathen vengeance" of their foes.

> "The praises high of God, let be
>   proclaimed in their word.
>   And let be ready in their hands,
>   a double-edged sword."

But Mercy could not stay, and woke at last to consciousness in the Putnam house. The vision encouraged her, but wiser heads recalled that Satan delighted in his disguise as an Angel of Light. The shining figure had appeared to the afflicted before—they called him the "white man"—and had sometimes warned them how long the respites between their fits would last.[1]

In the Visible World, Rev. Samuel Parris's salary again fell due, and again remained unpaid for the third quarter in a row.[2]

***

Salem Village

Stephen Bittford woke one midnight near the beginning of April to see the forms of Rebecca Nurse and both Proctors in his room at James Darling's house. As they disappeared, he felt (as he later reported) "a very great pain in my neck and could not stir my head nor speak a word." He wasn't sure the three caused this but he couldn't turn his neck for two or three days.[3]

April 2, 1692 • Saturday
Salem Village

The Elizabeth Proctor specter continued to torture Abigail Williams at the parsonage, pinching the girl "grievously" and tearing at her bowels. The real Proctor household, meanwhile, had trouble with their maid.[4]

When John Proctor took Mary Warren home after her testimony against Rebecca Nurse, he kept her hard at work under stern watch until the girl's convulsions stopped again. He probably beat her as threatened, and so shook her back
to conscious attention. The Proctors refused to accept Mary's interpretation of her
ailments and curtly informed her that if she ran into fire or water during a spell,
they would not try to stop her. Proctor may even have threatened to burn the fits
from her with fire tongs.

Once he exclaimed, "If you are afflicted, I wish you were more afflicted, and
you and all."

"Master," Mary asked, "what makes you say so?"

"Because you go to bring out innocent persons."

"That could not be," said Mary.[5]

When Mary's seizures did stop, she tacked up a note at the Meeting House one
Sabbath eve to request prayers of thanks for this deliverance. Such notes for
prayers were common and would continue to be so for generations, but her employers were displeased. That night Elizabeth Proctor (or her spirit) rousted Mary
from bed with sharp words on the subject.[6]

April 3, 1692 • Sunday
Salem Village

Samuel Parris read Mary Warren's note to his surprised congregation, who questioned the girl after services.

"The afflicted persons did but dissemble," she explained; but if she meant the
victims were deceived by false visions that they refused to question, some church-
goers took it to mean they lied. Although Mary could examine her situation more
calmly now and realize what was illusion, the other afflicted were still embroiled
in all the old painful confusions and suspicions. (Mercy Lewis, for one, was still
hounded by little Dorcas Good with her devilish book.) A few of the afflicted began to suspect Mary, whose freedom from torment may have rankled those still
suffering—especially if other folk began to doubt the girls' symptoms. The
specters had told them, after all, that their torments would end if they signed
the Devil's book, or even only touched it. (The Devil's book not only mocked the
Scriptural Book of Life and a church's record book that members signed on joining, but suggested Andros's hated requirement that those taking oaths place a
hand on a Bible to "swear by the Book.") Now, here was Mary, free from pain.[7]

April 4, 1692 • Monday
Ipswich

Ipswich officials took further depositions in the case of Rachel Clenton.[8]

Salem Town

Captain Jonathan Walcott and his uncle Lieutenant Nathaniel Ingersoll, meanwhile, journeyed from the Village to Salem town and swore a complaint against Elizabeth Proctor and Sarah Cloyse for tormenting Abigail Williams, Mary Walcott (Captain Jonathan's daughter), Ann Putnam Jr., Mercy Lewis (Sarah Cloyse's niece), and a new sufferer, John Indian (Parris's other slave, a grown man). John Hathorne and Jonathan Corwin began writing arrest warrants and warnings for witnesses, but then realized the scale of this crisis was too extensive to handle on a purely local basis. The magistrates set aside the paperwork until they could consult with the government in Boston.[9]

Salem Village

Back at the Village parsonage, Abigail Williams recognized not only Elizabeth Proctor among the menacing specters, but her husband John as well. "What?" said the girl. "Are you come, too? You can pinch as well as your wife."[10]

Cambridge

The Boston area ministers held their usual meeting at Harvard College in Cambridge to discuss, among other matters, the idea of reformation. They noted that several churches had renewed their covenants, and unanimously agreed this also required a renewal of obligations among members.[11]

April 5, 1692 • Tuesday
Salem Village

Still proceeding with the normal concerns of life in Salem Village, a committee of nine, including Israel Porter and Edward Bishop (who were or soon would be associated with the accused) paid Jacob Barney £7 for a two-acre lot on Ryal Side next door to Dr. William Griggs as the site for a future schoolhouse.[12]

Cambridge

In Cambridge, Assistant Governor Thomas Danforth presided, as a local magistrate, over a perfectly ordinary court session for Middlesex County.[13]

Boston

Across the Charles River in Boston, Deodat Lawson, home once more, finished writing an account of what he had witnessed in Salem Village and brought it up to date with a few more incidents heard "from persons of undoubted reputation and credit." Printer Benjamin Harrison rushed it to press and soon had copies for sale at his shop, under the title *A Brief and True Narrative of Some Remarkable Passages Relating to Sundry Persons Afflicted by Witchcraft, at Salem Village which Happened from the Nineteenth of March, to the Fifth of April, 1692.*[14]

By order of Governor Simon Bradstreet and the Council, meanwhile, Boston prison keeper John Arnold spent ten shillings on two blankets for Sarah Good's infant.[15]

April 6, 1692 • Wednesday
Salem Village

Evening brought spectral attacks on Thomas Putnam's household, and against Abigail Williams at the parsonage. She beat her breast and wailed to her uncle, Rev. Samuel Parris, that Goodman Proctor pinched her.[16]

South of the Village, farmer Benjamin Gould was startled by specters of his neighbors Giles and Martha Corey staring at him from his bedside. As soon as he saw them, they vanished, and Gould felt two sharp pinches in his side.[17]

April 7, 1692 • Thursday
Salem Village

On the second night, Benjamin Gould was surrounded in bed not only by the spectral Coreys, but also by the forms of the Proctors, Sarah Cloyse, her sister Rebecca Nurse, and Dr. William Griggs's wife Rachel—Elizabeth Hubbard's aunt. This encounter left Gould with such a pain in his foot he could not force a shoe on it for two or three days thereafter.[18]

April 8, 1692 • Friday
Salem Town

Once word reached Salem that members of the Governor's Council of Assistants would attend the next witchcraft hearing, John Hathorne and Jonathan Corwin completed the arrest warrant for Elizabeth Proctor and Sarah Cloyse, and issued it to Marshal George Herrick. The magistrates arranged for court to sit in Salem town for the visitors' convenience and put Samuel Parris in charge of notes.[19]

April 9, 1692 • Saturday
Salem Village

Despite all warrants, the spectral Sarah Cloyse continued to plague Abigail Williams.[20]

April 10, 1692 • Sunday
Salem Village

Salem Village's Sabbath meeting was interrupted when the Cloyse specter drew blood as it bit and pinched John Indian.[21]

Between or after services, Ephraim Sheldon observed fellow Maine refugee Mercy Lewis in a seizure at Ingersoll's, and heard her name Goody Cloyse. But when she came to herself and he asked her whom she saw, she said that she had seen nobody. Not even "Goody Nurse?" other bystanders asked, "Or Goody Cloyse? Goody Corey?" But Mercy only repeated that she had seen nobody.[22]

Abigail Williams, on the other hand, seemed quite sure she saw the specters of Goodwives Cloyse, Nurse, Corey, and Good. Both Abigail and Mary Walcott also saw the shining angel whose presence frightened the witches.[23]

Boston

Services were calmer in Boston where Cotton Mather preached on Romans 13:11 at Second Church. "'It is high time to awake out of sleep,'" he quoted, as he presented his plan "for the revival of practical Godliness." It comprised sixteen aspects of a moderate, honest, and observant Christian life. The congregation voted for it unanimously.[24]

Mather had the manuscript of this sermon, and two more from the January 14 fast, ready for publication under the title *A Midnight Cry*. The pamphlet urged folk to shake off their spiritual and moral apathy in this dangerous time—so dangerous that it might (possibly) be the end of time and the beginning of final reckoning. He took the risk of making a qualified prediction: "The time of the end seems just going to lay its arrest upon us, and we are doubtless very near the last hours of the Wicked One whom our Lord shall destroy with the brightness of His coming." Mather listed Witchcraft among fires, raids, and pestilence as only one of many ills. The "prodigies of wickedness" among the rising generation were more alarming. (He soon delivered a series of sermons on the description of the Last Judgment in Matthew 25—where individuals are damned not for their sins, but for the good they *neglected* to do.)[25]

April 11, 1692 • Monday
Salem Town

With the latest suspects in custody at Salem town by eleven o'clock, the Governor's Counsel convened in the meeting house (which was larger than the Town House). Aged Governor Bradstreet remained in Boston, but Deputy Governor Thomas Danforth and four assistants had traveled to Salem: James Russell, Isaac Addington, Samuel Sewall, and Samuel Appleton. Danforth, landowner and long-time public servant, was generally respected by the various political factions—although he had refused to serve under Andros, and had received death threats during King Philip's War when he tried to protect the Christian Indians. The assistants would ordinarily have been the court to try capital cases, such as witchcraft, under the old charter. For today's preliminary proceedings, the out-of-town assistants presumably observed while John Hathorne and Jonathan Corwin presided as local magistrates.[26]

Rev. Nicholas Noyes delivered the opening prayer and the examinations began, with Rev. Samuel Parris taking notes. "'Twas awful to see how the afflicted persons were agitated," Assistant Sewall would write in his diary, and as an afterthought add the half-Latin comment, "Vae, Vae, Vae, Witchcraft" ("Woe, Woe, Woe, Witchcraft") in the margin.[27]

Elizabeth Hubbard remained in a trance the entire time, unable to speak even when the magistrates addressed her. The other afflicted witnesses were as discordant as usual.[28]

"John," Hathorne* inquired. "Who hurt you?"

"Goody Proctor first," said John Indian, "and then Goody Cloyse."

"What did she do to you?"

"She brought the book to me."

"John! Tell the truth. Who hurts you? *Have* you been hurt?"

First an unknown gentlewoman hurt him, he explained, then Goody Cloyse, then Goody Proctor. Mostly the latter two came, by day, to throttle him when he refused to sign the book.

"Do you know Goody Cloyse and Goody Proctor?"

"Yes," said John pointing her out, "here is Goody Cloyse."

"When did I hurt thee?" she demanded.

"A great many times."

"Oh!" she exclaimed. "You are a grievous liar!"

"What did this Goody Cloyse do to you?" asked one of the magistrates.

She pinched and bit him till the blood came, John explained, "yesterday at meeting," and many times before.

Mary Walcott convulsed. She had trouble speaking even between seizures but managed to say that Goody Cloyse hurt her now. She had brought Walcott the book, and had said that the girl need only touch it to be well again. Sometimes Goodwives Nurse and Corey, and many others whom Mary did not know, accompanied her.

Abigail Williams described the crowd of about forty witches who took communion, with the afflicted's own blood served by she-deacons Good and Cloyse, in her uncle's pasture. Both Abigail and Mary Walcott related their sightings of the angel. "A fine grave man," Mercy described him, "and when he came, he made all

---

*The questioner is presumably Hathorne, although not named.

the witches to tremble." Abigail agreed that they saw him at Ingersoll's, as well as "Goody Cloyse, Goody Nurse, Goody Corey, and Goody Good."

This was too much for the real Sarah Cloyse. She asked for water, then slumped on the seat in a faint. Several of the afflicted winced and writhed. "Oh," they cried. "Her spirit is gone to prison to her sister Nurse."

The court turned its attention to the second suspect.[29]

"Elizabeth Proctor! You understand whereof you are charged, viz. to be guilty of sundry acts of witchcraft. What say you to it? Speak the truth." The magistrate also warned the afflicted sternly: "And so you that are afflicted, you must speak the truth, as you will answer it before God another day! Mary Walcott! Doth this woman hurt you?"

"I never saw her so as to be hurt by her," said Mary.

"Mercy Lewis! Does she hurt you?" Neither Mercy* nor Ann Putnam Jr. could make a sound, and Abigail Williams's hand was jammed forcibly into her mouth by unseen powers.

"John! Does she hurt you?"

"This is the woman that came in her shift and choked me," said John Indian.

"Did she ever bring the book?"

"Yes, sir."

"What to do?"

"To write."

"What, this woman?"

"Yes, sir."

"Are you sure of it?"

"Yes, sir."

In the audience John Proctor muttered that if he had John Indian in his custody, he would soon beat the Devil out of him.[30]

The court tried to question Abigail Williams and Ann Putnam Jr. again, but neither could speak. "What do you say, Goody Proctor, to these things?"

"I take God in Heaven to be my witness," she said, "that I know nothing of it, no more than the child unborn." (A baby might not be born elect, but it certainly had not had the opportunity to commit any sins.)

"Ann Putnam! Did this woman hurt you?"

"Yes, sir, a great many times." Ann and the other girls fell in convulsions as Goody Proctor looked their way.

"She does not bring the book to you, does she?" asked the magistrate.

---

*"Mary Lewis" in the original, corrected here to Mercy—although Mercy did have a sister Mary.

"Yes, sir, often, and saith she hath made her maid set her hand to it." (So now Mary Warren was suspected as well.)

"What would she have you do with it?"

"To write in it and I shall be well," said Abigail. She turned to Goody Proctor. "Did not you tell me that your maid had written?"

"Dear child," said Elizabeth Proctor. "It is not so. There is another judgment, dear child." Lying was an even more serious matter before God than before the courts.

But Abigail and Ann struggled, writhed, and twitched. They said, "Look you, there is Goody Proctor upon the beam," before their voices strangled off again. When they recovered they both blamed Goodman Proctor, calling him a wizard. Nearly all of the afflicted were seized with fits—except Elizabeth Hubbard, who was still entranced.

"Ann Putnam! Who hurt you?"

"Goodman Proctor and his wife, too!"

The afflicted, it seemed, could see the disembodied Proctor spirits move among them. "There is Proctor going to take up Mrs. Pope's feet," a girl cried, and immediately the woman's feet were jerked up.

By now the real John Proctor was in custody. "What do you say, Goodman Proctor, to these things?" a magistrate inquired.

"I know not. I am innocent," he protested.

"There is Goodman Proctor," cried Abigail, "going to Mrs. Pope," and Mrs. Pope convulsed.

"You see," said the court. "The Devil will deceive you. The children could see what you were going to do before the woman was hurt. I would advise you to repent, for the Devil is bringing you out."

"There is Goodman Proctor," shouted Abigail, "going to hurt Goody Bibber." At that point Sarah Bibber fell convulsing as the specters raged among them, seizing Mary Walcott and others.

When this turmoil calmed, the court took other evidence, such as Benjamin Gould's sighting of the accused and Goody Griggs, but Elizabeth Hubbard was still in a trance and did not respond when her aunt was named.

Striving against the specter of Elizabeth Proctor, Abigail Williams and young Ann Putnam each tried to hit the woman herself only to find their blows repelled. Abigail swung her fist at Goody Proctor's head, but as her arm arced closer, her hand opened and the force of the swing slowed like something in a dream until the blow landed with the lightest touch of her outspread fingers on the woman's hood. Even so, Abigail shrieked, "Oh! My fingers, my fingers, my fingers burn!" And Ann Putnam collapsed, her head pierced by pain.[31]

At some point in these examinations, the magistrates tried the folk test of having the accused recite the Lord's Prayer. One of the defendants misquoted the petition "deliver us from evil," saying instead "deliver us from all evil." They let her try again and this time she said, "hollowed be thy name," instead of "hallowed," thus reversing the prayer's meaning.[32]

After the senior Salem minister John Higginson closed the proceedings with a prayer, Sarah Cloyse and the Proctors were taken around the block to the jail. This left the Proctor children in the care of the no-longer-afflicted (but now suspected) Mary Warren and their thirty-three-year-old brother Benjamin, the eldest surviving child of John's first marriage. He was well used to tending the farm and had, furthermore, "helped bring up all my father's children by all his wives," as he would recall, "one after another." The youngest was three years old and, as it happened, Elizabeth had apparently only recently conceived the Proctor's last child.[33]

As the sun set at quarter past five, it was already evening before some of the witnesses and onlookers got home to the Village. Mary Walcott rode pillion behind her brother Jonathan and saw the specter of Elizabeth Proctor—which had never bothered her before. It shadowed them from Widow Gedney's tavern* in Salem town to the Village outskirts, where Jonathan paused for refreshment at Phillip's ordinary.[34]

Also among the crowd riding home were John Indian and Edward Bishop (the school committee man). Earlier in the day Bishop had seen John Indian have a seizure at a Salem inn. As Bishop shared Proctor's opinion of the slave, he clouted John into a more orderly state. Now, riding home behind another man, John again convulsed and clamped a firm hold with his teeth on the other man's back to keep from falling off the horse. His wrists, it was discovered, were unaccountably bound. Bishop whacked John with his stick until the fit ceased and John promised it wouldn't happen again. Bishop growled that he didn't doubt it, and added that given the opportunity he could likewise cure *all* the afflicted.

The road split north of Phillip's—one route leading to the middle of the Village, the other east toward Ryal Side. Once the cavalcade divided and Bishop headed east toward home, one of the afflicted cried out against him. And those who had cut John's hands free—for the tight knot gouged his flesh—later deduced that the incident with the cord happened just as one of the prisoners had her own hands tied back in Salem.[35]

April 12, 1692 • Tuesday
Salem Town

The local Salem magistrates held another examination, presumably of John Proctor and presumably in Salem. A dog, perhaps Rev. Samuel Parris's own, reclined

---

*The centrally located Ship Tavern is sometimes called "Widow Gedney's" as it was jointly inherited by Susanna (Clark) Gedney and her brother in law Bartholomew, the magistrate. However, their sister-in-law Mary (Pateshall) Gedney, widow of Eleazer, was also licensed to sell drink out-of-doors from her home near the Mill Dam in order to support her children. Both businesses billed the Province for "entertainment of jurors and witnesses."

under the table on which he wrote, for people took their dogs everywhere (even to Sabbath meetings).[36]

During a lull, while Marshal George Herrick went elsewhere to see about Proctor and the other prisoners, Parris tried to set his notes in order. "I met with nothing but interruptions," he wrote. When Abigail Williams, Mary Walcott, and John Indian entered the room, they and the other afflicted took up the cry, "There is Goodman Proctor!" "There is Goodman Proctor in the magistrate's lap," Abigail added before convulsing. Mary Walcott, on the other hand, sat down and calmly began to knit. At first she seemed entirely unaware when Parris and the others questioned her. Later, still composed, she confirmed that Proctor was on the magistrate's lap.

John Indian shouted at the dog under the table to come away, for Goodman Proctor was on its back. Then John stared at an invisible Sarah Cloyse. "Oh, you old witch," he cried, and fell in such violent convulsions that the marshal and three other men could hardly hold him. Mary Walcott, still knitting, glanced calmly at the struggle. Goodman Proctor caused it, she observed, with the help of his wife and Goody Cloyse.

The turmoil fueled by John Indian and by Abigail stopped all proceedings. They were sent out to recover, and so that Parris could bring his notes up to date. Mary Walcott remained where she was, knitting all the while. As Parris finished, the girl gave a little start. "There," said Mary. "Goody Cloyse has pinched me now."

Parris read the sheet aloud to the marshal and when he ended, Mary stopped knitting and became agitated. "Oh, yonder is Goodman Proctor and his wife, and Goody Nurse and Goody Corey and Goody Cloyse and Good's child. Oh, Goodman Proctor is going to choke me." She gagged as if choked.

All the suspects whose specters plagued Mary Walcott—including little Dorcas Good—were sent to Boston prison today (or at least their bills began this date). Dorcas would at least be with her mother again. Sometimes relatives were allowed to accompany prisoners in transit to save the cost of hiring another horse and deputy. Giles Corey rode south with Martha as far as the ferry. He lacked the money to cross, however, so they parted, he promising to be with her the following week.[37]

***

Rowley

Shortly after the first court was held in Salem, Frances Wycomb of Rowley became afflicted and remained so into the summer. The seventeen-year-old daughter of one of the town's leading citizens, already adjusting to a new stepmother, now found her throat choked and lungs pressed by the form of her widowed neighbor Margaret Scott, but whether in person or in specter, the girl was none too sure.[38]

April 13, 1692 • Wednesday
Salem Village

Specters of Rebecca Nurse, Martha Corey, and Elizabeth Proctor continued to harass Abigail Williams. The girl defied Nurse's attempts to make her leap into the fire, and resisted signing the witches' book, though she feared that Goody Corey might disembowel her. Meanwhile, the specters of Giles Corey and Abigail Hobbs, a wild young woman of Topsfield, pursued Ann Putnam Jr.[39]

The two-month-old daughter of Constable John and Hannah Putnam was taken with convulsions this night. Some time earlier, after Rebecca Nurse and Sarah Cloyse were arrested, John had remarked that he was not surprised they were witches, for their mother (Joanna Towne) had also been one. He was shortly after "taken with strange kinds of fits," but soon recovered. However, the baby sickened next, and now seemed to be dying. Although it was after nightfall, the couple sent immediately for John's mother and a doctor. When Mother Putnam saw the child, she said she feared there was an evil hand upon it, and the doctor agreed.[40]

April 14, 1692 • Thursday
Salem Village

Martha Corey's shape still tried to force the book on Abigail Williams, while Abigail Hobbs's specter tormented Mary Walcott, and that of Giles Corey beat Mercy Lewis until she thought her back would break.[41]

April 15, 1692 • Friday
Salem Village

Constable John Putnam's infant daughter died. The heartbroken parents suspected Rebecca Nurse's revenge for John's earlier gossip.[42]

April 16, 1692 • Saturday
Salem Village

By now the afflicted were tormented by two new specters: Goodwife Bridget Bishop from Salem town and Mary Warren, the Proctors' once afflicted maid who had recanted.[43]

April 17, 1692 • Sunday
Salem Village

The vengeful shape of Abigail Hobbs choked and pinched four Village girls who refused to sign her book—Mercy Lewis, Mary Walcott, Ann Putnam, and Elizabeth

Hubbard. Abigail Hobbs, a fourteen-year-old living with her family just over the Topsfield line, had told people for over a year that she had sold herself to the Devil. They had thought this behavior was nothing more than a tasteless jest, like the time she mocked baptism by flicking water in her stepmother's face, or publicly talked back to her, then pointed to an invisible "old Nick" perched on the bedstead. Abigail had worked in Casco Bay some years earlier when Burroughs was there, before the area's destruction. Unlike everyone else who feared guerrilla attacks, Abigail rambled the hills and fields at all hours of the day and night, protected, she said, by the Devil's power.[44]

Goodwife Deliverance Hobbs—Abigail's long-suffering stepmother—was also afflicted in the Salem Village meeting house. "Come away," a voice called to her, although the only specters that she saw were birds, dogs, and cats swarming both inside and outside the building. As she later told Abigail, she suspected Goody Wildes of Topsfield was behind it.[45]

April 18, 1692 • Monday
Salem Village

Ezekiel Cheever and John Putnam Jr. entered official complaints against Giles Corey, Abigail Hobbs, Bridget Bishop, and Mary Warren for tormenting Ann Putnam Jr., Mercy Lewis, Mary Walcott, and Elizabeth Hubbard. Marshall George Herrick arrested the four suspects and took them to Ingersoll's before the day was out.[46]

Nevertheless, Bridget Bishop's specter appeared to Mercy Lewis at Thomas Putnam's this evening, and hinted that Bishop's master—the Devil—made her tell more about her deeds than she had wanted.[47]

April 19, 1692 • Tuesday
Salem Village

Court sat at Salem Village with John Hathorne and Jonathan Corwin presiding as usual, and Rev. Samuel Parris and Ezekiel Cheever appointed to take notes. When the magistrates read the charges of witchcraft and admonished him to tell the truth, Giles Corey replied, "I hope through the goodness of God I shall, for that matter I never had no hand in, in my life."[48]

All the girls—except for Elizabeth Hubbard whose seizures prevented speech—testified how he tormented them. Less dramatically, Benjamin Gould described his injured foot, but added that he could not be certain Corey's specter caused the pain. (He also had seen Goody Rachel Griggs's specter, but apparently no action was taken against her. Whether the charge against a particular suspect was pursued or dismissed as illogical seemed to depend on the authorities' existing opinions about that person.)[49] The principal questioner was presumably Hathorne, although he was named only in Bridget Bishop's examination.[49]

"I never did hurt them," Giles protested.

"It is your appearance hurts them they charge you," said Hathorne. "Tell us what have you done."

"I have done nothing to damage them."

"Have you never entered into contract with the Devil?"

"I never did."

"What temptations have you had?"

"I never had temptations in my life."

"What?" Hathorne exclaimed. "Have you done it without temptations?" A life without any temptation was an incredulous notion. Was the man that cold-blooded?

"What was that reason that you were frightened in the cow house?" Sarah Bibber interrupted, then convulsed. Her husband John, his daughter, and Samuel Braybrook all testified how they heard Corey make such a statement that very morning. Corey denied it, but one of the magistrates reminded him that these witnesses referred to his bodily person, not simply to a specter.

"I never saw nothing but my cattle."

Several people contradicted Giles's assertion, and the court demanded to know what had frightened him.

"I do not know that ever I spoke the word in my life."

"Tell the truth. What was it frightened you?"

"I do not know anything that frightened me." He waved his arms in angry emphasis and the afflicted felt pinched, so the court ordered his hands tied.

"What!" demanded Hathorne. "Is it not enough to act witchcraft at other times, but you must do it *now* in the face of authority?"

"I am a poor creature," said Corey, "and cannot help it." He shook his head and the afflicted's heads jerked.

"Why do you tell such wicked lies against witnesses that heard you speak after this manner this very morning?" asked the magistrate, returning to the question of the cow house specter.

"I never saw anything but a black hog."

The magistrates produced the testimony that Giles had given about his wife on the day of Rebecca Nurse's examination, and asked about the time he was stopped in prayer. "What stopped you?"

"I cannot tell. My wife came towards me and found fault with me for saying, 'living to God and dying to sin.'" (The Gospel woman had presumably corrected a quotation from the Westminster Catechism, where God's grace enables its recipient "to die unto sin, and live unto righteousness.")[50]

"What was it frightened you in the barn?"

"I know nothing that frightened me there."

"Why, here are three witnesses that heard you say so today."

"I do not remember it."

Thomas Gould testified that Corey said "he knew enough against his wife to do her business," and the court wanted to know just what that knowledge was.

"Why, that of living to God and dying to sin," said Corey.

Marshal George Herrick and Bibber's daughter corroborated Gould's claim, but Corey snapped, "I have said what I can say to that."

"What was that about your ox?" asked the court, referring to the deposition about the lame ox.

"I thought he was hipped."

"What ointment was that your wife had when she was seized? You said it was ointment she made by Major Gedney's direction." Corey denied this and said it came from Goody Bibber.

"It is not like that ointment," Goody Bibber objected. (If the two women had traded home remedies, it was no longer safe to admit it.)

"You said you knew, upon your own knowledge, that she had it of Major Gedney," said the court, but Corey denied that, too. "Did you not say, when you went to the ferry with your wife, you would not go over to Boston now, for you should come yourself next week?" Was this remark of Giles's an appointment or a prophecy?"

"I would not go over because I had not money."

The court ordered one of his hands untied (perhaps to test the effect), and several of the afflicted convulsed as soon as it was free. He cocked his head and the girls' heads tipped grotesquely sideways. Exasperated, he sucked in his cheeks and the girls' cheeks pulled in.

John and Sarah Bibber told how Corey once spoke of temptations to make away with himself.

"How doth that agree with what you said, that you had no temptations?"

"I meant temptations to witchcraft," said Corey.

"If you can give way to self-murder, that will make way to temptation to witchcraft."

Several witnesses corroborated his suicidal threats and added that he had threatened to hold his son responsible—probably John Parker or Henry Crosby, the sons-in-law siding against him and Martha. Goody Bibber said Corey had called her husband a "damned, devilish rogue," which was, in effect, the charge against Corey. He was never one to mince words, and several others testified to the "vile expressions" that he hurled against them. With bad feelings all around, Giles Corey was committed to jail.

Abigail Hobbs had long jested about her association with the Devil, but none of those ordinarily afflicted showed any signs of discomfort when she was led in and told to answer the charges.[51]

"I will speak the truth," she said. "I have seen sights and been scared. I have been very wicked. I hope I shall be better, if God will help me."

"What sights did you see?" asked Hathorne.

"I have seen dogs and many creatures."

"What dogs do you mean? Ordinary dogs?"

"I mean the Devil." He appeared to her once, she explained, in the woods during the day "at the Eastward at Casco Bay" three or four years earlier. He looked like a man and promised her fine things if she did as he ordered.

"What would he have you do?"

"Why, he would have me be a witch."

"Would he have you make a covenant with him?"

"Yes."

"And did you make a covenant with him?"

"Yes, I did, but I hope God will forgive me."

"The Lord give you repentance."

She had seen the cats and dogs then, she said, and even at home in Topsfield. One cat pestered her to put her hand to a book, but she refused, since she had already done this with the Devil's book. Some men-specters also brought a book.

"What?" asked the bench. "Would they have you put your hand to their book, too?"

"Yes," she agreed, but not for her to worship them as the court suspected. "They would have me make a bargain for so long, and do what they would have me do." She had contracted to serve them variously two or three or four years, she said vaguely, periods of servitude which were nearly expired. They had promised her fine clothes (as yet undelivered) and had ordered her to hurt folks like Mercy Lewis and Ann Putnam Jr.

"What did you do to them when you hurt them?"

"I pinched them."

"How did you pinch them? Do you go in your own person to them?"

"No."

"Doth the Devil go for you?"

"Yes."

"And what doth he take—your spirit with him?"

"No. I am as at other times, but the Devil has my consent and goes and hurts them." But she did *not* hurt her mother last Lord's Day; Goody Wildes of Topsfield did that, as her mother had told her. Abigail never saw Wildes among the witches, however, only Sarah Good—who also hounded her with a book—and one other woman whom she did not know. She herself never attended any of the great witch meetings in the Village, but only heard of the hurt done there.

"But you know your shape appeared and hurt the people here?"

"Yes."

"How did you know?"

"The Devil told me if I gave consent he would do it in my shape." That was about a fortnight ago, she said (contradicting her earlier statement that she had seen the Devil only once, in Maine). This time he appeared "like a black man" wearing a hat. She denied letting familiars suckle from her body, despite the court's persistent questioning. "They do not come to my body. They come only in sight." They did speak to her, however, as other folks did.

"What? Do they speak to you as other folks?"

"Yes, almost."

The magistrates continued, but Abigail no longer heard them. Mary Walcott, Mercy Lewis, Betty Hubbard, Abigail Williams, and Ann Putnam Jr. could all see Sarah Good's and Sarah Osborne's specters jam their fingers into Abigail Hobbs's ears to block out the questions. Soon she was also unable to see, though her eyes were wide open. After a time she said, "Sarah Good saith I shall not speak," and then went mute, which put an end to the examination. After she was taken out, Mercy Lewis, Abigail Williams, and Ann Putnam Jr. repeatedly expressed sorrow for her state. Not once during this examination had any specter tried to hurt them. Not once had Abigail Hobbs tried to deny their charges.

But when Mary Warren approached the bar and pleaded innocence, the afflicted had such severe seizures that only Elizabeth Hubbard could speak to accuse her.[52]

"What do you say for yourself? Are you guilty or not?" Hathorne demanded.

"I am innocent."

"You were a little while ago an afflicted person," Hathorne reminded Mary. "Now you are an afflicter. How comes this to pass?"

"I look up to God, and take it to be a great mercy of God."

"What? Do you take it to be a great mercy to afflict others?"

Elizabeth Hubbard testified that soon after Mary Warren first recovered, she had said "that the afflicted persons did dissemble." Then all the afflicted convulsed, including Mrs. Bethshua Pope—who hadn't before—and John Indian.

"Well, here was one just now," said a magistrate referring to Abigail Hobbs, "that was a tormentor in her apparition, and she owns that she had made a league with the Devil."

It all became too much for Mary Warren and she crumpled to the floor. The girls shouted that Goody Corey and the Proctors had struck her down to prevent confession. Mary writhed, unable to see, hear, or speak. "I will speak," she said at last, then she wrung her hands and cried, "Oh! I am sorry for it, I am sorry for it!" But the seizures clamped down and gritted her teeth together when she tried to talk. She convulsed violently. "Oh, Lord help me! Oh, good Lord, save me!" she cried, strangled. Then she managed to say, "I will tell, I will tell," but fainted. She woke muttering, "I will tell, they did, they did, they did," but collapsed again. "I will tell. They brought me to it," she said at last, but the frightening seizures silenced her again and the court ordered her removed for the time being. This allowed her to ponder the certain effects of trying to recant, and the possibility that the Devil had her in his snare after all.

While Mary Warren calmed, Bridget Bishop of Salem town was led in and the afflicted were immediately tormented in the usual manner. Thrice married, the second husband abusive, she had been held on a witchcraft charge before in 1679 but apparently nothing came of it. (Wonn, an African slave belonging to John Ingersoll, one of Deacon Nathaniel's nephews, had claimed her specter pinched him, stole eggs, and spooked a team of horses.) She denied the present charge as well.[53]

"I am innocent. I know nothing of it. I have done no witchcraft. I take all these people," she added, glancing back and forth across the audience, "to witness that I am clear." The pain of the afflicted matched the motions of her head and eyes, and several identified her with the harmful specter. "I never saw these persons before, nor I never was in this place before. I am as innocent as the child unborn." (Stories about Bridget—married to Edward, a sawyer of Salem town—had been confused with stories about Sarah Bishop of Salem Village—married to farmer and school committee man Edward Bishop Jr., who had beaten John Indian.)

Even if Bridget herself never visited the Village, her specter had been reported there. Mary Walcott described how, when she had recently pointed out the accused's specter, her brother Jonathan had struck at it with his sword and torn its coat (meaning its petticoat or skirt). Mary had heard it tear.

"Is not your coat cut?" Hathorne asked the defendant. She said it was not, but the court checked and found a two-way rent—not exactly like a blade's slash. Jonathan Walcott said he had flourished the sword while it was still in its scabbard. Perhaps that explained the look of the tear.

"They say you bewitched your first husband to death," the magistrate said, referring to Samuel Wasselbee.

"If it please your worship, I know nothing of it."

With certainty, the afflicted charged her with hurting *them*, of bringing the Devil's book and otherwise tempting them to sin. She shook her head angrily, saying it was all false, and the afflicted's heads wrenched back and forth.

Samuel Braybrook said she told him earlier that although she had been suspected of being a witch these ten years, she was not, so the Devil could not hurt her.

"I am no witch," she repeated to the court.

"Why, if you have not wrote in the book, yet tell me how far you have gone? Have you naught to do with familiar spirits? What contract have you made with the Devil?"

"I have made no contract with the Devil. I never saw him in my life."

"She calls the Devil her god!" cried Ann Putnam Jr.

Hathorne badgered Goody Bishop to tell the truth while the afflicted shouted accusations.

"I am not come here to say I am a witch to take away my life," she snapped.

Then who did do it? Hathorne wanted to know, for the specter *looked* like her. But she continued to deny the accusation, and to deny knowing anyone present, even while her every motion appeared to produce painful reactions.

"Do you not see how they are tormented?" Hathorne exclaimed. "Why you seem to act witchcraft before us, by the motion of your body, which seems to have influence upon the afflicted."

"I know nothing of it. I am innocent to a witch. I know not what a witch is."

"How do you know then, that you are not a witch?"

"I do not know what you say."

"How can you know you are no witch," he rephrased the question, "and yet not know what a witch is?"

"I am clear. If I were any such person," she said menacingly, "*you* should know it."

"You may threaten," said Hathorne, "but you can do no more than you are permitted." He seemed to think God would not allow the witches to hurt him even if they could hurt mere girls, women, and Indian slaves.

"I am innocent of a witch," she repeated.

"What do you say of the murders you are charged with?"

"I hope," she answered, "I am not guilty of murder," and gazed upward to emphasize her innocence. But the eyes of the afflicted rolled back at the same time and spoiled the effect.

When he asked if she knew that some of the other accused had confessed today, she snapped that she did not. Whereupon John Hutchinson and John Lewis said they themselves had told her about Abigail Hobbs and Mary Warren.

"Why look you," exclaimed Hathorne, "you are taken now in a flat lie!"

"I did not hear them," she said, but her explanations and professions of innocence did not impress the court.

Bridget Bishop was led away as five of the afflicted wailed that *she* was the woman who hurt them. Didn't it bother her to see how they suffered? Samuel Gould asked her after the examination, while Will Good, free of wife and children, loitered close enough to hear.

"No," she answered, she was not troubled for them.

But didn't she think, Samuel persisted, that they really were bewitched? She didn't know what to think, she said.[54]

The court recalled Mary Warren, but she was no better and immediately convulsed. She *was* able to deny signing or touching the Devil's book before her seizures again got her sent outside for air. When she was brought back, it was only more of the same, so the magistrates and ministers questioned her privately without the audience or the noisy witnesses.[55]

"She said I shall not speak a word," Mary gasped. (Elizabeth Proctor had certainly not wanted her maid to testify like this.) "But I will. I will speak, Satan. She saith she will kill me. Oh! She says she owes me a spite and will claw me off. Avoid Satan, for the name of God avoid," she shouted, then fell writhing. "Will ye? I will prevent ye in the name of God—"

"Tell us," asked the magistrates, "how far have ye yielded?" But the fits took her again. "What did they say you should do and you would be well?" But her teeth clamped her lips to prevent speech, and the court abandoned its fruitless questioning.

Salem Town

After the magistrates (and their horses) refreshed themselves with five shillings worth of food and drink at Ingersoll's, the prisoners were taken to Salem jail. There Giles Corey's threatening specter appeared to Mary Warren in a locked room (*not* a cell). When more witches were caught in the Village, it said, they too would be put in Salem jail, where they would most certainly torment *her*. He also meant to "fit her for it" himself in revenge for something she once said that caused Proctor to charge more for a meadow than Corey was willing to pay.[56]

April 20, 1692 • Wednesday
Salem Town

When the magistrates questioned Mary Warren in Salem prison, she told them how averse her master Proctor was about putting up bills for public prayers, and how he brought her the Devil's book, which she now admitted signing. But, she protested, she had not known at the time *what* book it was. She had learned the Proctors were witches only when they told her so—at least Goody Proctor had admitted as much when she rousted Mary from bed the night after Mary posted the bill. On the following night her mistress declared that her stepson John and Mary herself would both be accused as witches.[57]

When Mary described Giles Corey's specter from the night before, she suffered "a dreadful fit." That was Corey's doing too, she said when she recovered. She described the specter's clothes—the color of its hat and coat, the cord around its waist, the white cap on its head, and the chains that bound it. (Mary must have seen Corey the day before. It would have been more unusual if he had been able to change his outfit and the notes do not say what, if anything, was different about it.) The magistrates sent for Corey, "who was then in close prison" elsewhere in the building, to confront Mary's charge. No sooner did the old man enter and face the girl, than she convulsed. The real Giles Corey, as all could see, was dressed exactly as Mary Warren had said.

Also questioned in Salem prison, Abigail Hobbs added to her confession. When she had worked in Casco Bay, she was friends with a young woman from Jersey named Judah White, who worked for Joseph Ingersoll (another nephew of Nathaniel Ingersoll). Just yesterday, said Abigail, on her way to be examined, she had encountered the shapes of this Judah, who worked in Boston now, and of Sarah Good. They urged her to flee and to tell the court nothing. Abigail refused but noticed the fine clothes Judah wore—such as the Devil had promised her and never delivered—"a sad colored* silk mantle, with a top knot and an hood."[58]

And yes, the Devil, disguised as a man, made her afflict Ann Putnam Jr., Mercy Lewis, and Abigail Williams. He brought wooden images and thorns for her to stab them with. She now admitted attending the great witch meeting in Parris's pasture and partaking of the red sacrament.

Topsfield

On this night of the full moon, the forms of Mercy Lewis (one of the afflicted girls) and Goodwife Sarah Wildes woke Deliverance Hobbs, Abigail's stepmother, and nearly tore her to pieces.[59]

Salem Village

Even so, a specter of Goody Hobbs herself appeared to Abigail Williams. "I have signed the book and have ease," it said. "Now do you sign, and so shall you have ease." Ann Putnam Jr. also spied a new specter. "Oh, dreadful, dreadful!" she cried. "Here is a minister come. What? Are ministers witches, too? Whence come you?" she asked the spirit. "And what is your name? For I will complain of you though you be a minister, if you be a wizard."

---

*A "sad" color is a dark, subdued tone.

Although racked and gagged, she refused to sign his book. Not even if he tore her to pieces! she shouted. How dare he recruit children's souls for Satan when he ought to teach them fear of God!

The specter finally identified itself as George Burroughs, the Village's former minister. He had killed his first two wives, he boasted, and had also killed Deodat Lawson's wife and child in retaliation for Lawson's chaplain service Eastward. Burroughs had bewitched many soldiers also, and it was he, rather than the Devil, who had recruited Abigail Hobbs. He was more than a witch, he declared, *he* was a conjurer.[60]

Similarly, around midnight, Mercy Lewis—unaware that Goody Hobbs had seen *her* specter—was harassed by the spirit of "an old, very gray headed man" identifying itself as George Jacobs Sr., a Salem farmer in Northfields. When she refused to sign his book, he beat her with his walking stick and warned her that he had killed his own first wife years ago.[61]

April 21, 1692 • Thursday
Ipswich

In Ipswich, the case against Rachel Clenton continued as Constable William Baker received a warrant to bring in more witnesses.[62]

Salem Town

In Salem, John Putnam Jr., Benjamin Hutchinson, Thomas Putnam, and another Village farmer, John Buxton, swore out complaints on behalf of Ann Putnam Jr., Mercy Lewis, Mary Walcott, and Abigail Williams. The magistrates forthwith issued arrest warrants for Sarah Wildes, William and Deliverance Hobbs, Nehemiah Abbott Jr., and Mary Esty (sister of Rebecca Nurse and Sarah Cloyse), all of Topsfield; Mary Black (Nathaniel Putnam's slave), and Edward and Sarah Bishop of Salem Village; and Mary English (wife of merchant and selectman Philip) of Salem town. Marshal George Herrick was ordered to bring them all to Ingersoll's by ten o'clock the following morning.[63]

Apparently speaking for other Villagers as well as for himself, Thomas Putnam wrote to John Hathorne and Jonathan Corwin to warn of matters that "we conceive you have not heard, which are high and dreadful—of a wheel within a wheel at which our ears do tingle." The letter did not specify what complicated events the Biblical allusion referred to, but it was probably the presence of a minister among the specter witches.[64]

The Salem magistrates, with Rev. Nicholas Noyes attending, again questioned Mary Warren in jail. Perhaps doubting her story of the Devil's book, they showed her a Bible and asked if *it* were like the Proctors' book in which she had seen a "flourish." (Families commonly recorded lists of births, marriages, and deaths on their Bibles' blank leaves.) But Mary said it was not the same. Had her mistress brought the book? they asked. It was her master, she said, and she did not sign but made a mark. Bit by bit, the story emerged from the relentless questions.[65]

Mary had been eating buttered bread and cider alone one day, when John and Elizabeth Proctor entered with a volume similar to a Bible. They held it out open and asked her to read a passage from it. The first word was "Moses," but she could not discern the next, so her master handed her the book. As soon as her fingertip touched the page, a black mark appeared under it on the paper. Mary trembled, realizing she had been deceived. She moved her finger to another line, but found her hand drawn back involuntarily to touch that black mark. It was not a blood stain and there was nothing visible on her hands but sweat and maybe butter. Whatever had made the mark also smudged her bread when next she touched it.

She cried that she was undone body and soul, but the magistrates insisted that she must have voluntarily touched the book, or the Devil would never have been able to do all that he was doing with her specter. For the ease of her body, they lamented, she had surrendered her soul. But the Proctors had *tortured* her, she said, and threatened to drown her, to burn her with hot tongs, to run her through hedges.

The real Proctors were jailed in Boston prison, but their specters now attacked and Mary convulsed. "I will tell, I will tell! Thou wicked creature, it is you stopped my mouth, but I will confess the little that I have to confess." Did she mean Goodwife Proctor? inquired the magistrates. Mary addressed the specter with rude familiarly as "Betty Proctor," and continued to berate it. "It shall be known, thou wretch. Has't thou undone me body and soul?" The specter snarled that it ought to have forced Mary to make a more thorough league with the Devil.

The Proctors didn't want anyone to know what went on in their household. Why there were times when her master threatened suicide just to be free of his wife's quarreling. Goody Proctor had books all over the house and even carried one in her pocket when visiting her sister in nearby Reading. She had once hinted that Mary might have realized the truth sooner if she paid attention to what books they were. The magistrates were still none too sure that the Devil's book had deceived an unwitting Mary, but she denied giving the Devil permission to afflict with her shape, and denied sticking pins into images. The Proctors, she said, spoke of image magic, but she never saw images in their house. Goody Proctor had used a foul-smelling green salve—it had come from her mother, Mrs. Bassett of Lynn—on Mary for some past ailment, but that was the only ointment.

Salem Village

Benjamin Hutchinson, Joseph's son and Deacon Ingersoll's foster son, returned to Salem Village between eleven o'clock and noon, when Abigail Williams met him outside Ingersoll's. She told him that George Burroughs's specter had boasted to her about killing two wives of his own and one of Rev. Lawson's, and about lifting the heaviest gun in Casco Bay with one hand. Moreover, the spirit of that "little black minister" even then watched them from the road "just where the cart wheel went along." Hutchinson had a "three-grained iron fork" in his hand and hurled it at the spot indicated by Abigail. She fell in a "little fit" and then said, "You have torn his coat, for I heard it tear."[66]

"Whereabouts?" asked Hutchinson.

"On one side." Undeterred, Burroughs's shape preceded them into Ingersoll's great room, where Abigail, trailing Hutchinson, spied it. "There he stands!" she shouted.

"Where? Where?" asked Hutchinson. He drew his rapier but the specter disappeared before he could take action.

"There is a gray cat," said Abigail, and Hutchinson stabbed where she pointed. Abigail convulsed. "You killed her," she said when she recovered, "and immediately Sarah Good came and carried her away."

After Lecture, around four o'clock, specters of William and Deliverance Hobbs attacked Abigail Williams and Mary Walcott in Ingersoll's. Goody Hobbs's specter bit Mary's foot and both girls saw the shapes sidle past the table. Benjamin Hutchinson whacked his rapier where the girls pointed.

"Oh," they said, "you have struck her on the right side," next to her eye. But the room was thronged with witches, and Hutchinson and Ely Putnam continued to stab here and there as directed. "You have killed a great black woman of Stonington," said the girls, "and an Indian that comes with her, for the floor is all covered with blood." These Connecticut specters escaped before expiring, however, because Mary and Abigail, looking outside, spied three dead altogether among the great company of witches on the hill north of the meeting house.[67]

Topsfield

Four of those recently accused lived even further north of the Village in Topsfield where Sarah Wildes's son Ephraim was constable. After Marshal George Herrick arrested Goody Wildes, he ordered her astonished son to arrest William and Deliverance Hobbs as well. Ephraim did, though troubled all the while by the knowledge of his own mother's certain innocence. Goody Hobbs did not sympathize, but glared at him maliciously. "One might almost see revenge in her face," Constable Wildes would recall.[68]

Salem Town

According to later family traditions (which are by no means ironclad), Mary English was not arrested until eleven o'clock at night. The sound of the front door's knocker woke the family. When they heard a servant climb the stairs, Philip thought the interruption must be an urgent business matter. But the officers marched into their chamber on the servant's heels, hardly giving Philip time to find his clothes. Mary English remained in bed. The law drew open the bed curtains, read her the warrant, and ordered her up. She refused. None of the men dared force the issue, so they left a guard outside the house. Once morning arrived, the officers again ordered her up. Again, Mary refused: it was not her usual hour. When that hour did come, she dressed, breakfasted with her husband and children, spoke with all the house servants, and only then consented to go.[69]

April 22, 1692 • Friday
Salem Village

Before court convened at Salem Village, the afflicted saw all the area witches flock to Rev. Parris's pasture. They tried to drag the girls along with them, and neighbors struck where the afflicted said the pursuing specters were. Bolder than the rest, Abigail Williams ran from her uncle's parsonage to speak with the crowd. From what the afflicted reported, and what "confessors" later corroborated, the meeting seemed to have gone as follows.[70]

Whole families flew from Andover led by Martha Carrier, who shared a pole with Ann Foster and Mary Lacy. But the pole broke and old Goody Foster grabbed Carrier around the neck to save herself. Even then she hurt her leg, for she flew not in spirit, like the more practiced Carrier, but bodily and hidden by a spell of invisibility. They sat under a tree at the edge of the pasture by a sandy cart track marked with horses' hoof prints, picnicked on bread and cheese brought in their pockets, and refreshed themselves with water from a nearby stream. They watched as the others assembled—witches who had been arrested, those who yet ran free, witches from all the region. But even the attending witches were deceived about the numbers present. Some saw only a few men among the company, yet William Barker of Andover spied 105 swordsmen armed with rapiers loitering by the meeting house. Three ministers arrived—the short, dark-haired George Burroughs, a gray headed man, and another. One of these was Rev. John Busse, who brought the wine from Boston, a sometime preacher and physician in Wells, Maine, and other frontier posts.

As the court began its duties, two companies of witches mustered to the beat of a drum. Burroughs called them to order with a trumpet blast, and then delivered a sermon reminding them of their task to replace God's churches with the Devil's. Begin here in Salem Village, where people were already divided, he said, then spread throughout New England to establish the Devil's Kingdom, where they would live in gallant equality with neither shame nor fear. At noon Burroughs administered the Devil's mocking, scarlet sacrament which female deacons Rebecca

Nurse, Sarah Good, Sarah Osborn, and Sarah Wildes distributed among the communicants. After the ceremony the witches lunched on ordinary brown bread and cider around a table in the pasture. Burroughs sat at its head with a man in a white high-crowned hat who may have been the Devil himself. For Satan had arrived with the Andover witches and was present to read a list of seventy-two recruits. Membership was now over three hundred and they would all, the Devil promised (again mocking Scripture), have crowns in Hell. But Burroughs and Carrier, *they* would be King and Queen of Hell.

Back in the Visible World, more spectators than ever packed the Village meeting house by ten o'clock. So many perched in the windows that they blocked most of the light and left Parris to make his notes in an artificial dusk. They were aware, from the afflicteds' reactions, of the spectral turmoil in the minister's pasture, and alarmed by the sound of a trumpet. They heard it clearly, yet no one ever learned who really blew it.[71]

To test the afflicted, Hathorne and Corwin decided to bring in the suspects without naming them. When asked to identify Goodwife Deliverance Hobbs, some of the girls were dumbstruck, but Ann Putnam Jr. named and accused her, and John Indian said Deliverance had choked him. Goody Hobbs denied hurting anyone or allowing the Devil to use her specter to do so.[72]

"It is said you were afflicted," said Hathorne.* "How came that about?"

"I have seen sundry sights."

"What sights?"

"Last Lord's Day in this meeting house, and out of the door, I saw a great many birds, cats, and dogs, and heard a voice say, 'Come away.'" Since then she had seen the shapes of people, "Goody Wildes, and the shape of Mercy Lewis."

"What is that? Did either of them hurt you?"

"None but Goody Wildes, who tore me almost to pieces." No specter tried to make her sign or even tempt her to join. They only hurt her. (The real Mercy Lewis was still afflicted—she had obviously not signed the Devil's book to gain ease— so the magistrates did not pursue this talk of her specter. But neither did they seem to consider that if Goody Hobbs misidentified the spirit she might have misnamed others, or that the specter's likeness was the Devil's illusion.)

"Is it not a solemn thing," said Hathorne, "that the last Lord's Day you were tormented, and now you are become a tormentor, so that you have changed sides? How comes this to pass?"

"There is Goody Hobbs upon the beam!" Abigail Williams and Ann Putnam Jr. interrupted. "She is not at the bar." Everyone else saw the woman's body, but the two girls saw only her specter taunting from overhead. The magistrates demanded an explanation, but she insisted, "I have done nothing."

---

*The principal questioner is presumably Hathorne, although he is not named.

"What? Have you resolved you will not confess? Hath anybody threatened you if you do confess? You can tell how this change comes."

She insisted she had done nothing, but if she glanced at John Indian or the others, they convulsed noisily—leaving the magistrates even less inclined to believe her. Weakening, Deliverance admitted signing the book, and the afflicted stilled, as if the confession had broken the specters' powers to hurt.

"Well, the Lord open your heart to confess the truth. Who brought the book to you?"

"It was Goody Wildes." Osborn came too, the night before last, and both threatened to tear her apart if she disobeyed. Wildes brought the pen and ink plus images to stick pins in.

"How many images did you use?" asked the magistrate.

"But two. Three."

"Nay, here is more afflicted by you. You said more. Well, tell us the truth. Recollect yourself."

"I am amazed."

"Can you remember how many were brought?"

"Not well, but several were brought."

"Did not they bring the image of John Nichol's child?"

"Yes."

"Did you not hurt that child?"

"Yes."

"Where be those images? At your house?"

"No, they carried them away again." A tall, dark man was with them, she added, wearing a high-crowned hat. (A specter in a white, high-crowned hat was even then in the pasture across the road.)

The magistrates, thinking of Benjamin Hutchinson's rapier, asked if she had been hurt the day before. She said she had felt a sharp pain in her right side—it was still sore—and something dusty in her eye. She pointed, and the marshall saw there was indeed a mark in her eye. The court sent her out to be searched privately by some women for the other wound, which they found. Deliverance Hobbs too was held for trial.

The examination of weaver Nehemiah Abbott Jr. began like all the others with his declaration of innocence. But when the magistrate* asked the afflicted to identify the defendant, only Ann Putnam Jr. could name him with certainty (though Mary Walcott recognized him from his specter). Abbott denied hurting them despite Ann's insistence.[73]

---

*Presumably Hathorne.

"He is upon the beam," she added.

The court reminded him that Goody Hobbs's specter had also been seen and *she* had just confessed.

"If I should confess this," said Abbott, "I must confess what is false." The magistrates persisted as usual but Abbott held firm. "I speak before God that I am clean from this accusation."

"What? In all respects?"

"Yes, in all respects."

Hathorne and Corwin asked the afflicted again if they were sure this man was the same one who hurt them. Some said he was, but others could not open their mouths. "Charge him not unless it be he," one magistrate admonished them.

"This is the man," some said, but others could say only that, "He is very like him."

"How did you know his name?" Hathorne asked Ann Putnam.

"He did not tell me himself, but other witches told me. It *is* the same man." She then convulsed.

Mary Walcott allowed that Abbott was very like the man, but Mercy Lewis said flatly he was *not* the same, though they all agreed the apparition had a growth—"a bunch on his eyes."

"Be you the man?" Ann Putnam asked through the strains of her seizure. "Ay, do you say you be the man? Did you put a mist before my eyes?"

Their doubt was enough that the magistrates sent Abbott out for a time to await further questioning.

William Hobbs, husband of Satan's recent recruit, Deliverance, and father of self-confessed witch Abigail, was next to be questioned, and all the afflicted except Goody Bibber said he hurt them. Because witchcraft was viewed as a corruption that could be taught, a witch's family members risked suspicion.[74]

"I can speak in the presence of God safely, as I must look to give account another day," Hobbs declared, "that I am clear as a new born babe."

"Have you never hurt these?" inquired Hathorne,[*] indicating the afflicted, who winced at Hobbs's every glance. But even as he denied involvement, Abigail Williams saw his spirit spring from his body and stride toward the witnesses. She shouted a warning to Mercy Lewis, who fell in a fit, and then to Mary Walcott, who also convulsed.

"How can you be clear," demanded the court over the shouts of the writhing afflicted, "when the children saw something come from you and afflict these persons?"

---

*Presumably Hathorne.

Hobbs insisted he performed no witchcraft, and the court asked if perhaps he called it "overlooking" (meaning the evil eye), for indeed, the afflicted fell whenever he looked at them.

"I hurt none of them." Hobbs remained as adamant as Abbott had, but the magistrates were not as inclined to doubt the accusations. The afflicted still convulsed, and the magistrates harped on the question.

"It was none of I," Hobbs said.

But the magistrates were still impressed that the afflicted had been able to see his spirit *before* it hurt them, and with that subject reintroduced, the phenomenon repeated itself. "Can you now deny it?" Hathorne asked.

"I can deny it to my dying day."

Hobbs had not, it seemed, attended public religious meetings for some while. "Because I was not well," he said. "I had a distemper that none knows." He denied avoiding Scripture readings at home, but, as Nathaniel Ingersoll and Thomas Haynes testified, his own daughter Abigail had said this was so.

The court noted how the afflicted calmed when the confessions of Hobbs's wife and daughter eased the girls' torments, "and so would you, if you would confess. Can you still deny that you are guilty?"

"I am not guilty."

"If you put away God's ordinances," said the magistrate, meaning public worship, "no wonder that the Devil prevails with you to keep his council. Have you never had any apparition?"

"No, sir."

"Did you never pray to the Devil that your daughter might confess no more?"

"No, sir."

"Who do you worship?"

"I hope I worship God only."

"*Where?*" Hathorne asked sarcastically. Not in the meeting house, it would seem.

"In my heart."

"But God requires outward worship."

Hobbs at last agreed that such apathy might give the Devil an advantage over him. But, no, he had not known his daughter was a witch, nor did he think so now. Certainly, something more than ordinary ailed the afflicted, but it was none of his doing, so he could not guess what caused it. The confessions of his wife and daughter weighed heavily against William. How could he *not* be aware of the diabolical doings perpetrated by two members of his own household? The magistrates asked about a rumor that he had threatened to kill his wife if she didn't sign the Devil's book, and that she did sign just when her specter began to torment the Parris household. "Did you not say so?" asked the court.

"I never said so," said William Hobbs, but he too, was committed to jail.

As a young woman, Sarah Wildes had been considered flashy and forward. Now long married, she was still resented by the family of her husband's first wife. When she entered the court room, the afflicted spied her spirit above them on the beam. They all convulsed intensely, even Goody Bibber, who had never seen that specter before.[75]

"What do you say to this? Are you guilty or not?"

"I am not guilty, sir."

But most of the afflicted identified her with the tormenting specter. "Here is a clear evidence," said Hathorne, indicating the notes of Deliverance Hobbs's examination, "that you have been not only a tormentor, but that you have caused one to sign the book the night before last. What do you say to this?"

"I never saw the book in my life, and I never saw these persons before."

With some of the afflicted in seizures, the magistrates demanded to know how she could deny what everyone could *see*. Had she consented to their being hurt?

"Never in my life."

Someone accused Goody Wildes of hurting John Herrick's mother, and she denied that, too, although a Captain How testified to confirm it. (This was likely Mary Reddington, Herrick's mother-in-law and sister of John Wildes's first wife. Mary had long suspected Sarah of witchcraft.) The afflicted watched her specter frolic on the beam above, but Sarah Wildes herself was held for trial. Constable Ephraim Wildes, watching as his mother was led away, was certain that Deliverance Hobbs had accused his mother from the spite she bore him for her own arrest. He hadn't forgotten Goody Hobbs's vengeful look when he apprehended her.[76]

Mary Esty was the sister of the imprisoned Rebecca Nurse and Sarah Cloyse, the third suspected daughter of their late suspected mother. When she was led in, the afflicted's seizures rendered them speechless. Abigail Williams at last identified her as the Goody Esty who hurt her. Mary Walcott and Ann Putnam said likewise and John Indian added that he had seen her with Goody Hobbs.[77]

"I can say before Christ Jesus, I am free," she said. But when the magistrates interrupted her repetitions of innocence to ask the afflicted if Goody Esty had brought them the book, they only strangled wordlessly.

"What have you done to these children?" Hathorne demanded.

"I know nothing."

"How can you say you know nothing when you see these tormented?"

"Would you have me accuse myself?" she objected.

"Yes, if you be guilty," said one magistrate while the other asked, "How far have you complied with Satan whereby he takes this advantage of you?"

"Sir, I never complied, but prayed against him all my days. I have no compliance with Satan in this. What would you have me do?"

"Confess, if you be guilty."

"I will say it, if it was my last time—I am clear of this sin."

"Are you certain this is the woman?" the magistrates asked the afflicted, but all were speechless from convulsions.

"It was like her," young Ann Putnam managed to say, "and she told me her name."

When the defendant declined to guess whether the afflicted were actually bewitched or not, the magistrate sarcastically remarked that he couldn't see why she should pretend *not* to know. Others had confessed that they themselves bewitched them.

"Well, sir," said Goody Esty, "would you have me confess that I never knew?" She clasped her hands as she spoke, and Mercy Lewis found herself unable to part her own until the officers made the defendant loosen her grip.

"Look," said one of the magistrates, "now your hands are open, her hands are open."

But the other asked the afflicted again, "Is this the woman?"

The afflicted could not speak, however. They could only gesture until Ann Putnam, and then Betty Hubbard, found their voices. "Oh, Goody Esty, Goody Esty. You are the woman, you are the woman."

The accused drooped her head, and the girls' necks snapped forward. "Put up her head," ordered the court, "for while her head is lowered, the necks of these are broken."

What, Hathorne asked Goody Esty, had she thought of the goings-on before her sisters' arrests? Did she think it witchcraft then?

"I cannot tell."

"Why do you not think it is witchcraft?"

"It is an evil spirit, but whether it be witchcraft, I do not know."

The afflicted cried out that she had brought them the book, and fell in more fits as Mary Esty was committed to prison until her trial.

Edward and Sarah Bishop and Mary English also proclaimed their innocence, but all were held for trial. (Unfortunately, their examination notes did not survive.)

Edward Bishop had beaten John Indian on April 11, and had offered to flog the other afflicted to their senses. His wife Sarah was a stepdaughter of the accused

Sarah Wildes and half-sister to Constable Ephraim Wildes. The Bishops ran an un-licensed tavern in their home in the Ryal Side section of the Village. People loi-tered there at all hours to drink and to gamble at the tabletop game of shovel board. If neighbors complained, the Bishops turned mean. Edward was repeatedly in court for selling liquor without a license, and once for letting his children "abuse" the neighbors' swine in retaliation. Two years earlier, Christian Trask had worked up the courage to face them directly—during the encounter she threw a shovel board set in the fire—but the situation continued. Goody Trask became dis-tracted, certain Goody Bishop had bewitched her. She had seizures in the meeting house and spoke of suicide and murder. After a month's decline she stabbed her-self to death through the windpipe, severing her jugular, with a pair of short-bladed sewing scissors. Sarah Bishop was not charged with witchcraft then, how-ever. (Her father-in-law was constable and her husband was on the coroner's jury.) But even before this, when the Bishops argued publicly, her husband had implied that Sarah was so familiar with the Devil that she sat up nights chatting with the fiend. (Nevertheless, Sarah had joined the Salem Village Church in 1690.) More re-cently, when Sarah Bishop's specter set upon their neighbor Elizabeth Hubbard, Elizabeth told potter James Kettle that the specter promised a whole kiln-full of his pots would be ruined, and so they were.[78]

Mistress Mary English, an accomplished woman who owned a good deal of in-herited property in Salem, handled some of her husband's business in his ab-sences, and probably ran the shop in their house. Some poorer neighbors thought her too much the great lady, but her own kin were a formidable lot. Only seven years earlier, her brother William Hollingsworth had fought off the constable with an ax when the latter tried to arrest him for debt, while William's widowed mother Eleanor clouted the lawman from behind. (One of the afflicted may have even accused widow Hollingsworth later this summer, until informed the woman was three years dead.) For now, Mary English was held for tormenting Elizabeth Hubbard.[79]

After several had been questioned, Nehemiah Abbott was led back, but the spec-tators blocking the windows made the room too dim for anyone to see his features clearly. So the court moved outdoors into daylight, where the afflicted calmed and observed the defendant with quiet attention. All agreed that while Abbott was sim-ilar to the specter, he was not the same, perhaps their description had been more detailed than most. Abbott "was a hilly-faced man and stood shaded by reason of his own hair," Parris wrote, but he lacked the wen next to his eye the specter had. Hathorne and Corwin therefore dismissed Nehemiah Abbott who, unlike any of the other suspects so far, was free to go. The magistrates evidently concluded from this that they could indeed separate the obviously innocent from the probably guilty.[80]

Mary Black, a slave belonging to Nathaniel Putnam,* answered the charges ambiguously, repeating "I cannot tell," but she denied hurting the afflicted or knowing who did.[81]

Her master related an incident from a year earlier when she had sat next to a certain man. (The notes are unfortunately vague.)

"What did the man say to you?" Hathorne inquired.

"He said nothing."

"Doth this Negro hurt you?" the magistrates asked the afflicted. Several said she did. "Why do you hurt them?" Hathorne asked Mary.

"I do not hurt them." She fumbled nervously with her clothing.

"Do you prick sticks?" he demanded, thinking of the wooden images that Goody Hobbs had mentioned.

"No, I pin my neckcloth."

"Well take out a pin and pin it again." She did so, and as the sharp point pierced the cloth, the girls shrieked in pain. Abigail Williams felt jabbed in her stomach, and Mercy Lewis in her foot. The court saw blood flow from Mary Walcott's arm. Mary Black was held for trial.

While the specters nooned in Parris's pasture, court officials and invited ministers dined at Ingersoll's (adding sixteen shillings to the county's bill. (Hay, oats, and miscellaneous refreshments added another ten.) At day's end, while Nehemiah Abbott returned home, Marshal Herrick took the eight suspects to Salem prison. There the specters found Deliverance Hobbs, as she said later, and offered to share their feast of savory roasted and boiled meats with her, *if* she signed the book. At the time others were sure they heard more than just her voice coming from the room.†[82]

Ipswich

Meanwhile, at two o'clock that afternoon, Major Samuel Appleton had presided over another local court at Ipswich in Major John Sparks's house for the "clearing up of ye grounds of suspicion of Rachel Clenton's being a witch." She would, however, remain in jail.[83]

---

*Upham, with no source, says Mary Black worked for Nathaniel's son Benjamin.

†"Room," not cell.

April 23, 1692 • Saturday
Salem Village

Ann Putnam Jr. pleaded for mercy from the shape of John Willard as it tried to make her sign his book. The real Willard, with other neighbors, had once helped the Putnam household during her afflictions. He had also served as deputy to arrest a few suspects, and had been overheard to say, "Hang them! They are all witches." He resigned, however, when more and more people he thought innocent were accused.[84]

Salem Town

Questioned further in Salem prison, Deliverance Hobbs admitted she was a covenanting witch. Yes, she had signed the book. Yes, her spirit had slipped from custody to attend the witch meeting in Parris's pasture. But no, she did not eat or drink that Hellish sacrament. She described Burroughs, the man with the white high-crowned hat, and the women deacons. The specters blinded her, she said, after Abigail Williams ran out to speak with them. As Goody Hobbs confessed, her stepdaughter Abigail was brought into the room and immediately fell in a seizure. It was, said Deliverance, Giles Corey and a gentlewoman of Boston trying to break her daughter's neck.[85]

St. John, Acadia

On the same day, a hesitant Captain John Alden returned to Acadia's Commander Joseph Robineau de Villebon at St. John—six months late and with only six of the fifty-nine promised French soldiers. After reporting to Villebon, he landed the six on a nearby island, then sailed for Boston with the two men Villebon had sent to guard him. Furious at the paltry results of so much effort, and at the treachery of a prisoner on parole, the Commander sent Nelson and Tyng to Canada, and outfitted a privateer to prey on English ships. One of the returned soldiers told Villebon that Alden had refused to bring some of the others who wanted to come back. (The French were certain their soldiers were being sold as bond servants, although at least some were Protestant French who preferred to worship in Protestant territory.)[86]

April 24, 1692 • Sunday
Salem

During the Sabbath meeting in Salem town, Susanna Sheldon (Ephraim's sister) saw Philip English—or his specter—climb over the side of his pew and, joined by a Boston woman, torment her. On the way home she met him near William Shaw's place with the book in his hand and the Devil by his side, for such the dark-haired man in the tall-crowned hat surely was. War had driven the Sheldons from Maine to Salem Village, where Susanna's brother Nathaniel suddenly died "distracted." Her father had also died of a cut knee only the December before. The Sheldons lived just south of the Nurse holdings, but apparently Susanna worked for William Shaw, or for one of his neighbors, down by Proctor's Brook.[87]

Resenting the hostility of his sons-in-law Crosby and Parker, who had aligned against him and Martha, Giles Corey made a new will witnessed by Salem jailer William Dounton. Corey left everything—buildings, land, livestock, moveables, money, and apparel—to his other, more sympathetic, sons-in-law William Cleeves of Beverly and John Moulton of Salem. He made no mention, however, of his wife Martha; but whether from resentment or from despair of her survival is anyone's guess.[88]

Salem Village

In the Village, the specter of widow Dorcas Hoar of Beverly attacked Elizabeth Hubbard and Ann Putnam Jr. Abigail Williams recognized it as the first specter to torment her—even before Tituba's. John Willard's shape returned and hurt Ann Putnam so badly that everyone around the girl heard her cry his name.[89]

When he was first suspected, Willard had asked Bray Wilkins, his wife's grandfather and the patriarch of their settlement at Will's Hill, to pray with him in this time of trouble. Bray, on his way out the door, agreed to do so that evening but, between one thing and another, he returned late and forgot. It seemed to him afterward that Willard had looked particularly annoyed with him.[90]

April 25, 1692 • Monday
Salem Village

The real John Willard confronted Ann Putnam Jr. at her father's house, but she was convinced he was the same as the apparition. While he tried to state his case, she pleaded desperately for him to stop hurting her, and promised not to complain if he would only *stop*.[91]

Stamford, Connecticut

Meanwhile, in Stamford, Connecticut—some 250 miles as the crow flies from Salem Village—David and Abigail Westcott's French servant girl, Katherine Branch, felt a prickling and pinching in her breast while gathering herbs. For two days she would weep and fall to the floor. For thirteen more, a spectral cat, alternately cajoling and threatening, pursued her. In the weeks to come, she woke one night screaming, "A witch, a witch!" A woman's specter prowled about for the next few days until Kate identified it as that of Goodwife Elizabeth Clauson. Neighbors would describe Goody Clauson either as peaceful, even under provocation, or as belligerent and given to throwing stones. After the Westcotts had argued with her in the past over a flax-spinning job, their daughter Johannah had seemed violently bewitched.

Soon Kate showed all the usual signs of spectral torture plus alarming, if temporary, swellings. During lighter moments she rode an invisible horse and turned cartwheels with invisible witches. Some doubted the girl. Mrs. Sarah Bates, the local midwife-healer, said the fits likely had a natural cause, and thought she saw the girl laugh into her pillow. Others, after listening to Kate's tales of being possessed by a cat devil, began to see strange lights also.[92]

Boston

Life proceeded more normally in Boston where eight companies of militia trained on the Common. Rev. Deodat Lawson delivered the closing prayer to the bloodied troops (for the mock skirmish had gotten out of hand toward evening) and Samuel Sewall treated his South Company to drinks.[93]

Salem Town

Philip English's specter tormented Susanna Sheldon in Salem during the day. Two women and the dark-haired Devil assailed her in the evening. When Susanna refused to touch their book and demanded to know their names, one woman said she was "old man Buckley's wife" from Salem Village and the other was her daughter. The Devil had given the Buckley specter two familiars to suckle—like hairless kittens with human ears, as Susanna described them. Again she spurned the book and the Devil smacked her on the head in parting.[94]

April 26, 1692 • Tuesday
Salem

Susanna Sheldon saw yet another female specter, who laughed at her from the dooryard before capering inside with a book. Although the specter identified itself as Goodwife Whits of Boston, Susanna refused to sign. She refused again when specters of Goody Buckley and her daughter returned with their copy. Exasperated, Buckley snatched her from the doorstep into the air, and dropped her in William Shaw's woodlot. At least that was where Shaw's son, William Jr., found her, screaming and flailing among the sticks as if fighting someone unseen.[95]

Boston

In Boston, court sat for Suffolk county to hear ordinary cases of debt, theft, damaged cargo, and the selling of liquor without a license. The only unusual business before the court was that of a man who broke *into* jail to be with his woman.[96]

April 27, 1692 • Wednesday
Maine

A French sloop off the Maine coast began firing on English shipping, to Captain Elisha Hutchinson's alarm. As he reported to the legislature, the frontier people complained enough when attacked (there had been a skirmish near Andover) but no one wanted to feed or to house the often unruly and demanding militia. Some towns had taken it upon themselves to send the men home for want of provisions. Hutchinson's men had corn enough for only ten more days, even though there was plenty of corn for sale in the markets.[97]

Salem

The Devil in the high-crowned hat—accompanied by the specters of Mary English, Giles Corey, and Bridget Bishop—returned to Susanna Sheldon. They all suckled their familiars—a yellow bird, a pair of turtles, and a snake, respectively—while they hounded her. But although they also bit her viciously, Susanna would not sign their infernal book.[98]

April 28, 1692 • Thursday
Salem Village

This morning the specters of Goodman Corey and Mrs. English forbade Susanna Sheldon to eat anything. When she put a spoonful in her mouth, Corey cuffed her ear and choked her. She would eat, he jeered, only when he told her to eat. Then he prevented her from unclasping her hands for a good quarter hour, during which Philip English tormented her to sign the book.[99]

John Willard's specter accosted Ann Putnam Jr., after three or four days of relative peace, with the ghosts of his murder victims: his first wife in a winding sheet, and Ann's *own sister* Sarah, spectrally whipped to death at the age of six weeks. Willard threatened to kill Ann, too, if she would not sign.[100]

April 29, 1692 • Friday
Boston

With so many prisoners brought from Salem, Boston jailer John Arnold had to make extensive repairs both to the jail, where most of the accused and confessed witches were confined, and to the prison keeper's house, where he lived and where better accommodations were available for a higher price. (Some prisoners might have been in the Devil's pocket, but they were gentry after all.) Besides boards and nails, he spent eight shillings on four new locks.[101]

Meanwhile, the young minister Cotton Mather reserved the day for private prayers in his North End study. He recounted the problems of the land and its inhabitants, especially the "horrible enchantments and possessions broke forth upon Salem Village, things of a most prodigious aspect," and asked God how he might best help, how he might be useful. In Mather's opinion, spectral evidence alone was not enough to convict a suspect, for demons could appear in the guise of innocent people. He also thought the afflicted should be allowed to recover with the aid of prayer and fasting in quieter surroundings. He had, at the outset, offered to care for up to six of the afflicted as he had for the Goodwin girl in 1689, but the offer was declined.

On a more personal note he also prayed for his own neglected health, which had so far kept him from traveling to Salem. He still felt feverish after two bouts of flu and after all the extra work that had fallen to him in his father's long absence. Yet even now the elder Mather, Governor Phips, and the new Charter were homeward bound, and for all this Cotton Mather thanked God.[102]

Salem

In Salem, however, specters of Goody Bishop, Mrs. English, both Coreys, and the Devil flocked about Susanna Sheldon. Martha Corey shamelessly suckled a hairless black pig familiar before the specters all knelt in prayer to the Devil. The Bridget Bishop specter confided that it had killed several women including John Trask's wife. (Susanna did not know that Trask suspected Sarah, not Bridget Bishop, of his wife's death.)[103]

April 30, 1692 • Saturday
Salem Town

As more and different specters continued to haunt the girls, Jonathan Walcott and Thomas Putnam of Salem Village swore a complaint against Rev. George Burroughs of Wells, Maine; Lydia Dustin of Reading; Susanna Martin of Amesbury; Dorcas Hoar and Sarah Morrell of Beverly; and Philip English (husband of Mary English) of Salem for tormenting Mary Walcott, Mercy Lewis, Abigail Williams, Ann Putnam Jr., Elizabeth Hubbard, and the newly afflicted girl Susanna Sheldon. (Martha Corey's specter choked Susanna whenever she tried to eat today.)

Hathorne and Corwin issued warrants for all the suspects, sent for Burroughs from the Eastward, and ordered that the rest be brought before them at Ingersoll's by ten o'clock the following Monday.[104]

Philip English got wind of his impending arrest, however, and fled, hiding in the home of a Boston business associate, George Hollard.[105]

Tonight, Goody Sarah Bibber woke just in time to see the form of Sarah Good slide back her bed curtains. Staring fixedly at Bibber's four-year-old child, the specter peeled back the sheets—whereupon the child had such violent convulsions that John and Sarah Bibber could hardly hold it.[106]

Salisbury

Near the end of April, probably around the time of Susanna Martin's arrest, Joseph Ring of Salisbury saw her shape at his bedside and felt pinched. But instead of afflicting him, this pinch released Joseph from a spell of speechlessness that had gripped him since August. Even before that last mute episode, for two years, as he said when able to speak, witches kept snatching him away to observe their meetings, and would then stop his speech to keep the secret.[107]

5

MAY 1692

I have beheld most strange things, scarce credible but to the spectators.

—Thomas Newton

May 1, 1692 • Sunday
Salem Village

A new specter attacked Elizabeth Hubbard this Sabbath: Goodwife Rebecca Jacobs, the daughter-in-law of old George Jacobs, Sr. She was known to have been mentally unbalanced for a dozen years and more.[1]

May 2, 1692 • Monday
Salem Village

Almanacs predicted unseasonable warmth and possible thunder as the court convened at ten o'clock. Only half of the suspects were in the village. Susanna Martin was en route; Philip English remained in hiding (the magistrates issued a second arrest warrant for him); and George Burroughs was still in Maine. Hathorne and

Corwin, with Samuel Parris and perhaps another scribe ready to take notes, began without them.[2]

Sarah Morrell, daughter of Jersey immigrants Peter and Mary Morrell, had lived with her family in Falmouth, Maine, before it burned. She, her sister, and her mother somehow avoided the capture of Fort Loyal, where her father was taken, and moved to Beverly to await his eventual return from Canada. (The Robert Morrell family who lived for a time in Thomas Putnam's household in the Village were possibly kin.) Either Sarah or her sister Mary was in court the summer before on a charge of fornication. Now Sarah was accused of witchcraft and, after questioning, was held for trial.[3]

Eighty-year-old widow Lydia Dustin (whose examination is also lost) had been long suspected a witch, even though she was a member of the Reading Church. Ten years earlier, a furiously drunken neighbor had hurled rocks at her daughter's house while denouncing that "old crooked-back witch, your mother, you, and all your company of witches!" Goody Dustin was today held for tormenting a new afflicted witness, Mrs. Mary Marshall of Reading.[4]

Dorcas Hoar, a widow known to tell fortunes, was one member of a rowdy Beverly family, in court earlier for stealing from their neighbors, which included Rev. John Hale. (The Hoars' accomplice was the minister's maid who silenced the Hale children by threatening to kill them or to set the Devil on them and their parents.) After the Hoars were fined for theft, they clubbed Hale's cow to death and threw rocks against his house on nights when he was away and his family was alone. Even so, Dorcas's husband William had, for a time, been paid to sweep the meeting house and to ring its bell. The winter before her arrest he died in an "untimely" fashion and, although the coroner's jury found nothing unusual, people wondered if she might have been responsible. "She choked her own husband," said Elizabeth Hubbard. She had also lately choked a woman in Boston, said Ann Putnam Jr. and Abigail Williams.[5]

"Why do you pinch me?" Elizabeth cried. People saw a pinch mark on her, and Marshal Herrick verified that Goody Hoar had squeezed her fingers together at just that time. She denied ever seeing these afflicted people before, denied threatening suicide, and denied bringing Susanna Sheldon the Devil's book with or without cats, much less pretending to be Goody Buckley! But the magistrates, convinced by the physical pain of the afflicted, overlooked the inaccurate details of their visions.

"Oh! You are liars," Goody Hoar exclaimed, when several of the girls claimed to see the Devil whisper in her ear, "and God will stop the mouths of liars."

"You are not to speak after this manner in the court," the magistrate reprimanded.

"I will speak the truth as long as I live."

But the girls heard the Devil warn the defendant not to confess. Goody Bibber, calm before, verified this and convulsed.

The magistrate asked about the two black cats that her specter suckled, but she denied having any familiars. "You do not call them cats," he suggested. "What are they that suck you?"

"I never sucked none, but my child."

He inquired of Goody Buckley, whom her specter had pretended to be. "I never knew her," she said. But Goodman Buckley said that Goody Hoar often visited their house. "I know you," she replied, "but not the woman."

"You said you did not know the name," said the magistrate. Several people verified that Goody Hoar "disowned that she knew the name."

"I did not know the name so as to go to the woman."

Susanna Sheldon and Abigail Williams clamored that a bluebird had just flown into the defendant's back. Marshal George Herrick batted at the spot where that specter had disappeared. No one else saw the bird but several in the audience had a start when a large miller moth fluttered across the room.

"What do you see, Goody Bibber?" asked the magistrate, but she stared upward, dumbstruck. "What?" he said, rounding on Goody Hoar. "Can you have no heart to confess?"

Again she denied having anything to do with witchcraft, the Devil, or his book. "I have no book, but the Lord's book."

"What *lord's* book?" asked the magistrate, knowing Satan was called the Lord of Hell.

"The Lord's book," she repeated.

"Oh, there is one whispering in her ears!" cried some of the afflicted.

"There is somebody will rub your ears shortly," Goody Hoar muttered, and instantly Mercy Lewis and the others felt their ears burn.

"Why do you threaten they should be rubbed?" asked the magistrate.

"I did not speak a word of rubbing," she said, but many had heard the remark and testified to it. "My meaning was God would bring things to light," she explained.

"Your meaning for God to bring the thing to light would be to deliver these poor afflicted ones. That would not rub them," one magistrate observed.

"This is unusual impudence, to threaten before authority," said the other. "Who hurts them now?"

"I know not."

"They were rubbed *after* you had threatened them," he reminded her.

The court ordered a touch test by which the hurtful power projected onto the victim by the witch's gaze could be made to flow back into its sender through her touch. The magistrates forgot that this was folk magic and had Mary Walcott, Abigail Williams, and Elizabeth Hubbard brought, supported by officers, toward Dorcas Hoar. But they were seemingly repelled and could not get near enough to touch her.[6]

"What is the reason these cannot come near you?" demanded the court.

"I cannot help it. I do them no wrong. They may come if they will."

"Why, you see they cannot come near you."

"I do them no wrong."

But Dorcas Hoar was held for trial.[7]

Susanna Martin, a sharp-tongued widow of about seventy, had been suspected of witchcraft for over thirty years and possibly longer since, when young, she had worked for a Goody Batcheler, also accused of witchcraft. Susanna's husband George had sued William Sargent Jr. in 1669 for saying she had borne and then strangled a bastard before her marriage. The jury cleared her of the slander, but the magistrates required a £100 bond that she appear before the Court of Assistants to answer a charge of witchcraft. Little more came of it, however, or of other suits against slanders that her son George was a bastard and her son Richard her imp. (Richard, however, for reasons no longer clear, once hurled his old father to the ground, stripped him of his clothes and threatened him with an ax.) The Martins had also disputed her father's will when Susanna's widowed stepmother left most of the property to a granddaughter. They accused the magistrate Captain Thomas Bradbury, of forging the document, but Bradbury's reputation was impeccable and the Martins gained only ill will.[8]

Today, Amesbury constable Orlando Bagley escorted Goody Martin the twenty miles to Salem Village. They arrived late, and the afflicted convulsed as soon as she entered the meeting house. Those who could speak accused her, except for Elizabeth Hubbard and John Indian who said she had never hurt them. Before they collapsed, Mercy Lewis pointed wordlessly and Ann Putnam Jr. threw her glove in a fit at the defendant. Goody Martin, from derision or nerves, laughed at the spectacle.[9]

"What? Do you laugh at it?"

"Well I may laugh at such folly."

"Is this folly?" demanded the magistrate. "The hurt of these persons?"

"I never hurt man, woman, or child," she said.

"She hath hurt *me* a great many times," Mercy Lewis cried in anguish, "and pulls me down."

Goody Martin laughed again, and the onlookers thought her utterly heartless.

When others said she hurt them, she denied working witchcraft or consenting that her specter be used. She had no idea what ailed these people.

"But what do you think ails them?"

"I don't desire to spend my judgment upon it."

"Don't you think they are bewitched?"

"No," she said. "I do not think they are."

"Tell us your thoughts about them then."

"No, my thoughts are my own when they are in," she answered defiantly, "but when they are out they are another's. Their master—"

"Their master?" the court interrupted. "Who do you think is their master?"

"If they be dealing in the black art, you may know as well as I," she snapped, suggesting that the afflicted were themselves witches and that the court was as ignorant as she about the matter. Susanna herself had nothing to do with it. "I desire to lead myself according to the Word of God."

"Is this according to God's Word?" the magistrate asked, indicating the afflicted.

"If I were such a person, I would tell you the truth."

Her specter again tormented the afflicted, and when asked about that, she answered, "How do I know? He that appeared in the shape of Samuel, a glorified saint, may appear in anyone's shape." But the magistrates would not contemplate a parallel as appropriate as the false specter raised for King Saul by the Witch of Endor. The afflicted's present extreme suffering was more influential on the court than Susanna's pointed Biblical challenge to its one-sided interpretation of events.[10]

"Do you believe these do not say true?" asked the bench.

"They may lie, for aught I know."

"May not you lie?"

"I dare not tell a lie if it would save my life."

"Then you will speak the truth?"

"I have spoke nothing else. I would do them any good."

"I do not think you have such affections for them whom just now you insinuated had the Devil for their master."

Elizabeth Hubbard flinched and murmured to Marshal Herrick that Susanna Martin pinched her hand. Other afflicted shouted that her spirit was on the beam.

"Pray God discover you," said the magistrate, "if you be guilty."

"Amen, amen," she snapped back. "A false tongue will never make a guilty person."

"You have been a long time coming to the court today," exclaimed Mercy Lewis. "You can come fast enough in the night."

"No, sweetheart," Goody Martin said sarcastically. Mercy and most of the others convulsed, which seemed to upset the accused enough that she gnawed her lip.

"It was that woman!" cried John Indian, now in violent seizures. "She bites. *She bites.*"

"Have you not compassion for these afflicted?" exclaimed the magistrates.

"No. I have none."

The court again attempted a touch test, once more lapsing into folk magic that had neither legal nor religious approval. But Abigail Williams, Mary Walcott, and Goody Bibber were all repelled. John Indian shouted that he would kill her if he could get close enough, but some invisible force threw him down before he reached her. It seemed as if a devil were right there in the courtroom among them all. "What is the reason these cannot come near you?" asked the court.

"I cannot tell," said Goody Martin. "It may be the Devil bears me more malice than another." She suspected they could approach if they wanted to, and offered to approach them herself, but the offer was ignored.

"Do you not see how God evidently discovers you?"

"No. Not a bit for that."

"All the congregation think so."

"Let them think what they will." But the frantic accusations and stubbornly irregular proceedings drowned out the defendant's sharp defiance and insistence on her own innocence. Susanna Martin was committed to prison all the same.[11]

Court ran later than usual, and the prisoners were kept overnight at Salem Village, probably in the watchhouse across from the ordinary. Ingersoll provided dinner for the magistrates, the marshal and his men, and for their horses, as well as three shillings worth of drink for the guards during the night.[12]

Sarah Good's specter finally attacked Sarah Bibber, who had earlier seen that shape hurt only others. Now, panicked, she felt nearly suffocated, all breath pressed from her lungs. The specter also made the baby cry and writhe so that John Bibber had to snatch it as it slipped from Sarah's helpless grasp. Even then the child's seizures were so terrifyingly violent that the desperate father kept losing hold.[13]

Meanwhile, the specter of a little, black-bearded man in dark clothing appeared to Elizabeth Hubbard, introduced itself as Burroughs, and presented a book from its pocket. She saw the blood-red writing and refused to touch the thing, so the specter pinched her twice before leaving.[14]

Wells, Maine

Eastward, Elisha Hutchinson again ordered Marshal Jonathan Partridge of New Hampshire to arrest Rev. George Burroughs. Partridge objected to the long journey from Wells to Salem. Hutchinson insisted, but said he might pass the prisoner from one lawman to another and avoid making the whole trip himself.

According to tradition, the law arrived at Burroughs's house in Wells while the family was at the table, with no warning and little explanation, to seize the suspect before he could finish his meal. Further lore added a tempest that overtook the guards and their prisoner on the road south. Thunder, lightning, and falling trees struck terror in horse and rider alike, yet when it was over, Burroughs was with them still. Instead of taking this as a sign of good faith, the men thought the Devil had unsuccessfully fought to free him. Surviving contemporary records mention none of this, however.[15]

Burroughs was the only suspect arrested in Maine during the witch panic, but people even there were nervous. Goodwife Sarah Keene of Kittery worried about the notion that one could be a witch and *not even know it*, about the wart under her breast, and about what the neighbors might think if they knew.[16]

May 3, 1692 • Tuesday
Salem Village

The Burroughs specter appeared to Elizabeth Hubbard again. Instead of trying to hurt her, it bragged that Burroughs was more than a wizard. He was a *conjurer*.[17]

The guards breakfasted at Ingersoll's before escorting the four prisoners—Sarah Morrell, Lydia Dustin, Dorcas Hoar, and Susanna Martin—by horsecart directly to Boston where the jailkeeper began their bills backdated to the day of their examinations.[18]

Salem Town

Once Goody Hobbs confessed, the afflicted no longer saw her specter, but later when she tried to deny the confession, her shape became maliciously active again. The magistrates, questioning her in the Salem jail, wanted to know what she was up to.[19]

"Nothing at all."

"But have you not since been tempted?"

"Yes, sir. But I have not done it, nor will do it."

"Here is a great change since we last spoke to you, for now you afflict and torment again. Now tell us the truth. Who tempted you to sign again?"

"It was Goody Oliver," she said, referring to Bridget Bishop whose second husband had been Thomas Oliver. Dorcas did not sign, however. Neither did she consent to hurt the afflicted again. But the magistrates' barrage of questions rattled her into agreement. She named other witches, suspects already arrested, but she did not identify the man with the wen. As for allowing a specter to hurt these children in her likeness she said "I do not know that I did." The interview ended with increasing confusion on both sides.[20]

Will's Hill

Meanwhile, in the westernmost part of Salem Village at Will's Hill, various members of the Wilkins family, including old Bray and his wife Anna, prepared for an Election Day trip to Boston. John Willard asked Henry Wilkins Sr., his wife's uncle, to accompany him. Henry agreed, seeing how earnest his kinsman was about it. But once Willard left, Henry noticed his sixteen-year-old son seemed troubled. "Willard ought to be hanged!" Daniel blurted. His father was amazed at his son's violent outburst, for Daniel had never talked like that.[21]

This evening, Mary Walcott endured the torments of Rebecca Nurse's shape, and heard it boast of murdering several neighbors.* And when Ann Putnam Jr. again refused the book that George Burroughs's specter brought this same evening, it warned her that Burroughs's two dead wives might appear but not to believe their lies. The wives' ghosts frightened the girl more than the minister's specter had, for they looked like corpses swathed in winding sheets. Even so, they flushed red as they accused their husband of cruelty and reminded him that when they reached Heaven, he would be in Hell. Burroughs vanished at that sort of incendiary talk. The ghosts, now pale as whitewash, told Ann how he had murdered the first in the Salem Village parsonage by stabbing her under the arm. She pulled aside her sheet to reveal the spot. He killed the second, they claimed, in a boat, aided by his present wife "because they would have one another." They pleaded for Ann to tell the magistrates despite their husband's dire threats. Later, other ghosts appeared to Ann: Deodat Lawson's first wife and their child, as well as Goody Fuller.† Burroughs had murdered them all.[22]

May 4, 1692 • Wednesday
Salem

As Rebecca Nurse's specter plagued Abigail Williams, the real George Burroughs arrived in Salem, escorted by Marshal Partridge the whole way from Maine.[23]

Boston

The magistrates were in Boston, however, for Election Day. There, two military companies marched in attendance and Rev. Joshua Moody delivered the Election

---

*The Nurse specter bragged of killing Benjamin Holten; John Harrod ("old Goodman Harwood"); Benjamin Porter; Rebecca Shepard—probably Rebecca (Putnam) (Fuller) Shepard; and several more.

†Burroughs's wives were Hannah (Fisher), Sarah (Ruck) (Hathorne?), and the living wife Mary (——). Goody Fuller may have been Rebecca (Putnam) (Fuller) Shepard.

Day sermon. Moody used the text I Samuel 12:7, a passage where the prophet Samuel—the same later counterfeited by the witch of Endor—reminded his people of God's many favors, before criticizing them for placing more trust in an earthly king than in the Lord God.

Simon Bradstreet was reelected acting governor, and Thomas Danforth confirmed as deputy governor. Only one incumbent lost his place. William Stoughton, Samuel Sewall, John Hathorne, and Jonathan Corwin were among the eighteen assistants reelected, as was Sir William Phips (whose royal appointment made him governor regardless of today's election). Simon Bradstreet served beer, cider, and wine, and the officials went off to dine at Wing's tavern.[24]

The Wilkins family, meanwhile, were invited to have their noon meal at the home of Goody Wilkins's brother, Lieutenant Richard Way, along with Rev. Deodat and Deborah Lawson. Bray's son Henry Wilkins Sr. and John Willard arrived after the other guests. When they entered, Willard looked at Bray with an odd expression that the old man feared was the evil eye. Stepping into the next room, Bray felt suddenly and utterly wretched. "I cannot express the misery I was in," he would later testify, "for my water was suddenly stopped and I had no benefit of nature, but was like a man on a rack." He told his wife that he suspected Willard for his agony, and this idea grew with his pain. Someone sent for a neighborhood woman skilled in healing. She did what she could, but to no effect. Had any "evil persons" damaged him? she asked. Bray wasn't sure, but was afraid they had. The woman agreed that she feared so, too.[25]

Salem Town

Around this time, Mary Warren, still in Salem jail, bemoaned her lot in the presence of several fellow prisoners whom she had once accused. Edward and Sarah Bishop, Mary Esty, and Mary English often heard her say the magistrates might as well question Keyser's daughter, a witless Salem girl "distracted many years," and take what *she* said seriously. "When I was afflicted," admitted Mary Warren, "I thought I saw the apparitions of a hundred persons." But she was too distempered then to know what she said, and when she was well, she could not remember what she had seen. The afflicted, Mary declared, simply did not know what was real and what was illusion.[26]

May 5, 1692 • Thursday
Salem Town

The Rev. George Burroughs was being kept apart from the other Salem prisoners in an upstairs room of Thomas Beadle's tavern when Eleazar Keyser (a brother of the distracted girl) dropped by. He fell into conversation with Captain Daniel King, a militia leader who had served in the frontier wars Eastward. King urged Keyser to talk with Burroughs, but Keyser nervously declined with the excuse that it was not his place to "discourse" with "a learned man" like Burroughs.

"I believe he is a child of God," King exclaimed, "a choice child of God" and God would reveal Burroughs's innocence.

Keyser admitted he feared that Burroughs was actually "the ringleader" of all the witches, to King's infuriated disgust.

Later that afternoon Keyser let curiosity overcome fear and did visit the prisoner. Burroughs, not caring to be an oddity for sightseers, stared back at Keyser in a way that further unnerved him. That night Keyser saw a dozen quivering globs of light like shining jellyfish in his dark room. When they disappeared, he noticed a glow, and, peering up the chimney, saw a light the size of his hand shimmer above the bar support. The maid saw it too, but his wife saw nothing.[27]

May 6, 1692 • Friday
Boston

The General Court, sitting in Boston since the election, recommended a Public Fast for May 26 to petition Heaven's mercies for persecuted Protestants abroad, for the success of New England's summer crops, and for the setbacks of their enemies everywhere. On a more mundane level the court put Samuel Sewall in charge of finances to keep the Castle armed and ready.[28]

While in Boston, assistants Hathorne and Corwin issued *another* arrest warrant for Philip English. This likely coincided with a search of George Hollard's house near the tide mill at the edge of the North End, but English successfully eluded the officers behind a sack of dirty laundry—the one place they did not look.[29]

Salem

At nine o'clock this evening Margaret Jacobs saw the specter of Alice Parker (a Salem town woman) in Northfields, where Margaret lived in her grandfather George Jacobs Sr.'s household between Salem town and the Village.[30]

Will's Hill

Bray Wilkins, still suffering from three or four days of urinary problems, risked the thirty-mile horseback ride home from Boston. When he arrived at Will's Hill, he found his grandson Daniel seriously ill of unknown causes.[31]

May 7, 1692 • Saturday
Salem Village

This evening Burroughs's specter slyly approached Mercy Lewis with an unfamiliar volume and claimed there was no harm touching this one which had been in his study back when she worked for him. Mercy didn't recognize it. He owned many books that she had never seen, the spirit countered, then bragged he could raise the Devil, had recruited Abigail Hobbs, and had already bewitched Mr. Shepard's daughter.* Mercy demanded to know how he could wreak all this havoc if he were bodily confined in Salem. The specter replied that the Devil was his servant whom he sent to do mischief disguised as himself. Burroughs's specter tortured Mercy until she thought she would be racked in pieces, yet she would not sign his book.[32]

May 8, 1692 • Sunday
Salem Village

For sacrament Sabbath, Samuel Parris addressed the Villagers on the topical text I Corinthians 10:21: "Ye cannot drink the cup of the Lord, and the cup of Devils; ye cannot be partakers of the Lord's Table and the Table of Devils." True enough as metaphor, this passage now seemed, according to recent testimony, to have a literal reality.[33]

Abigail Williams, Ann Putnam Jr., Mercy Lewis, and Mary Walcott were in a particularly bad state. Sabbath or not, Thomas Putnam and John Putnam Jr. traveled to the magistrates Hathorne and Corwin in Salem town. They swore a complaint against widow Bethia Carter, her daughter Bethia Jr., and widow Ann Sears all of Woburn, and Sarah Dustin (Lydia's daughter) of Reading.[34]

Besides these suspects' specters, another of "an old gray-headed man with a great nose" brought the book to Ann Putnam. He told her that he was "old Father Pharaoh" from Lynn, and everyone—even her father Thomas—respectfully called him "Father." Ann refused to believe him. (The real Thomas Farrar was a known drunkard of occasional violence.)[35]

Burroughs's specter, who had earlier threatened to starve or to choke Susanna Sheldon, now promised to kill her if she testified against him.[36]

May 9, 1692 • Monday
Salem Village

Before the examination, Burroughs's specter abducted Mercy Lewis and brought her to "an exceeding[ly] high mountain." He showed her all the kingdoms of earth—just as Satan had to Christ—and promised her *all* of them, if only she would sign. When she replied that they were not his to give, he threatened to break her neck, to hurl her down onto one hundred pitchforks for her defiance. Before court convened, the specter also accosted Susanna Sheldon at Ingersoll's, and boasted

*John Shepard's daughter Elizabeth, died January 1690/91, age three, "at Captain Putnam's."

of the three children whom he had killed in Maine, including two of his own, as well as his two wives—one smothered, the other choked.[37]

Constable Ephraim Bock brought the Woburn suspects, Ann Sears and the two Bethia Carters, to Ingersoll's. George Burroughs was brought up from Salem town, but Constable John Parker didn't bring Sarah Dustin over from Reading until noon.[38]

Examinations were likely held in the meeting house to accommodate the usual crowds. Because of the extra gravity of a minister accused of collaborating with the Devil, Assistants William Stoughton and Samuel Sewall joined Hathorne and Corwin to question George Burroughs. Rev. Samuel Parris took notes. They first spoke to the accused minister privately (probably at Ingersoll's) away from the afflicted. He was rumored never to take communion. Not being ordained, Burroughs could not himself administer the Lord's Supper, yet he was still a full member of the Roxbury Church, and had been in Boston and Charlestown on several sacrament Sabbaths. According to the notes, "he owned that none of his children but the eldest was baptized." (Perhaps this was a confusion about the children of his various marriages, for baptismal records still exist for five of the older children. The younger children were not yet baptized.) He admitted that his Maine home had toads but not ghosts. He vehemently denied his rumored cruelty to his wives.[39]

When Burroughs was led into the courtroom, most of the afflicted were tormented. Susanna Sheldon testified that Burroughs's dead wives said he had murdered them, and when the court ordered Burroughs to look at Susanna, she fell as if struck. So did most of the other afflicted when he glanced at them. Mercy Lewis suffered "a dreadful and tedious fit" before her deposition could be read. The other girls—Mary Walcott, Elizabeth Hubbard, Susanna Sheldon, and Ann Putnam Jr.—likewise convulsed as the court read their testimonies aloud, and as the people heard of Burroughs's tortures and temptations, of his magical boasts and mountaintop promises. In the flood of detail and amid the traumatic spectacle of the afflicted, the magistrates overlooked or ignored the contradictions in the stories given by the supposed ghosts of Burroughs's wives. For these specters told Susanna Sheldon that he had smothered and choked them, but told Ann Putnam that he had stabbed and strangled them.[40]

When asked what he thought of it all, Burroughs admitted that it was "an amazing and humbling Providence," but he understood none of it. "Some of you may observe," he added, "that when they begin to name my name, they cannot name it." In Burroughs's view this meant the accusers could not really identify him, but from the court's perspective he collaborated with invisible forces to interfere with the witnesses. After more testimony about his wives' ghosts, the afflicted convulsed so severely that some were taken outside to recover.

The court heard depositions from Abigail and Deliverance Hobbs concerning his poppets, his recruiting, and the witch meetings, and from Eleazar Keyser, whose suspicions had been followed by inexplicable lights. Captain Simon Willard (a brother of the Boston minister), John Wheldon, and Captain Jonathan Putnam related incidents from their military service Eastward in 1689. At that time, the story was all over Casco Bay about how Burroughs, though smaller and slighter than most other men, could aim one-handed a certain heavy fowling piece with a seven-foot barrel. They hadn't actually seen him do it, but Willard saw the gun— a type used in besieged blockhouses—and couldn't steady it even with two hands. Captain William Wormall and John Brown said they had heard that Burroughs could lift a full barrel of cider or molasses from a canoe and carry it ashore by himself. They hadn't witnessed this feat either, but had heard Burroughs himself say he nearly strained his leg doing it on the slippery shore. Burroughs denied the barrel story entirely, and explained that he had held the gun behind its lock and braced the stock against his breast (still a considerable feat).[41]

George Burroughs, bewildered and besieged but not yet vanquished, was held for trial, as were most of the day's defendants (for whom no notes survive).

Ann Sears had raised a family in Lancaster, Massachusetts, with her first husband Jacob Farrar until the town's destruction during King Philip's War. They and most of their surviving children relocated to Woburn, where Farrar died a few years later, and where Ann married John Sears.[42]

Lydia's daughter, Sarah Dustin, single even in her thirties, and a member of a long-suspected family, was brought in about noon by Constable John Parker. She was accused of tormenting a new girl, Elizabeth Weston (daughter of John Weston of Reading), and held for trial.[43]

Bethia Carter, not long widowed, had been given to gossip about other people's marital woes, perhaps because her own marriage was so unhappy. (Her husband Joseph had apparently raped the neighbor's slave woman.) As a girl in Lynn she and her sister had thought themselves bewitched by the healer Goody Burt (Elizabeth Proctor's grandmother).[44]

Although Constable Bock reported that he had brought all the Woburn suspects as ordered, twenty-one-year old Bethia Carter Jr. was not jailed with the rest. She apparently remained free for a few days more, or perhaps she, like Nehemiah Abbott, was simply released.[45]

On the other hand, twenty-year-old Sarah Churchill, a Maine refugee who perhaps had attended court as an afflicted witness, was examined by the magistrates and held for trial. (Her late grandfather, John Boynton, had been prominent in Saco, Maine, though once outlawed there for threatening to kill a man and anyone who tried to stop him. Her mother, Eleanor, who had been fined by a Maine court in 1667 for bearing a bastard, now lived in Marblehead with her husband Arthur Churchill, whom Sarah carefully avoided calling father.) Sarah had worked as a servant to George Jacobs Sr., until her convulsions interfered with her work—to old Jacob's disgust. ("Bitch witch," he had spat.) But she, like Mary Warren, tried to change her story and was sharply questioned about the reversal. The magistrates, confident that they understood events, disregarded not only the protests of the accused, but any deviation in word or deed of the afflicted. By the time the court finished questioning Sarah, she knew only that they would not believe her new story and threatened to jail her with Burroughs and his like, so she "confessed" to witchcraft. If her pain was gone she must have cooperated with the Devil. Besides, her specter tormented Mercy Lewis, Ann Putnam Jr., and Elizabeth Hubbard. Sarah said her name was in the Devil's book twice, along with her master, his son, and his granddaughter. Sarah convulsed tonight at Ingersoll's, which Mary Warren interpreted as the work of an old man leaning on two canes—Sarah's master, George Jacobs Sr.[46]

Jacobs's specter also beat Mercy Lewis at Ingersoll's until she thought her joints would be pulled apart, while John Willard's shape tormented Susanna Sheldon. His murder victims trailed behind him, all clamoring for Susanna to tell Hathorne about their plight.* Willard flourished a knife and threatened to cut her throat if she did. The specter of Elizabeth Coleson, Lydia Dustin's granddaughter, was more subtle and only offered a black coin as bribe to touch the book.[47]

May 10, 1692 • Tuesday
Salem

The ghosts swarmed back to Susanna Sheldon come morning, crying for vengeance, while Willard's specter continued to threaten mayhem if she testified. Then the radiant man appeared and made Willard vanish. This angel promised her safe conduct to and from court, but could not, he said, protect her during the

---

*The ghosts were of William Shaw's first wife (Elizabeth [Fraile] Shaw), widow Cooke, Goodman Jons, and his child.

upcoming examination. Two hours later, when Willard's dead wives and other victims returned, the angel named the ghosts and showed her their wounds. Southwark's had a pitchfork tine imbedded in his left side under his shroud. (The same ghosts as before plus "Southerek," perhaps Josiah Southwick who died sometime in 1692, and was kin to John Willard.)[48]

So while the latest prisoners were taken straight to Boston in Ingersoll's hired horsecart, the Salem magistrates ordered Constable John Putnam to arrest John Willard. (But when Putnam arrived at Willard's house in Boxford, the suspect had fled.) Partly due to Sarah Churchill's confession, Hathorne and Corwin also issued arrest warrants for George Jacobs Sr. and his granddaughter Margaret (although not for his son George Jr.). Constable Joseph Neal brought both suspects to Thomas Beadle's tavern* in Salem town, for today the witnesses rather than the magistrates did the journeying.[49]

Salem Town

George Jacobs Sr. entered the courtroom on his two sticks and confronted his accusers confidently. "Well, let us hear who are they, and what are they."[50]

"Abigail Williams—" the magistrate began, but Jacobs guffawed at the name and they pounced on that.

"Because I am falsely accused," the old man explained. "Your worships, all of you, do you think this is true?"

They wanted to know what *he* thought about it, but the questioning went nowhere. "Why should we not ask you? Sarah Churchill accuseth you. There she is," said the magistrate, indicating Jacobs's servant.

"I am as innocent as the child born tonight," Jacobs protested. "I have lived thirty-three years here in Salem."

"What then?" asked the court dismissively, for some of those years were turbulent.[51]

He would accept this charge, Jacobs told Sarah, "if you can *prove* that I am guilty."

"Last night I was afflicted at Deacon Ingersoll's," said Sarah, "and Mary Warren said it was a man with two staves. It was my master."

"Pray do not accuse me," said Jacobs. "I am as clear as your worships. You must do right judgments."

When Sarah told of a time that he hurt her by the river, and how he brought the book to her, Jacobs protested again. "The Devil can go in any shape." But the court

---

*The location of Jacobs's examination is not noted. Ingersoll's bill omits this date, the second exam would be at Beadles, and Willard's warrant ordered he be taken to Beadle's (a block east of Salem Common). Jonathan Corwin's house, still extant, is traditionally identified as the scene of preliminary hearings. Rural magistrates had to use their homes but surviving bills indicate Corwin and Hathorne rented public rooms at county expense.

ignored this defense, as they had from the very first day when Sarah Osborne made the same objection.

"Look here," the magistrate rounded on him. "She accuseth you to your face. She chargeth you that you hurt her twice. Is it not true?"

"What would you have me say? I never wronged no man in word nor deed."

"Here are three evidences," said the magistrate, as the afflicted convulsed.

"You tax me for a wizard!" Jacobs exploded. "You may as well tax me for a buzzard! I have done no harm."

But the girls' torments counted greatly against him, even though he repeated the still-ignored challenge to the legitimacy of such evidence: "The Devil can take any likeness." *Any* person might be counterfeited.

"Not without their consent," the magistrate snapped.

"Please, your worship. It is untrue. I never showed the book. I am as silly about these things as the child born last night."

"That is your saying," said the magistrate. "You argue you have lived so long, but what then? Cain might live so long before he killed Abel, and you might live long before the Devil had so prevailed on you."

"You had as good confess," Sarah interrupted, "if you are guilty."

"Have you heard that I have any witchcraft?" he asked her.

"I know you lived a wicked life."

"Let her make it out," he said disgustedly.

"Doth he ever pray in his family?" the court asked Sarah.

"Not unless by himself."

"Why do you not pray in your family?" the magistrate asked him.

"I cannot read."

"Well, but you may pray for all that. Can you say the Lord's Prayer? Let us hear you." Jacobs attempted to recite that basic Christian prayer, but made miss after miss.

He objected to Sarah's story that he had persuaded his son and granddaughter to sign the Devil's book, or that he had pestered her with it. "One in my likeness. The Devil may present my likeness."

They ignored the old man's repeated protest. (To accept it would be to doubt nearly all the evidence.) "Were you not frightened, Sarah Churchill, when the representation of your master came to you?"

"Yes."

"Well burn me or hang me!" Jacobs declared. "I will stand in the truth of Christ! I know nothing of it."

Knowing or unknowing, Jacobs was held for further questioning, but there was apparently no time to question Margaret.[52]

At some point during a lull in the proceedings, Goodwives Sarah Ingersoll, the Deacon's niece who lived around the corner from Beadle's Tavern, and Ann Andrews, George Jacobs's daughter, encountered Sarah Churchill outside the court-

room. She had undone herself, the girl sobbed, belying herself and others with her story of signing the Devil's book. Goody Ingersoll said that she had believed the girl's original confession. "No, no, no!" wailed Sarah. "I never did." But why, asked the women, would she lie if she lied to condemn herself? "They" threatened her, she said, threatened to imprison her with Burroughs and the rest. She paced back and forth, wringing her hands. She lied, she repeated, afraid *not* to confess after holding to her original story for so long. Besides, if she told Rev. Noyes only once that she put her hand to the Devil's book, he would believe her. If she told him the truth a hundred times now, he would not. (Known as a genial, charitable bachelor fond of puns and poetry, Noyes saw no humor in the present situation.)[53]

Boston

In Boston, John Arnold ordered three more large locks for his prison, and noted that Sarah Osborn, ill to begin with, had died, probably of "jail fever," after a confinement of nine weeks and two days, leaving a bill of £1-3-0. The witch scare had turned deadly even before the trials began.[54]

Salem

By evening, the Willard and Coles specters, accompanied by an old man and several animal familiars, flocked back to Susanna Sheldon. They all tried to tempt her with money to sign the book. Even the Devil in the high-crowned hat was there, to whom the others knelt before they all vanished.[55]

May 11, 1692 • Wednesday
Salem Town

The specters of John Willard and an old man, skimming over the river on something shaped like a dish, followed Susanna Sheldon to court. The real Willard had not been found, however, although the specter continued to torment Elizabeth Hubbard throughout the day.[56]

George Jacobs Sr. was questioned further at Thomas Beadle's Tavern, where the afflicted fell screaming as soon as he entered. Ann Putnam Jr. said he promised that she would be as well as his granddaughter Margaret if Ann but signed his book. Elizabeth Hubbard was not hurt by Jacobs's specter until today, but Mary Walcott was sure he was the same who beat her with one of his walking sticks. Jacobs denied everything.[57]

Mercy Lewis tried to approach him, but fell writhing some steps away. When the court read her testimony about his spectral activities, he exclaimed, "Why, it is false! I know not of it, any more than the child that was born tonight."

"Yes, you told me so," Ann Putnam contradicted, "that you had been so this forty years." Then she and Abigail Williams each discovered a pin stuck in their respective hands and blamed Jacobs.

"Are you not the man that made a disturbance at a lecture in Salem?" one of the magistrates asked.

"No great disturbance," he half admitted, then got to the point. "Do you think I use witchcraft?"

"Yes, indeed."

"No," said Jacobs. "I use none of them."

But again he was held, not for further questioning this time, but for trial.[58]

The court questioned Margaret Jacobs next. Because she had recovered from her spectral torments, the afflicted were certain she had succumbed and joined the witches. Her family had urged her not to confess to what she had *not* done, but Margaret was already scared witless, especially when the afflicted convulsed in their usual spectacular fashion. She had no idea what caused their fearsome seizures, but the authorities insisted that *she* must be causing it or the girls would not fall at her approach. All she later remembered were threats of imprisonment and hanging if she would not confess, but the promise of her life if she would. The court meant only that confession would save her spiritual life, her soul. (Witchcraft was a capital crime, and "confessors" were spared so that they—like other conspirators—could testify against their fellow criminals. The reprieve would only be temporary, but not all the defendants seemed to understand this.) Out of fear, Margaret "confessed" and lied to save her life. She agreed with whatever the court presupposed and implicated her grandfather Jacobs, Rev. George Burroughs, John Willard, and a Salem woman, Alice Parker.[59]

Joseph Flint slipped from the audience to the next room, where George Jacobs Sr. was being held, to tell him what had just happened. Margaret was charged not to confess, said Jacobs. Who charged her? Flint asked, for the specters reputedly demanded the witches' silence. Jacob paused. If Margaret were innocent, he said at last, and yet confessed, she would be an accessory to her own death.[60]

Preparing for future trials, the local authorities began to record testimony, either in court or, in cases of illness, at the deponents' own homes, about Burroughs, Susanna Martin, and others.[61]

Mercy Lewis had glimpsed John Willard's specter among the witches for weeks without harm, but today it throttled and threatened her. Around the same time, sixteen-year-old John DeRich, knowing old Jacobs was in prison, nonetheless found himself harried by Jacobs's specter. It knocked him into the river with its staff, and would have drowned him if a neighbor hadn't come to the rescue.[62]

In Salem jail, meanwhile, Abigail Hobbs swore that Burroughs had tried to make her sign his book. But Margaret Jacobs was sleepless with fear that the Devil would fetch her away for telling "such horrid lies." She did not, however, deny her confession just yet.[63]

May 12, 1692 • Thursday
Salem Town

Constable John Putnam Jr. admitted to the authorities that, try as he might, he could not find John Willard.[64]

The magistrates questioned Abigail Hobbs in Salem prison and garnered details of the image magic that Burroughs used to kill his Maine neighbors. This time Abigail mostly answered, "I don't know." She did say she had been a witch for six years and had made two covenants with the Devil. The first was for two years and the second for four—more like a servant's contract than the eternal and final sale that the Devil would require.[65]

The magistrates also questioned the wavering Mary Warren again about signing the Devil's book. "I did not know it then," she gabbled, "but I know it now to be sure. It was the Devil's book in the first place to be sure. I did set my hand to the Devil's book. I have considered of it since you were here last and it was the Devil's book my master Proctor brought to me, and he told me if I would set my hand to that book, I should believe."[66]

She denied consenting to the children's torment, digressed to Proctor's doubts about her fits, and then admitted hurting the girls with image magic. Her mistress had brought her a doll representing either Abigail Williams or Ann Putnam Jr. Goodwives Alice Parker and Ann Pudeator of Salem also brought such poppets and, when their specters visited her in prison, hinted that they would soon be there themselves. But of her mistress's book of magic, she knew nothing.

The Reverends John Higginson and John Hale entered to observe, and the scribe read his notes aloud for them. When he reached the testimony about Goody Parker, Mary fell in "dreadful fits," as she did a little later when Hathorne merely mentioned Parker's name. Parker's biting specter, she reported, boasted to her of the folk that it killed at sea or in the harbor, of drowning Goody Orne's son before his mother's own door, and of striking Mary's own sister dumb. Now Ann Pudeator's specter joined the bragging to announce that she had poisoned her own husband, and had nearly killed John Turner (who lived in what would later be called the House of Seven Gables) by tossing him on his head from a cherry tree. But she could not bewitch Mr. Corwin's mare to prevent his attendance in court at Salem Village. And even Burroughs could not hobble Hathorne's horse to keep him from Boston, much less bewitch Hathorne himself. (Mary said Ann Pudeator killed James Cloyse's child.)[67]

The severity of Mary's fits prompted Hathorne and Corwin to issue warrants for Ann Pudeator and Alice Parker "for sundry acts of witchcraft by them committed this day." When Marshal Herrick and his men went to arrest Ann Pudeator, the nurse tending her dying neighbor Goody Neal commented, "You are come too late." For Jeremiah Neal's wife, ill from smallpox, was now plagued with a flux as well, ever since Goody Pudeator had borrowed her mortar. Ann, who had once lived in Maine with her first husband, was now the widow of a second husband, whose first wife had died under curious circumstances while in Ann's care. Sarah Churchill said Goody Pudeator had brought her the Devil's book (but the notes to the accused's examination are lost). Ann Pudeator was included among the other prisoners next sent to Boston.[68]

Alice Parker lived by the shore with her fisherman husband John in a good-sized house that they rented from Mary English. Alice may have suffered from paralyzing fits of catalepsy, but she denied being a witch.[69]

"You told her this day," said the magistrate, meaning what the specter told Mary Warren, "you cast away Thomas Westgate."

"I know nothing of it," Goody Parker protested, but the court cited more disasters. "I never spoke a word to her in my life," she insisted.

Mary sought to strike her, but could not get within reach and only crumpled backward. Margaret Jacobs, still among the afflicted, accused Parker to her face of appearing "in apparition" in Northfields the Friday before.

Marshal Herrick added that when he had arrested Goody Parker, she said "there were threescore witches of the company."

She did not deny or explain this remark but claimed not to remember how many she had said. John Louder, who had recently been chased across Salem Common by her specter, had overheard the exchange and now verified Herrick's quotation of threescore (or sixty) witches.[70]

Mary Warren related, between convulsions, how her father got on Goody Parker's bad side after he had neglected a promise to mow Parker's grass (to harvest her hay) for lack of time. Parker came to the Warren house and said that "he had better he had done it." Shortly after, Mary's sister, and then their mother, fell ill. The mother died and her sister lost the power of speech. Now Mary accused Alice Parker of bringing poppets and a needle, and of threatening to run the needle through Mary's heart if she refused to torment the poppets. As she said this, Mary looked the accused square in the eye and convulsed.

Goody Parker declared that she hoped God would open the earth and swallow her up if one word of this were true. But the court was not impressed, for the magistrates could see, as the scribe noted, the results of witchcraft torturing the witnesses all the while. As far as Mary was concerned, the specter stepped from Parker's body to batter her while boasting of attending the diabolical meeting in Parris's pasture.

Rev. Nicholas Noyes reminded the accused of an earlier occasion when she was ill, and he spoke with her about witchcraft rumors. She told him then that if she were as free from other sins as from witchcraft, she would not need to ask God's mercy.

Mary Warren's seizures were so severe that her tongue, stretched far out of her mouth, turned black. Goody Parker, patience gone, snapped that the girl's tongue would be blacker before she died. When the court asked why she persisted in afflicting the innocent, she answered, "If I do, the Lord forgive me."

The magistrates issued a mittimus—a written order to send or receive prisoners—transferring eleven suspects to Boston jail: George Jacobs Sr., Giles Corey, William Hobbs, Edward and Sarah Bishop, Bridget Bishop, Sarah Wildes, Mary Black, Mary English, Alice Parker, and Ann Pudeator.[71]

Salem Village

This evening the specter of Sarah Buckley, whom the Dorcas Hoar specter had impersonated, choked and pinched Mary Walcott. It twisted the girl's neck again and again, vowing to kill her that very night. Mary gasped that she did not fear the threat, for she knew God's power was greater than the Devil's.

Will's Hill

Mercy Lewis accompanied some neighbors to call on the ailing Bray Wilkins at Will's Hill. For Bray Wilkins still suffered blockage, young Daniel's health worsened, and no one knew John Willard's whereabouts. When Mercy entered, the attending family and neighbors asked if she could see anything. "Yes," she said, looking into the Invisible World. "They are looking for John Willard, but there he is upon his grandfather's belly." She saw Goody Buckley too, pressing on the old man who was suffering a "grievous pain in the small of [his] belly." (Young Ann Putnam arriving soon after, verified the specters' identities.) John Putnam whacked at the invisible witches and Mercy convulsed. Bray's son Benjamin would recall that this counterattack would give the old man an immediate, if temporary, relief. Bray himself, however, would remember that his problems continued all the while Willard was loose.[72]

May 13, 1692 • Friday
Salem Town

The specter of Abigail Soames, a thirty-seven-year-old single woman from Gloucester, now of Salem, so tortured Mary Warren that Hathorne and Corwin issued a warrant for her at once. Constable Peter Osgood immediately fetched the suspect from the home of Samuel and Elizabeth Gaskill, where she lived and worked west of town. Mary Warren, meanwhile, was taken from prison to Thomas Beadle's tavern, where the pursuing specter bit her as she entered the gate. The biting and jabbing sensations continued, and when the defendant arrived, Mary collapsed, crying that this was the same woman whose specter hurt her.[73]

The court, suspecting image magic, had the suspect's clothes searched and found "a great crotching needle" in her apron. Abigail Soames denied knowing how the crochet hook got there, but Mary's pains ceased, Rev. Noyes noticed, once the object had been confiscated. Mary explained that she had never before seen the woman, only her specter who identified itself as Abigail Soames (living at the Gaskills' and bedridden for a year) whose brother was the Boston cooper John Soames. The magistrates asked the suspect if he were her brother, but she snapped that she would tell them nothing since all Mary Warren said was false (whatever the court might think about it). John *was* her brother, however, as well as being a Quaker twice arrested and whipped some fifteen years earlier under now defunct laws. Abigail Soames, her brother Nathaniel, and others from Gloucester had been reprimanded a dozen years back for not attending public worship.[74]

When Mary Warren said the Soames specter had bragged of helping kill some-one named Southwick,* Abigail turned to stare at her. This sent Mary into such a severe seizure that, according to the scribe, "the like was never seen on any of the afflicted."

Goody Gaskill testified that Abigail had been bedridden much of the past thir-teen months. Mary Warren chimed in to say she went out only at night, and Goody Gaskill had to agree, that it usually was at night. Soames's specter, Mary went on, tried to convince her not to tell just how sickly Abigail was, but insisted she was Mary's god.

"Mary Warren," asked a magistrate, "is this true?"

"It is nothing but the truth."

When the court asked Abigail who hurt the writhing girls, she replied, "It was the Enemy hurt her," meaning Satan. "I have been myself distracted many a time," she explained, "and my senses have gone from me, and I thought I have seen many a body hurt me, and might have accused many as well as she doth. I really thought I had seen many persons at my mother's camp at Gloucester, and they greatly afflicted me as I thought." (When she and her brothers neglected public worship in 1681, court records noted, "She hath been in a distracted condition about this two months, and her brother Nathaniel hath been forced to make it his whole employment to look after her.")[75]

---

*Perhaps the same Josiah Southwick as on May 10, likely a fellow Quaker.

The court ordered a touch test to bring Mary Warren out of a fit. Mary calmed as soon as Abigail took her hand as if all the spectral poison had been drained away, the intention of the test, but the first time that the notes indicate it gave any relief. This was done three times in all, for Mary fell whenever the magistrates ordered her to face the accused—she saw Abigail's spirit stride forward to shove her away. During the touch tests Mary's eyes clamped shut, but she could, she said, feel something soft in her hand. (She seemed to forget that the afflicted had earlier calmed each other with a touch.)[76]

"It was distraction in talking," Abigail Soames said more than once, but her explanation went unheeded. She began to laugh as she spoke and the seeming callousness worsened Mary's seizures.

Did she think witchcraft caused the fits? the court demanded. Did she believe there *were* witches?

Abigail said she knew nothing about it. It was the Enemy or some wicked person. Mary, passing in and out of trances, reported that Soames's specter threatened to bring an awl (a thin bladed tool used to punch holes) and to stab Mary's heart that very night. Abigail merely looked at her accuser and Mary felt a heavy blow slam her backward. Staggering, she burst into tears while Abigail burst into laughter. Mary's crying mouth twisted, mimicking the motions of Abigail's lips. But when the court ordered Abigail to look at Mary—for sometimes a second look undid the first—she flatly refused. The magistrates demanded she turn her head and face the girl, which she did, but with her eyes tightly shut. They made her touch Mary, who recovered at once. Abigail, her defiance defeated, opened her eyes and Mary collapsed at her glance.

"In this manner," the scribe wrote, "she practiced her witchcrafts several times before the court." Mary, seeing Abigail stand with one foot behind the other leg, found her own legs clamped across each other with such force that the strongest men present could not straighten them without risk of broken bones. (This may have also been the time an unidentified specter dragged Mary under the table.)[77]

Abigail Soames was held for acts of witchcraft against Mary Warren, but Mary's torments did not cease. After the examination the shapes of Proctor, Nurse, and Burroughs besieged her. When Burroughs bit her, witnesses saw the teethmarks quite clearly.

Margaret Jacobs broke down and wept. Burroughs, she said, had just told her that her Grandfather Jacobs would hang. Whether this weeping admission happened in court or back in jail, Margaret was still reporting specters. Soon, however, the reality and consequences of what she had said, and the unreality of what she had claimed, overwhelmed her. Fearing the Devil and damnation more than she feared the magistrates, she denied her earlier confession. The magistrates took her recanting to indicate not innocence but a stubborn relapse. They assigned her "to close prison"—to be locked in one room with no time outside in the prison yard, much less going out to testify against others in court. Margaret's relief was great regardless, because she knew she had chosen well.[78]

***

Boston

Sometime before the end of May, maidservant Mercy Short was sent on an errand to Boston jail. The young woman had been orphaned three winters earlier when she saw her mother, father, and three siblings killed during the French and Indian raid on Salmon Falls, New Hampshire. The raiders had marched Mercy Short and her remaining brothers and sisters as captives of war through the snow to Canada. Most of them were eventually ransomed by Phips's fleet after the Quebec expedition the following autumn, and brought to Boston.[79]

Mercy's errand was probably to distribute her mistress's charity of food and clothing to the prisoners. Whether the witchcraft suspects were to be included among the recipients or not, they made Mercy nervous. When Sarah Good asked her for tobacco, Mercy snatched a handful of shavings from the floor and hurled them at the woman while shouting, "That's tobacco good enough for you." Sarah Good replied with "ill words" and Mercy left, upset enough to fall into fits and torments soon after.

Mercy would suffer from them for several weeks that summer, as acutely hurt as any in Essex County. In addition, she would be unable to eat for as long as twelve days. Rev. Cotton Mather and other North End neighbors would pray for Mercy again and again, with Mather cautioning the others not to reveal any suspects' names that Mercy might cry during her seizures.[80]

May 14, 1692 • Saturday
Salem Village

Young Ann Putnam had seen, but not been harmed by, the specter of Elizabeth Hart for some time. The real Goody Hart, wife of a Lynn farmer, visited the girl as Martha Corey and Willard had earlier, and sought to resolve the accusations with reason. Her results were equally unsuccessful, for her specter began to torment Ann. Today, Nathaniel Ingersoll and Thomas Putnam entered complaints against Elizabeth Hart and Thomas Farrar Sr. of Lynn; two suspects from Reading— Elizabeth Coleson and Bethia Carter Jr. (for a second time); and several from Salem Village—George Jacobs Jr. with his wife Rebecca, and her brother Daniel Andrews, plus Sarah Buckley and her daughter Mary Witheredge.[81]

Will's Hill

Meanwhile, at Will's Hill, John Willard's afflicted nephew Daniel Wilkins was struck speechless at ten o'clock in the morning. He refused to eat and spat out whatever the family tried to spoonfeed him. Frightened, they consulted a "French" doctor, who, hearing of the problem, sent word that no medicine could help Daniel because his illness definitely resulted from witchcraft. When Mercy Lewis and another afflicted girl visited this evening, she saw John Willard's specter attack both old Bray and young Daniel, and heard it vow to kill Daniel in two days if it could.[82]

Boston

Late in the afternoon while this spiritual battle raged, a small convoy sailed into Boston Harbor. The fleet was headed by the frigate *Nonsuch* bearing Governor Sir William Phips and Rev. Increase Mather with the charter that made Massachusetts a legal political entity once again. The magistrates received them in the candlelit Town House at the head of King Street where Phips promised that, as God had sent him to New England, he would uphold the old laws and liberties as before. (Or so some interpreted it. The Charter allowed only those laws that did not conflict with English law.) Phips began to read his official commission when he noticed the sun was setting, and postponed the remainder rather than infringe on the Sabbath. The eight Boston militia companies omitted the celebratory volleys, but escorted Phips and Mather to their North End homes and to their waiting families.[83]

May 15, 1692 • Sunday
Boston

Boston's North Church welcomed back its senior minister, Increase Mather. His son, Cotton, though far from well, delivered the morning sermon on the subject of "Our Lord's passing over the waters."[84]

Salem

Salem Village's meeting, however, was interrupted when Sarah Buckley's specter attacked Mary Walcott. The specters of George and Rebecca Jacobs, Margaret's parents, tormented Susanna Sheldon during the day as well, presumably in Salem town.[85]

Andover

Miles away in Andover's meeting house, long-time witch suspect Martha Carrier (or her specter) accosted eleven-year-old Phebe Chandler. The angry woman's shape shook the girl's shoulder during the singing of a psalm and demanded to know where she lived. Phebe avoided answering. (Phebe's father kept a tavern at the sign of the Horseshoe in the southern part of town, and the Carriers lived just over the line in Billerica. Phebe and Martha were, moreover, related by marriage. Martha and her family had stayed with mutual relatives just up the road from Phebe during the smallpox epidemic.)[86]

Salem

Marshal George Herrick wrote a return for his arrests of Elizabeth Hart and Thomas Farrar of Lynn, but Daniel Andrews and his brother-in-law George Jacobs Jr. had escaped "out of the country." When Constable Jonathan Putnam and his men arrived at the younger Jacobs's house, his wife Rebecca was alone with the four youngest children. (The four youngest living Jacobs children were George, age 15; John, 13; Jonathan, 11; and Joseph, 2½. Just possibly there was another younger child.) Goody Jacobs had been unbalanced for the past dozen years. Her own mother said she was "a woman crazed, distracted, and broken in her mind." The constable arrested her, although he had trouble persuading her to accompany them until he promised she could soon return. She may have taken the youngest child with her as it was apparently still nursing. The rest she had to leave behind. Her children ran after her crying, a long way down the road to the Village, until the cavalcade outdistanced them and disappeared. The Jacobs boys had relatives nearby (their maternal uncle [and landlord], Daniel Andrews, lived just up the road), but it was neighbors (their nearer neighbors were Peter Cloyse and Jonathan Putnam) who took them in.[87]

John Willard was still at large. Even though it was the Sabbath, Bray Wilkins's son Benjamin Wilkins Sr. and neighbor Thomas Fuller Jr. appeared before Hathorne and Corwin to submit a complaint against John Willard for tormenting Bray and Daniel Wilkins, among others. The magistrates issued a second warrant requiring whatever lawman found Willard to pass him from town to town until he reached Salem.[88]

Will's Hill

Both Bray and Daniel continued in sore straits. Ann Putnam Jr. was taken to Will's Hill this evening and saw Willard's specter afflict not only Bray and Daniel, but also Rebecca, Daniel's older sister. Ann heard the specter swear to kill Daniel, even if it had to get the power from Rev. Burroughs to do it.[89]

May 16, 1692 • Monday
Salem

Specters of George and Rebecca Jacobs threatened to stab Susanna Sheldon if she didn't cooperate. She was wounded on her left side by the Jacobses, she said, and on her back by Elizabeth Coleson. Reading constable John Parker reported to the Salem magistrates that he could not find Elizabeth Coleson, and guessed she had fled, perhaps to take ship at Boston.[90]

Andover

Phebe Chandler, carrying beer to the farm hands in Andover, heard Martha Carrier's voice in the bushes by the path demanding to know where the girl was going. Phebe ran and told the laborers what had happened. About two hours later, when she passed the same spot on the same errand, she heard Carrier's voice above her threatening to poison the girl within a few days. Perhaps because of this, Phebe left to visit her sister Allen's farm up the road nearby. (Phebe's widowed half-sister Elizabeth lived with her widowed mother-in-law Faith Allen, Martha Carrier's mother. Elizabeth's husband, Andrew Allen, had died of smallpox two winters earlier when Martha's family temporarily moved in, bringing the infection with them.)[91]

Boston

With the Sabbath over, the new Charter government officially began. Eight Boston and two Charlestown militia companies escorted Phips and the assistants to the Council Chamber of the Boston Town House for a reading of the Charter and of the commissions. Thus, Phips was proclaimed governor of Massachusetts, vice admiral, and commander-in-chief of all New England militias. William Stoughton was named lieutenant governor, and Isaac Addington was appointed secretary of the province. The new officeholders were sworn in, but the only other business of the day was their decision that all other civil and military officers would continue until further notice.[92]

Assistants would be called councilors under the new government. Before Samuel Sewall could take his councilor's oath, however, his brothers-in-law from Newbury surprised him with news that his elderly father was dangerously ill. They all left immediately, passed at sunset through Ipswich (where they saw a rainbow), and arrived in Newbury to find the elder Sewall recovering.[93]

Will's Hill

This same evening, the scene at Henry Wilkin's house at Will's Hill was entirely different as family and neighbors watched Daniel Wilkins struggle for breath. Mercy Lewis and Mary Walcott saw John Willard's specter choke the boy while Goody Buckley's shape pressed on his chest. Both threatened to kill him in three hour's time. Henry and Benjamin Wilkins and neighbor Thomas Flint saw only Daniel, gasping until he died. ("Bewitched to death," Samuel Parris wrote in his church record.)[94]

Lancaster

No later than today, the real John Willard was discovered, forty miles west of home, hoeing a field in Lancaster on the Nashua River, where he owned land. In Salem at the same moment, the afflicted exclaimed, "Now Willard is taken!" Or so the time would seem to correspond when events were known.[95]

May 17, 1692 • Tuesday
Salem Village

Five suspects were in custody at Ingersoll's when Marshal George Herrick arrived in Salem Village: Rebecca Jacobs, Sarah Buckley, Mary Witheredge, Elizabeth Hart, and Thomas Farrar Sr. As soon as Herrick locked them in the watchhouse, Constable John Putnam rode up with John Willard and the afflicted screamed in pain until Herrick pinioned Willard.[96]

Ezekiel Cheever handed the marshal a troubling paper written by Benjamin Wilkins on behalf of his bereaved family and their neighbors. It recounted his nephew Daniel's deathbed sufferings, and asked that a jury of inquest examine the body "to prevent any further murder in the afflicted creatures who continue in a lamentable condition." Seven neighbors, three constables, and Marshal Herrick signed it, adding a note that Parris was absent in Salem.

Constable John Putnam straightaway ordered twelve local men* to view the body of Daniel Wilkins. They discovered many bruises on the back of the corpse, and broken skin in several places. Daniel's back was punctured all over by something like a small awl, and one side of his neck was bruised from ear to throat. When they turned the corpse over again, it gushed blood—whether from mouth or from nose or from both they couldn't tell. There was no swelling or purging to suggest poison. From this physical evidence and from what they had heard, the jury concluded that Daniel's demise was "an unnatural death by some cruel hands of witchcraft or diabolical act."[97]

Although Willard was physically apprehended, his specter tried to strangle Sarah Bibber, Mary Walcott, and Mercy Lewis in Ingersoll's chamber, and kept attacking them until Herrick shackled Willard's body. At the same time that Willard was chained, old Bray Wilkins finally had relief from his painful two-week urinary problem; too much relief, he thought, for he was hard put to keep dry.[98]

Wherever Susanna Sheldon was, the specter of Elizabeth Coleson Jr. tormented her. Hathorne and Corwin issued another arrest warrant for the elusive Reading woman, now suspected of hiding in Charlestown.[99]

---

*Nathaniel Putnam, Thomas Fuller Sr., Jonathan Walcott Sr., Nathaniel Ingersoll, Thomas Flint, William Way, Thomas Fuller, Joseph Herrick, Thomas Haynes, Edward Putnam, Daniel Rea, John Putnam Jr.

Boston

Samuel Sewall was still absent on family matters, but most of the council met with Governor Phips in Boston at one o'clock. They confirmed the Fast Order for May 26, ordered the establishment of a committee to supply the Eastward militia, and optimistically dismissed the brigantine *William and Mary* from guarding the coast, now that the frigate *Nonsuch* was available.[100]

May 18, 1692 • Wednesday
Salem Village

With Rev. Samuel Parris and Ezekiel Cheever ready to take notes, John Hathorne and Jonathan Corwin sat in Salem Village to hear the postponed cases. (Parris and Cheever had written the earlier transcriptions from their shorthand on full sheets of paper with generous margins. Today, by contrast, Parris's final notes for Sarah Buckley crowded a card no larger than a man's hand.)[101]

Elizabeth Hart, wife of Lynn farmer Isaac Hart, was bold enough to have confronted Ann Putnam Jr. directly when the girl accused her of witchcraft, and outspoken enough that the Lynn Church had reprimanded her in 1655 for calling her fellow members fools and lackwits. She was examined and held for tormenting Mary Warren.[102]

Thomas Farrar Sr., a seventy-five-year-old farmer, was a member of the Lynn Church, although denied the sacrament from time to time for drunkenness. (Waking from a befuddled sleep at a neighbor's house, Farrar thought himself home and staggered up, mumbling about good and evil angels until he blundered into a corner behind an open door. He thought he had found the privy.) Thomas could also be violent, as when he struck a pregnant woman, throwing her from her horse. Two of his children had once thought themselves bewitched by Goody Burt. Now his son was a selectman and the old man had a front seat in the meeting house, the better to hear from. But Thomas Farrar Sr. was also held for trial.[103]

Sarah Buckley and her shoemaker husband William had lived variously in Ipswich, where she had grown up in a respected family; in Marblehead, where William lost his house and land for debts owed to Simon Bradstreet; and in Salem Village, where they lost household goods in order to pay the debts of a dead son. Sarah was a member of the Salem Church, but Susanna Sheldon's recent confusion of Buckley's specter with Dorcas Hoar's had helped neither woman. Susanna and some of the others were speechless when they first confronted Goody Buckley, but Abigail Williams could talk—and did.[104]

"This is the woman that hath bit me with her scragged teeth a great many times."

Others testified to the specter's activity among themselves and against the Wilkins family. Mary Warren had seen Goody Buckley in a crowd of witches trying to lure her to the sacrament in Parris's pasture. Ann Putnam Jr., convulsing, was carried to Goody Buckley, who was forced to grasp Ann's arm—whereupon the girl recovered. Since the same phenomena happened with Susanna Sheldon *and* Mary Warren, the magistrates urged the defendant to confess. While Susanna Sheldon watched the Devil whisper in the defendant's ear, Goody Buckley insisted on her innocence, but was held for trial nonetheless.[105]

Mary Witheredge, living in the Village with her parents, William and Sarah Buckley (and her own two small children), since the death of her husband Sylvester Witheredge, was held for acts of witchcraft against Elizabeth Hubbard, who convulsed and strangled whenever the defendant looked at her.[106]

The afflicted did not recognize Rebecca Jacobs at first, until one of them—probably Elizabeth Hubbard—cried, "Don't you know Jacobs, the old witch?" and instantly convulsed. Already distracted, Goody Jacobs broke down and confessed not only to hurting the girls, but also to covenanting with the Devil, and perhaps also to killing her own child. (She would speak of this often in prison. Two-year-old Mary had drowned accidentally in a well seven years earlier.)[107]

Another active specter was that of Roger Toothaker, a farmer and folk-healer from nearby Billerica whose specialty was the detection and punishment of *maleficium*. Roger had lived in Salem apart from his family for about eight years, while the Billerica selectmen had to provide his wife with charity and to see to the apprenticing of his children. Hathorn and Corwin had issued his arrest warrant early enough that Constable Joseph Neale fetched Toothaker from town to the Village for questioning the same day. His examination is lost, but he had made no secret that he practiced countermagic and had even killed a suspected witch (possibly Mattheas Button) by it.[108]

John Willard was led in, a black-haired man of average height. All the afflicted but John Indian fell into "miserable fits," which reoccurred when Willard looked at them while the officer read his warrant.[109]

"Here is a return of the warrant that you were fled from authority," said the magistrate. "That is acknowledgment of guilt, but yet, notwithstanding this, we require you to confess the truth in this matter."

"I shall, as I hope I shall be assisted by the Lord of Heaven," said Willard. "And for my going away I was afrighted, and I thought by my withdrawing it might be better. I fear not but the Lord in his due time will make me as white as snow." He denied hurting the afflicted in person or by apparition despite their identification of him.

"Well, they charge you not only with this," said the court, "but with dreadful murders, and I doubt not, if you be guilty, God will not suffer evidences to be wanting."

The girls' convulsions during the reading of testimony seemed to be such an evidence. If Willard wanted God's mercy, said the magistrate, then he ought to confess.

"Sir," said Willard, "as for the sins I am guilty of, if the minister asked me, I am ready to confess."

"If you have thus revolted from God, you are a dreadful sinner."

Willard gnawed his lip. "Oh, he bites me!" cried Mary Warren and Ann Putnam Jr.

"Open your mouth," ordered the magistrates. "Don't bite your lips."

"I will stand with my mouth open, or I will keep it shut," Willard replied. "I will stand anyhow, if you will tell me how."

After hearing depositions about his afflicted kin, Willard commented that only someone pledged "to Hell from their cradle would be guilty of such things."

They asked if he bewitched his grandfather in retaliation for the old man's prayers that "the Kingdom of Satan be thrown down." Willard "began a large oration" (as Parris noted it) but the magistrate cut him short. "We do not send for you to preach."

Benjamin Wilkins told how Willard beat his own wife so hard he broke the sticks with which he hit her. "There are a great many lies told," Willard protested. "I could desire my wife might be called." But Margaret* was not summoned. Instead, Peter Prescott testified that he had heard Willard himself say he beat her.[110]

---

*Margaret (Wilkins) Willard was the daughter of Thomas and Hannah (Nichols) Wilkins and granddaughter of Bray Wilkins.

It was odd that "one of your confidence and ability to speak," said the magistrate, would have "no more courage than to run away. By your running away you tell all that you are afraid."

Willard begged his neighbor Aaron Way to speak for him. "If I must speak, I will," Way said reluctantly. "I can say you have been very cruel to poor creatures."

When the magistrates suggested the touch test, Ann Putnam Jr. volunteered, to Willard's dismay. *Anyone* but her, he said.

"Oh! He cuts me," yelled John Indian, and Susanna Sheldon saw the Devil whisper in Willard's ear.

"What do you say to this?" the magistrate demanded.

"Sir, I heard nothing, nor see nothing."

Susanna Sheldon tried to approach Willard, but collapsed. He grasped her hand—"with a great deal of do," as Parris observed—but the fit continued as she kept shouting, "Oh, John Willard, John Willard!"

"What was the reason you could not come near him?" the court asked when she revived.

"A black man stood between us."

"They cannot come near any that are accused," Willard protested.

"Why do you say so?" asked the magistrate. "They could come near Nehemiah Abbott. The children could talk with him."

The constable and others took firm hold of Willard's hands, so when Mary Warren was the next to have a seizure, she was carried to him without trouble and recovered when he clasped her arm.

"Why was it not before so with Susanna Sheldon?" Willard asked her.

"Because the standers-by you did not clasp your hand before." The constable and his men agreed, forgetting Susanna Sheldon's reported devil.

Many of the afflicted now saw the ghosts of Willard's murder victims crowd among them.

"Do you think these are bewitched?" the magistrates asked him.

"Yes, I really believe it."

"Well," said the magistrate, overlooking that the suspects were not even indicted, "others they have accused, it is found true that they are the guilty persons. Why should it be false in you?" Why should the court believe him in light of his reputation for "cruelty to man and beast," his flight from the law, and his specter raging among the afflicted? "If you can find it in your heart to repent, it is possible you may obtain mercy, and therefore bethink yourself."

"Sir, I cannot confess that I do not know."

"Well," said the magistrate, "if these things are true, Heaven and Earth will rise up against you."

Still protesting his innocence, Willard attempted the Lord's Prayer test, but botched it almost at once by adding the phrase "Maker of Heaven and Earth." He started again and missed another phrase. "It is a strange thing," he said. "I can say it at another time. I think I am bewitched as well as they." He laughed, but no one else did. On the third try he got as far as "trespass against" before omitting "us." On the fourth attempt, being pressed, he exclaimed, "Well, this is a strange thing! I cannot say it." And at the fifth failure he cried, "Well, it is these wicked ones that do so overcome me!"

Joshua Rea Sr. testified that only the night before Willard had said that he hoped he would confess despite his hard heart. Whatever he had meant then, Willard insisted on his innocence now.

"Do you not see God will not suffer you to pray to him?" asked the magistrate, falling into the popular superstition himself. "Are you not sensible of it?"

"Why it is a strange thing," Willard admitted.

"No, it is no strange thing that God will not suffer a wizard to pray to him. There is also a jury of inquest for murder that will bear hard against you. Therefore, confess. Have you never wished harm to your neighbors?"

"No, never since I had being."

"Well, confess and give glory to God. Take counsel whilst it is offered."

"I desire to harken to all good council, but if it was the last time I was to speak," Willard declared, "I am innocent."

But the court thought otherwise and held him for tormenting Mercy Lewis, Ann Putnam Jr., Susanna Sheldon, Abigail Williams, Elizabeth Hubbard, and probably Mrs. Ann Putnam and Mary Walcott as well.[111]

In contrast, the case of Mary Esty—who had been in Salem jail nearly a month—was now reexamined. This time only Mercy Lewis said that the defendant's specter tormented her. The others were no longer certain, so the magistrates released Goody Esty to the custody of her greatly relieved family. Then the court drew up the mittimus to transfer Elizabeth Hart, Thomas Farrar Sr., and Roger Toothaker to the Boston prison, and assigned them for the night to the Village watchhouse.[112]

Salem Town

Rev. Burroughs's specter appeared around this time in Mary Warren's cell, and summoned his witches* with a trumpet blast. He tried to lure Mary to their meeting in Parris's pasture, while Nurse and Good, calling themselves deacons, offered her sweet bread and wine. It was really blood, they said, better than real wine, but Mary refused despite their temptations and tortures.[113]

---

*Burroughs called Abigail Soames, Goodman Proctor, Goodwives Nurse, Proctor, Parker, Pudeator, and Darling (or Downing).

May 19, 1692 • Thursday
Salem Village

After the guards breakfasted at Ingersoll's and collected their horses from his pasture, they carted the prisoners from the Salem Village watchhouse to Boston. There John Arnold began their room and board bills with the date on the mittimus, the day before their actual arrival.[114]

The moon turned full tonight, though it may have been hidden by clouds since almanacs predicted thunder. Mercy Lewis—still tormented by the shape of Mary Esty—was now living in the household of Constable John Putnam, cousin and nearest neighbor of her former employer Thomas. John and Hannah's infant daughter had died the month before, of witchcraft the family thought. Perhaps Mercy's move was intended to relieve Mrs. Ann Putnam of the girl's care, since Ann Sr.'s fits had returned during Willard's examination. Mercy's own torments had continued unabated since Goody Esty's release, and now the neighbors were worried.[115]

May 20, 1692 • Friday
Andover

In Andover, Phebe Chandler remembered the spectral threats of poison and found her right hand and part of her face painfully swollen. This would continue for several days, along with pressure on her chest and legs that sometimes made it hard to walk.[116]

Salem Village

The magistrates sat in Salem Village again, where they and their attendants refreshed themselves with five shillings worth of Ingersoll's cider, and recorded depositions against Sarah Bishop and Roger Toothaker.[117]

Constable John Putnam was likely in attendance, for he was away from home when Mercy Lewis's afflictions returned and pinned her wordless in bed. After an hour of watching her silent duress, Hannah Putnam asked Samuel Abbey when he stopped by at nine o'clock to fetch her niece Ann, so the girl could see whose specter hurt Mercy. Abbey collected Ann Putnam Jr., her twenty-year-old cousin Sarah Trask (who was not afflicted), and Abigail Williams. Mary Esty's specter shadowed them on the way back, according to Ann and Abigail, and told them that it was taking revenge on Mercy for holding to her accusation. At the constable's house, both girls saw the specters of Esty, Willard, and Witheredge choke and batter Mercy. These three immediately attacked Ann and Abigail, and Mary Walcott, too, when she later entered. Esty, said Mary Walcott, had blinded them all to the truth before; all except Mercy Lewis, whom Esty now tried to choke with a chain.[118]

Mercy's torment continued for hours. "Dear Lord, receive my soul," she gasped once, and, "Lord, let them not kill me quite." She regained consciousness long enough to tell Abbey and the others that Esty had sworn to kill her before midnight. "Pray for the salvation of my soul," she cried as she again convulsed, "for they will kill me!" With Daniel Wilkins's death so recent, this prediction seemed all too likely.

Boston

In Boston, meanwhile, Phips and Stoughton called an emergency four o'clock council meeting. Three French privateers had captured a local coasting vessel and two fishing shallops, so the Council ordered the *William and Mary* refitted and back on active duty to assist the *Nonsuch*. Unfortunately, Captain Short had ignored Phips's order to keep his men on board ready for action. Once granted shore leave, many sailors simply did not return, so the *Nonsuch* was too undermanned to sail. Therefore, without asking Phips, Short sent press gangs to scour Boston for local volunteers, willing or unwilling.[119]

Salem Village

Back at the Village, concerned neighbors flocked to Mercy Lewis's bedside. By the time Constable John Putnam returned home with Marshal George Herrick and Benjamin Hutchinson, she seemed nearly dead. The three men concluded that the only chance of saving Mercy was to arrest Goody Esty as soon as possible; they left immediately to find the magistrates. Putnam and Hutchinson located Hathorne in Salem and filed a complaint against Mary Esty for tormenting Mercy Lewis, Mary Walcott, Ann Putnam Jr., and Abigail Williams. As soon as he had the arrest warrant, Marshal Herrick headed north to Topsfield, mindful of the specter's midnight deadline.[120]

The Putnams and assorted neighbors sat with Mercy all night as she hovered in a daze at death's door. Elizabeth Hubbard arrived later to join the other afflicted girls. All saw and were attacked by the same specters plus three more: the Proctors' daughter Sarah, her aunt Sarah Bassett of Lynn, and widow Susanna Roots of Beverly. (And if not at the Putnam household, then elsewhere that night, Susanna Sheldon and her neighbor Elizabeth Booth—daughter of a twice-widowed mother whose family had fallen on hard times—were tortured by a spectral Sarah Proctor, both Proctor parents, and Daniel Andrews.)*[121]

---

*Elizabeth Hubbard apparently arrived later as she is not named in the complaint Putnam and Hutchinson just went off to enter, but is in the one entered May 21. Susanna Sheldon and Elizabeth Booth are not in the May 21 warrant unless as "etc."

Marshal Herrick returned at midnight, while Mercy was in the midst of a violent seizure, to report that the Esty woman was safely in custody. Esty's specter, however, taunted Mercy with a corpse's winding sheet. "I had rather go into the winding sheet than set my hand to the book," said Mercy. Her convulsions continued all night. She grew weaker and weaker, her life apparently draining away, like Daniel Wilkins's. She felt nauseated and found no sleep until daybreak.

May 21, 1692 • Saturday
Salem

Mercy seemed barely alive when the neighbors finally left. Someone must have informed the authorities, who ordered chains for Goodwife Mary Esty. Not until the suspect was clapped in irons did Mercy begin to recover after two days and one night of almost continual seizures.[122]

Thomas and John Putnam entered a complaint before magistrates Hathorne and Corwin against widow Susanna Roots, Sarah Proctor, and Sarah Bassett for tormenting Mary Walcott, Abigail Williams, Mercy Lewis, Ann Putnam Jr., "etc." The "etc." may have included Susanna Sheldon, haunted today by Sarah Proctor's specter with the Devil's book. Sarah and the fugitives Daniel Andrews and George Jacobs Jr. struck Susanna deaf, dumb, and blind, and left her in a darkness deeper than the oncoming night.[123]

May 22, 1692 • Sunday
Boston

In Boston, Rev. Increase Mather delivered his first sermon after homecoming to his North End congregation. He spoke on the text Psalm 121:8, "The Lord shall prosper their going out and their coming in from this time forth, forevermore." His son Cotton, with a hand still shaky from a winter and spring of colds, took notes as his father assured the congregation of God's continued loving protection for His people—even when "there is a power of devils in our air that are seeking to hurt us."[124]

Salem Village

In Salem, Susanna Sheldon finally regained her speech, sight and hearing at ten o'clock only to see Philip English's specter with a knife at her throat to make her sign the book. But the ghost of Joseph Rabson interrupted to accuse English of drowning him when his boat capsized, and to tell Susanna that he would not let her rest until she told Hathorne about his murder. (By now, every disastrous death on land or sea was blamed on the witches.) When English threatened to cut her

legs off, the shining man appeared and urged her to tell all in court on the morrow. English stormed off then, vowing to kill the governor, his "greatest enemy,"
and other Boston folk if he were captured.[125]

May 23, 1692 • Monday
Salem Village

Almanacs predicted a dry, windy, and "pretty hot" day, in the course of which the
magistrates and their horses consumed three shillings worth of food and drink at
Ingersoll's. They originally intended to question Mary Esty at Beadle's in Salem
town, but so many others had been complained of since her rearrest that the court
convened back at the Village. The magistrates examined and held Sarah Bassett of
Lynn, Elizabeth Proctor's sister-in-law, and probably Susanna Roots of Beverly as
well. The only surviving testimony is from Goody Roots's fellow boarder, who noticed that she avoided family prayers, and was overheard talking nights with five
or six other voices in what ought to have been an empty room.[126]

The magistrates questioned Mary Esty again. Most of the evidence this time concerned the near death of Mercy Lewis (now recovered enough to testify) and the
girls' pain during the examination. All the afflicted witnesses were choked speechless from opening prayers onward but still managed to accuse Goody Esty of stabbing them with a spindle (the iron spike that held wool for spinning). After a spindle vanished from a house in the Village, one of the afflicted saw the specters jab
her with it. She lunged and wrenched it from the spirit's grasp, whereupon the
spectral weapon became visible to everyone else. It was the same as the missing
one. Someone safely locked it away, yet it disappeared once more, only to be seen
again in spectral hands.[127]

During the day more specters must have assaulted the afflicted, for Nathaniel
Ingersoll and Thomas Rayment made complaints against Benjamin Proctor and his
aunt Mary DeRich, and against Sarah Pease (wife of Robert the weaver) for tormenting Abigail Williams, Mary Warren, Elizabeth Hubbard, and others. Constable
John Putnam arrested Benjamin Proctor (leaving the family in the care of his
twenty-four-year-old half-brother John Jr.) and Goody DeRich, while Constable
Peter Osgood fetched Goody Pease. All were questioned before the day was out
(although no notes survive) because Hathorne and Corwin had to be away the rest
of the week. They ordered several prisoners transferred to Boston: Mary Esty, Abigail Soames, Susanna Roots, Sarah Bassett, Mary DeRich, Benjamin Proctor, and
Mrs. Elizabeth Cary (who began as a member of the audience and ended among
the accused).[128]

Captain Nathaniel Cary, a wealthy Charlestown shipmaster, had heard that the afflicted had named his wife among the witches. "Much disturbed" by the accusation
but confident that the misunderstanding could be resolved, they arrived in the Village unannounced to see for themselves.* Captain Cary (as he later remembered
the day) found the proceedings stylized and unconvincing. He watched the Lord's
Prayer test and touch test skeptically, noted how the defendants had their hands
held still, and observed how the accused were ordered to face the magistrates lest
their gazes produce fits in the accusers. He thought the magistrates were too quick
to call a girl dumbstruck if she only stared speechlessly at a person after recovering from a fit of seizures, and much too eager to pronounce a collapsed girl cured
when the accused touched her. The captain saw no visible change at all. The afflicted were three young women of about eighteen, and two ten-year-old girls
(one of whom saw more of the invisible goings-on than the others). In their quieter moments the afflicted noticed Mrs. Cary and asked her name.[129]

Meanwhile, through his old acquaintance Rev. John Hale, Captain Cary tried to
arrange for a private talk with Abigail Williams in her uncle's parsonage. But the
best that Hale could manage was an interview with her at Ingersoll's. John Indian
was waiting on customers when the Carys entered the ordinary, so the captain
bought him some cider and asked about his afflictions. The slave showed them
scars that he said witchcraft had caused (though Cary thought they looked too old)
and described his wife Tituba's imprisonment.

Then Abigail and the other afflicted entered. All convulsed so badly that three
women were sent for to keep the girls from hurting themselves. They tumbled on
the floor—"like swine," thought Captain Cary—while those in the room tensed to
hear what they might say. "Cary," they cried against Elizabeth, and immediately
Hathorne and Corwin, who were in a nearby chamber (waiting, Captain Cary
thought), ordered that she be brought before them.

The ten-year-olds were the most afflicted, but Mrs. Cary protested her innocence, and tried to explain that she had never heard of the girls before this day.
But the magistrates made her stand, arms outstretched, and forbade her husband
to help support even one of them. (He did not explain why this was different from
the others, whose hands were held still.) Weeping, she asked her husband to wipe

---

*Cary, writing later, dated the event May 24, but Hathorne and Corwin were in Boston
then and there were no examinations at the Village. Ingersoll's bill shows activity on May
23, the prison census says Mrs. Cary was ordered to Boston May 23, and Hammond says she
was committed to Cambridge jail and in irons on May 24. Cary said they arrived in time to
get good seats for the beginning of court, which would have begun at 10 A.M. according to
the warrants, although they had to come up from Charlestown.

the tears and sweat from her face, which he did. But when, feeling faint, she asked to lean against him, Hathorne refused to allow it. If she had strength enough to torment, he said, then she had strength enough to stand. Captain Cary tried to protest, but was told he would be put from the room if he were not silent.

John Indian joined the afflicted, "fell down and tumbled about like a hog, but said nothing." When the magistrates asked the girls who afflicted John Indian, they said that Mrs. Cary's specter sprawled over him. The magistrates ordered the touch test but required that Mrs. Cary's head be turned so her gaze would not make matters worse. The officers guided her toward the writhing John Indian, who grabbed her hand and pulled her down on the floor with him "in a barbarous manner." His hand was forcibly removed and hers touched on it to cure him.

Furious, Captain Cary declared that he hoped God would take vengeance on the court to deliver the Carys from such unmerciful men. But Mrs. Cary was held for trial, and it was only with some effort and expense that her husband was able to hire her a private room for the night, a room but no bed.

This same night, by Proctor's Creek, specters of Sarah Proctor, her parents, and her aunt Mary DeRich tormented Elizabeth Booth. Jade, snarled Mary, how dare Elizabeth insult her niece? It was just as well, Sarah added, that Elizabeth had *not* gone to the Village today.[130]

Boston

Acting on the Governor's orders, Boston prisonkeeper Arnold spent £2-5-0 on shackles—enough for ten prisoners. The government, however, was so hard-pressed for money that Samuel Sewall loaned them £200 in bills of credit, which the government accepted, though it would have preferred hard money.[131]

May 24, 1692 • Tuesday
Boston

The guards had a last drink at Ingersoll's, then carted the latest batch of prisoners from Salem Village to Boston's prison. Ahead of them, having started from Salem town, magistrates John Hathorne and Jonathan Corwin pressed on to attend a meeting of the governor and council scheduled for two o'clock that afternoon in Boston's Town House.[132]

When the councilors did gather and Samuel Sewall took his delayed oath, they considered the appointments of sheriffs, justices, and other civil officers. It was now the prerogative of the royal governor to fill these posts with the council's consent, but on this occasion Phips let the council nominate officers. He also announced that the General Court would convene in Boston on June 8. Everyone seemed to overlook that only the General Court was supposed to institute the judiciary. (Because of this technicality, the special court has often been called illegal. However, if the government had observed all the legalities, the same men would have been in charge anyway.)[133]

Boston

While the magistrates mulled over nominations for judgeships, Mary Warren rebuffed two choking specters: Mary Ireson, a Lynn woman, and Mary Toothaker, wife of Roger Toothaker (already in Boston jail) and sister of Martha Carrier. This specter brought not only the book, but also a winding sheet, a basin, and grave cloths (all equipment for preparing a corpse) and threatened to kill Mary Warren if she didn't sign. "Who are you?" bystanders heard Mary Warren ask the invisible presences. "What is your name? What? Toothaker? Doctor Toothaker's wife? I won't. I won't. I will not touch that book!"[134]

May 25, 1692 • Wednesday
Boston

Still in Boston, Hathorne and Corwin signed and dated a mittimus committing Martha Corey, John and Elizabeth Proctor, Rebecca Nurse, Dorcas Good, and Sarah Cloyse to the Boston jail—a technicality, since they were already there.[135]

Cambridge

Captain Cary had managed to have his wife transferred to the Cambridge jail in their own county of Middlesex. After her first night there, Elizabeth was unexpectedly shackled with eight pounds of iron chains. Overcome by it all, she suffered convulsions so severe that her husband feared she would die before another night passed. He pleaded that the irons be removed, but nothing that he said could change the order.[136]

Salem

Meanwhile, Joseph and Priscilla Bayley of Newbury journeyed to Boston by way of Salem Village, both on one horse, she riding pillion behind him. He was a brother of the Rev. James Bayley, who had served eight uncomfortable years with the Village congregation, and she was a daughter of Captain John Putnam Sr. As they came in sight of the Proctors' house, Joseph felt a hard blow to his chest "which caused great pain in my stomach and amazement in my head." Yet, he saw no one but his wife behind him.[137]

Passing the house, he saw John Proctor looking out the window while Elizabeth stood just outside the door. Joseph remarked on this as both Proctors were supposed to be in jail; yet when Priscilla turned in her sideways seat, she saw only "a little maid at the door" (probably three-year-old Abigail). But Joseph saw no girl at all, only Goody Proctor. A half-mile farther, he found himself utterly unable to speak, until his wife had him raise his hand if he could hear her. This motion broke the spell, but as soon as they reached the fork in the road, another painful blow slammed his chest and nearly knocked him from the horse. Dismounting, he noticed an unknown woman some three hundred feet away.* Again, Priscilla saw no one, and once back in the saddle, Joseph spied only a cow where the woman had been. They reached Boston without further incident. (But once they returned home to Newbury, he would feel "pinched and nipped by something invisible for some time.")

May 26, 1692 • Thursday
Salem Village

On this Lecture Day, the first official public fast under the new charter, people from other towns apparently attended the Salem Village observances, for Mrs. Mary Marshall of nearby Reading was there when she, Mary Walcott, Mercy Lewis, and Ann Putnam Jr. were attacked by specters. While Marshal Herrick and Constable Joseph Neal watched, the afflicted named their tormentors as Mrs. Bradbury of Salisbury, Goody Rice of Reading, Goody Read of Marblehead, and Goody Fosdick of Malden. The last spirit boasted that she had also hurt the black woman belonging to Mr. Tufts of Malden. (Peter Tufts was kin by marriage to the Putnams).[138]

May 27, 1692 • Friday
Boston

The governor and council at last reestablished the law courts when Phips approved all the nominations presented him. Secretary Isaac Addington and the councilors became justices of the peace (as part of their offices) along with other magistrates, including former deputy governor, Thomas Danforth for Middlesex, and John Higginson Jr. and Dudley Bradstreet for Essex County.[139]

As an increasingly hot summer began, throngs of prisoners crowded the jails. Rather than name a Superior Court, which could sit only at certain intervals, Phips instituted a Court of Oyer and Terminer (to hear and determine). This judicial body would proceed against all manner of crimes in Suffolk, Essex, and Middlesex counties, and would apply "the law and custom of England" rather than the Massachusetts laws of the old charter. Lieutenant Governor William Stoughton of Dorchester became chief justice over Justices Nathaniel Saltonstall of

---

*I. e. "twenty poles" away (330'), a pole or rod being 5½ yards.

Haverhill; Wait-Still Winthrop, Peter Sergeant, John Richards, and Samuel Sewall of Boston; and Bartholomew Gedney, John Hathorne, and Jonathan Corwin of Salem. Any five or more could hear a case as long as their number included Stoughton, Gedney, or Richards.[140]

The judges were, by trade, merchants and landowners. John Richards had worked his way up from the station of servant, while William Stoughton had inherited many of his acres. Nathaniel Saltonstall and Wait-Still Winthrop were active militia leaders. Winthrop and Bartholomew Gedney were trained physicians. Samuel Sewall and Stoughton were educated at Harvard, which Winthrop had attended for only a year. Sewall had considered the ministry but entered business. Stoughton, the only bachelor, had also studied in England at Oxford and had preached successfully both in old and New England. But he left the pulpit (without ever being ordained) to enter a life of politics and managed to participate in every new government, including Andros's. This involvement hurt his popularity after the revolution, though not as much as his friend Joseph Dudley's. (Peter Sergeant, on the other hand, helped to jail Dudley.) Stoughton, Gedney, and Winthrop all served as councilors and judges under Andros, when Sewall had declined office.[141]

The clerk of this court was Stephen Sewall of Salem (Samuel's brother and Betty Parris's host). Thomas Newton, an Anglican born and educated in England, was appointed King's attorney general, a post that he had also held under Andros (when he had likely prosecuted Goody Glover for witchcraft). Newton had represented the Crown in the New York case that resulted in Jacob Leisler's and Jacob Milborne's executions for high treason. Twenty-five-year-old George Corwin of Salem (nephew of Justices Corwin and Winthrop, son-in-law of Justice Gedney) became sheriff of Essex County, replacing the old office of marshal (although George Herrick would continue his duties as deputy sheriff).[142]

Stamford, Connecticut

Meanwhile in Connecticut, Sergeant Daniel Westcott initiated legal proceedings on behalf of his maid Katherine Branch. The commissioners (local magistrates) questioned Kate, who described the torments that she had endured from the shapes of Elizabeth Clauson, Mercy Desborough, and another woman nicknamed Goody Hipshod.[143]

May 28, 1692 • Saturday
Salem Town

Today's date appeared on the surviving complaint against Mrs. Elizabeth Cary that Thomas Putnam and Benjamin Hutchinson had entered in Salem (Hathorne and

Corwin were apparently back in town) on behalf of Abigail Williams, Mary Walcott, and Mercy Lewis. The complaint did not include Thomas's daughter Ann
who, by Captain Cary's description, was among the afflicted.[144]

John Holten and Jonathan Walcott also entered complaints on behalf of all four
girls against several more: Martha Carrier of Andover; Elizabeth Fosdick of Malden;
Wilmot Read of Marblehead; Sarah Rice of Reading; Elizabeth How of Ipswich;
Captain John Alden of Boston (back from Eastward); William Proctor (son of John
and Elizabeth) of Salem; Captain John Flood of Rumney Marsh (whose militia had
been too late to save York, Maine, the winter before); Mary Toothaker of Billerica
(the deserted wife of the jailed Dr. Roger Toothaker and sister of Martha Carrier),
with a Toothaker daughter whose name is lost (perhaps Mary); and Arthur Abbott,
who lived at the border of Ipswich, Topsfield, and Wenham. All were to be
brought to Ingersoll's on the following Tuesday by ten o'clock.[145]

Boston

Samuel Wheelright and three other men from Wells, Maine, were in Boston with
Captain James Converse of the Wells garrison to petition the legislature. Not only
was their village beset by the long frontier war, they said, but it was also devoid of
a pastor. Without naming their imprisoned Rev. George Burroughs, they asked the
General Court to send them someone who could minister to both town and garrison, in which case the court might help pay his services as chaplain.[146]

Stamford, Connecticut

In Connecticut, meantime, magistrates questioned Elizabeth Clauson and Mercy
Desborough. Kate Branch testified to spectral tortures and fainted repeatedly at
Goody Desborough's glance. Goody Clauson was sure it was all part of a nine-
year-old grudge that Kate's master Daniel Westcott bore her. A committee of
women searched the defendants' bodies for witch marks and found an excrescence on Desborough's privates, but only a wart on Clauson's arm. Both were held
for trial.[147]

May 29, 1692 • Sunday
Ipswich

Almanacs predicted hot, dry weather, and, Sabbath or not, the law was busy. Marblehead's constable arrested Wilmot Read, while Reading's arrested Sarah Rice.
Constable Ephraim Wildes of Topsfield located Elizabeth How in Ipswich at the
home of her brother-in-law Captain John How, and served her the warrant. Perhaps because her own husband James was blind, Goody How asked Captain How

to accompany her to Salem Village. He refused. For any other charge, he said, but not for witchcraft, not even for £10. (It was bad enough that Rebecca Nurse was his wife's aunt.)[148]

But curiosity overcame fear and he offered to come if Goody How told him how long she had been a witch and just what mischief she had done. This only angered her, but she asked him to come along the next day at least. No, he said, on Monday he must be in Ipswich.

Salem Village

Elizabeth Hubbard and Mary Walcott skipped the meeting at Salem Village to visit James Holten nearby. Holten had painful stomach cramps that the girls diagnosed as the work of John and Elizabeth Proctor pressing on him while aided by their children William and Sarah. Immediately, the specters attacked the girls. Seeing them convulse, Holten realized his own pain had ceased. After services Clement Coldrum gave Elizabeth a ride home behind him on his horse. (He lived in Gloucester, but the local goings-on apparently drew the curious.) Elizabeth urged him to ride faster, for the woods were full of devils. "There," she said, pointing, "and there they be." Coldrum saw nothing, but galloped the horse anyway until she said they had outdistanced them. As Elizabeth seemed oddly calm, he asked if she weren't afraid of the Devil. "Oh, no," she replied. She could talk to the Devil now as easily as to Coldrum. Later, when neighbor James Kettle visited her uncle Dr. Griggs's house, Elizabeth admitted she had not been to meeting, but only to James Holten's. Furthermore, Kettle would remember, "I found her to speak several untruths in denying the Sabbath Day."[149]

Elsewhere, Rebecca Nurse's specter tormented Abigail Williams, while Elizabeth How's attacked Mercy Lewis and probably Mary Walcott. However, two unnamed but "much afflicted" women in Topsfield could not be certain Goody How hurt them despite their suspicions.[150]

May 30, 1692 • Monday
Boston

After a month of hiding in Boston at his friend George Hollard's house, Philip English was finally taken into custody. Deputy Marshall Jacob Manning, still using the old terms of office, reported that the marshal general had committed English to the marshal of Essex.[151]

Salem Town

Nathaniel Putnam and Joseph Whipple of Salem Village entered a complaint against Elizabeth Fosdick (who had already been named in the multisuspect complaint of May 28), and against Elizabeth Paine, both of Malden, for bewitching Mercy Lewis and Mary Warren. Hathorne and Corwin issued no warrant, however, but busied themselves with depositions against Bridget Bishop.[152]

Ipswich

Susanna Sheldon, nearly dragged into a Salem pond by the specter of Elizabeth How, was not the only one to fear that woman. The defendant's brother-in-law Captain John How, having returned from Ipswich, stood in his dooryard admiring his pigs while chatting with a neighbor. With a piercing squeal, a sow suddenly leapt a yard in the air and fell motionless. Captain How was sure that witchcraft had killed the animal, and although the neighbor laughed at the thought, the sow was dead indeed. The neighbor then suggested cutting off the sow's ear (for countermagic). As Captain How sliced the ear, his hand that held the knife went numb. He was certain his sister-in-law Elizabeth was responsible, his conviction only hardening as the pain in his hand continued day after day, disabling him from work.[153]

Cambridge

Away from these little sorceries, the Boston area ministers met at Harvard College in Cambridge to discuss English affairs in light of Increase Mather's firsthand reports from England.[154]

May 31, 1692 • Tuesday
Salem Village

Court convened in the Salem Village meeting house before John Hathorne, Jonathan Corwin, and perhaps one of the new justices, Bartholomew Gedney. Rev. Samuel Parris took notes, and Attorney General Thomas Newton observed. Newton had seen witch trials before but something was alarmingly different about today's proceedings. "I have beheld most strange things," he would write this evening, "scarce credible but to the spectators."[155]

Rev. Henry Gibbs of Watertown and Boston also watched today's "remarkable and prodigious passages," and "wondered at what I saw, but how to judge and conclude, I am at a loss." Gibbs was a stepson of Jonathan Corwin and a grandson of the Boston widow Mrs. Mary Thatcher. (Mrs. Thatcher was not only embroiled in property disputes and plagued with a larcenous servant, but was also accused of bewitching the afflicted. Her own maid, perhaps Bridget Denmark, had confessed to witchcraft and probably accused her mistress. So far, however, the authorities did not take these charges seriously, for, from the start, not all accusations were believed.)[156]

Philip English was examined, and held for tormenting Mary Walcott and Elizabeth Booth. His flight could not have helped his case, but, except for spectral threats against the afflicted, the only surviving depositions were from William Beale of Marblehead. Back in 1690, according to Beale, English had tried "in a fawning and flattering manner" to buy his favorable testimony in a property dispute with Richard Read, and did not hide his anger at Beale's refusal. Later in the year, when English had Read arrested, Beale not only testified on the latter's behalf, but found and fetched another witness, Thomas Farrar Sr. of Lynn (Old Father Pharaoh). As these two witnesses rode along Lynn Common, Beale's nose suddenly gushed blood over his clothes and over his horse's mane. Later, when he was painfully ill in 1691, he saw the form of Philip English materialize in his sickroom.* Beale survived this too, but his son, apparently healed of smallpox, died the very morning of his father's vision.[157]

Besides his international shipping business and a thriving trade in Jersey bond servants, English bought, sold, mortgaged, and repossessed many properties in the Salem area. Like other Jerseymen trained under different laws, he was quick to sue for debt, even when the debtor thought he had made arrangements to pay. Many locals distrusted his honesty and also wondered how far they could trust the French among them, even if they were Protestants. Seafaring Jerseymen considered themselves nonresidents when Salem tax collectors came around, even though their wives and children lived ashore. The town had no end of trouble getting the Jerseymen's share from English when he was constable in charge of tax collection. English may have been gentry, but he was not popular in Salem.[158]

Constable John Parker of Reading brought in Goodwife Sarah Rice, an old friend of suspect Lydia Dustin. Goody Mary Toothaker and her daughter were probably also questioned (although no papers for their examinations survived).† William Proctor was scheduled for questioning today, and Captain John Flood as well. The latter had unsuccessfully represented Carr and Putnam heirs when they contested their father George Carr's will, and had, moreover, been unable to save the people of York, Maine, from frontier attack.[159]

The afflicted were agitated from the beginning. "Wenches," thought Captain John Alden, "who played their juggling tricks, falling down, crying out, and staring in

---

*The sickroom apparition had legs of "very great stature" but whether English himself was tall or the specter loomed larger than life is unclear.

†The earliest extant examination for Mary Toothaker is dated July 30, 1692.

people's faces." When the magistrates asked who in the room hurt them, one girl pointed wordlessly to Captain John Hill, another military man. But after the officer who helped support her whispered in her ear, she cried, "Alden." She had never before seen Alden in the flesh, she admitted, so the officer told her which man here was Alden.

As with Nehemiah Abbott's case, everyone was ordered outside into daylight and stood in a ring in the street. "There stands Alden," said the same girl, "a bold fellow with his hat on before the judges. He sells powder and shot to the Indians and French, and lies with Indian squaws, and has Indian papooses." Because his specter menaced the girls with his sword, this was confiscated while he waited some hours in Marshal Herrick's custody for the rest of his case to be heard.[160]

Alden had, as former hostage Mark Emerson charged, sold supplies to French and Indian settlements Down-East, as did other Boston merchants including Governor Phips. Men drafted for militia duty Eastward had resented him and his trading success even before the expensive and disastrous Port Royal venture that left Alden's own son captive. People recalled how, while acting on government orders, he had tried to remove the cannon from Marblehead's fort to Boston, and how a mob of angry townsfolk, men and women alike, had thwarted him. Some of the French prizes that he captured as a privateer, moreover, had been seized earlier by the French from New England owners, who wanted them back. But the courts had ruled that the vessels were Alden's by the fortunes of war.[161]

While Alden considered his situation, the magistrates questioned Elizabeth How. The afflicted collapsed at her glance and identified her with their spectral tormentor.[162]

"If it was the last moment I was to live," said Goody How, "God knows I am innocent of anything of this nature."

"Is this the first time that ever you were accused?"

"Yes, sir."

"Do not you know that one at Ipswich hath accused you?" the magistrate countered. (The Perley family had suspected her and confronted her when their little girl fell ill.)[163]

While the afflicted described How's attacks, the court saw fresh bruises and scratches on their arms and a pin stuck in young Ann Putnam's hand.

Goody How denied it all, from apparitions to image magic. "You would not have me confess that which I know not."

In looking about the room she caught Mary Warren's eye and the girl collapsed violently, followed by Mary Walcott. The court ordered Goody How to touch and to revive the fallen, who were more than ever aware of the rampaging specter. Susanna Sheldon also convulsed and had to be restored by the prisoner's touch after she said the accused was the same who carried her off the day before.

"You said you never heard before of these people," said a magistrate.

"Not before the warrant was served upon me last Sabbath day," she answered.

"Oh, she bites!" shouted John Indian, who fell writhing until her touch revived him.

"What do you say to such things? They cannot come to you."

"Sir, I am not able to give any account of it."

"Can not you tell what keeps them off from your body?"

"I cannot tell. I know not what it is."

"That is strange that you should do these things, and not be able to tell *how*," the court said with a mixture of sarcasm and pun before holding Elizabeth How for trial.[164]

Various ailing relatives of Martha Carrier were so relieved by word of her arrest that they were already regaining their health. In court the afflicted identified her in the midst of their convulsions. "She bites me, pinches me, and tells me she would cut my throat if I did not sign her book," said Susanna Sheldon, who also spied the Devil whispering to the defendant. "She looks upon the black man."[165]

"What black man is that?" asked the magistrate.

"I know none," said Goody Carrier, but the girls clamored one was there.

"What black man did you see?" the magistrate demanded.

"I saw no black man but your own presence," she snapped. (The justice was presumably Hathorne, for black hair ran in his family.)[166]

"Can you look upon these and *not* knock them down?" he asked.

"They will dissemble if I look upon them," she said bluntly and some of the afflicted fell at her glance, or at her remark.

"You see? You look upon them and they fall down."

"It is false. The Devil is a liar. I looked upon none since I came into the room but you."

"I wonder," Susanna Sheldon murmured in a trance. "What? Could you murder *thirteen* persons?" All the afflicted screamed in terror as they saw the advancing ghosts of thirteen people killed in Andover.

"It is a shameful thing," Martha Carrier told the magistrates, "that you should mind these folks that are out of their wits."

"Do you not see them?" Hathorne asked, meaning the ghosts.

"If I do speak, you will not believe me."

"You *do* see them!" the afflicted cried.

"You lie," she said. "I am wronged."

But the afflicted saw both ghosts and the Devil at the prisoner's ear, and convulsed. Mercy Lewis recovered at Goody Carrier's touch, but the seizures of the rest were "so great there was no enduring of it." As it was, no further business could be done. So the court, in an attempt to quell her dangerous specter, hurried Martha Carrier away, bound hand and foot. Once this was done, the afflicted, whom the magistrates and audience had thought "almost killed," felt a "strange and sudden ease" and recovered at last.[167]

Wilmot Read, wife of fisherman Samuel Read, lived uphill behind Rev. Samuel Cheever near the Marblehead meeting house. She was well known to be sour-natured—"grouty," as Marbleheaders put it—and rash enough (by tradition) to wish other people's children ill by hoping that a "bloody cleaver" be found in their cradle. Her mere presence sent the afflicted into turmoil. She brought the book, said some, and often hurt them. Ann Putnam Jr., however, testified that while she often saw the specter hurt others, it had never hurt her. But after hearing the testimony, Ann saw Goody Read's spirit disembody itself and advance, book in hand. Several sufferers were repelled when the court tried the touch test. They all had to be carried to the woman for relief, even John Indian. Although the magistrates repeatedly and relentlessly asked Goody Read what she thought ailed these people, she could only reply, "I cannot tell." When asked if they might be bewitched, she said again, "I cannot tell," and when pressed for her opinion, answered, "My opinion is they are in a sad condition." Goody Read's condition promised to be sadder still as she, like the rest of today's accused, was held for trial.[168]

When Captain John Alden was brought back into the meeting house, the court compelled him to stand upon a chair so everyone could see him. Marshal Herrick held his hands still to prevent magical pinches. From this awkward position, Alden asked why the court thought he would come all the way to the Village to afflict people whom he did not know. When Bartholomew Gedney, the newly appointed councilor and special court judge, urged Alden to confess and to give glory to God, Alden replied that he would give glory to God by *not* gratifying the Devil (as telling lies would do) and challenged anyone to bring *real* proof against him. Gedney allowed that he had known Alden for years, been to sea with him, and always considered him honest. But now he was not so sure.[169]

When Alden looked at his accusers as ordered, they convulsed. Alden glared at Gedney and asked why *he* did not fall, but Gedney did not answer. While the afflicted were carried to Alden for his touch, he said that it was an odd Providence of God to allow "these creatures to accuse innocent persons."

But Rev. Nicholas Noyes interrupted, asking sarcastically why Alden should speak of God, who governed the world in peace and order, so unlike the turmoils Alden presumably caused. Noyes went on at length, giving the defendant no way to get a word in edgewise. There must be a "lying spirit" in the girls, Alden at last told Gedney, "for I can assure you that there is not a word of truth in all these say of me." But he was committed to Marshal George Herrick. No bail was accepted. Instead, he and Sarah Rice, and most likely the others, were assigned to Boston prison.[170]

Arthur Abbott (not related to the fortunate Nehemiah Abbott) was "complained of by many," and was apparently jailed, yet he appears to have been free to return home at some later date.[171]

William Proctor was held for tormenting Elizabeth Hubbard and Mary Warren during his examination (which is lost).* Like everyone else today, he insisted on his innocence. Yet the court had him bound neck and heels. This was an unusual procedure, although Redcoat officers had punished their soldiers in this way. He was ordered to remain so for twenty-four hours or until he confessed. (Before either happened, William's nose gushed blood from the strain, and some unnamed person untied him.)[172]

The court also recorded a deposition against Rebecca Nurse from Mrs. Ann Putnam Sr. She had been free from witch specters—though not from ghosts—since March. Yet, as her words were read aloud before her swearing to them, Nurse's specter came back with a vengeance. It tackled her right in court before the eyes of her daughter Ann, who saw not only Nurse's specter, but those of Sarah Cloyse and Martha Corey as well.[173]

Salem Town

The magistrates and their attendants refreshed themselves at Ingersoll's, and then rode back to Salem town where Attorney General Thomas Newton wrote a report to Isaac Addington, secretary of the province. Newton particularly noted that the status of the accused did not save them from the accusations of the afflicted. Witch suspects occupied all ranks. He enclosed a list of prisoners whom he wished transferred from Boston to Salem, where the Court of Oyer and Terminer would sit, and

---

*Ingersoll's bill lists William Proctor's examination as May 21—which probably should be May 31 as the written sequence suggests.

asked that the confessors, Tituba and Mrs. Thatcher's maid, be kept separately from the others as evidence.* "I fear we shall not this week try all that we have sent for," Newton wrote, "by reason the trials will be tedious, and the afflicted persons cannot readily give their testimonies, being struck dumb and senseless for a season at the name of the accused."[174]

Boston

Meanwhile, in Boston, Judge John Richards requested the opinion of his minister, Cotton Mather, on the trying of witches. Mather had been ill earlier and unable to offer advice, but today, as an expert in the spiritual realm, he wrote a list of points to consider. He urged Richards to be very careful how much importance he attached to specters. Unlike Hathorne and others, Cotton Mather assumed from the first that tormenting spirits could be disguised devils. Malicious people might be impersonated more often than others, but that was no proof of their compact with the Devil. To assume so would lead to no end of trouble.[175]

For proof was no easy matter. "Albeit the business of this witchcraft be very much transacted upon the stage of imagination," Mather warned, drawing from his experience with the Goodwin children, it "yet may not be called imaginary. The effects are dreadfully real. Our dear neighbors are most really tormented."

"A credible confession" was one proof of guilt, and Mather trusted that the judges could determine what was legally credible and what was "the result of only a delirious brain, or a discontented heart." He did not approve of torture for confessions (like being tied neck and heels), but thought "cross and swift questions" might confuse anyone who tried to lie.

Without a confession several factors might be suspicious, though certainly not proof: humanly impossible knowledge or accomplishments; a wound on a suspect matching one given a specter; a surgeon's diagnosis of witch marks; the presence of poppets; or the failure of the Lord's Prayer test. But the court should *never* admit the latter as evidence (as the Salem courts were doing), or forget (as they also did) that the Devil could cause *any* of this with *no* intermediary witches at all thereby potentially invalidating all the evidence.

Mather felt that actual use of witchcraft had begun the present troubles, but it was also possible for a devil to lure complaining, discontented folk with promises and threats, so that many might succumb not for greed or for revenge, but for the sake of peace. With this possibility in mind, it would be more merciful, Mather thought, to enforce lesser punishments than the death penalty, depending on the degree of involvement and on the depth of repentance, even though this contradicted the present law. He left it up to the court's good judgment to untangle the situation.

---

*The prisoners to be transferred were the Proctors, Good, Nurse, Willard, Martin, Bridget Bishop, Alice Parker, and Tituba.

6

JUNE 1692

> 'Tis an undoubted and a notorious thing, that
> a Demon may, by God's permission, appear
> even to ill purposes, in the shape of an inno-
> cent, yea, a virtuous man.
>
> —"The Return of Several Ministers"

June 1, 1692 • Wednesday
Salem Town

Magistrates John Hathorne and Jonathan Corwin interviewed the Hobbs women and others in Salem and learned how George Burroughs's specter had buffeted them for revealing so much. Even during testimony Rebecca Nurse's specter attacked the women, and Philip English's stabbed a pin into Mary Warren's hand.[1]

On the same day prisoner Mary English deposed that, about a month earlier, she had heard the confessor Mary Warren exclaim repeatedly that she and the other afflicted were so distempered and distracted that they did not know *what* they said in their fits. (But now Mary Warren seemed thoroughly distracted once more).[2]

Susanna Churchill, confused and browbeaten, confessed to Hathorne and Corwin and to the King's Attorney Thomas Newton, that she had signed the book that

Pudeator's specter had brought. Before that, she was afflicted and unable to work, to the disgust of her master, old Jacobs. He beat her, she signed, and now Goody Pudeator made her stick pins into dolls while Goody Bishop boasted of her murder victims.[3]

Ordinarily, capital cases were tried in Boston before the highest court. The special Court of Oyer and Terminer, however, was to convene in the affected county, so the justices would have spent the day traveling to Salem for the morrow's sitting. In preparation, several prisoners were carted from the Boston jail to the Salem jail: John and Elizabeth Proctor, Susanna Martin, Alice Parker, Rebecca Nurse, Bridget Bishop, John Willard, Tituba, and Sarah Good. (Sarah's infant had already died, and little Dorcas stayed behind in Boston prison.)[4]

While the real Rebecca Nurse was in transit, her specter again threatened to murder Mrs. Ann Putnam. Shrouded ghosts of Mrs. Putnam's sister, Mary Bayley, along with three of her children and six Barker nieces and nephews, all accused Nurse, Cary, and an unidentified deaf woman in Boston of killing them.[5]

Stamford, Connecticut

In Connecticut, Mercy Desborough, confined in the county jail, requested the water test (based on the folk belief that a witch would float even if bound hand and foot). It was not legal, but she was certain of her innocence.[6]

June 2, 1692 • Thursday
Salem Village

First thing this morning, ghosts of Samuel Fuller and Lydia Wilkins loomed by Mrs. Ann Putnam's bed. They, like the witches, threatened to tear her into pieces if she wouldn't tell Hathorne that Willard had murdered them. And if Hathorne didn't believe her, they might just materialize in court! Willard's specter also came by to boast of the victims that he and William Hobbs had killed—mostly her own and neighborhood children. Joseph Fuller's ghost accosted her later to accuse Goody Corey. It was, by all reports, a busy time in Mrs. Putnam's bed chamber.[7]

Also, in the course of the day, Joanna Chibbun* saw apparitions of Sarah Good and her dead infant daughter. Her own mother had murdered her, the child's ghost cried. Sarah explained that she did so only because she could not care for it, but when her baby called her a witch, Sarah snarled that she had already given this child to the Devil. Goodman Harwood's glaring ghost materialized later, trailed by the shape of Rebecca Nurse. It was Nurse who had killed him, he said, by pushing him from a cart.[8]

---

*This name is given as "Joanna Chibbun" and "Johanna Childin." Might she be Susanna Sheldon?

Salem Town

Preliminary testimony began in Salem at eight o'clock in the morning and concerned Nurse, Willard, How, Parker, and possibly others. John Hathorne and
Jonathan Corwin, as local magistrates, finally wrote arrest warrants for Elizabeth
Fosdick and Elizabeth Paine after a three-day delay (probably because Peter Tufts
of Malden arrived in person to complain of their bewitching his "Negro woman").[9]

At ten o'clock in the jail, a jury of nine women and surgeon John Barton
searched the bodies of Rebecca Nurse, Alice Parker, Sarah Good, Elizabeth Proctor, and Susanna Martin for witch marks. They found that Bishop, Proctor, and
Nurse each had an odd "excrescence of flesh" on their privates, all strangely alike
yet unlike anything natural. But the eldest woman, a skilled midwife, disagreed.
The marks looked natural to her, especially after Goody Nurse explained her difficult birthings.[10]

The two-story Salem Town House (built in part by fugitive brick mason Daniel
Andrews) stood in the center of the street around the block from the jail and just
uphill from the meeting house. Rev. Nicholas Noyes lived across the way to the
south, while Bridget Bishop's former home stood northward. The Latin grammar
school occupied the Town House's ground floor with a courtroom above, where
the first Court of Oyer and Terminer now convened. Chief Justice William
Stoughton presided, with Samuel Sewall, John Hathorne, Bartholomew Gedney,
and (as five or more were required) probably John Richards and Nathaniel Saltonstall.[11]

Their first case was that of Bridget Bishop, and matters went badly for her from
the start. As guards escorted her from prison through the town center, she glanced
toward the meeting house just as something crashed inside the empty building. On
inspection, a nail-studded board was found wrenched from place and lying a good
distance from where it had been, though the building was, admittedly, in need of
repair.[12]

Once Bridget Bishop was arraigned on the Grand Jury's several indictments of
tormenting the afflicted at her examination, she pleaded not guilty and put herself
on trial by God and by country. She was allowed to challenge any members of the
trial jury whom she thought might not be impartial. (Abashed, few defendants
took advantage of this right.) She had been suspected for years of practicing witchcraft, and had been charged with it in 1679 after Wonn (probably "Juan"), a black
slave belonging to John Ingersoll (Deacon Nathaniel's brother), was plagued by
Bridget's apparition. Goody Oliver, as she was then known, was allowed to give
bond, rather than being compelled to wait in prison for the next sitting of the Court
of Assistants, which let her go.[13]

Back in 1660, as Bridget Playfer of St. Mary-in-the-Marsh, County Norwich, England, she had married a Samuel Wasselbee, had a son, and was widowed (some
now thought she had killed her husband). She then emigrated to Boston (where

she bore Wasselbee's posthumous daughter) and finally settled in Salem as the second wife of Thomas Oliver. They had a daughter Christian, who by 1692 was herself married and a mother. (The Wasselbee children had apparently died young.) But when Christian was less than a year old, her parents' quarrels were already so violent and so public that both Olivers were sentenced to be whipped or fined. Neighbors testified how Bridget's face was sometimes bloody and sometimes black and blue, though she managed to land a few blows against Thomas also. Nine years later, in 1677, they were back in court for once again making their battles public—and on a Lord's Day, too. ("Old rogue!" she had shouted at him. "Old Devil!") They were both sentenced either to pay a fine or to stand in the marketplace on Lecture Day wearing papers inscribed with the offense on their foreheads. Thomas's daughter Mary, from his first marriage, paid her father's fine, but left her stepmother to the public's humiliating gaze.[14]

Around 1682, a Goody Whatford accused Bridget of stealing a spoon and received the rough side of her tongue for it. Soon after, glowing specters of Bridget and Goody Parker came in the night and pulled Goody Whatford from her bed to the beach. Before they could drown her, she managed to call on God and the apparitions fled. But ever since, she had been distracted and crazed, "a vexation to herself, and all about her." In the summer of 1687, Bridget, now married to Edward Bishop, was accused of stealing and selling a mill brass (a bearing) from Thomas Stacey's mill. She claimed that she and her daughter had found it in a corner of the garden, but the daughter, who had tried to sell it, said it had been about the house since her father's time, though the inventory of Thomas Oliver's estate does not list a mill brass. Bridget was jailed in Salem from the December to the March session. Then Thomas Stacey claimed she had made peace with him the summer before, weeping on her knees for his forgiveness. This infuriated Bridget all the more. After the miller's son testified about the brass, he was flung about his own yard by an invisible presence.[15]

Now, in 1692, she was on trial again. Testimony began with the afflicted, who related under oath how the defendant constantly urged them to sign the book, how she snatched one girl from her spinning wheel and nearly drowned her, how her victims' ghosts accused her of murder, and how at her May 3 examination she struck them with her eye beams and twisted them by subtle motions of her own body. The torture began again as they spoke of it. Goody Deliverance Hobbs, badly tormented after her confession, said Bishop not only beat her with iron rods to make her sign that book, but also shared the Devil's bloody sacrament in Parris's pasture. The afflicted, as the court knew, referred to Bishop's specter, but, like nearly everyone else, they did not always bother to distinguish between the accused and an apparition of the accused. Furthermore, in all the confusion, no one seemed to notice that spectral murders attributed to Goody Bridget Bishop actually stemmed from gossip about Goody ·Sarah Bishop.[16]

Except for the afflicted's own testimony and some corroboration from observers who verified that the former had suffered fits on certain occasions and at those times had accused certain persons, most testimony concerned long-standing suspicions. Her neighbors' unease caused several nightmares (as later centuries would understand it) after arguments with her. In them, Bridget's form, dressed in her favorite red bodice, and accompanied by a light of no discernible source, entered dark, locked bedchambers to hurt the dreamer. Thus, John Cook was whacked on the side of his head; Samuel Gray and William Stacey each "woke" to find her trying to insert something into their mouths; and Richard Coman found her sprawled crushingly on his chest depriving him of breath enough even to wake his sleeping wife beside him. The specter vanished once the victim spoke. In Samuel Gray's case this caused or coincided with, his infant's shrieking in its cradle. The child, healthy earlier, pined and died within months.[17]

When John Louder had worked at the Ship Tavern for John and Susanna Gedney, whose orchard bordered the Oliver's, Louder quarreled with Bridget Oliver after her fowls scratched up the Gedney garden. Soon after, her specter sat on his stomach one night and tried to throttle him. When he and Mistress Gedney accosted her in the orchard and demanded an explanation, Goody Oliver denied it and became threatening when he insisted it was true. Louder took sick, and while staying home alone from an afternoon Sabbath service, encountered a black pig in the locked tavern. Once that animal disappeared, a black-furred, chicken-footed imp leaped in the window and spoke from a disturbingly human face. "I am a messenger sent to you," it said, "for I understand you are troubled in mind, and if you will be ruled by me, you shall want for nothing in this world." Louder twice drove the imp from the house before he crept to the backyard and spied Goody Oliver walking in her orchard. He returned indoors and saw the imp ready to spring. "The whole armor of God be between me and you!" Louder cried (using a Biblical metaphor as a charm). The imp deflected its course to fly away over the apple tree, scattering fruit as it went. This all left Louder dumbstruck for a good three days. Goody Bishop interrupted his testimony to deny she ever knew this Louder, but it was well known that they had lived in adjoining households for years and had quarreled more than once.[18]

William Stacey had suspected Goody Bishop for at least fourteen years, ever since she had visited during his bout with smallpox and "professed," as he recalled it, "a great love for this deponent in his affliction more than ordinary." Coins disappeared from his pocket after she paid him for work. His cart became stuck in a hole right after he told her how some folk suspected she was a witch, only there was no hole. He then talked so much about the time her specter invaded his room that the real Bridget complained he caused her more mischief than anyone else. After Stacey testified about her stealing his father's brass, he got tossed against a stone wall and down a bank one night. After that, his cart collapsed entirely the next time he passed her. But worse yet, his daughter Priscilla, a healthy child, fell ill and died within two weeks.[19]

Samuel Shattuck was a dyer and shopkeeper by trade, a Quaker by conviction, and brother by marriage to the jailed Abigail Soames. In 1661 his father, also named Samuel, had brought to Massachusetts King Charles II's order that revoked the death penalty for repeat Quaker proselytizers. But if the Friends disagreed with their neighbors on religious details, they agreed on the threat of witchcraft. Shattuck testified how in 1680 Goody Oliver frequently came to his house "in a smooth flattering manner" on odd trivial errands just at the time that his eldest child "was taken in a very drooping condition." The oftener she visited, the worse four-year-old Samuel Jr. became, his face bruised from unexplained falls. Bridget brought a pair of sleeves to dye, and later, as if running out of excuses, a few scraps of lace so short they appeared useless. Then the two pence she paid for the job disappeared from a locked box, though Shattuck's assistant vowed he put it safely away. Samuel Jr. began to have seizures, his face contorting, gasping for air. Between episodes he mostly cried until he cried himself to sleep. "His understanding decayed," said his father, and "ever since he has been stupefied and void of reason."[20]

After a year and a half of this, a stranger (as Shattuck put it) remarked that if anyone were bewitched, Sam Jr. was, and probably by a neighbor. "She has had a falling out with your wife," he said over Shattuck's mild protests, "and said in her heart: your wife is a proud woman, and she would bring down her pride in this child." Shattuck recalled an angry exchange between the women, and listened to the stranger's solution: to "fetch blood" from the suspect—just a scratch on the face, enough to break the spell. Shattuck entrusted his boy to the stranger and gave him a coin to buy cider from her as an excuse to get close. Bridget, however, ordered the stranger away from her door—she was not licensed to sell anything—and snatched up a spade to make him go. As he retreated, she spied the boy by the porch. "Thou rogue," she said and slapped Sam Jr.'s face, leaving bloody scratches. "What, dost thou bring this fellow here to plague me?" So blood was drawn on Shattuck's own child.

Sam Jr., now about sixteen, still suffered violent convulsions and needed constant watching lest he tumble into fire or water. Either he ran restlessly and aimlessly about, or teetered back and forth across a plank, seemingly unable to step off safely though it lay flat on the ground. His parents consulted physicians and surgeons, all of whom diagnosed the evil hand of witchcraft. Samuel and Sarah Shattuck were certain that Goody Oliver, now Goody Bishop, was the cause.

Goodwife Naomi Maule, of another Quaker family, testified that Goody Bishop, as both she and her husband Thomas believed, had caused one of their children to die.[21]

John and Rebecca Bly once bought a sow from Edward Bishop, who had them pay a third party to whom he owed money; this was an arrangement that Bridget disagreed with loudly. After the sow farrowed, the animal acted deaf and blind, banged her head against the fence, and foamed at the mouth if her young tried to suckle. Neighbor Goody Henderson, whose cattle had acted similarly Eastward, recommended that they mix red ochre in milk and feed it to the afflicted animal. Before recovering, however, the sow broke loose and charged up and down the street between the Blys' house and the Bishops' house for two hours. The Blys had no doubt who caused the trouble, for when John and his son William had repaired the Oliver house seven years earlier, they had discovered, on removing a wall, several poppets made of rags and hog bristles stuck full of headless pins, pointing outward.[22]

The court questioned Bridget Bishop about those poppets, but did not accept whatever she answered. Several times, they noted, she was caught in lies and inconsistencies. The disasters that followed her quarrels seemed too many for coincidence, especially in context with the observed convulsions of the afflicted in court. The justices as a whole (for they would not be of a single mind about the proceedings as they progressed) overlooked the fact that no single act of witchcraft had been positively proven to have been caused by the defendant, much less observed by two witnesses, except by the afflicted who could see the Invisible World. The magistrates also overlooked that several of the deponents and their neighbors themselves admitted to using charms and spells. Whether the neighborhood disasters were actually caused by witchcraft or not, they were *not* the crimes in Bridget's indictments.[23]

She was, in fact, indicted for tormenting Abigail Williams, Ann Putnam Jr., Mercy Lewis, Mary Walcott, and Elizabeth Hubbard. But if the spoken evidence did not prove this, the courtroom seizures did, at least to the court's satisfaction. Before the jury deliberated, Chief Justice William Stoughton advised them to ignore the obvious good health of the afflicted (for despite the severity of their fits, they were surprisingly hale when free of them), even though the indictment referred to them in the usual way as "pined, consumed, [and] wasted" by witchcraft. The point was, Stoughton told them, whether they had suffered such tortures, as everyone present had observed, that would *ordinarily* tend to pine and to consume. This, said Stoughton, was the sense of the law. With such instructions, the jury found Bridget Bishop guilty.[24]

Salem Town

At four o'clock, the same committee of one male surgeon and nine matrons examined Bridget Bishop, Rebecca Nurse, Elizabeth Proctor, and Susanna Martin. The obvious excrescences of the morning were not to be found, only a bit of dried skin where some had been observed. Furthermore, Goody Martin's breasts, full and firm at ten o'clock, were now "all lank and pendant."[25]

Fairfield, Connecticut

A special court also sat at Fairfield, Connecticut, to hear the Desborough and Clauson cases. Neighbors testified about disagreements that were followed by sick livestock or sick children. Some testified to possibly incriminating remarks made by Mercy Desborough while in prison, but the gist of the evidence was unclear. Because Goody Desborough had demanded the disputed water test, the local officials allowed it. Both defendants were bound hand and foot in a crouching position and tossed into water, yet they bobbed about like corks—or witches—even when the men tried to push them under. (Fortunately magistrates like Deputy Governor William Jones considered ducking "superstitious and unwarrantable.") Mercy still refused to confess or to name other witches as urged. Stephen Clauson produced a petition from himself and eighty neighbors, including magistrates, testifying to his wife Elizabeth's good character. She was *not*, they said, contentious, malicious, or a busybody. With the jury thoroughly confused, the magistrates referred the case to the next General Court.[26]

June 3, 1692 • Friday
Salem Town

Goody Bibber repelled John Proctor's specter and its proffered cup of blood. The Grand Jury heard evidence about Willard and Nurse. However, Rev. Samuel Philips and Rev. Edward Payson of Rowley, among others, testified *for* Goody How.[27]

Five days after the first complaint against them, Elizabeth Paine and Elizabeth Fosdick of Malden were delivered from Middlesex County to the Sheriff of Essex. Goody Paine, midwife and gossip, had been a center of turbulence before, accused (but found not guilty) both of public drunkenness, and of composing the probably bawdy verses that circulated when the long-widowed Rev. Wigglesworth married his nineteen-year-old maidservant.[28]

Goody Fosdick's husband was a man whose speech, in his younger days at least, could lapse into virulent obscenity. (But their cases are lost, though their arrest was mainly for bewitching Peter Tufts's "Negro woman." This was perhaps Nannee, whose owner, kin by marriage to the Putnams, was in court years earlier for excessively flogging a freeborn manservant. The Putnam family's witchcraft fears had extended beyond Salem.)[29]

June 4, 1692 • Saturday
Salem Town

Edward Putnam and Thomas Rayment of Salem Village entered a complaint against Mary Ireson of Lynn for tormenting Mary Warren, Susanna Sheldon, Mary Walcott, "and others."[30]

Gedney, Hathorne, and Corwin, acting as local magistrates, conducted an ex-amination of Job Tookey, laborer and waterman of Beverly. Referring to the other suspects, he had declared (as others overheard it) that he sided with Rev. Bur-roughs, that he could speak with the Devil as easily as he could with them, and that he was not the Devil's servant for the Devil was his. Shortly after this, the af-flicted (some of whom also claimed to chat with the Devil) said Tookey hurt them both in person and through his apparition. They said he boasted that "he had learning and could raise the Devil when he pleased," for he was "not only a wiz-ard but a murderer, too."

They were tormented as usual during his examination and terrified by the sight of five ghosts—two men, two women, and a child—crying, "Vengeance! Vengeance!" for Tookey had killed them all. When asked what child that might be, the real Job Tookey replied, "It was John Trask's child," which agreed with Ann Putnam Jr.'s testimony. He was held for further questioning.[31]

Tookey was no stranger to the Salem jail. Ten years earlier, he had fallen into debt after an accident left his right hand useless for over six months. Richard Knott, physician and entrepreneur, had him jailed for refusing to work for him as promised, and for owing £9 payable in silver or in fish. Knott said Tookey was lazy and defiant. Tookey said Knott beat him and kept changing the terms of employ-ment. Knott visited the prison to mock Tookey's educated background and minis-ter father, and to threaten to sell him as a bond servant to Virginia. However, Knott withdrew the suit after three months.[32]

Salem jail, as Tookey described it in 1682 when it was far less crowded, was "a sad, dolesome, stinking place," where he was "almost poisoned with the stink of my own dung and the stink of the prison."[33]

June 5, 1692 • Sunday
Boston

The congregation of Boston's North Church, which today included Governor Phips, heard Cotton Mather deliver a sermon, "Good Men Described" (especially good magistrates). God requires us to cultivate an excellent spirit, said Mather, to glorify God by all our ordinary acts, and to aspire—despite the scoffs of brutes and devils—to be "a saint on earth" (not just in the hereafter), to be like the angels, the very "angels that are now invisibly present here." We must seek occasions of use-fulness in small ways or great, to the neighborhood and to the larger community. "A good man . . . has not a spirit that will permit him to follow a multitude in the doing of evil" even if it means standing alone. "It is true, every public servant must carry two handkerchiefs about him, one to wipe off the sweat of travail, another to wipe off the spit of reproach." Attempting this, the good may bewail the sinful-ness of their souls, yet never despise them. "Oh, how loth he is to sell that soul for a song!" But the ungodly, "if the Devil tender them a little bit of money, or frolick, they'll sell their souls unto him, by rebellions, like the sin of witchcraft. Whereas, if the Devil offer unto a good man all the pleasures, and profits, and honors of the world, he will not sin for the sake thereof, and wrong his own soul. 'No,' he says to the Devil. 'Thy offers perish with thee; my soul is too excellent a thing for thee to have it so.'"[34]

***

Pentegoet

By early June, a war party of about four hundred gathered at the Baron de St. Castine's station at Pentegoet on the Penobscot River. The Abenaki, who had taken York the January before, were there, along with Micmacs, Malecetes, Penobscots, and others under leaders like the Sagamore Madockawando, St. Castine's father-in-law. The Sieur de la Broquerie and other French officers led about twenty Canadian troops accompanied by a few Jesuit missionaries. A similar force under the Penobscot chief Agamagus, whom the English called Moxus, had attacked Wells in a four-day siege the year before, killed all the cattle, but failed to take the blockhouses commanded by Captain James Converse. "My brother Moxus has missed it now," Madockawando was reported to have said, "but I will go myself the next year, and have the dog [Captain James] Converse out of his hole."[35]

June 6, 1692 • Monday
Salem Town

Mary Ireson's examination was scheduled for ten o'clock at Beadle's Tavern in Salem, Bartholomew Gedney presiding, along with Hathorne and Corwin. Salem clothier Simon Willard, a brother of Rev. Samuel Willard of Boston, and the same Lieutenant Simon Willard who had testified about Rev. Burroughs and the gun, took notes. The afflicted fell in fits and blamed Goody Ireson even during the opening prayer before the defendant's arrival.[36]

Mary Ireson's sister and uncle had accompanied her to court. As an experiment the justices presented Goody Ireson's sister, who was *not* under arrest, and asked the afflicted if this were the woman who hurt them. No, they replied, "it was she that had a hood on," meaning the actual prisoner whose features were shadowed by a riding hood.

"Do you not see how you are discovered?" the court asked the defendant.

Goody Ireson admitted that "she had been of a bad temper," and perhaps that sin had left her vulnerable. But she was not answerable to the sin of witchcraft.

Elizabeth Booth, Susanna Sheldon, Mary Warren, and Mary Walcott all fell at her glance and recovered at her touch several tedious times. Each, while conscious, reported the defendant's specter tormenting the others. All were certain that this was the woman whose specter had attacked them earlier. They described how the specter repeatedly brought them the Devil's book to sign—even, Susanna Sheldon claimed, during the examination when it threatened to tear out Susanna's throat.

The accused, perhaps in shock, stared with eyes "fixed," and the afflicted cried that she was watching the Devil as he ordered her not to confess.

"Confess," Mary Ireson's own uncle urged, "and *break* the snare of the Devil."

But Mary allowed that she knew not if she were in it. Might she "be a witch and not know it?" she asked. The justices said no, but the most Goody Ireson would concede (Willard wrote) was that "she could not confess till she had more light." So, still in the dark about the matter, Goody Ireson was held for future trial.

Another specter had also targeted the afflicted: the magistrates issued a warrant to arrest Ann Dolliver of Gloucester for tormenting Mary Walcott and Susanna Sheldon this day. As Dolliver was living in Salem with her father, Rev. John Higginson, Constable Peter Osgood was able to fetch her forthwith from her task of spinning. About ten years earlier she had married the improvident mariner William Dolliver, who quickly spent most of her money. After he left for parts unknown, she and her child returned to her father's Salem household. Rev. Higginson petitioned the courts to have the remainder of her marriage portion taken from her absent husband's power and put into his own hands for the maintenance of Ann and her child. (He could hardly provide for himself since the town owed him so much back pay.) As there were eventually three Dolliver grandchildren, Ann's move did not solve the problem. Rev. Higginson, like others, would eventually refer to his daughter as ruled "by overbearing melancholy, crazed in her understanding." Some of Ann Dolliver's Gloucester neighbors had thought her uncanny, knowing too much of what went on in other people's homes, but others defended her reputation.[37]

Mistress Dolliver (for even abandoned, Ann had status above goodwife) was questioned by Gedney, Hathorne, and Corwin. (Her brother John was a magistrate but apparently was not presiding.) When asked if she had ever performed witchcraft, Ann replied, "Not with intent to hurt anybody." When urged to confess further, she demanded, "Where be my accusers? I am not willing to accuse myself." But before the afflicted were brought back in, Mrs. Dolliver admitted that sometimes she had stayed out in the woods all night, once because she had become faint and had been unable to make her way home. She alluded to a disagreement with her mother (stepmother, that is) but denied being frightened by a "black thing" or by any spirit. She reminded the court that if the Devil could assume the form of a man, "she knew not a spirit from a man in the night."

When Susannah Sheldon, Mary Walcott, and Mary Warren were called in, they fell and insisted that the defendant was the woman who had hurt them earlier that

day. Her clothes were different, but her face was the same. Some of them also reported the ghost of a recently dead child crying for vengeance against Dolliver,
who "had pressed the breath from its body" over the course of several hours. Ann
had also, the specter informed them, tried to kill her own father, Rev. Higginson,
"for she had more spite at him than she had at the child." She also tormented folks
with wax poppets kept "in a secret place."

Mrs. Dolliver admitted that she did have one—well, two—wax poppets. About
fourteen years earlier, *she* had felt pinched and thinking *herself* bewitched, had
"read in a book that told her that was the way to afflict them that had afflicted her."
(In other words, she had used the images for countermagic.)

No, she didn't use them this morning, the only things she pinned were her
clothes. No, she had not been at Thomas Putnam's house, and she had visited
Goody Nurse only once when Ann had lost her way taking the long road round
to avoid the ferryman, "the ugly fellow." She had admitted enough about poppets, however, that she could shake hands with the afflicted with no harm, even
though they saw the Devil standing by her. Ann Dolliver was jailed to await
trial.

Boston

Under crown orders, the man-of-war *Conception,* recently captured from the
French, arrived at Boston from Virginia under Governor Phips's command, to
guard the coast from the French.[38]

June 7, 1692 • Tuesday
Salem Town

John Hathorne, Bartholomew Gedney, and Jonathan Corwin again questioned Job
Tookey, while Salem merchant William Murray took notes. Tookey answered
mainly in negatives.[39]

"Did you not say the other day," asked one magistrate, "that you saw the Devil?"

"I knew not then what I said," Tookey answered.

When the afflicted* did not fall at his glance, their eyes saw into the Invisible
World, for this court was attended by several shrouded ghosts—two children,
three men and three women—all glaring redly at their murderer. One was Andrew
Woodbury, another, Mary Warren reported, was Gamaliel Hawkins, lately dead in
Barbados after Tookey thrust a great pin through the heart of his image. Elizabeth
Booth pointed, speechless, where the Trask child's ghost in its little winding sheet
stood on the magistrate's table wailing for vengeance. Being set on by specters,
Mary Warren blamed not only Tookey but Mr. Busse as well. John Busse was a

---

*The afflicted said Tookey bewitched a Betty Hews (who was not necessarily in court).

physician and preacher active in Wells and Oyster River (when the towns were not burnt out by frontier raids). He was in Boston now, and had been reported at the great witch meeting.[40]

June 8, 1692 • Wednesday
Salem

Today the ghost of George Needham told Elizabeth Booth that Martha Corey had killed him because he did not mend her linen wheel. The late Thomas Gould Sr. added that Martha had killed him after he told her that "she did not do well by Goodman Parker's children" (her stepgrandchildren).[41]

Boston

The General Court convened this morning in Boston for the first time under the new charter, both council, in their capacity as upper house, and representatives, as lower house. He gathered them, said Governor Phips, to settle the government according to the charter; to nominate and appoint officers; to enact laws; to establish permanent courts; and to grant money for defense against French and Indian enemies. Indeed, Phips optimistically assured the members of the legislature that he wished only to serve them and would pass whatever bills they offered as long as they were consistent with the Crown's honor and interest. "And whenever you have settled such a body of good laws, that no person coming after me may make you uneasy, I shall desire not one day longer to continue in the government."[42]

Chief Justice and Lieutenant Governor William Stoughton signed and sealed the death warrant for Bridget Bishop, instructing Sheriff George Corwin to hang her Friday next. Stoughton's fellow jurist Nathaniel Saltonstall, present at the Legislature today, resigned from the Court of Oyer and Terminer around this time, presumably over the handling of the Bishop case. (As the months passed, he would remain "very much dissatisfied with the proceedings." The afflicted, moreover, would soon report seeing his specter.)[43]

June 9, 1692 • Thursday
Boston

The General Court discussed the collection of back taxes, administered justice of the peace oaths to the councilors, and heard Increase Mather report on his English negotiations. Most attended the afternoon lecture on leadership that Cotton Mather delivered, "Good Things Propounded." A good magistrate should hinder wickedness and propagate what was laudable. He should consider himself made

for his people instead of the reverse, and should be offered the proper respect for his efforts in return. A good minister, likewise, should be a good shepherd and a shining light to his people, who oughtn't expect him to sink into poverty while they withheld his salary as if it were alms. As for justice, Mather commented that "when things are misapplied, so that the innocent are condemned and the guilty acquitted, what is there to be seen, but, an abomination to the Lord!" And concerning the religious toleration now law under the new charter, he observed that (although an antireligious life was "abominably criminal") a man's nonconformity to a specific "way of worship" should "not break the terms on which he is to enjoy the benefits of human society. A man has a right unto his life, his estate, his liberty, and his family." Persecution only repelled people and made even the best cause appear evil. "Leave the otherwise-minded unto God."[44]

Salem Town

Elsewhere, Elizabeth Woodwell and Mary Walcott both saw Giles Corey enter the Salem meeting house and sit through the lecture in the center of the men's section by the post—even though his body was safely locked in prison.[45]

June 10, 1692 • Friday
Salem Town

On Midsummer's Day, the sun entered the sign of Cancer, and the local almanac predicted a moist, windy season (which would, in fact, be hot and dry).[46]

Some time between eight o'clock and noon, Sheriff George Corwin and his men took Bridget Bishop from Salem prison to be hanged. Salem had no regular place of execution, since all prior capital cases had been tried in Boston and the condemned executed there. For now, Salem officials chose a spot of common pasture at the edge of town—away from the center of things, yet visible to passers-by. Like later condemned witches, Bridget Bishop was transported in a cart flanked by guards and mounted officers in a procession that drew onlookers as it passed from the jail, down Prison Lane, to the main street. They proceeded southwest out of town where the road angled toward Salem Village and Boston, and the North River bent sharply to run between bedrock hills. A stream flowed from the height on the south into a salt marsh pool that met the river bend. The crowd headed north, crossing the stream on a causeway and bridge between the pool and the river (shallow now as its waters drained away to low tide). The procession turned left off the main road to a track that climbed the ledge above the salt marsh pool. Several of the afflicted were present, beaten, they said, by old Jacobs's specter, leaning on the Devil so it could use one of its staves as a club.[47]

Either a temporary structure or one of the few trees that grew from the clefts in the rock served as the gallows. With a noose about her neck, hands fastened behind, and legs and petticoats tied close, Bridget, protesting her innocence to the last, was blindfolded and placed half way up a ladder. She was either pushed off, or the ladder itself kicked away to let Bridget's body, her neck rigidly suspended, fall with sudden sharpness. If the neck did not break at once, as it seldom did, death took its time. In these cases, the face beneath the hood suffused dark red from the dammed up blood that wept from eyes, nose, and mouth. Starved lungs rasped loudly for the air they could no longer breathe. The whole body thrashed against its bonds as it convulsed uncontrollably, clenching and unclenching in every part, expelling waste. After a last jerk, the body stilled, empty of life at last. Bridget's corpse was buried nearby.[48]

John Hale (the Beverly minister) was present, perhaps requested to deliver prayers at the gallows for the condemned. After the execution he heard Quaker Thomas Maule declare that *he* certainly believed Bridget Bishop was a witch. She had bewitched one of his children to death, said Maule. And one thing he would *never* do was pray with the condemned at her execution, not even if asked. She covenanted with the Devil and forsook God, Maule concluded in his unorthodox manner, and *that* was the Unforgivable sin that Christians must not pray for.[49]

Later in the day as required, Sheriff George Corwin appeared before the clerk of the court, to write his official return. "I have taken the body of the within named Bridget Bishop . . . and caused the said Bishop to be hanged by the neck until she was dead."[50]

Boston

At the General Court in Boston, Phips ordered a committee of nine (Secretary Isaac Addington, plus the Oyer and Terminer judges) to consider a revision of local laws. (Nathaniel Saltonstall had resigned by then, replaced by John Foster, a Boston merchant.)[51]

Wells, Maine

Wells, meanwhile, bereft of its minister due to witchcraft charges, and of many other inhabitants due to the ravages of frontier war, was guarded by Captain James Converse and fifteen men quartered in Joseph Storer's garrison, the largest and strongest of the town's seven fortified houses. Two sloops and a shallop arrived today* with ammunition, supplies, and fifteen more men. But

---

*Dates for the attack on Wells are usually given as June 10 and 11 Old Style. Concerning the first day, Cotton Mather wrote, "But now Reader, the longest day of the year is to come on, and if I mistake not, the bravest act in the War fell out upon it." June 10 was the solstice by Old Style dating. The second day was "the Lord's day," but Sunday fell on June 12, not 11. A Sabbath, it would seem, is more easily noted than a solstice.

the village's terrified cattle ran home bleeding from the woods where they grazed loose. Realizing trouble was afoot, Converse moored both sloops together in the deep water of the winding tidal creek that bordered Wells and set a watch for the night.[52]

June 11, 1692 • Saturday
Wells, Maine

It was hardly daylight when French and Indian forces surrounded John Diamond between Storer's garrison and the creek. He claimed there were double the actual number of defenders. Yet, even that was no threat to the hundreds of besiegers, who now verbally divided the expected plunder and captives. A French officer exhorted his men to attack and to win, but spoke in English for its effect on the besieged.

As soon as Captain Converse and his men repelled the first assault on the garrisons, the attackers turned to the sloops at the creek's bend. But the sailors swabbed out the fire arrows, and the tide caught the siege-engine, rigged from a farm cart, that the attackers pushed onto the wide mud flats. Night passed with shouts and shots, and a brief flank attack by Converse's men.[53]

Boston

The day was more peaceful in Boston, where John Higginson Jr. (the Salem minister's son) and Dudley Bradstreet (the former governor's son) were sworn in at the general court as justices of the peace for Essex County.[54]

June 12, 1692 • Sunday
Wells, Maine

After a brief silence this Sabbath morning, the full French and Indian force marched on the Wells garrisons. It was so formidable a sight some English murmured of surrender, until Captain Converse threatened to kill the next coward who spoke so. The attackers formed three ranks, shouted, "Fire, and fall on, brave boys!" three times in English, and then fired all at once. But the people in the garrisons, including the women, kept up a steady fire until the attackers again turned to the creek.[55]

The wind drove their raft of "combustible matter" away from the sloops and capsized it against the opposite shore. The attackers crossed the river to slaughter all the cattle that they could find. They fired a last volley at the sloops that killed one man, then sent out a flag of truce. Despite insults, Converse refused to budge from his defenses. "Damn ye," cried one of the enemy, "we'll cut you as small as tobacco before tomorrow morning."

By now the Algonquin leaders, unlike the French officers, felt it unlucky to continue. The besiegers stayed beyond gunshot in sight of the English to slice and to singe the captive John Diamond. Then they shot at the garrisons off and on until ten o'clock at night.

June 13, 1692 • Monday
Wells, Maine

Once it was clear the attackers had left Wells, men from the garrisons and sloops ventured cautiously among the clutter of corpses. They found, besides Diamond's mutilated remains, the body of a French officer—Lieutenant General the Sieur de la Broquerie. He wore a pouch of religious items about his neck, papers of indulgence and the like, the English assumed, mere amulets, none of which had prevented his being shot through the head.[56]

Boston

News of Wells arrived in Boston while the General Court was debating back taxes. Phips informed his council that the Piscataqua region's militia had already sent their neighbors help. The governor then ordered Major Samuel Appleton to detach part of his Essex regiment to relieve the depleted Piscataqua garrison. Phips also placed an embargo on all ships and vessels in Massachusetts harbors. As long as the French were about, *no one* was to sail anywhere until further notice.[57]

Fairfield, Connecticut

In Connecticut, Kate Branch named yet another Fairfield specter: Goody Miller. (She and her husband fled over the New York border to her brothers in Bedford. None of the New York authorities cooperated with extradition requests.)[58]

June 14, 1692 • Tuesday
Boston

The General Court finally passed its first law under the new charter: all arrears in public assessments intended for defense against Indians and French (due since October 1689) were to be collected by November 1, 1692.[59]

***

Wells, Maine

If Rev. George Burroughs's wife was still in Wells, the siege convinced her to decamp. Mary Burroughs packed or sold everything, including her husband's library, and loaned the proceeds at interest. She left with her baby Mary and abandoned her seven stepchildren. The eldest was only sixteen, so they "were generally unable to shift for themselves" in that dangerous region without so much as a keepsake from their father, much less any money. The family owned property in Falmouth, Maine, and in England, but, after the recent fires and confusions, no longer had the papers to prove it.[60]

June 15, 1692 • Wednesday
Boston

The General Court decided, for the time being, to retain all laws in force under the former charter as long as they did not contradict the new charter or English law. England demanded that colonial law must not be "repugnant to, but as near as may be agreeable to the laws of . . . England." The King's ministers had made sure Increase Mather understood that the "repugnancy clause" could cancel the new charter—an ominous prospect much on the legislator's minds. Although the English Common Law's treatment of convicted felons differed from Massachusetts law, witchcraft was definitely a capital crime in England and therefore also in New England. As dealings with the Invisible World were uncertain at the best of times, Governor Phips had consulted the local Congregational ministers* for their expertise on the subject. Today, Cotton Mather submitted their reply, "The Return of Several Ministers."[61]

They acknowledged the severity of the afflicted's suffering, as well as the presence of knowledgeable magistrates to deal with it, but cautioned against acceptance of spectral evidence "lest by too much credulity for things received only upon the Devil's authority, there be a door opened for a long train of miserable consequences." The ministers recommended the standard law books of Perkins and Bernard, but rejected the folk tests as too often "abused by the Devil's legerdemains." The ministers hoped questioning might take place in as calm a setting as possible with due consideration for the accused. Furthermore, "there may be matters of inquiry which do not amount unto matters of presumption, and there may be matters of presumption which yet may not be reckoned matters of conviction." The appearance of the accused as a specter seen by the afflicted was *not* proof of guilt, for "'tis an undoubted and a notorious thing, that a Demon may, by God's permission, appear even to ill purposes, in the shape of an innocent, yea, a virtuous man." Eliminating such testimony could well end this "dreadful calamity" of accusations. With that in mind, the court might carry out "the speedy and

---

*The ministers who later signed the introduction to Increase Mather's *Cases of Conscience*, and who apparently contributed to the "Return" that Cotton Mather wrote, were: James Allen, John Bailey, and Samuel Willard of Boston; Nehemiah Walter of Roxbury; Charles Morton of Charlestown; Michael Wigglesworth of Medford; Samuel Angier of Newton; Jabez Fox of Woburn; Samuel Whiting Sr. of Lynn; Joseph Gerrish of Wenham; Samuel Philips of Rowley; William Hubbard of Ipswich and John Wise of Ipswich's Chebago section; and Joseph Capen of Topsfield.

vigorous prosecution of such as have rendered themselves obnoxious according to the direction given in the laws of God and the wholesome statutes of the English nation, for the detection of witchcrafts."

June 16, 1692 • Thursday
Boston

"Dr." Roger Toothaker, folk-healer, self-styled killer of witches, now a suspect, died in Boston jail. According to the coroner's jury called to examine the body at the prison, Toothaker's death was natural. (Whether his body went to a pauper's grave or not is unknown. If Toothaker's family wanted it back, they would probably have had to pay his jail bill first.)[62]

June 17, 1692 • Friday
Boston

Cloudy, hot, and dry, read the almanacs. It was becoming an alarmingly dry summer for crops.[63]

Recognizing that taxes for many public expenses (including ministers' rates) had been left in arrears even longer than defense taxes, the General Court ordered their collection by December 10. They also ordered a Thanksgiving on July 14 to celebrate, among other things, the Governor's safe arrival.[64]

June 18, 1692 • Saturday
Salem Village

As the moon turned full, Constable Jonathan Putnam, a near neighbor to the accused Cloyse, Andrews, and younger Jacobs households, felt inexplicably and wretchedly ill. Mercy Lewis was sent for, with her spectral sight, but went mute as soon as she crossed his threshold. Jonathan's father John Putnam Sr. was there, along with Rev. Samuel Parris and others, to observe what happened. Someone suggested she hold up her hand if she saw any specters tormenting Jonathan. Mercy, still speechless, lifted her hand and passed into a trance. When she recovered, she said the specters were Rebecca Nurse and Martha Carrier.[65]

Boston

Lydia and Sarah Dustin, mother and daughter, were transferred from the Boston* to the Cambridge prison in their home county of Middlesex. Several other prisoners were removed and sent back to Salem: George Burroughs, George Jacobs Sr.,

---

*The Boston bill reads June 19, but that was a Sabbath. Boston bills tend to be padded by a day, and Dustin's Cambridge bill begins June 18.

Giles and Martha Corey, Ann Pudeator, Sarah Cloyse, Sarah Wildes, Susanna Root, and Dorcas Hoar.[66]

***

Salem Town

Some time before the next trials, Marshall George Herrick, Constable Joseph Neal, and jailer William Dounton searched George Jacobs Sr. for witch marks in the Salem prison. They discovered an apparently insensible quarter-inch excrescence on his right shoulder and lanced it but no matter ran out. Another search by a seven-man committee found no marks on Rev. Burroughs, but three on Jacobs: on his right hip, his right shoulder blade, and inside his right cheek. The committee found two of the three insensible to probing pins.[67]

Some time in June, Dorcas Hoar's grown grandson John Lovett visited her in one of the prisons, perhaps to deliver provisions, for her family, unlike others, saw that she was fed and clothed. She worried who might witness against her. He said he could think of none (ignoring all the neighbors from whom the Hoars had stolen). Maybe Goodman Whitred, she went on, about that cow. Well, perhaps him, agreed Lovett.[68]

June 19, 1692 • Sunday
Salem Village

In Salem Village, Rev. Samuel Parris delivered another sacrament sermon apparently referring to God as "the Father of mercies, and the God of all comfort. Which comforteth us in all our tribulation, that we may be able to comfort them which are in any affliction." (He filed his notes with "loose papers," now lost).* Members who were kin to the accused, however, felt no comfort.[69]

June 20, 1692 • Monday
Ipswich

Rev. William Hubbard of Ipswich, who had signed "The Return of Several Ministers," deposed on behalf of the accused Sarah Buckley. He had known her since she came from England a half century before and had always thought her a good woman.[70]

June 21, 1692 • Tuesday
Salem Village

A newly afflicted person, Daniel Rea's eleven-year-old daughter Jemima, suffered repeated attacks from the specters of Goodwives Nurse and Black and neighbor

---

*The text in the printed edition is given as "2 Cant. 1." The ms. appears to be "2 Cor. 1" and 2 Corinthians:1 seems to make more sense than Canticles 2:1.

Goody Cloyse. Or so her attendants gathered from Jemima's one-sided conversation, as they tried to hold her still during six or seven consecutive seizures. "What?" she raved. "You cannot do it alone, and you brought this woman to help you? Why do you bring her? She was never complained of." This was Goody Black, she explained after she recovered, and the Devil himself would reveal that Goody Cloyse was indeed a witch.[71]

Salem

Neighbors visiting William Shaw's house found Susanna Sheldon convulsing, tortured by specters that had tied her hands so tightly her rescuers had to cut the string to free her. The girl blamed it all on Goody Dustin's specter. This may have been when her rescuers found Susanna hanging from a hook, close to expiring, but that happened four times in all, twice blamed on Dustin and twice on Good. Household items, moreover, turned up in odd places: a broom in an apple tree; a shirt and a milk tub in the woods.[72]

June 22, 1692 • Wednesday
Hartford, Connecticut

Connecticut's General Court at Hartford authorized their own Court of Oyer and Terminer, come September, to deal with the growing number of witchcraft cases in Fairfield.[73]

June 23, 1692 • Thursday
Boston

While the Massachusetts General Court continued to debate taxes, almanacs speculated that thunder and wind would bring rain. The weather, however, remained obstinately dry.[74]

***
Andover

Around this time thirty-year-old Timothy Swan began to feel stabbed and burned. According to later testimony, it would appear that a whole pack of witches swarmed into his father's house* to attack Swan, sometimes bodily in invisible disguise, sometimes in spirit. They were mostly women: Toothaker, Post, Lacy, Foster, and others. But Martha Carrier brought her sons as well as her daughter, and

---

*Court documents list the Swans in Andover, but they lived just over the Merrimack River in Haverhill.

Richard Carrier burnt Swan with a tobacco pipe and stabbed his knee with a hot iron spindle. The Devil, in the shape of a dark-haired man in a high-crowned hat, brought the spindle, but on other occasions the witches simply used poppets from a distance.[75]

(Some of the confessors later said they tormented Swan "for the sake of one of their partners who had some offense offered her by the said Swan," while others declared they acted "in the behalf of some of their confederates." The only specified quarrel was with old Mrs. Bradbury, but it may be significant that six years earlier Elizabeth Emerson, "singlewoman," named Timothy Swan as the father of her child, and that Elizabeth was kin to the Toothaker and Carrier families. When that paternity case went before the local magistrate, Nathaniel Saltonstall, Timothy denied everything, but was ordered to pay child support, which he did: late, seldom, and in goods as worthless as rusty hardware and broken harnesses. Yet, the court did not believe Elizabeth's charge of rape either, because she did not report it immediately and because, as she claimed, she conceived from that one occasion. Few besides her mother believed she was a virgin when Swan pulled her upstairs in her own home and had his way with one arm pressed across her throat to prevent outcry. In 1691 Elizabeth bore twins (sired by another), which the neighbors found sewn in a bag buried shallowly in the garden. She said they were stillborn, but other details that she provided seemed so unlikely that she was convicted of murder on September 22, 1691. Because of the intercharter situation, however, the sentence had not yet been pronounced, and she still waited in the Boston prison. If she were not the "confederate" referred to, she was likely not the only object of Swan's attentions either.)[76]

June 24, 1692 • Friday
Boston

The General Court ordered the towns to chose commissioners to list, to assess, and to tax all male inhabitants over age sixteen. The court set an abundance of shipping taxes (with a £20 fine for would-be smugglers). Then it extended hearty thanks to Increase Mather for the years spent obtaining the Charter (for which he was considerably out of pocket) but added that, due to war expenses, the government could not reimburse him just yet.[77]

Salem Town

John Proctor's specter pestered Abigail Hobbs with the book even in prison. Better to afflict than be afflicted, he said, and promised she would not hang. He made her touch the book and gave her a poppet and thorn with which to hurt Ann Putnam Jr.[78]

June 25, 1692 • Saturday
Boston

Governor Phips and council received two petitions composed by Boston's Baptist minister, William Milborne, one signed by himself "and several others" (now unknown). Like the earlier "Return of Several Ministers," the petitions objected to the use of spectral evidence in the trials, for fear it mostly served to condemn the innocent. "A woeful chain of consequences will undoubtedly follow. . . . [We] therefore request that the validity of specter testimony may be weighed in the balance of your grace and solid judgments, it being the womb that hath brought forth inextricable damage and misery to this province, and to order by your votes that no more credence be given thereto than the word of God alloweth."[79]

The council took offense at this unsolicited opinion and at its "very high reflections upon the administration of public justice." Governor Phips signed a warrant for Rev. Milborne to answer for the "scandalous and seditious paper." The Suffolk sheriff brought him before the council straightaway, and Milborne admitted he had indeed written both papers and had signed one. The council ordered him to appear before the Superior Court at its next sitting (after one was established). In the interim he had to post a £200 bond plus two sureties to guarantee his court appearance, or wait in jail. (In Andros's day, Milborne and Phips had petitioned for justice together, and Milborne's brother Jacob was executed in New York for defying the royal governor. The prosecuting attorney in that case was Thomas Newton, now king's attorney for the Court of Oyer and Terminer.)

Salem Town

In Salem meanwhile, more of Elizabeth How's former Ipswich neighbors deposed in her behalf before the court.[80]

June 26, 1692 • Sunday
Salem

Neighbors discovered Susanna Sheldon choking on the floor with her head jammed behind a chest, hands tied so tightly with a wheel band that it had to be cut to free her. Susanna blamed Sarah Good for this attack.[81]

June 27, 1692 • Monday
Boston

The General Court established a naval office to oversee and to tax shipping, and granted the governor power to march local militia in aid of neighboring provinces.

The Crown had already made Phips the military head of New England, yet each province expected a say in what its men would do, and preferred to recognize his military title only in the field. Phips was also under royal orders to build a fort at Pemaquid, a task all the more urgent after the Wells attack. The legislature also passed an act to incorporate Harvard College and to reorganize its governing boards into one corporation of president, treasurer, and eight fellows.[82]

Cambridge

Harvard's former rector (now president), Increase Mather, and several of the fellows were even then in the college library at Cambridge, attending the monthly meeting of congregational ministers. They discussed the state of overseas Protestantism in the light of Mather's recent sojourn, and then set a question for the next meeting: "Whether the devils may not sometimes have a permission to represent an innocent person as tormenting such as are under diabolical molestations?" Their "Return of Several Ministers" had said as much already, but after the government's reaction to Rev. Milborne's petition they may have wanted a consensus on the question.[83]

Salem

Elsewhere, Rebecca Nurse's specter tormented Goody Sarah Bibber, while Elizabeth Proctor's assailed Elizabeth Booth. The girl and her mother had not believed she was a witch before, it hissed, but now she would *make* them know it.[84]

June 28, 1692 • Tuesday
Salem Town

Sarah Good's trial began at nine o'clock in the Salem Town House.* It was yet another sorrow in a life of declining fortune: the father's suicide, the stepfather's grip on her inheritance, the first husband's death and debts, and the present husband's apparent inability to earn a living. Sarah's cumulative anger alarmed people—especially if cattle deaths followed.[85]

Samuel and Mary Abbey had taken in the homeless Will and Sarah Good, then ejected them after six months of Sarah's turbulence "for quietness sake." After Sarah's "spitefully and maliciously" expressed resentment to the Abbeys and to their children, the Abbeys' cattle began to sicken until seventeen head died in two years, as well as some sheep and hogs. A year ago May, when Will Good told

---

*The exact order of the trials is unclear. Calef lists the trials of Good, Martin, Nurse, How, and Wildes all under June 30, but Cotton Mather gives June 29, for Susanna Martin. Not all five cases could be heard in one day, and some testimony is dated after June 30.

Sarah about the losses, she declared that she didn't care if Abbey lost *all* his cattle, as Will told Samuel Abbey.[86]

One of Thomas Gadge's cows also died around the time that the Abbeys evicted the Goods. Gadge's wife had refused to let Sarah so much as set foot in their house for there was smallpox in the area and she feared Sarah might be carrying it. When Sarah's kinsman Zachariah Herrick not only refused her houseroom but also hustled her and her pipe off his property, she snapped that such behavior might just cost him two of his best cows. And sure enough, two of his best cattle were mysteriously replaced by lesser beasts.[87]

Now, in 1692, her four-year-old daughter Dorcas was alone in jail on suspicion of witchcraft, her infant daughter was dead, and her husband was testifying against her. All the spectral evidence from the examination would have been brought against her, plus reports of her specter's activities since (some of it from the confessors Deliverance and Abigail Hobbs). But it was the observable testimony of the afflicted that the court seemed to value the most: their suffering throughout the last five months (including seizures in the courtroom).[88]

During the trial (according to a later critic) one of the afflicted roused from a fit claiming that Good had stabbed her in the breast with a knife, and had broken its blade in the process. A sliver of metal was found in her clothes, but an unnamed young man volunteered that *he* had discarded a fragment from a broken knife blade in the presence of the same witness only the day before. He produced the damaged knife, which the court now compared with the sliver. It fit exactly. However, this was not the first time the specters had reportedly used physical objects to hurt their victims. The magistrates dismissed the young man with a warning to be truthful, and allowed the afflicted witness to continue her testimony.[89]

Sarah Good's luck did not improve; the jury found her guilty of witchcraft.

The court also recorded testimony against Tituba, and for Elizabeth How from her ninety-four-year-old father-in-law. Unlike some, her family did not desert her, for while she was confined to Boston prison, her blind husband, James How Jr., accompanied by a sighted daughter, made the long trip from Ipswich to Boston twice weekly with food and money. As they would later recall, this cost him about five shillings a week, not counting lost time and the expense of a horse.[90]

Rebecca Nurse petitioned for a second panel of women to examine her for witchmarks. Marks found by the other panel on the morning of June 2 disappeared by the same afternoon. She suggested Mrs. Higginson (the minister's wife, whose step-daughter Ann Dolliver was a prisoner), Mrs. Porter, and the midwives Mrs. Buckstone and Mrs. Woodbury. (But whether the court allowed this request is unknown.)[91]

Salisbury

Constable William Baker rode from Salem to Salisbury to arrest seventy-year-old Mistress Mary Bradbury. Wife of the prominent Captain Thomas Bradbury (whom Susanna Martin suspected of tampering with her father's will), she was related by marriage to the Nurse, Esty, Cloyse, Wildes, and Bishop families, and her daughter Elizabeth was married to John Busse, whose specter had brought wine to the great witch meeting. Mrs. Bradbury's own specter had been seen among the gang attacking Timothy Swan. Most of the surviving testimony against her would come from the Carrs, Mrs. Ann Putnam's kin.[92]

Baker also arrested Sarah Davis "betwixt Wenham and Ipswich," presumably for witchcraft. (It may be significant in light of the spectral witches' revenge on Swan, that a Sarah Davis of Haverhill had been found guilty of fornication in 1682, and that Timothy's brother-in-law Nathaniel Ayer was ordered to pay child support. Robert Swan, Timothy's father, had been furious with the presiding magistrate, Nathaniel Saltonstall (lately retired from the witchcraft court), for his sharpness toward Ayer and toward another Swan son-in-law in a similar case, and for what Swan viewed as lenience toward Sarah. Sarah had said that Major Saltonstall was like a father to her, but she was still fined a stiff fifty shillings. Unfortunately, the current witchcraft case is lost.)[93]

Boston

In Boston, meanwhile, the General Court reestablished a schedule of regular, quarterly, lower court sittings—the General Sessions of the Peace—for the several counties. The court specified that, as before, all jurors were to be chosen from freeholders according to the property qualifications specified in the new charter. Church membership was *not* a requirement.[94]

Stamford, Connecticut

Connecticut magistrate Jonathan Sellick questioned the still afflicted Katherine Branch at his home in Stamford before her master and various onlookers. She answered calmly, but collapsed in a seizure as soon as she left his house. The men carried her back inside, stiff as a board. But once this passed, she writhed backward in an arc. "You kill me, Goody Clauson, you kill me!" she cried. Two men together could not straighten even her arm from the invisible force that seemed to clutch it.[95]

All night long Kate argued with the specters of Elizabeth Clauson, Mercy Desborough, Goody Miller, old Mary Staples (who, in 1654, had sued the party who had called her a witch), Staples's married daughter Mary Hary, and her granddaughter Hannah Hary. "What creature is that with a great head and wings and no body and all black? Hannah, is that your father? I believe it is, for you are a witch." To drown the specters' comments, Katherine jigged about the room, singing prayers and verses from *The New England Primer* (including "A Dialogue Between Christ, Youth, and the Devil"). Some of the men tried to cut a lock of her hair for a counterspell, but they could hardly get near her. The one time anyone caught her, he could not keep hold due to the great strength in this apparently frail girl.

June 29, 1692 • Wednesday
Salem Village

Ann Douglas, once employed by Joseph Putnam's widowed mother Mary, returned to the house of her father, John Darling, after she lost her own husband. It was probably here that her infant daughter died today. Killed "by witchcraft, I doubt not," Rev. Samuel Parris noted in his records.[96]

Salem Town

The Grand Jury considered evidence concerning Susanna Martin, and the Court of Oyer and Terminer began her trial "by adjournment." Many attended from Boston, including Rev. Deodat Lawson. Goody Martin pleaded not guilty to the charges, and the afflicted, as usual, choked and convulsed. The judges, thought Lawson, needed patience to garner their testimony between apparent spectral attacks. He observed how grotesquely twisted the afflicted were, as if every joint were dislocated, and how they vomited blood. (Some, not sure what the mess was, dabbed a finger in the gore to check. It *was* blood.) The court read the account of her May 2 examination, wherein she laughed at the accusations as folly, while her evil eye battered the afflicted—even when they had not seemed aware she was looking at them.[97]

Now neighbors testified, not in evidence of the specific charges against her, but to determine character and probability. Lieutenant John Allen of Salisbury had refused to let his ox carry a load for Goody Martin, because he had wanted the animal put to grass after a big timber-hauling job. They argued about this in the road, she muttering that his oxen would be of little more use to him, he calling her a witch and nearly tossing her in the brook. Later, when Allen went to collect his rested oxen from their meadow by Salisbury Beach, he found only hoofprints leading to the mouth of the Merrimack River. All sixteen had swum to Plum Island, where they charged madly up and down its long length eluding capture for days. Two older beasts left the maddened herd, but fourteen plunged into the ocean and swam for the horizon. Only one turned back, charging over the island again and across the Newbury marshes to the woods by the Artichoke River. He eventually came home, but the other thirteen's drowned carcasses washed up all along Cape Ann.[98]

For a quarter of a century folk suffered cattle deaths following "Martin's discontents"—if they refused her beef or tried to pay her with an animal that she didn't want. One of her sons traded a cow to a neighbor against Martin's wishes and the beast, gentle before, acted crazed all the way to the ferry, breaking all ropes to plunge into the river.[99]

Twice, Goody Martin's specter stalked middle-aged farm hand Bernard Peach. Once it twisted him backward in a hoop until he bit its hand. No one else saw that apparition, but Peach found a drop of blood on the snow-covered doorstep, the footprints of a woman, and unmarked whiteness beyond. Another time, after Peach refused to help the real Goody Martin with corn husking, her specter and that of another crept upon him in the barn. He swung his quarter staff, hitting mostly the beams, but landed one blow on Susanna's specter. Goody Martin was soon after rumored to be unwell, but Peach did not check if it were due to his blow.[100]

Jarvis Ring of Salisbury reported being held motionless by something in the dark seven years before. He saw it only once; it was the specter of Susanna Martin, who forthwith bit his little finger. The wound never properly healed and the marks were still visible.[101]

When Susanna Martin was acquitted of the earlier witchcraft charge, Robert Downer was rash enough to tell her that in his view she *was* guilty. Her retort, something about a she-devil fetching him away, was followed with a night attack by a cat-like creature. Similarly, when John Kimball, who already had doubts about his cattle's deaths, argued with her over the sale of a puppy, she muttered, "If I live, I'll give him puppies enough." One evening as he ran home from the woods trying to elude the "force" that overtook him there during a squall, a small puppy-like creature nearly tripped him. It disappeared when he chopped at it with the ax that he carried, but only to be replaced by a larger, fiercer dog. This lunged for his throat, veered over his shoulder, and circled about until the frantic Kimball called on God and Christ, whereon the creature vanished. Both men kept the embarrassing encounters to themselves, and in both cases the Martins seemed to know all about it anyway.[102]

John Pressy deposed how, twenty-four years back, he became lost in familiar territory near the Martins' land in the dusk of a Sabbath eve. A moving light as big as a bushel basket accosted him and ruffled like a turkey cock when he prodded it with his stick. He panicked, whacked at it to no effect, then veered off, and fell into a hole that he never could find afterwards. The light disappeared, but he spied Susanna Martin watching him, and later heard the woman was ill. He was too frightened to ask if it were from his blows or not.[103]

William Brown of Salisbury described how his wife Elizabeth had been a sober, sensible woman until twenty-odd years before when she saw Susanna Martin vanish. After that, she felt prickling on her legs every time Goody Martin came by feigning neighborliness. The pain rose to her stomach like a knot of nails, then into her throat like a pullet's egg. "Witch," she cried, "you shan't choke me!" The church prayed and fasted on her behalf, and Goody Brown recovered to testify against Susanna in the earlier trial. Although acquitted, Susanna let her displeasure be known, which reduced Elizabeth to a flood of tears. Within two months, William Brown returned home from a journey to find his wife distracted, raving that they were divorced. And so she remained, healthy in body, distempered and frenzied in mind. No doctor could help, but all concluded she was bewitched.[104]

Joseph Ring of Salisbury (Jarvis's brother) had for two years been abducted intermittently to witch meetings, where he saw Susanna Martin. Each time, as he said on his return, he felt a blow on his back that left him paralyzed, able only to watch the witches feast and dance. Others verified that he had certainly been absent on those occasions. He had even been observed on the road and then vanished from view. From the previous August to April, he had been utterly mute, the power of speech returning only with Goody Martin's arrest. Furthermore, while Joseph was Eastward with the militia (after Casco Bay Fort was taken), he had gambled himself two shillings in debt to Thomas Hardy of Great Island in the Piscataqua. Convinced that Hardy had contrived the debt to gain power over his soul, Joseph kept encountering the man (or his specter) on the road among men and women on horseback, or with Goody Martin and others chatting and drinking cider in the woods before turning into black swine. Hardy wanted him to write something in a book and promised fine things in return, but the inkhorn was full of blood. Joseph, though scared witless by "most dreadful shapes, noises, and screeching," refused.[105]

Even when not perceived as menacing, Goody Martin often seemed uncanny, spooking the livestock. Nathaniel Clark and Joseph Knight, looking for stray horses in the woods, saw her carrying a dog under one arm. Yet, when they passed, the thing was only a keg. For commenting on this to her, they wasted the better part of the day chasing the horses round and round a knoll. Susanna, meanwhile, paused at Clark's house, where his dog bit her. "A churl," she muttered, "like its master."[106]

Sarah Atkins of Newbury testified how Susanna Martin had walked from Amesbury to visit her at a time when roads were so muddy that foot traffic seemed hardly possible. Goody Atkins shooed her children from the hearth, but Goody Martin flourished her petticoats and said she was quite dry. Even the soles of her shoes seemed dry, thought Goody Atkins, who exclaimed that such weather would have her wet to the knee. But Susanna only replied that she, for one, "scorned to have a draggled tail."[107]

Susanna Martin denied she ever used witchcraft and when the court asked what she had to say for herself, she declared she had "led a most virtuous and holy life." The court, like her neighbors, thought otherwise, and the jury found the still defiant Susanna Martin guilty.[108]

Most of the evidence against Rebecca Nurse came from the afflicted, with various unafflicted observers (like Rev. Samuel Parris) verifying that the girls and women had suffered convulsions on specific dates during which they had accused the defendant. There were more spectral attacks during court. Goody Sarah Bibber clutched her knee and cried that Nurse pricked her, but Rebecca's daughter-in-law Sarah Nurse saw Goody Bibber take pins from her own clothing and jab herself with them.[109]

Countering spectral reports from the ghosts of murder victims, John Putnam Sr. and his wife Rebecca, who had expressed their suspicions of the defendant earlier, testified that when their son-in-law John Fuller and daughter Rebecca Shepard had died of a sudden malignant fever, *no one* suspected witchcraft.[110]

But widow Sarah Holten was convinced that Rebecca Nurse's malice had killed her husband Benjamin three years earlier. He had been perfectly healthy until his pigs strayed—with their sharp trotters and rooting snouts—into the Nurses' field. Rebecca stormed to the Holten house "railing and scolding," ready to have her son shoot the pigs. According to Goody Holten, her husband was calm and polite throughout, but afterward suffered blindness, stomach pain, and choking spells. Doctors could do nothing and he soon died. Nathaniel and Hannah Ingersoll added that, while Holten *had* died in violent fits, they heard nothing of witchcraft suspicions at the time. Nathaniel Putnam said that, in all the forty years he had known her, Goody Nurse had acted like a good Christian woman. Although she occasionally disagreed with her neighbors, he never before heard anyone suspect her of witchcraft.[111]

Abigail and Deliverance Hobbs were brought in to tell of seeing "Deacon" Nurse at the Devil's sacraments. Rebecca Nurse, at the bar, turned toward her fellow prisoners in surprise. "What? Do you bring her?" she asked. "She is one of us."[112]

Balancing Mrs. Ann Putnam's accounts of her fits at the hands of specters like Goody Nurse was John Tarbell's description of how Mrs. Ann Putnam Sr. and Mercy Lewis each thought the other had identified the apparition first. Other kin and neighbors likewise cast doubt on the spectral evidence reported by various afflicted witnesses. In addition, the defendant's daughters, Rebecca Preston and Mary Tarbell, testified that their mother had endured for many years an unspecified "infirmity" that the jury of women had assumed was a witchmark. Israel and Elizabeth Porter described their March visit when Rebecca Nurse showed concern for the afflicted and surprise that they had accused her. Her brother-in-law Peter Cloyse (whose wife Sarah was under arrest) and Daniel Andrews (who had fled his own arrest warrant but apparently had returned) sent word that "we, if called thereto, are ready to testify on oath" about the same.[113]

There were twenty written depositions in all, plus more testimony delivered, as in other cases, viva voce. (Not specified in the surviving testimony, but sure to be resented in light of recent frontier attacks, was the Nurses' hiring a substitute for their son Benjamin's militia duty—the same Benjamin who would have shot the Holten's pigs.)[114]

The jury returned a verdict of *not* guilty. As soon as foreman Thomas Fisk announced this, the afflicted shrieked, startling—even after all they had witnessed before—not only the audience but also the officials.[115]

Court apparently recessed at this point. As the judges left the bench, one remarked that he was not satisfied with the verdict, and another replied that they would indict her anew for the latest afflictions. When court reconvened, Chief Justice William Stoughton told the jury that, while he would not try to impose upon them, the jurors had, nevertheless, heard what the accused said when she referred to the confessing Hobbs woman as "one of us." The jury, already concerned about the recent effects of the verdict on the afflicted, asked that they be allowed to reconsider. But as they could not agree how to interpret Goody Nurse's words, they came back to the courtroom and asked her directly. Was she identifying herself with Hobbs as a fellow witch or as simply one of the accused? Goody Nurse stood at the bar feeling miserable, confused, and unwell. The jury repeated her remark and its question, but she made no answer, saying nothing at all in her defense. So the jury brought a second, revised verdict of guilty. It was only afterward when the matter was explained to her, that Goody Nurse, hard of hearing, realized she had simply not heard the question and so lost her opportunity to speak. Even with so many testifying on her behalf, she now faced hanging.

June 30, 1692 • Thursday
Salem Town

Elizabeth How pleaded not guilty before the Court of Oyer and Terminer, but the afflicted could not bear for her even to look at them. Their depositions were interrupted by swoons and seizures that the accused was obliged to cure with her touch. (The court felt that the afflicted could discern her touch from anyone else's, but was not so sure about the murder victims' ghosts that the afflicted reported as present in the room.)[116]

At least a dozen people testified on Elizabeth How's behalf, including her ninety-four-year-old father-in-law, who described how tenderly she cared for her blind husband. But there were also the suspicions of her brother-in-law, Captain James How, who had offered her no help at all during her arrest.[117]

Timothy Perley's family had, in fact, suspected Goody How for over ten years. The Perleys were sure she had made their cows die after a quarrel. Worse yet, their ten-year-old daughter had been afflicted, wasting away to skin and bone for two years until she died. The ministers of Rowley, Samuel Phillips and Edward Payson, testified that, although the parents had summoned them at the onset of the girl's fits, they never heard or saw her accuse Goody How. In fact, they had both been present when the real Goody How took the girl's hand and asked if she had ever been hurt by her. The girl said that she never had and if ever she said so, she hadn't been aware of it. Indeed, Rev. Phillips overheard the girl's own brother try unsuccessfully to nudge her into saying that Goody How was a witch.[118]

But the dead girl's father insisted that he had to admonish her often for accusing Goody How. The ministers' conclusions evidently meant less to the court than the bereaved parents' interpretation of events and the physician's diagnosis of "an evil hand."

Witch rumors dogged Goody How even when she asked to join the Ipswich Church. She spoke of this gossip to Goody Safford, took her hand, and confided, "I believe you are not ignorant of the great scandal that I lie under by an evil report raised upon me." Goody Safford *was* aware already and afraid of the woman, yet soon insisted on Goody How's admission to the church "beyond reason and all persuasion," even publicly at a church meeting. After the application was defeated, she continued to rave nonstop for two hours that How was a precious saint, and then fell into a brief trance. "Ha! I was mistaken," she said. How was no saint but a witch, who would give Safford and her child no peace until her testimony secured How's church membership.[119]

The real Elizabeth How expressed sorrow for Goody Safford. But the sick woman no longer believed her, for now she saw How's specter, along with Goody Oliver's, repeatedly slip into the room between the clapboards.

Other neighbors and kin who had opposed Goody How's admission were soon plagued with misfortune. The Perleys' cow ran mad and died in a pond. The Fosters' mare was found bruised and wearied as if beaten. The elder who had recorded Goody How's conversion account inexplicably lost large quantities of drink from seemingly untouched barrels, and his daughter fell into a trance after eating an apple that How gave her. The hired man who delivered rotten fence posts provided by John Perley thought Goody How's earlier remarks about the wood's quality a prophecy (rather than an observation on Perley's dependability). Taken together, the mass of otherwise trivial events seemed suspicious.[120]

Finding her field trampled by an ox belonging to Nehemiah Abbott (himself recently arrested on charges of witchcraft but then released), Goody How had exclaimed that she hoped it would choke; and so the ox did, choking to death on a turnip. More of Abbott's animals perished or were injured, as did Isaac Cummings Sr.'s mare after he refused to lend her to Goodman How. Within a few days Isaac found the mare wasted, galled, and bruised, her face scorched from the bridle, lips swollen, and mouth so raw that her tongue was black and blue. Surely the beast was hag-rid (ridden hard all night by witches). Isaac and his brother-in-law Thomas Andrews treated the mare for bott and belly-ache. When that didn't work, Cummings agreed to Andrews's suggestion of countermagic. A long-stemmed pipe of burning tobacco, inserted in the animal's rectum, sent blue flame like a grass fire over her rump and flared toward the rafters. What they tried the next day, a Sabbath, Isaac Cummings refused to say, but that evening a neighbor advised they cut a piece from the animal. Perhaps tomorrow, Cummings said, but as soon as they left the barn, the mare fell down dead.[121]

Elizabeth How, despite the support of her family and her ministers, was found guilty.

The Grand Jury heard evidence about John and Elizabeth Proctor, Martha Corey, and against Sarah Wildes. Sarah Wildes of Topsfield, stepmother of suspect Sarah Bishop, may have been tried today. Except for testimony from the afflicted, most evidence against her came from the family of her husband's first wife, Priscilla Gould. For their sister was not even seven months dead when John Wildes married Sarah, who, they knew, had once been whipped for fornication and yet had the brass to flaunt finery above her station, or nearly so.[122]

Sixteen years before, the late wife's sister, Mary Reddington of Topsfield was convinced Sarah Wildes had bewitched her, as she told Rev. John Hale. And one of the late Priscilla's eight children told his aunt that his stepmother, Sarah, was a witch. Rev. Hale, summoned to testify about this matter, recalled how the stepson Jonathan Wildes behaved so strangely that several area ministers were asked to Ipswich to pray for him. Some of those ministers thought him mentally distracted; one theorized possession by a devil (without a witch's agency); while the rest suspected he faked the whole thing. But nothing more came of the accusation, and Jonathan died soon after in the frontier wars.[123]

Since then, Sarah's husband John Wildes had threatened to sue John Reddington if his wife did not stop her slanders. Sarah's son Ephraim, now constable, stopped courting a Symmonds girl when her family sided with the Reddingtons.

Ephraim was sure that the testimony was retaliation for this, as he suspected Goody Hobbs's stories of his mother's presence at the witch meetings were revenge for his arresting her.[124]

When Ephraim was only nine and unable to stop them, the brothers John and Joseph Andrews "borrowed" a scythe that Sarah Wildes did not want to lend them. Later, when they tried to transport a heavy load of hay cut with that scythe, the oxen refused to move and a cart wheel fell off. The brothers unloaded the hay fork by fork in order to fix the cart. After even more delays, the oxen spooked at the sight of a dog-like thing, then stampeded halfway into a stream, where the hay spilled into the water.[125]

The Andrews brothers' sister, Elizabeth Symmonds, quarreled with Goody Wildes about this hay, then felt a cat walk across her in the night, only she didn't own a cat. Mary Reddington was pulled backward off a horse into a brook, and others had their stock die the usual way.[126]

Overwhelmed by long-standing suspicions, Sarah Wildes was found guilty.

At some point during this series of trials, one of the afflicted identified her spectral attacker as Rev. Willard of Boston. Samuel Willard, in a recent series of sermons about the Devil's wiles, repeated his opinion that devils could impersonate the innocent and, to further destroy lives and reputations, could and *would* do so even without witches. The public roundly criticized Willard for his attitude and efforts, but on this occasion the judges trusted their own opinion of the man. The court told the girl that she was mistaken and sent her from the room. *John* Willard was a suspect, after all (and possibly distant kin to the minister). Although the judges did not always agree with one another, they all apparently trusted Rev. Samuel Willard.[127]

Boston

Tonight Captain Richard Short, ostensibly looking for sailors from the *Nonsuch*, led a shore patrol through Boston. Yet somehow they ended up in the chambers of legislators who had protested Short's press-gangs. At about eleven o'clock, "ancient" John Tompson, representative for Middleborough, was roused from bed in the Green Dragon and herded downstairs in his nightshirt to face a furious Captain Short. "Old rogue!" the captain shouted to Tompson's protests. "Assembly dog!" Short's wounded hand was well enough to land several blows on the landlord of the Dragon and on Tompson. The patrol dragged the old man into the unlighted streets, then left him to pick his way back barefoot under the dark of the moon.[128]

By midnight, Short's patrol broke through the latched door of Peter Woodbury's rented chamber and caned the Beverly representative four blows before he could even get out of bed. They left him for a time, then surged back, struck him with eight more blows to the head, buffeted him downstairs, then dragged him through the dark streets, and left him sick, sore, and bloody. (Short's warrant officers would later testify to his "abusing their Majesties subjects on shore," but the paper is torn and only a fragment survives referring to an incident of "beating and confining the Minister.")[129]

***

Salem Village

Although John Willard remained in prison, his specter stalked his relatives, especially young Samuel Wilkins. (His father had died a few years back while watching Christ and the Devil contend for his soul.) In late June and early July, while tying the fast-breaking threads of his loom, Samuel felt pains jab and slash his hand. Later, someone in a black hat jumped him from behind, knocking him from his horse into Forest River while Wilkins was returning from a trip to Marblehead. The unknown figure dashed for the woods, but trailed him half-seen all the way home across Salem. Samuel recognized it as John Willard when it reappeared another day, and then again at his bedside with a spectral couple, all three threatening to carry Samuel away before morning.[130]

7

JULY 1692

What god do witches pray to?

—Salem Magistrates

***
Gloucester

One night near the end of June or near the beginning of July, Ebenezer Babson's family began to hear running footsteps outside their house in the remote section of east Gloucester. (Single at age twenty-four, Babson lived in the family homestead with his widowed mother Eleanor, an unmarried sister, and possibly a married sister with her husband and infant son.)[1]

July 1, 1692 • Friday
Salem Village

Salem Village had not paid a salary to Samuel Parris for a full year and did not pay him today either.[2]

Salem Town

Thomas Putnam and John Putnam Jr. complained to the local magistrates against Mrs. Margaret Hawkes of Salem, "late of Barbados," and against her slave Candy for tormenting Mary Walcott, Mary Warren, and Ann Putnam Jr. Thomas Andrews, who had worked the charm on Isaac Cumming's mare, further explained that incident to the court, and the Grand Jury also heard testimony against Martha Carrier.[3]

July 2, 1692 • Saturday
Boston

Mindful of its scanty treasury, the General Court declared all bills of credit issued by the old government still valid in order to keep them in circulation. They also ordered that all their previous decisions about militia, taxes, and the rest, be printed and a copy sent to each town.[4]

Salem Town

The Grand Jury heard testimony against Dorcas Hoar, and the local magistrates questioned Ann Pudeator a second time. She had already been questioned on May 12 and sent to Boston prison. (Perhaps, like Mary Esty, she had been released and apprehended again on a second charge after her neighbor's recent death.) Now she was back before the magistrates in Beadle's tavern, while Simon Willard took notes.[5]

Sarah Churchill told how Goody Pudeator's specter brought her the Devil's book to sign, but said she hadn't seen the woman since. The court ordered the defendant to look at her accuser. "You did bring me the book," said Sarah. "It was at Goodman Jacobs's."

"I never saw the woman before now," Goody Pudeator protested.

"The maid charged you with bringing her the book at the last examination," the magistrate reminded her.

"I never saw the Devil's book, nor knew that he had one."

Neighbor Jeremiah Neal testified that Goody Pudeator was ill carriaged, even threatening. "Since my wife has been sick of the smallpox, this woman has come to my house pretending kindness, and I was glad to see it." But after she borrowed the mortar used to prepare medicine, his wife contracted a flux, on top of everything else, and then died.

The magistrates wanted an explanation for the numerous partial jars of different ointments in her house that Constable Joseph Neale (the dead woman's brother-in-law) had noticed—more than usual for common household salves.

"I never had ointment, nor oil, but neat's foot oil in my house since my husband died." (Rendered from the hooves of cattle, this was a common household leather conditioner.)

"But what was in these things the constable speaks of?"

"It was grease, to make soap of."

They asked why one substance was divided among so many containers when one would hold it, but her answers were vague. They dropped the matter, although it was well known that imps liked to nest in such foul places.

Sarah Bibber allowed she had never seen the defendant before. Elizabeth Hubbard and Mary Walcott had seen her (or her specter), however. Ann Putnam Jr. said she had seen the defendant only since last coming to town, then fell in a fit. Goody Pudeator had to cure her with a touch to the wrist, then do the same for Mary Warren who had two seizures one right after the other. (Mary, no longer trying to recant her confession, was allowed out of jail at least long enough to testify.) For these torments, Ann Pudeator was again held for trial.[6]

The magistrates also questioned aged Mary Bradbury of Salisbury whose specter had been so busy directing the attacks against Timothy Swan. The afflicted witnesses—Elizabeth Hubbard, Sarah Bibber, Mary Walcott, Mary Warren, and young Ann Putnam—all identified the defendant with one of the tormenting specters and fell at her every glance. In addition, Mary Walcott and Ann Putnam Jr. saw the ghost of Ann's uncle, John Carr, appear in the courtroom. Wrapped in a winding sheet, it accused Mistress Bradbury (who had thwarted his desire to marry one of her granddaughters) of murdering him. For the apparent torments in court, Mary Bradbury was held for trial.[7]

A specter of the accused slave Candy, meanwhile, attacked Mary Walcott and Ann Putnam Jr.[8]

July 3, 1692 • Sunday
Salem Town

Salem town's church observed the Lord's Supper this Sabbath. After the morning service the elders formally asked the full (voting) members whether or not sister Nurse ought still to be a communing member of their congregation. Rebecca had joined twenty years earlier with no whisper of objection against her, but now civil law had (seemingly) proved that her allegiance lay with the forces of evil. Therefore, as it was hardly appropriate that she join in the Lord's sacrament (communion) if her true loyalty were with the Devil, the vote to excommunicate her was unanimous.[9]

Brought from jail to the meeting house that afternoon, Rebecca Nurse heard Rev. Nicholas Noyes formally pronounce the decision. (The genial conversationalist known for easy wit and obliging friendship was eclipsed by his conviction that the

Devil was actively infiltrating his church.) Rebecca heard Noyes enumerate her sins and offenses, then declare, on behalf of the whole church and in the name of Christ, that she was spiritually unclean and was to be severed from the very ordinances that she had previously abused. She who had so scorned the church would be alone before the Devil and his wiles. (Yet, there was still the chance that the truly elect might learn a lesson from this ordeal and be saved at the Last Judgment.) During her March examination, Rebecca had reminded the magistrates: "You do not know my heart." Now, with her church believing her to be the worst sort of evildoer, she had to remind herself that God *did* know her heart.

Ordinarily, an excommunicated person would retain family fellowship and civil rights, or would even be reinstated after a sincere change of heart and behavior. Rebecca Nurse, however, was under a civil death sentence.[10]

July 4, 1692 • Monday
Boston

In Boston, Representatives Woodbury (Peter) and Tompson presented their accounts of Captain Short's shocking attacks, and swore to them before Justice William Stoughton who, as it happened, owned the Green Dragon, where Tompson was assaulted.[11]

Salem Town

Magistrates Bartholomew Gedney and John Hathorne, meantime, questioned the slave woman Candy in Salem, while Rev. Nicholas Noyes observed.[12]

"Candy! Are you a witch?"

"Candy no witch in her country. Candy's mother no witch. Candy no witch Barbados. This country, mistress give Candy witch."

"Did your mistress make you a witch in this country?" the magistrate asked. (Mrs. Hawkes was probably present, though her examination has not survived.)

"Yes, in this country, mistress give Candy witch."

"What did your mistress do to make you a witch?"

"Mistress bring book, and pen, and ink, make Candy write in it" (by making a mark), she explained.

"How did you afflict or hurt these folks? Where are the poppets you did it with?" She said she would demonstrate if allowed to get them. And the court did permit her to fetch the things from her lodgings under guard. She soon returned with a handkerchief knotted around a piece of cheese and a piece of grass, plus two rags (one tied once and the other twice). Mary Warren, as well as Deliverance and Abigail Hobbs, convulsed when they saw the articles. Terror-stricken, the afflicted cried that specters of the Devil, Mrs. Hawkes, and Candy were hurting them by pinching the rags.

The magistrates ordered the knots (which seemed to represent the afflicted) untied, but that gave no relief at all. They made Candy eat the grass blade, but nothing happened. They experimented with the cloths, perhaps to see if the objects contained power whether or not Candy held them, although in doing so the magistrates themselves attempted magic. They burnt a rag, but this only made the afflicted feel burnt. When the justices plunged the rags into water, two of the women choked and struggled as if drowning, while the third ran from the building toward the river, guards in pursuit.

In the face of all this turmoil and apparent evidence, Mrs. Hawkes confessed. Both she and her slave were held for trial.[13]

Many people disagreed with the court's verdict against Rebecca Nurse. Thirty-nine neighbors, believing her innocent, had signed a petition on her behalf. They included Daniel Andrews (still in danger of arrest); Sarah Holten (who had testified about her husband's death after a quarrel with Rebecca); Daniel Rea (whose own daughter Jemima had been afflicted by Rebecca's specter); Samuel Sibley (whose wife had made the witch-cake charm back in February); and seven Putnams (Benjamin, Jonathan, Joseph, Lydia, Nathaniel, Rebecca, and Sarah.[14]

The Nurse family persuaded Thomas Fisk, the jury foreman of Rebecca's case, to write a statement explaining why they had reconvened for further deliberations, and how they had understood her remark to mean that the Hobbs woman was a fellow witch.

Rebecca Nurse herself composed her own statement to explain that she had referred to Goody Hobbs and her daughter as fellow *prisoners*, and as such her remark was not a legal source (she thought) of evidence against her. "And I being something hard of hearing, and full of grief, none informing me how the court took up my words, and therefore had not opportunity to declare what I intended, when I said they were of our company."

Her family took the documentation to Boston around this time and presented it to Governor Phips. After considering the petitions for Goody Nurse, Phips granted her a reprieve shortly after her excommunication. (However, the afflicted were tormented anew at this development.)[15]

Boston

Today, Phips and his councilors spent the afternoon in the Boston Town House Council Chamber authorizing payment for the Eastward soldiers, for the Castle Island garrison, and for the seamen in vessels impressed for the trip to Maine.[16]

Salem Town

Tonight, in jail, Candy's throat burned as if scorched by the grass that she had swallowed.[17]

July 5, 1692 • Tuesday
Will's Hill

For all that the Wilkins family had endured, not everyone thought John Willard the cause. Old Bray Wilkins, however, argued with friends that the testimony of the afflicted, plus the coroner's inquest on the late Daniel Wilkins, were enough to condemn Willard, over and above anything that he or his son Benjamin had said. Within a quarter hour after this statement, Bray was again in painful misery, which would last twenty-four hours, and during which he would pass bloody urine.[18]

Boston

The General Court ended its session in Boston and parted until October. But, in the North End, Mercy Short was still afflicted and the attending neighbors, including Cotton Mather (who took notes), heard her long one-sided conversations with the specters. "Well, if you do burn me," she snapped to the invisible Devil (who appeared to her like a combination of Rev. George Burroughs and an Abenaki) "I had better burn for an hour or two here than in Hell forever." (After her capture by the Indians in 1690, Mercy had likely seen a man actually burned to death.) "What? Will you burn all Boston and I shall be burnt in that fire? No, 'tis not in your power. I hope God won't let you do that."

Between eleven o'clock and midnight, a fire broke out in Mercy's North End neighborhood at the King's Head tavern, only a block behind the Mathers's north meeting house. Twenty buildings burned before the bucket brigades contained the blaze. For a time it seemed as if the whole town would perish in flames.[19]

July 6, 1692 • Wednesday
Cambridge

Local almanacs printed the date for Harvard College's Commencement in larger type than even court dates. (The word was always capitalized, the closest Massachusetts had to a holiday.) Not only the faculty and families of the graduates attended, but also the governor with other notables and as many alumni as could make the journey, including most of the area's ministers and magistrates. (Governor Phips was not an alumnus and had not learned to read until age twenty-one.) Several hundred people, including enterprising hucksters, crowded Cambridge yearly and sometimes became rowdy. Harvard limited wine consumption to one gallon per student and three for degree takers, but banned a certain potent plum cake entirely.

This year President Increase Mather was back from England to lead the exercises, much of them in Latin, in the Cambridge meeting house, for the College had no building large enough to accommodate the audience. Morning was devoted to those taking Bachelors degrees, afternoon to Masters of Art. In between, college officials, alumni, and distinguished guests enjoyed a commencement dinner, traditionally paid for by the graduates, in the College Hall. In the presence of Lieutenant Governor William Stoughton, Chief Justice of the witchcraft court, a class of six took their Bachelor's degrees this morning—including Zachariah Alden, son of witch suspect Captain John.[20]

July 7, 1692 • Thursday
Boston

Phips commissioned Anthony Checkley as the king's attorney general for the Court of Oyer and Terminer, replacing Thomas Newton, who left to become secretary of New Hampshire. Checkley, a merchant and military man, had been attorney general in 1689.[21]

Topsfield

Goodwife Margaret Reddington fell "exceedingly" ill this afternoon in Topsfield. She saw her jailed kinswoman Mary Esty enter the room and offer her "fresh meat." But Goody Reddington did not trust her and said it "t'was not fit for dogs." Goody Esty vanished in a huff at the refusal.[22]

Gloucester

Returning home late one evening around this time, Ebenezer Babson saw two men run from the door of his east Gloucester home into a cornfield. No one inside the house had noticed strangers about, but Babson fetched his gun. He walked only a few steps when two men bolted from behind a log and into a swamp. "The man of the house is come now," he heard them say, "else we might have taken the house." They spoke English, but the French and Indian attackers had shouted English threats only a few weeks before at Wells. Immediately, the household evacuated to the nearest garrison. No sooner did they crowd inside, than everyone heard stamping footsteps outside. Again, Babson ran out with his gun, and again saw two men running downhill into a swamp.[23]

July 8, 1692 • Friday
Boston

Governor Phips and his council, unaware of a possible invasion of Gloucester, continued to organize the Maine expedition. Phips announced he would lead it himself and, advised by Majors Hutchinson, Winthrop, and Walley, ordered 500 more militia to active duty: 300 from Suffolk, Middlesex, and Essex counties; 200 from Plymouth, Barnstable, and Bristol. They put a committee of four in charge of provisions, with orders to impress food if necessary from ship or shore (pork, beef, peas, wheat, biscuit, flour, Indian corn, etc.) and to impress the men and boats required to move the supplies to the ships. The council also appointed John James as chaplain for the soldiers and for the inhabitants of Wells, Rev. George Burroughs's former home.[24]

Andover

Timothy Swan experienced a particularly severe spell of stabbing, burning pain in his knee. It seemed to him to be the work of the Lacys, Fosters, Carriers, and Mrs. Bradbury whose specters also invaded Andover to pinch and choke Elizabeth, wife of Joseph Ballard, before downing stolen cider in the orchard.[25]

July 9, 1692 • Saturday
Gloucester

Two nights after moving into the Gloucester garrison, Ebenezer Babson spied two Frenchmen near a fresh meadow running full tilt toward him. He saw the bright gleam of a gun on one man's back and raced back to the garrison. The others there did not see his pursuers, but heard pounding feet outside.[26]

July 10, 1692 • Sunday
Gloucester

The inhabitants crowding the east Gloucester garrison heard hollow thuds at a distance, as if someone were heaving rocks against the side of a barn.[27]

July 11, 1692 • Monday
Gloucester

Ebenezer Babson and John Brown, on patrol beyond the garrison, came within gunshot of three strangers and fired on them. But the strangers dodged away among the cornstalks and bushes (as would others over the next few nights).[28]

July 12, 1692 • Tuesday
Boston

Almanacs predicted misty mornings, but if there was any promised thunder, it did not bring the needed rain.[29]

William Stoughton signed a warrant for executions the following Tuesday morning: Sarah Good, Susanna Martin, Elizabeth How, Sarah Wildes, and Rebecca Nurse—for whom all the petitions and attempted reprieves had come to nothing. (The self-made Phips was more confident commanding in the field or at sea than among politicians. After Nurse's specter had resumed tormenting the afflicted, "some [unnamed] Salem gentlemen" (according to a later source) persuaded Phips to revoke his order.)[30]

July 13, 1692 • Wednesday
Boston

Eight armed militia companies drilled on Boston Common with the right-hand file of each company drawn off for service Eastward—all ignorant of the invaders sighted in Gloucester.[31]

Andover

Captain Dudley Bradstreet returned home to Andover from Boston and received payment from the selectmen for serving as representative to the General Court.

The selectmen also paid widow Rebecca Johnson six shillings, nine pence of her yearly forty shillings salary "for sweeping the meeting house and ringing the bell in the year 1691."[32]

July 14, 1692 • Thursday
Boston

By order of Governor Phips, this Lecture Day was a public thanksgiving for the successful defense of Wells and for the safe arrival of himself and Increase Mather. The governor invited Boston's ship carpenters, his former colleagues, to a feast celebrating God's blessings on his life. To some people's annoyance Sir William never hid his lowly origins (which everyone knew) but instead gloried in them.[33]

Gloucester

The east Gloucester folk did not attend lecture, much less keep a thanksgiving, for the neighborhood was still crammed inside the garrison. Today, most of the men marched out to confront the besiegers (who scattered) and chase them through cornfields and wooded swamps, losing them, reencountering them unexpectedly, then losing them again. Several strangers fell as if shot, but then either leapt up and escaped or disappeared. The Gloucester men heard a "great discoursing" in an unknown language from the swamp, and later saw several skulking figures in the corn near the garrison, but got no clear shot at any of them.[34]

Andover

Meanwhile, in Andover this evening, Elizabeth Ballard's torments continued. She felt pinched and found it hard to breathe from the pressure on her throat and stomach. (Later, it would seem as if the house were full of spectral witches drinking stolen cider between tortures. At some point in Goody Ballard's illness, her husband sent a mounted messenger to Salem Village asking that Ann Putnam Jr. and Mary Walcott be allowed to come see what in the Invisible World ailed his wife. Once in Andover, as before at Will's Hill, Ann and Mary saw, named, and were tortured by the guilty specters. But naming the witches did not stop the torments, for as more and more Andover families consulted the girls, the fits and "spectral sight" spread to other young people of those households.)[35]

July 15, 1692 • Friday
Gloucester

At daybreak the east Gloucester folk saw a man walk from the swamp to the garrison fence, then run away after Isaac Prince fired a load of swan shot at him. As it was obvious they needed help, Babson slipped out toward Gloucester Harbor two-and-a-half miles away. After a half mile he heard gunfire. A bullet whizzed past his ear, clipped the top from a pine bush beside him, and smacked into a hemlock. Looking back, he saw four armed men running toward him. He dashed for the bushes, turned and fired, then ran all the way to town.

While Babson's story was sent on to the authorities, six men accompanied him back to the garrison. They found the broken pine on the way and dug the bullet from the hemlock for a memento. Nearer the garrison they found men's tracks, half-glimpsed an Indian watching them and then a Frenchman, but got no clear shot at either. Various scouting parties from the garrison also saw the strangers: one Indian wore a blue shirt, white breeches, and something tied around his head.[36]

Boston

In Boston, the government received a letter from the Lords of the Privy Council requiring ousted Governor Andros's back pay. Governor Phips, facing more immediate problems, ordered his war council to impress four sloops to help transport soldiers Eastward if the soldiers could be impressed. Phips, as head of the combined militias, had ordered a muster of Boston's companies to recruit for the ships patrolling the coast (and for his own privateers while they were at it). But today's turnout was woefully thin. So many men were already Eastward or in the ships that even Captain Short's relentless press-gangs had problems. It was rumored in New York that press-masters were being knocked down in Boston streets at high noon.[37]

Salem Village

Widow Ann Foster of Andover, meanwhile, was examined in Salem Village (probably on Joseph Ballard's complaint). Seven years earlier, when her aged husband Andrew Sr.* died, she inherited three cows; twelve sheep; supplies of grain, wood, and cider; and a life interest in half the family home whose other half was occupied by her son Abraham and his family. The Fosters were no strangers to sorrow, however. A grandson (the one with three thumbs) had been shot, axed, and left for dead during a raid on Exeter. He recovered, but his mother, Ann's daughter, had her throat cut by her husband, who, after being haunted by her reproachful ghost, was hanged for the murder.[38]

At first Goody Foster denied the charges, but as Mary Warren, Mary Walcott, Elizabeth Hubbard, and Ann Putnam Jr. were spectrally choked and pinched, she agreed that yes, the Devil had appeared to her "almost half a year since." He took the form of a large-eyed, white-feathered bird that perched on a table and promised her prosperity. She knew who it was because it "vanished away black," and ever since she could afflict with her glance. However, it was Martha Carrier who persuaded her only three weeks ago to hurt these people. (The court already believed Martha to be Andover's principal witch.)[39]

The magistrates, and their horses, added fifteen shillings to the £8-10-9 county bill at Ingersoll's.[40]

Andover

On the same day, the specter of Mary Lacy Jr., Goody Foster's granddaughter, tortured Timothy Swan.[41]

July 16, 1692 • Saturday
Salem Town

The Salem magistrates continued to question Ann Foster in prison while Rev. John Hale observed. She held to her confession—the magistrates hardly listened

---

*Andrew Foster and Andrew Allen (Martha Carrier's father) both appear in the lists of the Scottish Charitable Society.

to denials in any case—but added that she had actually served the Devil for six years, not six months. Goody Carrier had threatened to tear her apart if she wouldn't join. Once in, Ann bewitched her neighbor John Lovejoy's hog to death. She used poppets and pins on Carrier's orders to sicken Andrew Allen's children (one of whom died) as well as Timothy Swan and some Salem Village people, but she threw a knotted rag into the fire to torment Goody Bibber. When Foster and Carrier had flown to the Village witch meeting two months back to hear Rev. Burroughs, they merely sat on sticks and said "journey" to make them fly (much as Tituba, Osborn, and Good had traveled in February).[42]

The magistrates had no more time but said Hale might stay and talk with Goody Foster. She answered his questions about the Village meeting, describing an impromptu picnic of bread and cheese under a tree. Then, after a little time, she admitted that "she had some trouble upon her spirit." She feared that George Burroughs and Martha Carrier would kill her, she confided, because she had confessed and implicated them. They had appeared to her—Hale knew their bodies were confined in other parts of the prison—and threatened to stab her to death with "a sharp pointed iron like a spindle, but four square."[43]

July 17, 1692 • Sunday
Gloucester

The Gloucester garrison still could not shoot the strangers who encircled them. On one foray, Richard Dolliver and Benjamin Ellery spied eleven men walking back and forth by John Row's deserted house, clubbing it now and again with a stick. Even the folk back at the garrison house heard that racket. Dolliver scattered them with a shot, but again hit no one.[44]

Between nine o'clock and midnight, the full moon was almost totally eclipsed, just as the almanacs foretold. Because the moon was in Aquarius, a sign ruled by Saturn, almanacs speculated that the celestial event might portend death and pestilence. But as Saturn also referred to old age, perhaps the eclipse referred only to the deaths of aged and eminent persons.[45]

July 18, 1692 • Monday
Salem

Goodwife Ann Foster continued her confession in Salem, further implicating Martha Carrier, who often accompanied the Devil. At the great Village witch meeting Goody Foster had heard of 305 witches working to ruin the country, beginning with Salem Village. The Devil had reneged on his promised prosperity, but still had power over her because she no longer found spiritual profit from attending proper religious meetings.[46]

Gloucester

As provisioning the Maine expedition continued, Phips and his council removed the embargo that had kept all vessels in port since June 13. Major
Samuel Appleton, however, sent sixty men from Ipswich to join more militia at
Gloucester Harbor, and then to march through the woods to relieve the east
Gloucester garrison. Hearing gunfire as soon as they arrived, the militia rushed
the swamp. John Day, one of the newcomers, pursued a man with bushy black
hair and a blue shirt until he lost him in the thickly wooded upland. Day returned to examine the man's tracks in the swamp's miry ground, but found no
tracks at all.[47]

Lancaster

In Lancaster, where John Willard had been caught, Peter Joslyn returned home
from work to find his six-year-old son kidnapped, and his wife, three other children, and a boarder dead from an Indian raid.[48]

Haverhill

It was probably around this time that some farmers were similarly killed in the
meadows on the north bank of the Merrimack River. Raiders certainly struck
Haverhill today and left a woman dead. Matthew Herriman, also of Haverhill and
brother-in-law to the afflicted Timothy Swan, felt oddly unwell and only dozed fit-
fully as he listened to the night's driving wind and rain.[49]

July 19, 1692 • Tuesday
Haverhill

Matthew Herriman woke to the dog days of summer with a tongue so sore it felt
as if a horse's bit pressed across it, only to discover there had been no rain at all.
The land was as dry as ever.

Goodwife Mary Emerson dropped in at first light, before five o'clock, to borrow
fire. Herriman knew Goody Emerson was the late Roger Toothaker's daughter and
Martha Carrier's niece. Her mother and sister were already jailed and Mary herself
was rumored to have killed a witch by magic.[50]

Salem Town

Between eight o'clock and noon, Sheriff George Corwin transported Rebecca
Nurse, Susanna Martin, Elizabeth How, Sarah Good, and Sarah Wildes—all praying that God would prove their innocence—from prison by cart through the streets

of Salem to be hanged. Quiet housewives or turbulent scolds, well-to-do or in rags, all five women now faced a painful, public death.

It was customary for the dying to attempt facing death in a spirit of forgiveness lest their souls appear before Heavenly judgment seething hatred. Sarah Good would have none of it. At the gallows Rev. Nicholas Noyes urged her to confess what the courts had seemingly proven and at least not die a liar. When she denied the guilt, Noyes said she *knew* she was a witch.[51]

"You are a liar," she snapped. "I am no more a witch than you are a wizard, and if you take away my life God will give you blood to drink." (The folk curse was loosely based on a verse in Revelation. People later remembered it when Noyes, it was said, died bleeding at the mouth when a blood vessel burst in his head.)

Rumors hinted that the Devil might attempt a last-minute rescue of his followers, but all five hanged as scheduled on the ledge above the tidal pool.[52]

Joseph Ballard probably witnessed the executions on his way from Andover. Soon after, he entered a complaint in Salem before Magistrates Gedney, Corwin, Hathorne, and Higginson against Mary Lacy and her daughter Mary Jr. for tormenting his wife Elizabeth with "strange pains and pressures." He even put up a £100 bond "on condition to prosecute." (Plaintiffs customarily did this in civil suits, the sum forfeit if the plaintiff didn't appear in court, but this is the first recorded bond in these witch cases where the accusations seem to have been treated as a public emergency.) The magistrates issued a warrant for only Goody Lacy, however, and not for her daughter.[53]

The bodies of the dead, meantime, were buried (if only temporarily) near the rocky execution site. By family tradition the Nurses waited for darkness (sunset was about a quarter after seven) then rowed up the North River to the bend by the ledge and exhumed Rebecca's body. According to another tradition Caleb Buffum (a distant relative) noticed this effort from his home nearby and helped carry the remains to the shore. From there a small craft could slip downstream past town on the midnight's high tide, then north up the estuary to Crane River and along its narrowing length to the Nurses' land, where they buried her privately on homeground.[54]

July 20, 1692 • Wednesday
Salem Town

Goodwife Mary Lacy of Andover, arrested and brought before the Salem magistrates, confessed. She admitted she had flown to the Salem Village witch meeting with Carrier, but insisted that her mother, Ann Foster, did *not* take part but only watched from a distance. At first Elizabeth Hubbard and Mary Lewis had seizures whenever Goody Lacy looked at them during questioning. But after she confessed, she shook their hands with no ill effect. It was then that Gedney, Hathorne, Corwin, and Higginson issued an arrest warrant for Lacy's daughter Mary Jr.[55]

Salem Village

In the course of the day Mary Walcott felt the usual afflictions, as did Abigail Williams at home in the Village parsonage. This time Abigail's aunt, Mrs. Elizabeth Parris, also felt an alarming (but undescribed) ailment—spectral tortures some thought.[56]

Boston

Samuel Sewall wrote a business letter to his cousin Edward Hull, then related news of the repulse Eastward and of the governor's expedition. "Are much perplexed per witchcrafts," he added. "Six persons have already been condemned and executed at Salem." Condemned, that is, by himself (among others), although he was by no means as sure of the proceedings as Chief Justice William Stoughton. Sewall could hardly bring himself to write about the matter, even in his otherwise copious diary. "'Tis a very dry time," he concluded.[57]

Sewall also attended a private fast of friends on behalf of the imprisoned John Alden at the captain's own home in Boston. While the Reverends Samuel Willard, James Allen, Cotton Mather, and others offered prayers and appropriate readings, the long drought broke in "a brave shower of rain." They concluded about five o'clock singing the first part of Psalm 103.[58]

> O thou my soul Jehovah bless,
>> And all things that in me,
> Most inward are, in humbleness
>> His Holy-Name bless ye . . .
> For He it is who pardoneth
>> All thine infirmities.
> Who thy life from distruction
>> Redeems: Who croweneth thee
> With His tender compassion
>> And kind benignity. . .

The unsung verses, as Judge Sewall and the others knew, reminded them that God had not dealt with them according to their sins, but with more mercy than they deserved.

> The Lord is merciful also,
>> He's very gracious
> And unto anger He is slow
>> In mercy plenteous . . .

***
Boston

Cotton Mather and his Boston neighbors continued to observe Mercy Short. The Devil, it seemed, wheedled her with promises of a husband and fine clothes—tempting bribes for a girl nearly eighteen who had lost half her family in the frontier war.[59]

"An husband!" she scoffed. "What? A devil! I shall then be finely fitted with an husband. No, I hope the blessed Lord Jesus Christ will marry my soul to Himself yet, before he has done with me, as poor a wretch as I am!

"Fine clothes! What! Such as your friend Sarah Good had, who hardly had rags to cover her! Pray, why did you not provide better for her then?

"Never die? What? Is my life in your hands? No, if it had, you had killed me long before this time! What's that? So you can! Do it then if you can!" she taunted. "Come, I dare you! Here I challenge you to do it. Kill me if you can!"

They scuffled, but the specters retreated. "Poor fool! But hark ye! If you can keep your servants alive, the more false wretch you, to let the halter choke the witches that were hanged t'other day, though you promised them that when the halters were about their necks, you would come and rescue them!"

Salem Town

One evening around this time, as Samuel Pickworth walked along the west side of Salem Common, he saw Goody Pudeator near Captain Higginson's home. The woman herself was locked in Salem jail, but, swift as a bird, her specter skimmed past Pickworth along the Common's edge and ducked into her house.[60]

July 21, 1692 • Thursday
Boston

Governor William Phips called a meeting of the council in his own North End home to authorize payment for enough food and clothing to last 800 militiamen two months; payment for the carters, porters, and laborers hauling it all to the warships; and payment to the owners of the brigantine *William and Mary*.[61]

Andover

Andover Constable Ephraim Foster (no relation to Ann Foster) arrested Mary Lacy Jr., and had her searched for poppets in the presence of witnesses—two women and two men. He found a parcel of rags, yarn, tape, and quills tied together. No one in the family knew what it was, so he took it as possible evidence.[62]

Salem Town

Magistrates Gedney, Hathorne, Corwin, and Higginson questioned Ann Foster for a fourth time, probably at Beadle's in Salem. They read her earlier confession and she agreed to it. The witches' meetings, she added, were for plotting how to afflict folk and "to set up the Devil's Kingdom." She signed the confession with a mark. Higginson's own sister, Ann Dolliver, had been accused and arrested, but as a group the magistrates accepted the defendants' frightened confessions as fact and saw their inconsistencies as evasions.[63]

"Your daughter here," said a magistrate, "hath confessed some things that you did not tell us of" (such as Goodwife Mary Lacy's presence at the witch meeting).

"I did not know it," or know her daughter *was* a witch. Mary Warren and Goody Lacy herself countered Goody Foster's protests.

"Oh, mother! We have forsaken Christ and the Devil hath got hold of us. How shall we get clear of this evil one?"

A magistrate reminded Goody Foster that she could not be free of that snare if her heart and mouth remained stubbornly closed. She muttered something and the afflicted saw the Devil whisper to her.

"I did not see the Devil," said Goody Foster. "I was praying to the Lord."

"What lord?"

"To God."

"What god do witches pray to?"

"I cannot tell, the Lord help me."

Bit by bit, in answer to the court's questions, her daughter described how she had flown in the Devil's arms to Newbury Falls* three or four years earlier and had witnessed him baptize six witches. As he dipped their heads, he declared that Mistress Bradbury, Goody How, and Goody Nurse were his forever and ever. She did not know the other three, but they were among the chiefs and higher powers.[64]

The older women were removed for the questioning of Mary Lacy Jr., whose presence made Mary Warren convulse violently.

"How dare you come in here," a magistrate demanded, "and bring the Devil with you to afflict these poor creatures."

"I know nothing of it," said Mary, but her touch on Warren's arm ended the seizure.

"You are here accused for practicing witchcraft upon Goody Ballard. Which way do you do it?"

"I cannot tell. Where is my mother that made me a witch and I knew it not?"

"Can you look on Mary Warren and not hurt her? Look upon her now in a friendly way." She tried, but Warren collapsed. "Do you acknowledge now you are a witch?"

---

*The baptisms occurred at Newbury Falls, or the Falls River. This is the Parker Falls River in Newbury's South Byfield section.

"Yes," said Mary, and began to confess, answering their questions briefly at first, then adding and altering details. She was at home one night the week before when the Devil appeared in the guise of a horse, though sometimes he came as a round gray thing. "He bid me to be afraid of nothing, and he would not bring me out. But he had proved a liar from the beginning." She neither signed his book nor submitted to baptism, and refused to kill a certain tinker in town. But she afflicted folk and worshipped the Devil, who told her that he was a god who could grant abundance on earth and glory hereafter. In the Devil's earthly kingdom "we should have happy days, and it would be better times for me if I would obey him."

The magistrates reminded her that she must freely confess what she knew. By repenting, she might still escape the Devil's power. "The Lord help me!" she cried, and admitted the Devil had actually come a whole *year* earlier, maybe a year and a quarter. Her mother often wished the Devil would take her. Mary admitted running away from home a year ago for two days at the Devil's prompting. Now she afflicted folk by squeezing things. She said the Devil convulsed Mary Warren, but soon admitted hurting Warren, Timothy Swan, Elizabeth Ballard, and James Fry's child. Richard Carrier, Martha's son, encouraged her, she said, to avenge Fry's beating of Richard's younger brother Andrew.

Mary Warren convulsed at the sight of a man's specter on the magistrates' table. Mary Lacy identified it as Richard Carrier and thought his "unhappy" brother Andrew was also involved. She hinted that Richard's mother had given him something that he must never show anyone. "It is a writing," she explained after some prompting, "that the Devil gave to Goody Carrier, and she has been a witch ever since she lived at Billerica." (Martha Allen had married Thomas Carrier, "alias Morgan," in Billerica in 1674 shortly after the local midwife ascertained that Martha was indeed with child, two months before Richard's birth.)[65]

Mary described Martha Carrier's murders of several women and children stabbed to death with pins and needles, plus "two brothers of her own and a brother-in-law: Andrew Allen, John Allen, and James Holt." (Martha's brothers and many others had died of smallpox in 1690, a time when Andover's selectmen warned the Carriers to keep away even from the meeting house lest they spread the infection.)[66]

But young Mary Lacy knew no more about the mysterious document, only that Richard, "a wicked wretch," told her that it would make him as powerful as his mother. Goody Carrier, in the shape of a bird or black cat, urged them on witchly expeditions (she gave Grandmother Foster no peace until she complied) as on Thanksgiving night when the whole family tormented Elizabeth Ballard and drank her cider. Mary flew to the Village meeting not by anointing herself as the magistrates suggested, but perched on a hand pole carried by the Devil. At first she said the only man there was the Devil, then said only Richard Carrier. When the magistrates reminded her of the minister her mother and grandmother had reported, she added that there was one, "and I think he is now in prison."

"Were there not two ministers there?" a magistrate asked. She couldn't tell, but he persisted until she agreed that Burroughs was there.

She saw the red wine served in earthen cups and the "reddish" brown bread, insufficient to serve the throng of Hellish communicants. The Devil called the names of seventy-seven witches and exhorted them to do his will. He promised that "they should obtain crowns in Hell" (a parody of Heavenly crowns), but Goody Carrier would be "a Queen in Hell" and George Burroughs, "a pretty little man," would be King.[67]

"Do you hear the Devil hurts in the shape of any person without their consents?" asked a magistrate.

"No," said Mary, confirming the court's theory.

One magistrate, recalling that the Village meeting had occurred at noon, asked why no one saw her if she attended bodily. "Sometimes we leave our bodies at home," she said, "but at other times we go in our bodies and the Devil puts a mist before their eyes and will not let them see us." Thus she traveled to Ballard's and drank stolen cider, while Goody Carrier, who left her body home asleep, did not. At other times, however, Carrier and her imps took Mary's spirit with them on journeys that she remembered the next morning upon waking. But if bodies shielded by invisibility were struck, they could be hurt as her mother's and grandmother's had been.

"And why will they venture again after they are hurt?"

"The Devil makes them go again, and tells them that if they will not, he will afflict them worse."

By now, Mary Warren was convinced enough of Mary Lacy's repentance to take her hand without harm, both weeping as Lacy begged forgiveness.

The magistrates decided to question all three generations together. "Here is a poor miserable child, a wretched mother, and grandmother," one of them observed.

"Oh, mother!" young Mary cried over and over, "why did you give me to the Devil?" Her mother apologized—the Devil tempted her to it—but Mary pressed her to repent. "Oh, mother, your wishes are now come to pass, for [you] have often wished that the Devil would fetch me away alive. Oh, my heart will break within me. Oh, that mother should have ever given me to the Devil." She burst into tears. "Oh, Lord comfort me, and bring out all that are witches."

Then Goodwife Ann Foster was led forward. "Oh, grandmother, why did you give me to the Devil? Why did you persuade me? And oh, grandmother, do not you deny it. You have been a very bad woman in your time, I must needs say."

One of the magistrates observed that Mary's outburst seemed to show a repentance that might yet free her from the Devil's snares. "But as for you, old woman," he rounded on Goody Foster, "though you have shown something of relenting, yet you retain a lie in the mouth."

While her own granddaughter nattered at her to tell all, Goody Foster at last said that Martha Carrier had killed the Fry, Osgood, and Holt children; that Toothaker's wife and daughter had been with the witches; and that Richard Carrier was "naught" (i.e. no good). Ann couldn't remember if she saw him at the great meeting, but her granddaughter chimed in to say he was there and she hoped he would be arrested.

Goody Lacy Sr. said she knew Richard was a witch, for he boasted he could make cattle drop dead in their tracks if he wanted. He and his mother, moreover, collaborated in murder. When the court got back to Goody Foster, she owned to six years involvement, but said the Devil had prevented her from talking about it earlier.

After the court read Mary Jr.'s confession aloud, her mother and grandmother agreed to its details: how they had signed the Devil's book with blood red ink at the Village meeting.

"They used a pen," the granddaughter volunteered.

While Mary Warren flinched away from Richard Carrier's specter, the mother and grandmother both insisted that the Devil had forced them to afflict, even though they were often hurt in the process. Mary Jr. interrupted to say that her grandmother had been a witch for seven years, and the old woman replied that she didn't know if it were true, but it might be.

While the three generations of women were sent to Salem jail, the magistrates issued an arrest warrant for Richard and Andrew Carrier.[68]

July 22, 1692 • Friday
Salem Town

Andover Constable Joseph Ballard, whose wife was still ill, brought eighteen-year-old Richard and sixteen-year-old Andrew Carrier to Thomas Beadle's in Salem before the same four magistrates. Both denied their guilt over and over, Andrew so frightened that he stuttered. Both Mary Lacy Sr. and Jr. were present with the afflicted, who saw both the Devil and Martha Carrier on the table preventing the brothers' confessions. Mary Lacy Jr. was not reluctant to speak, however, so the magistrates questioned her as an eyewitness and former accomplice. She told how they all rode on poles with the Devil, who provided them with hot irons and other weapons, to Timothy Swan's chamber. Richard, she said, traveled bodily but took only his spirit inside. They all tortured Swan on "Mrs. Bradbury's account, for a quarrel she had with him" over thatching a house.[69]

Goody Lacy denied actually hurting Swan despite her daughter's insistence— "Yes, mother. Do not deny it"—and said the Devil and his imps had wielded the hot irons, though she alluded to image magic.

"Now, Richard Carrier," said the court, "what say you to these two evidences that saw you with Timothy Swan?"

Richard still protested, so Mary Jr. described the expedition to Ballard's house a fortnight before and Richard's boastful death threats. He had a heart hard as a rock to deny it, she said, for he had made his own brother a witch, the same Andrew whose specter even now tortured the witnesses. The afflicted's convulsions were worse than ever, and blood ran from Mary Warren's mouth.

To stop this extreme reaction, the court removed the brothers to another chamber. According to fellow prisoner John Proctor, the two "would not confess anything till they tied them neck and heels till the blood was ready to come out of their noses." The old Body of Liberties allowed a certain amount of force in capital cases when a criminal concealed his accomplices' names, but this was legal only *after* a trial found the defendant guilty, and the Carriers hadn't even been indicted. Faced with the continued torments of the afflicted, the magistrates apparently felt that British law did not forbid such methods, the same that former governor Andros had used to punish rebellious soldiers.[70]

"Richard," said the magistrate when the young man was led back, "though you have been very obstinate, yet tell us how long ago it is since you were taken in this snare?"

"A year last May and no more," said Richard. Walking home from town one night, he met a dark man in a high-crowned hat who claimed to be Christ and who promised him new clothes and a horse in exchange for his service. Richard believed this offer and so made a red mark with a stick in the man's little red book. This spirit appeared a second time last January as a yellow bird and promised to fulfill the bargain yet. But it also told Richard that he would soon have to afflict and got Richard's permission to torment Goody Ballard. He began to hurt Swan about a month ago on behalf of Mrs. Bradbury, and twice attended witch meetings at Salem Village with Mary Lacy Jr. He admitted stealing cider from Ballard's cellar in spirit and drinking it in Ballard's orchard.

"He went in his spirit," interrupted Mary Lacy Jr., "and his body lay dead the while out of doors."

Richard agreed and told how his mother occasionally accompanied them. Once since her arrest Martha's spirit appeared to them as a cat. At the meeting in Parris's pasture he heard Sarah Good speak of more than one minister involved: Burroughs ("He is a little man") and some other. Then everyone set their hands and seals to the Devil's great book. "The engagement was to afflict persons and overcome the kingdom of Christ, and set up the Devil's kingdom, and we were to have happy days."

Yes, said young Mary Lacy, and the Devil wanted them to convert as many to witchcraft as they could. She knew Martha Toothaker (now Martha Emerson) and her mother were witches. "That Toothaker that died in prison was one, too," Richard added.[71]

Now Mary Lacy, like her former victims, fell in a seizure. It was Toothaker on her, said Richard. He also named several more witches at the Village meetings (people already arrested) and told how a drum signaled the gathering. Mary, meanwhile, convulsed again and accused Richard of cursing her.[72]

Richard admitted afflicting several people, including Mrs. Parris, by pretending that a rolled-up handkerchief was the victim. "The Devil doth it sometimes. Sometimes the Devil stirred me up to hurt the minister's wife." He described his baptism at the falls in Newbury along with Mrs. Bradbury, Goody Nurse, and Goody How, who all signed the book. But despite the Devil's promises, they all feared discovery. "And the Devil threatens if I come not unto this quarrel, he will tear me in pieces." Apparently, no one asked why Richard and the others had to sign the Devil's various books so often, but the afflicted were sufficiently convinced of Richard's confession to abide the touch of his hand while he asked their forgiveness.

When Andrew was brought in and told of his brother's confession, he agreed to most of its details except that he knew nothing of the document the Devil gave their mother, who in turn passed it on to Richard. Andrew signed the Devil's book in Deacon Fry's orchard one night in the presence of his mother and brother, and promised to serve five years in return for a house and land in Andover. However, he hadn't known the man was the Devil when this happened.

The magistrates committed the brothers to jail, and issued an arrest warrant for Toothaker's daughter Martha, wife of Joseph Emerson of Haverhill.[73]

Before the five condemned were executed on July 19, they had all prayed that God reveal their innocence to the world. But now these other five from Andover not only "confessed" to their own witchcraft, but also agreed that the executed women had been busily involved in the Devil's work after all. It took little time for this news to spread. Nevertheless, 115 friends of Mary Bradbury, including William and Elizabeth Carr (in opposition to their kin), and Jarvis Ring (who had testified against Susanna Martin) signed a petition testifying to Mrs. Bradbury's good character.[74]

July 23, 1692 • Saturday
Salem Town

Constable William Starling and two deputies delivered Martha (Toothaker) Emerson from Haverhill to Salem, where Major Gedney and the other magistrates questioned her. The recent confessors were now among the afflicted witnesses, but she was specifically accused of hurting Mary Warren and Mary Lacy Jr.[75]

"I never saw them," Goody Emerson protested.

Richard Carrier said he saw her spirit hurt both of them the day before, though he had not seen her at the witch meetings. Goodwife Lacy insisted that both

Martha Emerson and her mother Mary Toothaker *had* attended. Mary Warren and Mary Lacy Jr., meanwhile, convulsed at the defendant's glance (though young Lacy was cured by a touch to her wrist) as did two others. Goody Emerson continued to deny everything.

Mary Warren said the accused's specter boasted of harnessing a man with an enchanted bridle, which matched Matthew Herriman's testimony of feeling hag-ridden the Monday before. Seizures prevented further speech, but she managed to answer the magistrates by raising her hand to indicate that, yes, Herriman was the man whom Emerson's specter had mentioned.

Martha Emerson protested, but the court reminded her that her own father, Roger Toothaker, had described teaching her to kill a witch by heating a sealed bottle of urine from an afflicted person. Goody Emerson admitted doing this (which was countermagic of the same sort as Mary Sibley's witch-cake, only deadly). Having confessed to one detail, she now admitted all. When the magistrates asked who had prevented her from confessing sooner, she said her aunt, Martha Carrier, and Goody Green of Haverhill. They were before her now, she said, Green furious at her refusal to lie. It was Green with her pet pig who had tried to entice her a fortnight ago to join their company of devils.

Martha Emerson was held for tormenting Mary Warren, but she soon changed her story and again claimed innocence. She thought a confession would save her, she said, but she could no longer lie in the face of God, who had, after all, kept her from actually committing the sin of witchcraft. "Though he slay me," she quoted from Job, "I will trust him." The court noted her protest, but kept her jailed.[76]

In Salem prison, meanwhile, John Proctor completed a letter to several Boston ministers: Increase Mather, James Allen, Joshua Moody, James Bailey, and Samuel Willard. On behalf of himself and the other accused, he begged their help in obtaining more objective trials. The accused knew themselves to be innocent, but the Devil so deluded and enraged "the magistrates, ministers, juries, and all the people in general" that the defendants were as good as condemned before trial. The five recent confessors had accused several others of attending the Devil's sacrament. But Proctor knew that the Carrier boys, like his own son William, had not "confessed" until they were tied neck and heels. Many prisoners were, furthermore, "undone" in their estates. Proctor begged the Boston ministers to use their influence to replace the magistrates with more impartial parties or, better yet, to have the trials held at Boston. He asked that the ministers pray for the accused, and at least attend a trial to see for themselves what was happening.[77]

July 24, 1692 • Sunday
Salem Village

The almanac predicted foggy mornings as Samuel Parris baptized William and Persis Way's six-month-old daughter Abigail, born last January just before the afflictions began.[78]

July 25, 1692 • Monday
New Haven, Connecticut

In Connecticut, New Haven magistrates heard the case of Winifred Benham, suspected of witchcraft by her Wallingford neighbors, a charge she vigorously denied. (Her husband Joseph had loaded two bullets into his gun when Hannah Parker came around with her accusation and said he'd shoot her if she said that again.) For now, the magistrates ordered everyone to appear before the November county court.[79]

Boston

In Massachusetts, the governor and council appointed a committee to oversee the recruits' pay and billeting expenses. Phips also commissioned Benjamin Church, who had made a name as an Indian fighter in King Phillip's War, as Major of Militia, his second in command.[80]

Gloucester

The presence of more than sixty men at the Gloucester garrison, meanwhile, apparently discouraged the skulking strangers and allowed the locals to return home. Ebenezer Babson, searching the woods for his strayed cattle, spied three of the interlopers on a rocky point above the sea. He crept to within forty yards, aimed, and squeezed the trigger. The musket misfired over and over as the three strolled toward him. One carried a gun on his back but, except for a glance, they paid him no heed and calmly disappeared among the brush. Babson snapped his musket a few more times, then retreated home, where, when he tested it, the gun never once misfired. This was not the last odd event in Gloucester, and many concluded that the mysterious figures so many people had seen were not real French and Indians after all, but specters. "The Devil and his agents," Gloucester's minister, John Emerson, wrote, "were the cause of all the molestations which at this time befell the town."[81]

Rowley

Near nightfall, nineteen-year-old Mary Daniel of Rowley—single, and probably a servant to Daniel Wycomb—fell suddenly ill. When she lay down to rest she saw the specter of an angry woman who "beat, pinched, and afflicted" her, all the while railing at the girl for telling something she shouldn't have.[82]

July 26, 1692 • Tuesday
Boston

Not everyone in Boston jail was accused of witchcraft. Jean Reux was a ship-master charged by his ship's owners with scuttling their vessel the January before on Naushon Island. He and two other French Canadians were locked in a small room during the nights, though not shackled, and allowed in the common dungeon by day. When the jailer's assistants unlocked the cell this morning, they found the small room empty, its window grate cut into pieces. Reux had already escaped once and been captured, but although prisonkeeper John Arnold searched for them with the required hue and cry, no one saw or heard a sign of them.[83]

Governor Phips ordered the Boston regiment's officers to arrest the men who had failed to appear as ordered on July 15, to fine them each twenty shillings, and to haul any who refused to pay aboard the *Nonsuch*. Those who volunteered to privateer in one of his own vessels, however, could share the plunder. The fine was supposed to be only five shillings, and some merchants who refused to pay were offended to be threatened as if they were only common sailors. (When these vessels did arrive Eastward, they captured a French flyboat bound for Canada, laden with £12,000 worth of wine, brandy, textiles, and ready-made clothing.)[84]

Salem Town

A court of General Sessions for Essex County, postponed from its usual June sitting, convened at Salem with Bartholomew Gedney, John Hathorne, Jonathan Corwin, John Higginson Jr., Daniel Epps, Thomas Wade, and Daniel Pierce presiding. They considered only mundane matters like the illegal selling of ale, and the proper licensing of innholders Walter Phillips, Nathaniel Ingersoll, Mary Gedney, Samuel and Thomas Beadle, and Samuel Shattuck. Hannah Shattuck was also granted a retail license, for besides operating the dyeworks, the Shattucks sold a variety of goods, including refreshments to the courts.[85]

Andover

The arrests and confessions of the five Andover suspects did not stop Elizabeth Ballard's fevered torments. Specters of Mary Bradbury and Mary Bridges were apparently active, for Bradbury's apparition continued to harass Timothy Swan this evening, as witnessed by Mary Walcott and Ann Putnam Jr.[86]

Rowley

In Rowley, Mary felt the soles of her feet prickle as she sat in a chair by the fire, then saw the form of neighbor Margaret Scott. The specter jerked the chair and Mary over backward, which hurt her so, she lost her voice from terror. In some of the resulting seizures Mary fell senseless, dead to everything. But in others she saw Widow Scott and Goody Jackson looming over her.[87]

July 27, 1692 • Wednesday
Rowley

Mary Daniel woke, once more able to speak (although her seizures would continue for some days).[88]

Andover

Unlike most of the dry summer, a good rain fell. Yet even with this relief, Elizabeth Ballard, the constable's afflicted wife, died of lingering fever in Andover.[89]

July 28, 1692 • Thursday
Ipswich

Despite Timothy Swan's torments, efforts still continued to vindicate Mary Bradbury. She herself wrote to the authorities from jail to insist she despised the Devil and his works, and had always tried to lead a good and upright life, "human frailties and unavoidable infirmities excepted." The best proof of this was the opinion of her "brethren and neighbors that know me."[90]

Salisbury

To this her husband added how she had been for fifty years a "loving and faithful wife," a good mother to their eleven children and four grandchildren, and a cheerful charitable neighbor. The infirmities of age and the miseries of her present situation, however, prevented her from speaking as freely on her own behalf as others could.[91]

Andover

Newly bereaved Constable Ballard of Andover set out with an arrest warrant for Mary Bridges Sr., whose specter still afflicted Timothy Swan. Through her husband John the blacksmith, she was kin to Ann Pudeator and Sarah Cloyse. She was perhaps questioned locally by Justice Dudley Bradstreet (as other local suspects may

have been) before being sent to Salem. If so, the other civil and religious leaders of the community and as many neighbors as could fit likely crowded in to hear. Rev. Francis Dane, for one, had heard no local witchcraft rumors (except against his niece, Martha Carrier). But the convulsions of the afflicted and the apparent sincerity of their visions were too convincing to ignore.

In public and in private, suspects found themselves questioned by neighbors and, often, by their own shocked families, who argued with "extreem urgency" for them to confess. "You *are* a witch!" one would exclaim (as Dane reported). "You *are* guilty!" While another demanded, "*Who* afflicts this maid?" Threats of prison and the general confusion drove more and more to confess, partly in desperation, and partly because they began to believe themselves guilty, their admission verifying what others suspected. After being told repeatedly "that she certainly *was* a witch, and so made to believe it," Goodwife Bridges confessed to witchcraft.[92]

July 29, 1692 • Friday
Salem Town

Mary Bridges Sr. was probably questioned today in Salem, still holding to her confession. But she was not the last suspect. Magistrates Gedney, Hathorne, Corwin, and Higginson then issued arrest warrants to the Haverhill constable for Goodwives Mary Green and Hannah Bromage.[93]

Will's Hill

Up in Will's Hill this evening, Rebecca Wilkins saw the specter of her jailed uncle John Willard lurking in a corner, threatening to afflict her again, as indeed she was.[94]

July 30, 1692 • Saturday
Salem Town

Constable William Starling and three deputies transported Mary Green and Hannah Bromage from Haverhill to Salem for questioning, accompanied the whole way by Goody Green's husband.[95]

The four Salem magistrates questioned these two women and Mary Toothaker while William Murray took notes. The examination of Goody Green, wife of Haverhill weaver Peter Green and owner of a real or spectral pig, is lost. Apparently kin to Mary Bradbury, Mary Green had grown up in Hampton, New Hampshire, except for a year or more of her girlhood thirty years earlier, which she had spent in Charlestown and Lynn while various physicians and folk healers tried to mend her "very dangerous sore leg." One healer diagnosed the malady as the

King's Evil (scrofula), and Mary lost a five-inch sliver of bone from that "bad and desperate wound," but did not, at least, die of infection.[96]

Since the complaint against Mary Toothaker was dated two months before on May 28, there was either an uncharacteristic delay or this was a second examination. By now, her husband Roger had died in prison, her daughter Martha Emerson had confessed, and most of the country believed her sister Martha Carrier aspired to be queen of Hell. While Goody Toothaker insisted on her innocence, the afflicted writhed at her merest glance, the accused-turned-confessor Goody Bridges urged her to confess as well, and the court demanded an explanation for the convulsions.[97]

She was, Mary Toothaker said, under a great discontent for fear of Indian raids and often dreamt of fighting them off. But when the court asked if the Devil might have taken advantage of this fear to tempt her, she said she would confess if she could, but something in her breast prevented her. She often *tried* to pray, she added, but could not say much beyond "Lord, be merciful to me a sinner," for what little good that did. She began to gasp. Perhaps the Devil hindered her, she said, for her breath was often stopped as it was now. Two years ago, she went on, the Devil had appeared to her as "a tawny man" (like an Indian) and had promised to protect her from Indians so that she and her son might have happy days. He had also promised that the court would find her innocent. She did not sign the Devil's book, but rubbed a mark on the white of some birch bark that he brought her. Yes, he had promised her safety from Indians, she gasped, again fighting the Devil's attempts to stop her breath, for it was her fear of them that drove her to sign.

Now she prayed to the Devil, Goody Toothaker said, went in spirit to all those witch meetings with her sisters, and tormented Timothy Swan with Goodwives Bridges, Bromage, Green, and others. The Devil was so subtle he deluded her even by Scripture. Because the Psalm (perhaps Psalm 59) said, "Let my enemies be confounded," she wished destruction of all those who spread witch reports against her. She agreed that the Devil stood on the table by her when the afflicted reported him there. She described the witches' meetings, their plans to enthrone Satan, and the elderly woman Mrs. Bradbury, who had recruited them to hurt Swan. It was true her late husband spoke with their daughter about killing a suspected witch named Button. (A cunning man like Roger was perilously close to being a witch himself.) Father and daughter studied a number of magic texts, "especially one book that treated of the twelve signs," but as for her daughter's being a witch, Goody Toothaker never suspected it before this summer.

Hannah Bromage had inherited a house from her first husband (she and her second husband rented it out) but her three children from that earlier marriage had all died. So far, only Ann Putnam Jr. and Mary Walcott had accused her. With those two absent, the other afflicted were asked to look at the defendant and to take her hand, which they did easily. But as soon as Ann and Mary were brought in and Goody Bromage glanced at them, their seizures began again and stopped only at her touch. Ann also convulsed when the clerk read her testimony, tormented, Mary Walcott said, by Bromage's specter. Goody Bridges accused the defendant of helping to afflict Goody Ballard to death. As Ann Putnam suffered a violent seizure, Goodwives Lacy and Bridges said that Bromage's specter stabbed the girl with a spear. Until she confessed, Goodwife Mary Bridges told the defendant, the Devil would not leave her.[98]

Half convinced of her own guilt, Goody Bromage admitted to feeling a spiritual deadness toward religious services for some six weeks. A thought had come into her head: "I can help thee with strength." But she was unsure of its source and replied, "Avoid Satan." The magistrate asked in what form the Devil came to her, but she said only that the Devil was in her heart, and admitted no more, though there had been enough excitement to hold her for tormenting Mary Warren.

Ipswich

Constable Starling took the prisoners north to Ipswich jail, Peter Green still accompanying his wife as far as he was able. He would not get home until Monday.[99]

Cambridge

Meanwhile, Captain Nathaniel Cary of Charlestown, whose wife Elizabeth had been arrested in May, continued to work on her behalf. Although he managed to have her transferred to the Cambridge jail in their own Middlesex County, his several petitions failed to obtain a change of venue to Middlesex as well. Cary was not encouraged by the courts that he attended in Salem. If she were moved there for trial, he told his wife, she would *never* return. So working in secret with the help of friends, including Rev. Samuel Willard's son John (not to be confused with the suspected witch John Willard), Cary arranged for Elizabeth's escape today and sent her south. He stayed behind and was arrested. Because of the jailbreak the law confiscated some of his goods, but freed Cary himself after only half a day. Cary slipped away to join his wife in Rhode Island. Then they headed for New York to avoid further pursuit.[100]

Will's Hill

At Will's Hill, Rebecca Wilkins* again saw the specter of her jailed uncle John Willard which pulled her by the ear and tried to choke her.[101]

July 31, 1692 • Sunday
Salem Village

Willard's specter attacked Rebecca Wilkins again on the way to meeting. It was sacrament Sabbath and, if she and her family continued on, they heard Rev. Parris speak on John 6:48: "I am the bread of life." (But again, Parris's notes for it are lost.)[102]

Andover

In Andover, before the minister arrived to begin the morning service, young Phebe Chandler (recently summoned as a witness in Martha Carrier's trial), noticed Richard Carrier watching her. The real Richard was locked in jail, but her fear of his specter made Phebe's hand ache again, her stomach burn, and her ears deaf even to the prayers and singing until the Psalm ended.[103]

Rowley

In Rowley, meanwhile, four or five specters, including Margaret Scott's, shadowed Mary Daniel.[104]

---

*She said this happened July 29 but also said the following day was Sabbath, so it has to be today.

8

AUGUST 1692

Hell is a terrible place; I know there is no coming out.

—Mercy Short

August 1, 1692 • Monday
Cambridge

Increase Mather and seven other Congregational ministers (Cotton Mather was absent) met at the Harvard College library in Cambridge to discuss their scheduled topic: Could devils impersonate the innocent? Unanimously, they agreed that devils *could* falsely represent anyone. But the ministers still felt it happened only rarely and was less likely in cases severe enough to reach court. Either way, their conclusion was no help to the petitioning Proctors. Even if influential, ministers had no more legal authority than other private citizens. Their advice to the government in the "Return of Several Ministers," although requested, was largely ignored. Nevertheless, they urged Increase Mather to compose a thorough examination of spectral evidence.[1]

Billerica

Raiders, meanwhile, attacked north Billerica near the Andover border, killing the women and children of the Shed and Dutton families while the men were in the fields. This news was bound to alarm widow Toothaker, so terrified of Indians that she confessed she had allied herself with the Devil in exchange for his protection. Had she been at home instead of in jail, she too would have been targeted by that raid.[2]

***

Casco Bay

Around the beginning of August, Governor Phips and his forces sailed Eastward to build Fort William Henry at Pemmaquid. Critics objected that the fort would protect only one harbor and would be useless either as a refuge for locals or as a posting station for troops. But, long before the summer's attacks, King William had ordered its construction to show France that England would not abandon the area. Phip's fleet paused at the ruins of Casco Fort to salvage the cannon and to bury the weathered bones of its inhabitants. Later, when sailing past his boyhood home near the Kennebec, Phips took the occasion (as was his habit) to address his crew:

> Young men, it was upon that hill that I kept sheep a few years ago, and since you see that Almighty God has brought me to something, do you learn to fear God, and be honest, and mind your business, and follow no bad courses, and you don't know what you may come to!

Mindful of earthly business, Phips brought fur trapping equipment to make spare time profitable as well.[3]

August 2, 1692 • Tuesday
Salem Town

The Court of Oyer and Terminer sat again at Salem* to try Martha Carrier, John and Elizabeth Proctor, John Willard, George Jacobs Sr., and George Burroughs.[4]

Martha Carrier's trial began at ten o'clock in the morning with the defendant pleading not guilty to the indictments. But several of the afflicted, when called in, suffered seizures with all the usual appearance of the invisible tortures that they

---

*Calef dates all six trials August 5. Surviving warrants and Cotton Mather's more contemporary account place Carrier's trial on August 2. Some testimony was given August 3.

blamed on Carrier. The court had heard depositions about similar events during her examination in May when the convulsions were so bad that the afflicted thought themselves dying and the defendant was bound to subdue her rampaging spirit. Her lack of sympathy for them was also noted.[5]

So many testified Goody Carrier was a witch—Goody Foster and both Mary Lacys described the witch meetings—that the judges found it unnecessary for the defendant's sons to depose against her also. This was convenient for the court since the sons had been tied neck and heels before confessing. All had agreed that the Devil promised Carrier that she would be queen of Hell.[6]

Benjamin and Sarah Abbott told of a boundary dispute between them and the Carriers a year ago March. It so angered Martha Carrier that she vowed she would stick as close to Abbott as bark to a tree. He would be sorry for this before seven years were out, she railed, for not even Doctor Prescott would be able to cure him. She would hold his nose as close to the grindstone as it had ever been since his name was Abbott. Soon after, several of his cattle fell ill and died. Abbott himself felt terrible pain in his side. His foot became infected, gushing several gallons of corruption (it seemed) when Doctor Prescott lanced it. Another sore appeared on his groin and needed lancing, followed by another and another until Carrier's arrest. Only then did Abbott begin to heal, and he had been well ever since.[7]

Goody Carrier's nephew Allen Toothaker, all too aware that his mother, sister, and late father were witch suspects, also testified against his aunt. When he sided with Benjamin Abbott in that boundary dispute, he said, his cousin Richard Carrier grabbed him by the hair and threw him down. Then Aunt Carrier's specter sat on his chest until he told Richard that he yielded. Whenever Allen quarreled with her, she clapped her hands at him and said he would get no good from it. Then a cow or two would die. She also told him that his wound, received while fighting Eastward, would never heal. Indeed, he could probe a knitting needle into it four inches deep. But as soon as his aunt was arrested, it began to mend and was now perfectly well.[8]

John Rogers and Samuel Preston described their animals' illnesses and deaths after arguments with, or outright threats from, Martha Carrier. Phebe Chandler, verified by her mother Bridget, told of her ailments that followed Goody Carrier's odd (perhaps spectral) behavior, and how Richard Carrier's specter terrorized her one Sabbath meeting.[9]

The afflicted convulsed throughout the trial. At one point, the court was surprised to see Susanna Sheldon's hands tied with a wheel band so tightly it had to be cut.[10]

Martha Carrier remained defiant, exasperated by the afflicted witnesses. When told that her specter was twisting their necks nearly around she snapped, "It's no matter though their necks had been twisted quite off!" The jury eventually found Martha Carrier guilty as charged.[11]

At some point during the day John Proctor signed a new will in Salem jail, one that omitted his wife Elizabeth (so perhaps their trials occurred today and left him with no hope that either would survive, or their marriage was as unhappy as rumored). He divided his seventy-five acres equally among the children of his three marriages and named his eldest sons Benjamin and John Jr. as executors.[12]

Most of the surviving testimony against John Proctor was from the afflicted, especially his servant Mary Warren, who no longer tried to protest that she was out of her head when she accused anyone. James Holten related how his own pain ceased once Proctor's specter turned from him to the afflicted girls—or so they told him; he hadn't seen it. Nevertheless, Holten and nineteen other neighbors signed a petition on behalf of John and Elizabeth Proctor to say that none of them had ever suspected the couple of witchcraft. Thirty-two friends and kin from Ipswich, where John grew up, presented another petition, probably composed by Rev. John Wise. Besides vouching for the defendants' characters, the document noted that Satan once counterfeited a specter of the holy prophet Samuel.[13]

But neither scriptural example, nor the opinion of so many supporters prevailed. The jury found John Proctor guilty.

Most of the surviving testimony against Elizabeth Proctor dealt with tortures that her specter had inflicted since late winter on various girls, women, and a few men like John Indian and Stephen Billford. Several of the afflicted spoke of her murder victims' ghosts yearning for justice. Elizabeth Booth said the ghost of her stepfather, Michael Schafflin, told her that Goody Proctor had killed him from spite because the family wouldn't send for her when he first became ill. The defendant had also clashed with Doctor Zerubabel Endicott over medical matters.[14]

Daniel Elliott and William Rayment described the confusion among the afflicted at the beginning of the outbreak, their uncertainty whether they saw specters or not, and how bystanders suggested names for what they might have seen. But that testimony, favorable to the defendant, paled beside whatever Arthur Abbott related about the goings-on at the Proctor house. (His account, now lost, was sensational enough for Abbott's local magistrate, Samuel Appleton, to later accuse him of bearing false witness.)[15]

In spite of the petitions and testimony in her favor, Elizabeth Proctor, like her husband, was found guilty. However, as she pleaded for a delay on the grounds of pregnancy, her execution was postponed until after she gave birth.[16]

Andover

On the same day in Andover, Mary Walcott, Ann Putnam Jr., and Timothy Swan entered a complaint before Justice of the Peace Dudley Bradstreet against Mary Post of Rowley, Goodwife Mary Bridges's grown daughter. Swan even put up a £20 bond to prosecute, and Bradstreet issued a warrant for Rowley Constable Joseph Jewett to bring the suspect to the Salem magistrates. (Like her mother, Mary Post would confess. She admitted she tormented Swan and covenanted with the Devil.)[17]

Ipswich

Meanwhile, John Shepard of Rowley, formerly of Salem Village, broke his sister-in-law Mary Green out of Ipswich jail and put Constable William Baker to a shilling's expense finding and catching her.[18]

August 3, 1692 • Wednesday
Salem Town

Testimony continued in Salem against Martha Carrier, and various folk swore to their depositions about Mary Esty and Rev. George Burroughs before the Grand Jury. John DeRich wrote of his May encounters with George Jacobs Sr. and, while doing so, he again felt afflicted by Jacobs's specter. (John's mother, Mary DeRich, had been arrested May 23 with his Proctor kin.)[19]

Andover

Mary Walcott, Ann Putnam Jr., and Timothy Swan were so badly tormented in Andover by Mary Clark's specter that Timothy's father Robert and brother John entered a complaint against her before Justice Bradstreet and put up a bond to prosecute.[20]

Reading

Edward Marshall died of natural causes in Reading, leaving his fearful wife Mary widowed for a second time. She had felt afflicted since her neighbor Lydia Dustin's arrest in May. All the Dustins and their friends made her nervous. After Edward's death Rev. Jonathan Pearpont tried to console Mistress Marshall with the Psalm's reminder that God protected widows (either Psalm 68:5 or 146:9). But then Mary

Coleson, Mary Taylor, and Jane Lilly came by to comment that God was no substitute for a *real* husband.[21]

August 4, 1692 • Thursday
Salem Town

As soon as he received the Andover warrant, Haverhill Constable William Starling arrested Mistress Mary Clark. He and two deputies brought her to Salem, where she faced John Hathorne and the other justices, the usual afflicted, and several recent confessors. Mary Walcott identified her as the tormenting specter, then convulsed at her glance. After several others collapsed, the magistrates badgered Mistress Clark to confess "for the good of her soul." She utterly denied the charge. They asked the constable about her reputation, but Starling could vouch for none of the rumors. The justices asked Mary Walcott if she could be mistaken about the defendant's identity.[22]

"This is the very woman I saw afflict Timothy Swan," Mary Walcott declared, "and she has afflicted me several times." She had another seizure as the specter attacked Elizabeth Hubbard and Ann Putnam Jr. Mistress Clark stared at the girls when they made this claim, whereupon they convulsed again and came up pierced with pins. One stuck in Mary Walcott's arm, another angled in Mary Warren's throat and chin (Rev. Nicholas Noyes managed to extract it) and four bristled from Susanna Sheldon's hand. (During one examination, according to Deodat Lawson, an afflicted girl "had a pin run through both her upper and her lower lip when she was called to speak." Amazingly, the wound never festered.)[23]

Attempting the Lord's Prayer test, Mary Clark "erred much." Richard Carrier said that she had been among those baptized with him at Newbury Falls. Mary Post, another confessor, said that she saw Clark at the Village witch meeting *and* saw her afflict Timothy Swan. Her specter, Ann Putnam Jr. reported, had identified itself as "Mistress Mary Clark" and admitted that people had called her only "Goody Clark" not long ago, before her husband rose in the world. Her specter often pinched, choked, and clouted her in the face, Ann went on, and stabbed Timothy Swan with a ragged spear as long as her hand. Ragged like a file, Ann explained, when the justices puzzled over her description.

Besides accusing Mrs. Clark of stabbing pins into her, Susanna Sheldon also blamed Mr. Usher. (Hezekiah Usher, a Boston merchant charged by several with spectral crimes, was arrested at some point, but managed to substitute house arrest for prison. Usher's life was already unhappy: his wife had left him for her native England. He thought her too worldly; she thought him too unorthodox.)[24]

The Grand Jury heard witnesses against Mary Esty, Martha Corey, and George Jacobs Sr. Marshal George Herrick swore to finding an odd insensible excrescence on Jacobs's shoulder.[25]

Rowley

Mary Daniel made a deposition in Rowley about Margaret Scott's specter tormenting her the week before.[26]

Boston

Meanwhile, news of an earthquake in Jamaica stunned Massachusetts. Although
the place was reputed to be little better than Sodom and Gomorrah, and was a
known nest for pirates, many New Englanders had kin and business contacts
there. On June 7, a fine fair day, the sea suddenly swelled far up above the anchored ships in Port Royal Harbor, then crashed upon the town, drowning 1,700
people under five fathoms of water. Boston was relieved to hear that no New England ships were lost, and that the local Puritan minister had escaped alive. But the
whole disaster was so bizarre that it seemed like something from the Book of Revelation.[27]

Consequently, Boston's afternoon lecture became a fast observance. Rev. Cotton Mather, the week's speaker, chose a text from Revelation 12:12. "Woe to the
Inhabitants of the Earth, and of the Sea; for the Devil is come down unto you, having great wrath; because he knoweth, that he hath but a short time."[28]

The end of time, passing references aside, was ordinarily an uncommon sermon subject since the date of its occurrence was unknown. Yet all the varied
prophecies had unnerving parallels in current events: persecution of Protestants in
Europe, attacks from Canada, earthquakes in Jamaica, and witchcraft in Massachusetts. The last seemed especially like Hell's last great war. If that were true, so
was the rest of the prophecy—the Devil's defeat. Since even Satan was not as powerful as God, the present afflictions were more likely a last-ditch skirmish of an already defeated enemy.

Nevertheless, the present problems were deadly serious: the plot against Christianity detailed in recent confessions, and the real pains and deaths suffered by the
afflicted (plus a rash of suicides). Mather was convinced real witches *were* at work.
He trusted the judges' perceptions and accepted the reported confessions. However, he again cautioned against the use of spectral evidence. There were simply
too many people being accused, and too many of them had led obviously pious
lives. "The whole business is become hereupon so snarled, and the determination
of the question one way or another, so dismal, that our honorable judges have a
room for Jehoshaphat's exclamation, 'We know not what to do!'" The judges had
requested prayers on their behalf that they might proceed fairly, but for now, "the
Devil improves the darkness of this affair, to push us into a blind man's buffet, and
we are even ready to be sinfully, yea, hotly, and madly, mauling one another in
the dark." (But the judges were in Salem and did not hear or later heed Mather's
astute and impassioned warning.)[29]

The torments of the afflicted, as Cotton Mather described them from second-hand reports, matched the severity of the Goodwin children's seizures, which he had witnessed a few years earlier. Whatever the problem's cause, its effects in many cases *were* real and physical. Recent observers reported the scratch and bite marks on the skin of the afflicted (the sorts of lesions that could appear spontaneously, self-induced by the victims' own unconscious fears). Others saw blood gush from the girls' mouths, saw their bodies distort and disjoint during convulsions, or struggle as if with something invisible. Events were uncanny enough to convince observers even when the specifics were not always consistent, as when a "biting witch" was found to be toothless. Some viewers described coins, earlier reported lost, falling from the air into the hands of the afflicted as a spectral bribe. Some afflicted had confessed to signing the Devil's book just to gain relief from torment only to find themselves jailed with other witch suspects. But others, who did not sign, had developed an alarmingly casual attitude toward the Devil. They also saw and heard ghosts; discerned the living's secret thoughts; knew who approached unannounced when unable to see them; and knew what clothes they wore. Some people were sure the afflicted lied, while others thought that if they knew these things, *they* must be witches themselves.[30]

Cotton Mather's involvement, since his offer to house some of the afflicted had been refused, was limited to pastoral visits with the ailing Mercy Short, and to weekly private sessions of prayer and fasting. He, like others, may have been troubled by the repeated claims of innocence from the last five to be hanged. Now, however, the five new Andover witches' thorough confessions and their assertion that the other five and more were indeed guilty seemed to answer his doubts. Hell did have its local adherents, but they were beginning to defect.[31]

August 5, 1692 • Friday
Salem Town

Cotton Mather remained in Boston writing letters. But Increase Mather and Deodat Lawson joined the "vast concourse of people" who journeyed from Boston this morning to attend Rev. George Burroughs's trial in Salem.[32]

John Willard may have been tried already and condemned by the testimony of the afflicted, by the physical symptoms of his frightened relatives, and by the dramatic death of his nephew Daniel Wilkins. Willard's running away looked all the more suspicious now. People recalled his hints of secret powers and his jests that the Devil stalked him. His inlaws told how his wife Mary had to hide from him all night under the stairs after one beating, wondering if she would ever recover. She then escaped on horseback to her own kin while John ran about like one distracted. Neighbors had also helped Mary return to her family after inexplicable noises frightened her.[33]

Mary, however, had been providing for him in prison, even while he was far away in Boston. She also petitioned the government on her husband's behalf, if only because the household could not raise enough corn for their own bread without a man around.[34]

Willard's reported cruelty and his nephew's actual death outweighed all his protests of innocence. The jury found John Willard guilty as charged.

George Jacobs Sr. was perhaps tried this morning and also found guilty. The surviving testimony is mostly from the afflicted, including his servant Sarah Churchill (whom his specter, and probably the man himself, had beaten with a walking stick).

Young John DeRich, chased into the river by old Jacobs's specter, also told of several ghosts who accused Jacobs and other witches of killing them. The ghost of Mary Warren's mother appeared with the shining angel, said DeRich (veering off the subject), and told him that Goodwives Parker and Oliver had murdered her. According to his testimony, Martha Corey, the Proctors and their children, the Englishes, the Hobbs women, Goody Pease, and a woman named Mary from the upper end of Boston (who had a crooked neck and only one eye) tormented DeRich daily.[35]

"Well, burn me or hang me, I will stand in the truth of Christ!" George Jacobs Sr. had exclaimed at his initial examination. Nevertheless, he was found guilty of witchcraft.[36]

Rev. George Burroughs was tried in the afternoon, in time for Reverends Increase Mather, Deodat Lawson, and others to arrive from Boston, and John Hale from nearby Beverly. A larger than usual audience crowded the court room because this defendant was feared to be the earthly leader of an active plot to infiltrate and destroy New England's churches. Far worse than the menace of a neighborhood witch, this man—entrusted with his community's spiritual welfare—was suspected of plotting with the forces of evil against his own people, and this at a time when the area was under constant threat of foreign attack, and the civil government was so precariously new and untried.

Nevertheless, Burroughs exercised his right to challenge prospective jurors and actually rejected several of them.[37]

The afflicted testified how his specter had tormented them for so long, especially at his prior examination; how he pressured them to sign his book; and how he bragged that, as a conjurer, he outranked the mere witches whom he summoned to his meetings. The afflicted often accused his specter of biting. They displayed teeth marks on their arms that observers thought matched the pattern of Burroughs's own teeth.[38]

The delivery of this testimony was as sensational as its content, for seizures again and again choked the afflicted speechless. As their behavior resembled something invisible throttling their answers, Chief Justice William Stoughton asked Burroughs who he thought hindered the witnesses. Burroughs replied that it was the Devil. "How comes the Devil so loath to have any testimony born against you?" Stoughton demanded.

Burroughs had no answer to that query.

Suddenly, the afflicted froze in a trance—all staring fixedly at one spot between themselves and the defendant at the bar. They neither moved nor blinked nor answered the judges' repeated questions. But when they recovered, they recoiled in horror and the court immediately separated them for questioning. Each, without the prodding of the others, described the four ghosts that she had seen glaring redly at Burroughs and accusing him of their murders: Burroughs's first two wives, and the wife and daughter of Rev. Deodat Lawson (who was in the audience).

Visibly appalled, Burroughs denied that he could see them. (For some reason this spectral evidence was not included against him.)[39]

Eight confessors told how Burroughs had lured them to join the witches with fair promises. They described how he led the witch meetings; how he made them torment others with poppets and thorns; and how he encouraged them to conquer Salem Village secretly. Their testimony, too, was probably interrupted, for the confessing witches were subject to seizures ever since their confessions.[40]

Some thought that Burroughs neglected prayer and other religious ordinances—a circumstance more sinister than careless, hinting his allegiance was to the Devil. According to the notes of his May examination, "he owned that none of his children but the eldest was baptized." As a full church member, he was entitled to have them baptized, although he could not administer this sacrament himself since he was not ordained. Perhaps he had meant that the very youngest were not, for records still exist proving that at least four of his eight children *had* been baptized. Decades later, his supposedly neglected children would protest that he not only upheld religion at home, but also composed "solemn and savory written instructions from prison" to them.[41]

Although Burroughs was noticeably short for a grown man, he was surprisingly strong for his size. Nine people testified to feats of extraordinary lifting at Casco Bay during the 1689 campaign, some seen, others heard secondhand—from Burroughs himself, among others. He had reportedly held a heavy gun with a seven-foot barrel in one hand and, at another time, had lifted singlehandedly a full molasses barrel from an unsteady canoe. At his May examination, the notes of which were before the judges, Burroughs had denied the barrel story entirely and had explained that he held the gun before its lock and braced its butt against his chest.

Now, however, he claimed that an Indian steadied the gun barrel for him. But no one else remembered an Indian, and this only echoed the specters seen by widow Toothaker and the Gloucester men. Another witness repeated gossip that Burroughs stuck his right index finger into the gun barrel and so lifted it, but the court ignored this version.[42]

People said that he had treated his late wives harshly, bringing them "to the point of death" by his "barbarous usage," and then made any witness swear not to talk about it. Back in 1680, when he and his first wife Hannah had boarded with John Putnam Sr. in Salem Village, Burroughs had tried, according to his temporary landlord's testimony to make her sign and seal a written promise not to tell his secrets. The Putnams thought her dutiful, yet Burroughs was sharp with her all the same. (After Hannah died in 1681, John loaned Burroughs money for her funeral, then sued him for repayment. John, advised by his brother Thomas Putnam, even had Burroughs arrested for the debt in 1683 on the same day the Village was about to settle the minister's own belated pay.)[43]

Burroughs's second wife Sarah was possibly Judge Hathorne's sister-in-law by her first marriage.* She was too afraid of her husband to write her own father, John Ruck, according to neighbor Mary Webber, who wrote for her. Goody Webber described the apparitions that Mrs. Burroughs and her black woman servant had reported in the Casco Bay house: the white calf that Burroughs chased down the stairs, and the unseen thing that stood by Mrs. Burroughs's bedside and breathed on her. Hannah Harris, once a maid in that household, said her master always knew whatever Mrs. Burroughs told her in his absence, for he would repeat it on his return. And if he hadn't kept his wife standing at the door while he argued with her when she ought to have been in bed recovering from childbirth, she mightn't have died. Sarah's own stepdaughter thought so.[44]

Thomas Ruck, Sarah's brother, told of a strawberrying expedition when he and his sister had shared a horse, while her husband had accompanied them on foot. When Burroughs stepped off the road into the bushes and then did not return, Sarah took the opportunity to confide in her brother on the ride back. They were nearly home when Burroughs was suddenly beside them with a basket of berries and began a spate of criticism for his wife's remarks. He knew their thoughts, he said, noting their surprise. Even the Devil, Ruck countered, could not know that, but Burroughs answered, "My god makes known your thoughts unto me." As this remark sounded most unlike a Christian concept of God, the court asked Burroughs to answer Ruck's accusation. Without explaining how it altered the situation, Burroughs said his brother-in-law had left a man to wait for him while they went ahead with the horse. Ruck insisted there

---

*William Hathorne's widow, Sarah, is often said to be the same Sarah (Ruck) who married George Burroughs, but this has not been proven.

was no one else, and when the court asked Burroughs what the man's name was, he could not answer that either. All observed that "his countenance was much altered." Now it seemed that Burroughs had stepped off the road to become invisible (as many of the confessors said they could do) so he could spy on his wife.[45]

Burroughs spoke up several times during the proceedings, only to have his explanations sound like weak excuses or outright contradictions. He hinted that the witnesses were not all as honest as they should be, and handed in a paper for the jury to consider. It stated that there never had been any such persons as witches, because it was impossible for one to make an actual contract with the Devil, much less send devils to do one's will. The judges, however, recognized the argument as an uncredited quotation from Thomas Ady's book, *A Candle in the Dark*. The judges, and other educated men in the audience, were familiar with this controversial work. It argued that not only were the methods used to detect witchcraft too uncertain to trust, but that the current definition of witches and their reputed powers had *no* scriptural basis. What English Bibles translated as "witch" was not the same as what English law defined.

Burroughs denied taking any of it from a book, but after more questioning said he had transcribed it from a written copy given to him by a gentleman. The court was left wondering why he would bother to obscure the quotation's obvious source. (Burroughs's case seemed riddled with misunderstandings. Perhaps he tried not to say too much, or to say anything the court could misapply. Perhaps he customarily trimmed the truth. In any case, all his attempts to offer an explanation or defense were understood as mere "contradictions and falsehoods.")[46]

Burroughs still insisted on his own innocence even after the jury brought in a verdict of guilty, still denying involvement in witchcraft. Rev. Increase Mather, watching from the audience, didn't believe a word of it. "Had I been one of the judges," he later wrote, "I could not have acquitted him."[47]

Burroughs justified the judges and jury for condemning him based on the testimony marshaled against him, but, he added, he would die due to *false* witnesses. This statement disturbed Rev. John Hale enough to seek out one of the confessors who had claimed that Burroughs led the witch meetings (perhaps one of the Lacys or old Ann Foster who was still oppressed by the fear that Burroughs meant to kill her for her testimony). "You are one that bring this man to death," Hale reminded her. "If you have charged any thing upon him that is not true, recall it before it be too late, while he is alive." But she answered only that she had nothing of the sort for which to blame herself.[48]

While he was in Salem, Increase Mather also spoke with some of the jailed suspects. Several not only told him that they were indeed witches, but also detailed
the times and circumstances of their witchly deeds.[49]

Margaret Scott of Rowley had been arrested and was examined in Salem. Her
specter had bedeviled Captain Daniel Wycomb's family and neighbors for some
time. In addition, one of the confessors (identified by Rev. John Hale only as M.
G.) testified that she and widow Scott had made themselves invisible and crept up
on Captain Wycomb to whack him with a stick. Captain Wycomb declared that he
had indeed felt "a sore blow as if with a great stick, but saw no body."

Widow Scott denied hitting him, but "M. G., the confessor, very boldly looked up
in her face and said, "G[oody] S[cott], you know you did strike him, and I saw you
do it." She then went on to describe the circumstances of the episode. Margaret Scott
was held for tormenting Mary Daniel and Wycomb's daughter Frances.[50]

August 6–7, 1692 • Saturday–Sunday
Andover

In Andover, ten-year-old Sarah Phelps, a cousin of Phebe Chandler and a niece of
the late Elizabeth Ballard, was tormented from Saturday night on into the Sabbath.[51]

August 8, 1692 • Monday
Reading

While Sarah Phelps's seizures continued in Andover, thirty-four-year-old William
Hooper died at home in nearby Reading, probably another victim of the fevers plaguing the region. Almanacs predicted a hot dry week. In fact, it would be so hot that the
bodies of those who died in the night would have to be buried the following day, for
they simply "could not be kept." Hooper's family had enough time to acquire "several gallons of wine" for the funeral while his body lay in the house. The gathered kin
included Hooper's sister Sarah, now married to her second husband Samuel Wardwell—a farmer, carpenter, and fortuneteller. Others who may have been present were
the deceased's sisters Hannah (sister-in-law to Constable Joseph Ballard), and Ruth
(wife to Abraham Walcott of Salem Village, kinsman of the afflicted Mary Walcott). In-
law Mary Taylor was *not* present. She had been entrusted with a Hooper infant to wet
nurse, but William, dissatisfied, had taken it back from her.

After nightfall, the family discovered the wine missing, and heard shouts outside in the darkness. Later, when they realized the roof was on fire, they heard

more shouts—gloating cries of triumph it seemed. Whether the house was entirely destroyed or not is unclear, but there it was, flaming in the night with the corpse of its former master inside.[52]

August 9, 1692 • Tuesday
Salisbury

While the afflicted in Salem swore to their depositions against Mary Bradbury's spectral acts, her husband, Captain Thomas Bradbury, busied himself with pen and ink in Salisbury. He wrote a fair copy of a second letter composed by Robert Pike (the first is lost) to Judge Jonathan Corwin. As Salisbury's assistant in the General Court, Pike had taken depositions against Susanna Martin (hanged on July 19). Now, he spoke his mind.[53]

He accepted that the afflicted saw and felt what they reported, but thought that they were deluded by false specters. If human sleight of hand could create illusions, so much more could the Prince of Lies. Even if actual witches *were* thus represented, there was no way to discern which apparitions were real and which resulted from the Devil's lies.

Pike lamented the dangerous idea that the Devil needed people's permission to use their spectral appearances. A devil had once disguised itself as the Prophet Samuel. Recent reports of ghosts and bilocation were just such diabolical shams. Once deceived, the afflicted and the confessors were in the Devil's power, tormented at his whim to make them accuse others. Some people thought the afflicted faked their fits and visions. Pike did not, but either way, the testimony was based on a lie—their own or the Devil's.

While Scripture demanded that a witch be put to death, he wrote, it also required that the innocent be spared. Proof of any crime required corroborating testimony from two or more witnesses. But even that safeguard was untrustworthy, for the afflicted witnesses would have to judge what was suspicious in the Invisible World, which only they could see. Pike himself had not observed the afflicted's actions, only heard of them, but these included feats of perception far beyond what God allowed. The Devil hurt the afflicted, and the Devil told them lies.

But did the Prince of Lies act at the behest of a human witch as afflicted and confessors claimed? Pike did not trust their testimony. Why would a witch reveal herself by using magic in court? Surely the Devil hadn't turned reformer. (Unfortunately, whatever Jonathan Corwin might have thought of Pike's two letters is not recorded.)

Boxford

But most people accepted the afflictions at face value. Sixteen-year-old Martha Sprague's torments began early in the month at Boxford, just east of Andover. As a stepdaughter of Moses Tyler, she was kin to Mary Bridges, Mary Post, and other Tyler women, along with assorted Jacksons, Hows, and Cloyses.[54]

Andover

Ephraim Davis's child also began to show symptoms in Andover, and the two visiting Salem Village girls, Mary Walcott and Ann Putnam Jr., were afflicted again along with Sarah Phelps. This apparently happened at the home of Sarah's uncle, John Chandler, the scene of a dramatic spectacle that involved the spear-wielding specters of Martha Carrier's children, assorted Toothakers, Daniel Eames, and some of Rev. Francis Dane's kinswomen.[55]

Besides Timothy Swan, two more grown men were afflicted by this time: Benjamin Abbott (a witness against Martha Carrier), and Lawrence Lacy (husband of confessor of Mary Lacy Sr. and father of Mary Jr.).[56]

August 10, 1692 • Wednesday
Andover

Twenty-two-year-old Elizabeth Johnson Jr. was, as her grandfather Rev. Dane would say, "but simplish at the best." But when officers came to arrest her, neighbors snickered that her mother would be next. Goodwife Abigail Faulkner was furious to hear her sister and niece treated so, and blamed the afflicted. (And indeed, the afflicted were tormented all the while the prisoners were being brought in. Goody Faulkner would be arrested soon after.)[57]

Elizabeth (or Betty) Johnson, and Sarah and Thomas Carrier all confessed to Justice Dudley Bradstreet in Andover. They related how Martha Carrier, rather than the Devil, had baptized them. Seven-year-old Sarah said her mother made her a witch at age six by bringing her the red book to touch, but baptized her in Andrew Foster's pasture the day before Martha went to prison. Just last night, her mother gave her a spear, but Sarah already knew how to hurt by pinching and did so, with Betty Johnson's help, to Sarah Phelps and Ann Putnam Jr.[58]

Ten-year-old Thomas Carrier said he had been a witch only a week since his mother, heralded by a talking yellow bird, appeared with the book and threatened him into obedience. She pulled off his clothes, dunked him in the Shawsheen River saying he was hers forever and ever, then ordered him to torment the Walcott, Putnam, and Phelps girls. He was at John Chandler's as well, in a company of ten that included two women from Ipswich.[59]

Betty Johnson said that Martha Carrier brought her the book, too, told her that she would be saved if she became a witch, and then baptized her with young Sarah Carrier. Betty confessed to attending the great Village witch meeting, and to hurting the girls and men by using the same spear on Benjamin Abbott as on young Ann Putnam.[60]

Justice Bradstreet had his doubts. He collected the examination notes to send with the prisoners to Salem and added a letter admitting that, other than requiring bonds from complainants, he had no experience with such proceedings. His notes only summarized the confessions but made no reference to the crowded circumstances of the questioning. However obvious it seemed at the time, "they were too much urged to confess," Rev. Francis Dane would later write, especially the children. As for his simple granddaughter, Betty, "I fear the common speech that was frequently spread among us of their liberty if they would confess, and the like expression used by some, have brought many into a snare" of false confession.[61]

Dane's own daughter, Abigail Faulkner Sr., was probably also questioned with the children, but she did not confess. "Several that came before me," her father would write, ". . . spake with much sobriety, professing their innocency" even in the face of so many urging them to confess. "We thought we did do well in so doing," Dane would admit, "yet they stood their ground professing they knew nothing, never saw the Devil, never made a covenant with him."

However, "the conceit of specter evidence as an infallible mark did too far prevail with us. . . . Hence we so easily parted with our children when we knew nothing in their lives . . . to suspect them. . . . Hence such strange breeches in families."[62]

Returning from Andover that evening, Ann Putnam Jr. encountered the angry specter of Abigail Faulkner Sr. (Betty Johnson's aunt) which pulled Ann from her horse. The same apparition was also reported during the night's turmoil at Captain Thomas Chandler's garrison. (Thomas, the father of John and William Chandler, was active in Andover's militia, a frequent representative to the General Court. He owned considerable land in town, including the acres his sons farmed, as well as an iron works on the Shawsheen River.)[63]

August 11, 1692 • Thursday
Salem Town

The latest Andover suspects, now including Goody Faulkner, were questioned in Salem by Justices Hathorne, Corwin, and Higginson, as Simon Willard took notes.

Sarah Phelps and Martha Sprague joined the usual afflicted, while Richard Carrier and Mary Lacy Jr. still witnessed among the confessors. The Carrier children enlarged on their original statements. Thomas's notes are lost, but Sarah said that she had been a witch since age six.[64]

"How old are you now?"

"Near eight years old, brother Richard says. I shall be eight years old in November next." She didn't see the Devil when she was baptized in Andrew Foster's pasture, only Betty Johnson with her Toothaker kin. They promised Sarah a black dog, but never gave her one. She didn't use poppets to afflict, for her mother carried her in spirit to pinch the victims directly.

"How did your mother carry you when she was in prison?" asked a justice. (Sarah's reported activities were all recent.)

"She came like a black cat," said the girl. Earlier, she said that a cat had threatened to tear her apart if she would not sign the book.

"How did you know that it was your mother?"

"The cat told me," said Sarah. She related how she hurt the Phelps girl on Saturday with a wooden spear as long as her finger—the spear that the Devil gave to Betty Johnson. But no, Sarah did not attend the great witch meeting.

Betty Johnson said that Martha Carrier and the Devil bullied her into signing the Devil's book (by scratching it with her finger) four years ago at Carrier's house. They also promised she would not be discovered and would have a shilling besides, though she never did see any money. But she hadn't afflicted anyone until her baptism three years past, she said (contradicting what she had told Bradstreet), when the Devil dipped her head in Carrier's well. He looked like a man then, but later appeared as two black cats. She saw Goodwives Carrier and Toothaker with two of her children and Captain Flood at the Village meeting. (John Flood, the militia leader who had failed to save York, Maine, the January before, was included in the same May 28 complaint as Martha Carrier.) As Betty named them, she saw their specters appear and heard them threaten dismemberment. There were six score (one hundred-twenty) at that meeting, Betty went on, including a short minister.[65]

Her first victim had been either Benjamin Abbott or Lawrence Lacy, and then Sarah Phelps. Betty herself sat on Goodman Lacy's stomach to hurt him, but the Toothakers, Carriers, Daniel Eames, Captain Flood, and the Lacy women also hurt folk, she said. All of them had worked against the late Goody Ballard. They used poppets, Betty explained, producing three of them for the court. One was a piece of birch bark. The second had four strips of cloth each representing a victim—Lawrence Lacy and Ephraim Davis's child, with two others—wound around a center of thread. The third poppet was two strips of cloth rolled up and fastened by three pins to afflict

Benjamin Abbott, James Fry's children, and Abraham Foster's children. Ann Putnam she hurt with a spear. The justices asked if the spear was wood or iron, but she answered vaguely that either would do. Richard Carrier and Mary Lacy Jr. both verified seeing their mothers and Goody Toothaker with those very poppets.

When asked where her familiars drank, Betty presented a knuckle with a red place on it, and said there were two other spots. Some women searched her at the justices' order and found the two, both small, one behind her arm.

Betty's aunt Abigail, wife of Francis Faulkner and daughter to Rev. Dane, would not confess. The afflicted convulsed as soon as she entered the room, and again when she looked at them to deny the charge.[66]

"I know nothing of it," she said.

"Do you not see?" exclaimed a justice.

"Yes, but it is the Devil does it in my shape."

Her specter had shadowed them for months, said Mary Walcott and Ann Putnam Jr., but didn't hurt them until recently. "She pulled me off my horse," said Ann. They both collapsed at Goody Faulkner's glance and recovered at her touch.

Betty Johnson urged her aunt "to confess the truth for the credit of her town." Goody Faulkner refused. God did not require her to confess what she was *not* guilty of. She worried a handkerchief as she spoke.

The justices noticed, after Sarah Phelps said the woman hurt her, that the afflicted reacted every time Goody Faulkner squeezed the cloth. They took it from her and set it on their table, but the seizures continued. The girls cried that the specters of Daniel Eames and Captain Flood were working the handkerchief.

Goody Faulkner said that she was sorry they were afflicted, but the justices saw her dry eyes and lack of emotion. (Everyone knew witches could not cry.) Until the defendant's touch again restored her, Mary Warren's convulsions were so bad she seemed to be dragged under the table. When the girls first came to Andover, Goody Faulkner remarked, her gaze had not produced fits. That, the girls countered, was *before* she began to afflict them. Someone told how Goody Faulkner was suspected of conjuring with a sieve, but she denied it. That matter was already cleared up, she said. Nevertheless, the court held her for tormenting Martha Sprague and Sarah Phelps.[67]

Pemaquid, Maine

Far Eastward at Pemaquid, Governor William Phips and his men saw the arrival of the mast fleet, guarded by a forty-gun man-of-war, sent from London to collect tall timber for the Royal Navy's shipwrights. The fleet brought John Usher, a Boston bookseller, once treasurer under Andros and now lieutenant governor of New Hampshire. Usher was, in fact, in charge, for Governor Samuel Allen stayed in England. (Usher's brother, the merchant, Hezekiah, escaped from the province after two weeks of house arrest in Boston for witchcraft, probably for New Hampshire.) The fleet also brought news of an English naval victory over France in May, and the foiling of a plot to restore King James. This cheered the New Englanders, but the Canadian French were still active. Phips ordered Major Benjamin Church to lead his men to the Penobscot and Kennebec Rivers and to retaliate for recent raids by destroying the locals' corn and other provisions. He could kill at his discretion, but was to bring all captives—men, women, and children—safely to Phips, and generally to keep a rein on his men.[68]

Phips, meanwhile, saw to the building of Fort William Henry. It was to be a stone square over 700 feet around, with walls six feet thick at the level of the twenty-eight gun ports. The south wall would face the sea and a twenty-nine-foot-high round tower would rise to the west.[69]

August 12, 1692 • Friday
Salem

With the date of the next executions set for a week away, George Jacobs Sr. dictated a new will to replace the one he had drawn in January. Again, he left the use of his homestead to his wife Mary, though only during her widowhood this time. Then it would pass to his grandson George because his son, the boy's father, had escaped to who knew where. He eliminated a bequest to his daughter Ann and to her husband John Andrews, who had been of little or no help lately. Then he had the scribe write between the lines to add a legacy of £10 in silver for his granddaughter Margaret, who had repented her accusations and confession.[70]

Whether or not she would live to inherit the sum was as uncertain as whether there would be much left to inherit. After old Jacobs was condemned, but before his execution, Sheriff George Corwin confiscated £79-13-0 worth of his farm and domestic goods. The sheriff's men took five cows, five swine, one mare, and assorted fowls. They hauled off eight loads of hay, enough apples to make twelve barrels of cider, and sixty bushels of Indian corn. They took twelve shillings in coin, a gold thumb ring, £10 worth of bedding, two brass kettles, and a quantity of pewter and furniture. His wife's wedding ring (technically her husband's property) was among the "abundance of small things . . . took clear away," though she would, with some difficulty, retrieve it. They also raided the pantry, for Mary Jacobs had to buy back some of her own provisions. But the supply was scant and she was fortunate to find neighbors willing to help her as her relatives apparently were not.[71]

The 1641 "Body of Liberties" had forbidden such confiscations, but that law contradicted English Common Law, and the new Charter forbade any local law "repugnant" to English law. Now the Crown government was required to confiscate a convicted felon's personal goods. In witchcraft cases this did *not* include the felon's land or his widow's dower. (There is no record that widow Susanna Martin's goods were taken. The other executed women had been married, and everything a married woman owned, except for her clothes, belonged to her husband.)

Ordinarily, nothing was to be taken until a defendant was convicted. The goods were supposed to support the imprisoned felon and his family, then pass to the Crown after the felon's death. The sheriff was to inventory the goods, and to require that the family find sureties against "embezzlement" lest the property disappear by sale or gift before the government collected it. If they couldn't pay the bond, then the sheriff was to remove the goods into the town's custody.[72]

Just when Proctor's possessions were taken is uncertain. (His July 23 reference to "undone" estates may have meant neglected farms.) He and his wife, however, were probably indicted by then, as they had faced the Grand Jury on June 30. They were both still alive when Sheriff Corwin confiscated many of Proctor's possessions, either after their conviction, or because the family could not pay the newly required sureties. At some point Corwin sold some of Proctor's cattle at half their market value; and slaughtered, salted, and shipped the rest in casks to the West Indies. His actions were apparently within British law, but the distressed families thought him *far* too thorough. Proctor's children would tell how the Sheriff's men dumped beer from a barrel to take the barrel, and emptied broth from a pot to seize the pot.[73]

Daniel Eames's vengeful specter was busy this evening. It fell upon Mary Lacy Jr. and Betty Johnson in the Salem jail. It also struck in Andover against Timothy Swan, the Ingalls's child, Mary Walcott, Mary Warren, and Ann Putnam Jr.[74]

August 13, 1692 • Saturday
Salem Town

One almanac predicted refreshing winds which, if true, would have been a relief this sweltering week.[75]

Daniel Eames lived with his wife and children in his parents' household and worked the family farm in Boxford, near the Andover line. He had been absent from his family recently, and was given to shocking language when at home (or at least made careless references to the Devil). His specter had tormented the afflicted for some time, and now he was under arrest.[76]

John Higginson Jr. and other Salem magistrates interviewed several of the confessing witches about Eames. Betty Johnson related how she had accompanied his spirit by night when he afflicted the Phelps child by pinching and stabbing a poppet. His specter had also hurt Betty herself and young Mary Lacy in prison the day before—an incident that Richard Carrier verified. Likewise Mary Walcott described her own torments in Andover, seconded by Ann Putnam Jr. and Mary Warren.

All of the afflicted fell when officers brought Daniel Eames into the room.

"What? Do you act your witchcraft before us?" exclaimed one of the magistrates.

Eames denied the charge, and denied running away, although he had been "southward" for two or three months. "He that is the Great Judge," he said (meaning God), "knows that I never did covenant with the Devil. I do not know anything of it. I never signed to no book, nor never [saw] Satan or any of his instruments that I know of."

But when Eames turned toward the afflicted, five of them collapsed and needed his touch to revive them.

He admitted that he had once dreamed that some witches tried to tempt him "to sign to Satan, but I resisted."

"Are you certain you were asleep?" a magistrate asked.

"I was asleep, to be sure."

Neighbor Samuel Farnum related local gossip that Eames had followed the Devil over Five Mile Pond. Daniel tried to explain what that incident had really been about, but to no avail. The most wrongdoing he would admit to was the time when, "as a little boy" he had drunk a bottle of his father's rum.

Mary Warren insisted that Eames was the same as the specter that had afflicted her during Goody Faulkner's examination. When questioned directly, the confessors Mary Post and Goodwife Mary Bridges both said that they knew who he was ("He is my height," said Mary Post), but neither believed he was a witch. Ann Putnam Jr., however, insisted that Eames had been made a witch "at a brook."

Bridges (perhaps Mary's husband John) was certain Eames himself had boasted of going about with the Devil on the Sabbath.

"I did not know but I might say so," Eames said cautiously, "but I belie myself."

However, Betty Johnson saw the shape of a young man near Eames with the black man (the Devil). Both she and Mary Lacy Jr. identified the specter as one seen before with the defendant's specter, Abigail Faulkner's nephew Dean* Robinson: the Lacys' near neighbor, and Rev. Dane's grandson.[77]

Lynn

Some time in August, Elizabeth Wellman of Lynn saw Sarah Cole, the cooper's wife, walking ahead of her through the open woods. Sarah wore "the skirt of her garment" (the topmost of several petticoats) over her neck like a shawl, and was accompanied by "a black thing of considerable bigness." The creature disappeared near a fallen tree. Goody Cole walked on, turned to face Goody Wellman, swung her clasped hands together twice over her head, and vanished.[78]

---

*The family name was spelled as both "Dean" and "Dane."

August 14, 1692 • Sunday
Salem Village

Lately, certain members of the Salem Village Church seemed always absent from worship: John and Mary Tarbell, Samuel and Mary Nurse, and Peter Cloyse—all kin to the executed Rebecca Nurse and her sisters. After services, the church members (the men) remained to discuss the situation. They chose a committee, comprised of Rev. Samuel Parris, both deacons, and Nathaniel Putnam, to speak with the absentees.[79]

August 15, 1692 • Monday
Rowley and Boxford

The specter of Margaret Scott pinched and choked Sarah Coleman in Rowley, while the apparition of Samuel Wardwell began to torment Martha Sprague in Boxford.[80]

August 16, 1692 • Tuesday
Cambridge

Increase Mather and Samuel Sewall, among other worthies, were in Cambridge for the funeral of thirty-five-year-old Rev. Nathaniel Gookin who died yesterday (possibly of the fever that was going around). It was so hot that the body of Captain Ruggles was also buried today, before his friend Sewall even knew of the death, though he died only the night before.[81]

August 17, 1692 • Wednesday
Boston

Rev. William Milborne's June 25 petition had nettled the governor's council, but now some of its members felt uneasy about the trials. John Foster had asked the advice of Cotton Mather, who replied today by letter. Spectral evidence, Mather repeated yet again, was *not* enough to prove a suspect's guilt, since it was well known that devils could assume any appearance they pleased, even Cotton Mather's. Optimistically he assumed, however, that the judges also had sufficient evidence of a more mundane sort against the accused.[82]

Since the problem was to prove that a human had *deliberately* communed with the Devil (wrote Mather), it must be remembered that the Devil could be busy with an involuntary subject. No one could trust the touch test, for the accused might be victimized by devils as much as the afflicted were. Therefore, Mather hoped that the judges would dismiss any case they might doubt, or at least would accept bail for those with only spectral evidence against them. Even if some were convicted on spectral evidence alone, mightn't exile be sufficient penalty? He would accept such a penalty himself if his specter were seen. Although he knew there was no law to cover this approach, he knew the death penalty had been relaxed before and could be again.

Mather cited a 1645 English Court of Oyer and Terminer for witchcraft, when Parliament appointed clergymen to the bench. That court had convicted no one of the crime and, even if some guilty escaped then, the troubles immediately ceased. (But there was no precedence in Massachusetts for ministers to hold public office while still serving as ministers.)*

Neither this or Mather's other suggestions were acted on.

Boxford

In the two weeks between John Willard's condemnation and the execution date, his wife Margaret somehow managed to "obtain a replevin for him for a little time." (A personal replevin would temporarily reprieve him from prison.) However, the necessary papers had not yet reached Salem. So Goody Willard made her way from Boxford to Salem, hired a horse, and headed for Boston to see for herself about the delay, however, to no avail.[83]

August 18, 1692 • Thursday
Andover

On complaint of Timothy Swan, Mary Walcott, and Ann Putnam Jr., Justice Dudley Bradstreet issued an arrest warrant for Frances Hutchins and Ruth Wilford of Haverhill, and ordered Constable William Starling to take them to Salem. Mrs. Hutchins, a well-to-do widow, had managed her late husband's business during his last, infirm years, even suing debtors when necessary. Forty years earlier she and three other women (including Rev. Nicholas Noyes's mother) were brought to court for violating the sumptuary laws by wearing expensive silk hoods. They were found to have sufficient means to wear silk, however, and Mrs. Hutchins, moreover, deposed that "she was brought up above the ordinary rank." Her son Samuel represented Haverhill in the General Court. Unfortunately her examination is lost.[84]

---

*Stoughton had preached, but was never ordained and retired from the pulpit before seeking public office. John Woodbridge was minister of Newbury for years, retired after parish quarrels, and only then became a magistrate.

Salem Town

On the eve of the executions, Margaret Jacobs received permission to speak with Rev. George Burroughs. She poured out her shame for bearing false witness against him, John Willard, and her own grandfather. She begged Burroughs for forgiveness, which he granted along with his prayers.[85]

Andover

But while Burroughs prayed in the Salem jail, others, including the visiting Salem Village girls, observed his specter conduct a sacramental witch meeting in Andover near John Chandler's home. After the bloody bread and wine, they saw this apparition of Burroughs bid his followers farewell and exhort them to abide by their faith in the Devil by not confessing.[86]

August 19, 1692 • Friday
Salem Town

Haverhill Constable William Starling arrested Mrs. Frances Hutchins, but found no sign of Ruth Wilford. On borrowed horses he set out for Salem with his prisoner and a deputy. Similarly, Rebecca Eames, wife of the Boxford selectman Robert Eames and mother of the accused Daniel Eames, had been arrested and was also en route to Salem for questioning.[87]

But most of the day's traffic were folk heading to the latest executions. Only the local justices (Hathorne, Gedney, and Corwin) might have been present, however. Stoughton and Sewall were in Watertown trying to mediate a dispute among church members as long and virulent—thought not spectral—as that of Salem Village.[88]

Today's hangings attracted an even greater crowd than the previous ones, partly because of Rev. George Burroughs's presence among the condemned. Several other ministers and former ministers attended: Rev. Nicholas Noyes of Salem; John Hale of Beverly; as well as Zachariah Symms, Samuel Cheever, and Cotton Mather from Boston. This was apparently Mather's first trip to Salem this year.

"It would break an heart of stone," Cotton Mather soon wrote, "to have seen what I have lately seen; even poor children . . . from seven to twenty, more or less, confessing their familiarity with devils, but at the same time, in doleful, bitter lamentations . . . expostulating with their execrable parents for devoting them to the Devil in their infancy." Perhaps Martha Carrier's children pleaded with her one last time to confess—a bitter farewell indeed.[89]

John Proctor, waiting in the Salem jail, did not feel spiritually ready to face death and divine judgment. He asked Rev. Noyes to pray with him, but Noyes refused sharply, exasperated that Proctor still would not confess.[90]

When the five condemned—Rev. George Burroughs, Martha Carrier, John Willard, George Jacobs Sr., and John Proctor (three farmers, a minister, and another minister's niece)—were taken away, Elizabeth Proctor remained behind in prison. Her own execution was postponed until after the birth of her child some months in the future, should she survive the ordeal of childbirth in the squalor of the crowded jail.[91]

While the crowd moved through town toward the place of execution, on foot and on horseback behind the slow cart carrying the condemned, it met the Boxford lawmen with Rebecca Eames. Not wanting to miss the executions, her guards left Goody Eames at "the house below the hill" belonging to John Macarter, and joined the throng.[92]

All the condemned insisted that they were innocent, including Martha Carrier, whom the crowd thought one of the most guilty. They earnestly requested that Cotton Mather pray with them, which he (unlike Noyes) did. They asked that their sins and their accusers' sins all be forgiven, and that theirs would be the last innocent blood shed.

Their sincerity and general conduct, especially that of Proctor and Willard, impressed many onlookers. Rev. Burroughs, contained to the last, spoke of his innocence as he stood on the ladder and prayed so movingly that some wept to hear him. He concluded with the Lord's Prayer, appropriate in itself but also a reference to its use as a folk test in the trials. His perfect recitation "did much move unthinking persons" in the crowd (as Samuel Sewall would later put it) even though the disputed Lord's Prayer test could, at best, only indicate possibility, not proof. Some onlookers began to doubt and to question his guilt, but the afflicted said that the Devil stood by him to prompt the lines.[93]

After Burroughs was dead, the people, who had done nothing to help the man at his trial, became restive and angry. Cotton Mather, who had calmed mobs before, spoke to them from his horseback vantage point to remind them (according to a later source) "that the Devil has often been transformed into an angel of light." (Neither the Devil or folk tests were reliable.)[94]

The hangings continued as, one after another, the four men and one woman had their lives strangled to an end. The bodies were buried near the site, some possibly temporarily if the families were to remove them later. Stories circulated of a common grave, where the corpses were so hastily and shallowly covered that Burroughs's chin and hand, and someone else's foot remained above ground.[95]

The crowd broke up and the constables collected Rebecca Eames. Goody Macarter, having just viewed five witches hanged outside her back door, in the unwelcome presence of a stranger whom she believed to be another witch, found a pin run into her foot and was sure specters had done it.[96]

Once before the Salem magistrates, with the executions fresh in her mind, and likely already sharply questioned in Andover, Goody Eames confessed. The Devil had appeared to her as an ugly colt accompanied by a ragged girl a month back, she said, no, two months, three—seven years ago actually. She had promised him allegiance in exchange for "power to avenge herself on them that offended her." Now, at his bidding, "I afflict Mary Warren and another fair face." She said she hurt Timothy Swan with an awl, yet knew nothing of the spear of which the girls complained.[97]

"But can you ask them forgiveness?" asked a magistrate.

"I will fall down on my knees to ask it of them!" she exclaimed. But she would not say she had signed away body and soul in the Devil's book, or on a birch rind, or on anything else. The Devil in the form of a horse carried her spirit about to afflict, but they went alone. The afflicted reminded the court that they had seen the specter of her son Daniel.

"Did you not say," a justice asked, "the Devil baptized your son Daniel?"

"He told me so."

"But did you not touch the book, nor lay your hand on book nor paper?"

"I laid my hand on nothing without it was a piece of board."

"And did you lay your hand on the board when he bid you?"

"Yes."

Mary Lacy Jr. said that Goody Eames's specter boasted how she gave Daniel to the Devil when her son was only two. The defendant remembered none of this, but was able, at the court's order, to take successfully the Warren and Lacy girls by the hand and to ask their forgiveness without sending them into fits. If she did give Daniel to the Devil, she said, it must have been "in an angry fit," (thinking of such curses as, "Devil take you"). "I do not know that he is a witch, but I am afraid he is."

Mary Lacy saw and heard Daniel's specter beside his mother, urging her not to confess. But Goody Eames saw only "a burling* thing before her." She also denied baptizing Daniel in Five Mile Pond as Mary alleged. The reason that she suspected Daniel, Rebecca Eames explained, was because of the "dreadful bad words" and evil wishes that he used when angry.

If she had dedicated twenty-eight-year-old Daniel when he was two, someone pointed out, then she must have been a witch even longer than she had admitted. She stuck to the seven years, but told of feeling discontented ever since, for the Devil lurked about daily disguised as a rat or mouse. Rebecca alluded to a rumor that Sarah Parker was a witch, but could say only that she had heard that the Devil once kissed Sarah after she was crossed in love. As for hurting Timothy Swan, only her son Daniel had helped with that (contradicting her earlier statement that she and the Devil went alone to afflict). She hoped he would confess.

---

*"Burling" might be boiling.

Had she been at the executions that morning? a magistrate asked. She saw a few folk, Rebecca said, when she was in the house below the hill. The woman of the house had a pin stuck in her foot, but *that* was none of her doing. She had consented to other afflictions, but only during the last three months. The Devil had not required it earlier.

"But doth not the Devil threaten to tear you in pieces if you do not do what he says?"

"Yes, he threatens to tear me in pieces."

"But did you use to go to meeting on Sabbath days?"

"Yes, but not so often as I should have done."

Rebecca Eames was held for trial. Too rattled to recall a word of what she had just told the court, or what anyone had said to her, she remembered hearing only the name of Queen Mary—for the court acted in the names of their Majesties, King William and Queen Mary. (Worse yet, fellow prisoners Abigail Hobbs and Mary Lacy Jr. would hound her to confess for the next four days. *They* knew she was an old witch, they said, spitting in her face, and Goody Eames would soon hang like the others.)[98]

After sunset, kin of the dead may have recovered some of the bodies. (Family traditions would tell of John Proctor's and old George Jacobs's bodies being brought home for burial near their houses. George Jacobs Jr. was still out of the country, but someone, grandson George perhaps, may have transported old Jacobs's corpse home across Northfields. For, in the nineteenth century, a lone grave on the Jacobs's farm would be opened to reveal the skeleton of a very old, utterly toothless man.)[99]

August 20, 1692 • Saturday
Salem Town

Margaret Jacobs wrote her father from Salem prison to beg his prayers that they might have "a joyous and happy meeting in Heaven." She knew not how soon she too might be executed "by means of the afflicted persons." Grandfather was dead "and all his estate seized for the King" (though not, in fact, his real estate). At least she had not continued in the wretched lie of her false confession, but because the magistrates would not believe her when she told the truth, she remained in this "loathsome dungeon." Mother (also imprisoned since May for witchcraft) "is very crazy," but sent love to her husband and to her brother, Margaret's uncle Daniel Andrews.[100]

(Margaret's father George Jr. had fled "out of the country" when he and his brother-in-law were accused in May. But Daniel Andrews had returned to the area before mid-July, when he signed a petition in favor of Rebecca Nurse. However, he evidently did little for his Jacobs kin.)[101]

Giles Corey's specter barged into the house in Northfields where John DeRich worked, and took, over John's objections, some platters for a witches' feast. Fortunately, Corey returned them an hour later, presumably before John's employers knew about it, but *not* before the other servants noticed their absence.[102]

Haverhill

Constable William Starling finally caught the elusive Ruth Wilford and had her under lock and key in time for Sabbath.[103]

August 21, 1692 • Sunday
Salem Village

In Salem Village this Sabbath, Jane Hutchinson, Benjamin's wife, endured violent pain throughout her body, the worst of it in her head and teeth. The agony began soon after the last execution, and was now so intense that her husband fetched Mary Walcott. Mary reported old Sarah Buckley and her widowed daughter Mary Witheridge to be working on Goody Hutchinson. Just knowing the cause relieved Jane a bit, but her husband also told the sheriff what harm his prisoners' specters were causing. Once the women were fettered, Jane Hutchinson felt "tolerable well."[104]

Boston

The Sunday before their trials, Philip and Mary English escaped from Boston and headed for New York. Because the affluent English had put up a £4,000 bond, he and his wife were allowed to rent better quarters in the Boston jailer's own house, and to have Philip's six-year-old daughter Susanna stay with them. (This was a daughter born during their marriage, but apparently *not* to Mary.)* According to later family lore, the Reverends Samuel Willard and Joshua Moody engineered their flight after the latter preached pointedly on Matthew 10:23: "They that are persecuted in one city, let them flee to another." The Englishes may have taken their eldest daughter Mary with them, but arranged for four other children to board in Boston during their absence. Susanna stayed in the household of fellow prisoner Captain John Alden.[105]

Moody and Willard may well have had a hand in the Englishes' escape. Gossip called Rev. Moody's wife a witch. Rev. Willard's son John helped Nathaniel and Elizabeth Cary escape. All summer, Willard's sermons described the Devil as

---

*The printed Salem Vital Records list all the English children as Mary's, but the daughter Susanna, when deposing about her father's estate in 1738, referred to Philip and Mary as "my father Philip English and wife." Novelist Nathaniel Hawthorne knew the family story that Philip had illegitimate sons, but heard it from a branch of the family descended from Susanna.

ravening after souls like a man-eating lion and urged compassion for the accused, because the Devil delighted in lies and slanders. Willard also criticized the legal handling of the cases, certain that it only made matters worse. The three judges who belonged to his congregation—Samuel Sewall, Peter Sergeant, and Wait-Still Winthrop—apparently ignored his advice, but other people took loud and angry offense at his objections.[106]

Little was done to recapture the fugitives now in New York, but English worried about his properties. He knew their flight forfeited his £4,000 bond, but thought that would be the only loss, since neither he nor his wife had been tried or convicted. But escape was a crime in itself, subject to forfeitures, and in any case the government was hard pressed to provide for the growing prison population, which would number about a hundred. (Fortunately, the court seems to have omitted the proper outlawry proceedings against English and against Nathaniel Cary—otherwise their lands would also have been at risk.)[107]

Salem

Soon after, Sheriff George Corwin and his men confiscated all they could lay their hands on from English's Salem home and warehouses—a windfall total of £1,183-2-0. Besides his furniture, plate, and personal wine cellar, they took clapboards, cordage, lumber, grain, cod, and cod hooks from the warehouses. They seized yardgoods, women's shoes, and three gross of thimbles from the shop in the house. They took six swine, and the bob-tailed cow from the yard. All this, according to English, was "squandered," mostly to feed the imprisoned witch suspects. Neighbors scavenged among the rest. (Descendants would tell of two hundred sheep seized from Salem's great pasture, family portraits from the house, and seven vessels from the harbor—not listed in English's own account.)[108]

August 22, 1692 • Monday
Salem

Sabbath over, Constable William Starling finally got Ruth Wilford to Salem with the help of a hired deputy and a couple of hired horses. Between the Wilford and Hutchins women, Starling was out of pocket £1-8-0. Goody Wilford was likely examined today (but the notes are lost).[109]

August 23, 1692 • Tuesday
Ipswich

The almanacs predicted a clear, bright day and before it was over, Goody Mary Green escaped the Ipswich jail a second time, again aided by her brother-in-law John Shepard.[110]

***
Boston

The Devil continued to harass Mercy Short in Boston. He was God, he claimed, he was Christ. He would carry her to Heaven. "It makes me think of Goody Carrier," Mercy punned. "Pray, whither did you *carry* her?" The Devil had long since been tossed from Heaven for his pride, she continued. "They that follow you will mistake the way to Heaven, I'll promise 'em. He that has the Devil for his leader must be content with Hell for his lodgings."

Earlier, the Devil had assured her that there was no Hell, but now he bluffed that one might come and go from there at will. "Ye lying wretch! I have catched you in an hundred lies," said Mercy. "Pray then, let Sarah Good come. If I could see her, I am confident she would tell me that Hell is a terrible place; I know there is no coming out."

Cotton Mather, who took notes of Mercy's conversations, continued to pray for her, as did many of the neighbors, until the seizures and visions subsided. Her weeks of affliction included a twelve-day fast, but at some point in late summer, the problems lessened. When the specters departed they left her temporarily blind as if lightning had struck her. Mercy's sight returned within a few days. Although still sickly, she resumed normal life for the time being.[111]

August 24, 1692 • Wednesday
Ipswich

Constable William Baker recaptured Goody Green after searching for her a night and a day, and once again returned her to Ipswich jail.[112]

Boston

A group of fifteen French and Indian hostages, including children, arrived in Boston from the Eastward. Jean de St. Aubin, who had traded with the *Bostonaise* in the past, was among them with his family.[113]

August 25, 1692 • Thursday
Boston

The weekly lecture was hosted, in Boston, by the First Church, where it was observed as a fast on behalf of the witchcraft cases and the continuing effects of drought.[114]

Salem

Several Andover area girls continued to be haunted by suspects related to confessor Mary Bridges, the Hows, Sarah Cloyse, and Rev. Francis Dane.

Constable Ephraim Foster escorted Goody Bridges's five daughters and step-daughters to Salem, all accused of tormenting their sixteen-year-old stepcousin Martha Sprague and the constable's thirteen-year-old daughter Rose. (Rebecca Eames was Rose's grandmother and the recently hanged Elizabeth How a great aunt.) Martha and Rose joined the afflicted witnesses and confessors who included Mary Warren, Richard Carrier, and the defendants' own sister Mary Post.[115]

Faced by Justices Gedney, Hathorne, Corwin, and Higginson, *all* the sisters confessed.* (They had probably already been questioned in Andover.) The older ones held out longer before joining the "witnesses" to urge the next sister also to confess. Simon Willard, the day's scribe, noted that the defendants answered the questions dry-eyed, as the afflicted fell at their glance and recovered at their touch. But once the accused confessed and convinced the afflicted of their repentance, they could take their accusers' hands with no ill effect. The defendants burst into tears at this not unexpected turn of events, and confessed to all accusations—time, place, and incident—sobbing over and over, "Yes, I did. I am sorry for it. Pray forgive me."[116]

They all said that the Devil had appeared to them, and each admitted to tormenting people and to attending witch meetings, especially the one at Chandler's a week earlier. Yet, if the questions were the same, their stories were all slightly different. They encountered the Devil as a pig, a cat, a yellow bird, a white bird, a bear, and a dark man (who sometimes claimed to be Jesus). He brought an inkwell full of some red liquid when Susanna Post signed. But Hannah Post cut her own fingertip to sign in blood and even showed the court her scar.

The sisters implicated more suspects. Some, like Abigail Faulkner, were already under arrest; others, like Sarah Bridges's aunt Elizabeth How, were dead. But Susanna Post named three laborers: John Howard, Elizabeth How's brother John Jackson Sr., and his son John Jr.

Hannah Post was herself afflicted after she confessed. She said that she saw the specter of Martha Emerson now, and admitted to being struck by the constable at the Tyler's house last week while invisible.

Thirteen-year-old Mary Bridges Jr. said that her sisters helped her hurt folk with image magic, but would not say she had learned it from witches. She did it when the Devil ordered, but the dead had taught her how.

According to Sarah Bridges, only one innocent man had been imprisoned with the real witches: Abbott of Ipswich (Arthur Abbott, not the "hilly-faced" Nehemiah of Topsfield, who was likewise released.) The magistrates, aware of changing public sentiment, also asked if she thought the afflicted were witches. Ah, no, said Sarah. They were honest people who helped expose *real* witches.

As these confessions seemed to verify other suspicions, Joseph Tyler of Boxford (Martha Sprague's stepbrother), and Andover constable Ephraim Foster entered

---

*The order of examination seems to be Hannah Post, Sarah Bridges, Mary Bridges Jr., and Susanna Post.

complaints against John Jackson (Sr. *and* Jr.) and John Howard for tormenting Martha Sprague and the constable's daughter Rose Foster.

Andover

But this action did not ease the girls' torments. After the men returned to Andover, they both saw Abigail Martin afflicted (by specters from the Barker and Marston families, she said). Sixteen-year-old Martha Sprague saw this, too. Consequently, Abigail's father Samuel Martin and Martha's stepfather Moses Tyler filed complaints locally against William Barker Sr. and his nieces Mary Barker and Goodwife Mary Marston. Justice Dudley Bradstreet addressed the warrant to Constable Ephraim Foster who lived in the same neighborhood near the Boxford line as the suspects, but no arrests were made just yet.[117]

August 26, 1692 • Friday
Rowley

While John Jackson's specter again throttled Martha Sprague in Boxford this evening, the man himself was at work in Rowley for Captain Wycomb. (Wycomb's own daughter had been afflicted by Margaret Scott's specter.) Nevertheless, Jackson, his son, and the other suspect, John Howard, were soon in the custody of Deputy Sheriff George Herrick.[118]

August 26–27, 1692 • Friday–Saturday
Quebec, Canada

John Nelson, meanwhile, was still a hostage in Quebec. Due to his status as a gentleman, his skill in languages, and his reputation for kindness to French captives in Boston, he lived in the chateau of the governor himself: Louis de Baude, Count de Frontenac. Nelson was forbidden to write letters, but was allowed to walk about town under guard.[119]

Two weeks earlier, Nelson had seen two men-of-war sail into Quebec from France with the yearly supply fleet. Through daily business conversations with various Canadians and with Sachem Madockawando of the Penobscots (for Nelson spoke Algonquin as well as French), he learned of France's latest plan against New England. With the season too late to attack Hudson Bay as planned, the two men-of-war under Pierre d'Iberville would now sail a few hundred Canadian soldiers around Acadia to join St. Castine, Madockawando, and 200 to 300 of their men. This force would commandeer all smaller vessels from Port Royal down the coast, and would then attack Wells, the Isles of Shoals, Piscataqua, and eventually Boston.

Nelson found a pair of French soldiers, Arnaud DuVignon and Francois Albert, who were preparing to desert south to New York with a party of escaping Dutch and English hostages. He bribed them with thirteen French crowns to take a letter to Boston, and wrote a warning over August 26 and 27. His guard discovered the first attempt and confiscated his inkhorn. He finished the second in bed under the sheets whenever the guard left the room. The French ships needed another twelve to fifteen days of preparation, Nelson wrote, and a month more to reach New England. His messengers could walk the distance in about twenty-two days, but his part in this warning *must* be kept secret.

August 27, 1692 • Saturday
Salem

Hathorne and the other justices convened in Salem, probably at Thomas Beadle's tavern, with Simon Willard taking notes.[120]

"He is coming!" the afflicted shouted, and convulsed even before the senior John Jackson entered the room. He had suffered odd moods ever since a summer of deep and nearly fatal melancholy in his youth. Later, he quarreled with his wife, who soon after froze to death in a spring snow storm while crossing the Rowley Marshes to her father's house. Jackson had been strangely unwilling to look for her then. But whatever he did, from eating to working, he *over*did; and whatever he decided, whether foolish or the present knowledge of his own innocence, remained firm.[121]

Martha Sprague, Rose Foster, and Mary Warren all said Jackson hurt them. "I desire to cry to God to keep both me and mine from this sin," he replied. "I never did it since the day I was born."

"If you be innocent," said a justice, "you can look upon them that are afflicted." But when Jackson tried, Martha Sprague and Mary Warren fell over and had to be revived by his touch. "Look, how you afflict them," chided the justice.

"No, indeed. I never did it."

Hannah Post, Mary Walcott, and Ann Putnam Jr. related his and his son's spectral behavior at John Chandler's the night before the last executions: drinking, then tipping his hat to George Burroughs before hastening away. The court ordered that he look at Hannah Post after she testified, but he could not bring himself to gaze directly. He looked down instead, the result being that she was less afflicted than usual. But the Putnam and Walcott girls fell writhing, as did Sarah Bridges when she was brought in. Sarah did not recognize him when she recovered, but Mary Lacy Jr. did. "Yes, I saw him last night," she said, then convulsed.[122]

Richard Carrier also said that he saw Jackson last night. Jackson protested that he was in Rowley working at Captain Wycomb's then. *These* people, he added, were not in their right minds. Whereupon Mary Warren fell as if struck, saying he hit her on the head. Onlookers saw something cloud-like drift from her head cloth, and what that could be if it were *not* spectral they could not tell. Jackson was carried off to jail, still firmly unrepentant and denying any devilish baptism.[123]

The convulsions began all over again as soon as twenty-two-year old John Jackson Jr. entered. "Can you tell why these fall down?" a magistrate asked. But John volunteered only that his Aunt How had bewitched him four years earlier. The Devil had appeared to him then as a black man, he added, and had lurked about keeping him awake nights, but neither brought the book nor baptized him. John was baptized only once, in Rev. Phillip's meeting house. The Devil mentioned a book, however, when he appeared looking like cats and like John's own Aunt How.[124]

The defendant spoke hesitantly and the afflicted cried that John's father stood by him invisibly demanding he not confess. John agreed, burst into tears, and blubbered that his father had bewitched him.

"Was your Aunt How a witch?" asked a magistrate. (She had already been hanged for that crime.)

"Yes, she afflicted me. When I was at work in the field she come and looked upon me, and tore down the fence, and my head fell of aching. When she looked on me, there was a black spot on my hat as if it was burnt."

"But you say your Aunt How and your father bewitched you. When did your father bewitch you?" He would not answer, so the court called witnesses: the afflicted. All claimed to have seen him torment them the night before, and all fell writhing. John had to revive them with his touch, and made a good deal of noise about it. "Much like a fool," Simon Willard noted.

John Howard was trusted enough in 1684 to be in charge of sweeping the Rowley meeting house and ringing its bell. His examination (which is lost) probably went the same as the others', for he was taken to Ipswich jail with the Jacksons where prisonkeeper Thomas Fossey began their bills. (At some point during their stay there, blacksmith Thomas Manning would fit the three with fetters, an expense of five shillings apiece.)[125]

While in Salem, Martha Sprague and Rose Foster felt pinched and choked by the specters of William Barker Sr., Mary Marston, and Mary Barker.[126]

Boxford and Andover

Abigail Martin was also tormented, though whether or not she went to Salem is unclear, since all the girls were afflicted at the Tyler house in Boxford come evening. Warrants for the Barker and Marston suspects had been issued on Thursday, yet the law, so busy of late, had not hurried to catch them. Barker spent all of this Saturday harvesting his hay and English corn just over the line in Andover.[127]

August 28, 1692 • Sunday
Salem

The dog days ended as Sirius moved on, but the drought did not. By order of governor and council, Massachusetts observed this Sabbath as a day of fasting and prayer "to seek mercy from God in relation to the present afflicted state of things in both Englands" (as the Salem Church put it), "and an exhortation by repeated prayer and fasting to keep the wheel of prayer in continual motion . . . 'til our God hath spoke peace to us."[128]

Andover

But there was no peace in Andover for Abigail Martin or Rose Foster, both tormented by specters of their neighbors Mary Marston and Mary Barker.[129]

Reading

Nor was there peace for widow Mary Marshall, harassed by shapes in Reading. One of these, she assumed, was her neighbor Mary Taylor.[130]

Lynn

Nor was there peace in Lynn. Sarah Cole, second wife of the cooper John, had a visit from her Salem sister-in-law, also named Sarah and married to tailor Abraham Cole. The guest praised her hostess's children in a fulsome manner that their mother thought suspicious. (As many cultures agreed, such praise in a time of high infant mortality only attracted evil spirits and reflected the praiser's envy.) Sure enough, both Cole children took sick—four-year-old Samuel and two-year-old Anna, who saw her aunt's threatening specter. The frightened mother found pins jabbed into her daughter's skin among the bites and scratches, and saw blood stream from her nose after an invisible blow.[131]

The Cole family had other trouble around this time. John the cooper discussed his intention to join the Lynn church with his neighbor John Brown near the end of August. "All church members were devils," Sarah interrupted (as

Brown would remember it), and "her husband was going to be a devil, too."
Brown admonished her for such an accusation, but Goody Cole did not reply.
She only "looked steadfastly" at Brown, who soon after fell ill. He had also quarreled with her over a fine for damages done by her pigs. After that incident, a
perfectly good Indian pudding, made of corn meal and molasses, turned as red
as blood pudding.[132]

August 29, 1692 • Monday
Salem

Constable Ephraim Foster rounded up William Barker Sr. and his nieces Mary
Barker and Goodwife Mary Marston, then brought them from Andover to Salem,
along with their accusers to be questioned* before Justices Bartholomew Gedney,
John Hathorne, Jonathan Corwin, and John Higginson, Jr.[133]

Mary Barker, the thirteen-year-old daughter of an Andover church deacon, felt
relatively confident during the trip that she would be freed after questioning (by
Gedney, Hathorne, and Corwin). But although she first denied the charges, she
soon confessed and blamed Goodwives Faulkner and Johnson of forcing her, by
threats of dismemberment, to sign the Devil's book last summer. Now she tormented the girls at the Devil's command, and had attended the Salem Village witch
meeting. The court asked why Mary hadn't admitted to baptism in Five Mile Pond,
as her specter had boasted to Martha Sprague. Mary, beginning to suffer hysterical
symptoms, replied that "there was such a load and weight at her stomach that hindered her from speaking." She had given herself up body and soul to the Devil,
she continued, for his promise to forgive all her sins. But now she felt lost from
God and from all good people. The only recent demonic apparition was a fly that
ordered her to afflict "these poor creatures." She had thought herself "brave and
clever" before when the Devil promised concealment, but now she was terribly
sorry. If she remembered any more, she would tell them.[134]

Goodwife Mary Marston (when questioned by Gedney, Hathorne, and Higginson)
denied hurting the afflicted directly, but said that she gave the Devil permission to do
it for her a week ago last Monday. But as Abigail Martin and Martha Sprague choked
and writhed before her, she amended the story. Last *winter* when her husband John
was absent and she home alone, a dark man appeared in the room to bid her serve

---

*The order of these examinations is unclear. The different combinations of justices listed
suggest a certain coming and going. Barker's specter ceased to afflict after his confession,
but it was still active at the end of Mary Marston's examination.

and believe in him. He brought pen, ink, and a book of papers sewn together, which she marked. Only then did he reveal that he was the Devil. He promised that she would be happy, yet turned threatening when she refused his will.[135]

But no, her involvement *really* started three years past during a bout of melancholy following her mother's death. Although the Devil had taught her to afflict from a distance by squeezing her hands, she still traveled in spirit to hurt the folks at the Tylers' home and at Salem with William and Mary Barker. Despite her confession, the girls continued to fall at her glance over and over, and require her touch to revive them. The Devil and William Barker's specter stood by her, claimed young Mary Lacy and Martha Sprague. Goody Marston admitted to riding a pole to the Village meeting, but said no more. The specters, Martha Sprague reported, would not let her.

William Barker likewise confessed to the signing, the torments, and the meetings when Gedney, Hathorne, Corwin, and Higginson questioned him. The Devil had come to him three years earlier in the guise of a black man with one cloven foot. When Barker pleaded his large family and many debts, the Devil promised smoothly to pay what was owed and to let Baker's family live comfortably thereafter. The Devil's plan, explained Barker, was to replace Christianity with Devil worship beginning at Salem Village, because folk there were already divided against their minister. Satan promised that his followers would live bravely, in equality, with no future resurrection or judgment, no punishment or even shame for sin. Baker identified Mr. Busse as the ringleader of the Village witch meeting (rather than George Burroughs), and said that the attending grandees told him there were 307 witches in the country (only the Connecticut ones no longer traveled up here to afflict). All the witches were furious that the afflicted were exposing them and wanted the afflicted to be thought witches. But they were *not*, said Barker. The afflicted were innocent and performed a good service. Only the guilty were being jailed. Barker asked pardon of the afflicted which they granted. As expected, his glance no longer hurt them.[136]

Samuel Martin and Moses Tyler entered complaints before Salem justices Gedney, Hathorne, and Higginson, against widow Elizabeth Johnson and her daughter Abigail for afflicting Martha Sprague and Samuel's daughter Abigail Martin. (When Goody Johnson's son brought her news of this menacing development, she was not much surprised, but remarked that "she was sure *she* was no witch.")[137]

August 30, 1692 • Tuesday
Andover

Andover Constable John Ballard, recently widowed by alleged witchcraft, arrested Elizabeth and Abigail Johnson—his minister's daughter and granddaughter. The constable thought it uncanny that Goody Johnson knew why he arrived at her door, though the neighbors had snickered for weeks over the possibility.[138]

Salem

The usual magistrates questioned the two suspects in Salem while Simon Willard took notes. Like her older simple sister Betty, eleven-year-old Abigail Johnson, confessed, probably snared by the fact that she once lived with her kinswoman Martha Carrier.[139]

Elizabeth Johnson Sr., not long widowed, had been sued with her son Francis a year back for a debt owed by her husband's estate, and had to put up a £100 bond to avoid arrest. Unlike her sister Abigail Faulkner, Elizabeth was (as her father, Rev. Francis Dane, would write) "weak, incapacious, [and] fearful." Now, confronted by the afflicted, she confessed. Goody Johnson was unsure when she became a witch, but thought it was since her other daughter's arrest three weeks earlier. The Devil woke her one night for permission to afflict with her specter, but she didn't sign anything.[140]

"Come, be thorough," said a justice. "In all likelihood you have been long in this snare."

"Sundry years," she said. "Pray for me for it is true. I have been long in this snare," but not for more than three or four years. The Devil came in the guise of a white bird to her house by day at first, then in the likeness of a dark man. Yes, she had signed the book with a black smudge from her finger.

"How long has the child that is here been a witch?" asked a justice, referring to Abigail.

"Five years I suppose," for she "lived at Goody Carrier's."

The court wanted to know more about how the Devil recruited her. Was William Barker there?

"No, he has not been, oh, so long. It was my sister Abigail Faulkner—"Goody Johnson suddenly reacted, as if to a specter.

"Who stands before you now? Is it not the sister Faulkner?"

"Yes. She threatens to tear me in pieces if I confess." Her vengeful sister had been a witch no longer than herself, she said, for both were baptized in Five Mile Pond with many others, including their blind cousin James How (devoted husband to, and now widower of, the hanged Elizabeth).

"But did you give the children to the Devil?"

"No," she said and turned to her daughter Abigail. "I do not know that this girl is a witch."

"What number of witches be there in all?"

"It may be . . . I do not know." She named some of the other suspects attending the witch meetings, and thought Mr. Busse had brought the wine.

"How did it taste?"

"It has been bitter to me, I am sure."

"But why," one of the justices thought to ask about the witches, "do they afflict now [when] they are daily brought out?"

"The Devil makes them do it."

"Come," another prodded, "you that have been a witch so long—you do not thoroughly confess. You know who you have afflicted." She admitted to hurting Sarah Phelps and three of Samuel Martin's children, but her sister and Sarah Parker had helped.

"Then do you know Sarah Parker to be [a] witch?"

"I know she afflicted those, or else I afflicted none." But she wasn't sure about all of her victims. "I know not what my spirit did," for when it was out of her body, she was left "in a cold, dampish, melancholy condition."

The court still wanted to know how long Goody Johnson had been a witch. She tried to subtract the numbers in her head and estimated that twenty-five years back,* after three of her children had been born, the Devil had appeared as a black bird. But she did not sign until a year later with her sister Abigail Falkner. She was to serve the Devil thirty years in return for glory, happiness, and joy, but all he gave her was a familiar like a brown puppy. Elizabeth did not know her son Stephen was a witch, she said, watching an apparition form before her eyes. The afflicted saw this vision too, certain it was Stephen. They accepted Goody Johnson's confession and took her hand unharmed.[141]

The accused sister, Goody Abigail Faulkner Sr., was brought from Salem prison to face the magistrates again. She still insisted on her innocence, but did admit anger toward the neighbors for laughing at her niece, and against the afflicted for accusing her family. But maybe, she said as her confidence weakened, this was enough to let the Devil in. She *had* squeezed her hands together in anger, but did not afflict the girls. The Devil did. Except, perhaps, she said, breaking down at last, at Captain Thomas Chandler's garrison home the night after Justice Dudley Bradstreet questioned her niece.[142]

---

*She and Stephen Johnson Sr. married in 1661, and in 1662 confessed to fornication before their marriage.

Unlike the Andover women, who were conscience-stricken after their false confessions, William Barker Sr. wrote a further statement from prison. He added 500 swashbuckling "blades" armed with rapiers to the Salem Village meeting, and blamed his signing of the Devil's book on fellow prisoners Abigail Faulkner and Elizabeth Johnson.[143]

August 31, 1692 • Wednesday
Salem

Rebecca Eames had confessed on August 19 after viewing the hangings. Now, after days of harassment from fellow prisoners Abigail Hobbs and Mary Lacy Jr., she confessed more. She was indeed baptized in Five Mile Pond, Rebecca told Hathorne and Corwin, with her son Daniel, who had been a wizard for thirteen years. They had both tormented Timothy Swan in Andover with Widow Toothaker and Goody Faulkner. Goody Eames herself had been a witch for twenty-six years, after smudging a black fingerprint in the Devil's book. When she realized what she had done, she was filled with such a horror of conscience that she fetched a rope to hang herself and a razor to slit her throat. It was her great sin of adultery! she blurted. *That* was how the Devil got hold over her, for he promised that no one would find out.[144]

(Whether Rebecca's adultery was committed or only contemplated is not clear. Her husband would eventually take Zerubabel Endicott—who had testified against Mary Bradbury—to court on the matter, but Endicott would deny everything.)[145]

Salem Village

In Salem Village, which was calmer now that the turmoil had moved to Andover, the church committee (assigned to see why certain members avoided meeting) decided to wait before proceeding further. Samuel Nurse and his wife did, sometimes, attend, they found. Tarbell was "sick, unmeet for discourse," while Peter Cloyse was hardly at home since he was in Ipswich so often visiting his jailed wife.[146]

Boxford

Apparitions of widow Mary Parker, William Barker's son Will Jr. and members of the Wardwell family hounded Martha Sprague, Sarah Phelps, and Rose Foster (the Andover constable's daughter) at the Tyler household. Invisible witches forced the girls to frolic with them hour after hour until the girls thought they would die.[147]

Andover

Rose's mother Hannah, daughter of confessor Rebecca Eames and sister of foul-mouthed Daniel, was similarly forced by specters to dance about her own home today.[148]

The specter of Samuel Wardwell was especially active, for he was arrested by evening, leaving his wife Sarah alone with seven children and the knowledge that Martha Sprague's accusation had taken her husband away. Goody Wardwell caught one of the children into her arms and, in a rush of anger, turned the hug into a squeeze. Martha Sprague and Rose Foster, meanwhile, felt Goody Wardwell's specter torture her and, before long, Sarah and her two oldest children were arrested as well.[149]

9

SEPTEMBER 1692

I question not but your honors ... would not be guilty of innocent blood for the world. But by my own innocency, I know you are in the wrong way. ... I cannot, I dare not, belie my own soul.

—Mary Esty to the Judges

September 1, 1692 • Thursday
Salem Town

By morning, four of the Wardwell family (the five youngest children had to shift for themselves) were in Constable Ephraim Foster's custody and on the road from Andover to Salem: Samuel, his wife Sarah, their nineteen-year-old daughter, Mercy, and Sarah's twenty-one-year old daughter, Sarah Hawkes. (Young Sarah was the only child of her mother's first marriage to wealthy Adam Hawkes, whose grandchildren were as old as his bride.) Through her Hooper brothers and sisters, Goodwife Sarah Wardwell was kin to the Ballards and Walcotts, and it was her late brother William Hooper whose house had burned while his corpse lay inside. Thirteen years earlier, their mother Elizabeth had been called a witch, but that led only to a slander suit against the accuser.[1]

Foster also arrested two fourteen-year-old Andover boys: William Barker Jr. (whose father had confessed) and Rev. Francis Dane's grandson, Stephen Johnson (whose mother, sisters, and aunt were already in prison).[2]

The suspects had likely been questioned earlier in Andover. In Salem they faced Justices Gedney, Hathorne, Corwin, and Higginson. The afflicted witnesses included not only Martha Sprague, Abigail Martin, and Rose Foster, but the confessors Sarah Bridges, Hannah Post, Mary Warren, and Mary Lacy Jr. All the accused confessed, though the elder Wardwells pleaded innocence longer.[3]

Samuel Wardwell, carpenter and farmer, was well known for his fortune telling. After first denying the charge, he said that he fell into the Devil's snare from discontent at the amount of work that he could do, and from his habit of telling fortunes—some of which came true. He would also bid the Devil to take stray beasts that trampled his fields. Perhaps that invoked Satan.

Constable Ephraim Foster (whose wife had been forced to dance by specters) told the court how Wardwell once said that he could will cattle to come to him. Cautioned to be truthful, Wardwell allowed that twenty years before, when twenty-six and newly spurned in love by one of the Barker girls, he had seen cats and the form of a man behind Captain Bradstreet's house. The stranger called himself a Prince of the Air and promised that Wardwell would live comfortably and be captain of the militia (instead of Dudley Bradstreet) in return for service and honor. Wardwell had signed this Devil's book with a black square, and had agreed to covenant until the age of sixty. About a week later, the man reappeared to repeat the same claims and promises, but had yet to fulfill any of them. The Devil became angry when Wardwell insisted on family prayer, but forced him to afflict only during the last fortnight. By pinching his coat and buttons, said Wardwell, he commissioned the Devil to torment. Martha Sprague was the first victim, but two Reading women (Mary Lily* and Hannah Tyler) helped, all at the Devil's orders.[4]

Sarah Hawkes, like her stepfather, had meddled with fortune telling and had turned the sieve and shears the previous winter. Because of this dabbling, she said, the Devil came and made her scrawl allegiance on a paper that hung before her in midair. First, he appeared as "a black man"† (as he did when he baptized her in Five Mile Pond last month), then as a shadow, but now he took her thoughts away. She had seen a dozen strangers fly on poles to the great meeting in Salem Village. Most were women but "one of the men was tall, the other short and fat." (Riding through the air on a pole or broomstick was rare in English witch cases. Tituba had

---

*Examination notes say "Mary Lilly," but Jane Lilly would be arrested.
†"Black" could refer to hair, skin, clothing, or just a shadowy figure.

mentioned it at the first examination, and now the court apparently questioned every Andover suspect about the practice as stories of the great witch meetings grew. The specters *had* to have flown in order to travel so far so quickly.) Sarah's specter was also at Moses Tyler's house with other witches to make their victims sing and dance. She implicated all the other defendants including her own family.

The afflicted were in constant turmoil during today's examinations, falling at a suspect's glance and reviving at a touch. Martha Sprague and Rose Foster also convulsed when Sarah Hawkes fumbled off her glove. Sarah agreed she worked magic with the glove and, when touching Martha to revive her, gripped her wrist so tightly that it swelled. A second, lighter touch relieved the painful swelling. Despite all that she admitted, the afflicted still reacted as if she were concealing something. When she entered the building and climbed the stairs, said Sarah, "she had a mind to confess but now cannot." Once she "remembered" she had renounced her former baptism, the afflicted were no longer repelled, and Sarah took their hands freely.[5]

Sarah Hawkes's younger half-sister, Mercy Wardwell, was courted earlier in the summer by a young man whom she did not love. When she declined his offer of marriage, he threatened to drown himself. Other people assured her that she would never find such another to love her. The Devil, she now said, appeared to her as the disconsolate suitor or as a dog, and, occasionally, even claimed to be God or Christ. She promised to serve him for twenty years and sealed the vow with a red mark on a scrap of paper. He wished her to curse and to lie and to bid the Devil take this and that in anger. She and her family, she said, hurt the Sprague and Foster girls. Then Mercy Wardwell fell silent a moment and gazed at the table. She said that "when she looked down upon the table, she could confess nothing." Nevertheless, she described hurting Timothy Swan, and being baptized by the Devil at home, her face plunged in a pail of water. But the afflicted continued to be repelled until Gedney asked Mercy if the Devil had made her renounce her former baptism. Once she admitted this, the other girls—as with her sister—were able to take her hand safely.[6]

Goodwife Sarah Wardwell, with a noticeable lack of emotion, finally agreed that the Devil had come as a man six years earlier, had promised her anything she wanted "as clothing and the like," and had presented a paper for her to mark. Why, asked the magistrates, did she not weep to admit such a thing? She could not weep, she explained, for she had given herself body and soul to the Devil, who rebaptized her face down in the Shawsheen River. She walked home alone after that, but rode to

the Village meeting on the same pole with Carrier, Foster, and a Goody Laurence.* Daughter Sarah Hawkes had also admitted to this trip, but her mother did not think she could have been involved more than a month. Goody Wardwell certainly had not known her husband was a witch until *after* she joined. In court, her glance had struck down confessors Sarah Bridges and Hannah Post as well as the other afflicted Andover and Salem girls. Goody Wardwell admitted magically pinching Martha Sprague the evening before in anger that the girl's accusation had gotten her husband arrested. Now she was sorry for all her misdeeds and renounced the Devil.[7]

The two fourteen-year-old boys likewise confessed. Each described how he hurt Martha Sprague by squeezing his own hands together. But while Will Barker Jr., whose father had confessed on Monday, did not deny the accusations of the afflicted, he also said that he did not remember doing any of it. Will first saw the Devil in dog shape six days earlier while fetching home cows from the evening woods. After a sleepless night Will met the black man—a man dressed in black, he explained, with perhaps black skin as well. The boy promised him loyalty in exchange for a suit of clothes (which he never received) and dipped his fingertip into an inkwell of red stuff that the Devil brought. He marked his fingerprint on the offered page, but hadn't been rebaptized. Martha Sprague, tormented by his glance all along, insisted that he had flown on a pole to Five Mile Pond with Goody Parker for the rite. Breathless with fear, his stomach in knots, Will struggled to confess as desired. Once he told the court how the Devil dipped his head into the pond and made him renounce his first baptism, saying he forgot before, his stomach felt better, and he could take the afflicted's hands. He hated the Devil, he said, as he too, implicated the other suspects.[8]

Stephen Johnson, Elizabeth's son and Rev. Dane's grandson, said that the Devil came to him at midsummer when Stephen was alone hilling corn. On the first day he appeared as a talking speckled bird somewhat smaller than a pigeon, and on the second as a black cat. On the third day he came as a man, and asked him to sign the book. He produced only a sheet of paper, however, which Stephen marked with a fingerprint of his own blood, promising to afflict for a year in exchange for French fall shoes, which he never received.

After a day working for Benjamin Abbott, Stephen had stripped for a swim in the Shawsheen River when the Devil appeared, accompanied by two men and two

---

*"Goody Laurence" might be Goody Mary Lacy, wife of Laurence Lacy, whose last name was variously spelled Lahauce and Lahorse.

maids. He told the boy that he must be rebaptized, then "took him up and flung in his whole body over the bank into the water." But now Stephen was sorry and renounced the Devil.[9]

Once the four younger suspects confessed, they, at least, were able to take the afflicted by the hand with no ill effect. Today's confessors were held not only for tormenting the afflicted, but also for covenanting with the Devil.

Yet, the afflicted were *still* troubled. The shape of Henry Salter went after Mary Walcott, while widow Mary Parker's tormented Martha Sprague and Goodwife Hannah Bixby (kin to the Danes and Abbotts and aunt of the afflicted Phelps children).[10]

Boston

In Boston, some of the high court judges enjoyed the happier events of their own lives. Samuel Sewall attended the wedding of Major John Richards and Mistress Anne Winthrop (Wait-Still Winthrop's sister). Justice William Stoughton performed the civil ceremony, "at the house of Madame Usher," Sewall's distant kin. (Sewall managed Bridget Usher's Boston property while she lived in England, estranged from her husband Hezekiah who was currently in hiding from a witchcraft charge.)[11]

Sewall did not describe the festivities, but other weddings he attended included the singing of Psalms as well as refreshments. At a later occasion, Sewall made note of "bride-cake, good wine, burgundy and canary, good beer, oranges, pears." (Doubtless the celebration was more restrained than the prolonged merrymaking in rowdy Marblehead. There the guests would march around the marriage bed throwing old shoes and stockings at the bride and groom within it.)[12]

September 2, 1692 • Friday
Salem Town

Widow Mary Parker of Andover was well provided for by her late husband's will. She was, however, related by marriage to the Mrs. Frances Hutchins arrested earlier. Mary's daughter Sarah was also arrested around now, the young woman whom Rebecca Eames said the Devil had kissed.[13]

Magistrates Gedney, Hathorne, Corwin, and Higginson presided, while Salem merchant William Murray took notes. Several of the afflicted (Mary Warren, Sarah Churchill, Hannah Post, Sarah Bridges, and Mercy Wardwell) fell writhing as soon as Parker's name was announced, before she even entered the room. Goody Parker had to revive them with her touch before questioning could even begin. She denied hurting Martha Sprague and Sarah Phelps, and denied being in the Devil's snare. But Martha Sprague was certain this was the same person as the tormenting specter, even though, as the defendant noted, "There is another of the same name in Andover"—her sister-in-law.

Martha collapsed when the defendant looked at her, and no sooner was she revived than Mary Lacy Jr. did the same, followed, twice, by Mercy Wardwell. William Barker insisted Parker went with him the evening before to afflict Martha Sprague. (Sr. or Jr. is not specified in the record, but as both had confessed, neither ought to have had a still-active specter.) Mercy Wardwell recovered enough to identify the defendant as one of Timothy Swan's tormentors, and Mary Warren convulsed so violently that blood ran from her mouth. Attendants found a pin jabbed into her hand as well, but managed to drag her to Goody Parker to be touched. It was *this* Mary Parker, said Warren, once she could speak, who tormented her. She had seen her spirit, perched on a beam above the court, at one of the examinations in Salem Village. However, Mary Parker seems to have resisted confessing, an increasing rarity at this feverish point in the witch panic.[14]

Boston

Cotton Mather, like his father and most of the ministers, questioned the court's use of spectral evidence. He had advised caution all summer, prayed with the condemned as well as for the afflicted, and prayed privately to God "for a good issue of the calamities wherein He had permitted the evil angels to ensnare this miserable country." Mather also delivered a sermon to the witch suspects in Boston prison on Acts 24:25, an episode where a wrongly accused Paul is sent from pillar to post seeking justice in the Roman courts, for Cotton knew that innocent people had been accused along with those that seemed most guilty.[15]

But if some were innocent, Mather nevertheless believed that *something* diabolical was happening, and that the condemned parties were genuinely guilty. The sometimes furious reactions of the trials' opponents now alarmed him. Having calmed the potentially dangerous mob that might have turned on Andros in 1689, Mather worried that instead of leading to a reform of court methods, the present discontent would halt *all* hope of orderly procedure. It might even lead to violence against the judges. "The honorable judges," he wrote, were "men of an excellent spirit" who did not undertake their task lightly. Indeed, those whom he knew personally had begun "this thorny business" with "a very great aversion" (as far as he could see), and continued it with "heart-breaking solicitudes." He trusted that they, at least, could sift fact from confusion to reach the truth, that they could recognize a non-witch if and when they tried one.

Since no one else seemed to be doing so, Mather had begun to write his own account of the trials. Deodat Lawson's *A Brief and True Narrative of Some Remarkable Passages Relating to Sundry Persons Afflicted by Witchcraft* covered only the earliest events. Increase Mather's work in progress focused on spectral evidence.

Cotton Mather decided to present the court's view of the extensively tangled problem. He had not attended any of the trials himself, but those who had been there, such as his father, Increase, told him that the defendants had been found guilty by more than spectral evidence.

So, trusting in the judges' good sense, and encouraged by "the advice of others," he sent a preliminary portion of his book to Chief Justice William Stoughton. The manuscript included the fact of present tensions and accused innocents, though he respectfully asked Stoughton to verify this. (Rev. William Milborne had been arrested after writing a more direct criticism in June.) "A distinct account of the trials which have passed" would, he hoped, illustrate the actual problems that the court faced, and "vindicate the country, as well as the judges and juries." He asked if Stoughton or the other judges might write a few lines signifying their approval.[16]

Stoughton did approve the project, but—as he was the judge most certain that an innocent person's appearance could *not* be counterfeited as a tormenting specter—he apparently disregarded all the manuscript's politely phrased precautions. Mather, receiving no contradiction or complaint, unfortunately did not look more directly into the matter himself.

A few streets away, Edward Randolph, surveyor general of customs and New England's longtime nemesis, cornered Governor Phips in his own coach house. Years before, when Randolph arrived to dissolve the Bay's original Charter, he had sailed on Phips's borrowed treasure-seeking ship. (Its near piratical crew had harassed him the whole way.) Some years later, after Phips had acquired his treasure, his knighthood, and the office of Provost Marshall General of the Dominion, the two had argued on a Boston street when Randolph prevented Phips from assuming that office. Now Randolph was assigned to check customs violations from the Carolinas northward. He had already heard from the royally appointed Collector of Customs Jahleel Brenton about how the local Naval Office prevented Brenton from fulfilling his duty.

Phips insisted local commerce was no concern of the commissioners of trade. (Massachusetts law ignored British regulations to exempt certain goods and coastal traders from taxation.) The encounter ended with ill feelings all around. It was true that Phips sat as an admiralty judge on cases involving his own prize ships, that his officers did not enforce all the customary taxes, and that he paid the seamen pressed to his service with shares from the captured prizes. (It was also true that Brenton, as Randolph had already heard, overcharged on the fees, then kept the difference, plus some of the Crown's share as well.)[17]

September 3, 1692 • Saturday
Gloucester

Even with spectral French and Indian forces absent, Gloucester remained beset. If Eleanor Babson had lived with her son and son-in-law's family out at the remote farm before, she had perhaps moved back to Gloucester Harbor by now. For something was tormenting both her and her neighbor, Mistress Mary Sargent, wife of the local justice of the peace. Someone, probably Eleanor's son Ebenezer Babson, invited some of the visionary girls to view and diagnose the ailing women. When they arrived, the afflicted girls reported the specters of Goodwives Margaret Prince and Elizabeth Dicer torturing both women.[18]

Salem Town

While Ebenezer rode to Salem with the returning girls, Elizabeth Hubbard confided that Goody Prince's specter had said that she (Elizabeth) would be unable to testify against her in court. Nevertheless, Babson filed complaints against Prince and Dicer, and posted a bond to prosecute. Magistrates Gedney, Hathorne, and Corwin at once issued an arrest warrant to Gloucester's constable, Thomas Riggs Jr.[19]

September 4, 1692 • Sunday
Reading

Mary Walcott felt nearly choked to death in Salem by Henry Salter's specter. And Sabbath or not, Constable John Parker of Reading had arrest warrants to serve Jane Lilly, Mary Taylor, and probably also Mary Coleson, the schoolmaster's wife. When he told Goodwife Mary Taylor that the complainant was her neighbor Mrs. Mary Marshall, Goody Taylor was furious. "Whoever lived to see would find Mrs. Marshall's case like Mary Warren's," she flared, for they had long been at odds. "There was a hot pot now, and a hotter pot preparing for her."[20]

The constable also went after Mary Coleson's daughter Elizabeth, who, although complained of in mid-May, had hidden herself so well that many thought she had gone abroad. Now the authorities suspected that she was hiding in the house of her grandmother, Lydia Dustin, herself arrested late April. Constable Parker proceeded to the Dustin house with William Arnall and Arnall's dog. Parker found the outer front door open and the inner door locked. As Arnall stepped into the entry, both men heard another door open inside the closed room.[21]

Arnall dashed around the building in time to see Elizabeth Coleson sprint from the back door toward the neighbor's field. She needn't run, he shouted, for they would surely catch her. Elizabeth, saving her breath, did not speak, but only shook her hand, as if striking at him, Arnall thought. She tripped, fell, sprang up, and, petticoats and all, still eluded him. Arnall set his dog on her, but the dog only loped around the woman and would not touch her. Elizabeth ran behind a stone wall backed by a few bushes, Arnall close behind. Yet, when he reached the wall, he saw no one, either in the next field or among the bushes. He jogged toward a nearby fence and came face to face with a large cat. Fearing this animal was the witch, he called his dog, but the dog headed in the opposite direction. Arnall struck with his stick and the cat streaked under the fence and out of sight. That was the last Arnall and Parker saw of either Elizabeth Coleson or the cat that day.

September 5, 1692 • Monday
Boston

When the governor and council met in Boston's Town House, it was nothing but expenses: £8 to Mary Matson for nursing two wounded men from the *Conception* since June; £15 to James Maxwell, the legislature's doorkeeper and messenger; £8-17-0 to Boston's selectmen for the new warning beacon on Beacon Hill.[22]

Cambridge

The ministers gathered as usual at Harvard College, with Rev. Samuel Willard as moderator, to discuss improvements for the institution. Several of the men present were also members of Harvard's new corporation, which also met today for the granting of degrees. As part of making the college a university, the corporation voted Baccalaureates for John Leverett and William Brattle, once tutors there, and a *Gradum Doctoratus in Theologia* to President Increase Mather. (The faction that still resented him for not retrieving the old charter intact would call the degree stolen and self proclaimed.)[23]

Salem

In Salem, Hathorne, Higginson, and the other magistrates questioned two women from Gloucester and three from Reading, while Simon Willard took notes and Rev. Nicholas Noyes, Eleazer Keyser, and Ebenezer Babson observed. The afflicted now included Elizabeth Hubbard, Mrs. Mary Marshall, eighteen-year-old Elizabeth and fourteen-year-old Alice Booth and their new sister-in-law Elizabeth, the sixteen-year-old wife of their brother George. (Young Goody Booth, sister of the late Daniel Wilkins of Will's Hill, was presently four months gone with child—only *two* months after her wedding.) They were joined by confessors Hannah and Susanna Post, Mary Lacy Jr., Sarah Churchill, Mary Warren, and Samuel Wardwell. Most convulsed at the sight of the defendants and required repeated application of the touch test.[24]

Elizabeth Dicer had been fined thirteen years past for calling Mary English's mother "a black-mouthed witch and a thief." She was married to William Dicer, a refugee from Saco who now worked as a mariner out of Boston, but she was arrested in Gloucester, where her married daughter lived. The notes to her case are lost, but she, too, was held for trial.[25]

Over thirty years before, gossip had hinted that Margaret Prince of Gloucester was a witch, until she sued the source for slander. She was now recently widowed after decades of abuse from a drunken husband.[26]

"Margaret Prince," said Hathorne, "you are complained of for afflicting the widow Babson and William Sargent's wife of Cape Ann. What say you?"

"I am innocent."

Asked what he knew of the defendant, Sargent said that his sister was "grievously afflicted and the afflicted person said that this woman hurt her." He, however, had always heard that her reputation "was well and good."

Elizabeth Booth and Mary Warren, meanwhile, fell convulsing and needed Goody Prince's touch to revive. The court asked Elizabeth Booth and her younger sister-in-law Goodwife Elizabeth Booth if they had seen the defendant.

"No," they said. "Not before." But they and two others fell in fits needing Prince to revive them. Now all said she hurt them. They also said that they saw the Devil on the table, then stood transfixed at the apparition of a coffin.

Elizabeth Hubbard claimed that Goody Prince's specter had boasted of killing Mrs. Duncan of Cape Ann (Mrs. Sargent's mother who had recently died in July). The defendant exclaimed that she had never hurt Duncan, nor Babson, nor anyone, not "for a thousand worlds."

And at that, Elizabeth was struck dumb for a time, just as Prince's specter had said would happen, said Ebenezer Babson, just as the girl had told him.

Margaret Prince was held her for trial, but apparently she did not break down and confess.

The three Reading women—Jane Lilly, Mary Taylor, and Mary Coleson—were all kin or friends of old Lydia Dustin, and Mrs. Mary Marshall suspected them all.[27]

"Mrs. Marshall," asked John Hathorne, once Mary Taylor denied the charges, "did you accuse this woman?"[28]

"Yes," said Mrs. Marshall. "She has beat me, and come to persuade me to worship her god, and told me my God could not save me. And she has brought images to me."

The court ordered Goody Taylor to look squarely at her accuser, who convulsed. With such a "dangerous eye," the court observed, it was no wonder that folk thought her a witch. Even while she denied it, Hannah Post, young Mary Lacy, and Mary Warren had seizures and required her touch to recover. Goody Taylor denied the Devil's baptism, insisting she was baptized only once as a child in Charlestown. She knew nothing of witchcraft except, possibly, some ill will toward Mrs. Marshall for her complaint.

But Mrs. Marshall's brother, Major Jeremiah Swain, disagreed, and said that Taylor had out-and-out threatened not only his sister, but also his wife and others as well.

Although a confessed witch himself, Samuel Wardwell quizzed the defendant as sharply as the magistrates. Had she *never* fallen out with his brother William Hooper? he asked when Goody Taylor denied killing the man. A falling out was easily proved, added Major Swain. Yes, said Wardwell, for they had quarreled when Hooper reclaimed the child whom he had placed with her to wet nurse. Taylor insisted she was home when Hooper's house caught fire, but Wardwell wanted to know about the triumphal meeting afterward, when she, Jane Lilly, and another from Billerica gathered to drink. *Someone*, Major Swain added, drank that funeral wine. Surely, she remembered "the shock," said Wardwell cryptically, "and the shock, and the double shock." Killing Hooper was one shock, he explained to the court, torching the house was another. The "double shock," he hinted, just might be the destruction of Hooper's whole family.

Constable Parker reported Goody Taylor's obscure remarks about a hot pot now and a hotter pot later. She explained that, if Mrs. Marshall wronged her, Hell would be prepared for the liar. But her confidence ebbed and soon she confessed. When she found it difficult to talk, she asked the court's prayers that she might speak the truth, then agreed, after a fashion, that she began tormenting Mrs. Marshall a week ago Sabbath. The Devil that guides destiny, she said to Rev. Noyes and Mr. Keyser, brought her a birch rind to sign, and she promised him worship and honor. It all came of visiting Goody Dustin's house so much last winter. Once Taylor had made a fist and wished ill to Mrs. Marshall at Jane Lilly's house in the presence of Dustin and her daughter. Perhaps that had started it. Mary Taylor too, was held for trial.[29]

"Now you have the opportunity to tell the truth in this matter," the magistrates warned Jane Lilly as the afflicted convulsed. Goody Lilly said the truth was that she knew nothing of it *or* of being in the Devil's snare. When Mary Warren said that the defendant sometimes visited the Proctors' house, Goody Lilly denied anything to do with Proctor or his wife, even though Sarah Churchill swore she saw her visit them in prison. The defendant also denied burning Hooper's house, much less killing him with or without a spear as charged. Of *course*, she would speak the truth, she replied to the court's cautions, "for God was a God of Truth." But her voice went hoarse when she said this phrase. The Devil, Mary Warren reported, choked Goody Lilly when she tried to say, "God of Truth."[30]

Samuel Wardwell described the stolen wine and the five shouts of triumph. It was herself triumphing, he told Goody Lilly, as she ran off after setting Hooper's house ablaze. When Jane Lilly protested that she was home and had never inclined to witchcraft, Major Swain reminded her how often she had frequented Dustin's house. He and a neighbor John Brown knew she was a friend of the arrested Goody Rice as well. But Goody Lilly held to her innocence, for to confess to any of these false charges would deny truth and wrong her soul. Jane Lilly was held for tormenting Mrs. Marshall.[31]

Mrs. Marshall said that her afflictions started when Mary Coleson's mother, widow Lydia Dustin, was arrested. Although others entered the complaint against the old woman, Mrs. Marshall was sure that Goody Coleson's specter was after her for revenge. "These three," she said, "Taylor, Lilly, and Coleson, came to me and said [Rev.] Pierpont sang that Psalm [perhaps Psalm 68:5 or 146:9]: 'God will be a husband to the widow,' but He would be none to me, they said. They told me also, if I had served their god, my husband had been alive yet." (She was, in fact, *twice* widowed, losing both Thomas Clark and Edward Marshall.)[32]

The justices ordered the defendant and her accusers to face each other. Several fell and needed Mary Coleson's reviving touch, including Alice Booth and both Elizabeth Booths.

It was obvious, the justices declared, that the defendant acted witchcraft right before them, and that it seemed likely she had a hand in the deaths of William Hooper *and* Edward Marshall.

If she confessed, said Goody Coleson, she would rather be examined by herself before the magistrates, away from the noisy afflicted.

But this was not done, and the three Reading women were sent to jail in their own county of Middlesex in Cambridge, to join Mary Coleson's imprisoned kin.[33]

The specter of Joseph Emons of Manchester (perhaps the idle shoemaker once of Marblehead) afflicted Mary Warren, so Simon Willard the scribe and Eleazar Keyser, both present for Mary Taylor's examination, entered a complaint against him on Warren's behalf.[34]

Likewise, Thomas Dodd of Marblehead entered a complaint before Justice Higginson against Nicholas Frost, a turbulent Piscataqua mariner, whose shape hurt his daughter Johanna Dodd.[35]

The court completed odds and ends of business. William Barker Sr. signed his August 29 confession. Clerk of the Court Stephen Sewall issued warrants for witnesses to attend the Court of Oyer and Terminer the following day. Both Ipswich prison keeper Thomas Fosse and his wife Elizabeth testified to Mary Esty's good behavior while in his jail. John and Mary Arnold likewise deposed in favor of Goody Esty and her sister Sarah Cloyse for their time in Boston's prison.[36]

But specters of Giles Corey and Margaret Jacobs afflicted John DeRich (whose own mother was in Boston jail and would soon be transferred to Salem). Margaret, he said, threatened to skewer him and to cut him "with a knife bigger than an ordinary knife" for refusing to sign the Devil's book. "She hath done worse before." (Margaret Jacobs, in fact, was so seriously ill with "an imposthume in her head," [an abscess] that her case was postponed.)[37]

Boxford

Several invisible witches broke into Moses Tyler's house tonight, according to the afflicted, who reported the shape of Rev. Francis Dane eyeing them from among the other specters. Perhaps resentment over his decade-old salary dispute had resurfaced in his congregation in addition to the fact that his daughters, granddaughters, a grandson, and a niece were confessors, while two more nieces had been recently hanged: Elizabeth How and Martha Carrier (the supposed queen of Hell). As with others whose specters were seen, Dane had likely criticized the court proceedings.[38]

September 6, 1692 • Tuesday
Salem Town

The Court of Oyer and Terminer sat at noon in Salem to begin trying the cases of Dorcas Hoar, Alice Parker, Giles and Martha Corey, Mary Esty, Ann Pudeator, and Mary Bradbury (though the order and dates of the trials is not clear).[39]

Rev. John Hale of Beverly was summoned to testify concerning his longtime parishioner Dorcas Hoar. For years she had told gloomy prophecies of which child or spouse would die. Hale warned her against the practice, but she only seemed to renounce it. Then fourteen years ago last spring, in 1678, William and Dorcas Hoar, their grown children, and Hale's own maid servant Margaret Lord had systematically robbed the Hales not only of money, but also of clothing, food, small livestock, a necklace (one pearl at a time), the pudding bag, and flour by the pillowcase-ful. When the adult Hales were away, Margaret entertained Dorcas's daughters at the parsonage and terrorized the Hale children into silence. The maid showed his thirteen-year-old daughter Rebecca a book the size of a grammar and promised her that the Hoars could raise the Devil against her with it. Dorcas's daughters and Margaret also threatened her with a hot frying pan, dangled her over the well, and vowed to kill her parents if she told.[40]

When the Hales realized the extent of their losses, Margaret fled. Only then did Rebecca have the courage to tell her father about the threats. The Hoars were found guilty for their part in the thefts, and William Hoar openly threatened Rev. Hale. This was followed by thumps and blows against the Hale house (especially at night and when the master was away) all climaxed by the Hoar children clubbing Hale's white-faced cow to death. Rebecca remained terrified of the family until she found the Scripture: "Fear not them which can kill the body." But her father learned of this information from a friend only after the girl had died at age fifteen.

For all their talk of the Devil, no one was accused of witchcraft in 1678, neither maid nor neighbors. The book that Hale's daughter described contained some kind of diagrams, but inquiry about the volume went nowhere. Goody Hoar claimed that she had sold her copy, but continued to tell fortunes.

Hale had visited her in Boston prison this summer, and asked again about her divining. A shipmaster, she explained, had told her future back when she was first married: that she would live better after her husband died. As for telling Ensign Comings that his wife would die first, well, the woman had "a certain streak under the eye," and she *did* die. But Dorcas had never seen the Devil, only the ghost of Thomas Tuck trying to tell her about some land—and she ran away from *that*.

Other neighbors testified about her prophesies based on the lines and shapes of people's faces, for she practiced the art called physiognomy or metoposcopia. (This, like palmistry, was considered scientific by its practitioners, and dangerously enticing to devils by most ministers.) Goody Hoar had once gazed at Mary Gage's perfectly healthy nine-year-old son and remarked that he hadn't long to live. He died within weeks. When the bereaved mother asked her how she had known, Goody Hoar said that a doctor had taught her and that she owned a doctor's book. It was not surprising that when young David Balch died two years back, he had seen "a confederacy of witches" whispering at the foot of his sick bed: Goody Hoar, Goody Wildes with her daughter, and an unidentified Marblehead woman (perhaps Sarah Wildes's stepdaughter Sarah Bishop and Wilma Read).[41]

Neighbors Rachel Tuck and Hannah Cox related how they and various kin had taken turns sitting up nights three years past when Goody Hoar was ill. As sick as she was, somehow she disappeared from her bed and, when they rushed out to find her, *something* grabbed at the last one out. When they mustered the courage to return, there she was, seated on the steps, fully dressed in cloak and hat.[42]

William Hoar died just the winter before, "untimely" enough for a coroner's jury to examine the body. As John Richards recalled, the widow wrung her hands as the men entered to gaze at her husband's naked corpse. She stamped the floor in a passion. "You wicked wretches. What? Do you think I have murdered my husband?"[43]

Goody Hoar's hair was odd as well. Most of it was short and gray, but at the back of her head it grew darker in a snarled lock four feet, seven inches long. This would ordinarily be coiled under her cap, but once the court discovered, and measured, the oddity, the justices ordered the lock cut off. She protested and explained that she would die (or at least be sick) if it were removed. (Folk belief hinted that imps nested in such snarls and, moreover, that a witch's hair could *not* be cut.) But cut it they did, despite the impropriety of short hair on women, observing that it was as matted as an elf-lock. Even after the shearing of her hair, Goody Hoar was found guilty.[44]

Salem Village

Several more people were afflicted this evening by the specter of Alice Parker: Goody Sarah Bibber, Mary Walcott, Ann Putnam, Jr., and Mary Wardwell who was choked.[45]

September 7, 1692 • Wednesday
Boston

Today was the deadline for towns to submit their censuses of adult, taxable males to the General Court, but no one rushed to comply. (Salem Village's records remained blank all this summer, including July when commissioners were to have been chosen for the task.) The reluctance or confusion was province-wide, however, not just in the afflicted counties.[46]

Edward Randolph again accosted Governor Phips at his home in Boston's North End to complain about uncollected import-export taxes. Phips obliged him to wait at the door, but he was not easy to be rid of. Randolph thrust a copy of his instructions at Phips with a sharp warning and the latter's temper flared. Had Randolph not been a guest under his roof, the governor growled, he would receive a drubbing for such impudence.[47]

Salem

In Salem, the Grand Jury heard testimony concerning Ann Pudeator and Alice Parker of Salem, and Mary Bradbury of Salisbury. Rev. James Allen, Rev. John Pike, magistrate Robert Pike, and other Salisbury neighbors petitioned the court on behalf of Mrs. Bradbury.[48]

Alice Parker of Salem was cited anew for spectral attacks against Mary Warren and Mary Walcott on the day before. Goody Parker had been suspected of witchcraft for some time, and her specter reported by several confessors at the Devil's sacrament in Salem Village. Friction between her and the Warren family had flared after Mary's father neglected to mow Goody Parker's meadow as promised. The woman even came to his house, furious at the delay (which could ruin her crop). Soon after, both Mary's deaf-and-dumb sister *and* her mother fell ill and died.[49]

Other Salem neighbors found Alice Parker uncanny, especially those who had discovered her unconscious in the snow last January. Ten years before, Martha Dutch had observed what a great mercy it was that the local mariners managed to return safely home from sea, and hoped that her own husband would as well. But Goody Parker said, "No, never more in this world." And so, as widow Dutch now deposed, it was. More bluntly, Mary Warren accused the defendant of drowning several mariners, a whole crew even, and Goody Orne's son (washed up dead at his mother's own door).[50]

Alice's fisherman husband, John Parker, dallied in taverns more than she liked. John Westgate recalled how she once stormed into Samuel Beadle's to rail at her husband. When Westgate tried to intervene, she called him a rogue and told him to mind his own business. So he *knew* whose fault it was when, on the walk home later, a great spectral pig pursued him and his dog across Salem.[51]

Quaker Samuel Shattuck had a more damning tale to tell. His afflicted son, whose wits had been turned in 1680 by Bridget Bishop, was further tormented five years later by Goody Parker. She came to call and "fawned upon my wife with very smooth words." Doctors who examined the boy (his limbs and very vitals twisted, his neck and eyes turned awry) were sure he was bewitched. Some neighbors tried a folk remedy which was, although the court did not seem to notice, very close to the countermagic to which Martha Emerson had confessed. They clipped a lock of young Sam's hair one Saturday, said Shattuck, and dropped it in boiling water. The boy shrieked in pain. They then placed the hair in a skillet, but it fell out, though no one was near. They tried this tactic again and Goody Parker came to the door.[52]

As the magic was intended to draw out the witch, word spread that Goody Parker caused the boy's latest ailments. A few days later, Alice, her husband, and some other men confronted the Shattucks at their home. Samuel protested that *he* did not think her guilty, but she didn't believe him and cried, "You are a wicked man! The Lord avenge me of you, the Lord bring vengeance upon you for this wrong!"

Then why, asked one of the men, *did* she come to the house on Saturday?

Well, to sell chickens, she said. But, as Shattuck pointed out, she had had none with her. Because she sold them to a neighbor, she said. But the neighbor was present and claimed that he never bought any.

Pressed to explain those chickens, she said that her son took them to sea as provisions. But her son had gone to sea on *Friday*, her own husband said, so she could not have had any birds on Saturday.

Instead of answering, Goody Parker stalked into the child's sick room to tell Goody Shattuck that she was a wicked woman for her gossip. "I hope I shall see the downfall of you!" she shouted at her.

Not all the witnesses for Mary Esty's trial presented themselves by noon as ordered. Widow Mary Town composed an excuse to the court for her family's absence. They were all ill, she explained, herself, two sons and two daughters, "in a strange condition," bedridden, in fact, and unable to rise. Her daughter Rebecca, moreover, "hath strange fits. Sometimes she is knocked down of a sudden."[53]

Margaret Reddington, kin by marriage to the defendant (and to the Wildes family), did not decline the summons. Three years earlier, she had incautiously confided in Mary Esty about her infirmities, then "fell into a most solemn condition" soon after. Only last summer, a week before the July Thanksgiving, Esty's specter came around offering Goody Reddington tainted meat.[54]

The high court also took depositions about Mary Parker of Andover, while the local justices examined more new suspects: Rebecca Johnson, her daughter Rebecca, Henry Salter, and Mary Tyler.[55]

Since November 1690, Rebecca Johnson had swept the Andover meeting house and rung its bell for meetings and curfew, a job usually held by a man, but apparently suitable for a recent widow at forty shillings a year. Her sister-in-law Elizabeth Johnson and her nieces had confessed; her sister Sarah Cole was afflicted in Lynn; and her own daughter Rebecca Jr. (whose examination is lost) had just been implicated in fortune-telling. Before Hathorne, the other magistrates, and the scribe William Murray, widow Johnson denied practicing witchcraft. But she confirmed her daughter's attempt, the winter before, to divine whether or not her mother's brother-in-law, Moses Hagget (taken captive by the Indians), were dead. It took two people to balance the sieve, but it was the daughter who had learned the spell to recite from Rev. Barnard's maid servant. "'By Saint Peter and Saint Paul, if Hagget be dead, let this sieve turn round,' and so it did."[56]

As Widow Johnson looked at her accusers, young Goody Booth convulsed. Martha Sprague and Rose Foster saw the defendant's specter trounce her, and heard it vow to hurt the young woman's unborn child. Then the other girls convulsed and needed the defendant's touch to revive them. Abigail Martin and Alice Booth were likewise afflicted, with Alice adding that she had seen the woman's shape even at home during a witches' sacrament. Worse still, Rose Foster, Martha Sprague, and Alice Booth all saw the Devil stand beside widow Johnson and her daughter in the court room.[57]

Henry Salter, son of a drunken and neglectful father, had come from Charlestown to Andover as a servant when only a boy. Twice he had been whipped and placed in a leg-lock for running away. Then he and some other hired boys stole, were caught, broke out of the Ipswich jail, and were caught again. Now he farmed in Andover.[58]

In court he had the usual bad luck with eye beams, striking down Mary Warren, Rose Foster, Mary Lacy Jr., and Mary Walcott, who declared that he hurt her on Thursday and nearly choked her last Sabbath. She, Martha Sprague, and Hannah Post had also seen his specter attack Timothy Swan and others. Mary Warren agreed and said that his specter told her that his methods of witchcraft were conjuration by Bible and key, and by sieve and scissors. Right now, she saw the Devil behind him along with two women, a man, and a whole flock of little ones.

"When was it that company of witches were at your house and the white man drove them away?" someone asked Salter (referring to an otherwise lost episode involving the angel).

"I never knew of any such thing," he protested. But after a time he vaguely admitted to telling Goody Lovejoy something that he had since forgotten. He also admitted to lies and drunkenness, but *not* to witchcraft.

Salter, like the other three suspects examined today, were returned to prison to await their trials.[59]

The specter of Mary Tyler, Martha Sprague's step-aunt, was observed tormenting Constable Foster's wife Hannah as well as Ralph Farnum Sr. Farnum was kin to the Tylers and father-in-law of the Benjamin Abbott afflicted by Betty Johnson's specter.[60]

September 8, 1692 • Thursday
Andover

Arrests continued in Andover. One moment Mistress Mary Osgood was watching a stray cat from her door. Suddenly, the yard filled with the constable and his deputies who had come to take her, even though her husband, Captain John Osgood, was one of Andover's leading men, and her son Peter a constable in Salem. The law arrested several others around this time, such as Mrs. Osgood's niece-in-law Eunice Fry. (Her husband, Deacon John Fry, along with Dudley Bradstreet, represented the town in the General Court this year. The deacon was brother of the James Fry who beat Andrew Carrier.) Abigail Barker, sister-in-law to the confessor

William Barker Sr. and aunt to the confessing Barker cousins, was also taken in, as were Rev. Francis Dane's own daughter-in-law Deliverance Dane, and Goodwife Sarah Wilson.[61]

These latest suspects were first brought to the Andover meeting house—the only building large enough to hold all the thronging onlookers. (Earlier examinations may have been held here once the crowds became too large for the magistrate's house.) The afflicted, as the accused later wrote, were "falling into their fits at our coming into their presence, as they said," even before the junior minister, Thomas Barnard, offered the opening prayer. "We were blindfolded. . . . And some led us and laid our hands upon [the afflicted persons], and then they said they were well, and that we were guilty of afflicting them. Whereupon, we were all seized, as prisoners, by a warrant from the justice of the peace [Dudley Bradstreet] and forthwith carried to Salem."[62]

There must have been more to the examination than that. The women may have been among those who "with much sobriety" (according to Rev. Francis Dane) "stood their ground professing they knew nothing, never saw the Devil," even though (as Dane later admitted), "they were too much urged to confess."[63]

As Goodwife Mary Tyler later recalled, she was not really afraid at first because she knew she was innocent. But while she rode to Salem on horseback behind her brother-in-law John Bridges (who was also brother-in-law to Sarah Cloyse, and whose wife and daughters were already imprisoned for witchcraft) he badgered her to confess. Of *course* she was a witch, he told her, as anyone who saw and heard the afflicted would know. Hadn't her touch cured the girls? She insisted she knew nothing about witchcraft, and begged him to stop such talk.[64]

The cavalcade of prisoners and guards, accompanied by Captain Osgood, wound from Andover through Salem Village, and paused for refreshment at Phillips's ordinary. As they remounted to continue the journey, a party of afflicted witnesses overtook them. Although Mrs. Osgood merely glanced at the girls, they convulsed and cried out against her. The prisoners' party had to wait for the others to pass safely from sight before proceeding.[65]

Salem Town

Once in Salem, Goodwife Mary Tyler found herself flanked by John Bridges and Mr. John Emerson, a schoolmaster from Charlestown (nephew and namesake of Gloucester's minister, but no relation to Martha Emerson). Both were utterly convinced of her guilt and both were quick to contradict any denial.[66]

Not only was she a witch, said Emerson, batting at the air close to her face, but she saw the Devil before her very eyes. She wished herself in any dungeon rather than listen to this talk, but held her ground. "Well!" Emerson exclaimed. "I see you will not confess! Well! I will now leave you, and then you are undone, body and soul forever." When Bridges said her confession would not be a lie, she cried, "Good brother, do not say so, for I shall lie if I confess, and then who shall answer unto God for my lie?" But he countered that God would not have let "so many good men to be in such an error about it," and she would surely hang like the rest if she did not admit it, and on and on and on. Goody Tyler lost all confidence in her own mind and confessed to everything.

When Mrs. Mary Osgood faced Justices Hathorne, Higginson, and the rest, the afflicted convulsed time and again. Martha Sprague and Rose Foster both required her touch, then Hannah Post, Mary Lacy Jr., and Betty Johnson. Amid this apparent cause and effect, and the magistrates' accusing questions, Mrs. Osgood agreed that she was a witch, but could not remember when she became one. She certainly *did* know, the magistrates insisted, and she *must* tell.[67]

Frantic from the court's endless badgering, Mrs. Osgood racked her memory for likely details. She had walked in melancholy through her orchard, she said, brooding during an ill period eleven years ago after the birth of her last child. The sight of a cat distracted her attempt to pray to God, she added (thinking of that morning's stray, as she only later explained). So she prayed to the Devil who appeared as a dark man claiming to be God. He brought a book for her to blot with blood from her finger.

Two years ago, she had flown on a pole with Goodwives Tyler, Barker, and Fry to be baptized in Five Mile Pond. She tormented others by concentrating while pinching her bedclothes, which allowed the Devil to torture people in her shape, and by striking them with her eye as she did now in court and at Phillips's ordinary earlier. She admitted to hurting Martha Sprague, Rose Foster, and John Sawdy. (Thirteen-year-old John had been arrested at some unknown date and joined the accusing confessors.)[68]

"Do you know the Devil can take the shape of an innocent person and afflict?" asked a magistrate.

"I believe he cannot."

"Who taught you this way of witchcraft?"

"Satan," she answered. He had also promised her an "abundance of satisfaction and quietness in her future state," but actually she had lived "more miserably and more discontented since. When, last Monday, she and the others went invisibly to Moses Tyler's, she and Mrs. Dane even brought a shape of Rev. Dane so the victims would think their minister tormented them. It hadn't worked.

"What hindered you from accomplishing what you intended?"

"The Lord would not suffer it so to be, that the Devil should afflict in an innocent person's shape." Mrs. Osgood denied attending any of the witch meetings, but then said that the Devil was before her, insisting her confession was a lie. Nevertheless, she declared to the court, it was indeed true.

Something about her actions or about the afflicted's reactions must have seemed different. One of the magistrates asked her husband if he thought her "to be any ways discomposed." Having lived with her so long, said Captain Osgood, he did not think her at all discomposed, but rather had cause to believe her confession.

The magistrates, in the surviving scrap of Deliverance Dane's examination, were especially interested to learn why she and the other witches had brought Rev. Dane's specter with them to torment the afflicted. (Fortunately for her father-in-law, Francis Dane, the magistrates did not believe that he, unlike Rev. George Burroughs, was actually guilty.) Satan had them do it, she said, assuring them that "he would put a sham upon all these things and make people believe that [Dane] did afflict." Yes, she and Mrs. Osgood consented to this.[69]

Like Mrs. Dane, Sarah Wilson and Abigail Barker (whose examinations are lost) were held for covenanting with the Devil. Goody Barker was also held for tormenting Rose Foster and Ralph Farnum Sr. But, as she later explained, she and the rest of them accused others whom they never suspected simply because the magistrates kept repeating that they *did* know these things were true, and they *must* tell.[70]

All six Andover women confessed, along with a later defendant Eunice Fry (wife of the deacon who had quarreled with the Carrier brothers). Afterward, locked in prison, all were horrorstricken as each realized what she had done. Their confession, they later explained, "was no other than what was suggested to us by some gentlemen, they telling us that we were witches, and they knew it, and we knew it, which made us think that it was so. And our understandings, our reason, our faculties, almost gone, we were not capable of judging of our condition; as also the hard measures they used with us rendered us incapable of making our defense, but said anything and everything which they desired, and most of what we said, was but, in effect, a consenting to what they said."

The high court, meanwhile, took testimony concerning Martha Corey and Mary Bradbury, and sent Constable Ephraim Wildes with a second summons for Mary Town's family to present itself for Mary Esty's trial.[71]

Lynn

Sarah Cole of Lynn was home, sitting up close to midnight with her sick children. Suddenly, several people barged in: her sister-in-law Sarah Cole from Salem; the fugitive Elizabeth Coleson; the wife of John Wilkinson of Malden with one of her sisters;* and a ten-year-old girl whom Sarah didn't recognize. One of the women held a foot-long board as broad as her hand and studded with nails through one end. Sarah's two-year-old daughter Ann shrieked that she'd been hit by this board. Immediately, the intruders flickered sideways, like paper cut-outs, and disappeared. The distraught mother remembered how her sister-in-law had praised the children with a suspiciously effusive tone on Fast Day, and how their afflictions began soon after.[72]

September 9, 1692 • Friday
Salem Town

The Grand Jury heard testimony concerning Giles Corey. The court had summoned witnesses to testify about him and his wife, but if he were scheduled to stand trial today, he did not cooperate. Although pleading innocent to all the indictments as they were read, he refused to answer when asked the formality of how he would be tried. Giles was expected to answer, "By God and my country." Until he spoke those precise words, his case could not proceed. This situation, despite his not-guilty plea, was technically known as "standing mute" and, under English law, was punishable by *peine forte et dure* (pressing under heavy weights) until he cooperated. Perhaps he was threatened with this punishment today, but if so, it did no good. The court postponed Giles Corey's trial.[73]

Most of the surviving testimony against Martha Corey dealt with her specter's reported acts, especially during her examination when plenty of people witnessed the seizures that followed her every gesture. There was also Goody Corey's apparent foreknowledge when her neighbors came to check what clothes she wore, and the oddly sudden deaths that followed her quarrels.[74]

---

*John Wilkinson of Malden married Abigail Gowing. Her sisters were Mary Snow, wife of Samuel; Sarah Jenkins, wife of Ezekiel; Priscilla Robbins, wife of William; and Elizabeth Feltch, wife of John. Her sister-in-law was Johanna Gowing, wife of John. Joanna's maiden name may have been Darling, and in that case perhaps kin to the Salem Village Goody Mary Darling whose specter was sighted.

By now, the court had received a petition from Mary Esty and Sarah Cloyse, sisters of the executed Rebecca Nurse. They affirmed their innocence and made three requests. As they could not well speak for themselves and were not allowed council, would the judges please advise them? (Customarily, attorneys did not handle criminal cases until the eighteenth century. Judges were to guard the defendants' rights for, as in England, they took an active part in the proceedings.)[75]

"Whereas we are not conscious to ourselves of any guilt in the least degree of that crime whereof we are now accused," they asked that "those who have had the longest and best knowledge of us, being persons of good report, may be suffered to testify upon oath what they know concerning each of us: viz., Mr. Capen the pastor, and those of the town and church of Topsfield who are ready to say something."

They also asked "that the testimony of witches, or such as are afflicted as is supposed by witches, may not be improved to condemn us without other legal evidences concurring. We hope the honored court and jury will be so tender of the lives of such as we . . . as not to condemn them without a fair and equal hearing of what may be said for us as well as against us."

Evidently, Mary Town and her reluctant family made their way to Salem, for Esty's sister Sarah Cloyse was charged with tormenting her niece Rebecca Town (though little more seems to have been done about trying her).[76]

The evidence against her, Mary Esty thought, was no more than "wiles and subtlety": the spectral attacks that nearly killed Mercy Lewis after Goody Esty's short release from jail; Goody Reddington's old illness; the time something (or someone) pelted Samuel Smith with pebbles during a dark ride home from Goody Esty's after she had rebuked him for rudeness; and the committee of searchers who found a bump that they thought might be a witch's tit.[77]

Besides tormenting the various afflicted in the usual way, Ann Pudeator was also suspected of the slow death of constable Jeremiah Neal's wife, who had died between the defendant's first and second examinations.[78]

According to Mary Warren, Goody Pudeator had knocked young John Turner* headfirst from a cherry tree so that he lay unconscious for a dangerously long time, and was also responsible for the deaths of her own second husband and his first wife.[79]

Isabel, Jacob Pudeator's first wife, had been a notorious drunkard who pawned for drink whatever she could lift from home; who passed out in the streets; and who had threatened to burn the house down if her husband tried to stop her. Ja-

---

*John Turner recovered to live for years in his mansion now called the House of Seven Gables.

cob hired the widowed Ann Greenslett to help tend to his wife in her last delirious days, and both were present the night that Isabel died. It was unclear at the
time whether they merely offered her the rum and brandy that finally did her in,
whether she purloined it herself, or whether they forced it on her. At any rate, Isabel died suddenly; widow Ann Greenslett married Jacob Pudeator; and the matter reached court in November 1680. Little came of it, but a year later Jacob himself was presented for public drunkenness. The following year, Ann was widowed
again and in possession of considerable property.[80]

Samuel Pickworth related how Goody Pudeator's shape, while her body was in
prison, skimmed past him one evening. John Best Sr. told how his late wife, convinced years before that only Pudeator's death would stop her torment, was
pinched black and blue by the defendant's specter. His son John Jr. agreed and
added that when once he drove Goody Pudeator's cattle away from his father's,
the woman somehow knew about it, though he was alone in the woods at the
time. (Her collection of twenty small jars of unidentified greases was no help either.)[81]

Most of the extant testimony against Mrs. Mary Bradbury came from the Endicotts
and the Carrs (Mrs. Ann Putnam's brothers), though her specter seemed the prime
instigator against Timothy Swan. Samuel Endicott told how butter that he bought
from her to provision an ill-fated voyage turned rancid and maggoty. Then, during
a violent tempest in which the ship lost fifteen horses from the leaking hold, he
saw Bradbury's shape on the vessel. Long before that, when they were boys,
Samuel's brother Zerubabal, their father George, and Richard Carr saw Mrs. Bradbury enter her gate and round a corner one Sabbath noon. Immediately, a blue
(gray in color) boar ran out the gate and charged the horse that Carr and his son
were riding. Carr lost sight of the malevolent beast as the horse shied and stum-
bled. But the boys saw it dart into Mrs. Bradbury's window. "I am glad you see it
as well as I," Carr told the boys. He was at odds with Mrs. Bradbury, and was sure
she had transformed herself into the boar.[82]

When James Carr competed with one of Bradbury's sons in courting the same
woman, James was "taken after a strange manner as if [some] living creature did
run about every part of my body ready to tear me to pieces." Dr. Crosby was sure
James was "behagged" and already believed that "Mrs. Bradbury was a great deal
worse than Goody Martin." Crosby's physic did no good, until *after* James struck
back at a spectral cat.[83]

When John Carr died in 1689, some of his kin suspected Mrs. Bradbury's spectral hand in it. Mrs. Bradbury had rebuffed John in his courtship of her granddaughter—the girl was simply too young—and he thereafter grew melancholy,
and then "by degrees much crazed." (His brother William, however, never heard

John complain of Mrs. Bradbury and thought the death was natural.) However, John Carr's vengeful ghost had appeared to his niece, Ann Putnam Jr., at Mrs. Bradbury's initial examination, and Bradbury's specter had tormented young Ann since May. The girl was certain the woman killed her father's sheep and "that horse he took such delight in."[84]

Against this testimony, and the convulsions of the afflicted, stood several petitions presented in her favor by her husband, her minister, the local magistrates, and dozens of neighbors. Yet it was not enough to make the justices wonder if here was a righteous woman wrongly accused, much less convince the court of her innocence.[85]

September 10, 1692 • Saturday
Boston

Elizabeth Coleson still eluded capture. William Arnall thought she might be in Boston and sent a complaint to authorities there. Accordingly, Assistant John Joyliffe issued a warrant to the Suffolk sheriff for her arrest and removal, once captured, to Salem for trial.[86]

Salem Town

All six defendants tried this week—Martha Corey, Mary Esty, Alice Parker, Ann Pudeator, Dorcas Hoar, and Mary Bradbury—were found guilty of witchcraft and sentenced to hang.[87]

In addition, the Grand Jury heard evidence against the confessor Abigail Hobbs, and Ann Foster signed the written version of her July confession with a mark.[88]

Sarah Cole of Salem, the tailor's wife, unnerved more people than just her Lynn inlaws. Salem laborer William Bragg entered a complaint against her and against Hannah Carrol, wife of Salem wheelwright Nathaniel, for afflicting his son Henry. Bragg put up a bond to prosecute and the magistrates Gedney, Hathorne, Corwin, and Higginson issued the arrest warrants.[89]

Lynn

Meanwhile, the suspect's brother-in-law John Cole returned to Lynn and found his household in turmoil. Not only were the children ill, but there had been "strange sights" and sounds. He himself would soon see unexplained cats and dogs.[90]

Salem

Back in Salem, the specter of her stepgrandmother, Joan Penny of Gloucester, began to torment Mary, the daughter of Zebulon Hill. The girl's aunt was the afflicted widow Eleanor Babson and her uncle, the Captain John Hill of Beverly, for a moment mistaken for Captain Alden by one of the Salem Village girls.[91]

***

Salem Town

After the death sentences passed, Ann Pudeator petitioned the court to protest its use of such "altogether false and untrue" testimony as that of John Best Sr., who had been "whipped, and likewise recorded for a liar." (And so he had in 1683, after gossiping about how he thought the Beadle brothers had obtained the money to finance their taverns by running a burglary ring.)[92]

Mary Esty addressed a second petition to the governor, court, and ministers. "Knowing my own innocency . . . and seeing plainly the wiles and subtilty of my accusers [I] cannot but judge charitably of others that are going the same way of myself, if the Lord steps not mightily in." Therefore, "I petition not for my own life, for I know I must die, [but that] if it be possible, no more innocent blood may be shed, which undoubtedly cannot be avoided in the way and course you go in. I question not but your honors . . . would not be guilty of innocent blood for the world. But by my own innocency, I know you are in the wrong way." If they would only question the afflicted separately, and try some of the confessors, the court would surely find many had made false confessions. She and others were told that they could not confess because they were in the Devil's snare. But to say she was guilty, even to save her life, "I cannot, I dare not, belie my own soul."[93]

Dorcas Hoar, however, shorn like Sampson, broke down, confessed that she was indeed a witch, and started naming others. Nevertheless, she was still condemned. The law seized her estate soon after: two cows, an ox, a mare, four shoats, bed, bedding, and other household items.[94]

Mary Bradbury's supporters, having exhausted the possibilities of petitions, somehow broke the old woman out of jail and secreted her away. (And around this time her accuser Samuel Endicott left home and simply never returned. After seven years he would be declared legally dead.)[95]

September 11, 1692 • Sunday
Salem Village

Samuel Parris chose the text Revelation 17:14 for his morning and afternoon sermons in Salem Village: "These shall make war with the Lamb, and the Lamb shall overcome them." By this last great battle between Christ (the Lamb) and the Devil, as Parris noted in his manuscript, he refered to the trials, and specifically to Martha Corey. For although she was in full communion with the Village Church, nevertheless she had been pronounced guilty the day before of communing with the Devil.[96]

(The accumulating witch confessions seemed to verify the Hellish plot against New England's churches. By now Parris may have felt more personally besieged. On the one hand the confessions only emphasized that Parris's own divided community was the weak spot where the Devil's forces had infiltrated New England's spiritual defences. On the other hand remained the old opposition of the Nurse family and others who now opposed the trials' direction as well. Neither side was likely to let him forget that the problem had begun in his own household.)

The Devil, who despises religion, said Parris, will fight as long as he can. But he could not fight forever, not by specters and witchcraft, and not by the troops of "the bloody French Monarch" (who sent war parties to burn their towns here, and outlawed Protestantism abroad). Once it seemed that only foolish old women were suspected, but now the land was infested with a "marvelous number of witches abounding in all places" including their own Village.

"It may serve to reprove such as seem to be amazed at the war the Devil has raised amongst us by wizards and witches against the Lamb and His followers that they altogether deny it." (Certainly Rebecca Nurse's family denied this.) "If ever there were witches, men and women in covenant with the Devil, here are multitudes in New England."

"It calls us all to mourn that the Devil had had so many assistants from amongst us," he said, for it was not necessary to be a witch to assist the Devil. "It teacheth us the vileness of man's nature, that, if left to himself, will give help and assistance to the Devil against Christ," self defeating though that behavior was. Even non-witches abetted the Devil by their disobedience when they flouted Christ's ordinances, the laws of good society, and the magistrates who administered them. "Here are but two parties in the world, the Lamb and His followers, and the Dragon and his followers: and these are contrary one to another. Well, now they that are against the Lamb, against the peace and prosperity of Zion, the interest of Christ, they are for the Devil. Here are no neuters. Everyone is on one side or the other." He cited a variety of Biblical disasters that resulted from such rebellious acts.

"Hence," he warned, paraphrasing Romans 13:1 (and entirely out of patience with stubborn opposition during the crisis), "resisters of authority are resisters of God, because they resist the ordinance of God."

Yet the Devil could not win this war. "Fear none of those things which thou shalt suffer," Parris quoted from Revelation 2:10. "Behold, the Devil shall cast some of you into prison that ye may be tried, and ye shall have tribulation." But "be thou faithful unto death, and [earn] a crown of life." (The Nurse family, if present, could only brood on how Rebecca had been imprisoned in actuality, and on who had helped put her there.)

Then Parris proposed Martha Corey's excommunication, a mere formality if, as it seemed, she had joined the enemy's side (and an insulting betrayal if she had not). The members of the church showed where they stood in the fight and voted to excommunicate "by a general consent," but not a unanimous one.[97]

September 12, 1692 • Monday
Salem

Autumn began as the sun passed into Libra. Almanacs optimistically predicted cool rain with possible hail and snow before November was out. However, the day remained as drought-stricken as ever, while fifty or more witch specters crowded widow Schafflin's house on the outskirts of Salem to receive a diabolic sacrament. The widow's daughter Alice Booth and daughter-in-law Elizabeth Booth saw it all. They recognized thirteen witches led by Giles Corey, who presented the bread and wine. He tried to make the Booths take it, too, and afflicted them when they refused.[98]

Boston

Meeting in the Boston Town House, the governor and council authorized payment of £40-16-6 to Boston prisonkeeper John Arnold, and a loan of seven barrels of gunpowder for six months to Lieutenant Governor Usher of New Hampshire.[99]

September 13, 1692 • Tuesday
Salem Town

This week, the Court of Oyer and Terminer tried the cases of Ann Foster and her daughter Mary Lacy Sr., Wilmot Read, Samuel Wardwell, Margaret Scott, Rebecca Eames, Mary Parker, Abigail Faulkner, and Abigail Hobbs. (The schedule of trials is not clear, and not all the testimony has survived.)[100]

Mary Walcott, Elizabeth Hubbard, and Mary Warren told the Grand Jury how Ann Foster had tormented them during her July examination. Such observed afflictions and Goody Foster's own several confessions comprise the bulk of the surviving evidence against her. Her daughter and granddaughter, moreover, had confessed and had accused her. It was probably no help to her defense that so many of the Devil's baptisms took place in her son Andrew's pasture. If she held to her confession, it did her no good. Ann Foster was found guilty of witchcraft.[101]

Ballard's complaint that Goodwife Mary Lacy Sr. also bewitched his wife had led to Goody Lacy's arrest. Several of the afflicted told the Grand Jury how she had hurt them. But her own confessions offered the most elaborate description of witchly activities and the most damning evidence against herself. Once she came to trial, Mary Lacy Sr. would be found guilty.[102]

The court read Samuel Wardwell's confession to him for verification. Despite his testimony against Mary Taylor and Jane Lilly at their examinations, Wardwell had had a change of heart. He agreed that while the document recorded what he had said, he had lied. *None* of it was true. But it was all one, he said resignedly, for he knew that he would die for it now—whether he owned the confession or not. (Confession, after all, had not helped Ann Foster, or changed Goody Hoar's guilty verdict.)[103]

Wardwell's specter afflicted Martha Sprague in court and pulled her from her horse as she rode home to Andover. She, Rose Foster, and Rose's mother, Hannah (daughter of Rebecca Eames), were all afflicted by his specter today.[104]

As Mary Hill's torments continued, her father, Zebulon, made official complaint against Mary's stepgrandmother, Joan Penny. The law, however, did nothing just yet.[105]

Boston

What Captain John Alden learned about the trials during his fifteen weeks in Boston prison gave him no confidence at all. He somehow escaped captivity around this time—his money and connections could only help—and left the province for New York. (By tradition, he fled by way of relatives in Duxbury where he roused the household at midnight, claiming that the Devil was after him.)[106]

September 14, 1692 • Wednesday
Cambridge

The elusive Elizabeth Coleson, in hiding since mid-May, had been finally captured in Charlestown after seven days of hue and cry across Middlesex County. Even lacking the resources of Alden and the other wealthy defendants, she had managed to remain in hiding an astonishing four months. Sheriff Timothy Phillips brought her to Salem, where she was questioned, and assigned today to the Middlesex County prison in Cambridge with her mother Mary Coleson, aunt Sarah Dustin, and grandmother Lydia Dustin.[107]

Marblehead Constable James Smith appeared in court in Salem at seven A.M., as ordered, to report that he had warned the several witnesses against Wilmot Read. These presumably arrived at the stated hour of eight A.M., except for two who were at sea and one who was "not well."[108]

What survives of the evidence presented to the Grand Jury against Goody Read is mostly the afflicted's reports of her spectral torments. Three neighbors related an incident five years earlier that followed another neighbor's quarrel with the defendant over missing linens. Mrs. Syms, said Charity Pitman, was sure that Goody Read's maid stole them, and when she threatened to tell Justice Hathorne, Goody Read snapped that if Syms did, she would "never mingere, nor carcare" as the scribe translated the folk curse. (Wilmot probably used more earthy terms like never piss, nor shit). Sure enough, Mrs. Syms suffered blockage and "dry bellyache" for months, and never did recover until she left the area.[109]

Whatever the other witnesses may have said, Goody Read's reputation for ill temper was entrenched enough to outlast her for more than a century and a half. Wilmot was ill-tempered, "grouty" in the local dialect, even if she weren't magic. Her reputed habit of wishing a "bloody cleaver" be found in the cradles of other people's children was no help. People were sure they saw the cleaver's apparition over a child before it sickened. Others had churns of perfectly good milk turn so moldy that it looked like snarls of blue wool.[110]

Unfortunately, most of the testimony is lost, but Wilmot Read was found guilty of witchcraft.

Samuel Wardwell of Andover, his recantation ignored, was faced with testimony about his specter's work before, during, and since his recent examination up to the Tuesday attack on Martha Sprague. As with Dorcas Hoar, Wardwell's long history of fortune telling worked against him. "He was much addicted to that," said Thomas Chandler, "and made sport of it." Only last winter at Samuel Martin's house, in the presence of the now afflicted Abigail Martin, Wardwell had told John Farnum about a refusal in love, a trip south, a fall from his horse, and a gunshot wound—all of which happened. On the same occasion Wardwell amazed James Bridges by revealing he had loved a girl when only fourteen, something James had never told anyone. "I wonder how Wardwell could tell so true?" said James's father John Bridges (whose own wife and daughter were now suspects).[111]

Constable Ephraim Foster reported that his sister-in-law Dorothy Eames (whose mother Rebecca and brother Daniel were now under arrest) had definitely thought Wardwell a witch to know the future so accurately. And Wardwell himself had told Foster's wife that she would have five daughters and then bear a son—as indeed she had.* His method was to examine a subject's hand, then cast his eyes on the ground before making a pronouncement. He also boasted that he could call cattle to him at will. And according to Joseph Ballard, his brother-in-law Wardwell complained that Ballard accused him of bewitching the latter's ailing wife, but did so *before* Ballard even suspected magic.[112]

Samuel Wardwell was found guilty of witchcraft with the rest.

The Salem Village Church committee visited Martha Corey in Salem prison to inform her of the excommunication vote. Lieutenant Nathaniel Putnam, Deacons Nathaniel Ingersoll and Edward Putnam, and Rev. Samuel Parris found Goody Corey stubbornly unrepentant. "If thou shoulds't die a rebel in the fight" of the Devil against Christ, Parris had said in his sermon the Sunday before, "then thou art damned forever." But Goody Corey still insisted on her innocence. "We found [her] very obdurate," Parris wrote of the encounter, "justifying herself and condemning all that had done anything to her just discovery or condemnation. Whereupon after a little discourse (for her imperiousness would not suffer much), and after prayer (which she was willing to decline), the dreadful sentence of excommunication was pronounced against her."[113]

Fairfield, Connecticut

Connecticut's Court of Oyer and Terminer sat in Fairfield. Governor Robert Treat presided with seven other justices, including Major Nathan Gould, stepfather-in-law of the accused Mary Harvey. The Grand Jury found the charges against both Mercy Desborough and Elizabeth Clauson "*billa vera*"—the indictment was a "true bill" suitable for trial. Both women pleaded not guilty and asked for trials by jury.

The Grand Jury also recommended that Mary and Hannah Harvey as well as Mary Staples be arrested on witchcraft charges and be brought to trial. The justices, however, ordered only that anyone having evidence against them come forward within the next two days.[114]

September 15, 1692 • Thursday
Salem Town

The drought continued as the moon turned full again.[115]

In Salem, Goodwife Mary Marston, Stephen Johnson, and Mercy Wardwell all owned their previous confessions before Justice Higginson. Mercy signed with an "x," adding that she did *not* know if her parents were really witches.[116]

---

*Genealogies list Ephraim and Hannah's first six known children as Rose, Hannah, Hannah, Jemima, Ephraim, John, etc.

Rev. Samuel Parris swore to the accuracy of his notes to Sarah Buckley's examination, and several others from the Village swore to their May testimony against Goody Buckley and her daughter Mary Witheridge.[117]

Likewise, Thomas Greenslett, whose mother Ann Pudeator had just received the death sentence, testified about the late Rev. George Burroughs's supernatural strength, for Thomas had been discouraged from participating in Burroughs's trial. (Perhaps it seemed safer to testify against one of the accused, and better to do so after it was too late to change the verdict.)[118]

The Grand Jury heard testimony against widow Margaret Scott of Rowley (whose specter went after Mary Daniel), Mary Warren, Elizabeth Hubbard, and Frances Wycomb during the proceedings. Ann Putnam Jr. saw this assault but was not hurt by it.[119]

Frances's father, Daniel Wycomb, testified how, five years past, Goody Scott had stopped by his house to ask if she might glean in his field. (It was the right of the poor to collect harvest leftovers, though Goody Scott owned land and her own grown children might have helped her. She had been widowed since 1657; two years before that, her husband Benjamin was "fined and admonished for theft.") Since Wycomb had not harvested yet, he asked that she wait for him to get the corn in first.[120]

Perhaps, she countered, he would *not* get his corn in tonight.

He insisted that he would, but his nervous wife gave Goody Scott some corn and the old woman left.

Wycomb drove his cart to the field, but once it was loaded, the oxen refused to pull it, they would only back up or go in any direction but the *right* one. The cart stayed in the field all night. Next morning, the oxen drew the load home with ease.

Six years past, widow Scott had asked Thomas Nelson for some wood and, being in debt to her for ten shillings, he offered ten shillings' worth of wood to clear the debt. She was *not* willing and, by the end of their argument, left with neither fuel nor money. Soon after, two of Nelson's cows died, one first rearing on her hind legs, the other found dead with her head caught under a plank. Furthermore, the late Robert Shillito had often complained of Goody Scott's hurting him, Philip and Sarah Nelson now testified, and had declared to the last that he would never be well as long as Scott lived.[121]

The Grand Jury also considered testimony against Rebecca Eames who, rattled by the August 19 executions seen on her way to court, had lost her wits under the clamor of the afflicted and had confessed without knowing what she said.[122]

The court probably made a second attempt to try Giles Corey, who stubbornly "stood mute." Nothing that the court said changed his mind, so he was taken back to prison. There his old friend Captain Thomas Gardner and others argued that answering the plea would be for Corey's own good.[123]

Deputy Sheriff George Herrick arrested Sarah Cole of Salem and left her under guard prior to examination.[124]

Lynn

In Lynn, the suspect Sarah Cole's niece suffered the last seizure to be caused by her aunt's specter. She had already experienced bites, scratches, pin jabs, and spectacular nosebleeds.[125]

Andover

Another nest of suspects was named in Andover, all or most of them the children of confessors. (At some point Nathaniel Dane's manservant was arrested for witchcraft as well.) This time the accused were questioned at the home of Rev. Thomas Barnard, Andover's junior minister, probably because the senior minister, Francis Dane, had been seen among the specters and was related to so many of the suspects. (Around this time Justice Dudley Bradstreet refused to grant any more warrants. Shortly after he took this stand, the afflicted claimed that he and his wife Ann had killed nine people by magic. The Bradstreets escaped to parts unknown, as did a "Mr. St[evens]" of Andover.) Young Sarah had difficulty speaking, and the afflicted saw Johanna Tyler's specter hinder her words.[126]

September 16, 1692 • Friday
Boston

Unaware of the latest French invasion plans, Governor Phips informed his council that he would sail for Pemmaquid this very day to settle a garrison there. He left orders for Captain Richard Short to follow in the *Nonsuch*, but apparently missed the eight o'clock tide, for he remained in town overnight.[127]

Salem Town

Salem magistrates John Higginson Jr. and Captain Thomas Wade, meanwhile, examined the newest Andover suspects: Dorothy and Abigail Faulkner (daughters of Abigail Faulkner Sr. and granddaughters of Rev. Francis Dane); Martha and Johanna Tyler (daughters of Mary Tyler and stepcousins of Martha Sprague); Sarah Wilson Jr.; and Joseph Draper.[128]

All of them, even her own daughters, said that Goody Faulkner had made them witches. It happened two months before, said Johanna Tyler, then she stopped, speechless. Something, she said at last, did not want her to confess, but it was Goody Faulkner and the Devil who made her sign the book. Now she could hurt people just by wishing it. Yes, she went to the meeting in Chandler's pasture. Yes, she afflicted Sarah Phelps and let the Devil use her shape to hinder Sarah Wilson's confession. But now she could speak no more, for Goody Faulkner's specter was on the table before her.[129]

William Barker Sr. owned to his confession before the Court of Oyer and Terminer; his son William Jr. swore to his accusation of Mary Parker; and Clerk of the Court Stephen Sewall handled more paperwork on Margaret Scott's case.[130]

Giles Corey was brought before the justices again and remained as tight-lipped as ever. His friend Captain Thomas Gardner had pleaded with him for *two* days, and still Corey would not cooperate. Consequently, for "standing mute," the court condemned Giles Corey to *pien-fort-et-dure* to make him enter a plea.* The old Province laws did not include pressing and even prohibited "barbarous tortures," but, under the new charter, English law now prevailed. Corey's survival depended on a quick answer, and perhaps he thought to bluff the court or to thumb his nose at it. Perhaps he mistakenly thought his land would be confiscated from his heirs if he were tried and found guilty. (Twenty years later, fellow members of the Salem Church would say that he bitterly regretted his refusal, but that story circulated later.)[131]

Fairfield, Connecticut

The Connecticut jury still could not reach a decision on the Clauson and Desborough cases. Kate Branch testified how Goody Clauson was the first to afflict her,

---

*Some dating is a guess. Defendants standing mute were traditionally asked three times how they would be tried before being sentenced to pressing. Corey was presumably first asked during the week before when he was originally scheduled for trial. Sewall said he was once pressed on Monday, September 19. Calef later said he was pressed September 16. As Calef probably took the date from a document, I assume Corey was condemned on the 16th after a third refusal to answer, and after Capt. Gardner spent two days arguing with him, then pressed on the 19th.

and Daniel Westcott described his family's problems after arguments with the defendant. But his wife, Abigail, now said she did not believe the accused were
witches, and complained that her husband would believe Kate before he would
believe her, the minister, *or* the magistrate. Others described times when they felt
sure Kate faked her symptoms: laughing into her pillow, or snapping out of a fit
with suspicious rapidity if a doubter tried to jab her with a pin.[132]

Testimony against Mercy Desborough involved confusion and bad dreams after
quarrels with her. But the woman had a shady past and had been in trouble with
the law before on an unrecorded matter. Mercy's father was in court for theft and
fraudulent business practices before he died and left his impoverished family on
public charity. Only one lone juror believed the women innocent. The court returned the defendants to jail, and ordered the jury to reconvene in Hartford when
the trials resumed in October.

Only two witnesses appeared against Mary Staples, Mary Harvey, and Hannah
Harvey. The court, including Major Gould, dismissed today's evidence as worthless (apparent dreams of witches dancing about a sickroom), acquitted the three
defendants by proclamation, and ordered everyone else to forbear future accusation and innuendo.

September 17, 1692 • Saturday
Salem Town

The Massachusetts Court of Oyer and Terminer finished the week's trials. The only
surviving testimony against widow Mary Parker of Andover was from the afflicted
and the confessors. Even less remains concerning Rev. Francis Dane's daughter,
Abigail Faulkner, who had eventually confessed. Rebecca Eames now denied *all*
her detailed confession. Ann Foster and her daughter Mary Lacy, Sr. may have
stuck to theirs. Nothing other than spectral evidence from the usual Salem Village
girls and the testimony of other confessors remains within the surviving records—
the word of afflicted people who, even if they changed their minds about the situation, would now find it dangerous to say so.[133]

Abigail Hobbs, known to be wild and strange, was one of the first confessors. She
stayed out in the woods all night unafraid because, as she told the Nichols girls a
whole year and a half before the arrests, she had sold herself to the "Old Boy."
Folk did not entirely believe her then, but all saw how rude and disobedient she
was toward her parents: bidding her stepmother hold her tongue and threatening
to raise the Devil if she did not. Since her imprisonment, she had provided considerable detail against Rev. George Burroughs.[134]

All nine were found guilty, and the Court of Oyer and Terminer sentenced them to death by hanging: Margaret Scott, Wilmot Read, Samuel Wardwell, Mary Parker, Abigail Faulkner, Rebecca Eames, Mary Lacy Sr., Ann Foster, and Abigail Hobbs. Not all of the condemned could be executed at one time, however, and Abigail Faulkner was temporarily excused due to pregnancy. The remaining untried cases would have to wait until the next scheduled court sitting on November 1.[135]

On the local level, Sarah Hawkes, stepdaughter of the condemned Samuel Wardwell, acknowledged her confession before Justice Higginson.[136]

Higginson probably also sat with Hathorne and the others who reexamined William Proctor, son of the executed John and the condemned Elizabeth, while William Murray took notes. William Proctor had been arrested on May 28 and questioned May 31. His specter had lately targeted Mary Warren again. When he looked at her as the charge was read, she fell as if struck. Revived by his touch, Mary testified that he "had almost murdered her to death this day by pains in all her bones and inwards also." William's specter also hurt Alice Booth and her sister Elizabeth (who saw William twisting a poppet), Elizabeth Hubbard, Ann Putnam Jr., Sarah Churchill, and another afflicted witness, Mary Pickworth. They revived, however, at Proctor's touch.[137]

Eastward

Governor Phips, meanwhile, sailed Eastward in the sloop *William and Mary*. He brought money for supplies and four whale boats for hunting beaver in the shallow creeks around Pemmaquid. (Edward Randolph suspected the province would be charged with the expense of this sideline if it proved unprofitable.)[138]

Randolph himself journeyed to Salem, where the deputy collector refused to show him the accounts, and eventually to Piscataqua. There he learned of the mast fleet's problems finding tall enough trees. The locals cut what they pleased and the Surveyor of their Majesties' Woods in New Hampshire and Maine (Jahleel Brenton again) never bothered to inspect the place. But this year people were afraid to enter the forest, and raiders killed the oxen needed to haul timber.[139]

Captain Richard Short may have provided Randolph's transportation, for he detoured to Piscataqua on his slow progress Eastward. He reached Pemmaquid four or five days after Phips, to the governor's disgust, for the delay foiled hope of a surprise attack on some of the off-shore islands.[140]

Phips's second-in-command, Benjamin Church, was also upset. In Admiral Phips's absence, he was forced to buy his men bread from the man-of-war *Conception*. When Phips *did* arrive, he brought only enough money to pay for the bread, but none for Church's own back pay or for recent out-of-pocket expenses.[141]

September 18, 1692 • Sunday
Salem Town

The Salem Town Church excommunicated Giles Corey. He had not been proven guilty of the crime of witchcraft. Yet, his refusal to stand trial seemed not the brave defiance of unfair practices that he perhaps meant it to be, but more an indication of guilt or even the crime of suicide. The congregation no doubt remembered his earlier threats to kill himself, and knew he was unlikely to survive the *pien-fort-et-dure* set for the morrow.[142]

Salem Village

Tonight, vengeful witch specters, including Giles Corey's, vowed to press Ann Putnam Jr. to death before the law pressed Corey. But the specters were unsuccessful and left her alone with a ghost in a winding sheet. Giles Corey had murdered him, said the ghost, pressed him to death with his feet before Ann was born, then covenanted with Satan to escape the murder charge. Now, when the court offered the easier death of hanging, Corey's heart was too hard to accept. "It must be done to him," said the ghost, "as he has done to me." When Ann's father, Thomas Putnam, heard, he marveled that no one had recalled the murder "all the while Giles Corey was in prison, and so often before the court."[143]

Seventeen winters before, Corey's hired man Jacob Goodale, "almost a natural fool," was found bruised and dazed. Mary Corey (Giles's second wife), and Jacob's brother Zachary got him to Salem on horseback to see Mrs. Mole, a local healer. They paused at Proctor's on the way, where John noticed Jacob's sad condition, and indeed, the man soon died. Doctor Zerubabel Endicott performed the autopsy and found "clodders of blood about his heart." A coroner's jury, which included Endicott and Francis Nurse, declared the man murdered. During the ensuing trial, Proctor testified that Corey himself said he had beaten Jacob. Elisha Kibbe related how he had tried to stop Corey, who must have struck Jacob Goodale about a hundred blows with a stout stick. But others were also accustomed to clouting Jacob—Corey's son-in-law John Parker and Jacob's own brother Zachary, for example. So Corey was not convicted of murder, but only heavily fined. Some grumbled that he had bought his way free. Goodale was beaten rather than pressed or kicked, as the ghost told Ann, but Thomas Putnam thought there might be a rough justice at work.[144]

September 19, 1692 • Monday
Salem Town

"About noon, at Salem," wrote Samuel Sewall, "Giles Corey was pressed to death for standing mute." For "two days, one after another," the court and his friend Captain Thomas Gardner had tried to make him change his mind, "but all in vain." Almanacs predicted a dry and windy day when Corey, as stubborn as ever, was taken from Salem jail, and (by tradition) led across the street to an open pasture. While the public watched, officers placed Corey face up on the ground, set flat boards across his body, and piled heavy stones on these, one after another. The idea was to make the prisoner talk, but after a certain point the pressure's damage would go beyond hope of healing. Giving in then would do the prisoner no good, for even if released, he would still die a lingering death from the crushing injuries.[145]

Preferring not to prolong his dying, Corey kept silent. He spoke only once (by tradition) to gasp, "More weight."* As Corey's tongue lolled from his mouth while he fought for his dying breaths, Sheriff George Corwin poked it back in with the tip of his walking stick. (This detail particularly impressed a small boy among the onlookers. In his old age he would tell another young lad about Corey's tongue and that lad, when old, would tell another boy, who in *his* old age would pass along the detail [now applied to Justice Hathorne] to a fourth, bringing the story into the twentieth century.)[146]

This was the last and only pressing in Massachusetts.

By tradition, Corey's body was buried in, or near, the crossroads by Butt's Brook (as if he were a suicide), though this resting place was not part of his home farm. Wherever the actual burial, his loyal sons-in-law William Cleeves and John Moulton probably handled it, since Corey had struck the other two ingrate heirs from his will. Moulton had paid some of the prison bills and had accompanied Giles and Martha as they shuttled from jail to jail.[147]

After Giles's death, Sheriff George Corwin arrived to seize Corey's goods or to collect £11-6-0 in hard money. Moulton found the cash to save the farm, but had to sell some livestock at a loss to raise the amount in time. His expenditures of time and money, however, only roused his neighbors' criticism.[148]

Musing on the day's events and the previous night's apparitions, Thomas Putnam wrote Judge Samuel Sewall to relate the parallels among the ghost's testimony, the old case of the hired man's death, and Corey's demise.[149]

September 20, 1692 • Tuesday
Salem Town

As nothing had apparently been done about Zebulon Hill's complaint against Goodwife Joan Penny for tormenting his daughter Mary, he put up a £100 bond of "current money" to prosecute. Justices Gedney, Hathorne, Corwin, and Higgins issued the desired warrants forthwith.[150]

---

*The cry, "More weight," is traditional to the punishment. John Milton used it metaphorically for asthma in his "Second Epitaph on Hobson." "As [if] he were pressed to death, he cried, 'More weight!'"

Boston

Judge Samuel Sewall wrote very little about the summer's trials in his diary, but he did note Giles Corey's death and today's receipt of Thomas Putnam's letter. "Now I hear from Salem that about eighteen years ago, he was suspected to have stamped and pressed a man to death, but that he was cleared. 'Twas not remembered 'till Ann Putnam was told of it by said Corey's specter the Sabbath day night before execution."[151]

Elsewhere in Boston, Cotton Mather wrote to the judge's brother Stephen Sewall, clerk of the Court of Oyer and Terminer. Mather asked, for a second time, to borrow the trial cases for "a half dozen, or if you please a dozen, of the principal witches that have been condemned" for the narrative that he was compiling. By now Governor Phips had approved of the project, too, though Mather also alluded to "all sorts of objections and objectors" against the trials. Mather evidently had a time limit. With only three weeks left before the manuscript's deadline, he rushed each essay to the printer for typesetting as soon as he finished revising it from his own past sermons and lectures.[152]

Stephen Sewall had already spoken to Mather about the events in court. Now Mather hoped Sewall would also write an eyewitness account of the confessors; the credibility of the witnesses and their testimony; the preternatural acts; and "the awe which is upon the hearts of your juries." For purposes of demonstration, to show what it was like to attend a trial (as he had not), he suggested that Stephen write as if Mather had to be convinced, as if he were a "witch advocate" or a materialist. "Address me as one that believed nothing reasonable," Mather exhorted.

September 21, 1692 • Wednesday
Salem Town

Although Joan Penny was, as Zebulon Hill's complaint against her noted, of Gloucester, she had land elsewhere. Ipswich Constable John Choate brought her to Salem for questioning.[153]

Goody Penny had been married earlier to Samuel Braybrook of Ipswich, a well-to-do if contentious man. They had no children together, but reared a nephew as well as Samuel's illegitimate daughter by a former maidservant. This daughter, Mehitable, was married and well provided for when her father died. She agreed when the probate court granted a life interest in Samuel's Wenham farm to her stepmother, Joan. But as soon as Joan married Thomas Penny of Gloucester, her stepdaughter Mehitable and her husband sued for the farm, and lost.[154]

Now Thomas Penny was dead, too, leaving most of his estate to "my beloved wife," also his executrix. He left £5 to his daughter Joan Kent and £2 to her grown son Thomas, but postponed its distribution for "one year after my decease at the discretion of my executrix." Even then, the town's selectmen were to manage the daughter's sum.[155]

Only a fragment of her examination notes survive. She evidently did not confess, and made her own generous emendation to the Lord's Prayer test. "When she came to 'Forgive us our trespasses, as we forgive them that trespass against us,'" wrote the scribe, "she said, 'So do I.'"[156]

Nevertheless, Joan Penny was held for trial, and Constable Choate and his assistants escorted her to Ipswich jail.[157]

A petition on behalf of the condemned Dorcas Hoar arrived in Boston addressed to Governor Phips, or, in his absence, to Lieutenant Governor William Stoughton. Signed by ministers John Hale and Nicholas Noyse, and schoolmasters John Emerson and Daniel Epps, it asked that Goody Hoar's execution be delayed at least a month, so she might "prepare for death and eternity." She was "in great distress of conscience," they wrote, but she had also confessed and revealed others. They hoped she could have this opportunity "to realize and perfect her repentance for the salvation of her soul." She might also serve as an example to encourage the *others* to confess as well—as long as her specter did not afflict anyone during that time.[158]

Phips was still away Eastward, but Stoughton granted the delay. "Accordingly," Samuel Sewall wrote in his diary, "an order is sent to the sheriff to forbear her execution, notwithstanding her being in the warrant to die tomorrow. This is the first condemned person who has confessed." (Perhaps Ann Foster, like Samuel Wardwell, did recant their confessions.)[159]

Reading

Tonight, in Reading, widow Mary Brown again felt tormented by the specter of Sarah Cole of Lynn. Outside, in the dark, stones thumped against her house and something like cats scampered across the roof. But whatever she spied lurking down by Ross Creek was more like a dog, or something larger.[160]

Wenham

While Mary Esty prepared her soul in Salem jail for her body's death, her specter appeared this evening to seventeen-year-old Mary Herrick in Wenham. "I am going upon the ladder to be hanged for a witch," said the apparition, "but I am innocent, and before a twelvemonth be past, you shall believe it." The girl told no one about this vision, but she began to be afflicted around this time.[161]

September 22, 1692 • Thursday
Salem Town

Leaving Dorcas Hoar behind in prison, with the others who had been condemned but not yet scheduled to die, eight victims were carted off to be hanged: Mary Esty, Alice Parker, Ann Pudeator, the recently widowed Martha Corey, Margaret Scott, Wilmot Read, Mary Parker, and Samuel Wardwell.[162]

As the crowd crossed the causeway over North River and turned up the steep path, the ox cart stuck. While men labored to move the wheels, the afflicted saw the Devil holding back the cart. But eventually the oxen heaved it forward and up to the ledge.

Many wept when Mary Esty spoke a last farewell to her husband, children, and friends. Martha Corey, Gospel woman to the last, repeated her plea of innocence from the ladder and, defiantly ignoring the common prejudice against women and public speaking, "concluded her life with an eminent prayer." Samuel Wardwell tried to state his innocence, but gagged on the waiting executioner's pipe smoke. The Devil, claimed the afflicted, directed the smoke to silence Wardwell.

After all eight had the breath permanently choked out of them, and their bodies hung lifeless, Rev. Nicholas Noyes remarked, "What a sad thing it is to see eight firebrands of Hell hanging there." (If Goody Whitford were in the crowd, she would have been more relieved than sad. Insane for ten years since a near drowning by the specters of Bridget Bishop and Alice Parker, she began to recover once those women were arrested. She mended even more rapidly after their deaths.)[163]

Boston

As Rev. Noyes and the rest turned from the hill, the sky was probably already darkening and the wind rising for a storm. It lowered in Boston, where Judge Samuel Sewall hosted a discussion "speaking about publishing some trials of the witches." Besides Cotton Mather, the group of six included Samuel's brother Stephen, who likely brought a selection of court papers (but no first-person account); Chief Justice William Stoughton; and Justices of the Peace John Hathorne and John Higginson Jr. All the men but Mather were eyewitnesses to the trials and examinations. They discussed the problems faced by the court: the seriousness of the charges; the multitudes of suspects to be dealt with (which included Higginson's own sister Ann Dolliver); and the severe effects of apparent magic on the afflicted.[164]

They must have considered the rising opposition to the witch trials, the "cloudy fury" alluded to but not fully described. (Boston merchant Thomas Brattle called the critics "men of a factious spirit, and never more in their element than when they are declaiming against men in public place, and contriving methods that tend to the disturbance of the common peace.") One purpose of the book was to "flatten that fury," as Cotton Mather had written to Stoughton, "which we now so much turn upon one another." They were all aware that if Massachusetts could not establish and keep civic order, England would send someone like Sir Edmund Andros to do it for them.[165]

The judges, Stoughton most especially, were certain their convictions were based on more than just spectral evidence. And again Cotton Mather simply chose to trust their judgment and accept their assertions as fact.

As they talked, rain fell heavily enough that Stoughton left early for his home in Dorchester on the mainland. The one road from Boston's peninsula ran over a narrow neck, and the highest tides of the month reached full flood shortly after five o'clock at sundown. Stoughton toiled on horseback through the rain well beyond the Neck's fortifications before realizing the way was impassable. Thus, the Sewalls were surprised by a dripping wet chief justice on their doorstep, and obliged to put him up for the night despite a houseful of visiting relations. Even so, the plentiful rain was an obvious blessing.[166]

That evening before retiring, Samuel Sewall read through 1 John:1. "God is light, and in Him is no darkness. If we say we have fellowship with Him, and walk in darkness, we lie and do not the truth." Apparently, Sewall had not done much to contradict Stoughton, yet he evidently felt some nagging doubt for his own part in the trials. "If we say that we have no sin," he read, "we deceive ourselves, and truth is not in us."[167]

September 23, 1692 • Friday
Boston

In Boston, Stoughton rose early and left before the Sewalls awoke.[168]

Springfield

Pierre La Moyne, Sieur d'Iberville finally sailed from Quebec for the rendezvous off Acadia. John Nelson's French messengers meanwhile (after a long pursuit including a canoe chase down Lake Champlain) had reached safety in Albany. Today, they delivered Nelson's letter to Major John Pyncheon at Springfield, Massachusetts, on the Connecticut River. He immediately sent them on to Boston.[169]

Gloucester

Mehitable Downing, Joan Penny's litigious stepdaughter, may have been arrested today, not for the first time. As a hired girl in her youth, she had set her master's house afire, either from spite (as he thought) or by accident when she dropped her pipe on the thatch. When she married John Downing, her father gave them a farm on the Gloucester border, but though the couple was well-off, the marriage was turbulent. Both had been charged with drunkenness and child neglect, and John had once obtained a court order to prevent his wife and David Gennet from carousing over rum together in his absences.[170]

***

Andover

Shortly after Mary Parker's hanging, Sheriff George Corwin sent an officer with confiscation orders to her Andover farm. Her sons John and Joseph explained that she had no estate. (She could not dispose of it during her lifetime, as it was to pass to the children on her death.) The officer seized corn, hay, and cattle anyway. The sons complained directly to Sheriff Corwin in Salem that the confiscated goods were theirs, *not* their mother's. Corwin (as the brothers later complained) demanded a further £10 and threatened to sell it all. They managed to settle with a promise of £6 payable within the month. (Some of this may have been for outstanding jail bills, but the Parkers, like others, severly doubted the legality of it all.)[171]

September 25, 1692 • Sunday
Boston

The arrival of letters from Nelson and Major Pyncheon detailing the French invasion disrupted Boston's Sabbath.[172]

September 26, 1692 • Monday
Boston

Lieutenant Governor William Stoughton and the council ordered that John Nelson's warning and John Pyncheon's suggestion be sent Eastward posthaste to Governor Phips and to New Hampshire's Lieutenant Governor John Usher.[173]

Lynn

If Sarah Cole of Lynn thought her sister-in-law the cause of her family's ailments, she, in turn, was suspected not only by Mrs. Mary Brown of Reading (beset by Sarah's specter today) but also by her own husband, John. Both husband and wife saw cats, dogs, and fireballs dart through their home. Tonight, John heard a thud against the wall of his house during evening prayers. Then he felt a blow against his head and side that left him so breathlessly dazed that he could not pray again for a quarter hour. Once he recovered and asked his wife, Sarah said she hadn't noticed a thing.[174]

Around this time, however, Sarah woke at night to find a ball of fire in the room. As she sprang from bed, the blazing object disappeared, leaving her in the dark with a strange dog looming by her. She grabbed a spade to hit it, but was herself knocked over. The dog vanished through a crack in the wall.[175]

September 27, 1692 • Tuesday
Ipswich

At Ipswich, a Quarterly Court of General Sessions for Essex County convened, presided over by Samuel Appleton, Daniel Epps, Daniel Pierce, John Higginson Jr., and Thomas Wade (and with Joseph Bailey, who had seen the Proctor specters in May, on the trial jury). Most of the cases dealt with the selling of liquor without a license. Lieutenant John Neal (who thought Ann Pudeator's magic had killed his wife) sued James Greenslett (one of Ann Pudeator's sons) for debt. This lawsuit was, however, dismissed.[176]

The court fined John Shepard of Rowley a stiff £30 plus costs for helping his sister-in-law Mary Green escape Ipswich jail, where she was being held on a witchcraft charge. He requested a reduction of the sum, for fines were supposed to be scaled to the payer's finances, and the justices altered it to £5 plus costs.[177]

One of Andover's selectmen, John Chandler, had a house often invaded by specters. A second, Dudley Bradstreet, was himself accused and in hiding. The remaining three—John Abbott Jr., Samuel Fry, and his brother-in-law John Asselbee (a brother of Rebecca Johnson and Sarah Cole of Lynn)—petitioned the court for advice. The four unprovided-for Wardwell children were in "a suffering condition" because their mother and older sisters were imprisoned and their father recently executed. The sheriff and his deputies, furthermore, had recently confiscated Samuel Wardwell's goods, cattle, hogs, horse, carpenter tools, eight loads of hay, and six acres of corn not yet harvested. The court allowed the selectmen to place the children with four different Andover families.[178]

Accordingly, fifteen-year-old Samuel Jr. was sent to stay with his uncle John Ballard for one year. Thirteen-year-old William was apprenticed until age twenty-one to learn weaving from selectman Samuel Fry. Five-year-old Eliakim was bound until age twenty-one to farmer Daniel Poor (a son-in-law of Mary Osgood), while baby Elizabeth went to John Stevens's family until age eighteen. All were to receive an apprentice's usual reward of clothing at their time's end.

September 28, 1692 • Wednesday
Ipswich

As long as John Shepard was in court, he entered the paperwork before Justice Thomas Wade for the Salem Village orchard that he had sold to Samuel Parris the previous January.[179]

Boston

Edward Randolph had been back in Boston for over a week, staying with the family of his absent friend John Usher, lieutenant governor of New Hampshire. Randolph had yet to examine Jahleel Brenton's books, but had heard a great deal about Brenton's irregular and arbitrary proceedings. For now, Randolph busied himself with writing critical letters to the Lords of Lrade on the local situation. (He did not, however, mention the witchcraft trials, even though his host's brother, Hezekiah, was still in hiding.)[180]

Randolph blamed the huge war debt on Phips, as if the "silly" Quebec expedition were Sir William's idea alone. He criticized the governor for not sending the two men-of-war now guarding Boston and Pemmaquid to intercept the French supply fleet that had just reprovisioned Quebec with enough food and soldiers for two or three years. (Phips had sent two smaller vessels which burned several houses along the Canadian coast, and then captured a French prize full of brandy and other goods at the mouth of the St. Lawrence.)[181]

September 29, 1692 • Thursday
Boston

Governor Phips returned to Boston from Pemmaquid at the dark of the moon, vexed over Captain Richard Short's delays; irritated by Randolph's continued adversarial presence; and aghast to find his wife named a witch. Lady Phips had signed, entirely without authority, a warrant to release a certain woman from prison. Perhaps the names William and Mary (Phips) were "accidentally" taken to mean the British monarchs. In any case, the prisoner was gone and nothing could be done but to discharge the jailer.[182]

***

Eastward

Rather than just wait for Canada to attack, Phips at some point contrived a plan to capture the Baron de St. Castine. Even Andros had been unable to remove him or his fort at Pentegoet which still served as a base for attacks against New England. No Englishman could get through unnoticed, but Nelson's two French army deserters Arnaud deVignon and Francois Albert, were willing to attempt the kidnapping. For guides, Phips recruited two recently captured Acadian prisoners-of-war: Jean de St. Aubin and his son-in-law Jaques Petipas. The two had enjoyed trading contacts with the English in the past, and their families were hostages now. Cotton Mather, present when Phips instructed the two deserters, wondered if they could be trusted to carry out a plan against their fellow French. Nevertheless, the French deserters set off with the Acadian guides and a few other men.[183]

September 30 1692 • Friday
Lynn

Sarah Cole's husband grew more and more nervous in Lynn, as nightly torments made him afraid to sleep in his own home. Once he spied a large cat staring at him through the front door and chased it into the cornfield near the house. John saw no more of the beast, but the cornstalks rustled and waved as if blown by a strong wind.[184]

The night was windless.

10

OCTOBER 1692

> *It were better that ten suspected witches should escape, than that one innocent person should be condemned.*
>
> —Rev. Increase Mather

***

Boston

A Boston man "of no small note" took his sick child all the way to Salem for spectral diagnosis. The afflicted said that Mrs. Cary and Mrs. Obinson caused the hurt. Mrs. Cary was in New York, but the anxious father entered a complaint against Mrs. Mary Obinson before the Boston justices as soon as he returned. Her childless marriage to tanner William Obinson was one long wrangle, and her contemptuous remarks about neighbors had brought her to court on other occasions. Even so, the justices denied the arrest warrant. When Increase Mather heard of the accusation, he confronted the father to demand whether the man did not think there was a God in Boston that he should go to the Devil in Salem for advice.[1]

Salem Village

After a Salem Village dog began acting strangely, the bewitched girls said that Mr. John Bradstreet's spirit rode and tormented the beast. The dog, though considered a victim, was killed. Bradstreet (a brother of Dudley Bradstreet) fled from Andover to Piscataqua.[2]

Andover

Another dog was shot to death after a convulsing Andover girl* claimed a dog specter afflicted her. This further exasperated Rev. Increase Mather. If the dog were an actual devil in disguise, he said, no one would have been able to kill it. As someone *had*, the dog was obviously an ordinary animal and therefore incapable of committing magic.[3]

Some Andover girls also accused a "worthy gentleman of Boston," who heard of the matter before it reached court. He obtained "a writ to arrest those accusers in a thousand pound action for defamation," and sent friends to warn them that they needed certain proof for their accusation. Faced with this aggressive response, the bewitched backed down and the matter ended.[4]

Gloucester

Nevertheless, some of the other afflicted girls were invited to use their spectral sight in Gloucester again, and what they saw there caused the arrest of four women. Three of these were likely Goodwife Mary Row (daughter of the jailed Margaret Prince), her stepmother-in-law, Rachel Vinson, and sister-in-law Phebe Day. Widow Vinson had been married to a first husband who drank; to a second so cruel that after he died (or decamped), she reverted to the first husband's surname; and a third whose earlier wife had been suspected of witchcraft. Phebe Day was both Sarah Bishop's sister and the executed Sarah Wildes's stepdaughter.[5]

Manchester

A woman's specter, wrapped in a white winding sheet, assaulted a young woman in the Pitman household in Manchester (just east of Beverly). The girl fought back and, as her father held her, snatched the edge of the sheet that only she could see. Witnesses heard a rip and suddenly she held a bit of torn cloth. Her father and the specter both grabbed for it. After a tussle the apparition vanished in defeat, leaving the father with a sore hand and a real piece of cloth as tangible evidence of the

---

*Calef said "the afflicted," Increase Mather said one girl.

struggle. (Or so folk said. Others were equally certain that the girl had been seen with the scrap of cloth the day before.)[6]

October 1, 1692 • Saturday
Reading & Lynn

Spectral sights and sounds so frightened widow Mary Brown of Reading that she finally made a complaint against Sarah Cole of Lynn. Benjamin Larrobe, whose relatives were refugees from Falmouth, Maine, entered the paperwork with a £100 bond to prosecute. The suspect's husband, John Cole, also continued to worry— wakeful through the rainy night with stomach cramps and a headache so bad it felt like twisted string tightening around his skull.[7]

October 3, 1692 • Monday
Cambridge

The ministers gathered at Harvard University postponed their discussion of church policy to hear Increase Mather's awaited essay against the court's use of spectral evidence: *Cases of Conscience Concerning Evil Spirits*. As the senior Mather was not present, the moderator, his son, Cotton, most likely read the report aloud.[8]

Its key argument was that the Devil could most certainly impersonate an innocent individual, living or dead, and use this sham to afflict others. The Witch of Endor's raising a false apparition of the Prophet Samuel was one example of this deception, as were more recent specters of angels and eminent ministers. There was no point in supposing that God would forbid Satan to ape the innocent (since equally evil non-spectral acts had occurred throughout history) or in supposing that devils lacked the will to perform this subterfuge (for their malice rejoiced in wronged reputations).

Although Scripture and history were full of magicians' illusions, it was well known that certain people *did* have real spectral sight. Some had it from the Devil. Others were plagued with it as the result of another's enchantment or by nature— like Laplanders, who bequeathed prophetic dreams to their children; or like local folk who, if entering a house where someone would soon die, were overwhelmed by the stench of a corpse that only they could smell.

Accusations were not proof, for even Christ and Martin Luther were denounced as wizards. Deathbed accusations were no better, for even if they did not lie, the dying could be deceived as much as the living. The afflicted, like Elizabeth Knapp of Groton, might be possessed by demons (rather than suffering bewitchment), as their violent symptoms suggested. Therefore, to consult them in their fits was to consult the ruling devils.

Demons also struck down the afflicted when they reacted to a suspect's apparent "eye poison." "Sight does not proceed from an emission of rays from the eye," Mather wrote, citing recent discoveries in the science of optics, "but by a reception of the visible species." Otherwise, everyone would feel the effects. Gossiping tongues did more damage than eyes.

Often enough the suspect's touch appeared to hurt rather than heal anyway, and the whole was the Devil's mockery of Christ's true healings. When magistrates used the touch test, they either deliberately risked the subject's health or played into the Devil's hands. Nothing in nature supported this test, since some people were cast into fits by the sight of cats, cheese, apples, or even their own children. It was all as meaningless as the recent episode with the dog in Andover.

In sum, evidence for witchcraft cases ought to be as clear as for other capital crimes, and *no* magical folk test was lawful for Christian use. As the legal authority Gaule had written, a confession would count as evidence (*if* the confessor were neither forced, possessed, nor insane) as would the testimony of two reliable witnesses verifying that the suspect said or did a thing impossible without the Devil's help.

Granted, there *were* dangerous witches who ought "to be exterminated," some of them in New England. Nevertheless, Increase Mather wrote, "It were better that ten suspected witches should escape, than that one innocent person should be condemned."[9]

All the listening ministers agreed and signed the statement: James Allen, John Bailey, and Samuel Willard of Boston; Charles Morton of Charlestown; Michael Wigglesworth of Malden; Jabez Fox of Woburn; and Nehemiah Walter of Roxbury.[10]

Soon after this meeting, Rev. Samuel Willard composed an introduction for the essay. "The more execrable the crime is, the more critical care is to be used in the exposing of the names, liberties, and lives of men (especially of a Godly conversation) to the imputation of it," he wrote. "In the case of witchcraft, we know that the Devil is the immediate agent in the mischief done, the consent or compact of the witch is the thing to be demonstrated." And spectral evidence did *not* do this.[11]

Several other ministers would add their names to the end of this introduction: William Hubbard of Ipswich, and John Wise of the Chebago section of Ipswich (who had petitioned for the Proctors); Samuel Whiting Sr. of Billerica; Samuel Angiers of Newton; Samuel Phillips of Rowley (who had testified in favor of the late Elizabeth How); Joseph Gerrish of Wenham (who had petitioned for Sarah Cloyse and Mary Esty); and Joseph Capen of Topsfield. Manuscript copies of the essay and introduction would be presented to Governor Phips, while others would circulate hand to hand. It was a stronger statement of the same advice offered all along, but now, perhaps, people might heed it.[12]

Salem Town

Acting as probate judge in Salem, Bartholomew Gedney considered and approved the late Thomas Penny's will. But the executrix and chief heir, Joan Penny, in prison on a witchcraft charge, was unable to deal with the estate. Therefore, her stepgrandson Josiah Kent, who was to receive only £2, petitioned to be made its administrator and claimed that, as sole male heir, he had been promised it all.[13]

Sarah Cole of Lynn, meanwhile, was arrested and examined late Monday before the Salem justices. Her statements, as recorded by Higginson, mostly concerned the spectral attacks from her sister-in-law, "Abraham Cole's wife," after that woman's suspiciously effusive praise of the defendant's children. She named the crowd of specters that had barged into her house, and described her son's and daughter's torments, the fireball, and the disappearing dog. Although Goody Cole sounded as afflicted as her accusers, Mary Warren convulsed twice and needed to be revived by her touch. Mary said that she had often seen Goody Cole's specter with Goody Hart and another woman, but was not hurt by her until tonight. Furthermore, the ghosts of a woman named Bates and of a child, both crying for vengeance, stood before the defendant now. Goody Cole admitted only that she and some others had toyed with a Venus Glass and egg to see "what trade their sweet hearts should be of," (as had some of the afflicted).[14]

Goody Cole was held for tormenting Mrs. Mary Brown on September 26 and was sent to the Middlesex jail in Cambridge. Her bill there began today, but she was still in Essex County tonight when her neighbor Abraham Wellman's cow acted wild and refused to be milked. She was "as gentle a cow as I would desire to set pail under," Wellman would say, but that was before Goody Cole coveted the beast. Now she ran at anyone's approach, and no one had so much as touched her in a week.[15]

October 4, 1692 • Tuesday
Lynn

The Wellman children were still unable to milk the cow this morning, or even get close to her. But once Sarah Cole was sent out of the area to prison, the animal began to calm, and was soon as gentle as she ever had been.[16]

October 5, 1692 • Wednesday
New York City, New York

Joseph Dudley, whose principal residence was in Massachusetts, had lost his post as New York's chief justice when Governor Benjamin Fletcher arrived in September. However, so many Massachusetts witch suspects were refugees there that Dudley (possibly acting for Phips) consulted New York's French and

Dutch ministers on the question of spectral evidence. Dudley himself had presided at the witchcraft trial of Mary Glover in 1688, which ended in her execution. He now submitted for their consideration eight questions in Latin, their common language.[17]

October 6, 1692 • Thursday
Salem Town

For the first time, six suspects, all minors from Andover, were released on bail from Salem prison. Abigail Faulkner Jr. and her sister Dorothy were freed after their uncle Nathaniel Dane and John Osgood Sr. (both of whom had wives still in jail) appeared before Jonathan Corwin and pledged £500 to keep the girls in their custody until the court required them.[18]

The girls' father, Francis Faulkner, joined with John Barker Sr. (Mary Barker's father) to put up a £500 bond for the release of Mary Lacy Jr., despite all her damaging testimony.[19]

Stephen and Abigail Johnson and Sarah Carrier were also freed on £500 bail, put up by their fathers, Francis Johnson and Thomas Carrier, acting with one Walter Wright.[20]

By now, Captain John Osgood and Deacon John Fry were heartbroken that they had earlier doubted their wives and frightened them into confessions. The petition for the confessors sent to Chief Justice William Stoughton around this time (and a copy to circulate) may have been the statement from six Andover women who told how they were scared so witless they admitted whatever was expected, and most of that was mere agreement with anything the court said.[21]

October 7, 1692 • Friday
Salem

Edward and Sarah Bishop (and William Barker Sr. as well, for all his earlier confessions and accusations) somehow escaped from jail, so the law confiscated cattle from their farms. Sheriff George Corwin had already taken some of Bishop's cattle for prison debts, but had spared a few for the family. These his men branded on the horn, while Edward Jr. (whose wife was a Putnam) held each cow steady. As he grappled with the fourth, a boil burst on his thigh making him wince at the sharp pain and lose hold of the beast. Word went around that his parents' specters made him feel the branding iron as punishment for his earlier slowness in finding favorable testimony for them. Today, the second son, Samuel the cordwainer (shoemaker), managed to borrow money to pay the fine rather than lose more to confiscation, the punishment for flight. Sheriff Corwin wrote him a receipt for £10 "in full satisfaction."[22]

Weymouth

Justice Samuel Sewall and Rev. Samuel Willard visited their newly widowed friend Rev. Samuel Torrey in Weymouth. When the conversation touched upon the trials, Torrey said that he thought the Court of Oyer and Terminer ought to continue, but only after correcting whatever was amiss in its proceedings. Thinking on this view, Willard and Sewall returned to Boston just before a fine rain began.[23]

October 8, 1692 • Saturday
Boston

While the chill rain continued under a north wind, Boston merchant and amateur astronomer Thomas Brattle wrote of his own dissatisfaction with the witchcraft courts. Although addressed to an unnamed "Reverend Sir," the letter was intended to circulate publicly.[24]

Brattle trusted the judges as individuals, but could see that they were not infallible. Their errors, moreover, tended to "pervert the great end of authority and government," especially now with so much noisy opposition from the sort who always criticized authority anyway.

When Brattle watched the look and touch tests applied in court, he noticed that the defendant's touch did not always "heal." Time, rather than touch, seemed to end the fit. Yet, even if the touch test *did* work, it was still sorcery. Some justices argued it was a scientific effect—that a witch's touch reabsorbed "the venomous and malignant particles that were ejected from the eye." But that was optical nonsense. The effect could not be natural or else the subject's glance would poison others, especially the "tender, fearful women" in the audience. Brattle was amazed that Rev. Nicholas Noyes, ordinarily "a learned, a charitable, and a good man," should so vehemently support the touch test.

Brattle had seen and heard the confessors several times, and felt that evil spirits deluded them. Their testimony was distracted, full of contradictions, and often interrupted by fits when, as the judges explained, "the Devil takes away their memory, and imposes on their brain." What they *could* remember was still from the Devil, so how could the court trust *any* of it, especially under oath? Anyone claiming to have renounced God could hardly be trusted to swear by God's name to tell the truth. This was just like the Groton case, where no one believed the girl's accusations after the Devil spoke through her. (Except, Brattle added, Chief Justice Stoughton, who still believed it.)

Witchmarks were useless, for who is unblemished? Tearlessness was no clue, for how many are impassive in calamity who weep for joy?

Legally, the indictments concerned the wasting and consuming acts of witchcraft against the body of a specific victim. But the evidence presented seldom dealt with the precise charge, except for information from the Invisible World, and most of *that* assumed the accused and their specters were the same. The justices may as well condemn a man for murder who pistols a shadow. If they were so sure the afflicted were accurate in their testimony and accusations, then why did no one issue warrants for Mrs. Thatcher, Justice Corwin's much accused mother-in-law? No one tried to catch Hezekiah Usher when he escaped, and no one tried to extradite Mrs. Cary or Mr. Alden from New York.

Granted, the courts were not alone in their opinions, Brattle wrote, citing those who sought spectral diagnosis for sick and dying kin. But now people of excellent reputation were accused. Some had fled; others had been confused into confession. Gossip said Andover held forty men who could raise the Devil as easily as any astrologer, but the truth was that only a few foolish girls had tried to divine by sieve and shears the previous winter.

Chief Justice Stoughton would admit no doubt and "is very impatient in hearing anything that looks another way." Yet, others had disagreed from the beginning: former Governor Simon Bradstreet and Thomas Danforth; Reverends Increase Mather, Samuel Willard, and most of the other ministers (except Hale, Noyes, and Parris); former Justice Thomas Graves; Nathaniel Byfield; and Francis Foxcroft, as well as "some of the Boston justices," who now considered resignation.

The next court would sit the first Tuesday in November. Perhaps, Brattle concluded, the General Court, which would convene shortly before that date, could change the proceedings?

That night the winds veered northwest, and the clouds dispersed, revealing a thin crescent moon just past its first quarter. Below this open sky, the soaked and dripping land began to freeze.[25]

October 9, 1692 • Sunday
Eastern Massachusetts

Sunrise revealed a landscape silvered by the year's first frost. A strong northwest wind blew all day, scattered the falling leaves, and hummed in the eaves of the meeting houses. The ministers, who had attended the Cambridge meeting earlier in the week, read the conclusions of *Cases of Conscience* to their several congregations.[26]

October 10, 1692 • Monday
Boston

The cold continued. A light snow fell on Boston as the Court of Oyer and Terminer sat to try a perfectly ordinary murder case (of a "French mulatto for shooting dead an English youth").[27]

By noon the sky was clear and the snow melted.

October 11, 1692 • Tuesday
New York City, New York

The congress of four New York ministers (Henry Seljins and Peter Peiretus of New York, Godfrey Dellius of New Albany, and Rudolph Varich of Flatbush) drew up eight Latin answers to Joseph Dudley's questions. The ministers agreed there always had been witches, but as "the formal essence of witchcraft consists in an alliance with the Devil" in order to work evil, it was this alliance and prior malice that had to be proven in court. While a servant of the Devil certainly would be malicious, not all evil thought was evident to the world, nor did all malicious expressions lead to evil deeds.[28]

"The Devil can assume the shape of a good man, and present this shape before the eyes of the afflicted as the source of the afflictions which they suffer." This was only one example of the many false accusations that the good had endured throughout history. Judges needed to avoid furthering the Devil's efforts to vex the afflicted and to ruin the innocent. That the afflicted did not physically decline despite their torments, could also be the Devil's doing. A certain man in New York, for example, wandered the mountains under every full moon. He took water but no food, and he was as hale as anyone.

Rev. John Miller, the Anglican chaplain to the King's troops in New York, also replied to the questions. He agreed with the other ministers' conclusions, but he also theorized that nonwitches might have their specters counterfeited as punishment for some other, as yet unknown, sin.[29]

Boston

In Boston, Samuel Sewall returned home from a funeral to peruse Samuel Willard's introduction to Increase Mather's *Cases of Conscience*. By now, both Sewall and Stoughton had also read galley proofs of Cotton Mather's *Wonders of the Invisible World*, for their letter verifying his account of the trials—or at least its "matters of fact and evidence"—was dated today. (Willard, meanwhile, was composing his own commentary on the matter.)[30]

October 12, 1692 • Wednesday
Boston

Delegates gathered in Boston from all over the Province for the General Court (though Lieutenant Governor William Stoughton was absent). They heard a report

---

*John Osgood, John Fry, Ebenezer Barker, and Nathaniel Dane for their wives; Joseph Wilson, John Bridges, Hope Tyler for their wives and children; John Marston for his wife who was Christopher Osgood's daughter.

from the committee to revise Massachusetts's laws, for this revision would be this session's great task.[31]

Nine Andover men* petitioned the legislature on behalf of their imprisoned wives and daughters, "a company of poor distressed creatures" beset by "inward grief" and "outward troubles." Lack of food and the winter's approach, they said, "may soon dispatch such out of the way that have not been used to such hardships." And the prison fees were likely to ruin their families. Might at least those "approved as penitent confessors" be sent home on bail to await trial?[32]

Indeed, Governor Phips decided to halt court proceedings until the Crown advised a course of action. He would allow no more arrests "without unavoidable necessity," no further proceedings against those already arrested, and no more printed discussions that only inflamed "needless disputes." Phips did not make his decision clear to the legislature, however, but only detailed it in a letter to William Blathwayt, clerk of the privy council.[33]

Phips himself was Eastward much of the summer and, on his return, found that the Devil had impersonated several doubtlessly innocent people. His political enemies tried to heap all the blame for the misfortune on him, he wrote, so in turn, he was placing the decision in their Majesties' hands.

In another letter, to the Earl of Nottingham, Phips reported on the work at Pemmaquid (without mentioning that it wasn't finished), and on the depredations of his 600 men against the French and Indians (omitting that the opponents amounted to a few scattered families). He reminded his lordship that, with ships and stores enough, the English might take Canada in the spring. Phips ended with a complaint against some few in New England, who "too much idolize the old Charter, and others who through envy seek my prejudice."[34]

Phips likely included a copy of Cotton Mather's *Wonders of the Invisible World*, and entrusted the package to the *Samuel and Henry*, bound for England. (Mather took the same opportunity and sent a copy to his London publisher John Dunton.)[35]

Both Increase and Cotton Mather's books were in press when Phips halted further publications, But each work circulated by mid-October, dated, as a technicality, 1693. Cotton Mather's *Wonders of the Invisible World* intended to illustrate the problems that the magistrates confronted, as well as to caution against dependence on spectral evidence. His intent was "to countermand the whole plot of the Devil against New England," but also to show readers abroad that New England was not overrun by the Devil, to calm the more tumultuous locals, and to discern a lesson in the events. He also hoped to clarify his own opinions. Gossip, Mather felt, misinterpreted his attempts at mediating contrary views, and made it seem that he opposed his father and the other ministers. Unfortunately, his haste in meeting the swift deadline left the book choppy and circuitous.[36]

For all its worldly lapses, wrote Mather, New England was surely resented by the Devil, who would have preferred to keep the New World for himself. First, he sent heathen Indians to attack the settlers, then (as a confessed witch prophesied forty years earlier) spectral forces, and now a storm of animosity that threatened to capsize the new government before it even started. Better to rely on charity and cooperation than on rage, he advised, better to ask, What might *I* have done to please the Devil?[37]

The many recent confessions seemed to confirm the accusations, especially in light of the afflicted's painful seizures. Nevertheless, some confessors admitted to using counterfeit images of the innocent. He quoted from *Cases of Conscience* about such fakery and reminded his readers that even Christ was accused of witchcraft.

Devils might impersonate the virtuous as a trial, or the uncharitable as a punishment. Foolish fortune-tellers attracted devils that they would not be easily rid of, and some of these would likely be revealed along with the activity of more deadly witches. But surely if anyone repented of such little sorceries to their minister, the matter should be kept quiet and *not* brought to law.

Yet, the present troubles could not be ignored. The guilty *must* be found and the afflicted *must* be delivered from their suffering. But neither the touch test nor spectral evidence should be used. (Earlier, he had thought such tests might indicate matters of suspicion. Now they seemed too dangerous.) Folk magic only drew in evil spirits, and it would be just like some wily conjurer to use a crowd of false specters to hide a few real ones. Accepting the Devil's spectral lies would condemn the innocent along with the guilty. Only evidence from the living, perceived by mortal human senses, should be admitted. Mather cautioned the judges not to prosecute the cases further than such evidence allowed. "A wise and a just magistrate," he advised, "may not do what he should leave undone, yet he may leave undone something that else he could do."

The book's main section covered the trials of Rev. George Burroughs, Bridget Bishop, Susanna Martin, Elizabeth How, and Martha Carrier. Using the incomplete material provided by Stephen Sewall, he quoted actual dialogue from the examinations (but none of the depositions in the defendants' favor.)* Cotton Mather had not attended any of the trials himself, but he had spoken with eyewitnesses, and was impressed especially by the confessors' stories and by the various accounts of people's recoveries after the deaths of the "witches" whom they had feared. Mather referred to similar incidents abroad, but also noted the Stockholm girl whose false accusation caused her own mother to be burnt for a witch, and who was herself executed as a murderer after confessing her deadly lie.[38]

However, Mather observed, people were more apt to cooperate unaware than to contract with the Devil deliberately. No earthly person or place, status, or sta-

---

*Mather wrote, "But I am forced to omit several passages in this, as well as in all the succeeding trials, because the scribes who took notice of them have not supplied me."

tion, was free of evil's influence. Even good and necessary actions could be skewed and corrupted. Those *not* accused of witchcraft needn't feel superior.

Cotton Mather's *Wonders of the Invisible World* appeared in print first, though his father's *Cases of Conscience* had circulated earlier in manuscript and been summarized from area pulpits. Both books warned that something devilishly dangerous was afoot. Both believed that many innocent people had been accused, but both assumed that those already tried and executed were actually guilty. Both believed the judges capable of common sense, even as both cautioned against accepting spectral evidence.[39]

The argument against spectral evidence was the heart of Increase Mather's book. Cotton's work repeated the same warning, but its purpose was to present the court's view of the witch problem. Given the shift in public opinion, Cotton feared that people would take a bare warning against spectral evidence as an excuse to ignore the whole problem. He hoped that his and his father's books would balance each other. Instead, many assumed they were in opposition. What readers *did* notice was Cotton's conviction that the Devil plotted against New England, and his calling Martha Carrier a "rampant hag."

Earlier, the public had clamored for the law to deal with the supposed plague of witches, and criticized Cotton Mather for concealing the names of accused persons. Now, many concluded that all the afflicted were always liars. Many took *Wonders of the Invisible World* to support everything the court did, and overlooked its warning against spectral evidence entirely. Chief Justice William Stoughton overlooked it, too, for although he did not change his mind about spectral evidence, he wrote a highly complimentary introduction for the book.[40]

Supposing that the Mathers were at odds over the trials, some people reprimanded Cotton for his supposed unfilial stand. This criticism surprised Increase, who had read and approved his son's work in manuscript. So he added a postscript to his own *Cases of Conscience*, as the printer finished setting the type. "Some I hear have taken up a notion, that the book newly published by my son, is contradictory to this of mine. 'Tis strange that such imaginations should enter into the minds of men."[41]

But once both books were available for comparison, all that most people noticed was that Cotton's name was not among those of the other ministers who had signed the introduction to Increase Mather's book.

October 13, 1692 • Thursday
Boston

The General Court defined nine "general privileges" to preserve such rights as no taxation without representation, due process of law, trial by jury, and the right of all (including slaves and foreigners) to justice under the law. And, as a reaction against the summer's confiscations, the General Court also revived the old law forbidding that practice. (But England, finding the change "repugnant," would cancel it.) The Upper House, now including Stoughton, also heard the treasurer's report describing how tax returns were far short of what they should be.[42]

October 14, 1692 • Friday
Boston

Phips signed the bill of rights and liberties into law, authorized payment to the head gunner of the Salem Fort, and assured Jahleel Brenton of cooperation in customs regulations.[43]

October 15, 1692 • Saturday
Salem Town

Mary Bridges Jr. was released from Salem prison on a bail of £500 pledged by her father John Bridges and John Osgood Sr., whose own wife Mary was still jailed.[44]

Ipswich

Arthur Abbott of Ipswich, himself once arrested and released, had testified against Elizabeth Proctor, and had then been taken to task by magistrate Samuel Appleton for bearing false witness. Now Abbott felt himself dying and sent for local magistrates Daniel Epps and Captain Thomas Wade to witness his will. Although he faced death and God's own judgment, Arthur nevertheless denied giving false testimony.[45]

Cambridge

Meanwhile, after attending a session of the Upper House concerning inheritance and debt, Judge Samuel Sewall visited Thomas Danforth in Cambridge. The former deputy governor had observed some of the earliest Salem examinations and, as a local magistrate, had jailed various suspects. But Danforth had long disagreed with the court's proceedings. He told Sewall that he thought the courts could not proceed until there was better agreement among the justices, the ministers, and the increasingly fractious people.[46]

October 16, 1692 • Sunday
Salem Village

Samuel Parris baptized Samuel Abbey's three-day-old son John in the Salem Village meeting house after services.[47]

October 17, 1692 • Monday
Hartford, Connecticut

Before resuming the trials of Goodwives Clauson and Desborough, Connecticut's General Court requested the local clergy's views. Reverends Timothy Wood-bridge and Joseph Eliot issued a statement in Hartford on behalf of the rest. The water ordeal, they wrote, was not only irrelevant but also sinful. Searching for ex-crescences was useless without a physician's knowledge. And it was only re-motely possible that the reported cattle deaths had any connection with the ac-cused. Katherine Branch's afflictions, furthermore, sounded like a combination of fakery and actual hysteria "improved by craft." If she thought they were caused by the person whose specter she saw, that was the Devil's deception. It was use-less as evidence.[48]

October 18, 1692 • Tuesday
Boston

While the Massachusetts General Court discussed debt laws, another petition from twenty-six Andover men, including Rev. Francis Dane, and Rev. Thomas Barnard (but not the fugitive Dudley Bradstreet) arrived. While real witchcraft must be dealt with, the petitioners felt that good Andover women had been misrepre-sented. Their confessions were due only to fear from "the extreme urgency that was used with some of them," and any accusations from "children and others who are under a diabolical influence" were invalid. If the court's methods did not change, the troubles would only continue.[49]

Phips informed the legislature that he would be absent for two or three days in the remote parts of the province. (Canadian forces were even then massing in Penobscot Bay.)[50]

October 19, 1692 • Wednesday
Salem Town

Because of the recent conflicting statements by and about the confessors, Increase Mather and Thomas Brattle again visited Salem prison. On an earlier trip, some of the prisoners had "freely and credibly acknowledged" their guilt to him, Increase Mather had written, and detailed "the time and occasion with the particular cir-cumstances of their Hellish obligations and abominations." Now, however, the older women all insisted that their confessions were false, frightened from them in weakness and confusion. They were badgered for details, said Mrs. Mary Osgood, until they invented what the magistrates expected to hear. They were told over and over that everyone knew they were witches (as Mrs. Deliverance Dane and Good-wives Abigail Barker, Mary Tyler, and Sarah Wilson said) until they half believed it themselves. Now they were appalled at those confessions and, as Goodwife Mary Marston summed it up, were burdened by their lies.[51]

But some of the younger women clung to their stories. Mary Post told Increase Mather how her spirit rode on a stick, and Sarah Churchill described how she stuck a poppet with thorns. Then she fell gasping in a seizure. Hannah Post informed Rev. Mather that Margaret Jacobs's specter, disguised as a two-year-old child, was choking Sarah.

Nevertheless, Abigail Hobbs and Mary Lacy Jr. had already told Mather and Brattle that all their testimony against Goody Eames was false,* based only on the Devil's illusions.[52]

Boston

Back in Boston, the General Court continued to receive petitions for the imprisoned. Not only was that good woman Elizabeth Hart in misery, wrote her son Thomas, but her husband was left "ancient and decrepit." Nicholas Rice of Reading reminded the court that his wife Sarah, whom he never suspected in all their twenty years together, had been imprisoned since May with nothing done about her case. "It is deplorable," Nicholas wrote, "that in old age the poor decrepit woman should lie under confinement so long in a stinking jail when her circumstances rather requires a nurse to attend her."[53]

The whole terrible problem dogged Samuel Sewall. In writing to his cousin Stark today, he added, "[I] desire your prayers for us relating to the witchcraft."[54]

October 20, 1692 • Thursday
Boston

Some people's growing irritation with the courts had flared at the publication of *Wonders of the Invisible World*, then focused on the book's author. Cotton Mather sent a copy to his uncle John Cotton of Plymouth. "With what sinful and raging asperity, I have since been treated," Mather wrote, "I had rather forget than relate." He had tried to mediate and to show both sides of the problem—for surely *something* was happening—and had been criticized for not opposing the alleged witches enough. Now he was blamed for not opposing the trials. He challenged "the fiercest of my accusers, to find the thousandth part of one wrong step taken by me, in all these matters." His critics spoke unconvincing "expressions of sweetness" to his face, while behind his back they spread "the great slander that I run against my own father, and all the ministers in the country." (His own exasperated temper would not let him think yet of what he had *not* done.)

---

*Rebecca Eames said that Hobbs and Lacy disowned their false accusations against her when Mather and Brattle were in Salem. Mary Lacy Jr. was apparently released on bail Oct. 6.

"I confess, things become every day more and more circumstanced, as if my opportunities of serving my neighbors were after a sort expiring; alas, that I have made no better use of them while I had 'em."[55]

Until recently, public opinion had been equally indignant against Rev. Samuel Willard for criticizing the court's methods. Willard's own book, *Some Miscellany Observations*, appeared around this time anonymously and under a false Philadelphia imprint (as if the fugitives had sent it).[56]

Willard wrote his argument as a debate between S. (for Salem), who accepted spectral evidence, and B. (for Boston), who did not. Both agreed that the crime of witchcraft was abominable and real.

S. argued that less evidence could be convictive, as no one was likely to witness an actual signing of the Devil's covenant.

But reason tells us, B. protested, that "the more horrid the crime is, the more cautious we ought to be making any guilty of it for it is one thing to be certain that there is witchcraft in the thing, and another to know who is concerned in it." With the defendants' lives at stake, B. accepted only a full confession (with no torture) *and* the usual two clear-minded witnesses—*not* the afflicted. Otherwise "there will be no security for innocence." The afflicted, at best, were deceived by the Devil's information, their memories fragmented by fits.

When S. suggested that God gave them the information to spoil the Devil's plot, B. refused to believe that God would require such pains and convulsions.

Their greatest disagreement was whether the Devil could use an innocent person's specter to torment others, or only that of a willing confederate. S. thought that God would not allow such goings-on, but B. reminded him that good people had suffered throughout history. Anyone could be accused, even S.

"I never fear it," exclaimed S. "God will never permit such a thing." Although he did not think *all* the accused were guilty, any criminal might claim a that devil in his likeness had committed his crime. With two witnesses, countered B., the real suspect's whereabouts could be established.

"You are an admirable advocate for the witches," said S. and reminded him of the confessors.

Even if the confessors spoke true, B. retorted, they would then be allied to the Father of Lies and could never be trusted.

October 21, 1692 • Friday
Salem Town

Samuel Sewall journeyed from Boston to Salem, where his brother Stephen languished under a month-long fever. Stephen, fearing he might die from the stubborn illness, was touched by his brother's arrival, and vowed "to serve God better, if his life be spared."[57]

October 22, 1692 • Saturday
Boston

In Boston, now that Governor Phips was back, the General Court passed an act determining how insolvent estates were to be distributed in ways fair to both debtors and widows. (As this act did not give precedence to debts owed to the Crown, the privy council would disallow it.) In an act of particular interest to Salem Village's quarrels, the court required that all leases, deeds, wills, and contracts be in writing and witnessed, along with any later changes or cancellations. The General Court also passed an act for the proper keeping of the Lord's Day (to which the Anglican privy council would *not* object). Attendance at "orthodox" services was not required, but nothing ("works of necessity and charity only excepted") was to interrupt the day.[58]

Phips and his councilors also instituted a Court of Oyer and Terminer for York County, Maine, to deal with all manner of crime. They appointed former Massachusetts King's Attorney Thomas Newton as one of its judges.[59]

October 23, 1692 • Sunday
Salem Village

Rev. Samuel Parris chose a text of reconciliation for his morning and afternoon sermons, Canticles 1:2. "Let him kiss me with the kisses of his mouth, for his love is better than wine." (Canticles, The Song of Solomon, celebrated earthly love, but selections from the poem were often used as metaphors for spiritual love.) The point was, Parris said, that "all true believers are urgently and fervently desirous of sensible and feeling manifestations of the love of Christ." There were kisses of subjection, treachery, and lust, he explained, but also kisses of affection, love, approval, and reconciliation. "Kisses are very sweet among true friends after some jars and differences, whereby they testify true reconciliation."[60]

After the service Aaron Way presented his month-old daughter Sarah for Parris to baptize, but the kin of the imprisoned and executed were in no mood for reconciliation. The Village "jars and differences" could not be easily solved.[61]

Boston

This evening, as tide and wind did not pause for Sabbath, Massachusetts agents Elisha Cooke and Thomas Oakes returned to Boston from England with Plymouth agent Rev. Ichabod Wiswell. They were all still upset about the new charter and their inability to persuade the Crown to change it.[62]

October 24, 1692 • Monday
Cambridge

While the governor and council met in Boston to discuss health regulations for slaughterhouses, Rev. Samuel Willard's son John appeared before the Middlesex county court to answer for helping Mrs. Elizabeth Cary break free from jail after she was charged with witchcraft. As no one spoke against him, John was cleared by proclamation.[63]

October 25, 1692 • Tuesday
Boston

The General Court was debating fire and health codes when it received word of three French warships off the coast. At once Governor Phips embargoed all unauthorized vessels. He ordered 120 more men Eastward and sent written orders to Captains Short and Fairfax—whose ships still guarded the unfinished fort at Pemaquid—to stay there and to fight if necessary.[64]

The enemy ships presumably included two men-of-war, but French plans had changed since John Nelson overheard them. It was nearly winter, and the Sieur d'Iberville lacked a pilot familiar with local waters. He sailed close enough to see the three English men-of-war and the mast fleet off Fort William Henry (but not close enough to see that the fort was unfinished), and then retired to Mt. Desert Island.[65]

October 26, 1692 • Wednesday
Boston

Almanacs predicted snow and clouds while the legislature wrestled with the problems of uncollected taxes, with the province's growing debt, and with Governor Benjamin Fletcher's assumption that New York owned Martha's Vineyard and Nantucket. The General Court received bills requesting a fast, and a convocation of ministers, so that by prayer and discussion "Satan's delusions" might be avoided, and the right way to proceed with the witchcraft cases might be found. Authorizing either request would be an admission that the courts had mishandled the cases. But the bill passed 33 to 29. The yeas included Captain Dudley Bradstreet (back from hiding) and Deputies Henry True and William Hutchins (son-in-law and son of the accused Misses Mary Bradbury and Frances Hutchins). As far as Judge Samuel Sewall could see, this seemed to mean that the Court of Oyer and Terminer was now dismissed. (But Phips still had not made his decision clear.)[66]

October 27, 1692 • Thursday
Boston

After a morning's debate on the payment of ministers and schoolmasters, Samuel Sewall and the other legislators heard Cotton Mather deliver Boston's lecture.

Mather's text was James 1:4 on steadfastness, which was, the verse explained, gained by successfully withstanding life's trials and tests of faith.[67]

Salem Village

In Salem Village, meanwhile, Mrs. Ann Putnam gave birth to her eighth child (six of whom still lived).[68]

***

Andover

Joseph Wilson of Andover petitioned for the release of his wife, Sarah, imprisoned fifteen weeks now, and of their daughter Sarah, jailed for six.[69]

October 28, 1692 • Friday
Fairfield, Connecticut

When Connecticut's witchcraft trials resumed in Fairfield, the jury found Elizabeth Clauson innocent, and the court ordered her freed on payment of fees. But the jury found Mercy Desborough guilty, and although the justices asked the jurymen to reconsider, they refused to change the verdict.[70]

Boston

Up in Boston, the General Court debated inheritance laws, appointed Anthony Checkley Attorney General, and discussed the establishment of regular courts. The day ended with a treat: a reception and refreshments in honor of the newly returned agents, Elisha Cooke and Thomas Oakes.[71]

Lieutenant Governor William Stoughton missed part of the session, however. Although the morning's high tide peaked just after ten o'clock, it was at the month's spring and storm-driven at that. The water was still rising as he set out in the rain for the legislature's nine o'clock sitting, and high enough to drench him as he crossed the narrow neck road from Dorchester. Wet through to the skin, and likely to catch his death of cold, Stoughton took to a borrowed bed at Boston, while his servant toiled back to Dorchester for dry clothes. (Others, not as lucky, drowned along the coast.) Presentable at last, Stoughton confronted Phips and the council to ask whether or not the Court of Oyer and Terminer would sit as scheduled on Tuesday. As before, he received no straight answer, only an uncomfortable silence that most took to mean the court would *not* sit.[72]

After a month's absence Eastward, Major General and Justice Wait-Still Winthrop, knowing none of this, sailed into Boston this stormy evening in time for the court date. No one had attacked Pemmaquid, but the French ships had not yet left the region. Nevertheless, the *Nonsuch* and *Conception* also returned to Boston against Phips's orders, if not today, then soon after.[73]

Furious at the disobedience, Phips met the two warships in the pilot boat. Captain Richard Short explained how he had waited until he was down to five days' worth of provisions before leaving. Phips thought this reason nothing more than a thin pretense, and reminded Short that he should have sent the purser for supplies. (Short's disgruntled officers would say that the captain was too often drunk to keep track of his stores.) In addition, Short had just lost the *Nonsuch*'s bow anchor and most of its chain. He thought, however, that they all faced a greater danger of foundering when Phips insisted on telling the pilot how to do his business. Phips ordered the men-of-war back to Pemmaquid directly. Convinced it was impossible to winter a ship safely in Maine's icebound waters, Short managed to dissuade the governor, and have the *Nonsuch* laid up for repair instead.[74]

October 29, 1692 • Saturday
Hartford, Connecticut

A committee of women in Connecticut swore to Secretary John Allen that, in searching Goodwives Elizabeth Clauson and Mercy Desborough for witch marks, they had discovered odd flaps of skin on both the suspects' "secret parts"—yet only *one* woman was found guilty. Even so, the jury held to its verdict, and Governor Treat signed Goody Desborough's death warrant. (After an appeal, however, three of the Hartford assistants would issue a reprieve and stay of execution until the next sitting of Connecticut's General Court's in May 1693.)[75]

Boston

In Boston, the Massachusetts General Court passed a list of thirteen capital offenses (which would eventually be disallowed by the privy council due to what they considered vague definitions). Some, like idolatry and blasphemy, though always capital crimes, had, in practice, only resulted in lesser penalties and that would not change. But witchcraft was definitely still a crime in England, and therefore in the provinces. "If any man or woman be a witch," the legislature decided, "that is, hath or consulteth with a familiar spirit, they shall be put to death." This definition was about the same wording as the 1641 "Body of Liberties" version of the law used during the summer's trials (though some, by now, noticed it was the *afflicted* who had contact with spirits).[76]

The Court of Oyer and Terminer was still officially scheduled to resume the following Tuesday to try the awaiting witchcraft cases. Worried that its demise would cause further problems, James Russel who, as an assistant, had observed the April 10 examinations of Sarah Cloyse and Elizabeth Proctor, asked outright whether the court would stand or fall. It must fall, Governor Phips replied, speaking plainly at last. (Chief Justice Stoughton was not in town that day to voice his opinion.)[77]

October 30, 1692 • Sunday
Salem Village

Rev. Samuel Parris baptized two more children of church members after services: three-day-old Abigail, daughter of Thomas and Ann Putnam (who thought the child's dead sister had been killed by witchcraft); and Jonathan, Rebecca Nurse's grandson (born the spring before to John and Mary Tarbell).[78]

Eastward

Eastward, the mast fleet and its men-of-war sailed home for England, leaving Pemmaquid unprotected in the absence of Captains Short and Fairfax.[79]

The French, however, though still at Mt. Desert Island, were distracted by the capture of Phips's two spies—Arnaud deVignon and Francois Albert (sent to kidnap the Baron de St. Castine). As Cotton Mather had suspected, their Acadian guides overpowered them and delivered the whole expedition to d'Iberville's forces. After a week of "interrogation" the spies told everything they knew about the kidnap plot, and about John Nelson's letter of warning as well. Being army deserters, the two were court-martialed, St. Castine, their intended victim, was among their judges. Then, to show the Indian allies how France dealt with traitors, the officers ordered the deserters' skulls smashed.

D'Iberville, apparently unaware of the English fleet's departure, abandoned his expedition in the face of approaching winter, and sailed for France (to the Abenakis' disappointment and to Frontenac's eventual fury). Acadian Commandant Villebon rewarded the guides with money to redeem their families and sent word to Quebec along with the other men involved in the kidnap plot. Frontenac ordered these men questioned further with thumb screws, then had them shot while John Nelson watched. Frontenac had already removed Nelson from the Chateau to prison, and very soon shipped him, Edward Tyng, and young John Alden to France. By January 1693, Nelson would be in the dungeons of the Chateau d'Angouleme, allowed no contact with anyone, and convinced that Phips had deliberately put him at risk with his foolish kidnapping plan. (Nelson would remain there for two years, and endure ten years of captivity in all before seeing home again.)[80]

October 31, 1692 • Monday
Boston

Just past the dark of the moon, the spring tides began to subside. So William Stoughton had dry passage to the Upper House's afternoon meeting to discuss the establishment of permanent courts.[81]

Salem Village

No one, including the government, knew when the trials *or* the delayed executions would resume. Families, like the province as a whole, grew more and more divided on the subject. In Salem Village, Thomas Putnam and his household were as convinced as ever of the spectral threat. His younger, wealthier, half-brother Joseph, on the other hand, who had taken notes at the first witch hearing, now opposed the trials. (His descendants would say that Joseph kept a horse saddled and ready for six months during the witch scare, and went about armed the whole time in order to flee or to fight back if any came to arrest him.)[82]

NOVEMBER 1692

And what grief of heart it brings to a tender conscience, to have been unwittingly encouraging of the sufferings of the innocent.

—Rev. John Hale

November 1, 1692 • Tuesday
Cambridge

The Quarterly Court for Middlesex County met only long enough to adjourn, and the Court of Oyer and Terminer did not sit at all.[1]

Boston

In Boston, the legislature considered matters of probate, weights and measures, and punishments for various non-capital offenses. Thieves, for example, were to pay their victims triple restitution, while fines for cursing and drunkenness would go to bolster a town's poor funds.[2]

Thomas Barrett of Chelmsford petitioned Governor Phips for the release of his daughter, Martha Sparks. Nothing else had been brought against her, Barrett wrote, since Justice Danforth had committed her a year and five days ago on a charge of witchcraft (months before the Salem Village outbreak). With Martha's husband Henry away soldiering Eastward, all care of the five-year-old and two-year-old Sparks children fell to their grandfather, Barrett. Not only were they "a considerable trouble and charge to him in his poor and mean condition," but his wife, their grandmother, had herself been bedridden for five years. (Fourteen years earlier, Martha had been convicted of beating her mother bloody, but now Barrett was desperate.) Would the court *please* release Goody Sparks to take care of her own children?[3]

Other folk in Chelmsford had been suspected. When someone struck at the invisible specter of a certain woman, its bewitched victim exclaimed, "You have made her forehead bleed." Neighbors checked the accused, found that her forehead *was* bloody, and told their minister. Rev. Thomas Clark, a classmate of the late Rev. George Burroughs's, went to see for himself. The woman explained how her cow had gored her during milking. The specter, Clark realized, had appeared to the girl just as this woman was actually wounded. However, as he could not believe the woman would collaborate with the Devil, the minister concluded that the apparition was Satan's ploy to incriminate the innocent. And so the matter ended, as it had not for Goody Sparks.[4]

November 2, 1692 • Wednesday
Boston

News of Little Compton's secession interrupted the General Court's debate on payment of schoolmasters and ministers. That town, on the eastern shore of Narraganset Bay, had been part of Plymouth Colony and therefore, under the new charter, part of Massachusetts. But Rhode Island's charter now included the eastern shore within its bounds as well. Little Compton's Quakers and Baptists did not consider a Congregational minister's pay a proper municipal expense. Three of them petitioned the Rhode Island assembly to resurvey the eastern bound to include their town. The assembly agreed, and notified Phips, who was anything but pleased. He sent Majors Hutchinson and Walley to forbid the conflicting survey, and sent the sheriff of Suffolk to arrest the ring leaders.[5]

November 3, 1692 • Thursday
Boston

The legislature decided which magistrates could perform marriages, and reconfirmed Andros's ruling that ministers could do so as well (as they had not been allowed in the earlier days of Puritan rule). Fees for the service, however, were not mentioned.[6]

Gloucester

But the Invisible World was still active. Lieutenant James Stevens of Gloucester sent for some of the afflicted girls to diagnose his ailing sister, Mary Fitch, wife of John Fitch. As the girls, including Elizabeth Hubbard, approached town over the Ipswich bridge, they convulsed at the sight of an unnamed old woman, but little came of this encounter. When they reached Mrs. Fitch's bedside, they saw the specters of Goodwives Esther Elwell, Abigail Row, and Rebecca Dike crouched on top of her. Lieutenant Stevens saw nothing, but heard his sister complain of being "squeezed to pieces." She felt a woman on the bed, Mary Fitch said, for when she reached out, her hand touched someone's invisible head and fingered not only the hair, but also a peg in the hair.[7]

November 4, 1692 • Friday
Boston

In a matter of particular interest to Salem Village (and Little Compton), the legislature passed laws concerning the towns' obligation to hire ministers and schoolmasters. Under pain of a £10 fine, every town of fifty or more households was to support its own schoolmaster. Towns of one hundred or more were to employ a grammar school master as well, a reputable person knowledgeable in Latin and Greek, to prepare such boys as might go on to the college.[8]

A town's minister was to be of good repute, "able, learned, and orthodox." But contrary to orthodox policy, he was to be chosen by a majority of the town's (male) inhabitants (as Salem Village had been allowed earlier), whether or not they were church members. All were to help pay his salary, and all contracts were to be honored. If there were no contracts or if one expired, the county's quarterly court could decide the matter, as it could other contractual disputes, and order compliance. But a town destitute of money or minister could also ask for help.

November 5, 1692 • Saturday
Boston

The General Court debated weights and measures, while the governor and council (William Stoughton again absent) conceded that all certificates from arriving vessels be delivered to Surveyor Jahleel Brenton, who would then return them to the local naval office.[9]

It was expected to be clear and frosty with the moon in its first quarter this Guy Fawkes Day. (The observance commemorated the failure of the 1605 Gunpowder Plot when Guy Fawkes, a Catholic, and others were discovered mining the parliament building as part of a wider plan to explode it with King James I and all of Parliament inside.) However, as popular customs tended toward incendiary, semipagan antics transferred from All-Hallows Eve, Samuel Sewall was relieved to note that Boston, at least, was not disturbed by bonfires this night.[10]

Ipswich

But specters caused disturbances throughout the day in Gloucester, according to the visionary girls who saw them throttle the suffering Mrs. Fitch. So Lieutenant James Stevens, his son William, and Mary Fitch's son Nathaniel Coit today entered a complaint in Ipswich against the three whose specters had been seen: Abigail Row (daughter, granddaughter, and stepgranddaughter of the accused Mary Row, Margaret Prince, and Rachel Vinson respectively); Rebecca Dike (a sister-in-law to the imprisoned Ann Dolliver); and another kinswoman, Esther Elwell. Despite Phips's ban on further arrests except in cases of "unavoidable necessity," the Ipswich justice of the peace, Thomas Wade, issued arrest warrants to Gloucester Constable Peter Coffin.[11]

Wenham

In Wenham, meanwhile, Mary Herrick was still shadowed after two months by several specters. These included the dead Mary Esty and the living Sarah Hale (wife of Beverly's minister John Hale, and cousin of Rev. Nicholas Noyes). Although the girl was not clear which specter actually hurt her earlier, Mrs. Hale most definitely choked, pinched, and jabbed the hapless girl today, while the ghost of Mary Esty watched.[12]

November 6, 1692 • Sunday
Boston

Domestic upset jarred Samuel Sewall's Sabbath. His four-year-old son Joseph (who would grow up to be a minister) acted badly at prayer time, and raised a bloody lump on his sister's forehead with a brass knob. The boy, looking as guilty as Adam in the garden, hid behind the cradle, but did not escape a whipping.[13]

November 7, 1692 • Monday
Andover

John and Joseph Parker of Andover, sons of the hanged Mary Parker, addressed a petition to the governor and council. They complained that the Essex sheriff had confiscated some of *their* property under the pretense that it had all belonged to their mother, and then demanded £10 when they protested.[14]

Boston

The General Court, meanwhile, debated the establishment of courts, while Phips, meeting with his council, lifted the two-week-old embargo that had kept ships in port safe from the marauding French fleet.[15]

Cambridge

With wet weather predicted, perhaps even snow, the ministers' association met at Harvard College to discuss church policy rather than current events.[16]

Gloucester

The afflicted girls, still in Gloucester, observed the specters of Goodwives Abigail Row, Rebecca Dike, and Esther Elwell continue to torment Mrs. Mary Fitch, even though the three accused women were confined in jail. They surrounded Mrs. Fitch, one on either side and another behind, choking the life out of her until she died this night.[17]

November 8, 1692 • Tuesday
Ipswich

Lieutenant James Stevens told the Ipswich magistrates, Daniel Epps and Thomas Wade, what his late sister had said about the apparitions as she lay dying. Elizabeth Hubbard also reported what she had seen in the Invisible World over the last five days. (But despite Mary Fitch's death, at some point Goodwives Elwell, Row, and Dike would be released on bail. Their kin, however, would still be in Ipswich jail come December.)[18]

Boston

After regulating casks of beef, pork, and tar, the General Court decided to keep all earlier decisions about the militia in force, and to affirm all former judgments passed during the interim government. This meant, among other things, that Elizabeth Emerson, convicted in 1691 of murdering her bastard twins, could now be hanged.[19]

November 9, 1692 • Wednesday
Salem

Daniel Epps testified on behalf of Arthur Abbott that, even on his death bed, the man insisted he had not lied about Elizabeth Proctor.[20]

Boston

Although the latest Canadian attack had come to nothing, the legislature extended the governor's powers to send troops into other provinces for another six months.[21]

November 10, 1692 • Thursday
Boston

Ignoring Jahleel Brenton, the General Court renewed the present excise taxes. The legislature also set licensing requirements for taverns. Anyone flouting the law (like Edward Bishop) would now be subject to a forty shilling fine—half to go to the informer and half to the town poor fund.[22]

November 11, 1692 • Friday
Boston

The Upper House debated the duties and obligations of town officers, and labored over the problem of tax assessments.[23]

November 12, 1692 • Saturday
Wenham

Clear and windy, said the almanacs. While the legislature in Boston considered an additional tax to cover war expenses, the ghost of Mary Esty appeared again to Mary Herrick in Wenham. As the accompanying specter of Mrs. Sarah Hale lit into the girl, the ghost seemed trying to speak. When they returned that night, the Hale shape continued to torture Mary. Did the girl think her a witch? the specter snarled.

"No," cried Mary. "You be the Devil!"

Now the silent ghost of Mary Esty spoke at last. She came to tell the girl again of her innocence and wrongful death. "Vengeance, vengeance!" she exclaimed, and bade the girl to report all the encounters to Rev. Hale and Rev. Gerrish. Then she, Mary Esty, would be able to rest, and the specter resembling Mrs. Hale would be powerless to hurt.[24]

November 13, 1692 • Sunday
Wenham

Mary Herrick approached her minister, Joseph Gerrish, and told him about the latest developments from the Invisible World.[25]

November 14, 1692 • Monday
Beverly

Although Thomas Brattle had listed John Hale among the supporters of the witch-craft trials in his October letter, Rev. Hale may have begun to doubt the proceedings as early as August. Rumors of his wife's specter (Sarah was about a month away from giving birth to her fourth child) would only have strengthened his doubts, for he was absolutely sure of her innocence. On this dark, cold day Hale and Gerrish listened to Mary Herrick's full story, while Gerrish took notes.[26]

There is "no truth more certain to a man, than that which he hath formerly doubted or denied, and is recovered from his error," Hale would later write. "And what grief of heart it brings to a tender conscience, to have been unwittingly encouraging of the sufferings of the innocent." If a lying devil could impersonate his innocent wife, he realized, devils could impersonate *any* of the accused.[27]

November 15, 1692 • Tuesday
Boston

After the Upper House's morning debate on county expenses (including those arising from the recent trials), some of the legislators attended a private thanks-giving arranged by Elisha Cooke for his recent safe return from England. He invited a number of worthies and their wives for prayers, sermons, psalms and an excellent dinner. Samuel Sewall attended, and noticed that neither Mather was present. Cooke made no secret of his dislike for the new charter, while Increase Mather resented being treated as if he had faced no obstacles dealing with two kings, a queen, and a parliament full of politicians. Since Cooke's return, there was talk of withholding Mather's Harvard salary, unless he moved from his beloved Boston to Cambridge. "The good Lord unite us," Sewall wrote in his diary, "and remove our animosities!"[28]

Andover

Meanwhile, Joseph Ballard, who had invited the afflicted girls to diagnose his dying wife in Andover, ended three-and-a-half months of widowhood by marrying Rebecca Orne. (Her Salem Village niece, Jemima Rea, had suffered seizures in June.)[29]

Fairfield, Connecticut

At the same time, Hugh Crotia of Stratford, Connecticut was caught leaving town, and arrested on a warrant of committing witchcraft against Eben Booth's hired girl. Hugh was rash enough to brag that he had sent the Devil to torment her and there was a rumor of doors and gates slamming as if something invisible had passed through them. But now, brought before authority in Fairfield, he admitted that he had said these things, but that he had lied. Yet he apparently admitted signing the Devil's book in blood five years earlier, and he may have attacked the girl himself. He did not send the Devil to Booth's, he said, but knew the Fiend had slammed the doors because the Devil himself told him so when he appeared in the form of a boy.[30]

November 16, 1692 • Wednesday
Boston

The Massachusetts General Court redefined the rights and duties of town governments, preserving a yearly March town meeting, and continued to debate the court system.[31]

November 17, 1692 • Thursday
Boston

Almanacs predicted snow or rain, while the Upper House discussed the proper number of representatives, and the continuing issue of taxes.[32]

***

Cambridge

Around mid-month, Rebecca Fox of Cambridge petitioned Governor Phips and Lieutenant Governor Stoughton on behalf of her daughter, Rebecca Jacobs. The daughter, imprisoned a good half year, was "well known to be a person crazed, distracted, and broken in mind." So her remarks about killing a child (two-year-old Mary, drowned in a well) must not be taken literally. Some prisoners, moreover, had already died in jail, Goody Fox pointed out, and others were dangerously ill.[33]

November 18, 1692 • Friday
Boston

The General Court passed an act concerning town bounds, and another allowing any whose consciences would not let them swear an oath (such as Quakers) to make a "Declaration of Fidelity" instead of the Crown's required Oath of Allegiance. (This declared that no foreign prince, law, or state—including the Vatican—had power in English realms, and renounced the idea that papal excommunication invalidated a monarch's rule.) The legislators also considered an act to raise money for various public works, such as the poor, bridges, and the many destitute prisoners.[34]

The governor and council dealt with £237-3-5 still owed to the Salem and Marblehead gentlemen who had outfitted a ketch to guard the coast during the old government. The governor and council instructed the Salem constable to pay this debt from whatever taxes he had so far collected, but not in bills of credit.[35]

November 19, 1692 • Saturday
Boston

Governor Phips, who began his career as a shipwright, gave Samuel Sewall the honor of driving a treenail into the brigantine that he was building. And Sewall, after driving the peg, invited Phips and others home for a glass of brandy.[36]

Besides his public duties as governor, admiral, and commander in chief, Phips continued with private ventures like the brigantine. It was common practice for Royal Navy captains to hire out their men to merchant vessels and privateers at twenty shillings a head, to be paid the captain from the sailor's wages. Phips, as admiral, had pressed some of Short's men to serve on his own ships for shares, thus paying the sailors but *not* Captain Short. Phips's reputation among the men was so high that some deserted their posts to work for him.[37]

Phips still wanted the *Nonsuch* and *Conception* back on guard at Pemmaquid. Captains Short and Fairfax, convinced that it was impossible to winter there safely, thought the order due to pique. But they did persuade Phips to let the men-of-war lay up in Boston until spring by promising to man a sloop for winter supply runs to Pemmaquid.[38]

November 20, 1692 • Sunday
Boston

Joseph Dudley was in Boston; perhaps bringing the New York ministers' reply. Although he was Anglican, he attended today's services in Rev. Samuel Willard's South Meeting House.

During the first prayer of the afternoon session in the Mathers' North meeting house, someone shouted, "Fire!" There was no fire, or any injuries from the resulting near-panic (except to Mercy Short's nerves). She had recovered from her summer's afflictions. Yet, the old melancholy closed in on her again, her spirits as depressed as the dark and fog-shrouded weather.[39]

November 21, 1692 • Monday
Boston

Mercy Short swooned and fell unconscious for several hours around this time. When she woke, her seizures were clearly back. Asleep or awake, she saw crowds of specters, as if she were in a dark cellar full of demons and witches. An extremely short man, no taller than an ordinary walking staff, approached her. His skin was tawny—like the Indians who had kidnapped her to Canada—and he wore a high-crowned hat over his straight black hair. But one of his feet was cloven. This was the Devil.

He offered her a book, long and thin like a trader's accounts, yet bound and clasped like a Bible. It was full of his witches' red scrawls and just touching it, he said, would ease her pain. The witches dashed it at her, so she would brush it accidentally while warding off the blow. But Mercy resisted, and refused his bribes of finery as well. This caused the little Devil's eyes to flash blindingly. The witch specters ignited like jets of flame and fell upon her, intending to set her burning at a stake, as one of her fellow captives had been on the march to Canada.[40]

November 22, 1692 • Tuesday
Boston

Samuel Sewall reserved part of the day for private prayer and fasting to ask God's pardon for the past and direction for the future. He prayed that the assembly might choose wisely and assist the new judges, and asked God to "save New England as to enemies and witchcrafts, and vindicate the late judges." Sewall now doubted the court's past actions, and had only the cold comfort that he had tried to do the right thing.[41]

After pondering all this, Sewall learned of Mercy Short's afflictions, for her relapse was already the talk of Boston.[42]

November 23–24, 1692 • Wednesday–Thursday
Boston

On Wednesday, the General Court discussed forms of oaths for officeholders, and the problem of counterfeiting. By Thursday, the court decided the penalty for clipping or counterfeiting coins would be double restitution and the loss of an ear. The court set standards of weights and measures, and equivalents for the many foreign coins in local circulation. The General Court also faced several petitions from various towns desiring clarification of the new tax requirements.[43]

November 25, 1692 • Friday
Boston

The Upper House reestablished the judicial system: from the local justices of the peace, through the quarter sessions, to the superior court. Essex County had just missed its scheduled Salem sitting for the second Tuesday in November. The next one would be in Ipswich on the last Tuesday in May. The legislators set a January date for Middlesex in Charlestown, and an April date for Suffolk in Boston.

They also determined "that it shall be in the liberty of every plaintiff or defendant in any of the said courts, to plead and defend his own cause in his proper person, or with the assistance of such as he shall procure, being a person not scandalous or otherwise offensive to the court." Jurymen need not be church members, but did have to own real estate worth four shillings per annum or a personal estate of £50 or more.[44]

The General Court also began to set a long list of court fees, and considered a petition from the Boston constables. The petitioners (including Robert Calef, who would become a vocal critic of the trials) asked for more time to collect all those back taxes, and pleaded "insupportable burdens" due to their "attendance in keeping the peace and serving of warrants" this past year.[45]

A short distance away in Boston's North End, Cotton Mather hastened through the lingering fog to attend to Mercy Short. As pastor, he was expected to visit and to comfort the sick. But opponents of his recent book found Mather's interest in Mercy's spectral ills troubling. Mather himself—besides seeing a chance to be useful—recognized the opportunity to study manifestations of the Invisible World firsthand.[46]

November 26, 1692 • Saturday
Boston

The General Court attempted to limit mackerel fishing, and regulate the scandal-ridden trade in pickled fish. Major Elisha Hutchinson reported to the governor and council on the situation in Little Compton, where the Massachusetts men had been met by "a considerable number of people, with clubs and staves in a tumultuous and riotous manner," uttering treasonous remarks against the King's authority. The council agreed that Sheriff Gookin needed help.[47]

November 28, 1692 • Monday
Boston

The legislature finished its list of court fees, and Governor Phips signed a sharp letter ordering the Little Compton rebels to desist.[48]

November 29, 1692 • Tuesday
Boston

The General Court debated forms of writs and warrants, and discussed how to assess and to collect money needed to operate the impoverished government. Phips announced a council meeting for the following Tuesday to appoint superior court judges.[49]

Meanwhile, Cotton Mather and several neighbors assembled to pray for Mercy Short. The girl seemed unaware of the people around her, reacting only to her invisible swarm of specters. Mather's sermon referred to the possessed boy cured by Christ. Whenever the evil spirit seized the lad, Mather reminded those assembled, it held him rigid or dashed him up and down (much like the afflicted in New England). The disciples had failed to cast out the fiend, because "this kind," as Christ explained, "cannot be driven out by anything but prayer and fasting." Mercy seemed oblivious to it all, yet she suddenly darted at Mather and ripped his Bible. The tear, he discovered later, pointed directly toward the sermon's text.[50]

November 30, 1692 • Wednesday
Boston

Benjamin Proctor left Boston prison, while the legislature discussed writs and warrants. Its members voted that each representative be paid three shillings a day while in court or in transit to a session, and set a fine of five shillings for absences.[51]

12

DECEMBER 1692

The confessors ... own, that they wronged me,
and what they said against me was false, that
they would not that I should have been put to
death for a thousand worlds.

—Abigail Faulkner Sr.

December 1, 1692 • Thursday
Boston

Both William Stoughton and Samuel Sewall were absent when the Upper House met, only to adjourn until the next morning.[1] Mercy Short, meanwhile, had no seizures. After a nine-day fast, she was able to eat a little—but only a very little.[2]

December 2, 1692 • Friday
Boston

Old Thomas Farrar of Lynn left Boston prison, while the Upper House passed bills defining fees for justices and other court officials.[3]

December 3, 1692 • Saturday
Boston

While the legislature continued to argue about money, Sarah Bassett and Sarah Rice were freed from Boston prison. Ann Sears likewise left Cambridge jail, until the next Middlesex court, on a £200 bond put up by her son-in-law John Horton of Lancaster and by Jonathan Prescott of Concord.[4]

Salem

Abigail Faulkner Sr., condemned to hang but reprieved until she could give birth, petitioned the governor from Salem prison for release. Five years earlier, she explained, her husband had suffered fits that clouded both memory and understanding. With God's help for her efforts, he had recovered, but now grief had brought the illness back. He and their six children, moreover, lacked all support.

Besides, the only evidence against her was spectral, and the word of "the confessors, which have lately since I was condemned owned to myself and others, and do still own, that they wronged me, and what they said against me was false, that they would not that I should have been put to death for a thousand worlds, for they never should have enjoyed themselves again in this world."[5]

December 4, 1692 • Sunday
Boston

Mercy Short was strong enough to walk the quarter mile from her employer's home to the north Meeting House in North Square for services. But her spectral tormentors found her there and blocked her senses to the outside world. Mercy's seizures returned by meeting's end. Several strong men tried to carry her home, but got no further than a nearby house, where a neighbor took her in, demons and all. Mercy would be unable to eat for another fifteen days.[6]

Salem Village

In Salem Village, Mrs. Bethshua Pope (allegedly the target of Martha Corey's torments the spring before) gave birth to her seventh child, Ebenezer.[7]

December 5, 1692 • Monday
Milton

Mary Watkins, once of Maine, now of Milton, Massachusetts, was discovered trying to strangle herself. She had been afflicted earlier and had accused "her dame Swift" of witchcraft and of murdering a child. Her employers were probably

Thomas Swift (deacon, selectmen, Indian agent, and quartermaster in the local militia) and his second wife Sarah.* They brooked no nonsense from their servant, and stopped her symptoms with threat of punishment. Mary retracted the accusations, but remained melancholy and then attempted suicide. Released from her noose, she immediately confessed to being a witch. So her rescuers hurried her before the local magistrates, who ordered her to Boston jail.[8]

Salem Town

Meanwhile, Rebecca Eames petitioned Governor Phips from Salem prison to insist on her own innocence. The testimony against her, she said, was the Devil's delusions. She remembered none of her confession and disowned it all. As she had told Thomas Brattle and Increase Mather, she was "hurried out of my senses" for four days by the afflicted, especially Abigail Hobbs and Mary Lacy Jr. Since then, even those two had admitted their charges were based on the Devil's lies.[9]

December 6, 1692 • Tuesday
Boston

Reports from Little Compton so angered the council that it recommended Sheriff Gookin be granted a military commission to subdue the rebels by arms if necessary. However, Captain Anthony Gullimore of Scituate volunteered to mediate in hopes of a peaceful settlement. The council accepted the offer, but sent eighty men to march with him.[10]

"A very cold dark day," Councilor Samuel Sewall observed in his diary. Almanacs predicted rain or even snow.[11]

Charlestown

Chelmsford mason Thomas Barrett appeared before Middlesex magistrates James Russell and Samuel Heyman with a £200 bond for the liberty of his daughter, Martha Sparks, then in Boston jail. Her husband Henry was still soldiering Eastward, and she would have to appear at the next county court, but at least now Martha could care for her children.[12]

Andover

And eight Andover men[†] again petitioned the governor and council to ask that their wives and daughters be allowed bail. Having hoped for a jail delivery before

---

*Mary lived at Unkity, i.e., Milton, and her mistress was Sarah (Clapp) Swift.

[†]John Osgood, Christopher Osgood, John Fry, Nathaniel Dane, Joseph Wilson, Hopestill Tyler, John Bridges, and Ebenezer Barker.

this, the petitioners now feared that some of the prisoners would perish as winter drew on.[13]

December 7, 1692 • Wednesday
Boston

The General Court decided on a salary of five shillings per day for members during sessions (instead of the original three shillings to match the fine for non-attendance). And eighteen councilors, including Samuel Sewall, met to cast ballots for judges of the newly reorganized courts. William Stoughton again became chief justice of the Superior Court with fifteen votes. Thomas Danforth, long in disagreement with Stoughton over the handling of the witchcraft cases, received twelve votes, John Richards seventeen, Wait-Still Winthrop and Samuel Sewall seven each. Justices chosen for each county's Inferior Court of Common Pleas included Samuel Appleton (who thought Arthur Abbott had given false witness against Elizabeth Proctor), Bartholomew Gedney, John Hathorne, and Jonathan Corwin for Essex.*[14]

Salem Village

Spurred on, perhaps, by the General Court's acts regulating deeds and contracts, Salem Village selectman Joseph Putnam posted a warning for a town meeting the following Tuesday. Those attending would choose a committee for next year, the notice read, and "consider what shall be done about our ministry house and land, it seeming to be conveyed away after a fraudulent manner." (The old controversy over whether giving Parris the parsonage outright had been legal or not was of greater concern than ever. Parris's opponents were not about to let the matter drop.)[15]

December 8, 1692 • Thursday
Charlestown

John Pierson and George Lilly, husbandmen of Lynn, appeared before the Middlesex magistrates with a £200 bond for the release of Pierson's sister, the widow Bethia Carter Sr. They pledged another £200, in company with George and Ruben Lilly, for the release of the latter's mother Jane Lilly.[16]

Salem

George Herrick of Salem, once Marshal, now Deputy Sheriff of Essex, addressed a floridly lettered petition to Phips, Stoughton, and the council asking

---

*Elizabeth Hoar, in Boston jail since 18 May, was also released today. Perhaps this is actually Elizabeth Heart, jailed on the same date.

to resign his post. For over nine months, he explained, he had been kept so busy serving warrants, apprehending and escorting suspects to and from various jails, and attending to their examinations and trials that he had to neglect his business (of upholstering) and was unable to support his own family. With the approach of winter he hoped that the government would offer them some relief, "for I have been bred a Gent' and not much used to work." In fact, he had spent £25 worth of his time and not yet been paid for it. (But the government did not accept his resignation, for Herrick would still be "under sheriff" the following June.)[17]

Boston

The General Court argued over poll taxes and issued a proclamation offering indemnity to any Little Compton rebels who submitted to the justice of the peace at Bristol.[18]

Because Thomas Danforth was unsure whether or not to accept his judgeship, Samuel Sewall invited him to dinner, so he and the Reverends Charles Morton and Increase Mather could urge Danforth to take it.[19]

December 9, 1692 • Friday
Boston

While Governor Phips and his council worried over unpaid wages owed to officers and men who had served Eastward under Andros years earlier, the government published the new acts dealing with writs, representatives, and court fees.[20]

***

Salem Town

Around this time of longest nights and shortest days, the elderly confessor Ann Foster died in jail, after twenty-one weeks imprisonment. Before he released her body, the jailer required £2-10-0 from her son Abraham, plus another £4 for provisions and other expenses.[21]

December 10, 1692 • Saturday
Boston

Samuel Rea of Salem put up a £50 bond before "one of the council" for the release of Dorcas Good, though her bill was not paid. The child had gone to jail in March as "hale and well as other children," but had spent the ensuing months chained and terrified, and apparently was never again in her right mind.[22]

According to the General Court's June decision, a town's back taxes, to cover expenses like the minister's salary, were to have been collected by today. Not all had complied (Salem Village certainly hadn't) so the legislature further debated assessments.[23]

December 11, 1692 • Sunday
Salem Village

For his sacrament sermon, Rev. Samuel Parris chose the text Ephesians 1:7 to expound on the ceremony as a symbol of forgiveness, "even the forgiveness of sins, according to His rich grace." (Parris recorded only the text. He still believed the executed "witches" had been guilty, but his notes do not reveal how the sermon may have referred to them. Their living relatives were in no mood for forgiveness.)[24]

December 12, 1692 • Monday
Boston

Still fearing French infiltration, the General Court required that the governor and council license all French (except for established Huguenot families) if they wished to settle on the coast or frontier, to open a shop, or to practice a trade.[25]

The Upper House, meanwhile, considered the legal definition of witchcraft.[26]

Ipswich

The Ipswich prison bill for Rowley laborer John Howard, arrested in August with the Jacksons, ended today. Prisonkeeper Thomas Fossey, however, wasn't paid the £2 that Howard owed.[27]

December 13, 1692 • Tuesday
Boston

The moon turned full, though rain or snow probably obscured it. During the morning the Upper House considered a bill against illegal imprisonment, and continued to administer oaths to various lower court justices.[28]

Salem Village

The Salem Village men gathered at noon in the meeting house to choose the next year's rates committee: Joseph Porter, Joseph Hutchinson, Thomas Wilkins, Zachariah Goodale, and Joseph Putnam. They neglected, however, to note their discussion of the dubious parsonage deed.[29]

***

Ipswich

Ten prisoners in the Ipswich jail petitioned the governor, council, and general assembly: widows Joan Penny, Rachel Vinson, and Margaret Prince, as well as Goodwives Mary Row and Phebe Day, all of Gloucester; Goodwife Elizabeth Dicer of
Piscataqua (who had been arrested in Gloucester); Goodwives Mehitable Downing and Rachel Haffield (Clenton before the divorce), both of Ipswich; Goodwives Mary Green and Hannah Bromage of Haverhill; "besides three or four men."
The older of them, the petitioners wrote, were near four score in age, some of the
younger were with child, and one nursed her ten-week-old infant. They feared
that they might perish if compelled to spend a winter where they were, being
"weak and infirm at best, and one [probably Rachel Clenton] fettered with irons
this half year and almost destroyed with so long an imprisonment."[30]

Boston

It was indeed cold enough that the government ordered the Boston prisonkeeper
to spend £16 on bedding, blankets, and clothes for the poorer prisoners in his
jail.[31]

December 14, 1692 • Wednesday
Salem Town

John Nichols (Bray Wilkins's son-in-law) and Joseph Towne (brother of Goodwives Nurse, Cloyse, and Esty) of Topsfield put up a £200 bond to release their
townsman William Hobbs.[32]

Boston

The Lower House passed their "act against conjuration, witchcraft, and dealing
with evil and wicked spirits," to which the governor and council consented. The
law stated that anyone who invoked, conjured, entertained, employed, fed, or rewarded an evil spirit; who exhumed a corpse (in whole or part) to use in magic;
or who used any means to waste, pine, consume, or lame any person (in whole or
part) would be put to death as felons along with their accomplices. Covenanting
with the Devil was *not* mentioned, but the definition followed the common understanding of witchcraft, and only enlarged upon the witchcraft category in October's list of capital crimes.[33]

But as a departure from the past, this law mitigated the penalties for lesser acts
of magic. Those now attempting by charms or sorceries to locate buried treasure,
precious ores, or lost articles; to compel another's love; to destroy or waste an-

other's cattle or goods; to try and bodily hurt (though not kill) another human even if unsuccessful, all such transgressors would be imprisoned for one year without bail. Once every quarter of that year, the prisoners would have to stand for six hours in the pillory at the county seat with the name of the crime inscribed in capital letters on papers pinned to their chests. A second such offense would merit them the death penalty as felons.[34]

Since forfeitures were once again forbidden (though England would not allow this decision to stand), the new witchcraft law made no specific provision to protect a widow's dower. Because of this omission the privy council would disallow the entire witchcraft act itself in 1695. As the legislature submitted no other version of the law, Massachusetts thereafter lacked any laws against witchcraft. (English courts, however, held witch trials until 1736.)[35]

Today, the General Court also passed an act for the "prevention of illegal imprisonment" by preserving the right of *habeus corpus*. (This too would be quashed by the privy council which did not believe that such rights extended into *any* of the colonies.)[36]

Cotton Mather, meanwhile, addressed John Richards about a church problem. Months earlier, Mather had proposed admitting adults of good reputation to baptism even when they didn't feel Grace enough for Communion and full membership. This "Halfway Covenant," used by some churches since 1662, was still controversial. Two influential members of North Church—one of them Richards—opposed the idea. People who came to Mather desiring baptism tearfully asserted that they would apply to another church *if* necessary. As Richards and Mather knew, several who had been lately condemned for witchcraft were church members. A church could attempt only so much purity and purification before making membership impossible and the congregation a hollow shell. So many had reported *devilish* baptism, Mather wrote, that North Church's reluctance to baptize seemed sinful. (Richards did not change his mind, but, appreciating Mather's tact, neither did he oppose widening the membership.)[37]

December 15, 1692 • Thursday
Salem Town

The Ipswich prisoners' petition had some effect, for Jonathan Corwin accepted a £200 bond from Gloucestermen Thomas Prince and Richard Tarr (Elizabeth Dicer's son-in-law) for the release of Prince's widowed mother Margaret.[38]

Boston

In Boston, meanwhile, the General Court was having a hard time collecting back taxes to pay for defense. Assessment lists had been due September 7, but, the court noted, the June act had "not been fully understood, or at least not attended."

Today's act was specific about who would be taxed (males sixteen and older); who would be exempt from the poll tax (settled ministers, grammar school masters, councilors, and college students); how various possessions would be valued; and at what rate the sum would be assessed (30 shillings per £100). For example, Rev. Samuel Parris was, as a settled minister, exempt from the 10 shilling poll tax, but would pay 6 shillings on the £20 assessed value of his slave John Indian.[39]

Boston also received more bad news from Jamaica. In addition to the 2,000 people killed in last summer's earthquake, 4,000 more had died of infections spawned by so many corpses.[40]

December 16, 1692 • Friday
Ipswich

Mary Green, though she had twice escaped, was released from Ipswich jail on a £200 bond offered by her husband, Peter Green, and James Sanders, both of Haverhill.[41]

Boston

The General Court published its acts concerning taxes, resident French inhabitants, *habeus corpus*, and the penalties for different degrees of witchcraft. Then, before recessing until February, and because of the crowded jails and numerous petitions, the court passed a supplementary act for a special sitting of the Superior Court at Salem on January 3. Dissolution of the Court of Oyer and Terminer had not removed existing and new witchcraft charges. And Governor Phips, after all of his prior hesitations, consented. But now he insisted that the judges *not* accept spectral evidence.[42]

The council met in Phips's home and decided on a £100 per annum salary for Stoughton as chief justice, and a £50 salary for the other supreme court justices.[43]

December 18, 1692 • Sunday
Boston

Captain John Alden was out of hiding and back in Boston. He did not, however, attend services at South Church, even though it was sacrament Sabbath there. At least young Susanna English would now have news of her father, the still self-exiled Philip English, for she continued to board with the Aldens.[44]

December 19, 1692 • Monday
Boston

For fifteen days, Mercy Short had eaten hardly at all: only a raw pear or apple every two or three days, a few chestnuts, a spoonful of hard cider, or a mouthful of cold water. When offered anything more substantial, she either convulsed or clamped her teeth against the food.[45]

As the specters batted at her, Mercy was sometimes aware of the real people in the room. She heard their voices faintly amid the witches' guttural threats or glimpsed dim hands before her face. When her perception of both worlds was clearer, she heard the specters gossip about the neighbors and brag of picking their pockets. When free of pain, Mercy turned frolicsome and witty with relief.

But even then she was unable to hear a word of religion. To her, silence punctuated prayers; Psalms sung by a roomful of people became a mime, even though Mercy could still hear any other sound. To lose the words of hope and comfort was too close to losing salvation, though at times, even prayers caused spectral torment. After leaving the house during one respite, Mercy returned to find Rev. Deodat Lawson waiting to speak with her.

"I am loath to go in," she said, "for I know he will fall into some good discourse, and then I am sure I shall go into a fit." Nevertheless, she entered the house where Lawson advised that she use her time to make peace with God and to pray for deliverance. Before he finished speaking, "she fell into a fearful fit of diabolical torture."[46]

Mercy's afflictions were observed not only by her host family, but also by neighbors who prayed with her daily, a changing group that sometimes included curiosity seekers. None of them saw the specters that she described, but all saw the girl's convulsions, saw the pins in her flesh at the end of bloody scratches, and saw her writhe on the floor, gasping for breath. The onlookers felt that, when they tried to lift her, a weight much greater than her own overpowered their efforts—as if something sat on her ribs. No one saw the poison that she said the specters forced on her, but everyone saw the same swelling reaction. No one saw flames when she said that the Devil burnt her, but they saw the burns and blisters. (While some faded in a few days under the usual home remedies, the more severe wounds seemed likely to remain for a lifetime.) No one saw the hot iron thrust down her throat, but all present saw the skin of her tongue and lips peel back and burn away.[47]

A few observers heard scratching sounds on Mercy's bed and on the nearby wall, and some smelled a brimstone stink in the room. But they all heard her side of the lengthy arguments, and assumed, from her reactions, that the singing of Psalms annoyed the specters. They knew when she was made deaf, for she heard nothing, even if they shouted into her ear. By following her nervous, darting glance, they thought they knew where the invisible specters were and sometimes struck at the spot—when her eyes didn't clamp shut to foil them. Some neighbors were scratched and jabbed themselves. Others made excuses to be elsewhere.

All of this turmoil was reported to (and some of it observed by) Cotton Mather, who kept notes of the case. Prayer groups visited Mercy daily, but how often Mather came is unclear. He visited some evenings and was present on the private fast days, but did most of his praying at home in his study. From spite, the Devil told Mercy that Mather did not pray at all, and made the minister appear monstrous to her.

Listening with the others to Mercy's arguments, Mather was amazed by the unschooled girl's erudition. He observed her wounds, scars, and burns with the eye of one who had studied medicine, and noticed that the devils made her fast after he mentioned a similar European fasting case. Her frolicsome periods, which she forgot on waking, surprised him the most. The specters stole a ring from his pocket during one of them. Mercy told him where they had hidden it, and warned him that they meant to get it off his hand again before he reached home. The spirits did not succeed, though Mather's finger did feel a bit numb.

Even during her antic times she craved the religious comforts that she could not hear. "Do . . . you know what," she begged. "Do what you used to do." But her visitor's confusing gestures only made her cry from frustration. Gradually, Mather discovered that she understood crucial words if they were spelled, and concepts if they were described. Once, Mercy asked him what to say the next time the Devil came.

"Mercy, tell 'em, that the Lord Jesus Christ has broke the old Serpent's head," said Mather, referring to the passage in Revelation that describes the Devil defeated and in retreat.

"What do you say?" asked Mercy.

"I say," Mather repeated, "tell 'em, that the Lord Jesus Christ has broken the old Serpent's head. Can you hear?"

"No, I can't hear a word."

"Well then, mind me and you shall know what you can't hear. A snake. Mercy, can you hear?"

"Yes."

"Well, an old snake. Can you hear?"

"Yes. Well, what of an old snake?"

"Why his head broke," said Mather, tapping his own forehead. "D'ye hear?"

"Yes. And what then?"

"Why, who broke it?" he asked pointing Heavenward. "D'ye mind?"

"Oh!" she said, recognizing the quotation. "I understand. Well, what else shall I tell them?"

On less troubled occasions she found her own comfort by leafing through a Bible or psalm book without looking, even in the dark, and by folding down a page to point out an encouraging passage when "it was darted into her mind that she had the place." (Some mistrusted the source of her revelations.)

She could be impertinent to the prayer groups and objected that several people had never prayed in their lives. She begged Mather to drive them away, but he refused. He had no way to know such a thing, and no intention of asking her about it.

"Well, it's no matter," she said. "Take but a candle then, and look in their faces, and you'll know by their blushing who they are. Turn them out that blush."

But Mather, who had his own doubts about curiosity seekers, only warned the company against a prayerless life.

More importantly, Mather warned the others not to repeat any names that Mercy might mention in her torments. Public opinion was largely against the accusers now. But he had said as much during her summer afflictions, when the situation was quite different—as he had before in the Goodwin case. "Had we not studiously suppressed all clamors and rumors that might have touched the reputation of people exhibited in this witchcraft," Mather wrote, "there might have ensued most uncomfortable uproars." (Some so named, he warned privately, like Secretary John Allen of Connecticut.)

Mercy's case was the talk of Boston anyway. "Rash people in the coffee-houses" waxed hostile and sarcastic, certain her fits were a lie. Word of this attitude got back to Mercy (the devils made sure she heard *all* the criticism), but she bore the animosity with her other trials.[48]

December 20, 1692 • Tuesday
Salem Town

Winter began as the sun passed into Capricorn. The weather was already cold, and almanacs predicted a good deal of "falling weather"—rain or snow or both.[49]

Eunice Fry and Mary Osgood of Andover were released from the risk of wintering in jail when their husbands, Deacon John Fry and Captain John Osgood, pledged a pair of £200 bonds before High Sheriff George Corwin in Salem.[50]

Boston

Meeting in the Boston Town House, Governor Phips and his council appointed Jonathan Ellatson as clerk of the new Superior Court, and ordered a committee, headed by William Stoughton, to examine Andros's and Usher's past-due accounts. Phips ordered the proposed Public Fast on behalf of all the recent troubles to be held December 29. But there was no mention of the requested convocation of ministers.[51]

December 21, 1692 • Wednesday
Salem Town

Samuel Hutchins, representative to the General Court for Haverhill, and Joseph Kingsbury of the same town, appeared in Salem before High Sheriff George Corwin with a £200 bond to free widow Frances Hutchins, the representative's mother.[52]

Boston

Watchers in Boston saw five to seven fireballs move about the dark sky around seven o'clock in the evening. The lights gleamed brightly, as Major General Wait-Still Winthrop observed, but did not stream like ordinary shooting stars.[53]

December 22, 1692 • Thursday
Boston

After the Boston lecture, Governor Phips formally appointed William Stoughton as chief justice of the Supreme Court, with John Richards, Wait-Still Winthrop, Samuel Sewall, and Thomas Danforth as justices, and Jonathan Ellatson as clerk. Each took his oath separately, promising to "impartially administer justice according to our best skill."

Afterwards, Sewall delivered the newly printed order for the Public Fast to his minister, Samuel Willard. Mrs. Willard commented "very sharply" on Captain John Alden's absence from the Lord's Supper the previous Sabbath. Her husband, after all, had spoken and acted for the accused. But Sewall was more concerned for his own daughter Betty, feverish and sick in bed.[54]

December 23, 1692 • Friday
Boston

Jonathan Ellatson, clerk of the court, ordered the various Essex County towns to select jurors for both Grand Jury and trial juries, and to send them to the next Court of Assizes and Goal Delivery to be held in Salem on January 3 at nine in the morning.[55]

Betty Sewall's illness, meanwhile, proved wholly material, for she began to recover after vomiting three sizable worms.[56]

December 24, 1692 • Saturday
Beverly

In Beverly, Sarah Hale gave birth to her fourth child, John, named for his father, Rev. John Hale, who was no doubt also relieved that the event had not occurred in prison.[57]

London, England

Overseas in London, John Dunton rushed to publish his own edition of Cotton Mather's *Wonders of the Invisible World*. Having received a copy from the author, Dutton had divided the sections among several different printing offices to speed the typesetting, and today advertised that the book would soon be available.[58]

December 25, 1692 • Sunday
Boston

Boston, meanwhile, expected cold, blusteringly wet weather. The witch specters, like Anglicans and Roman Catholics, apparently celebrated Christmas, for Mercy Short overheard them plan a dance. As soon as she reported this news to the prayer group, the members all heard the sound of bare feet pattering over the floor among them. Some were sure that they felt the dance's vibrations as well.[59]

Salem Village

After services in Salem Village, Rev. Samuel Parris announced a meeting of voting church members for the following day.[60]

December 26, 1692 • Monday
Salem Village

With Parris's salary a good year and a half in arrears, and a lower court about to sit at Salem, the Salem Village Church unanimously agreed to petition against the delinquent rates committee, for the new committee proved as uncooperative and ineffective as the old. The church members chose three to represent them in court: Lieutenant Nathaniel Putnam, Captain John Putnam, and Captain Jonathan Walcott.[61]

December 27, 1692 • Tuesday
Salem Town

The court of general sessions convened in Salem, with Bartholomew Gedney, John Hathorne, John Higginson Jr., Samuel Appleton, and Jonathan Corwin presiding. Nathaniel Putnam served on the Grand Jury and Captain John Putnam on the trial jury. The court decided several cases of theft and of selling liquor without a license. The justices fined Ezekiel Collins £3 for barging into the Gloucester home of William Sargent* late one night, and "abusing" both Sargent and his wife. (But the records do not indicate if this altercation had to do with past witch accusations or not.)[62]

And the magistrates considered the Salem Village Church's petition. "For several years past," they read, several Village inhabitants had paid none of their assigned share toward the minister's salary and the upkeep of church property. Others paid only "as little as they pleased," so that most of the rates remained uncollected. Those chosen to set the rates refused to do so. Consequently, not

---

*Two unrelated William Sargents lived in Gloucester. The wife of one of them was named as a victim in the complaint against Goodwives Prince and Dicer.

only were the fences about the ministry land neglected, but the meeting house it-self was also in disrepair. "By reason of broken windows, stopped-up some of them, by boards or otherwise, and others wide open, it is sometimes so cold that it makes it uncomfortable, and sometimes so dark that it is almost unuseful." The Village factions hardly spoke to each other. The minority opposition had drawn people to its side who would not ordinarily act so, while some simply stayed away and avoided voting "because they cannot bear the jars amongst us."[63]

The magistrates adjourned the matter to January 17, when they would sit in Salem Village itself.

At the same time, in Middlesex County, Chief Justice William Stoughton, Judge Samuel Sewall, and others spent the day in Watertown trying to resolve a bitter, pro-longed quarrel over where to build the new meeting house. Although lacking the recent divisive sorrows of Salem Village, the Watertown factions were just as stubborn. Initially, they did agree to abide by the decision of a mediation committee to be cho-sen by the governor and council (but later found reasons not to consent).[64]

December 28, 1692 • Wednesday
Boston

In Boston, the governor and council received more bills: £12-8-5 from surgeon Humphry Bradstreet for tending the soldiers Eastward; and £58-18-4 from Thomas Brattle and the rest of the debenture committee (which had parceled out pay-ments) for salaries, stationery costs, and room rent.[65]

December 29, 1692 • Thursday
London, England

John Dunton's edition of Cotton Mather's *Wonders of the Invisible World* went on sale in London. Eager readers who snapped up the book noticed that it contained an advertisement for Dunton's forthcoming edition of Increase Mather's *Cases of Conscience* as well.[66]

Lynn

Across the Atlantic, the town of Lynn chose its grand and petty jurors for the com-ing trials, including Benjamin Collins (whose wife Elizabeth was the widow of a Putnam).[67]

Boston

This Lecture Day was also a Public Fast across Massachusetts, or at least in towns that had heard of the proclamation.[68]

Besides joining the communal prayers for guidance in dealing with the present troubles, Mercy Short's Boston neighbors began a private three-day fast on her behalf. The specters told Mercy of the plan before her human friends did, and vowed to prevent it. The more faint-hearted withdrew when they heard of this threat. Even some who stayed were plagued by doubts. But others in town were angrily outspoken in their conviction that the whole thing was a sham. Mercy herself feared she was dying, and spoke often of her funeral.[69]

December 30, 1692 • Friday
Andover

Andover paid widow Rebecca Johnson, free on bail, for her past duties of sweeping the meeting house and ringing its bell. The town also reinstated her for the coming year, though she still had to appear at the next Superior Court to answer the witchcraft charge.[70]

Essex County

Several more Essex County town meetings chose jurors for that court: Andover, Wenham, Topsfield (which chose Rebecca Nurse's nephew, Ensign Jacob Towne), Salem (whose choices included two Village men who had signed the petition for Rebecca Nurse—Job Swinnerton and Captain Jonathan Putnam), and Marblehead (whose four choices included Wilmot Read's brother-in-law Richard Read, and William Beale, who had reported an apparition of Philip English).[71]

Salem Town

The quarterly court, meanwhile, continued in Salem. George and Elizabeth (Wilkins) Booth (both afflicted witnesses the summer before) confessed to fornication prior to their tardy marriage. The court fined them each forty shillings plus costs, though only George appeared. He explained that his wife was too ill to come (she was probably recovering from childbirth) and paid both fines. Her childless uncle and aunt Rogers had once adopted Elizabeth, but recent events prompted them to substitute her four-year-old brother Ebenezer as heir instead.[72]

Boston

And in Boston, the faithful neighbors continued their prayer and fasting for Mercy Short.[73]

December 31, 1692 • Saturday
Essex County

Haverhill, Rowley, Newbury, and Gloucester selected jurors for the January trials. Gloucester's three choices included William Stevens, kin of the lately afflicted and now deceased Mary Fitch.[74]

Boston

Also in preparation for the trials, William Stoughton signed a mittimus in Boston to transfer Lydia and Sarah Dustin, Mary and Elizabeth Coleson, and Sarah Cole from the Cambridge prison to Salem jail for the Tuesday sitting.[75]

Boston shopkeepers Nathaniel Williams and Samuel Checkley put up a £200 bond before Jonathan Richards for Captain John Alden, who was presumably still at large anyway.[76]

By the third day of the prayer circle's fast for Mercy Short, the girl neared despair from the specters' constant nattering. God had cast her off, they hissed, and Mercy was surely damned.[77]

"This is worse than all the rest!" she shrieked. "What? Must I be banished from the favor of God after all?"

She saw the specters flock about her, and as they pulled her away, she cried out for Rev. Mather. Someone ran to fetch him, as Mercy continued to fight back. Suddenly, the specters dropped their bluff and stormed out in a rage, admitting that they had no power over her.

When Cotton Mather arrived, he found Mercy dressed and apparently well, but very weak and faint. She told him what had happened. "Now go," she rejoiced, "and give to the great God the greatest thanks you can devise; for I am gloriously delivered! My troubles are gone, and I hope they'll visit me no more."

Thus, the year ended, with Mather and the praying neighbors offering their thanks to God for allowing them, this time, "to tread upon the lion, and to trample the dragon underfoot."

PART II

1693

13

JANUARY 1693

Our sin of ignorance, wherein we thought we did well, will not excuse us when we know we did amiss.

—Rev. Francis Dane

January 1, 1693 • Sunday
Salem Village

Readers of John Tully's new almanac saw, besides the forecast of rain or snow, both an advertisement for Cotton Mather's *Wonders of the Invisible World* and a woodcut of the Astrological Man of Signs adorned with symbols of the Zodiac.[1]

And in Salem village, Rev. Samuel Parris's salary again came due, and again went unpaid.[2]

January 2, 1693 • Monday
Essex County

In preparation for the morrow's trials, Ipswich and Beverly's town meetings chose jurors (including Robert Cue of Beverly, stepfather of the formerly afflicted Mary

Herrick). And at William Buckley's request, two ministers (Samuel Cheever of Marblehead and John Higginson of Salem) deposed on his wife Sarah Buckley's good character.[3]

Rev. Francis Dane, meanwhile, refuted various rumors about Andover in a letter to another minister. For all the recent talk of rampant sorcery, in his forty-year ministry he never saw or heard of anyone there using charms to call cattle, and only once heard of a divination by sieve, which, he assumed, stopped after he spoke against it. True, Goody Carrier (his niece) had been suspected earlier, but she was the *only* one. No one had suspected his daughter Elizabeth Johnson before spectral evidence was offered, and *her* daughter Elizabeth was "but simplish at the best."

"Had charity been put on, the Devil would not have had such an advantage against us," Dane wrote. The "conceit of specter evidence" allowed too many to be arrested. Those who confessed did so from fear and confusion, especially the children. "Our sin of ignorance, wherein we thought we did well, will not excuse us when we know we did amiss, but what ever might be a stumbling block to others must be removed, else we shall procure divine displeasure, and evils will unavoidably break in upon us."[4]

January 3, 1693 • Tuesday
Salem Town

The Superior Court of Judicature, Court of Assizes and General Goal Delivery began in Salem at nine o'clock on a fair and freezing morning, if the almanacs were right. (The court would sit for two weeks and would face more than fifty cases.)[5]

Chief Justice William Stoughton presided with Judges Thomas Danforth, Wait-Still Winthrop, John Richards, and Samuel Sewall. The first day seemed taken up with formally opening the court and swearing in the Grand Jury. This included Job Swinnerton of Salem Village and Richard Read of Marblehead, with foreman Robert Paine of Ipswich (a former minister turned farmer). Several bills of indictment were presented to them, and the court adjourned until nine the next morning.[6]

Some jurors asked the court how much importance they ought to give spectral evidence in the coming cases. "As much as of chips in wort," said one judge bluntly—of no worth at all.[7]

Meanwhile, Abigail Soames, Sarah Morrell, and Mary Black were moved from Boston jail to Salem. And Middlesex Sheriff Timothy Phillips hired five men and five horses, besides his own, to transport Lydia and Sarah Dustin, Mary and Elizabeth Coleson, Sarah Cole, and (perhaps) one other prisoner to the Salem court.[8]

Boston

Frictions continued in Boston, meanwhile, between Admiral (also Governor) Phips and Captain Richard Short. The latter had leased men to a merchant ship (in which Phips held shares) for a brief voyage. While these men were still absent, Phips ordered Short to provide *more* men to sail the *Mary* to Pemmaquid, and to reserve thirty-six others for imminent province business. Short claimed that he had no sailors to spare, though he had promised such runs in return for Phips's permission to winter Short's vessel in Boston. The captain muttered his discontent all evening, and was overheard to say that "he would go and huff the governor next morning."[9]

January 4, 1693 • Wednesday
Boston

In fact it was Phips who confronted Short at nine o'clock on Scarlet's Wharf with direct orders that the captain still refused. Short had enough men to rent for a fee, Phips reminded him. When he denied this charge, Phips called him a liar and told him that he wouldn't have so many desertions if he weren't so abusive. For all his boasts the night before, Short would later say that he had been ill several days, and troubled in his right hand again. Phips was the larger of the two men but both, being military gentlemen, wore swords and carried walking sticks. Short shook his stick for emphasis as he recounted grievances dating back to their Atlantic crossing the previous spring. When he waved it dangerously close to Phips's nose, the governor parried with a warning stroke that clipped the captain's hat and shoulder. Short hit back, wielding his cane left-handed. He struck head and body blows, but could not draw his sword before Phips compelled him to retreat step by step and tip backward over a cannon. Phips put Gunner Thomas Dobbins in charge of the *Nonsuch* and confined Short—his head still bleeding—in prison without bail or visitors. It was the common "nasty" jail at that, despite Short's rank and station, in an "open cold room in the worst of weather," he complained, "among witches, villains, negroes, and murderers."[10]

Salem Town

In the same hour that Phips drubbed Short, Superior Court began in Salem. The Grand Jury declared most cases *ignoramus* for lack of evidence, and found enough suspicion for the petty jury to try only four. The bewitched accusers were presumably present, but whatever they did was not recorded.[11]

Rebecca Jacobs, wife of the younger George, was the first on trial. Brought to the bar, she was arraigned on the indictment of tormenting Elizabeth Hubbard during her May 18 examination and at other times (but not for the other charge of covenanting with the Devil). Like all of the defendants during this sitting, Goody Jacobs pleaded not guilty, for she was not so distracted now as to plead otherwise. The jury found her not guilty and the court ordered her freed as soon as her fees were paid. (Her family apparently could not do so until March.)[12]

Rebecca's daughter Margaret Jacobs was indicted on two counts for spectral torments during her May 11 examination. She submitted a letter explaining her remorse at her earlier false confession. The same jury found her not guilty, and the court ordered her discharged on payment of jail fees. She, too, lacked the sum, however. (But after a month she was able to borrow the £3-12-0 from Beverly fisherman Philip Gammon, and leave prison at last.)[13]

A second jury considered the cases of Sarah Buckley and her widowed daughter Mary Witheridge, and found both not guilty. The court also ordered them freed on payment of fees.[14]

January 5, 1693 • Thursday
Salem Town

While the Grand Jury continued to work its way through the maze of cases, the various scribes swore to the accuracy of the examination notes that they had taken, and various witnesses swore to earlier testimony. The trial jury decided two more cases. Job Tookey, the Beverly waterman, was tried on only one of the three charges of spectral affliction and found not guilty. Hannah Tyler, "singlewoman," Mary Tyler's daughter, was likewise found not guilty of such torments or of a devilish covenant.[15]

January 6, 1693 • Friday
Salem Town

Four more defendants came to trial: Candy (the slave of Mrs. Hawkes whose own case was presumably declared *ignoramus*), Mary Marston, Elizabeth Johnson Sr., and Abigail Barker. All were indicted for tormenting the afflicted and, except for Candy, for covenanting with the Devil as well. Despite the defendants' earlier confessions the jury found them not guilty. All were to be freed on payment of fees, though whatever ailed Ralph Farnum, Abigail Barker's alleged victim, still plagued him.[16]

January 7, 1693 • Saturday
Salem Town

Simon Willard swore before the Grand Jury to the accuracy of his notes for the examinations of John Jackson Sr. *and* Jr. (whose cases were both declared *ignoramus*), and for Susanna Post, whose case was kept for future trial. The Grand

Jury also declared the cases of widow Rebecca Johnson and William Proctor *ignoramus*. Proctor's mother Elizabeth, close to giving birth, stayed behind in jail.[17]

Mary Tyler, wife of Hopestill, stood trial for tormenting Ralph Farnum Sr. and Hannah Foster (Ephraim's wife), and for covenanting with the Devil. Goody Tyler, too, was found not guilty and ordered freed on payment of fees.[18]

January 8, 1693 • Sunday
Andover

Although no one was found guilty of afflicting him, Ralph Farnum died today* in Andover.[19]

January 9, 1693 • Monday
Salem

The Trasks and the Corwins had long disputed the rights to a farm in the south of Salem. William Trask had sold the land forty years earlier, but *not* his wife's dower rights in it. Five owners later, the farm belonged to Jonathan Corwin (as he thought), who rented out the place. Tonight, egged on by his widowed mother, miller John Trask (the late William's son) proceeded to the farm after dusk with nine other men and three ox sleds to steal the farmhouse. So when Corwin's hired men returned that night, they found—instead of their one-room dwelling—only a heap of broken chimney bricks and deep sled tracks leading toward Trask's fulling mill.[20]

January 10, 1693 • Tuesday
Salem Town

The Court of Assizes began again in Salem with the same bench minus Wait-Still Winthrop, who did not serve this week.[21]

The Grand Jury considered evidence against Mary Bridges, whose case would be continued, and Martha Emerson, whose case was declared *ignoramus*.[22]

Sarah Wardwell (widowed since her husband's execution) and her two daughters came to trial. Goody Wardwell was indicted for covenanting with the Devil and for tormenting Martha Sprague (but not for afflicting Rose Foster as originally charged). Gossip said that the retraction of Sarah's earlier confession was only half-hearted, considering her late husband's fate after he changed his story. She pleaded not guilty, but the jury found otherwise: the *first* guilty verdict of this sitting.[23]

---

*Printed records give Ralph Farnum's death as Jan. 8, 1691/92. My guess is that it may be 1692/93 because a Ralph Farnum Sr. was alive in 1692 to be afflicted.

The daughters, Sarah Hawkes and Mercy Wardwell, were tried for covenanting with the Devil and for spectral torments. Unlike their mother, both were found not guilty and ordered freed on payment of fees.[24]

January 11, 1693 • Wednesday
Salem Town

Neighbors testified against Sarah Cole of Lynn, whose case was continued. But Mary Black, Nathaniel Putnam's slave, was cleared by proclamation.[25]

Elizabeth Johnson Jr., however, was found guilty of covenanting with the Devil and for tormenting Ann Putnam Jr. and so committed back to prison.[26]

Tonight the moon turned full and eclipsed behind the clouds. A flock of specters in the guise of Philip and Mary English, Goody Dustin, Elizabeth Johnson, (Sr. presumably), and "Old Pharaoh of Lynn" (Thomas Farrar) assailed Mercy Lewis. Mrs. English pushed the book at her jeering that the court would likely clear them all, so she might as well sign and be well.[27]

January 12, 1693 • Thursday
Salem Town

Almanacs predicted snow or rain as the Grand Jury considered evidence against the absent Philip English (still in New York). William Beal (called to serve on the trial juries) told of English's aggressive business tactics and the apparent spectral retaliation that had followed. Mercy Lewis, describing her torments from the evening before, felt a blow to the breast and strangled as she spoke. Even so, she thought the suspects would all be cleared. The English case, at least, went no further.[28]

Goodwife Mary Bridges Sr., her daughters Mary and Sarah Post, her stepdaughter Sarah Bridges, and Mrs. Mary Osgood were all indicted for covenanting with the Devil as well as for committing spectral torments. The juries found four of them not guilty, but determined that Mary Post was guilty.[29]

Despite her not guilty verdict, Chief Justice William Stoughton still had his doubts about Goody Bridges and required a £100 bond (put up the same day by her husband John and John Osgood) that she appear before the next Court of Assizes as proof of good behavior.[30]

Eunice Fry's trial was still in the future, but she was freed temporarily on £100 bail pledged by her husband James Fry and (again) John Osgood.[31]

The Ipswich prison bills for Rachel Clenton and for John Jackson Sr. and Jr. ended when the prisoners were probably transferred to Salem (where the Grand Jury would dismiss their cases).[32]

Salem Village

The Salem Village Church members met to discuss the lower court's action on their petition to make the rates committee do its duty. They elected agents to act for them: Nathaniel and John Putnam, Deacons Nathaniel Ingersoll and Edward Putnam, Captain Jonathan Walcott, and Ensign Thomas Flint.[33]

January 13, 1693 • Friday
Salem Town

At least six more prisoners were temporarily released on bail pledged before Chief Justice William Stoughton. William Barker Jr. and his cousin Mary were freed on £100 bond put up by her father, John Barker, and John Osgood. A like sum promised by Francis Faulkner and Joseph Marble freed the sisters Dorothy and Abigail Faulkner Jr. (whose mother was still under a death sentence). Although she had already been found not guilty, Joanna Tyler and her sister Martha were released on a £100 bond for good behavior provided by their father Hopestill and uncle John Bridges (who had apparently repented of badgering their mother into confessing). John Osgood and Joseph Wilson also offered a £100 bond for the latter's wife and daughter, Sarah Wilson Sr. and Jr.[34]

Mary Lacy Jr., out on bail since October 6, returned and pleaded not guilty to the indictments of covenanting with the Devil and of tormenting Timothy Swan. Although she had been confessor and accuser both, the jury found her not guilty and she was free to go—once her fees were paid.[35]

January 14, 1693 • Saturday
Salem Town

Mary Marston left prison around this time after a twenty-week stay. Sarah, wife of Salem tailor Abraham Cole, was bailed out with £50 put up by her husband before Justice John Hathorne. (The out-of-town judges must have left Salem to return home prior to Sabbath, because Stoughton set £100 bonds.)[36]

Besides one probate matter, the two-week session had heard over fifty witchcraft cases. It discarded thirty as *ignoramus*, including that of Sarah Cloyse (whose two sisters had hanged for witchcraft). Sarah's husband Peter soon moved them from Salem Village to Boston.[37]

Of the twenty-one defendants tried, only three were found guilty—Elizabeth Johnson Jr. and Mary Post ("two of . . . the most senseless and ignorant creatures that could be found," in Robert Calef's opinion), and Sarah Wardwell. Stoughton signed a warrant for their "speedy execution" (probably set for February 1) along with five others condemned under the old Court of Oyer and Terminer: Abigail

Hobbs, Mary Bradbury (who had escaped and was still in hiding), Abigail Faulkner Sr. and Elizabeth Proctor (who had both pleaded pregnancy, but had not yet given birth), and Dorcas Hoar (whose month reprieve to put her soul in order had long expired).[38]

King's Attorney Anthony Checkley relayed the court's decisions to Governor Phips, and added that he could see little or no difference in the cases of those cleared and those condemned. In Checkley's opinion, the three found guilty were as innocent as the rest. Phips had been in Rhode Island during the first week of the trials, making sure that that government knew where its boundaries lay. Now he mulled over Checkley's report, along with the news of Stoughton's execution warrant.[39]

January 15, 1693 • Sunday
Salem Village

Rev. Samuel Parris's sermon this sacrament Sabbath drew on the text I Corinthians 11:23–26 concerning sacramental bread and wine as a ceremony of Christ's own devising. "This do in remembrance of Me," Christ had said. No one is truly worthy of the sacrifice that the sacrament represents, said Parris, yet those called to partake must not refuse due to overimagined unworthiness—an excuse no one used to cease reading or praying. "This great and holy ordinance is not to be slighted, or neglected." Once eligible for communion, church members were not to partake or not at will. "Oh! It is a necessary duty, pray be entreated to attend it." (But Parris's opponents saw him as an insurmountable barrier between them and the Lord's Table.)[40]

After meeting, the members voted to take communion on the first Lord's Day of each month beginning in March, as most of the other churches did, instead of every six weeks or so as formerly. Then *everyone* (including the chronically absent members) would know the date ahead of time. (It would also be easier to get the bread from Salem.)[41]

January 16, 1693 • Monday
London, England

Cotton Mather's *Wonders of the Invisible World* sold rapidly in London, spurred by a prominent advertisement in today's issue of the *Athenian Mercury* magazine.[42]

Boston

In Boston, meanwhile, Captain Thomas Clarke arrived from New York to deliver a demand from Governor Benjamin Fletcher to turn over Martha's Vineyard, and to

extradite Abraham Gouverneur. Gouverneur had been condemned with Jacob
Leisler and Jacob Milborne in the revolt against Andros, but reprieved by the
Queen's proclamation of clemency. (His wife Mary was both Leisler's daughter
and Milborne's widow.) Nevertheless, he soon had to flee to Boston with little
more than the shirt on his back. Phips sympathized and in the course of their conversation either he or Gouverneur opined that Fletcher was interested only in
money, for Leisler's side had done no more wrong than King William. Gouverneur
repeated this remark in a letter to his parents. Fletcher intercepted it and concluded that Phips was inciting New York's malcontents. Once in Boston, Clarke
met with Lieutenant Governor John Usher of New Hampshire and with Joseph
Dudley, who, as former chief justice of New York, had helped condemn Leisler
and Gouveneur. Neither Usher nor Dudley was friendly with Phips, but they
arranged an interview with him for the following morning.[43]

January 17, 1693 • Tuesday
Boston

Phips received Captain Clarke at nine o'clock in the presence of John Usher, Rev.
Joshua Moody, and Phips's clerk, Benjamin Jackson. King William had recently
transferred command of Connecticut's militia from Phips to the governor of New
York for geographic reasons, but neglected to tell Phips. The extradition demand
and the troop takeover seemed all one with Fletcher's claim to Martha's Vineyard
(which he called "Martin's" Vineyard). The island had been absorbed by New York
a decade earlier, but was again part of Massachusetts under the new charter. Nevertheless, in the instructions read by Clarke, Fletcher informed Phips that he would assume its government in the spring.

And if the fugitive Gouverneur had misquoted Phips, Fletcher wrote, then of
course Phips would wish to apprehend him. But if Phips *had* said such things,
then "you have forgot your duty to the King and your manners to gentlemen."
Phips said that he would consider Fletcher's requests. But the messenger's repeated demands sounded like flaming insolence, and Clarke had to remind him
the words were Fletcher's. In *that* case, said Phips, the threats against Martha's
Vineyard seemed a direct challenge. If Fletcher came to the Vineyard, then Phips
would defend it.[44]

Salem Village

The predicted snow or cold rain, meanwhile, was making travel difficult. Even so,
the quarterly court for Essex reconvened in Salem Village at Ingersoll's ordinary,
with Bartholomew Gedney, John Hathorne, and Jonathan Corwin presiding. They
ordered John Pudney to be branded on the forehead with the letter "B" and to pay

triple restitution to John Trask, whose mill he had burgled. (Justice Corwin knew that this same Trask had stolen the house, but couldn't yet prove it.)[45]

The court determined that William Chandler (the afflicted Phebe's father) had not sold liquor illegally as charged. The justices renewed his license, as they did for Justice Gedney, who operated "at the sign of the Ship" in Salem. But various parties involved in other liquor license cases—like that of Edward Bishop—never came forward, though their names were called the required three times.[46]

The agents for the Village church, "several of the principal inhabitants," as the court record noted, presented their case against the delinquent rates committee, which was also present. The agents explained that since they could not legally convene to decide anything without that committee (which refused to do anything), they wanted the court to let them appoint a new one. Rev. Samuel Parris, referring to recent Village hardships, offered to abate £6 from each of his last two years' salaries. The magistrates postponed their decision to the following day.[47]

January 18, 1693 • Wednesday
Salem Town

Edward Bishop, back from hiding, attended the quarterly court session, which began at nine o'clock in the Salem Town House. He, among others, admitted to selling liquor without a license, and was fined ten shillings (a sum far below the General Court's recently required forty shillings), plus sixpence costs for Tuesday's default.[48]

The magistrates then handed down their postponed decision: the Salem Village rates committees for 1691 and 1692 had utterly neglected, even refused, to do their duty in collecting the minister's salary. Therefore, the court ordered Constable John Putnam to warn the inhabitants of a meeting in Salem Village at ten o'clock the following Wednesday, when the inhabitants would choose another rates committee.[49]

January 19, 1693 • Thursday
Boston

After Governor Phips and the council heard the Queen's ten-month-old letter (which had arrived by way of East Jersey) requiring that the province establish a proper post office, Phips had Captain Thomas Clarke brought in. The governor ordered him to repeat Fletcher's message to those present, but Clarke refused, claiming his instructions were private. Phips lost his temper, threatened the messenger with jail, and called him an "impudent, saucy, pitiful jackanapes." As an example of Clarke's disrespect, Phips flourished a political paper that called the Massachusetts governor a cowardly fool who deserved hanging. Unhesitatingly, Clarke named the piece's real author, but stuck to his refusal. Phips was only provoked further when William Stoughton, acting the contained, educated gentleman, took the messenger's part. Clarke found himself waiting in the hall outside the council chamber in the marshall's custody for half an hour while Phips and Stoughton continued their disagreement before releasing him.[50]

January 21, 1693 • Saturday
Boston

Captain Fairfax and other friends of the imprisoned Captain Short tried to get bail set for him, while Phips growled that Short was lucky not to be in irons. His supporters nearly obtained a writ of *habeus corpus* from "a judge" (under the circumstances Stoughton would have been a likely choice). But Phips transferred Short abruptly from the common jail to the more comfortable prisonkeeper's house and then removed him to the Castle in Boston Harbor.[51]

January 22, 1693, Sunday
Boston

Such thick, driving snow fell that even in Boston fewer than usual attended the meetings. Samuel Sewall and two of the family's maids managed to flounder the short distance through the drifts to South meeting house, but most women were marooned at home. Major General Wait-Still Winthrop stayed away in the afternoon, and old Governor Simon Bradstreet was too sick to venture out at all.[52]

January 23–24, 1693 • Monday–Tuesday
Boston

The almanacs predicted snow or sleet for most of the week.[53]

January 25, 1693 • Wednesday
Salem Village

As ordered, the Salem Village voters convened* in the meeting house at ten o'clock to select a new rates committee: Joseph Pope (whose wife was once afflicted), Joseph Holten Jr., James Smith, and two of Rebecca Nurse's sons-in-law, John Tarbell and Thomas Preston (who had also signed the first witchcraft complaint the previous year). Smith refused to serve.[54]

On the same day, Rev. Samuel Parris baptized Benjamin, the three-day-old son of Benjamin Putnam. The prevailing mood, however, was probably not overly cheerful.[55]

---

*The printed Salem Village records date this Jan. 15, 1693, but that was a Sunday. This seems to be the 25th, after the court order.

January 26, 1693 • Thursday
London, England

The King and his privy council considered Governor Phips's letter of October 12 requesting royal advice on the witchcraft cases. They approved Phips's "stopping the proceedings against the witches in New England." They ordered that "in all future proceedings against persons accused of witchcraft or of possession by the devil [thus lumping accused and afflicted together], all circumspection be used so far as may be without impediment to the ordinary course of justice." The King and council directed the Earl of Nottingham to compose the reply for one of the monarchs to sign.[56]

January 27, 1693 • Friday
Boston

Furious at Governor Fletcher's angry demands, Governor Phips fired an answer back to New York. He refused to extradite a pardoned man. "Your absurd abusive letter demonstrates that if I have forgotten my manners to gentlemen," wrote the self-made man, "I have forgotten what you never had." Fletcher would do better to attack their common enemy of Canada, he added, than to invade Martha's Vineyard.[57]

Elsewhere in Boston, old Governor Bradstreet took to his bed. (He would recover and would live another five years.) But now he revised his will and requested his friends' prayers.[58]

Salem Town

While the former governor contemplated the end of life, the widowed Elizabeth Proctor faced both birth and death in Salem prison, as she struggled to bear her child.* Birth was always dangerous, and far more so in the squalid jail (where people had already died of infectious fevers). But she did survive, with the baby's future to think about, and with her own execution to confront the following week; only the baby's unborn presence had so far delayed her own hanging. Elizabeth named the boy John, after his dead father, even though there was already a half-brother of the same name living.[59]

January 28, 1693 • Saturday
Cambridge

Sarah Cole of Lynn, Mary Toothaker, and Mary Tyler were shuttled back to Cambridge jail until the Superior Court for Middlesex County convened the following week.[60]

---

*Perley gives the birth date, but no source.

January 29, 1693 • Sunday
Boston

Almanacs expected snow, but instead a January thaw made this Sabbath sunny and unusually hot.[61]

January 30, 1693 • Monday
Boston

The governor and council worried over the committee's report on Lieutenant Governor John Usher's accounts, and proposed a Thanksgiving for February 23 to observe various "public mercies" at home and in England.[62]

***
Salem Town

The authorities ordered graves to be dug in Salem prior to the executions—no easy task in frostbound New England. Even if the thaw had melted the snow cover, the ground would still be iron hard. But the diggers persevered, for the hangings were probably scheduled for Wednesday, February 1.[63]

Boston

And all the while the workmen dug in Salem, William Phips pondered in Boston the matter of the upcoming executions, unable to ignore the attorney general's report on accepted evidence.[64]

January 31, 1693 • Tuesday
Charlestown

Superior court for Middlesex began at Charlestown just across the Charles River from Boston. Chief Justice William Stoughton, Justices Thomas Danforth, John Richards, Wait-Still Winthrop, and Samuel Sewall presided. The first day dealt mainly with swearing in the Grand Jury, and Simon Stone as its foreman, and with a few cases, such as Mary Toothaker's and Mary Taylor's. (Evidence against widow Toothaker and other Middlesex residents had been presented to, or at least sworn to, the Essex County grand jury a few weeks earlier.)[65]

While the juries decided on suits and appeals concerning the disposal of disputed-but-mundane cargo, the Dustin and Coleson women were brought directly to Charlestown from Salem. Sheriff Phillips, who had spent nine shillings for firewood to keep his prisoners warm, besides the hire of a guard, brought Sarah Cole, Mary Toothaker, and Mary Taylor from the Cambridge jail.[66]

Boston

Little had gone right lately for Phips, who was thoroughly tired of being opposed and patronized. After brooding on the situation, the governor decided to reassert himself by reprieving the condemned—at least until he heard from London as he had originally planned. Phips countermanded Stoughton's execution warrant (without telling the chief justice) and sent the reprieve to Salem.[67]

14

FEBRUARY 1693

> *Who it is obstructs the cause of Justice I know*
> *not, but thereby the Kingdom of Satan is ad-*
> *vanced.*
>
> —Chief Justice William Stoughton

February 1, 1693 • Wednesday
Charlestown

If the weather were as dry and windy as predicted, the estuary was choppy while the crowds crossed on the ferry from Boston to Charlestown. Court no sooner began when news arrived of Governor Phips's reprieves. Chief Justice William Stoughton was as furious as he was astonished.

"We were in a way to have cleared the land of these!" he exclaimed. "Who it is obstructs the cause of Justice I know not, but thereby the Kingdom of Satan is advanced. The Lord have mercy on this country."* Then he stormed from the court and refused to have any more to do with the session. (Whatever he said to Phips was not recorded, but the latter would refer to Stoughton as "enraged and filled with passionate anger.")[1]

Thomas Danforth took over as chief justice for the rest of the sitting. The court handled one probate case, cleared five or six witchcraft charges by proclamation, and tried five more. (The records list the cases in chronological order, but relate no further dates. The official record lists only Jan. 31 and Feb. 1 for this sitting. An anonymous account says "Mr. D———" headed the court "3 several days." Sewall was in Boston for a council meeting Feb. 2, but Jane Lilly was cleared by proclamation Feb. 3.)[2]

Martha Toothaker, widowed since her husband Roger's death in jail, was indicted for signing a covenant with the Devil on a piece of birch rind. She pleaded not guilty, contrary to her earlier confession, and, being so found by the jury, was ordered released on payment of fees. Mary Taylor of Reading was also indicted for a Hellish covenant, and Sarah Cole of Lynn for tormenting Mrs. Mary Brown of Reading. Both were found not guilty.[3]

The most talked-of case was Lydia Dustin's. Because of thirty-year-old gossip "that if there were a witch in the world, she was one," a great throng attended from Boston and elsewhere, perhaps including Boston Constable Robert Calef. She pleaded not guilty to the indictment of tormenting Mrs. Mary Marshall on May 2, 1692, and though thirty witnesses appeared against her with stories of odd events occurring after arguments, their evidence was wholly spectral. Instead of threats, Goody Dustin's responses now sounded more like Christian admonitions: reminders that God would not prosper those who wronged a widow.

Goody Dustin said little in her defense; yet, the jury found her not guilty and the court ordered her freed on payment of fees, which she could not afford. However, there may have been something in the evidence that made even Justice Danforth, who had so long disapproved of spectral evidence, doubt her actual innocence.

"Woman, woman," he admonished her (according to Calef), "repent! There are shrewd things come in against you."[4]

The last tried was Lydia's granddaughter Sarah Dustin, indicted for tormenting Elizabeth Weston of Reading. She, too, pleaded not guilty, and was so found.[5]

---

*Stoughton's remark combines two versions from Calef ("We were in a way to have cleared the land of these, etc., who it is obstructs the course of justice I know not; the Lord be merciful to the country."); and from "Further Account" ("That who it was that obstructed the execution of justice, or hindered those good proceedings they had made, he knew not, but thereby the Kingdom of Satan was advanced, etc. and the Lord have mercy on this country.").

The evening after Lydia Dustin's trial, a Boston man (perhaps Constable Robert Calef) met one of the judges "in a public place" and told him that some people who had attended both the Salem and Charlestown trials thought there was more evidence against Lydia Dustin than against *any* of those condemned in Salem. The judge agreed.[6]

February 2, 1693 • Thursday
Boston

Court may have recessed for a day, so the justices could serve as councilors in Boston, for at a meeting of the council, Governor Phips approved the order for a Public Fast later in the month. It would offer thanks for (among other things) the recent "restraint of enemies, with the check given to the formidable assaults of witchcrafts." Lieutenant Governor (and Chief Justice) William Stoughton did not agree with the description, but must have kept a stony silence, for the bill went to the printer unhindered.[7]

Andover

Nevertheless, the much-afflicted Timothy Swan died in Andover at age thirty of unstated causes, though he apparently suspected witchcraft until the end.[8]

February 3, 1693 • Friday
Charlestown

Jane Lilly was among those cleared by proclamation, as the court tidied up odds and ends of business in Charlestown.[9]

Salem Village

A town meeting notice for February 14 was posted in Salem Village, signed by Thomas Preston, Joseph Pope, Joseph Holten, and John Tarbell. The meeting was to consider who could vote and to void several votes from past meetings—Parris's salary, for one; and the gift of the ministry house, barn, and two acres, which "seem to be conveyed from us after a fraudulent manner."[10]

February 4, 1693 • Saturday
London, England

John Dunton advertised an abridged edition (minus its precautions) of Cotton Mather's *Wonders of the Invisible World*, in London's *Athenian Mercury* (which Dunton also published). The diarist John Evelyn, like much of England's reading public, marveled at the news contained in Mather's account, whole families in Massachusetts giving themselves to the Devil, it seemed, and threatening all hope of public order and safety.[11]

February 5, 1693 • Sunday
Salem Village

Salem Village remained at loggerheads. Thomas Wilkins (the late John Willard's father-in-law), Samuel Nurse, and John Tarbell (the late Rebecca Nurse's son and son-in-law respectively) had long avoided public worship and even (for they were full communing members) the Lord's Table. Peter Cloyse, numbered among the absentees the summer before, now lived in Boston since his wife's release.

The greater meaning of the sacrament was not to be slighted by personal quarrels, so this evening after services, "a general vote of the brotherhood" selected a committee to speak with the absentees privately: Rev. Samuel Parris, Deacons Nathaniel Ingersoll and Edward Putnam, Nathaniel Putnam, John Putnam Sr., and Bray Wilkins (father of the dissenting Thomas).[12]

February 6, 1693 • Monday
Salem Village

Under predictions of cloudy wet weather, Rev. Parris and the church committee visited each of the three local dissenters. None of them offered an explanation for his absence, but they agreed on a conference in the parsonage the following afternoon.[13]

February 7, 1693 • Tuesday
Salem Village

Almanacs again predicted snow or rain, but nothing deterred the three dissenting brethren who arrived at Rev. Parris's door early, around eleven in the morning. He spoke with them one at a time upstairs in his study, or rather he listened.

John Tarbell raged at Parris for over an hour on the idolatry of consulting the possessed, and on bearing false witness in court when describing the touch test. Had it not been for Parris, Tarbell lectured, his mother-in-law Rebecca Nurse might *still* be alive. Wiser men had admitted their past errors and present sorrow, but Parris, "that great persecutor," had not. Until he did, Tarbell, for one, refused to join him in communion, much less receive it from him.

Samuel Nurse continued in a similar vein for another hour until the church committee's scheduled arrival at one o'clock interrupted him. All Parris would, or could, say was that he did not yet see a reason to change his opinion. (After all, his niece Abigail Williams very likely still suffered alarming seizures.) If they wanted a debate, they would have to let him speak also. But Parris did not intend to argue now, so he and Nurse went back downstairs to the appointed meeting.

After the opening prayer Parris addressed the three dissenters to remind them that he and the committee were appointed by the church to inquire about their absences. He paused, but instead of repeating their earlier volley of complaints, the three men only asked for time to consider their response.

"You know, brethren, of your dissent," Parris prompted, "and doubtless you cannot be to seek of the reasons of it."

But all they did was agree to another meeting on February 16. Parris invited them to bring their absenting wives as well. As long as the committee knew ahead of time, he added, making sure that the dissenters knew he meant to follow the rules (for the church had authorized the committee to treat only with the brethren).[14]

February 8, 1693 • Wednesday
Boston

Governor Phips opened the General Court's new sitting at two o'clock, and the legislature again faced the pressing need for money to pay the soldiers.[15]

Salem Village

Peter Cloyse, meanwhile, arrived in Salem Village from Boston to accost Rev. Parris with the same objections as the other dissenters, and to receive much the same answer. He left, then returned shortly with the other three *and* William Way, another church member. Parris let them choose in what order they would discuss the matter with him up in his study. Demanding satisfaction, Cloyse came first, accompanied by Way and Thomas Wilkins. This conflict, Parris could now see, was not going to remain either a private personal dispute or a pastoral discussion between a brother and his minister—for Cloyse had brought formal witnesses. But while both were full church members, as required, one was also part of the dispute and so ineligible. They said that one would be enough when Parris pointed out this discrepancy, but he refused, which ended the meeting.[16]

February 9–10, 1693 • Thursday–Friday
Boston

The General Court debated the regulation of town matters and realized that, since taxes were trickling in so slowly, the government might have to borrow money.[17]

Mercy Short, well for about seven weeks, though frail and subject to fainting, felt uneasy again as the moon turned full. She kept catching whiffs of brimstone in the house.[18]

February 11, 1693 • Saturday
Boston

While the General Court discussed the bounty on wolves, Lydia and Sarah Dustin, Elizabeth Coleson, and Sarah Cole (all of them acquitted on the charge of witchcraft) were transferred from Boston to the Cambridge jail until their fines could be paid.[19]

February 12, 1693 • Sunday
Boston

Rev. Cotton Mather customarily observed his birthdays with thanks for his blessings and with a new diary volume. Thinking of his past poor health and his present age (thirty), he selected Psalm 102:24 for his sermon text: "I said, 'O my God, take me not away in the midst of my days.'"[20]

But the service did not go smoothly, for Mercy Short was overwhelmed by her specters before it ended. (She was again subject to all the old tortures and even some new ones. For the next week she would be unable to eat anything.)[21]

February 14, 1693 • Tuesday
Salem Village

While the General Court met in Boston to discuss the regulation of wolves, sailors, and vital records, the Salem Village men gathered in their meeting house at eleven o'clock. They decided that all ratable men living within the boundaries could nominate and appoint committees, and could vote in any public concern. Clearly, they considered the selection of ministers to be a "public" rather than a "church" matter (in accordance with the recent law). But whatever they may have discussed about Parris's salary or parsonage deed was, as usual, not recorded.[22]

February 15, 1693 • Wednesday
Boston

The legislature considered slight changes in various laws, including the one that Salem Village had used a day earlier.[23]

Governor Phips, meanwhile, wrote at length to the Earl of Nottingham about his troubles with Captain Short from the trip over to the January fight. Phips likely included in the package other letters from Gunner Thomas Dobbins and from the *Nonsuch*'s purser Matthew Cary, who described Short's drunken cruelties.[24]

February 16, 1693 • Thursday
Boston

The General Court determined that taxes would be levied at eighteen pence for every assessed pound, and granted Rev. Increase Mather £100 for his work at Harvard College. (His opponents would gossip that the sum was actually £500 and that he "huffed" at the amount. In fact, Increase had spent over £500 of his own money in England transacting province business. Nevertheless, the anti-Mather faction thought he shouldn't be paid anything unless he moved to Cambridge full time.)[25]

The governor and council, faced with the "extraordinary charges" left by the Court of Oyer and Terminer, authorized £40 partial payment to Salem tavern-keeper Mrs. Mary Gedney for providing refreshments to jurors and witnesses. The court also revised its letter to the queen, since the ship carrying it was still in port. After thanking the monarchs for the two frigates with the customary effusions, the General Court emphasized the war's great losses and costs, which would not improve as long as the French were active. The court hoped, too, that the province's inhabitants would not have to pay for Fort William Henry and its garrison, as the place was too remote to be useful. (This hope proved vain, however.)[26]

Salem Village

As planned, Samuel Nurse, John Tarbell, and Thomas Wilkins (but not their wives) met with Rev. Samuel Parris and the church committee in the parsonage to present their complaints. The three dissenters (Samuel Nurse read aloud) had long borne a "burden of great grievances by reason of some unwarrantable actings of Mr. Parris, as we esteem them."

They had proceeded in an orderly manner "to obtain satisfaction from him, and had taken steps thereunto, according to the advice of some neighboring elders" (other ministers). But Parris himself and this church committee had obstructed their efforts by demanding to know why they absented themselves from communion (an irregular proceeding to their minds, "because in this case we esteem ourselves to be the plaintiffs"). Since they had made the first move according to the rules as defined by Christ, they now wanted the freedom to continue. If there were any further obstruction, the three dissenters would take the matter before the whole church and even other outside parties. But beyond the hint of Parris's "unwarrantable actings," Nurse, Tarbell, and Wilkins still would not specify their complaints to the committee.

The cited rule in Matthew 18:15–16 advised any with a grievance to solve disputes privately with the party concerned. If that person would not listen, one should take two or three others to witness the negotiations. If the opponent still wouldn't listen, the problem could be presented to the church as a whole. If he wouldn't listen then, he was a lost cause.

Despite the dissenters' valid grief and anger over the trials and executions, their explanation did not jibe with events because there were two complaints in collision. Since the dissenters blamed Parris for the unfair deaths of their kin, they no doubt felt that his distribution of the sacraments showed more disrespect to the institution than their avoidance of it. But the church committee's visits concerning their absence had *preceded* rather than followed their complaint, and had actually begun in August. Even with the recent change in court procedure, Parris and the others still agreed with the court's earlier guilty verdicts, and Parris's niece was probably still afflicted.

Rather than keep their own pastor and church in the dark, said Parris, it would have been better to speak with him before consulting outsiders. The three men only pleaded ignorance, but it took a good deal of persuasion before they let Deacon Putnam even copy their paper of complaints. Parris later copied this document, and wrote an account of the meeting in the church records. Now that this was obviously a church matter, he also described the February 7 and 8 encounters.[27]

February 17, 1693 • Friday
Boston

Northward, ice was already breaking up on the Merrimack River. In Boston, the General Court passed bills requiring town clerks to keep a register of births and deaths, and changed the law concerning ministers. The general, ratable inhabitants of a place could choose their pastor (the bill now clarified) only when no gathered church was yet established, and then only with the advice of three neighboring ministers. When an already established church needed a new minister, the full communing members would find the candidate, then present him for final approval to those members of the general congregation who could vote in public matters (even if not in church matters). Furthermore, the law required (with a detail of even *more* interest to Salem Village) that if a town neglected to pay its minister as contracted, on complaint the local quarterly court could require the town's selectmen to fulfill the obligation, and could fine the delinquents on a rising scale. (The fines would go, *not* to the minister, but to the town's poor.)[28]

The governor's council again ordered town constables to collect back taxes, for the treasury had no money to pay the soldiers. Samuel Sewall, meanwhile, saw his former judicial colleague Nathaniel Saltonstall, noticeably the worse for drink, slumped on a bench across the council chamber. Sewall went over and struck up a conversation about a mutual friend and Saltonstall grew quite merry. But "his head and hand," Sewall observed, "were rendered less useful than at other times."[29]

February 18, 1693 • Saturday
Boston

The General Court concluded its session by extending the present rates of shipping duties and imports to the end of the following June. And the council met with the governor to consider a list of expenses submitted by the Wells garrison. They ordered partial payment, and reiterated the five shillings per diem wage to representatives while on duty.[30]

February 20, 1693 • Monday
Boston

Sabbath over, the representatives dispersed to their home communities (except for the Boston gentlemen who represented remote towns) while the council met with the governor to finish the correspondence for London.[31]

February 21, 1693 • Tuesday
Boston

The council faced John Usher's renewed request for back pay (earned years before when a councilor and treasurer under Andros, before he became Lieutenant Governor of New Hampshire) and postponed a decision by asking for an audit.[32]

As long as the ship *Walter and Thomas* was available to carry mail, Governor Phips wrote some thoughts of his own to the Earl of Nottingham. The governor was emboldened, perhaps, by Stoughton's absence from the council meeting while the latter recovered from a fall.[33]

Phips summarized the problems caused by the swarm of witchcraft cases begun before his arrival as governor and by his required absences Eastward. He emphasized that Lieutenant Governor William Stoughton, as Chief Justice, had headed the witchcraft court and had continued to accept spectral evidence, even after most people, including Phips, no longer trusted it. Therefore, he (Phips) ended the court and ordered the suspects released on bail. Only when the judges agreed to alter proceedings, because they had acted too harshly before, did he permit a special Superior Court for Essex. Although that session found only three persons guilty, Phips yet had doubts, especially after

Stoughton was so quick to sign eight execution warrants. So Phips reprieved them all until further notice. In spite of Stoughton's voluble disgust, the storm of accusations ceased once the courts changed their procedure and emphasis on spectral evidence.[34]

About six o'clock in the evening, a meteor blazed over Boston west to southeast and shot off seven or eight fire balls during the two minutes that it was visible.[35]

***

Boston

Mercy Short's North End neighbors may have seen the meteor on their way to pray with her. The regular weekly Young Folks meetings—one for young men, the other for young women—took turns watching with the neighbors in Mercy's "haunted chamber." There was someone by her nearly all the time.

Her first fast lasted about a week. Once she could eat again, it was only a mouthful every few days. If anyone offered her an apple or biscuit, it often disappeared—snatched by specters, Mercy said, watching them eat what they stole.

Others in the room during her torments felt themselves scratched, jabbed, or brushed by unseen entities. Ordinarily level-headed folk fainted in astonishment when they collided with spectral dogs and cats. Some men, striking their swords where the specters seemed to be were later spooked by apparitions while returning home. Although they kept these embarrassing encounters to themselves, Mercy soon discerned and revealed all, for the specters bragged of their retaliations. At this point Cotton Mather advised that those so afflicted use the Arms of the Church, faith, instead of sidearms, which only aggravated the situation.

Mercy continued her habit of leafing through a Bible without looking in order to find rebuttals to her devils' arguments. She was convinced that these impulses were communications from a helpful spirit, who stood by her, unseen, hardly heard.[36]

***

Salem Village

Some time in February, John Hadlock returned to Salem Village from his tour of duty Eastward, and reckoned with Francis Nurse for the remaining seven shillings owed for his service in Benjamin Nurse's stead. Francis paid all but four shillings, which Hadlock picked up a few days later from Benjamin Nurse, who had most benefited from the arrangement. Benjamin paid Hadlock himself on that occasion, and thought the business ended. (Hadlock, however, would eventually think otherwise.)[37]

February 22, 1693 • Wednesday
Salem Town

John Andrews, Salem shipwright, presented the will of his father-in-law George Jacobs Sr. to the Essex County probate court, "the other executor being beyond sea." George Jacobs Jr., the other executor, was still in hiding from a witchcraft charge. Shortly before his execution, George Jacobs Sr. had made a second will disinheriting his daughter Ann and her husband. The court had both wills at hand, but approved this, the earlier document.[38]

February 23, 1693 • Thursday
Massachusetts

This Lecture Day was also a Public Thanksgiving, when the churches offered thanks for the state of the British government, for the area's previous harvest and present health, for the safe return of those abroad on public business, and for the "restraint of enemies, with the check given to the formidable assaults of witchcrafts."[39]

February 24, 1693 • Friday
Boston

The governor and council faced a £2,400 debt (plus 7 percent annual interest) borrowed from four of the councilors to pay other debts in England and to feed the soldiers Eastward. They definitely needed the soldiers, for news arrived from New York of a French and Indian force attacking their Mohawk allies.[40]

Salem

Encouraged by his removal of the hired men's house, John Trask returned to the disputed "Corwin Farm" in Salem to cut and carry off timber, and not for the first time either.[41]

February 25, 1693 • Saturday
Andover

The much-tormented Rose Foster, daughter of Andover's Constable Ephraim Foster and granddaughter of the accused Rebecca Eames, died in Andover, aged fourteen, the apparent victim of spectral torments.[42]

February 27, 1693 • Monday
Boston

Governor Phips relaxed the ban on visitors to Captain Short at the Castle. Accordingly, the cook from the *Nonsuch* conferred with his former officer on how to get Short's supporters to England with him to confirm his version of the events.[43]

Samuel Parris (1653–1720). This may be a portrait of the Salem Village pastor in whose home the witchcraft panic began in 1692. (*Massachusetts Historical Society, Boston, Massachusetts.*)

These fragments of a green glass bottle, a blue decorated Rhenish stoneware jug, and the rim of a pewter plate with the monogram of Samuel and Elizabeth Parris, were excavated from the Salem Village parsonage site in Danvers. (*Richard B. Trask.*)

Salem Village Parsonage. (*Courtesy of the author.*)

Rev. Increase Mather (1639–1723), depicted in a portrait that he brought home from England along with the charter in 1692. He and his son Cotton were two of the most prominent Congregational clergymen of the period. (*Massachusetts Historical Society, Boston, Massachusetts.*)

Rev. Cotton Mather (1663–1723), here pictured three decades after the Salem trials. His book *Memorable Providences*, describing the suspected witchcraft of an Irish washerwoman in Boston, proved influential to a public that largely ignored his precautions in the witch scare of 1692. (*American Antiquarian Society, Worcester, Massachusetts.*)

Harvard College, Cambridge, Massachusetts. (*Courtesy of the author.*)

William Stoughton (1631–1701), career politician, was Chief Justice of both the Court of Oyer and Terminer and the Superior Court that succeeded it. (*Danvers Archival Center, Danvers, Massachusetts.*)

Samuel Sewall (1652–1701), merchant, diarist, and judge (here portrayed long after the trials), served on both the Court of Oyer and Terminer and the Superior Court and made a personal apology for his part in the witch trials. (The caps he and Stoughton wear in their portraits are not judicial, but were what old men wore over their bald spots.) (*Danvers Archival Center, Danvers, Massachusetts.*)

Town House, Boston. (*Courtesy of the author.*)

Wait Still Winthrop (1642-1717) was major general of the militia as well as judge in both the Court of Oyer and Terminer and the Superior Court. (*Boston Public Library Rare Books Department.*)

Isaac Addington (1645-1715), secretary of Massachusetts in 1692, was one of the four assistants who observed the April examinations of Sarah Cloyse and Elizabeth Proctor. (*New England Historic Genealogical Society.*)

Salem Village Parsonage site. This 1890s photo of Danvers, before suburbia hid the view, looks from the parsonage site, across the pasture where the spectral witches held their meeting, toward the hill where the Connecticut witches gathered, and the site of the first meetinghouse—here occupied by the white house above and to the right of the stone post. (*Danvers Archival Center, Danvers, Massachusetts.*)

George Jacobs Sr.'s house (rear), Salem. (*Courtesy of the author*.)

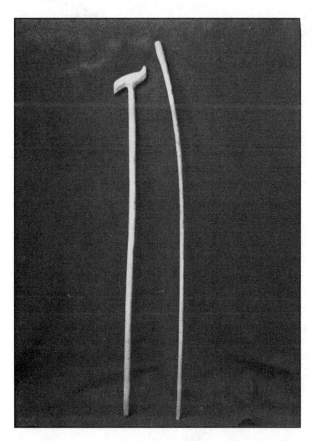

George Jacobs used and probably whittled these two handmade walking sticks, which his specter reportedly used to beat his maidservant. (*Peabody Essex Museum; glass negative 18,790*.)

Nurse Farm, Salem Village. (*Courtesy of the author.*)

This engraved brass sundial once marked the time at John Proctor's farm. (*Peabody Essex Museum; 4143.39.*)

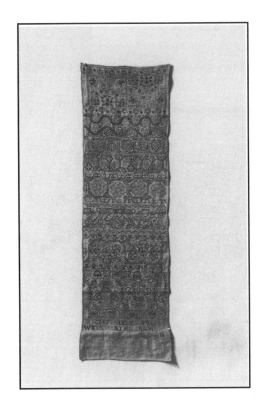

Mary (Hollingsworth) English stitched this intricate sampler as a girl in Salem. (*Peabody Essex Museum*.)

Phlip and Mary English's house, Salem town. (*Courtesy of the author*.)

Fort William Henry, Pemaquid (Maine). (*Courtesy of the author*.)

Salem Village meeting house. (*Courtesy of the author*.)

The Pope cabinet, housing ten small drawers for valuables behind its red and black painted door, was made in Salem in 1679 by the cabinetmaking shop of James Symonds as a wedding gift for a Quaker couple, Joseph and Bethshua (Folger) Pope of Salem Village, years before Mrs. Pope thought Rebecca Nurse bewitched her. (*Peabody Essex Museum; 138,011.*)

House of Judge Peter Sergeant, Boston. (*Courtesy of the author.*)

Regni *ANNÆ* Reginæ Decimo.

Province of the Massachusetts-Bay.

AN ACT,

Made and Passed by the Great and General Court or Assembly of Her Majesty's Province of the Massachusetts-Bay in New-England, Held at Boston the 17th Day of October, 1711.

An Act to Reverse the Attainders of *George Burroughs* and others for Witchcraft.

FOR AS MUCH *as in the Year of our Lord One Thousand Six Hundred Ninety Two, Several Towns within this Province were Infested with a horrible Witchcraft or Possession of Devils ; And at a Special Court of Oyer and Terminer holden at* Salem, *in the County of* Essex *in the same Year One Thousand Six Hundred Ninety Two,* George Burroughs *of Wells,* John Procter, George Jacob, John Willard, Giles Core, *and his Wife,* Rebecca Nurse, *and* Sarah Good, *all of* Salem *aforesaid* : Elizabeth How, *of* Ipswich, Mary Eastey, Sarah Wild *and* Abigail Hobbs *all of* Topsfield : Samuel Wardell, Mary Parker, Martha Carrier, Abigail Falkner, Anne Foster, Rebecca Eames, Mary Post, *and* Mary Lacey, *all of* Andover : Mary Bradbury *of* Salisbury : *and* Dorcas Hoar *of* Beverly ; *Were severally Indicted, Convicted and Attained of Witchcraft, and some of them put to Death, Others lying still under the like Sentence of the said Court, and liable to have the same Executed upon them.*

A   The

The 1711 reversal of attainder, of which the first page is pictured, exonerated twenty-two convicted people but omitted to state the names of five who were hanged—an omission not corrected until 2001. (*Danvers Archival Center, Danvers, Massachusetts.*)

15

MARCH 1693

By our maintaining and upholding differences amongst us, we do but gratify the Devil, that grand adversary of our souls.

—Salem Village dissenters' petition

March 1, 1693 • Wednesday
Boston

Captain Richard Short (and the government mail) was officially entrusted to Jeremiah Tay, commander of the merchant ship *Walter and Thomas*. Governor Phips ordered that Short be taken directly to the Earl of Nottingham, and warned Tay not to take aboard any men from the *Nonsuch*. Phips also sent Matthew Cary, the *Nonsuch*'s purser, to arrest several deserters then heading north to New Hampshire with horses and money provided by one of the ship owners (Nathaniel Byfield, one of Phips's political foes) and discharge papers dated January 3, the day before Short's arrest. Phips, however, was certain that Short had written them well *after* his suspension.[1]

March 2, 1693 • Thursday
Cambridge, Salem, & Boston

Elizabeth Coleson left the Cambridge jail, where her aged grandmother Lydia Dustin was seriously ill. Mary Post and Dorcas Hoar, both condemned but not executed, also left prison around this time. And Philip English presented (or sent) a petition to Governor Phips demanding back all his goods "illegally" seized the August before by Sheriff George Corwin.[2]

March 3, 1693 • Friday
Boston

The Upper House labored over tax assessments, and swore in members of the lower court for Suffolk County: John Foster, Peter Sergeant, and Isaac Addington.[3]

Nathaniel Saltonstall was again absent from the legislature. Samuel Sewall, disturbed by reports of his friend's drinking, composed a letter urging him to break off the habit. Saltonstall apparently felt that everyone was against him because he had not received a Superior Court judgeship. He also suspected that a faction at home wanted to replace him as major of Haverhill's militia. Sewall emphasized that *he* had not advised the governor to exclude Saltonstall, nor did he know who had. He also offered condolences for the troubles caused by past reports of Saltonstall's specter.[4]

March 4, 1693 • Saturday
Boston

The Upper House met at nine o'clock to suggest paying the governor £500 for his work on behalf of the Province, since the charter neglected to mention a salary for that office. Then, in its role as governor's council, the members selected a committee to peruse the war committee's accounts.[5]

March 5, 1693 • Sunday
Salem Village

Salem Village now observed communion on the first Sunday of the month like other congregations. Rev. Samuel Parris continued his series of sermons on I Corinthians 11:23–27 describing the Last Supper, a Passover seder the night before Christ's death. Parris compared the Paschal lamb with communion's "spiritual nourishment," and compared Passover at length with Christian symbolism. For the sacrificial lamb and the Israelites' Passover corresponded to Christ and the Lord's Supper. "This do in remembrance of me," Christ had said (in the sermon's text).

"Great and weighty things take up the mind and thoughts of wise and serious dying men," said Parris. "That then must needs be a most weighty and excellent ordinance that our Lord instituted with His departing breath." Therefore, he added (referring to the dissenters), surely God's command in Numbers 9:13—where anyone eligible for Passover who yet neglected it "shall be cut off from among his people"—applied to Christians as well.

"Now then," Parris concluded, "I entreat you meditate on these things, and see how you will excuse yourselves for neglecting this great ordinance."[6]

Piscataqua

Matthew Cary, purser of the *Nonsuch*, found and seized the four deserters at Piscataqua. But Lieutenant Governor John Usher of New Hampshire rescued them all and nearly jailed Cary.[7]

March 6, 1693 • Monday
Cambridge

The Boston area ministers met at Harvard to discuss just what power synods could wield over the affairs of individual churches like Salem Village's church. (They concluded that synods could only advise.)[8]

Eastward

After three days of trying to evade the *Nonsuch's* sloop, the *Walter and Thomas* paused at Gloucester, while Captain Short sent a messenger overland to retrieve his men from New Hampshire. (They would refuse, however, to leave the safety of Usher's jurisdiction.)[9]

Partly due to Captain Short, Governor Phips was absent from the council meeting, which was still embroiled in the question of tax assessments.[10]

Phips was in Boston, however, where he interviewed Essex sheriff George Corwin, who delivered the inventory of goods confiscated from Philip English. Although (as English himself would say) much of it had been "used to subsist the numerous company of prisoners," Corwin promised to return everything.[11]

March 7, 1693 • Tuesday
Boston

Governor Phips and the Upper House considered tax assessments, and ordered a vessel outfitted to guard Martha's Vineyard. He was no doubt pleased that the legislature agreed to grant him £500 to cover his expenses and service since his arrival.[12]

The spell of warm weather ended in "a sore storm of snow," as Sewall noted. He was also surprised to see Nathaniel Saltonstall in the council chamber. As he had not yet sent his letter, Sewall delivered it himself. Saltonstall took the advice in the spirit in which it was offered, thanked Sewall for his concern, and asked for his prayers.[13]

March 8, 1693 • Wednesday
Boston

Mercy Short was still violently besieged by specters urging her to sign the Devil's book, the third volume so far, two others being already full of signatures. She demanded that the specters let her see what they would have her sign, and then amazed the attending neighbors by apparently reading from the invisible book. Its contents sounded like a journal of the witches' meetings and their instructions for proselytizing, along with a list of recruits and their terms of service. Again, Cotton Mather warned against spreading reports of those names.

This evening Mather and others heard Mercy trying to spell a long, apparently unfamiliar word. "Quadragesima," he thought it was, referring to the forty days of Lent, which in 1693 had begun March 1. (Of course, Puritans did not observe Lent, but Mercy's Canadian captors did.) She also read an invisible passage (used to persuade converts) stating that even the apostles Paul and Silas had invoked the Devil, who then freed them from prison by earthquake. ("Horrible stuff!" thought Mather, recognizing the parody.)[14]

March 9, 1693 • Thursday
Boston

The Upper House, still busy with the tax committee, voted down a bill to divide Essex County. And the Sewall household was in an uproar after young Joseph swallowed a bullet.[15]

March 10, 1693 • Friday
Cambridge

It had been four weeks since her return to Cambridge jail after being declared not guilty of witchcraft. Old Lydia Dustin, still unable to pay her prison fees, died— and so ended her captivity.[16]

Little Compton

Little Compton, to the legislature's relief, finally agreed to readjust its boundary. Most of the rebels had accepted the terms of amnesty and the ringleaders were in custody. (One would escape to Rhode Island before trial, while a second would decamp afterward without paying his fine.)[17]

Piscataqua

Phips's men, meantime, arrested Captain Short's messenger on his return to Gloucester, but the *Walter and Thomas* escaped to sea and tacked toward Piscataqua. Informed of this development, Phips sent purser Cary to follow in his sloop and remind Tay *not* to allow the deserters to board. (But Usher's men would arrest Cary as soon as he landed.)[18]

March 11, 1693 • Saturday
Boston

After dealing with tax assessments in the Upper House, Samuel Sewall attended a sunset funeral for a four-year-old Holyoke twin, who had perished in a well. He returned home to find his own son had safely passed the bullet.[19]

March 13, 1693 • Monday
Boston

If Little Compton was no longer a problem, then New York was. The General Court read a letter from Queen Mary—sent October 11, 1692—requiring New England, Virginia, Maryland, and Pennsylvania to help New York defend Albany. (As this order was not reciprocal, none of the provinces cooperated. Sir William Penn would nearly be relieved of his post for his refusal.)[20]

Boston, meanwhile, held its annual town meeting to select local officers, thus ending Robert Calef's term as constable.[21]

Salem

And in Salem, miller John Trask received a writ from Jonathan Corwin ordering him to appear at the next county court (where Corwin would be a judge) to answer an action of trespass and the carrying away of a house and timber.[22]

***

Boston

At the beginning of the week, Mercy Short's guardian spirit encouraged her to be steadfast, for she would be free of her torments by the following Thursday evening. So Mercy asked that Cotton Mather and his brother Samuel be with her then.[23]

Around the same time, Cotton's wife Abigail had a bad fright in the entry of her own home. Near her time of giving birth, she felt "her bowels to turn within her" from fear when she saw "an horrible specter." Before and after this encounter, as Cotton learned later, the specters hounding Mercy had boasted that they meant to frighten Mrs. Mather in order to hurt her infant, if not herself as well.[24]

And all the while, the specters toyed with their own and stolen books. Governor Phips, at Mercy's request (and perhaps as a distraction to his troubles with Captain Short) visited the girl with Cotton Mather. She confided to them that she knew where the specters had recently lost the second of their three volumes: "in the cockloft of a garret belonging to the house of a person of quality."

Neither Phips nor Mather thought that the book had a tangible reality, and both knew that devils were liars. But after a few days, "upon mature consideration" (or because they could not stand the suspense), they found an excuse to send "a discreet servant" after the "book." The man no sooner climbed into the attic than a great black cat rushed over him and away, scaring him out of the attic for good. That household, furthermore, did not own a black cat or know anything about one.

The people attending to Mercy assured Mather that no one had told her anything about the incident, yet she seemed to know all about it. Mercy thought that the specters might soon lose the book again, but Cotton Mather could see they were only toying with him, and determined to ignore any further wild-goose chases.

Sometimes, after several hours in a senseless daze, Mercy described how specters carried her spirit to distant witch meetings. Many French Canadians and Indian Sagamores attended these events, she said (as a few of the confessed suspects had described earlier). Some of the attendees followed her back home and joined her usual tormentors. They showed Mercy certain religious books that they used at their meetings, and claimed that they stole the volumes from Cotton Mather's library whenever they wanted. Mercy, who had apparently never seen the minister's library, described the volumes in enough detail for him to locate and identify them later: an ordinary Catholic devotional and another for Holy Week. Over the next few days he kept finding the books misshelved or with their pages folded down. When he visited Mercy next, her specters bragged about how they stole the book again yesterday. Cotton was not convinced that the volumes had ever left the house, but he wondered about the similarities between Popish ceremony and devilish enchantment, between French attempts against Protestantism and Hell's assaults against New England.[25]

March 14, 1693 • Tuesday
Boston

Although her North End neighbors still prayed with, and for, Mercy Short, they no longer volunteered for the more time-consuming days of prayer and fasting. Remembering the apparent healing in sequences of three, Cotton Mather began a private fast of his own for her recovery.[26]

The governor and council met during the afternoon to authorize military aid to Connecticut and to urge the representatives to finish the tax assessment lists. Phips also wrote (for a second time) to Lieutenant Governor John Usher of New Hampshire asking for the *Nonsuch* deserters back, and criticizing Usher's lax sense of duty in taking them from the officer whom Phips had sent to retrieve them.[27]

March 16, 1693 • Thursday
Boston

When Cotton and Samuel Mather visited Mercy Short this evening, they found her free of pain, but still arguing with the Invisible World. Something prevented the specters from touching her, even though (as she later described it) the Devil was there to cuff and to kick his minions.

"Well, I see you are going," Mercy taunted. "What good counsel have you to give me, before you go?" She interrupted their snarled answer to advise them that even if the Devil were beyond help, the rest of them still had time to repent.

But the specters refused to listen. "Go and be damned!" they cried. "We can do no more."

"Oh, ye cursed wretches!" Mercy exclaimed. "Is *that* your blessing? Well after all the wrong that you have done to me, I do not wish that anyone of you may be damned. I wish you may *all* be saved, if that be possible. However, in the name of the blessed Lord Jesus Christ, be gone! And let me be no more troubled with you."

The specters rushed from the room in a torrent, leaving enough consternation in their apparent wake that another young woman fell in a faint as if struck. The fainter revived and everyone gave thanks for Mercy's deliverance. (And indeed, Mercy Short would never after be troubled in this way.)[28]

March 17, 1693 • Friday
Boston

William Stoughton was absent from this last day of the General Court. After the legislators voted for a total tax of £30,000, Rev. Samuel Willard offered the closing prayer, and the session dissolved about one o'clock.[29]

March 18, 1693 • Saturday
Hartford, Connecticut

When Mercy Short had repeated the names of her tormenting specters to the Mathers, they both kept the information to themselves unless it seemed wiser to warn the accused. Secretary John Allen of Connecticut, for one, wrote his thanks to Increase Mather: "As to what you mention, concerning the poor creature in your town that is afflicted, and mentioned my name to yourself and son, I return you hearty thanks for your intimation about it, and for your charity therein mentioned, and have great cause to bless God, who of his mercy hitherto, hath not let me fall into such an horrid evil."[30]

March 20, 1693 • Monday
Andover

Abigail Faulkner, free at last and back home in Andover, gave birth to a son whose presence had safely delayed her execution. She named him Ammiruhama—a combination of Hebrew names that means "My people have received mercy."[31]

Boston

Phips at last received news from the King that a British war fleet would arrive at Boston in late May or early June en route to attacking Canada. Today he acknowledged the order and promised to have reinforcements and supplies ready for this long-awaited expedition.[32]

March 22, 1693 • Wednesday
Boston

Samuel Sewall's chimney caught fire at noon, blazing alarmingly at the top and setting the wooden shingles afire, while the frantic family snatched their dinner from the hearth beneath. Fortunately, there was no more harm done than that, and the crisis soon ended. The Sewalls were able to sit down with their guests and to dine merrily on rescued Westfield pork.[33]

March 23, 1693 • Thursday
Boston

The governor and council discussed the establishment of a post office, as the queen had ordered, and assigned £29 to Benjamin Harris for printing the province's new laws.[34]

Cambridge

Sarah Cole of Lynn and Sarah Dustin, meanwhile, were released from Cambridge jail (where the latter's mother Lydia Dustin had recently died).[35]

March 27, 1693 • Monday
Salem Village

John Tarbell and Peter Cloyse arrived on Parris's doorstep at evening with Joseph Holten Sr., Joseph Putnam, and (soon after) William Osborn of Salem town. None of the last three, Parris noted, were members of the Village church so they could not serve as witnesses to a formal church complaint. The dissenters handed Parris an undated, unsigned petition addressed to himself and "to some others of the plantation" (meaning the settlement of Salem Village).

The petition requested a council of mutually chosen elders (other ministers) to hear the grievances between Parris and themselves. "Those uncomfortable differences" were "very dishonorable to God and a scandal to religion, and very uncomfortable to ourselves, and an ill example to those that may come after us. And by our maintaining and upholding differences amongst us, we do but gratify the Devil, that grand adversary of our souls."

It sounded like a pack of "confused calumnies" to Parris. And although it began with the opening, "We whose names are underwritten," there were no signatures, only a snipped-out space that might have once held two or three names.

Just who, asked Parris, was *this* from?

From all the plantation, they answered, a great many of them anyway, and it would be signed all in good time. So Parris slipped the paper into his pock-et. When the others demanded an answer, he told them that he would consider it.[36]

March 28, 1693 • Tuesday
Ipswich

Many Salem Villagers spent the day in Ipswich at the quarterly court (where Judge Jonathan Corwin lost his trespass suit against John Trask, but then appealed). Acting on behalf of their church, Nathaniel and John Putnam entered a complaint against the new rates committee for refusing to do its job. The rates committee members insisted on a jury, which found them guilty of negligence as charged—except for James Smith, who had refused to be part of the committee, and Joseph Holten, whose lameness kept him from the job. The losers had to pay £1 in costs plus a fine of forty shillings and twelve shillings and sixpence costs each (which would go to the Village poor fund). Unrepentant, Thomas Preston, John Tarbell, and Joseph Pope paid in full. The court ordered them to assess the Village inhabitants for the present and past two years for Rev. Parris's salary "per agreement," and to keep a written record of the sums. The court also disallowed the Village's vote to allow any ratable man a vote in any local matter.[37]

Salem Village

Returning to Salem Village that evening, John Tarbell, Peter Cloyse, and Joseph Hutchinson Sr. pounded on Parris's door for an answer to their petition. He found the visit disquieting, but all he would say was "I had not considered of it yet."[38]

Boston

In Boston, between four and five o'clock, Abigail Mather gave birth to a "comely and hearty" boy. As this infant was the couple's first son, they named him Increase after his paternal grandfather. But while Cotton Mather received his friends' good wishes on the child's birth, his father Increase received a strange, angry letter from a woman once suspected of witchcraft. In it she railed against Cotton and declared, "He little knew what might quickly befall some of his posterity." The Mathers remembered the spectral threats against the child and soon realized that, for all his apparent health, the baby was feeling noticeably uncomfortable.[39]

Piscataqua

Governor Phips, meanwhile, was in Piscataqua to retrieve Captain Short and the government mail. He sailed into the river about six in the evening under his Vice Admiral flag—just in time to see the *Walter and Thomas* flee back upstream. He found the vessel anchored in the harbor at Great Island but occupied by only a few sailors who claimed that they could not take his orders.[40]

March 29, 1693 • Wednesday
Great Island, New Hampshire

After a night ashore, Governor Phips found Captain Tay but *not* Short or the deserters. He took back his warrant entrusting Short to Tay, and ripped his seal and signature off to void it. Then, when Tay seemed likely to use the torn document as an example of unjust proceedings, Phips wrested that from him and demanded Short and his trunks. Tay claimed that the governor had no authority in New Hampshire—a view that Phips as "Admiral of New England" did *not* share. By noon, Phips had a blacksmith remove the hardware from the door of the *Walter and Thomas*'s great cabin, extracted Short's trunks, and sent them to Boston on the *Nonsuch*'s sloop. Short, the trunks, and the mail were still intended for England on another ship. However, Phips could not find Short or the deserters, and could not get a local warrant for their arrest. Instead, the gates of the fort were shut in his face and a file of musketeers sent to keep him out.[41]

March 30, 1693 • Thursday
Boston

The Council (minus the governor) set a schedule of postal rates, while the Mather infant became more and more unwell.[42]

March 31, 1693 • Friday
Boston

As their child continued to suffer, Cotton and Abigail Mather realized that their infant's bowels must be in some way blocked, for no wastes had passed. The parents applied what cures they could. Provident housewives knew any number of herbal remedies, and Cotton had studied medicine. They doubtless called in the family doctor. Nothing worked.[43]

APRIL 1693

*Shall we receive good at the hands of God and
shall we not receive evil?*

—Job 2:10

April 1, 1693 • Saturday
Boston

"The moans of your sick children," Cotton Mather would later write to other griev-
ing parents, "may be stabs to your hearts, and pierce and cut like daggers there."
The Mather baby's agony continued, tended by his parents, until ten o'clock on
Sabbath eve when he died, unbaptized.[1]

April 2, 1693 • Sunday
Boston

Sleepless and bereaved, Cotton Mather delivered morning and afternoon sermons
on the theme of loss in an effort to make some sense of his child's death—an all-

too-common occurrence. "Shall we receive good at the hands of God," Mather quoted from Job, "and shall we not receive evil?"[2]

Salem Village

Rev. Samuel Parris continued his series of communion sermons, this time focusing on the subject of bread. As bread is the most basic and necessary nourishment to one's body, so too is Christ, the bread of life, necessary for one's spiritual nourishment. "When you eat your daily bread, think as often of this bread you live without." he warned the congregation (especially the four displeased brethren who could partake but refused to do so). "Since Christ has appointed it, doubtless it cannot be unnecessary or indifferent."[3]

April 3, 1693 • Monday
Boston

An autopsy on Monday showed that the Mather child was internally malformed, unable to pass waste. Many sympathetic neighbors attended the burial on Copp's Hill. But later, as he worked on his account of Mercy Short's illness, Cotton Mather brooded on past spectral threats and on the ominous letter from a woman whose name he never did reveal. Lacking the heart to finish, he broke off the narrative in mid-sentence.[4]

April 14, 1693 • Friday
Salem Village

The "displeased brethren," meanwhile, harried Parris for answers, and for an outside mediating council. He refused to discuss it when they appeared unannounced at his door accompanied by Joseph Hutchinson and the widower Francis Nurse. They did, however, agree on a meeting with proper witnesses, after lecture on April 20.[5]

April 20, 1693 • Thursday
Salem Village

All four dissenters attended the meeting at Nathaniel Putnam's house: Jonathan Tarbell, Samuel Nurse, Thomas Wilkins, and even Peter Cloyse up from Boston. They brought two non-member supporters—Joseph Hutchinson and Israel Porter—the only people (Parris noticed) they associated with now. When they demanded an answer to their paper with the cut-off names, Parris pronounced it a libel. So the four produced another sheet with forty-two signatures: more than the church membership and every one of them, Parris observed as he read it, in the same hand. The four claimed not to know the original's whereabouts, but insisted that the men all signed their own names or had someone do it for them.

They also insisted that their complaint was a church matter despite the involvement of non-members at this stage. They blamed Parris for hindering their opening moves (during the noisy February encounters), and angrily refused to state their case before the present company. The dispute continued until nightfall. When everyone was about to leave, the four finally agreed to meet again the next morning.[6]

April 21, 1693 • Friday
Salem Village

Parris met the dissatisfied four an hour after sunrise at Ingersoll's ordinary with William and Aaron Way and the two deacons as mutually acceptable witnesses. Samuel Nurse, speaking plainly at last, read "a large scroll" of complaints. They avoided Sabbath meetings, he read, because the tumults of the possessed prevented their hearing the sermon, and because they feared the possessed would accuse them. They would not join Parris's prayers about the troubles because of the offensive way in which he described the events. They withdrew from communion because they could not accept it from a man who consulted and believed the possessed, who gave unsound evidence on oath, who would not explain what he had written for the court records, and who persisted in unsound doctrine.

The dissenters refused to let Parris see their list for himself, or even to let him copy it until he called a meeting of the whole church.[7]

April 25, 1693 • Tuesday
Boston

Chief Justice William Stoughton returned to the bench when Superior Court convened in Boston for Suffolk County, assisted by Justices Thomas Danforth, John Richards, and Samuel Sewall. Among the cases heard in the Town House, John Arnold appealed two rulings against him for neglect in "allowing" prisoners to escape from Boston jail (none of them witch suspects) and won.[8]

In addition, Grace, a slave whose newborn was found jammed down a privy, was found guilty of murder. Stoughton pronounced the formal sentence of death against her, and also against Elizabeth Emerson, who had waited in jail two years since being found guilty by the interim government of murdering her twins.[9]

When John Alden appeared as pledged, no one spoke against him. So the court dismissed the case by proclamation (ignoring his jail break and illegal flight).[10]

After two soldiers were found guilty of forging pay vouchers, an apologetic Mary Watkins was brought forward. The details of how she had accused her employer, Mrs. Swift, of witchcraft, then retracted the charge, attempted suicide, then accused herself confused the Grand Jury. The jurors questioned the justices and Mary herself on several points, deliberated, and then declared the charge *ignoramus*. The court sent them back to reconsider, but their verdict remained the same. The court ordered Mary to find sureties for good behavior, and to appear at the next Suffolk sitting. However, as kin and friends alike refused any contact with her, she could not fulfill the court's demand or pay her jail bill, so she returned to Boston prison.[11]

April 26, 1693 • Wednesday
Boston

Governor Phips wrote to Sheriff George Corwin a second time, sharply repeating his order to return all of Philip English's possessions. (As much of English's confiscated wealth had gone to feed the prisoners in 1692, the matter would drag through the courts for years.)[12]

April 30, 1693 • Sunday
Salem Village

After services, Rev. Samuel Parris informed the full church members of the recent dealings with the dissatisfied brethren, and recommended the Village church oblige them with a meeting, although "I do not understand their methods."[13]

17

MAY 1693

The general deportment of the said three dis-
pleased brethren was at this meeting exceeding
unchristian, both to [the] minister and the
other brethren.

—Rev. Samuel Parris

May 7, 1693 • Sunday
Salem Village

Samuel Parris's sacrament sermon enlarged upon Christ's command when offering the bread at the Last Supper: "Take. Eat." The significance was threefold, Parris explained: a command, a promise of benefit represented by the bread, and a duty. For this was no ordinary meal but a spiritual act. As Parris preached, "We must feed upon this wonderful gift as bequeathed to each of us." (But if the displeased brethren were present, they still refused to accept communion from him.)[1]

May 8, 1693 • Monday
Piscataqua

Six people—men, women, and children—were killed by Indian raiders near York, Maine. Another family had been attacked a few weeks earlier near Lamprey River in New Hampshire. Some were kidnapped but no one remained alive to explain what had happened.[2]

May 9, 1693 • Tuesday
Ipswich

Beginning today, Superior Court convened at Ipswich for Essex County. Only three justices presided—Thomas Danforth, John Richards, and Samuel Sewall, but *not* Chief Justice William Stoughton. Samuel Appleton served as foreman of the Grand Jury, which included William Chandler (father of the once-afflicted Phebe), while Jonathan Putnam of Salem Village was foreman of the trial jury.[3]

May 10, 1693 • Wednesday
Ipswich

During this session the court heard several cases of debt, rejected Judge Jonathan Corwin's appeal in his case against John Trask for trespass and for the theft of the hired men's house, and considered the last witch suspects. (At least two witchcraft cases were heard on May 10.) The Grand Jury dismissed most of them, including Tituba's. Only five (all from Andover) came to trial and at least three of these had already been before a Grand Jury in January. All, except for Mary Barker Jr., were indicted for covenanting with the Devil (though she had confessed to that crime as well). Susanna Post, her half-sister, Mary Bridges Jr. (whose mother was freed in January); Eunice Fry; William Barker Jr.; and his cousin Mary Barker Jr. were indicted for spectral torments. All were found not guilty and ordered freed—after payment of fees of course.[4]

May 12, 1693 • Friday
Hartford, Connecticut

The Connecticut General Court met to reconsider the condemned Mercy Desborough's fate. Three of the assistants—Samuel Willis, William Pitkin, and Nathaniel Stanley—reprieved her when they found that a new juror had been substituted in another's absence, for her trial had been conducted on two separate days over a month apart. It was a dangerous irregularity, said the three assistants, and the evidence against her was entirely spectral. None of it met the requirements stated by Perkins, Bernard, or Mather. As the assistants could legally reprieve Goody Desborough, they preferred to do so, rather than fall into "the miserable toil" plaguing Massachusetts. The court agreed. (Besides, the previous December, Rev. Gershom Bulkley, Mercy's former employer and a pro-Andros royalist, had written a pamphlet in her favor titled *Will and Doom*. This publication not only criticized the evidence brought against Mercy, but also cast doubt on the legality of Connecticut's government operating under its revoked charter. "Rebellion against the king is immediate rebellion against God," declared Bulkley, "and it is like the sin of witchcraft.")[5]

***

And so, depending on jail debts, Massachusetts released the remaining prisoners to make the best of their interrupted lives. Even those who were never indicted felt branded by events and feared future accusations. After all, the eight condemned to death but not yet executed were reprieved only temporarily.[6]

Even before her case reached the Grand Jury, Rebecca Johnson had resumed her old job of cleaning the Andover meeting house, a position that she would keep for years to come. Some, like Sarah Cloyse, had returned to fiercely protective families, or, like Eunice Fry and Mary Osgood, to once suspicious but now repentant husbands.[7]

Others lacked even that comfort. Elizabeth Proctor, condemned but freed with her newborn (*if* he survived), found her late husband's farm picked clean. John Proctor's will made no mention of his widow, so Elizabeth had not a penny from it, neither her widow's third nor the dowry that she had brought to the marriage. When she protested, her stepchildren ignored even her prenuptial contract and replied that she could not inherit, for, being condemned to hang, she was dead in the law.[8]

Widow Dorcas Hoar, also officially condemned, returned home to Beverly, but her livestock, along with her bed—bedding and all—had been taken for prison debts.[9]

Those with nothing to confiscate remained uneasily in jail, as their bills mounted. Margaret Jacobs was still in debt for the money used to pay the jailer. Tituba was sold outright to pay her bills, for Parris refused to take her back after she changed her story.[10]

Whoever paid Rachel Clenton's debts is not recorded, but she left prison for the solitude of the Ipswich marshes. She lived on Hog Island in a small house with a garden plot inherited from her mother. (Actually, her family had sold it thirty years before, and the land had changed hands since, but no one objected, and Goody Clenton died after only a few years.)[11]

Fugitives returned from exile.

The ancient Mary Bradbury rejoined her family and lived another seven years, until her death in 1700 at age eighty.[12]

Philip English considered staying in New York, but his wife Mary longed for home. They returned to Salem in the summer of 1693, and Philip found his wharves empty of vessels, his pastures bare of sheep, and his warehouses stocked with a single hogshead of malt (overlooked under a pile of wood shavings). Their great house was stripped, from the wine in the cellar to the thimbles in the corner shop. The family portraits were missing from the parlor and the bob-tailed cow from the yard. Philip recalled his scattered children to Salem (though he later sent the girls to a genteel boarding school in Boston). For now, he itemized his losses and prepared to sue his light-fingered neighbors.[13]

But the Englishes were not destitute. Philip still had trading contacts and several vessels full of goods that had remained at sea to avoid confiscation.

Mary DeRich's loss of her bed and cooking pot was far greater, because they were all she had, and because there were so few ways for a woman to earn money.[14]

Some prisoners, like Sarah Wardwell, returned to families broken by death. Some, like young Dorcas Good, came home but left their wits behind them. Others never returned at all—the nineteen hanged, the one pressed to death, the others dead of jail fever.[15]

May 18, 1693 • Thursday
Salem Village

Only three of the local dissatisfied brethren, Jonathan Tarbell, Thomas Wilkins, and Samuel Nurse, attended when Rev. Parris and twenty of the twenty-one other brethren gathered at the parsonage after lecture. "Brethren," Parris addressed the trio, "you desired the church to give you a meeting. Now here they are, and I have you to acquaint them with your reasons for desiring of it."

They came to give their charges against Parris, they said, now that they had witnesses to prove them. The other brethren objected with "much agitation," for both sides needed to prepare before either brought witness testimony. Over the dissenters' angry protests, the others voted that the dissenters' case would *not* be heard until they acted in an orderly manner.

The three clamored "loudly and fiercely" that since the church refused to hear them, they demanded an outside council. *This* church was incapable of judging them.

Then why, Nathaniel Putnam asked, had they wanted a church meeting?

They might explain that to a council, they hinted, but they absolutely *insisted* on one. The other brethren agreed, *if* it were done properly, and asked just who offended them besides Parris. They refused to say, but agreed that the pastor affronted all three equally. Parris offered to talk with them individually, but not to argue *en mass*. Samuel Nurse refused to talk with Parris alone *or* to set foot in his house again.

"The general deportment of the said three displeased brethren was at this meeting exceeding unchristian," Parris wrote that evening—his normally contained handwriting flaring across the page—"both to [the] minister and the other brethren; very irreverend towards him, and as rough towards them to the great grief of many, if not the whole church."[16]

May 25, 1693 • Thursday
Boston

Shortly after midnight, a fire broke out in a bakery and threatened the whole North End. Flames engulfed three houses before local volunteers stopped the blaze by blowing up two other houses with gunpowder in order to stop the blaze. (Unfortunately, one man broke his arm and falling timbers mortally wounded another.)[17]

May 31, 1693 • Wednesday
Boston

The legislature invited Rev. Increase Mather to deliver the Election Sermon—the annual event before the representatives (chosen by their towns' voters) voted for members of the governor's council. This election was the first under the new charter (for the King had appointed last year's council from Increase Mather's recommendations).

Now, Mather spoke on the qualities of good leaders, of men committed to upholding order and to protecting religion. Then the elder Mather offered a caution about the new power of "negative voice" (a veto) which the King had insisted his royal governors have. Mather had fought bitterly against including this veto in the new charter, but had been unable to prevent it. He hoped the legislators would not propose councilors that the governor could not accept "and so necessitate him to make use of his negative voice when he has no desire to use it." For "no governor can take such men into his counsel who are malcontents." He also hoped that Phips would "be a governor whose heart is engaged to seek not himself but the public good."[18]

Despite a general discontent with the handling of the witchcraft trials, William Stoughton, Thomas Danforth, John Richards, Wait-Still Winthrop, Bartholomew Gedney, John Hathorne, and Samuel Sewall were all reelected. (Elisha Cooke of the anti-Phips faction, whom Increase Mather had not recommended to the earlier legislature, was also elected, though by far fewer votes.) Nathaniel Saltonstall, who had resigned from the Court of Oyer and Terminer, was also voted in, but Dudley Bradstreet, himself accused of witchcraft, was not.[19]

18

JUNE 1693

I was sorry for their sorrow and temptations.

—Justice Samuel Sewall

June 1, 1693 • Thursday
Boston

While in England, Elisha Cooke had opposed the appointment of Sir William Phips as governor of Massachusetts. He made no secret that he disliked both Phips *and* the new charter. Governor Phips chose to rid himself of this "malcontent" and exercised his prerogative to veto Cooke's election. Predictably, Cooke and his supporters were furious. They blamed Increase Mather as well as Phips, convinced that Mather's Election Sermon remarks were a challenge rather than a caution for cooperation.[1]

June 4, 1693 • Sunday
Salem Village

Rev. Samuel Parris continued his sacrament sermons on the symbolism of Christ as the bread of life. "Oh, how necessary is bread to sustain life. Oh, how sweet and grateful to an hungry man. Why so Christ is to the needy soul." Yet some, Parris added pointedly, "turn their backs upon it as not worthy to be taken notice of."[2]

June 5, 1693 • Monday
Salem Town

Margaret Jacobs had worked in Marblehead since being cleared of the witchcraft charge the pervious winter, but she still owed Philip Gammon the £3-12-0 that he had loaned her to pay her jail fees. Today, he had her arrested for debt and brought to face the magistrates at the Ship Tavern in Salem. Her father, George Jacobs Jr., was back at last from hiding. Margaret pleaded with him to pay the debt "and not to go to court about it." But her father had to repeat "that he had not the money." George did, however, thank Gammon "for his kindness in lending" the sum and promised payment. He also tried to get a loan from Daniel Eames "to pay that honest debt," but whether her father was successful is not clear. (Just the £7 bond that the court had set for Margaret's release amounted to more than a year of her wages.)[3]

June 8, 1693 • Thursday
Boston

The day set for the executions of Elizabeth Emerson and Grace fell on a day that Rev. Cotton Mather was scheduled to take his turn with the weekly lecture. He had visited the two women in prison but neither seemed repentant of their respective infanticides. However, their situation might at least serve as a warning to others, so he spoke on the text Job 36:14 ("They die in youth, and their life is among the unclean.") If the condemned found no comfort in this message, the large audience was impressed, as was Samuel Sewall, who thought it "a very good sermon." At the end Mather read Elizabeth's own confession where she admitted to disobeying her parents, and to keeping "bad company." (The bad company included the long-afflicted and now dead Timothy Swan.)[4]

　　Meanwhile, the new government struggled against a faction that wanted the old charter back, and against another that wanted to revive the Dominion under a royal governor of unlimited power, Andros perhaps, but not Phips. Elisha Cooke was still furious that Governor Phips had vetoed his election to the council, and blamed it all on Increase Mather. Thomas Danforth tried to reconcile the two today, "but I think in vain," Samuel Sewall thought. (At least the situation in Massachusetts was nothing like New Hampshire's impasse, where the legislature utterly refused to work with royally-appointed Lieutenant Governor John Usher.)[5]

June 10 • Saturday
Salem

Exactly one year had passed since the hanging of Bridget Bishop.

June 11, 1693 • Sunday
Boston

A fleet of British warships under Rear Admiral Sir Francis Wheeler arrived off the coast and began moving into Boston Harbor. They had just failed to conquer Martinique and Guadeloupe, and had then proceeded north (by way of New York, where Captain Richard Short joined them), bound for Canada. Wheeler expected New England forces to join the British expedition.[6]

The fleet commanders invited Rev. Cotton Mather to deliver a sermon to the soldiers on one of the ships. Although a fisherman for Christ, Cotton was no sailor. Passing down the harbor in Governor Phips's own barge, Mather was suddenly and embarrassingly "taken so vehemently sick that my friends would not let me go further." He recovered once back on solid land, and was well enough to deliver the afternoon sermon in his own meeting house with Admiral Francis Wheeler and the other fleet captains in the congregation.[7]

However, the ships proved to be riddled with what was possibly yellow fever, the only trophy from the disastrous Caribbean expedition. Instead of the long-awaited help against Canada, the fleet was a deadly danger in itself. Now his embarrassing episode of seasickness seemed a gift from Cotton's guardian angel to keep him off a plague ship.[8]

June 12, 1693 • Monday
Boston

Samuel Sewall visited John Alden and his wife, and told them that "I was sorry for their sorrow and temptations [meaning their troubles], by reason of his imprisonment," Sewall wrote in his diary, "and that [I] was glad of his restoration."[9]

The council, in an attempt to prevent a plague, ordered accommodations on Long Island in Boston Harbor for the sick sailors and soldiers, and forbade any association between the local inhabitants and the troops.[10]

Cambridge

Similarly concerned, the monthly ministers' meeting at Harvard discussed just how much a minister was expected to risk his own health—and life—when visiting the sick during an epidemic.[11]

June 23, 1693 • Friday
Cambridge

Governor Phips and President Increase Mather hosted Sir Francis Wheeler and the frigate captains at a "treat" at Harvard. The sailors and soldiers of the fleet, unlike the officers, were still under orders to remain on board.[12]

June 25, 1693 • Sunday
Boston

If Cotton Mather had been unable to reach the fleet, others from Boston had ignored the ban on visiting the ships. Today, the town was "much startled" by the sudden death of a hired man from "fleet-fever," the first local death.[13]

June 26, 1693 • Monday
Topsfield

Mary Jacobs of Salem, widow of the hanged George Jacobs Sr., married John Wildes of Topsfield, whose late wife Sarah had also been executed for witchcraft.[14]

Salem

George Jacobs Jr. took over his late father's farm in Salem's Northfields—ignoring the fact that the probate court had allowed some of it to his sister and her husband.[15]

June 27, 1693 • Tuesday
Salem Town

Witnesses testified to Margaret Jacobs's good intent when the county court sat in the Salem Town House. Constable George Herrick *and* the plaintiff Philip Gammon both described how she and her father, George Jacobs Jr., intended to "pay that honest debt." The family was short of funds, and the farm hard pressed after so many confiscations. (Presumably, they were able to settle the matter, and prevent Margaret from returning to Salem jail.)[16]

June 29, 1693 • Thursday
Boston

The council considered a petition for a public fast, so that the people might pray for relief from the drought that threatened to ruin the crops, and from the "contagious and mortal sickness" spreading throughout the region. This epidemic was proving to be the worst anyone could remember—worse even than past outbreaks of smallpox. Victims turned yellowish during the first few days, Cotton Mather noted, then they began "vomiting and bleeding every way and so dying."[17]

June 30, 1693 • Friday
Boston

Gossip whispered that Elisha Cooke and Thomas Oakes (still angry at Rev. Increase Mather's Election Sermon remarks) had claimed that *they* could have gotten the old charter renewed, and that they thought that Mather had "betrayed the country." When Increase Mather confronted the two directly, they denied making either statement. "I declared myself willing to forgive the wrong they had done me," Mather noted, but he doubted their denial.[18]

19

JULY 1693

July 2, 1693 • Sunday
Salem Village

Communion, Rev. Samuel Parris reminded his congregation, was to be performed in Christ's memory. By doing so, Christians remembered and commemorated the sufferings and sorrows of the "torn, broken, and grievous death" that Christ had endured for the benefit of His people, the death by which He was able "to break the power of the Devil."

But, Parris reminded the congregation, "we have feeble and slippery memories, as to the greatest matters. We can remember our worldly business, our carnal interests, but we are ready to let slip the things of spiritual concernment."[1]

(The dissenters, if present, no doubt thought that their pastor had a slippery memory when it came to the grievous deaths of their own wrongly accused kin.)

July 5, 1693 • Wednesday
Cambridge

Harvard held its first Commencement as a university, the celebration dampened, perhaps, by the epidemic.[2]

July 6, 1693 • Thursday
Boston

Massachusetts observed a fast to pray for help against the continuing drought and the increasing epidemic. Boston's people gathered in the First Church's meeting house to hear Cotton Mather deliver a sermon "on what fears we may have at this time to quicken us; what hopes there are for us at this time to comfort us; and what prayers would be likely to turn our fears into hope."[3]

July 7, 1693 • Friday
Boston

The legislature considered a petition addressed to Governor Phips and the General Court by the dissatisfied brethren of Salem Village and their supporters. Due to some "very uncomfortable differences . . . chiefly relating to our present minister . . . whereby the name of God, the good of the church, and the peace of their majesties' good subjects is not a little disadvantaged," and because they despaired of obtaining satisfaction locally, the petitioners asked that the General Court, "out of compassion unto this distressed plantation," appoint a committee of "prudent and impartial persons" to advise them, so "that peace and truth (which are now so much wanting) may prevail among us." Fifty men's names followed, all written in the same hand as the rest of the document: names of the accused like Daniel Andrews and Edward Bishop; of the bereaved like Alexander Osborn and Francis Nurse; of Joseph Putnam (who had opposed his relatives' views in 1692); and also of Joseph Pope (whose wife Bethshua had been afflicted).

The legislature named a committee of four laymen and three ministers (Reverends Samuel Willard, Samuel Phillips, and Samuel Torrey) to investigate and to advise on the matter.[4]

(But this committee would not make peace between the Village factions. Parris and his supporters were aghast at such a public petition "scandalizing the church and minister as unpeaceable with their neighbors." Eventually, "several whose names were there and who subscribed do utterly disown any such speech or intention.")[5]

July 10, 1693 • Monday
Cambridge

The ministers' meeting at Harvard decided that even in a time of contagion, a minister had to attend sick folk who were in real distress of soul, but not those who simply wanted to chat. They also discussed the publishing of a history of New England. (This would become Cotton Mather's collection eventually published in London: *Magnalia Christi Americana*.)[6]

July 11, 1693 • Tuesday
Boston

At last, as Samuel Sewall observed, the thirsty land was relieved by a "plentiful shower of rain after much drought."[7]

July 13, 1693 • Thursday
Boston

The council received a dispatch advising them of a French incursion at Sandwich on Cape Cod. Despite the fleet, a French privateer from Martinique had landed 130 men. Fortunately, the local militia captured them all, and the *Nonsuch* took the ship after a day's chase. Later, Jean Reux, who had escaped Boston prison the previous summer, cruised the coast as a privateer prior to his recapture in New York.[8]

July 14, 1693 • Friday
Boston

Due to "deep poverty and want of friends," Mary Watkins (who had accused herself of witchcraft) was unable to produce the sureties to stand for her good behavior. Now, still in Boston prison, she was "very infirm and like to prove burdensome to the public." The court waived the required sureties, and Samuel Sewall wrote an order for her release which he signed along with Justices William Stoughton, Thomas Danforth, John Richards, and Wait-Still Winthrop. Mary still owed her jail fees, however. She had a modest inheritance that would have paid her debt *if* she could pry it from her brother-in-law's grasp.[9]

***

Boston

Governor Phips, meanwhile, was preoccupied with Admiral Francis Wheeler and the Royal Customs Collectors. Jahleel Brenton chafed at having to sue tax evaders as if he were a private party, but everyone else (including the rapacious Randolph) thought he overcharged the people and underpaid the king. The problem boiled over in July, when Brenton confiscated a cargo belonging to a friend of Phips. The ensuing discussion outside the locked warehouse ended when Phips cuffed Brenton about the wharf, while a delighted crowd shouted encouragement.[10]

July 19, 1693 • Wednesday
Salem

A whole year had passed since the executions of Sarah Good, Rebecca Nurse, Susanna Martin, Elizabeth How, and Sarah Wildes.

July 24, 1693 • Monday
Boston

"One of the fleet-women" died at a house ashore, Samuel Sewall wrote in his diary. Townsfolk were dying as well, and many of those who could afford it planned to move away from Boston until the sickness abated. Nathaniel Byfield, the representative for Bristol, informed Sewall that he meant to evacuate his wife and daughter to the country.[11]

July 26, 1693 • Wednesday
Boston

Among others, Dr. Thomas Pemberton, a surgeon, died of the fleet-fever, causing, as Rev. Samuel Willard noted in his prayers, great "consternation at the deaths."[12]

July 27, 1693 • Thursday
Boston

The members of Mather's congregation had received a building permit to enlarge the North meeting house "by a timber addition to be covered with shingles." Disastrously, Caleb Rawlings fell from the top of its steeple today, breaking his leg, arm, and neck.[13]

Notwithstanding the yellow fever, Admiral Wheeler still expected Governor Phips to accompany him against Placentia, Newfoundland, with a thousand men and a dozen ships. Phips, whose earlier Quebec expedition had been blighted by smallpox and late starts, claimed that he could not march the militia out of the province without the consent of the legislature, which had just dismissed. He wasn't able to prepare for such an expedition because the orders had come too late.

Wheeler didn't believe him for a minute, but with only 1,400 men remaining from his original 4,500, he could not attempt to attack Canada alone.[14]

Although Phips had written to the lords of the treasury the previous March about joining the British expedition, he may have only *just* received the actual orders. The monarchs' long-delayed letter concerning the witch trials arrived today. Phips took its vague caution as royal approval for what he had already done: reprieving the condemned. He could not legally expunge the sentences (only the Crown could do that) so he let the reprieves stand indefinitely. "Next to divine Providence," Phips wrote to England, "it is the stop to these proceedings which has averted the ruin of this province."[15]

20

AUGUST 1693

Our friends, relations, and kindred slight us to extremity.

—Mary Watkins and Susanna Davis

August 2, 1693 • Wednesday
Boston

Captain Richard Short, who had joined Admiral Wheeler's fleet at New York, had sent word to Governor Phips that he wanted his trunks back. But Short refused to put the request in writing (to prove his identity), as Phips demanded, much less venture ashore. So the trunks remained in storage. When Sir Francis's diminished fleet limped home today, Captain Short sailed with them, leaving his luggage behind in storage.[1]

With a heat wave worsening, the fleet-fever still raging among his own people, and Indian raids continuing on New England's frontier, Phips was now confronted by a messenger from the governor of New York demanding troops to help defend Albany.

"This put him into a ferment," the messenger wrote back to Governor Fletcher, while he waited for Phips to cool. "I found his reason drowned in passion and the storm increasing."

"Sir," a councilor explained later, "you must pardon him his dog days. He cannot help it." Although some of the better sort tolerate Phips for the sake of peace, the messenger wrote to Governor Fletcher, the rest ridicule him. His only friends are from the "mob," where "noise and strut pass for wit and prowess."[2]

August 4, 1693 • Friday
Eastward

At eight o'clock in the evening Governor Phips sailed from Boston for Pemaquid. A group of Maine Sagamores, fearing Iroquois attack and receiving no French help, had proposed peace.

After Canada's Abenaki allies made spring raids against New Hampshire, Maine, and western Massachusetts, Captain James Converse and his men had burnt what native villages and supplies that they could. Finding no armed opposition, they began building a fort at Saco. (It was here an Indian observed, "The French ministers were better than the English, for before the French came among them, there were a great many witches among the Indians, but now there were none, and there were much witches among the English ministers, as Burroughs, who was hanged for it.")[3]

August 6, 1693 • Sunday
Salem Village

Rev. Parris's sacrament sermon concentrated on the wine—"the most noble kind of drink," as bread was "the most noble kind of food." The wine signified Christ's blood and the suffering that He endured for His people. "Oh, remember the Devils cannot behold this but with terror and malice. But thou mayst behold with comfort and profit." To ignore or to slight this sacrament is to ignore and to slight the sufferings of Christ (which it represents) endured for us, His people. To contemplate those bloody wounds "accuseth us as the vile actors," Parris went on. "Our conscience tells us that our cruel hands have made these wounds, and the bloody instruments were of our own forging." (But if the dissatisfied brethren *were* present, they were likely thinking of the cruel hands that had caused the deaths of Rebecca Nurse and the others.)[4]

Boston

When Captain William Greenough died around four o'clock this afternoon of the fleet-fever, the weather was so hot that his body had to be buried the same evening at nine o'clock.[5]

August 7, 1693 • Monday
Boston

People were still dying of the epidemic, but at last the week's "excessive heat" broke. Cool air moved in, bringing much needed rain, just in time for Samuel Sewall's wife Hannah to give birth safely to a daughter.[6]

August 9, 1693 • Wednesday
Boston

The parched land at last received (as Sewall noted) "a plentiful rain after a long, distressing drought."[7]

Cambridge

The ministers' meeting at Harvard discussed a problem of concern to Salem Village: under what circumstances might a minister leave his congregation? They decided that such a serious matter should involve consultation with neighboring churches, not just the minister's own decision. "In case there be arisen those incurable prejudices, dissensions, animosities, and implacable offenses between a pastor and his people that all reverence for, and benefit by, his ministry is utterly to be despaired, he may be removed." (The pastoral bond was likewise broken "if a minister have a tolerable subsistence, wherewith he may after a Christian manner provide for his own, denied him.")[8]

August 11, 1693 • Friday
Pemaquid

Thirteen Sagamores, including Madockawando, representing their people from the Merrimack to the far Eastward, signed a treaty with Governor Phips in Fort William Henry at Pemaquid. They promised to change their allegiance from France to England, and to return all captives, and left three hostages as surety. Phips invited them to a feast on his frigate, after which, in a grand gesture of peace, they hurled their axes into the sea.[9]

August 13, 1693 • Sunday
Boston

With more and more people dying daily, and no one to help them pay their court and prison bills, Mary Watkins and another prisoner, Susanna Davis of Newbury, composed a petition dated today. They asked the Boston jail keeper "to provide master or masters to carry us [as bond servants] out of this country into Virginia, our friends, relations, and kindred slighting us to extremity." (Shortly after, Boston merchant John Winslow paid the jailkeeper £4-7-6 for the two women.)[10]

August 19, 1693 • Saturday
Salem

A full year had passed since the hangings of Rev. George Burroughs, John Proctor, John Willard, George Jacobs Sr., and Martha Carrier.

Boston

Governor Phips returned from the Eastward with the new treaty, the hostages, and the hope that his diplomacy would succeed where Admiral Wheeler's expedition had not. To counteract French influence, he also planned to send the tribes "supplies of necessities for life" until trade could be reestablished. To counteract Catholic influence he planned to send a Christian Indian missionary, Nahanton.[11]

SEPTEMBER 1693

A new storm of witchcraft [will] fall upon the country to chastise the iniquity that was used in the willful smothering and covering of the last.

—Mrs. Carver

September 3, 1693 • Sunday
Salem Village

Parris's sermon this communion Sabbath dealt with the cup of wine as representing the new covenant between God and His people—the covenant of grace. "This holy ordinance is not such an indifferent thing as many by their practices, in standing off from it, seem to imagine. Many dare not neglect praying, reading, and hearing, and yet too many dare neglect receiving." (Every congregation had members uncertain if they were spiritually worthy of communion and in need of encouragement. But Parris had the dissatisfied brethren boycotting the service as well.) "The greater the duty, the greater the sin in omitting of it," he said pointedly.[1]

***
Boston

The governor and the councilors were, so far, still well—but many were not. Twelve-year-old John Barnard Jr. (whose family attended the Mathers' church) burned with fever in his father's North Square home, each breath sword-sharp. On the third night young John saw their family doctor's wife enter and offer him some small dark pills. His fever cooled as she explained their application, and he was voluble with gratitude when his anxious father checked him the next morning. The elder Barnard feared that the fever had addled his son's wits, for no one had visited the house in the night. Yet, the boy remained lucid and healthy, and held to his story, so the family concluded that the figure may have been an angel in disguise.[2]

Such sightings required caution for Satan himself, as Cotton Mather (and others) warned, might transform "into an Angel of Light." Eight years earlier, Mather had glimpsed an angel during meditation. Now, privately contemplating angelic blessings, he may have seen the awe-inspiring figure again that September. But he kept the second experience even more private than the first, hardly alluding to it in his diary because angels "love secrecy in their administrations," and because one never knew about apparitions *or* public opinion.[3]

September 9, 1693 • Saturday
Salem Town

When Cotton Mather was invited to be guest preacher at the Salem Town church in September, he took the opportunity to research the witchcraft trials before time further blurred memory. He interviewed a Mrs. Carver,* who had seen "shining spirits" that she took to be good angels. She confided a number of secret things (which Cotton kept secret) and told him that "a new storm of witchcraft would fall upon the country to chastise the iniquity that was used in the willful smothering and covering of the last."

At some point during his stay in Salem, Mather discovered eighteen sheets of his sermon notes missing under suspicious circumstances. He wondered if the Invisible World were behind their loss.[4]

Boston

Meanwhile, Margaret Rule, a young member of Rev. Cotton Mather's congregation, fell afoul of a North End neighbor. The older woman, reputed to cure various hurts by muttering charms over them, had been imprisoned on suspicion of witchcraft at some earlier date. She threatened Margaret this evening, "bitterly." Margaret was the teenaged daughter of John and Emma Rule, driven with her parents from Saco,

---

*Perhaps Dorothy (Gardner) Carver, wife of Robert Carver, daughter of Thomas Gardner.

Maine, in her young childhood. Unlike Mercy Short's, her family was intact and fairly well-off. But like Mercy, Margaret grew troubled after the disturbing encounter.[5]

September 10, 1693, • Sunday
Salem Town

Undeterred by the loss of his notes, Rev. Cotton Mather remembered most of the three sermons and extemporized the rest, "so that the Devil got nothing."[6]

Boston

But if the Devil was thwarted in Salem, specters were active in Boston at the Mathers' North meeting house. There, "after some hours of previous disturbance" during Sabbath services, Margaret Rule "fell into odd fits" and had to be carried home. After only a few hours her seizures appeared quite "preternatural" and the neighbors, if not her family, remembered the altercation with the witch suspect the previous evening. Nevertheless, the Rules decided not to prosecute (the courts were unlikely to hear such cases now) and proceeded with Mather's recommendation of prayer.[7]

September 11, 1693 • Monday
Salem Village

Eleven displeased brethren wrote to the church at Malden (and possibly to other churches as well) asking for a council to solve their dispute with the Salem Village church. In the letter they denied sending the July petition to the governor and general court, even though their names were on it. (The Malden church informed the Village about this latest tactic.)[8]

Boston

When Rev. Cotton Mather returned home from Salem, he was surprised to hear of the new assault from the Invisible World. He knew only that the Rules lived in the North End and were reputedly "sober and honest."[9]

Margaret recognized four long-suspected women among the eight specters who tortured her at the command of a short, swarthy devil. They made her fast nine days and tried to force poison on her. They deafened her to religious words, but nights of prayer and psalms seemed to help, so local vigilant prayer groups took turns with her. They found pins stuck in her flesh after confiscating all pins from her clothing, and saw her body "monstrously inflamed" or blistered as if by poison. Some thought they smelled the reek of sulfur, or brushed against a solid invisible thing the size of a rat, or heard loud handclaps in her room. A half dozen grown men swore that they saw Margaret levitate off the bed entirely, lifted by a force stronger than they, combined, were able to muster.

Between seizures, Margaret argued with the specters and repeated their boastful plans. She told Cotton Mather that the specters bragged that *they* had stolen his sermon notes, but "they confess, they can't keep them always from you. You shall have them all brought you again." She also reported a plan to drown a certain North End youth, currently impressed on a man-of-war in the harbor. After the same young man nearly drowned trying to escape overboard, several tried to question Margaret as an oracle, which Cotton firmly forbade.

But Mather's own observations convinced him that her pains were real, whatever their cause. Her case entwined his pastoral duty and professional interests. He also knew that any association with it could be as dangerous to his reputation as a hike "over a rocky mountain filled with rattlesnakes," unless he could prove to others the accuracy of what he had observed for himself.

Yet, if he ignored the case, the names of suspects were sure to become common knowledge, and the girl's friends would encourage the spirits by consulting her spectral sight. All of this possible fervor could revive public accusations and bring on another "storm of witchcraft" that *must* be averted.[10]

September 13, 1693 • Wednesday
Boston

But other folk, like Robert Calef (textile merchant and former Boston constable) distrusted all of the afflicted, and thought that Rev. Cotton Mather's actions were a deliberate attempt to revive just such a storm. He already disliked everything about *both* Mathers, from the charter on down. Early in Mercy Short's illness, Calef and thirty to forty others thronged her room for a prayer service, led by Reverends Increase and Cotton Mather. That evening, the patient suffered only mild seizures, which interfered with her breathing. Otherwise, she was still and light headed, slow to speak and unable to hear religious words. The ministers paraphrased much of what they said, so that she could understand. Calef thought their approach was little better than charms and spells.[11]

Margaret Rule fainted—so still that Cotton put his hand to her face to determine if she were still breathing, then fanned his hat above her head to stir some air in the packed room. The crowd was *not* about to leave, but at least, Mather hoped, they would see for themselves that there was *no* fraud. Something caught his attention at the opposite end of the pillow from her head. As he reached out, he touched, but could not see, a rat-like thing that squirmed swiftly away. Others had felt it earlier, but Cotton reassured Margaret that it might yet be only fancy and imagination.

Increase prayed for general guidance, and ended with the wish that if there were "any evil instruments" involved, God would reveal them. The Mathers avoided calling the specters "witches," since they believed that the apparitions were more likely to be disguised devils, even if human witches were involved. The Mathers ordered Margaret *not* to name her tormentors, even if she thought that she recognized them. Before the ministers left, the Mathers asked after Margaret's health (for her fast had just begun) and learned that she had swallowed only a single spoonful of medicinal rum, then felt worse afterward. She still had trouble breathing, but only the Mathers left.

The crowd stayed.[12]

But Boston still endured physical ills as well. Samuel Sewall's little daughter Jane, barely a month old, died shortly after midnight.[13]

September 15, 1693 • Friday
Boston

Samuel and Hannah Sewall buried their baby. Rev. Willard's son John (who had helped the Carys escape the year before) carried her body to the family tomb.[14]

September 19, 1693 • Tuesday
Salem

A year had passed since Giles Corey had been pressed to death.

Boston

Rev. Cotton Mather visited Margaret Rule again after her fast had ended. He no longer wasted prayers in a room mobbed with curiosity seekers but, he assured Margaret, he prayed for her at home. As they spoke alone for half an hour, this occasion was probably when Margaret identified the specters to him, since there was no one else to overhear. He recognized the names of long-suspected neighbors, names that he had kept silent when critics said his silence obstructed justice. Again, he bade Margaret to conceal their identity, and warned her that some visitors came only to prove her a fraud.[15]

After Mather left, some ten people trailed in over the course of the evening and Margaret's seizures returned. She was screaming and gasping when Robert Calef entered, but once she recovered, she grew merry and talkative. She tidied herself, joked with an old sweetheart, and complained that some folk thought she lied. Her attendants told Calef that her joints sometimes twisted and locked, and that her head sometimes pressed so hard to the pillow no one could lift it. Calef and a few others grabbed her head and neck to try, but as she was not convulsing, they had no trouble moving it. Margaret's friends had to shoo them out.[16]

Calef wrote and circulated an account of his two visits to Margaret. In *his* version, Cotton Mather nattered on and on with leading questions about witches to a half-dressed, rum-soaked girl, who either muttered monosyllables or flirted. When she faked unconsciousness (wrote Calef), Cotton pretended to revive her by fondling her breasts and stomach, a process that the minister repeated in pursuit of the invisible rat. Then Increase, after also groping for the rat, droned a half hour of prayers full of witches and devils. During the second visit (Calef continued), Margaret screamed as well as flirted, but seemed altogether too healthy to be in any real distress.[17]

To the Mathers' pained fury, Calef's version spread quickly, raising salacious snickers and loud indignation at the witch persecutions' supposed revival. Calef's remarks, said Cotton Mather, were at best, fragments taken out of context that contradicted what he had advised for years. And how could anyone believe that a person with lascivious designs against the girl would commit them before forty witnesses?[18]

Mather declined his friends' advice to refuse his next turn at Lecture to protest the insults of "some" in the First Church's congregation. But he later referred to the "pernicious libels" from his own pulpit.[19]

September 22, 1693 • Friday
Salem

A full year had passed since the last executions for witchcraft had hanged Martha Corey, Mary Esty, Alice Parker, Ann Pudeator, Margaret Scott, Wilmot Read, Samuel Wardwell, and Mary Parker.

September 25, 1693 • Monday
Boston

Wait-Still Winthrop (former Oyer and Terminer judge) was a physician as well as a merchant, and was known for treating the needy at no charge. But when his own children fell ill of the epidemic, nothing he did was enough to help them. Today his nine-year-old son, William, died of the "bloody flux."[20]

September 27, 1693 • Wednesday
Boston

Only two days after his brother's death, four-year-old Joseph Winthrop died, also of "bloody flux."[21]

September 29, 1693 • Friday
Boston

After Rev. Cotton Mather threatened to sue for slander, Robert Calef wrote him the first in a series of letters expressing surprise. They agreed to meet and to discuss their differences at John Wilkins's book store, but the minister was soon diverted by more important issues.[22]

OCTOBER 1693

It is not a little our frequent and daily grief to consider what amazing confused noises (by the by) we hear go of us.

—Rev. Samuel Parris

October 1, 1693 • Sunday
Salem Village

Rev. Samuel Parris's sacrament sermon noted that the Lord's Supper was to be observed in memory of Christ, a remembrance not "to be concealed in our hearts, but to be declared and published as an open profession of Christ in our lives." This declaration could be discerned in our "grateful and joyous remembrance" and "an industrious endeavor to shun sin and to please God in all things." Of course, Satan tries "to overthrow these holy purposes." Where "Christ designs the conjunction and concord of [church] members, . . . the Devil endeavors the distraction and discord of members; one for that way, another for this." And "only by pride commeth contention." Will they turn their backs on communion as if ashamed, as if "Christ's death had no virtue in it," or as if they themselves "had not any interest in it?" (The displeased brethren and their supporters must have remained stubbornly un-moved. Parris recorded more extensive notes for this sermon than he usually did.)[1]

October 3, 1693 • Tuesday
Charlestown

Rev. Cotton Mather's young daughter, Mary, became dangerously feverish. Her parents took her, at some point, out of Boston to her maternal grandparents' home in Charlestown, where she lay burning, "with a vomiting, and with worms."[2]

October 5, 1693 • Thursday
Charlestown

Rev. Cotton Mather could hardly compose his mind to pray until evening. He man-aged to hope that his children would be happy in heaven, even if they could not be in their parents' earthly care. Ironically, Cotton's lost sermons returned as pre-dicted, this same evening. The pages had been found scattered through the streets of Lynn, but he could hardly think of their odd reappearance as he sat up all night with his suffering child.[3]

October 6, 1693 • Friday
Charlestown

Mary Mather died at six o'clock in the morning, just shy of two years old.[4]

October 7, 1693 • Saturday
Boston

Cotton Mather buried his daughter in the family plot in the North burying ground with "an honorable attendance at the funeral," including Rev. Samuel Willard, one of the four who helped carry the little coffin.

"Gone, but not lost," Cotton wrote on the grave stone.[5]

October 10, 1693 • Tuesday
Boston

While Boston's militia mustered on the Common, Rev. Cotton Mather prayed and fasted alone in his study for the "many humbling circumstances, both as to my sins, and as to my sorrows," especially the recent deaths, but also "the cursed re-proaches" against himself and his family from "this unruly, ungodly, ungrateful people."[6]

He visited Margaret Rule later to pray with her and to remind the Lord that, as Margaret's minister, he had a better right to demand her deliverance than the Devil had to her damnation.

At home that sunset, Margaret saw a brilliant, white-clad figure. It offered comfort and advised her to treat Rev. Mather as a spiritual father. She addressed him so, when he visited that evening, before all the company, including, presumably, her own father.

Encouraged, but cautious, Mather observed three days of private prayer and fasting.[7]

October 13, 1693 • Friday
Salem Village

Rev. Samuel Parris received a letter from Rev. John Higginson of Salem advising the Village church to agree to a council (as the dissenting brethren desired). Rev. Samuel Willard of Boston's Second Church had passed along the news about the Village strife to the Reverends John Higginson and Nicholas Noyes of Salem and to Rev. John Hale of Beverly. So Parris and other voting church members met privately at Deacon Ingersoll's to discuss this development.[8]

October 14, 1693 • Saturday
Salem Village

Rev. Samuel Parris received a second letter urging a council, this time from the Reverends John Hale and Nicholas Noyes, who included further details and conditions.[9]

October 15, 1693 • Sunday
Salem Village

The full voting members of the Village church (the brethren) stayed behind after services ended to hear Rev. Samuel Parris explain about the letters from the Salem and Beverly ministers. The members decided to meet further about it at Parris's house.[10]

October 19, 1693 • Thursday
Salem Village

The day was so wet and stormy at three o'clock that afternoon that only twelve brethren attended the meeting at the Village parsonage. They read and debated the letters from the neighboring ministers, the various petitions, and the dissenting brethren's letters to other churches. The brethren decided, "unanimously" for once, to follow the ministers' advice and to call a council "in an orderly way." They selected a committee to inform the four dissenters, and to inform the church as a whole the following Lord's Day.[11]

October 22, 1693 • Sunday
Salem Village

The full members remained after the second service, so that Rev. Samuel Parris could inform them of the appointed meeting with the dissenting brethren. He supposed, he said, "that the great storm hindered them" from attending earlier, and hoped that they would be able to attend the meeting on the morrow.[12]

Boston

Margaret Rule now reported that the specters could not get near her, not even when the Devil struck and kicked them with a slave driver's fury. "You shan't be the last!" they snarled, and with a curse, left Margaret. She was still weak—quick to faint and slow to concentrate—but the spectral torments seemed over.[13]

October 23, 1693 • Monday
Salem Village

At two o'clock, about twenty church members assembled at Deacon Nathaniel Ingersoll's ordinary as planned. They recapitulated the problem and the decision to accept a council, where each side could present its case in an orderly manner with proper witnesses, so that they might know once and for all *exactly* with whom the dissatisfied brethren were dissatisfied.

The four dissenters arrived at three o'clock, and insisted on bringing non-members with them. Protesting the irregularity, Rev. Samuel Parris and the others at last agreed to include others *if* they were fully communing members of some other church. The dissenters produced Israel Porter, a Village man belonging to the church at Salem Town.

They met, Parris said, to call a council (for which the dissenters had long agitated), so they desired to know *exactly* the purpose of the council.

The dissenters said that their offense was against Rev. Parris, not against the church itself. They offered to read a paper detailing the complaints. "But," Parris wrote, "we answered we would not hear it unless they would leave it with us after it was read, or a copy of it, that we might consider of it." In turn, the church would provide a written list of its own complaints against *them*, so that each side would face the council knowing the specific charges ahead of time. The four absolutely refused and they all argued until near sunset. The meeting broke up with the dissenters declaring that they would have a council—whether the others agreed or not.

Parris, on behalf of the church, wrote a letter to Reverends Higginson, Noyes, and Hale agreeing to the council, and noted (with some irony) that he was glad to hear the dissenters had agreed to whatever the council decided. "It is not a little our frequent and daily grief to consider what amazing confused noises (by the by) we hear go of us." He insisted that the Village church had proceeded orderly, detailed the latest meetings, and asked for the ministers' prayers in this "bewildered case."[14]

23

NOVEMBER 1693

> *That there are witches is not the doubt, the Scriptures else were in vain which assigns their punishment to be by death. But what this witchcraft is, or wherein it does consist, seems to be the whole difficulty.*
>
> —Robert Calef

November 5, 1693 • Sunday
Salem Village

Rev. Samuel Parris's sacrament sermon dealt *not* with those who stayed away from the Lord's Supper, but with those hypocrites who partook of it "unworthy." Those who *outwardly* celebrated the Lord's Supper "and yet suffer divisions and schisms to reign among you," who slighted the poor and otherwise avoided living a Christian life, and offered a Judas-like betrayal of Christ's suffering. They merely went through the motions with the sacred symbolism of the bread and wine.[1]

After the services, the brethren chose members to inform the various dissenters of a meeting at Parris's on the 13th.[2]

November 13, 1693 • Monday
Salem Village

Peter Cloyse, Samuel Nurse, and John Tarbell (but *not* Thomas Wilkins) arrived at the parsonage for the one o'clock meeting. (Peter and Sarah Cloyse, as well as sons from both their previous marriages, and various kindred, had moved far west to Framingham.)[3]

After an opening prayer, Rev. Samuel Parris cautioned that all proceedings should "observe order and meetness," then reread the letters from the Salem and Beverly ministers. He asked again for a written and properly *signed* account of the dissenters' complaints and again they refused. The dissenting four wanted to bring in certain members of other churches waiting nearby as witnesses. The Village church refused "such innovations." The dissenters did read off a signed and dated petition offering to abide by "a council of indifferent persons" *if* "indifferently chosen," or chosen by the General Court. *Then* the four would produce a written list of complaints thirty days in advance, *if* the church promised to provide a written answer to them six days before the council met.

Was that all they would say? asked Parris. They said yes, and Cloyse fidgeted to be off. But Parris read a list of seventeen "Sundry Objections" against *them*. The dissenters' "precipitant, schematical and total withdrawing from the church (yea, and congregation)" caused the Village church to suffer "defamation abroad . . . [and] reproach and grief at home." And then they claimed "that they were forced to withdraw from all public worship" far earlier than they actually had. They clamored for the church to hear them, he read, but retreated to silence or ambiguity when they got their meeting. Instead of even *trying* to settle their differences locally, they blazed their complaints to the General Court itself, then *denied* their own petition which bore the names of many who never signed it. The dissenters circulated a "seditious libel" against their pastor, and generally made the Village an object of contempt. (The libel was probably the undated paper accusing Parris of trafficking with familiar spirits—the Biblical definition of witchcraft—and of deserving to be cast off by God.)[4]

November 24, 1693 • Friday
Boston

Robert Calef continued to spread innuendos against the Mathers until (according to Calef) both Increase and Cotton sued him for "scandalous libels." Having posted a bond to appear at the next county sitting, Calef wrote another letter to Cotton Mather today, as the season's first snow fell on Boston.

"That there are witches is not the doubt, the Scriptures else were in vain which assigns their punishment to be by death. But what this witchcraft is, or wherein it does consist, seems to be the whole difficulty." The only scripturally acceptable definition of witchcraft that he could locate in Mather's *Wonders of the Invisible World*, wrote Calef, was that of an anti-religious attitude. All the other definitions amounted to gross superstitions and lies. He signed off with mock humility, but Cotton received the letter calmly, and told the messenger that he had no reason to prosecute.[5]

November 25, 1693 • Saturday
Boston

Complaints about Gov. William Phips, meanwhile, headed toward London. Lieutenant Governor John Usher and Governor Benjamin Fletcher said that Phips had sent too few Massachusetts men to help guard their respective frontiers. Admiral Sir Francis Wheeler was offended that Phips would not attack Canada. The bruised Jahleel Brenton and Captain Richard Short related more personal complaints as well as charges of obstruction of duty. (In England at the time, Joseph Dudley encouraged it all, as he wanted the governorship for himself.)[6]

Phips was popular at home with the majority, but not with Elisha Cooke's anti-charter faction or with certain merchant-legislators who resented him as an upstart swamp-Yankee. Chief Justice William Stoughton, for one, had never gotten on with him, and Stoughton was a good friend of Joseph Dudley. Phips's supporters composed an address to the King asking that Phips *not* be removed from office. It passed the House of Representatives by only one vote, because many distant towns elected Boston merchants to represent them. Consequently, Phips proposed that legislators should actually *live* in the towns for which they spoke. Today, a bare majority of representatives voted in favor of the residence requirement.[7]

November 26, 1693 • Sunday
Salem Village

Meeting after services, Rev. Samuel Parris and the brethren composed a letter to Peter Cloyse, Samuel Nurse, and John Tarbell. They were willing to have a council to hear the dispute, as the Boston ministers advised. However, the Village church was *not* willing to accept the conditions petitioned for at the last meeting (the involvement of the General Court). The very least the dissenters could do was to provide the church with a signed list of complaints. The letter ended with a list of Biblical texts advising cooperation.[8]

November 28, 1693 • Tuesday
Boston

The council confronted the controversial residence requirement. Twenty-one members of the lower house who opposed the law signed a protest, declaring the requirement contrary to the charter, and contrary to the customs both of England and of Massachusetts. Jahleel Brenton and others claimed that it would ruin the Province, and Nathaniel Byfield called it an attempt to pack the legislature.

After hot debate, Governor Phips withdrew so his council could vote. The measure passed nine to eight (with Chief Justice William Stoughton opposing)* and became law despite complaints about having rustics for colleagues.[9]

---

*In favor: Thomas Danforth, John Richards, Wait-Still Winthrop, James Russell, John Hathorne, Samuel Sewall, Jonathan Corwin, John Foster, and Daniel Pierce. Against: William Stoughton, Bartholomew Gedney, John Walley, Isaac Addington, Peter Sergeant, Samuel Donnell, Nathaniel Thomas, and Charles Frost.

DECEMBER 1693

I suppose that some of our learned witlings of the coffee-house, for fear lest these proofs of an Invisible World should spoil some of their sport, will endeavor to turn them all into sport.

—Rev. Cotton Mather

December 3, 1693 • Sunday
Salem Village

Continuing his sacrament sermon series, Rev. Samuel Parris broached the subject of *how* one might know if one were worthy to take communion. "We are to strive and labor that not one, living, reigning, unwounded and unmortified sin may be brought in our bosoms to the Lord's Table." Participants must attend to the ordinance "regularly and suitably," with their inward and outward behavior "reverent, serious and composed," neither fidgeting nor napping, with a real desire for the soul's food. On the other hand, the impenitent "do come upon the peril of their own souls." And, he added meaningfully, "to eat with divisions and sinful prejudices, mars all our holy feasting."[1]

December 5, 1693 • Tuesday
Boston

The council considered, but did not decide on, a bill proposed by Elisha Cooke's anti-Mather party that would require the president of Harvard to live at the college full-time, and not just commute as Increase Mather was doing.[2]

The quarterly court for Suffolk County sat at Boston. As no one appeared against Robert Calef, the court dismissed the Mathers' case against him. Instead of arguing on Calef's terms, Rev. Cotton Mather was composing an account of Margaret Rule's afflictions (to circulate in manuscript): "Another Brand Plucked Out of the Burning, or, More Wonders of the Invisible World." The essay repeated his cautions, and remarked irritably on truth-twisting, anti-christian materialists: "I suppose that some of our learned witlings of the coffee-house, for fear lest these proofs of an Invisible World should spoil some of their sport, will endeavor to turn them all into sport."[3]

December 23, 1693 • Sunday
Boston

After snow storms that sank ships at sea, Governor Phips set sail yet again for the Eastward to oversee the frontier defenses—his second trip this month.[4]

December 26, 1693 • Wednesday
Salem Town

Salem's December County Court again ordered the Village rates committees to pay Rev. Samuel Parris his 1691 and 1692 salary. The committee again refused. (In contrast, Beverly had voted in October to bestow the ministry house *and* two acres upon Rev. John Hale in appreciation for his years of service.)[5]

***
Boston

While writing his account of Margaret Rule's affliction, Rev. Cotton Mather did *not* include the case of another young local woman, afflicted for only one day at year's end.* Before witnesses she screamed that a specter of Cotton Mather menaced her. But once she was herself again, she begged for the real Rev. Mather's prayers and assured him that the other specters could not make his "dead shape" harm her. For years, Mather had warned that the innocent could be represented spectrally. If God willed the ruin of his good name, Cotton prayed, so be it. But he would rather

---

*By Old Style dating, year's end could also be early 1694.

the afflicted woman *and* his name be preserved. One session of prayer was enough to cure her without relapse.

No word of the incident ever reached the cynical and opportunistic Robert Calef, who would certainly have used it gleefully against his perceived enemies, the Mathers.[6]

PART III

1694

JANUARY 1694

Sin is the Devil's vomit.

—Rev. Samuel Parris

**January 7, 1694 • Sunday,
Salem Village**

Rev. Samuel Parris continued his series of sacrament sermons on 1 Corinthians 11, concentrating today on verse 28: "Let a man therefore examine himself, and so let him eat of this bread and drink of this cup." When considering the Lord's Supper, said Parris, participants must examine their knowledge of the sacrament, their faith, and their repentance for "sin is the Devil's vomit, the soul's excrement."

Do those who partake truly confess, or do they cover their sins "by denying the evil that a man has done, or by extenuating the sin he has done, making a light matter of it in its own colors, or by hiding it from God, so as not to acknowledge it with godly grief and sorrow, or by living still in it and continuing therein impenitently?"[1]

January 11, 1694 • Thursday
Boston

Although Robert Calef did not hear of the spectral Cotton Mather, he did read "Another Brand Pluckt out of the Burning" and wrote to Rev. Cotton Mather. Again, he took offense at passages where Mather took offense at Calef. He enclosed a copy of his account of the visits to Margaret Rule, but insisted that *he* had not been there. His information had come from two reliable witnesses, Calef insisted, and was not as sensational as gossip implied. Mather's manuscript only confirmed Calef's fear that the Rule case would soon start another witch hunt. So would the Reverend Sir meet him at one of the bookshops and explain *how* Calef erred (*if* he did) by sound reason and Scripture—not by quoting heathen sources like Virgil.[2]

January 15, 1694 • Monday
Boston

Rev. Cotton Mather wrote a point-by-point rebuttal of Robert Calef's accusations. He reminded Calef that there were plenty of witnesses to what had *actually* happened at the Rule household, not the "little bits, scraps, and shreds" of information that Calef twisted out of context. Cotton declined public debate, but offered Calef the use of his substantial private library to peruse the comparative literature on the subject. Then, to show that he was not the only person to witness the supernatural, the minister included the statements of six men, who each swore that they had seen Margaret Rule levitate (in Mather's absence).[3]

Like a reoccurring nightmare, these controversies paralleled a dangerous illness in Mather's family—that of five-year-old Katherine, Cotton and Abigail's last living child. By mid-January her parents knew there was little hope of recovery, and Cotton could only resign her to God's protection once she slipped entirely from his own. But while the distraught father prayed, his daughter began "a critical and plentiful bleeding," then "recovered from that hour, unto the admiration of us all."[4]

January 17, 1694 • Wednesday
Boston

A January thaw had melted Boston docks free of sea-ice, as if it were already March, when Governor William Phips returned overland through Salem from a month Eastward.[5]

January 18, 1694 • Thursday
Boston

"I suppose," Robert Calef, sneering at the levitation report, wrote to Rev. Cotton Mather, "you expect I should believe it." But *he* was not a Papist to be so superstitious. He was surprised that Mather found his account of the visits to Margaret smutty, and hinted that he had heard *far* worse. Calef still wanted a public debate, and dismissed Mather's offer of his library: "I thank God I have the Bible."[6]

Governor Phips, meanwhile, wrote to the Earl of Nottingham that the Treaty of Pemaquid still held despite French efforts to break it. Furthermore, the still-loyal sachems had informed him that Quebec was suffering a smallpox epidemic.[7]

January 19, 1694 • Friday
Boston

Old Mrs. Elizabeth Prout, one of the Mathers' North End neighbors, died in Boston after such "sore conflicts of mind" that some thought witchcraft responsible. (However, neither Cotton Mather nor Robert Calef mentioned these public suspicions in their correspondence to each other.)[8]

26

fEBRUARY 1694

February 4, 1694 • Sunday
Salem Village

Rev. Samuel Parris continued his series on the spiritual self-examination required to be worthy of the Lord's Supper with the text 1 Corinthians 11:28: "We
should examine wherein we are most weak as to grace, and wherein we are
most strong as to sin." To neglect this scrutiny of ones' self "is a sign of un-
soundness and hypocrisy of heart" that cannot be hidden. "Shall not God search
this out? For He knoweth the secrets of our hearts." We must ponder privately
on this vital question, *now*, without delay, even—or *especially*—in time of affliction. "Oh, know we that our deceitful hearts, if it be possible, will herein
cheat us."[1]

February 19, 1694 • Monday
Boston

Robert Calef continued to badger Rev. Cotton Mather for an answer to his earlier letters. As far as Calef could see, the only evidence of being a witch that would convict a suspect now seemed to be a signed covenant with the Devil, which had no scriptural authority. If he erred in this understanding, would Rev. Mather *kindly* enlighten him with proper scriptural references? (Shortly after his daughter's recovery, Cotton began to compose a reply to Calef, turning his response into a more general essay on witchcraft, but it was far from complete.)[2]

February 24, 1694 • Saturday
Boston

The much-suspected, but never arrested, Mrs. Margaret Thatcher died in Boston.[3]

27

MARCH 1694

> *We have followed the example of Pagan and Papal Rome, thereby rendering us contemptible and base before all people.*
>
> —Robert Calef

March 4, 1694 • Sunday
Salem Village

Continuing with his sacrament series, Rev. Samuel Parris delivered a sermon on the next verse (1 Corinthians 11:29) concerning the bread and wine: "For he that eateth and drinketh unworthely, eateth and drinketh his own damnation because he discerneth not the Lord's body." Damnation here, explained Parris, meant "punishment, as the word often signifies." (This was the same reference that Mrs. Ann Putnam had shouted during Rebecca Nurse's examination.) An unworthy communicant still lacks grace, is still "dead in trespass and sins," or continues to sin despite "having had true grace wrought in his soul." This corrupted spiritual state only offers dishonor to the meaning of the sacrament.

Earlier, Parris had had to encourage members to participate, to remind them that they need not wait for perfection, or to criticize them for ignoring the cere-

mony. Although the dissenting brethren *still* stayed away, others seemed determined to join in, whether they had thought devoutly on the meaning of the sacrament or not. "See the great stupidity of such as think it enough to be communicants, howsoever they do communicate. Oh, there are them that will not be
withheld from this ordinance, but look upon such as oppose them herein to be
their worst enemies."[1]

After the services Parris baptized and received into full communion John
Wilkins, one of Bray Wilkins's many grandsons. Two years earlier John had testified to his belief that his first wife had been killed by the witchcraft of his cousin-
in-law John Willard.[2]

March 5, 1694 • Monday
Cambridge

Harvard's president, Increase Mather, and seven Fellows signed a proposal to collect "illustrious discoveries of the Divine Providence." They asked area ministers
to send them examples of "wonderful deliverances of the distressed, mercies to
the godly, judgments on the wicked, and more glorious fulfillments of either
promises or threatenings in the scriptures of truth, with apparitions, possessions,
enchantments, and all extraordinary things wherein the existence and agency of
the Invisible World is more sensibly demonstrated." (Little came of the project. It
mostly made such as Robert Calef suspicious of *any* interest in the Invisible
World.)[3]

March 8, 1694 • Thursday
Boston

Robert Calef had netted another correspondent, a Scottish chaplain named Stuart,
who was attached to one of the Navy frigates. (Calef's first letter to Stuart does not
survive, but it argued that the scriptural command that "thou shalt not suffer a
witch to live" referred only to the ancient Jews, not to seventeenth-century Christians.) In a lengthy discussion of the relative power of devils, Stuart argued mainly
from Scripture (as Calef had taunted Rev. Cotton Mather to do). Although the Bible
does not mention contracts with the Devil, Stuart wrote, it does mention both the
Devil *and* witches.[4]

March 20, 1694 • Tuesday
Boston

Robert Calef (citing Colossians 2:8) lectured Chaplain Stuart against accepting
mere philosophies rather than the Word of Christ, and accused his opponents of
believing that the Devil was God's equal. More importantly, he lamented the

witch-finding methods used in 1692. They had no scriptural authority, and by using them, in Calef's view, "we have followed the example of Pagan and Papal Rome, thereby rendering us contemptible and base before all people."[5]

Salem Village

The inhabitants of Salem Village gathered at noon in their meeting house to choose a new rates committee for the year: Nathaniel and Thomas Putnam, their kinsman Thomas Flint, Thomas Fuller, and Fuller's brother-in-law Henry Wilkins (father of the late bewitched Daniel).[6]

March 27, 1694 • Tuesday
Ipswich

Salem Village continued to quarrel. Even men who *agreed* on the church and witch trial disputes sued each other when the court of common pleas convened in Ipswich. Joshua Rea sued Ezekiel Cheever for trespass on land that they both claimed by a complication of marriage and inheritance, and lost.[7]

Acting as constable, John Tarbell (one of the dissenters) had attached two mares (as bond in another court case) from Joseph Porter, who sued him promptly for trespass and theft. Even with Joseph Putnam as surety, Porter lost.[8]

APRIL 1694

I thought it my duty to be no longer an idle spectator.

—Robert Calef

April 1, 1694 • Sunday
Salem Village

Rev. Samuel Parris spoke more sharply than usual to the communicants and congregation, as he continued his sacrament sermon text (1 Corinthians 11) to verse 30: "For this cause many are weak, and sick among you, and many sleep."

"The ordinances of God are great things, choice things," Parris reminded his listeners. "The abuse of them is therefore so much the greater, by how much the ordinances are more precious." Because "plagues and punishments are the worthy fruits of unworthy communicating at the Lord's Table," it is "for this cause many are weak and sickly among you, and many sleep," even die, spiritually *and* physically. Let us learn from these afflictions and learn how to guard our soul's health.[1]

April 2, 1694 • Monday
Boston

On the day that the Boston artillery company trained on the Common, John Richards (a former Oyer and Terminer Judge) "fell into an angry passion with his servant," was seized with "a fit of apoplexy" shortly after, and died suddenly, to everyone's amazement.[2]

April 3, 1694 • Tuesday
Boston

As far as anyone could tell, the late John Richards had been in good health before his unexpected death. When the body "was opened" this evening, the vitals all appeared "fair and sound."[3]

April 6, 1694 • Friday
Boston

John Richards was buried in the family tomb in the North burying place. Six colleagues, including William Stoughton, Thomas Danforth, Samuel Sewall, and Isaac Addington, carried his coffin. Wait-Still Winthrop helped escort the widow, while Boston's foot regiment accompanied the solemn procession as an honor guard. However, in the spring of 1694, the water table was so high that when the tomb was opened, all the coffins in it were afloat. The mourners had to wait for workmen to nail boards across the coffins "to prevent their floating up and down."[4]

April 8, 1694 • Sunday
Boston

"Two young women," communing members of the Mathers' church, "having been found guilty of consulting an ungodly fortune-teller in the neighborhood with desires to be informed of some secret and future things," apologized to the congregation, and were reconciled back into the church.[5]

April 9, 1694 • Monday
Boston

Governor William Phips sailed for the Eastward yet again.[6]

April 16, 1694 • Monday
Boston

Robert Calef continued to demand answers from Rev. Cotton Mather and accused the minister of the pagan notion that *all* evil came from the Devil, because "God did hurt to none, but good to all." He also claimed that Mather concealed the names of the accused only from cowardice of public opinion. "I thought it my duty," wrote Calef, "to be no longer an idle spectator." (He had done nothing to help in 1692 when serving as a constable.)

Despite the jibes, Mather did not respond. (When his son Increase had died Cotton had used the sermon text Job 2:10: "Shall we receive good at the hands of God, and shall we not receive evil?") For now, he sent Calef a copy, as a loan, of Richard Baxter's *The Certainty of the World of Spirits* and continued to compose his own views on witchcraft.[7]

April 21, 1694 • Saturday
Salem

Mary English gave birth to a son, Ebenezer. (She was apparently already ill from a consumption contracted, her descendants would say, as a fugitive. She soon died of it (although she was evidently alive as late as the end of March 1696 when her name appeared with her husband's in various lawsuits.)[8]

April 30, 1694 • Monday
Salem Village

A general meeting of Salem Village inhabitants gathered at eight o'clock in the morning in the meeting house, and voted that the disputed land along the Ipswich River did indeed belong to Salem Village. Then they appointed a committee—Nathaniel Putnam, John Putnam, Nathaniel Ingersoll, Thomas Flint, and Joseph Herrick—"to demand, sue for, and recover" in the name of the Village that land from any Topsfield claims. (Topsfield was already embroiled in a boundary dispute with Ipswich.) Although this motion passed "by general concurrence," Thomas Preston and Samuel Nurse, whose Topsfield kin claimed some of that land, asked specifically that their dissent be entered into the record.[9]

29

MAY 1694

Alas! We are all sinners.

—Rev. Samuel Parris

May 6, 1694 • Sunday
Salem Village

"For if we would judge ourselves, we should not be judged," Rev. Samuel Parris preached as he continued with his series on I Corinthians 11:31. We must judge and improve ourselves *now*, he exhorted his congregation, to avoid a rightful divine judgment of our uncorrected faults later. "If you die in this neglect, you will unavoidably fall under God's eternal judging of you to condemnation." We must conquer pride and face our sins impartially, he said, and correct the wrong done. We must admit this before other people if necessary—not just silently to God— even if it means punishment in this world. "We are wont to twit men in the teeth" by implying that they don't know themselves. But *do* we know ourselves? "Alas! We are all sinners."[1]

May 7, 1694 • Monday
Cambridge

This month's meeting of ministers at Harvard College discussed whether or not a pastor could "by himself suspend from the Lord's Table" a communicant suspected of some scandal until the matter could be resolved.[2]

May 15, 1694 • Tuesday
Ipswich

The Superior Court met in Ipswich for Essex County with Chief Justice William Stoughton and Justices Thomas Danforth and Samuel Sewall presiding. With Sheriff George Corwin's confiscations still in dispute, the court "adjusted the accounts of George Corwin," found them "to be just and true," and noted that the county still owed him £67-6-4. Furthermore, neither Corwin nor his heirs were liable for the money, goods, and chattels that he had seized or collected in the course of his office.[3]

May 23, 1694 • Wednesday
Boston

Governor William Phips returned from Pemaquid. The Eastward tribes still had not returned the English captives.[4]

May 30, 1694 • Wednesday
Boston

On this Election Day, several candidates who lived in Boston were chosen in violation of the new residency law—including Nathaniel Byfield for Bristol, and Samuel Legg for Marblehead. Governor Phips refused to let them take the oath of office. Legg declared to the House of Representatives that he would not leave unless the House itself rejected him. Getting wind of this defiance, Phips rushed over "in fury without his hat," as Byfield noticed. The governor said that he would welcome Legg if Boston (where he lived) had elected him, but if the House didn't turn Legg out, Phips *would*.[5]

JUNE 1694

We beseech you to study those things which make for peace and edification.

—Seven ministers to the
Salem Village church

June 3, 1694 • Sunday
Salem Village

Departing from his usual texts for a sacrament sermon, Rev. Samuel Parris, spoke from a passage in the Book of Job—a man who endured many afflictions—but the text notation is not clear and the pages are lost.[1]

June 10, 1694 • Sunday
Salem

Two years had passed since Bridget Bishop was hanged for witchcraft.

June 12, 1694 • Tuesday
Boston

While the sun eclipsed in a clear sky, Nathaniel Byfield wrote to Joseph Dudley to complain of Sir William Phips and the new residency law. Byfield was sure it was an illegal move to pack the assembly. (Dudley, no friend of Phips, was in England busy collecting depositions against the man whom he hoped to replace as governor. He had publicly stated before the lords of trade that Phips had not done one good thing as governor. Fortunately, someone else spoke up to remind the lords of the peace treaty with the Eastern Indians, which silenced Dudley for a time.)[2]

June 13, 1694 • Wednesday
Salem Village

Deputized by Sheriff George Corwin, Jonathan Putnam attached an orchard and two nurseries belonging to widower Francis Nurse as bond in a suite brought by John Hadlock. The latter claimed that he still had not been fully paid for performing Benjamin Nurse's military service in 1692. (Also in 1692, Jonathan Putnam had entered the complaint against Rebecca Nurse, then later helped petition on her behalf.)[3]

June 14, 1694 • Thursday
Salem

A council of ministers met at Salem to consider the problems in the Salem Village church: Samuel Willard and James Allen of Boston, John Higginson and Nicholas Noyes of Salem, John Hale of Beverly, Samuel Cheever of Marblehead, and Joseph Gerrish of Wenham. "Considering the sad effects likely to follow on the continuance of this fire of contention," they suggested that the two sides agree on a council of six churches to mediate (Noyes flatly refused to serve) and agree what their opposing charges were *before* it sat. "We beseech you to study those things which make for peace and edification."[4]

Boston

Abigail Mather gave birth safely to her fifth child who was named Abigail after her mother. (Unlike three of her older siblings, this daughter would survive and grow to adulthood.)[5]

June 17, 1694 • Sunday
Boston

"Baptized my little Abigail," Rev. Cotton Mather wrote in his church records.[6]

Salem Village

Having received the letter of advice from the committee of ministers, Rev. Samuel Parris notified the Village church members of its receipt this evening.[7]

June 21, 1694 • Thursday
Salem Village

The brethren of the Salem Village church discussed (but did not yet vote on) several points concerning the ministers' letter: whether they would comply with the advice, and whether the dissenters should pay the expenses of holding a council. They chose a committee (Nathaniel and John Putnam, Bray Wilkins, and the two deacons—Nathaniel Ingersoll and Edward Putnam) to assist Rev. Samuel Parris with the problem, so "that the whole church may not be oppressed otherwise with a multitude of meetings." Any brother could attend, and any "who can give any personal help for greater expedition" was most welcome, but the rest did not have to be present.[8]

June 22, 1694 • Friday
Boston

Although the Pemaquid treaty had held so far, there were rumors that it might be broken. The governor and council decided it would be best to renew old ties with the Mohawks and "other nations of the Western Indians."[9]

June 26, 1694 • Tuesday
Salem

Zerubabel Endicott of Topsfield appeared before the county court to answer for suspected adultery with former witch suspect Rebecca Eames. He denied everything, but the court (and Robert Eames) were not entirely convinced and required a £200 bond from Endicott for good behavior until the next sitting.[10]

Relatives, servants, and neighbors deposed that the Nurse family had paid John Hadlock in full for his military service on Benjamin Nurse's behalf, but the jury found for the plaintiff. Ordered to pay Hadlock £10-5-0 *and* the court costs, Francis Nurse (husband of the hanged Rebecca) appealed to the Superior Court.[11]

June 29, 1694 • Friday
Salem Village

Most of the voting brethren of the Salem Village church discussed again the seven ministers' letter of advice, "but concluded upon nothing," as Rev. Samuel Parris wrote. If anything, they were "rather further off from approbation of said advice than before." They decided only to pray and to fast about it on July 4. (The Village committee, meanwhile, posted a notice for an inhabitants' meeting on July 3 to select another committee "to take and get legal bills of sale" for the Village parsonage and its lands.)[12]

JULY 1694

> *You intend to serve yourself with the unthinking, who measure the sense of words by their jingle.*
>
> —Chaplain Stuart

July 3, 1694 • Tuesday
Salem Village

A "general meeting of the inhabitants of Salem Village . . . voted by a general concurrence" on a committee of three—Israel Porter, Thomas Flint, and Thomas Putnam—to get the bills of sale from Joseph Hutchinson Sr., Joseph Holten Sr., and Nathaniel Ingersoll for the parsonage house and land. They also empowered the committee to sue for the deeds if necessary.[1]

July 4, 1694 • Wednesday
Boston

News of an approaching ship carrying important letters for Governor Phips reached him in Cambridge during Harvard's Commencement exercises. The ship itself sailed into Boston harbor after dark, and a messenger from it delivered a packet to Phips that very evening. In a letter dated February 15, King William sent orders for Phips to come "home" to England to answer the many charges leveled against him by Jahleel Brenton and Captain Richard Short, including both their personal complaints and the charge that Phips had embezzled the "King's tenth" owed from the booty of captured privateers. (His accusers had wanted him suspended immediately and judged by a committee of his enemies, but the King allowed Phips to defend himself in person.)[2]

The messenger also brought a packet for the lieutenant governor. William Stoughton was to head the province in the governor's absence, and to collect depositions relating to the charges against Phips—depositions that Phips was not to "intermeddle" with.[3]

July 5, 1694 • Thursday
Boston

No doubt feeling great satisfaction at the turn of events, William Stoughton informed the council of the King's orders to Governor Phips and to himself. The council set aside the 17th to begin receiving evidence in the case.[4]

Salem Village

The brethren of the Salem Village church met at Nathaniel Putnam's house. Rev. Samuel Parris delivered a fast sermon on Psalm 5:8 ("Lead me, O Lord, in thy righteousness because of mine enemies: make thy way straight before my face"). Then, "after as much reasonings to and fro as time would allow" (for it was evening), they voted to read the seven ministers' advice to the whole congregation the following Sabbath. Any inhabitant could speak his piece on the matter later in the week at a general meeting, which "such neighbors as are in amity" could also attend. Not everyone agreed with this approach, and no one liked Parris's suggestion that messengers be sent to the dissatisfied brethren "in behalf of all of them." It was enough that Parris could notify the congregation on the following Sunday.[5]

July 12, 1694 • Thursday
Boston

Governor Phips wrote to the Earl of Nottingham that he had received the King's command, and would embark as soon as possible. First, however, he had to sail Eastward to secure the peace. (He had hopes of an expedition against Villebon's headquarters on the St. John River, which had supplied and armed war parties in the past. He had heard rumors, too, that some sort of attack was in the offing. Phips had ordered the *Nonsuch* to the St. John's River. But the frigate's new captain, recently sent from London to replace Phips's appointee Thomas Dobbins, claimed that he never saw the French vessel that resupplied Villebon, though his men thought it was about to attack.)[6]

July 13, 1694 • Friday
Salem Village

Church members and inhabitants (just who and how many were not recorded) met at Nathaniel Ingersoll's at noon with the dissenters. But again they "came to no agreement," for the dissenters refused to provide their specific charges until *after* the church chose a council to hear them.[7]

July 18, 1694 • Wednesday
Oyster River, New Hampshire

Although Lieutenant Villieu, the French officer of Indian affairs, had been unable to dissuade Madockawando's party from the Pemaquid treaty, his agents had since encouraged other sachems, who opposed it. Word of a planned attack was common knowledge in Quebec as early as May, even among the English hostages there, who could do nothing to help.[8]

Today, just before dawn, a French and Indian force attacked Oyster River, New Hampshire, slaughtering over fifty people before the settlement could defend itself. The attackers carried off about forty hostages, burnt thirteen homes, killed all the cattle that they could find, and destroyed the corn crop.[9]

July 19, 1694 • Thursday
Boston

Lieutenant Governor William Stoughton had begun collecting depositions against Governor Phips. The councilors cross-examined some of the witnesses, while Phips growled from the sidelines, unable to intervene. But the whole process was suspended today, so that the governor could deal with the attacks Eastward.[10]

Salem

Two years had passed since the executions of Sarah Good, Rebecca Nurse, Susanna Martin, Elizabeth How, and Sarah Wildes.

July 20, 1694 • Friday
Boston

Governor Phips sailed Eastward again knowing that this moment was the worst possible time for him to leave for England.[11]

New Hampshire's lieutenant governor, John Usher, had asked Phips for help, but the latter responded that he could not send troops out of the province without the consent of the legislature. He would, however, strengthen the adjoining frontiers and would see to the Eastward territories, which were part of Massachusetts. (In Phips's absence, Lieutenant Governor William Stoughton ordered militia to New Hampshire. Their home territory was at risk, and it was the height of the growing season, however, and the men refused to go.)[12]

July 21, 1694 • Saturday
Strawberry Bank, New Hampshire

The French and Indian raiders fell upon some men and women harvesting at a farm on the south bank of the Piscataqua, some distance from the relative safety of Strawberry Bank.[13]

July 25, 1694 • Wednesday
Boston

Stuart, the navy chaplain, ignored Robert Calef's letters until he learned that Calef was circulating their correspondence as if Stuart's silence meant agreement. This was the *end* of their debate, wrote Stuart. Calef twisted his statements. "You intend to serve yourself with the unthinking, who measure the sense of words by their jingle, not knowing how to weigh the things they signify" in order "to throw dirt at them that differ from you . . . in your overeager contention to maintain your principle."[14]

July 27, 1694 • Friday
Groton

Unseen, the enemy war party circled inland to enter Massachusetts and to fall on Groton at dawn. A hundred mounted militia rushed to the town's aid, but found no sign of the raiders or their thirteen captives—only twenty or so corpses.[15]

July 28, 1694 • Saturday
Boston

The night after the Groton attack, even Boston stood under alert. (There, Rev. Samuel Willard, once minister of Groton, faced the additional sorrow of his daughter Sarah's death at age one and a half.)[16]

July 29, 1694 • Sunday
Boston

Rev. Samuel Willard buried his little daughter Sarah just before sunset.[17]

32

AUGUST 1694

Witchcraft is manifestly a work of the flesh.

—Robert Calef

August 2, 1694 • Thursday
Boston

Governor Phips returned from Pemaquid, where not *one* Indian ally had shown up as promised. No one knew where the raiders were at present. The wind, meanwhile, blew from the north and east all night as the mist thickened to fog.[1]

August 5, 1694 • Sunday
Boston

An "abundance of rain" had fallen since Thursday, in downpours mixed with thunder and lightning. Now, after a night of strong wind, the Sabbath brought a "clear, hot, sunshiny day" good for the "languishing" crops of grass and Indian corn.[2]

August 6, 1694 • Monday
Boston

Accompanied by Rev. Benjamin Wadsworth of Boston's First Church as chaplain, Samuel Sewall and Major Penn Townsend set out on horseback for Albany. Massachusetts had commissioned Sewall and Townsend to join other delegates from New York, New Jersey, Connecticut, and the Five Nations to reaffirm their alliance against Canada.[3]

August 8, 1694 • Wednesday
Boston

The Royal Navy galley *Newport* arrived in Boston, having sailed from England with another frigate and two mast ships bound for Piscataqua. Perhaps this would be a help against the attacks.[4]

August 17, 1694 • Friday
Boston

Robert Calef wrote again to the chaplain Stuart expressing surprise at the latter's reaction and repeating his own view that devils could act only how and when God Himself decided. To believe otherwise was to consider Satan a god as well. "Witchcraft," he concluded, "is manifestly a work of the flesh." But Stuart refused to write any more letters and this correspondence ended.[5]

Intending to prevent any further witchcraft trials based on spectral evidence, Calef began to collect the grim particulars of the recent cases for publication. However, he did not let consistency or fact hinder his purpose. Like others, he now distrusted *any* interest in any aspect of the Invisible World (such as Harvard's planned collection of remarkables).[6]

August 19, 1694 • Sunday
Boston

Two years had passed since the executions of Rev. George Burroughs, John Proctor, John Willard, George Jacobs Sr., and Martha Carrier.

August 20, 1694 • Monday
Spruce Creek and York, Maine

The French and Indian force had worked northward into Maine, where they killed field workers at Spruce Creek and at York.[7]

August 24, 1694 • Friday
Kittery, Maine

The raiders turned south again toward the Piscataqua region and struck Kittery, where they killed or captured eight. One seven-year-old girl was found scalped the next day, but miraculously she was still alive and recovered.[8]

August 31, 1694 • Friday
Boston

Samuel Sewall, Major Penn Townsend, and Rev. Benjamin Wadsworth—having avoided bad weather, bears, and enemy forces—returned around noon from their expedition to New York. The conference had reaffirmed the old treaties (but, as it happened, Massachusetts would have to defend itself anyway).[9]

33

SEPTEMBER 1694

> *The English are in despair, for not even infants*
> *in the cradle were spared.*
>
> —Lieutenant Villieu

September 3, 1694 • Monday
Cambridge

The Congregational ministers' meeting at Harvard College debated whether angelic visions could appear visibly in their day and, if so, how to differentiate them from a devil's masquerade.[1]

Their concern was not merely abstract, for the Invisible World was still active in Boston. At some point this fall, a sixteen-year-old North End girl fell into trances during prayer meetings with other young women, and again when Rev. Cotton Mather questioned her. She pointed across the room to a glorious angel that only she could see, but Mather cautioned against devilish disguises. "Our friend Mather is apt to doubt we are good angels," the spirit told her. After uttering some incorrect prophecies, it left.[2]

Another young woman said that during prayer she heard a voice offering devout advice and news of neighbors' misdeeds. Cotton Mather told her to heed the written word of God rather than disembodied gossip. If she encouraged further contact, he said firmly, he would consider her as one with a familiar spirit (the definition of a witch).

The voice refused to speak with her after that, to Mather's relief, for this seemed an attempt to lead the girl straight into witchcraft.[3]

September 4, 1694 • Tuesday
Amesbury

The French and Indian raiders reentered Massachusetts, where they ambushed and killed Joseph Pike, deputy sheriff of Essex County, on the road between Amesbury and Haverhill.[4]

Lieutenant Villieu, hearing a false rumor of English warships heading for Quebec around this time, hurried to warn Frontenac in Montreal (and to present the governor with thirteen English scalps). Villieu was especially satisfied with the attack on Oyster River, "because," as he reported to France, "it breaks off all the talk of peace between our Indians and the English. The English are in despair, for not even infants in the cradle were spared."[5]

September 19, 1694 • Wednesday
Salem

Giles Corey had suffered death by pressing two years ago today.

September 20, 1694 • Thursday
Salem Village

The inhabitants of Salem Village gathered in their meeting house at two o'clock "to hear and consider" what Rev. Parris had to say "relating to our ministry house and land, and also to see if we can possibly agree together in peace and unity to settle peace amongst us by calling a council." But what *actually* happened about the land was not recorded.[6]

That same day Parris had received another letter from five area ministers: John Higginson of Salem, James Allen and Samuel Willard of Boston, Samuel Cheever of Marblehead, and Joseph Gerrish of Wenham. Concerned that the earlier advice had not been followed, they now intended to make their view clear: The Salem Village church was to join with the dissatisfied brethren to call a council of six churches (with no objections to anyone's choice), to determine a time and place for the council's meeting; and, after that was done, twenty days before the time appointed, the dissatisfied brethren were to give Rev. Parris "a true copy of those two papers of grievance which were showed to us." The area ministers feared "that longer delays will be of dangerous consequences to you in divers respects," and urged them to call a council before winter.[7]

Parris had prepared a statement to send to the dissenting brethren, which he now read to the assembly. "We have long discoursed of a council, and look upon yourselves as the only bar to it" (with the dissenters' refusal to state their grievances). "But that we might not contend forever," the rest were willing to choose a council forthwith (the church naming four other churches and the dissenters naming three) "and that you give us immediately your dissatisfactions signed under your hands." If they contained matters not suitable to an ecclesiastical council, these points would be eliminated or the council would fall.

Besides the pastor, twenty brethren were present and while the rest of the inhabitants observed, all voted to present this decision to the dissenters.[8]

September 22, 1694 • Saturday
Salem

Two years had passed since the executions of Martha Corey, Mary Esty, Alice Parker, Mary Parker, Ann Pudeator, Margaret Scott, Wilmot Read, and Samuel Wardwell.

September 29, 1694 • Saturday
Salem Village

Rev. Samuel Parris and twenty of the brethren formally voted to send the proposals, discussed at the inhabitants meeting on the 20th, to the dissenters.[9]

34

OCTOBER 1694

Respond not a scorner lest he hate thee.

—Proverbs 9:8

October 7, 1694 • Sunday
Salem Village

Rev. Samuel Parris based this month's sacrament sermon on Proverbs 9:1-8: "Wisdom hath builded her house," and "as for him who wanteth understanding, she saith to him, 'Come, eat of my bread, and drink of the wine which I have mingled.'" (The notes for this sermon, however, are lost, but the rest of the text continues: "Respond not a scorner lest he hate thee. Rebuke a wise man and he will love thee." At this point, no one in the Village seemed able to endure criticism. Parris, however, was apparently mulling over his own part in the 1692 witch scare, and reaching the uneasy conclusion that he may have been as gullible as Saul at Endor.)[1]

October 22, 1694 • Monday
Boston

Over the summer, the governor and council had received several petitions for tax relief. Today they read yet another, from Groton, so devastated by recent attacks.[2]

October 28, 1694 • Sunday
Boston

"A very high, boisterous, and cold northwest wind" heralded the beginning of winter.[3]

October 31, 1694 • Wednesday
Boston

The legislature addressed a plea to the King and Queen, describing their "deplorable state" since the series of attacks by the Eastward Indians. Massachusetts hardly had the troops to guard its own and New Hampshire's frontiers, so there was certainly none to spare to guard New York as ordered. (None of the other provinces sent troops either.) Therefore, would their majesties *please* not deprive Massachusetts of Phips as Governor at such a risky time?[4]

35

NOVEMBER 1694

God has been righteously spitting in my face.

—Rev. Samuel Parris

November 1, 1694 • Thursday
Boston

Thomas Dobbins (whom Governor Phips had once made captain of the *Nonsuch*) refused to pay bail (when he came to court on an unspecified charge). As the sheriff escorted him to prison, Governor Phips intervened personally, threatening to jail the sheriff if he so much as touched Dobbins. William Stoughton opposed the move, which (as Samuel Sewall noted) "occasioned very warm discourse between [Phips] and the lieutenant governor."[1]

November 2, 1694 • Friday
Salem Village

Fifteen brethren of the Salem Village church met with Rev. Samuel Parris at Nathaniel Ingersoll's. Having addressed a letter to the dissenters on October 29 about the terms of the council, they now "debated whether it was not high time" to call the dissenters to state their reasons for withdrawing from their communion—the other bone of contention. "By a universal vote" those present decided to have all the rest of the brethren on the following Sabbath decide whether to summon John Tarbell to state the dissenters' reasons.[2]

November 3, 1694 • Saturday
Boston

Governor William Phips adjourned the General Court until the following February, the last time before he left for England. Its members disputed on a technicality the phrasing that he had used (so they would be able to gather legally in case of emergency in his absence), and Phips had words with the Speaker of the House over a letter to Sir Henry Ashurst. The session ended on a strained note all around.[3]

November 4, 1694 • Sunday
Salem Village

Following the afternoon sermon, Rev. Samuel Parris proposed that the church members vote whether to require that the dissenting brethren be called to give the reasons for their dissent. No one spoke against the idea and, as far as Parris could see, all but Joshua Rea voted that Jonathan Tarbell should appear and state his reasons on the following Sabbath. Making sure, Parris asked if there were any objections, "but no dissent was manifested."[4]

November 7, 1694 • Wednesday
Boston

When court sat in Boston for Suffolk County, Thomas Dobbins again refused to pay bail. He claimed that he was in the sheriff's custody (though apparently he was not confined) and produced two warrants under the governor's hand and seal. Even so, Dobbins was taken to jail anyway, gripped between the sheriff and the prison keeper.[5]

November 9, 1694 • Friday
Boston

Lieutenant Governor William Stoughton and the council members gathered for a farewell dinner in honor of Governor Phips. Sir William, however, was so angry over the matter of Thomas Dobbins's arrest that he refused to attend. His empty chair stood like a reproach at the table head. Neither Increase nor Cotton Mather attended either, though Cotton, as he later told Sewall, "was sick of a grievous pain in his face."[6]

November 11, 1694 • Sunday
Salem Village

After giving the evening blessing, Rev. Samuel Parris formally called Jonathan Tarbell to come forward and state his case. Tarbell, however, was not there. Nathaniel Putnam had to explain that when he and Nathaniel Ingersoll had delivered the message to him, Tarbell had said that he would rather appear on a weekday than on the Lord's Day.[7]

November 15, 1694 • Thursday
Boston

The council met at Governor Phips's North End home to discuss the affidavits that his clerk, Benjamin Jackson, had taken in Phips's favor. Later, after the lecture, the council members debated this matter further in the Town House. Finally, Jackson's depositions were read aloud, and he swore to them, his oath delivered by Lieutenant Governor William Stoughton and the council. (Stoughton had amassed 109 pages *against* Phips.)[8]

November 17, 1694 • Saturday
Boston

Sir William Phips left his wife and his home at dusk. Accompanied by William Stoughton, Samuel Sewall, Rev. Cotton Mather, and most of the council, justices, captains of the frigates, and many other gentlemen, he made his way to the water stairs at Salutation Wharf. There he boarded his yacht, which took him to a ship in the harbor. As the castle guns fired a salute, Phips sailed into the darkening east, flags flying, his departure, like his arrival (Samuel Sewall recalled), crowded into a Sabbath eve.[9]

November 18, 1694 • Sunday
Salem Village

Jonathan Tarbell was absent from Salem Village's Sabbath services, but appeared once Rev. Samuel Parris finished the second, afternoon, sermon. When asked his reasons for withdrawing from the congregation, Tarbell produced a paper, "which he was urged to deliver to the pastor to communicate to the church."

Tarbell refused. "Who was the church's mouth?" he asked.

"The pastor."

The offense, said Tarbell, was *with* the pastor.

Was he offended by anyone else in the church? Parris demanded.

"No." Tarbell had a non-member, Joseph Hutchinson, read his paper. For all the secrecy about the exact charges, the complaints were the same as before—Parris's acceptance and encouragement of spectral evidence.

Then Parris read his own statement of "overtures for peace and reconciliation": his "Meditations for Peace," in which he admitted that the outbreak had begun in his own household, where some used diabolic means to raise spirits (for fortune telling and countermagic). He himself was wrong to accept the words of the possessed about what they perceived, for (he now realized) evil spirits could certainly counterfeit the innocent. He insisted, however, that he was careful in his court notes (which the magistrates had ordered him to take) and that when he spoke under oath about the accused, he referred to their specters (as had nearly everyone else, including the King). But he apologized for unwise statements in his sermons that year, and truly sympathized now with the accused and their kin. He asked their pardon and their prayers, for "God has been righteously spitting in my face."

Tarbell appeared "much affected" by Parris's confession. "If half so much had been said formerly, it had never come to this," he said, but added that the other dissenters must decide also.[10]

November 19, 1694 • Monday
Pemaquid, Maine

Bomaseen, chief of the Norridgewocks and one of the Sagamores who had signed the Pemaquid treaty, came to Fort William Henry commiserating with the late troubles. He said that he had just arrived from Canada. But surviving eyewitnesses had said that he led the attack on Oyster River. The fort's commander seized him and other Indians and sent them to Boston.[11]

(Bomaseen would remain in Boston jail, off and on, for about four years. Soon after he arrived, he quizzed Rev. Cotton Mather on the differences between the French Catholic and English Protestant versions of Christianity. The French, Bomaseen told Mather, had taught "that the mother of our blessed Savior was a French lady, and that they were Englishmen by whom our Savior was murdered, and that it was therefore a meritorious thing to destroy the English nation.")[12]

November 21, 1694 • Wednesday
Boston

While the weather stormed and rained, and while her mother and her husband Samuel prayed in the kitchen, Hannah Sewall gave birth to a daughter, Sarah. The birth was difficult, but all went well at last. As the storm intensified, the relieved family served the attending women a celebratory dinner of roast beef, mince pies, "good cheese," and tarts.[13]

November 26, 1694 • Monday
Salem Village

Not only church members, but also the congregation in general and several out-siders, filled the Village meeting house at two o'clock. Samuel Nurse, John Tarbell, and Thomas Wilkins only reluctantly let Rev. Samuel Parris touch a copy of their grievances. While Parris read it aloud to the gathering, Nurse checked what the minister said against the original to be sure no word was changed.

After Parris read in full the dissenters' charges of his uncharitable, unchristian behavior, he asked them if they were offended by any other than himself to with-draw from the church and from communion. When they assured him that they re-sented no one else, he read his "Meditations for Peace" again to admit his own gullibility, his family's use of forbidden magic, and God's rightful rebuke. He now believed that God "has suffered the evil angels to delude us on both hands, but how far on the one side or the other is much above me to say." What he himself did in 1692, "as I apprehended was my duty—however through weakness, igno-rance, etc., I may have been mistaken." Therefore, "I beg, entreat, and beseech you, that Satan, the Devil, the roaring lion, the old dragon, the enemy of all right-eousness, may no longer be served by us, by our envy and strifes," but that "we may on all hands forgive each other heartily, sincerely, and thoroughly, as we do hope and pray that God, for Christ's sake, would forgive each of ourselves."

This time Tarbell said that they would have to think about it, and they wanted a copy of the statement. Then, replied Parris, he needed a *signed* copy of their as-yet-anonymous list of complaints. It was like pulling teeth for them to agree and involved many whispered conversations, as Daniel Andrews and Thomas Preston relayed messages from the dissenters to Israel Porter, Joseph Hutchinson, and others.[14]

November 30, 1694 • Friday
Salem Village

The Salem Village inhabitants gathered in their meeting house at two o'clock and chose Thomas Putnam to continue keeping their record book, and voted again to empower the same committee as before to deal with the disputed Topsfield lands. Putnam repeated a long description of the Topsfield dispute in the record book, along with the vote to pursue that claim. This time, more men with Topsfield as-sociations made a point of dissenting from the move: Joshua Rea Sr.; the widowed Francis Nurse; his son, Samuel Nurse; and Francis's sons-in-law, John Tarbell and Thomas Preston.[15]

The church members also met at Rev. Samuel Parris's home the same day. Fran-cis Nurse and Jonathan Tarbell arrived near dusk with Joseph Putnam and Thomas Preston. They were *not* satisfied by Parris's paper, they said. They *still* wanted a church council according to the other ministers' advice.[16]

36

DECEMBER 1694

The pastor ... was even quite tired out.

—Rev. Samuel Parris

December 2, 1694 • Sunday
Salem Village

After the Sabbath services Rev. Parris informed the brethren of the latest developments and arranged for a meeting on the subject.[1]

December 4, 1694 • Tuesday
Boston

Lieutenant Governor William Stoughton took formal control of the government at
a meeting of the council in the Town House, as he became Acting Governor in
Phips's absence. He "made a brave speech" and took his oath of office. After handling the day's business, Stoughton invited the company to a "splendid treat"—a
celebratory dinner. Both Mathers and Rev. Willard attended.[2]

December 6, 1694 • Thursday
Salem Village

The brethren met at Deacon Edward Putnam's house and decided to meet with the dissenters on December 20 at Deacon Ingersoll's. All the church members would be there "excepting the pastor," as Rev. Samuel Parris wrote of himself, "who was even quite tired out, and also because he thought they might be more free in his absence."[3]

December 20, 1694 • Thursday
Salem Village

The brethren of the Salem Village church apparently met with the three local dissenters at Deacon Nathaniel Ingersoll's ordinary as planned. However, as Rev. Samuel Parris stayed away, no one kept notes of the meeting.[4]

December 25, 1694 • Tuesday
Boston

"Shops are open," Samuel Sewall observed, "men at work. Carts of pork, hay, coal, wood come to town as on other days."[5]

PART IV

1695

37

JANUARY 1695

> *Some of my husband's children and relations*
> *have brought upon me inconvenient and un-*
> *necessary charges.*
>
> —Mary Putnam

January 8, 1695 • Tuesday
Salem Village

Widowed Mrs. Mary Putnam, who had inherited jointly the family home with her son Joseph, had been unwell for some time, tended by Dr. William Griggs. Twenty-year-old Abigail Darling was at work in the house spinning thread when the old woman fell in her chamber and the household thought she had died. "Some run one way and some another," Abigail recalled, "to tell our neighbors that she was dead." But after a considerable time, Mrs. Putnam began to revive. She seemed to recognize her family, but was so weak and ill that they feared she would not last long.[1]

January 9, 1695 • Wednesday
Salem Village

Old Mrs. Putnam fainted away again, but was apparently rational and able to talk toward evening. As Abigail Darling passed in and out of the sickroom, she overheard the family (Joseph Putnam and his wife Elizabeth) worrying that his mother had no will. Mary Putnam seemed unwilling, but at last agreed to make one. (Her contentious stepsons Thomas and Edward Putnam had inherited ownership of the farms that their father had given them during his lifetime, but a man's estate was not completely distributed until *after* his widow's death.)[2]

January 10, 1695 • Thursday
Salem Village

Joseph and Elizabeth Putnam sent Abigail Darling and fellow servant Deborah Knight to work in an outbuilding for a time, before calling them both back to the sickroom. There Elizabeth's father, Israel Porter, steadied Mary Putnam's hand while she made a mark on a paper. Abigail and Deborah also signed (with marks) as witnesses, while Porter told them to take notice that their mistress was "sensible." But Abigail was none too sure the woman *was* sensible, and it bothered her that the family might expect her to testify to it.[3]

January 12, 1695 • Saturday
Salem Village

Leaving Mrs. Mary Putnam still unwell, Abigail Darling returned to her father's house, where she expressed her doubts about the will.[4]

January 14, 1695 • Monday
Salem Village

Joseph Putnam sent for Abigail Darling's widowed sister, Ann Douglas, today to help tend his mother. (Ann's child had died in 1692 when Rev. Samuel Parris, at least, had suspected witchcraft as the cause, and when Mary Walcott may have reported seeing the specter of a Goody Darling—probably Ann and Abigail's mother Mary.) Ann had worked for the widow before, and the old woman, "though sick and weak," recognized her former servant this evening.[5]

January 19, 1695 • Saturday
Salem Village

As Ann Douglas tended Mrs. Mary Putnam through this week of rain and snow, Ann thought that the old woman "continued pretty sensible." She was, however, still very weak and had taken to staring by the time Ann returned home to her father John Darling's house Saturday night.[6]

January 20, 1695 • Sunday
Salem Village

Elizabeth Putnam sent for Ann Douglas again, fearing her mother-in-law would again have fits.[7]

January 21, 1695 • Monday
Salem Village

Rev. Samuel Parris and the brethren met at John Putnam's and decided to offer a fresh proposal about a council to "our dissenting brethren and neighbors" at their *next* meeting.[8]

January 23, 1695 • Wednesday
Salem Village

After tending Mary Putnam since the previous Sunday, Ann Douglas felt ill herself, and frightened by the two or three fits that the patient now endured daily. When Thomas Putnam dropped by, Ann and the family asked him to fetch Sarah Cave to take over nursing duties. Thomas did, and Ann, relieved, returned home.[9]

January 27, 1695 • Sunday
Salem Village

Rev. Samuel Parris baptized and received into full communion Goodwife Mary Wheldon. Then, after the rest of the congregation left, he informed the full church members of the next meeting to discuss the dissenters and the proposed council.[10]

January 28, 1695 • Monday
Salem Village

Mrs. Mary Putnam continued to drift in and out of consciousness, sometimes "as decently and rationally" as ever (according to a son-in-law), and sometimes "stupefied" in her understanding (as Dr. William Griggs and her brother-in-law thought). Her daughter (by her first marriage) thought that her mother spoke very sensibly after other people who thought she had lost her reason had left the room, for her mind clouded only during the seizures. Perhaps the family worried about Abigail Darling's doubts about the old woman's state of mind, for the will that would be filed eventually was dated January 28, and witnessed *not* by Abigail

Darling but by George Jacobs (the younger), Sarah Cave (the third nurse), and Deborah Knight.[11]

In both cases Joseph Putnam's father-in-law, Israel Porter, wrote the document. ("I was desired to write it for her," Porter testified later.) He asked Mary what she wished to leave to her stepchildren. "Truly," she said (as Porter would relate), "I have done for them already according to my abilities, and if I should give them a small matter, it will but give offense, and to give them a great deal I don't know how Joseph can pay it, for there is a great deal to pay yet."[12]

(As her daughter Mary Lindall would recall, "some" told her mother "that her husband's children would trouble her son, but she could not believe it." When advised to leave them something, "she answered that there was nothing due to them. For, she said, she had given considerably already among them which she had not told any of it but to myself.")[13]

Porter suggested dividing £10 equally among them. "Aye," she said, "it is easy to write down a thousand, but where will it be had?" Porter went off to consult Joseph, who replied that whatever his mother wanted was fine by him. She still didn't like the latest idea. "While I was waiting I was informed," said Porter (but did not say by whom), "that I should set down five shillings apiece for three of them and ten for two of them. And her son should be executor to her will."

So Mary Putnam made her mark on what was apparently a second will that left ten shillings each to two of her stepdaughters, and only five shillings apiece to stepdaughter Deliverance Walcott (Mary Walcott's stepmother), and stepsons Thomas and Edward Putnam. "Unto all which I have done something already according to my ability and might, and would have done more but that some of my husband's children and relations have brought upon me inconvenient and unnecessary charges and disbursements at several times." Everything else was left to her son and executor Joseph (who was already wealthier than any of his brothers).[14]

(Although Joseph had taken notes at the first witch hearing in 1692, he soon opposed his half-brothers' views on the subject. He may well have taken the precaution of keeping a loaded pistol and a saddled horse ready during 1692 in case anyone accused him of witchcraft.)[15]

January 31, 1695 • Thursday
Salem Village

A "full meeting" of the Salem Village church crowded into the parsonage and, at long last, agreed to a council. "The third Tuesday in March next would be as convenient a time as we could pitch upon," Rev. Samuel Parris noted. The church members scheduled a general meeting for the next Lecture Day, so the rest of the Villagers could hear the seven ministers' June letter of advice. That evening, William Way and John Wilkins informed the dissenter Thomas Wilkins (their neighbor and kinsman) of the decision.[16]

FEBRUARY 1695

They openly charged the whole church as a nest of deceivers.

—Rev. Samuel Parris

February 7, 1695 • Thursday
Salem Village

Rev. Samuel Parris read the seven ministers' June 14 letter of advice to the Villagers gathered in the meeting house. Now that there would be a council, he asked that "the dissenting neighbors then present" for the written statement they wished to present. "This was much urged but to no purpose," Parris later wrote. The dissenters wanted the council members to be decided *before* they submitted their complaints, as recommended in the ministers' second letter of September 10. Since the dissenters themselves had procured the June letter, Parris retorted—and behind the backs of their fellow brethren, no less—they ought first to give their charges, "let them be what they would." *Then* both sides would nominate and vote on a council.

The dissenters refused.

In that case, said Parris, since the church had heard their reasons for withdrawing from fellowship, here was the list of complaints that the church intended to submit to the council. Parris read aloud the seventeen points of contention first presented in November 1693: the dubious signatures, the dissenters' rough and threatening attitude even toward "aged" brethren, and their clamorous refusal to settle the matter peacefully. Despite the claim that their discontent was with the minister alone, "they openly charged the whole church as a nest of deceivers."

"That is a large epistle," Thomas Wilkins scoffed.

So *that* was how it was, said Parris, and after such "a loud and long cry for a council, and yet now a declining of it."

As it was sunset, the meeting broke up, with Parris informing the dissenters that the church would hold a council on the third Tuesday of March, whether they cared to attend or not. Then most of the men stalked up the street to Ingersoll's ordinary.

After a time, Samuel Nurse and later Thomas Wilkins drifted into the taproom. Might they have time to consider the offer?

"We were," Parris told them, "even spent and tired out with the multitude of meetings which they had occasioned us." However, they appointed yet another church meeting for the following Tuesday.[1]

(It was perhaps after one of these February meetings that Thomas Preston encountered Joseph Putnam and inquired after his mother's health. "She was a very weak woman," said Joseph. "I question whether she will recover this sickness. Her fits have brought her very low. But yet she retains her sense and reason, I think, as well as she ever had.")[2]

February 12, 1695 • Tuesday
Salem Village

In "extreme cold," a few days after "a very extraordinary snow," the Village church brethren gathered at one o'clock in Nathaniel Putnam's house. The three local dissenters—Thomas Wilkins, Samuel Nurse, and John Tarbell—arrived late and kept going into corners for whispered conferences. They argued until nearly sunset over which churches should be part of the mediating council. Perhaps hoping that the men would ride to the nearby Topsfield meeting house once a week, Rev. Samuel Parris asked if dismission to another church would suit them.

Aye, snapped Tarbell (still thinking of the rates), if they could find a way to remove their livings, too.

The session ended with Parris writing letters in the name of the Village Church to Boston's North Church, and to the churches of Rowley, Malden, and Weymouth (but not Ipswich as the dissenters wanted). Parris requested that they send elders and messengers to help cool these "fires of strife, division, etc."[3]

Boston

Continued cold weather was always very hard on Mrs. Ann Moody. Today, she was struck with a palsy in her right side and rendered speechless. Rumors had once circulated that she was a witch, after her husband, Rev. Joshua Moody, had helped John and Mary English to escape jail.[4]

February 13, 1695 • Wednesday
London, England

Sir William Phips had crossed the winter Atlantic with his head full of plans for trade, war, salvaged treasure, and his own vindication. But his personal collisions with Jahleel Brenton and Captain Richard Short now overshadowed their own insubordination and conflict with authority, especially after they stretched the truth. (Short's two months in prison became nine in his depositions.) As soon as Phips landed in England, Joseph Dudley and Brenton had him arrested on a £2,000 suit (the exact charges are unclear). Sir Henry Ashurst offered to post bail, but the indignity, his friends later thought, weakened Phips's usual burly good health. He caught a cold, and was in a bad way from it at his February 13 hearing in the Council Chamber at Whitehall.[5]

February 18, 1695 • Monday
London, England

Sir William Phips's cold grew worse until even he, more at home outdoors, had to keep to his chamber. During this time "a very eminent person at Whitehall" honored him with a visit. The official urged Phips to "get well as fast as he could, for in one month's time he should be again dispatched away to his government of New England."

However, Phips's cold proved to be influenza, a new malady then gripping London. After only a few days of "malignant fever," Phips died suddenly, "to the extreme surprise of his friends."

(Immediately, Joseph Dudley maneuvered for the governorship of Massachusetts, but settled for the Isle of Wight when Ashurst obtained a reversal of attainder for the New York rebels whom Dudley had helped to condemn to death.)[6]

***

Boston

February brought "a very extraordinary storm of snow" to New England, and the completion of Rev. Cotton Mather's essay on witchcraft—thirty-two quarto pages intended for circulation. Mather sent it to Robert Calef by one of the Brattles with

the provision that he might peruse it for two weeks, but not copy it. Calef complied, but scribbled sarcasms in the margin as he read. Some of his comments were
questions answered in the next few pages, or rephrasings, intended as rebuttals,
of points that Mather had just made.[7]

A witch, Mather wrote, was a mortal cooperating with evil spirits in order to
work magic. This did not require a deliberate written or spoken agreement, or
even a complete understanding of the risks. Therefore, some may be witches
legally and be guilty of encouraging spectral harm, yet *not* deserve death. He accepted the reality of witchcraft because of scripture, history, and personal experience. But he knew also that many effects ascribed to witchcraft worked *within* the
mind of the afflicted. Many apparently bewitched people (and some apparent
witches, too) were actually possessed, so their perceptions and accusations could
not be trusted.

So why question any of them? Calef asked in the margin. He also dismissed
Mather's observations of symptoms as "easy tricks" or as "signs and lying wonders." He hooted at the minister's speculation on the possible manipulation of a
"Plastic Spirit"—a spiritual force that permeated the physical world as theorized by
the neo-Platonists of Cambridge University. "What's that? Sure some inkhorn
term."[8]

Devils, Mather continued, were not all powerful, but the disasters credited to
them were no more out of character than the horrors that humans committed.
They did not *need* witches' help to harm, but might hook them in as collaborators
just to damn them. (Why, that would mean the Devil cheats! Calef exclaimed from
the margin.) Mather cited past cases from sources that he trusted (here Calef called
Baxter crazy) and from his own experience. People distressed for their souls had
confided to him of their own attempted magic, and Cotton had recently advised a
young woman to ignore a disembodied voice. (Calef snorted that it was a pity that
this hadn't been done at Salem).[9]

February 26, 1695 • Tuesday
Boston

The Salem Village assessors (Thomas and Nathaniel Putnam, Thomas Fuller,
Thomas Flint, and Henry Wilkins) petitioned the General Court for help collecting the unpaid minister's rates. Although they could legally assess taxes, they
had no power to compel people to pay them. The Village was *still* part of Salem,
but Salem constables refused "to make distress upon the goods of any person
that did neglect or refuse to pay," unless the assessors accompanied them. (The
committee did not explain why they did not accompany the constables. The task
would not have been pleasant.) Furthermore, earlier rates committees "have
wholly neglected their duty" by refusing to collect the sums themselves, or to ask

the Salem constables to do it, or even to enter *what* the rates were in the Village record book.

Therefore, they asked the court to order the Salem constables to collect the Village taxes, and to require the rates committees to do their job and to make a proper public record of it.

The General Court allowed the petition.[10]

39

MARCH 1695

Going to the afflicted or possessed to have them divine who are witches by their spectral sight, is a great wickedness.

—Robert Calef

March 1, 1695 • Friday
Boston

Robert Calef returned Rev. Cotton Mather's marked-up manuscript essay on the nature of witchcraft. He then composed a letter to a "Mr. B." (one of the Brattles) complaining of his year-long wait for what turned out to be only "crude matter and impertinent absurdities." Calef itemized his objections, sneered at Mather's similes, doubted that "plastic spirit" was a real term, and consistently referred to Mather's thirty-two page manuscript as "four sheets." He condemned flatly Mather's views as "dangerous errors (if not heresies)" that could reignite the flames of witch persecutions all over again.[1]

Furious with the marred manuscript, Mather abandoned the farce of debate.

Salem Village

Rev. Samuel Parris and the church brethren met to pray at Ezekiel Cheever's house before the next sacrament Sunday. They also discussed the latest advice from the mediating churches, whether or not the committee should include representatives from the other two Boston Congregational churches, and whether the meeting should be postponed another two weeks. After only a little debate "we quickly assented," and shortly sent a messenger with letters to the other churches.[2]

***

Salem Village

Encountering Sarah Cave, Nathaniel and Hannah Ingersoll inquired about Mrs. Mary Putnam. They'd heard that she had made a will, they said.

Although she had apparently put her mark to two documents, Sarah replied that she knew nothing about a will, and did not think that her mistress was even able to make one.[3]

March 17, 1695 • Sunday
Salem Village

A "very sore storm of snow" fell all night and all today. "Mrs. Mary Putnam, widow," Rev. Samuel Parris wrote in his list of local deaths. Then he added the deaths of "a Negro woman of said Putnam's a few weeks ago," and "a child of the said Negro woman."[4]

Boston

When the afternoon service ended, the brethren of Boston's South Church chose two from their number to accompany Rev. Samuel Willard to the April council in Salem Village, "to see [Samuel Sewall noted] if [they] can put an end to their contentions." It was a troublesome time in Boston as well as in the Village, with people dying of illness or accident—a toddler scalded in a brewer's beer vat, a boy falling into a ship's hold, a woman falling from her horse. This night Sewall dreamed that all of his children except little Sarah were dead, "which did distress me sorely."[5]

March 18, 1695 • Monday
Boston

Robert Calef acted surprised at Rev. Cotton Mather's exasperation, but turned his attentions "to the ministers, whether English, French, or Dutch." Mather's views on

witchcraft, wrote Calef, had helped cause the late troubles, yet Mather's only answer to his reasonable queries were four sheets of quibbles. He implied that
Mather credited the Devil with God-like power. He also lectured the ministers
against the shocking belief that Scripture was insufficient to detect witches, and
against using folk tests and other methods that they already distrusted. "Going to
the afflicted or possessed to have them divine who are witches by their spectral
sight, is a great wickedness."

He sent this to Rev. Samuel Willard, who, like the rest, ignored it. Calef announced that he took their silence as consent, but they did not rise to that bait either.[6]

March 21, 1695 • Thursday
Salem Village

An inhabitants' meeting at Salem Village chose a rates committee for the current
year: Nathaniel and Thomas Putnam, Thomas Flint, Henry Wilkins, and Jacob
Fuller—the same men who had petitioned on the Village's behalf in February. Their
assessments to cover Rev. Samuel Parris's salary from July 1694 to July 1695 listed
the two wealthiest taxpayers as Joseph Porter (rated with his sons at £2-12-0) and
Joseph Putnam (at £2-4-0). Both were staunchly anti-Parris.[7]

March 29, 1695 • Friday
Boston

Alarming news from England spread throughout Boston: after only four day's illness, Queen Mary had died of smallpox on December 27.[8]

March 31, 1695 • Sunday
Salem Village

Middle-aged Thomas Fuller Jr. joined the Salem Village church and was received
into full communion.[9]

APRIL 1695

Considering the extreme trials and troubles which the dissatisfied brethren in the Church of Salem Village have undergone in the day of sore temptation which hath been upon them, we cannot but advise the church to treat them with bowels of much compassion.

—Increase Mather
and the council of mediators

April 3, 1695 • Wednesday
Salem Village

The long-awaited committee of mediators met in the Salem Village parsonage. In addition to ten laymen, there were seven ministers. Increase Mather, the moderator, represented Boston with Samuel Willard, James Allen, and Cotton Mather (to whom the dissenters, unlike Calef, did *not* object). Samuel Torrey traveled up from Weymouth, and Samuel Phillips and Edward Payson arrived from Rowley. Rev. Michael Wigglesworth of Malden was absent due to his wife's serious illness.[1]

April 4, 1695 • Thursday
Salem Village

After deliberating overnight, the panel of mediators listed their decisions and publicly read them aloud to the Villagers. The ministers felt that in 1692 Rev. Samuel

Parris, "then under the hurrying distractions of amazing afflictions," had indeed taken "sundry unwarrantable and uncomfortable steps." But his subsequent change of heart and apology ought to be considered, especially as he had otherwise fulfilled his pastoral duties and still had the majority's support. They did not think that all the charges against him were fair or accurate, but it would not reflect badly if he left this congregation for the sake of peace. They also persuaded Parris to apologize for his lack of "due exactness" in the many writings produced "in the late confusions." (Although he had then believed that the accused were guilty, his notes *do* appear to be accurate, but they were out of sight in the county's files.) Parris added an apology in the margin of the church records next to his "Meditations for Peace."

"Considering the extreme trials and troubles which the dissatisfied brethren in the Church of Salem Village have undergone in the day of sore temptation which hath been upon them, we cannot but advise the church to treat them with bowels of much compassion, instead of all more critical or rigorous proceedings against them, for the infirmities discovered by them in such an heart-breaking day." If the dissenters *still* could not abide Parris's ministry "in the remembrance of the disasters that have happened," the Village church should allow them to be dismissed to another church.[2]

April 5, 1695 • Friday
Boston

Thunder and lightning jolted Boston awake at daybreak, sounding at first (Samuel Sewall thought) like cannon-fire.[3]

April 9, 1695 • Tuesday
Boston

More news of Queen Mary's death arrived in Boston by returning ships, along with a report that King Louis XIV of France was dead as well. (However, *that* hope proved false.)[4]

April 29, 1695 • Monday
Boston

Samuel and Hannah Sewall invited their friends to a housewarming to celebrate their home's new wing. After wet, rainy weather, the day had begun "warm and sunshiny," but at two o'clock unexpected thunder and lightning swept over Boston. Sewall was standing in the kitchen with Cotton Mather, who had just remarked that it seemed as if lightning struck ministers' houses more often than others.

Suddenly, "a very extraordinary storm of hail" hit the house and smashed 480 of the diamond-shaped panes of new window glass. Hailstones as big as musket balls hurtled into the very center of the room, while outside they covered the ground (Sewall thought) like fallen blossoms. Astonished neighbors gaped at the ruin from the street.[5]

41

MAY 1695

For we have had three ministers removed already, and by every removal our differences have been rather aggravated.

—Pro-Parris petition

May 3, 1695 • Friday
Salem Town

While Deputy Sheriff George Herrick was helping to test a shipment of cannons at a Salem wharf, one of the great guns exploded. The blast injured several bystanders, and killed one man outright. Herrick was found badly torn and burned, his leg and thigh thrown some distance away. Although he lived nearby, he died before he could be carried home. (In 1692 Herrick had had to arrest and transport so many witch suspects that he had neglected his own upholstery business. Now he left a widow with three young unprovided-for children.)[1]

May 5, 1695 • Sunday
Boston

Now incoming ships brought news of Sir William Phips's death in February. "People are generally sad," Samuel Sewall thought—and apprehensive of who the next royal governor might be.[2]

May 6, 1695 • Monday
Cambridge

While Boston fired guns in mourning from the forts and Castle Island to honor the late Governor Phips, the area ministers met at Harvard College to ponder the unbrotherly mood of the churches at Watertown and Salem Village. They had received a petition signed by eighty-four Salem Villagers: men and women, church members and non-members, householders and boys of sixteen (old enough for the militia but not old enough to vote). Those who signed included the dissenting brethren, the Nurse family, Sarah Osborn's widowed husband Alexander *and* his new wife, as well as the accused Daniel Andrews, Sarah Buckley, and Edward Bishop. The petitioners had hoped that the ministers' conference would bring "an happy issue" to the "long and uncomfortable differences" relating to Rev. Samuel Parris. But they "now are utterly frustrated," for "instead of uniting, our rent is made worse and our breach made wider." Perhaps the mediators had lacked the time to truly understand the situation. Therefore, would the ministers hear the case again, or advise Parris "to dispose of himself elsewhere," or allow the petitioners to call a second minister of their own?[3]

Rev. Increase Mather and the eight other ministers present wrote to Samuel Parris and to the Village church and regretfully advised Parris to "come away from his present station" and the people to unite "as far as you can, in calling another minister." The ministers knew of "a probability of an opportunity" elsewhere for Parris, since "we do, with grief, see the door so far shut up among yourselves."[4]

Salem Town

Some Villagers had more personal problems as well. Today, Thomas Putnam entered a caveat in the Salem probate court asking that his stepmother's will not be approved until he could "declare and plead" against it.[5]

May 8, 1695 • Wednesday
Boston

Samuel Sewall visited the widowed Lady Mary Phips, "who takes on heavily for the death of Sir William." She thought that Lieutenant Governor William Stoughton and the council "were not so kind to him as they should have been."[6]

("The love, even to fondness, with which he always treated her," Rev. Cotton Mather would write of their marriage, "was a matter not only of observation, but even such admiration, that everyone said, 'The age afforded not a kinder husband!'" Lady Phips would commission a carved marble plaque to be placed over her husband's grave in the London church of St. Mary's Woolnoth. Flanked by cupids, and topped by a coat of arms, the plaque depicted a ship at sea and men diving for treasure—all watched over by the winged eye of Providence.)[7]

May 20, 1695 • Monday
Pemaquid

A fleet of canoes having arrived the previous night off Fort William Henry at Pemaquid, "old Sheepscot John" led a delegation of Abenaki to renew the treaty and to exchange captives. (There had been a mortal sickness among the tribes, weakening their forces.) The Abenaki released eight prisoners on the spot and agreed to a thirty-day truce, so Boston could send a committee to manage the exchange. (However, the Indians wanted Bomaseen returned, and the English demanded *all* of their captives back first. The delegations withdrew, and the English settlements went on alert.)[8]

Salem Town

George Jacobs Jr. (though Sr. since his father's execution), Sarah Cave, and Deborah Knight swore before Justice Stephen Sewall that they had witnessed Mary Putnam sign and seal her will, "and that she was then of a disposing mind to their best discerning."[9]

May 25, 1695 • Saturday
Boston

Samuel Sewall returned home from two weeks' absence on court business in Maine to find his family well, except for the baby, Sarah, born with some difficulty the November before.[10]

May 29, 1695 • Wednesday
Boston

This Election Day, Thomas Danforth received the most votes for council—seventy-nine to Acting Governor William Stoughton's seventy-one. Elisha Cooke, Wait-Still Winthrop, Bartholomew Gedney, John Hathorne, Jonathan Corwin, and Samuel Sewall were also reelected to the council, but Nathaniel Saltonstall was not.[11]

Rev. Samuel Willard hosted an Election Day dinner for Boston's ministers, but the arrival of Deacon Edward Putnam (heading a delegation from Salem Village with *another* petition opposing the *earlier* protest) interrupted the celebration. This one was signed by 105 men and women—church members and household-ers, *all* adults—protesting that the threatened loss of Rev. Samuel Parris would do nothing to unite the Village. "For we have had three ministers removed already," they wrote, "and by every removal our differences have been rather aggravated." Rather than "leave us as sheep without a shepherd, . . . we desire that [Rev.] Parris may continue in his present station."[12]

42

JUNE 1695

It seemeth very hard for flesh and blood to bear, that those that know not what an oath might mean in a word do swear away three or four hundred pounds from the right owners thereof.

—Thomas Putnam

June 3, 1695 • Monday
Salem Village

The Salem Village brethren met at eight o'clock in the morning at the parsonage, where Rev. Samuel Parris introduced two messengers from Suffield,* Massachusetts, west of the Connecticut River. (Suffield now lies on the Connecticut side of the border.)

Suffield needed a minister, said Parris. He was willing to go if, in his absence, the Village could agree on another minister.

"After several hours debate," the brethren and neighbors belonging to other churches "all declared an averseness to my motion," except "the four known dissenters." Since Parris was not free to leave *without* the church's consent, he thanked them and, "seeing they would not let me go, I pressed them to keep me, and make much of me."

The messengers made the long trip back to Suffield, and Parris wrote to inform Reverends Increase and Cotton Mather of this development.[1]

Salem Town

Thomas and Edward Putnam and their brother-in-law Jonathan Walcott petitioned Probate Judge Bartholomew Gedney to delay approving what their brother Joseph claimed was their late stepmother's will. Neither Joseph nor his mother had ever produced an accurate inventory of Thomas Putnam Sr.'s estate, which ought to have been done back in 1686 (after their father died). They desired "the liberty and opportunity to contest the aforesaid instrument before it pass the seal of your office."[2]

June 5, 1695 • Wednesday
Boston

The faction that most disliked the new charter still resented Rev. Increase Mather for not obtaining a better one. Today, the House of Representatives voted to pay the senior Mather a salary of £150 a year for his service as president of Harvard, but *only* if he moved to Cambridge full time.[3]

June 10, 1695 • Monday
Salem Town

By a providential accident (so he thought), Thomas Putnam happened to be in town, where he heard that his half-brother Joseph intended to have his mother's will probated with no prior warning that very day. Thomas was in town alone but wrote to Judge Bartholomew Gedney a petition on behalf of himself, his brother Edward, and their brother-in-law Jonathan Walcott. Thomas asked for a hearing where witnesses could testify "that our mother Putnam was not of a sound mind and memory for near three months before she last died, and that she had been looked upon by standers-by as dead several times before the date of the aforesaid instrument." He asked that Sarah Cave and Deborah Knight be called (but did *not* ask for the third witness, George Jacobs Jr.). "It seemeth very hard for flesh and blood to bear, that those that know not what an oath might mean in a word [do] swear away three or four hundred pounds from the right owners thereof." (Joseph might have wondered about Thomas's *sworn* testimony that had helped take away life instead of merely money.)[4]

Exactly three years to the day, Bridget Bishop had been hanged on such testimony at the edge of town.

June 17, 1695 • Monday
Salem Town

Witnesses on both sides of Mary Putnam's contested will gathered in Salem's Ship Tavern at two o'clock: family, servants, neighbors, and her physician. Abigail Darling (whose name was *not* on the current will) made it clear that she could not tell if Mrs. Putnam was "sensible" or not when Isaac Porter helped her sign the document. No witness statements survive from Sarah Cave or Deborah Knight (who were at least summoned), nor from George Jacobs Jr. Nathaniel and Hannah Ingersoll related that Sarah Cave had been unaware of *any* will (she had signed with only a mark) and had told them that she did not think that her mistress "was capable of making any." Nevertheless, Mary Putnam's will would be probated as it was.[5]

June 22, 1695 • Saturday
Boston

The Sewall household was roused in the night by the sudden illness of Hannah Sewall's widowed mother, Judith Hull ("my dear mother Hull," Samuel called her). Family and servants rallied around, and Sewall summoned the best doctor in the area, and also called for Rev. Samuel Willard. At her bedside, Samuel Sewall "took the opportunity to thank her for all her labors of love to me and mine, and asked her pardon of our undutifullness." She died just before sunset, to her family's "very surprising grief and sorrow."

The evening before, the family's Bible reading had just reached Revelation 16 with its description of death and destruction arriving unexpectedly, "like a thief." (Sewall may also have brooded on the sixth verse: "For they shed the blood of the saints and the prophets, and therefore Thou hast given them blood to drink.")[6]

June 25, 1695 • Tuesday
Salem Town

Philip and Mary English, as administrators of her uncle Richard Holingsworth's estate, lost a case against John Cromwell at the court of common pleas. The court of general sessions, meanwhile, sitting the same day, fined Edward Bishop Sr. of Salem Village five shillings for drunkenness.[7]

43

JULY 1695

I sought him, but I found him not.

—Canticles 3:1

July 7, 1695 • Sunday
Salem Village

For his communion sermon, Rev. Samuel Parris chose the text Canticles 3:1, part of an Old Testament love poem used commonly as a metaphor of spiritual yearning: "I sought him whom my soul loveth. I sought him, but I found him not." But the rest of the sermon, and its application to the Village church's attempts to approach God and Christ, is lost. The text alone stands at the end of Parris's only surviving notebook.[1]

July 19, 1695 • Friday
Salem Town

Three years had passed since Sarah Good, Rebecca Nurse, Susanna Martin, Elizabeth How, and Sarah Wildes had been executed for witchcraft.

July 26, 1695 • Friday
Boston

Samuel Sewall's four-year-old daughter, Mary, fell down a neighbor's cellar stairs, and gashed a two-inch wound against the stones. "Poor little Mary," her distressed father wrote in his diary. "The Lord sanctify to me this bloody accident."[2]

44

AUGUST 1695

The withdrawing of persons ... from the communion of the church at the Lord's table, does carry an high and hard imputation upon the church itself.

—Cambridge Association of Ministers

August 5, 1695 • Monday
Cambridge

Prompted, perhaps, by Salem Village's dissensions, the congregational ministers meeting at Harvard College discussed what duty a church had toward members "who upon private prejudices withdraw from the communion of the church.

"The withdrawing of persons thus irregularly from the communion of the church at the Lord's table, does carry an high and hard imputation upon the church itself." It was, moreover, "a sin against the Lord's commandment and their own covenant." The pastor should send for the person and try "to instruct and convince and admonish him," and in cases of "contumacious obstinacy . . . to deal with him as one unruly." However, the vigor with which such offenses were prosecuted should be balanced by "compassion toward the ignorant or injured" (as the mediators had advised Salem Village).[1]

Rev. Increase Mather, meanwhile, did not want to leave Boston *or* his North Church congregation. Today, he informed Harvard's corporation that it needed to find a successor, for he could no longer serve as president under the new requirement. The Fellows (unlike the representatives) voted to keep him and offered £70 plus money to buy a horse for the journey.[2]

Billerica

Widow Mary Toothaker had suffered nightmares of Indian attack long before her arrest for witchcraft. But today she and her neighbors felt more curiosity than fear when they saw mounted men ride into their neighborhood, for Indians seldom had horses. But this *was* a raiding party, and its swift assault killed fifteen people, including Mary Toothaker. Her youngest daughter Margaret's kidnapping was recorded in the town's death records.[3]

August 6, 1695 • Tuesday
Boston

Mrs. Mary Obinson, once named as a witch, had a violent falling out with her husband, William, a tanner. By two o'clock in the afternoon, she had had enough and marched up the street from her home near Boston Neck to justice Samuel Sewall's house, to report William's "ill usage." He "kicked [me] out of bed last night," she complained, allowed her water but no food, and wouldn't let her take her clothes.[4]

August 8, 1695 • Thursday
Boston

Little Sarah Sewall suffered a convulsion this morning. Hannah sent for Samuel and the doctor. Although the fit didn't last long, the child had "another sore fit" later that afternoon.[5]

August 9, 1695 • Friday
Boston

Sarah Sewall had another convulsion this morning in her mother's arms, but that would be the last for the time being.[6]

August 11, 1695 • Sunday
Boston

The North Church's congregation took up a collection of £80 toward ransoming "three young men in Turkish slavery," as Rev. Cotton Mather wrote in the church records. (Local mariners sailing abroad risked capture by pirates from Algeria and other Muslim nations as well as those from French possessions.)[7]

August 13, 1695 • Tuesday
Boston

Partly to honor his late mother-in-law, Samuel Sewall held a private fast in his new (and newly repaired) chamber. Several ministers and several councilors attended, though Sewall worried that he ought to have invited all of the councilors then in Boston. When he set the tune to sing Psalm 27, he burst into tears. ("Hear, oh Lord, when I cry unto thee. . . . When my father and mother forsake me, then the Lord will take me up.") Sewall "could scarce continue singing."[8]

August 19, 1695 • Monday
Salem Town

Three years had passed since the hangings of Rev. George Burroughs, John Proctor, John Willard, George Jacobs Sr., and Martha Carrier.

SEPTEMBER 1695

*The way of the Devil is to hide or justify the
sin, as if it were for fear of disparaging the
goodness of the persons that committed it.*

—Richard Baxter

September 19, 1695 • Thursday
Salem Town

Giles Corey had died by pressing three years past.

September 20, 1695 • Friday
Boston

Robert Calef once again addressed Rev. Samuel Willard claiming that, despite the
ministers' "consent" to his views, he needed to correct Willard's *Some Miscellany
Observations*. As "seasonable and well-designed" as it was, it did not object
enough to spectral evidence.

Calef was also upset by Harvard's proposal to collect "remarkables" that Willard
(a Fellow) had signed. So Calef submitted a few "remarkables" of his own: Judge

John Richard's sudden death, the deaths of Judge Wait-Still Winthrop's children, or the exploding cannon at Salem "where that furious marshall [George Herrick] was rent to pieces." And after a man fell to his death trying to hang the new bell in the North meeting house, Calef gloated inaccurately, wasn't the first death that bell tolled the child of Cotton Mather? And Mather, Calef declared, "by printing and speaking, had had as great a hand in procuring the late actions as any, if not the greatest." But *most* remarkable was the plague of false accusations that executed twenty and imprisoned hundreds more until ministers and magistrates were accused.

Calef, who had dismissed Baxter before, now quoted him: "The way of God is to shame the sinner, how good soever in other respects. But the way of the Devil is to hide or justify the sin, as if it were for fear of disparaging the goodness of the persons that committed it." Calef ended with the hope "that all that have had a hand in any horrid and bloody practices may be brought to give glory to God, and take the due shame to themselves."[1]

After Willard read this scolding, he told the messenger that his answer was in Proverbs 26:4: "Answer not a fool according to his folly lest thou also be like unto him."[2]

At some point this year, Calef wrote Rev. Cotton Mather again for Scriptural proof of witchcraft. He quoted extensively from Baxter (for he still had Mather's copy) but now scorned the author. If Mather meant to pervert Calef's Christianity with such a book, he would not succeed. All Baxter's talk of angels smacked of Popery, and if *that* were acceptable, why not "the pagan, Indian, and diabolists' faith?" Modern education propagated heathen ideas once wisely forbidden to Christian scholars, Calef wrote, so now even ministers, corrupted by the likes of Virgil and Ovid, assumed that the Devil and witches had God's own power. Mather should repent his pagan ways.[3]

Although he learned of Calef's stinging sneers to Willard about the dead baby, Mather did not answer the letter.[4]

September 17, 1695 • Tuesday
Boston

Boston troops mustered with a great firing of guns on the Common—where "many Gentlemen and Gentlewomen" dined under tents—while former Governor Simon Bradstreet prepared to move back to Salem. Samuel Sewall entertained him and Mrs. Bradstreet with wine and fruit, before the festivities proceeded to the fine brick mansion of Madam Ann Richards (Judge John Richard's widow). There, Lieutenant Governor William Stoughton and other councilors made a formal farewell to the old statesman. On the way, a message arrived that ten of the twenty-four men stationed at Pemaquid had been shot, four mortally, while rowing a barge of wood to the fort.[5]

September 22, 1695 • Sunday
Salem Town

Three years had passed since the executions of Martha Corey, Mary Esty, Alice Parker, Mary Parker, Ann Pudeator, Margaret Scott, Wilmot Read, and Samuel Wardwell.

September 24, 1695 • Tuesday
Newbury

At an Essex County court—with Bartholomew Gedney, John Hathorne, Samuel Appleton, and Jonathan Corwin presiding—Salem Village sued Topsfield over the disputed boundaries. The Village won in one dispute and lost in another. As usual, no one was satisfied.[6]

46

OCTOBER 1695

> *Brother Cloyse brought me back the letter* . . .
> *saying it was a letter of recommendation and*
> *not of dismission that he desired.*
>
> —Rev. Samuel Parris

October 5, 1695 • Saturday
Salem Village

Peter Cloyse returned to the Village from Framingham in order to transfer his and his wife Sarah's membership from the Village church to the nearer church in Marlborough.[1]

October 7, 1695 • Monday
Newbury

Indian raiders entered John Brown's house in Newbury, killed several people, and kidnapped nine more. A rescue party caught up with the band that night, but the raiders escaped over the river, after first clubbing all of their captives in the head.

Only one boy, who had received a glancing blow survived. The rest died over the course of the next year, "their very brains working out at their wounds."[2]

October 10, 1695 • Thursday
Salem Village

Having received approval for Peter and Sarah Cloyse's transfer from the "major part" of the Salem Village church members the previous Sunday, Rev. Samuel Parris wrote the required letter of dismission to the Marlborough church. He left it for Cloyse at John Tarbell's house, only to have Cloyse appear at his door again on Thursday. "Brother Cloyse brought me back the letter . . . saying it was a letter of recommendation and not of dismission that he desired." (Dismission was appropriate, but Cloyse was not accepting more than the bare minimum from Parris.)[3]

October 24, 1695 • Thursday
Salem Village

While Massachusetts observed a fast on behalf of the captives taken in Billerica and Newbury, Salem Village was no nearer agreement. Besides feeling a neighborly concern, folk in the outlying settlements must have wondered who among them might be targeted next.[4]

NOVEMBER 1695

Departed by death.

—Rev. Samuel Parris

November 22, 1695 • Friday
Salem Village

Rev. Samuel Parris added the name of his staunch opponent Francis Nurse to his list of "Persons departed by death in Salem Village," as well as the old man's age of "77." Francis's children buried their patriarch in the family burying ground down the western slope beyond the house, next to his beloved and unjustly killed Rebecca.[1]

DECEMBER 1695

Unbelief and rebellious living, ... was the sin of witchcraft before Him and His light.

—Thomas Maule

December 12, 1695 • Thursday
Salem Town

Salem shopkeeper Thomas Maule had begun writing a book in 1690 to defend Quakerism and to criticize its critics. After 1692 he revised the manuscript to declare that the witchcraft trials were God's punishment on Massachusetts for its earlier persecution of Quakers. When no Boston printer would touch it, he sent the manuscript to New York for publication. By the fall of 1695, copies of *Truth Held Forth and Maintained* reached Boston and Salem.[1]

Maule and a few other Quakers had attempted countermagic against a suspected New Hampshire witch in 1682. In 1692 he had thought that Bridget Bishop had magically killed his child, and had berated Rev. John Hale at her execution for praying with such a sinner. Now Maule criticized the trials for their disruption of public order, but contended that at least *some* of the people executed *were* guilty.[2]

Only those committing murder by witchcraft ought to die, however, for "it is better that one hundred witches should live, than that one person be put to death for a witch which is not a witch." Yet, some of the accused, he wrote, had been rightly condemned in 1692. The stored-up sin of the foolish who persisted in seeking God the wrong way (in other words, non-Quakers) not only left them open to the Devil's power, but also had flared into the witchcraft epidemic. They will be judged on their "unbelief and rebellious living, which was the sin of witchcraft before Him and His light." That several of the condemned were members of the orthodox churches was no surprise. The Devil could use a *witch's* specter without consent, "but to act and do such wickedness in the form, shape, and likeness of God's faithful children [Quakers] is that which I cannot believe." He also pronounced the afflicted liars, and the confessors foolish with fear. The government, he wrote (for, like Robert Calef, he didn't count Rev. George Burroughs), stopped the trials only when one of its hireling priests* was represented spectrally.[3]

Boston

Once copies circulated in Massachusetts, non-Quakers found themselves (accusers and accused) denounced as witches, their ministers charged with simony, and the symbolism of their religion a target of contempt. Personal innuendos, and a gossiping delight in non-Quakers' misfortunes, obscured Maule's point that persecution was the Devil's work.[4]

Today, Lieutenant Governor William Stoughton and the council ordered Maule jailed and the remaining thirty copies of his book confiscated.[5]

December 13, 1695 • Friday
Salem Village

The Salem Village rates committee set an assessment to pay Rev. Samuel Parris for the current year. The two wealthiest ratepayers were Nathaniel Putnam (a pro-Parris member of the committee), and his anti-Parris nephew Joseph Putnam.[6]

December 14, 1695 • Saturday
Boston

The House of Representatives resolved to inquire into Thomas Maule's "evil work," which was "stuffed with many notorious and pernicious lies and scandals" to slander their forefathers, their religion, and themselves.[7]

---

*Maule says someone reported the specter of the "Lynn priest"—Rev. Jeremiah Shepard.

Salem

Sheriff George Corwin had seen to the arrest of Thomas Maule. Today Jeremiah Neale, deputy sheriff and jailer, escorted the prisoner to Boston.[8]

December 19, 1695 • Thursday
Boston

Thomas Maule marched before the council with a Bible under his arm, and acted surprised that no one argued religion but instead complained of personal slanders. He backed down on some details and eventually admitted that the work was his—barring typographical errors. The angry council ordered the confiscated copies burned in Boston and Salem, and Maule demanded a jury trial in his own county.

Judge Samuel Sewall set a £200 bond for him to appear at the next Essex County court, and two Boston sympathizers stood surety for Maule: shopkeeper Thomas Bannister and clothier Robert Calef.[9]

PART V

1696

49

JANUARY 1696

> *The Lord bring light and comfort out of this*
> *dark and dreadful cloud.*
>
> —Justice Samuel Sewall

January 6, 1696 • Monday
Boston

Samuel Sewall kept a day of private fasting and prayer, concerned for his family (his wife's pregnancy, his son's future trade), his government (the as-yet-unknown new governor, upsets at home and abroad), and his own thinning hair.[1]

January 13, 1696 • Monday
Boston

After visiting an ailing Thomas Danforth in Cambridge, Samuel Sewall returned home in the dark, crossing the ice-filled Charles River by boat, to find his family in an uproar. His fifteen-year-old daughter Betty was in floods of tears. She feared that her sins were not pardoned, she explained finally, and that she would go to

Hell. (Her fears had been heightened when she read some less-than-comforting sermons—one by Rev. Cotton Mather.) Her parents sent for Rev. Samuel Willard to pray with the girl, which seemed to help. "The Lord bring light and comfort out of this dark and dreadful cloud," Sewall wrote in his diary.[2]

January 31, 1696 • Friday
Salem Village

Rev. Samuel Parris listed the death of the "wife to John Martin, not sick a fortnight," then ceased to record Village births and deaths. His own son Thomas may have died around this time, and his niece Abigail Williams, haunted to the end, apparently died before the end of 1697 if not sooner, no older than seventeen. The Suffield post was lost to him, the Village was no closer to agreement, and his wife, Elizabeth, was very likely already mortally ill.[3]

50

FEBRUARY 1696

Oh, the Lord is laying of me low!

—Rev. Cotton Mather

February 12, 1696 • Wednesday
Boston

Rev. Cotton Mather observed his birthday by keeping a "secret thanksgiving" of prayer in his study for all that the Lord had granted him.[1]

February 22, 1696 • Saturday
Boston

Today, Rev. Cotton Mather kept a private day of humiliation to pray over his shortcomings. Compared to what he ought to be, he felt *vile* in heart and life. He prayed that he might be both good *and* useful, but brooded over the possible consequences of his faults: "Oh, the Lord is laying of me low!"[2]

On the same day, young Betty Sewall woke full of "disquiet" for the state of her soul. As she told her father, she still feared that she was damned. Samuel "answered her fears as well as [he] could," and prayed with her. (Betty's tearful terrors would continue, off and on, for months. Samuel eventually sent her to stay with his brother Stephen in Salem for the following autumn.)[3]

February 25, 1696 • Tuesday
Boston

A fierce snow storm swept Massachusetts, freezing to death at least one man near Boston.[4]

February 26, 1696 • Wednesday
Boston

The snow storm postponed today's opening of the General Court, for only ten legislators appeared and at least forty were required.[5]

Salem Town

Snow or no snow, Constable John Woodwell presented a writ to former Essex County sheriff, George Corwin. Philip English was suing Corwin again. In spite of the 1694 Supreme Court ruling that the sheriff had been following orders when he confiscated goods in 1692, English was *not* about to let the matter drop. Corwin or "others employed by him," the warrant read, had taken "from or near about the dwelling house of said English a certain cow with bob tail, dark colored, and five swine, viz. a large sow and four shoats" without English's "leave or license sometime in August 1692, and doth yet detain the same, though demand hath been made for them." (The confiscations related to English's flight from jail. Just possibly, the bob-tailed cow and the swine—the shoats would have grown up years ago—represented payment for part of the £67-6-4 that the government owed Corwin.)

Nevertheless, the writ demanded goods valuing £15 as a bond for Corwin to appear at the next Essex County court, or, lacking that, Corwin himself bodily. Although he was only thirty years old—today was his birthday—Corwin was not a well man, and he had neither the money nor the goods on hand to post bail. Therefore, the constable "for want of goods seized the body of the within mentioned Captain George Corwin and delivered" him to the jailer. So English had the satisfaction of seeing Corwin in custody, as well as the additional pleasure of knowing that Rev. Nicholas Noyes was dangerously ill around the same time.

(One of Corwin's relatives likely provided the bail to release him from Salem prison. Not feeling able to handle the matter himself, George appointed Joseph Neal to act as his attorney in the case.)[6]

February 28, 1696 • Friday
Boston

Inadvertently, Rev. Cotton Mather omitted the name of his infant daughter Mehitable while praying for his family early this morning. He corrected this oversight and blamed himself for such a foolish omission. But no sooner had he finished than he learned that Mehitable had died an hour before, quite unexpectedly, in her nurse's arms. (Her mother Abigail's reaction is not recorded.) Her stunned father found it very hard to accept this death as God's will.[7]

February 29, 1696 • Saturday
Boston

After the burial of his daughter, Mehitable, Cotton Mather found some comfort in the thought that at least her soul must be safe in Heaven with other good spirits. "Four of mine are now flown thither before me." (Later, he and Abigail would learn that the nurse had actually "overlaid" the baby—rolled on and smothered Mehitable in bed.)[8]

51

MARCH 1696

> *To be a Christian, and a minister too, oh! 'tis no easy matter.*
>
> —Rev. Cotton Mather

March 24, 1696 • Tuesday
Salem Village

A Salem Village's inhabitants' meeting chose a rates committee more amenable to Rev. Samuel Parris: John and Thomas Putnam, John Dale, Benjamin Wilkins, and John Walcott. However, the constables were of little help in collecting the sums.[1]

March 28, 1696 • Saturday
Boston

Among his prayers, Rev. Cotton Mather prayed for fellow minister Nicholas Noyes, who was "dangerously ill" in Salem. "To be a Christian, and a minister too, oh! 'tis no easy matter."[2]

March 31, 1696 • Tuesday
Ipswich

Although Joseph Putnam had been one of Salem's constables in 1693, he had refused to collect the rates for Rev. Samuel Parris's unpaid salary, so the Village rates committee sued Joseph. Today's county court at Ipswich ordered a Salem town constable to do the job by "distress" if necessary.[3]

52

APRIL 1696

Let the church be provided for, and myself be
fairly dealt with ... [and] I shall readily gratify
those who are so earnest for my giving way
—Rev. Samuel Parris

April 2, 1696 • Thursday
Boston

Massachusetts observed a public fast to pray for relief in this time of famine. The Boston congregations also planned to make collections to aid the poor, an idea that Rev. Cotton Mather especially urged. After he delivered his sermon, with an assurance that the famine "should not overwhelm us," the North Church collected the largest contribution in Boston: over £55.[1]

April 9, 1696 • Thursday
Salem Village

The latest lawsuit had done nothing to solve Salem Village's quarrels. Matters were in such a state that Justice Bartholomew Gedney offered to serve as moderator, if

Rev. Samuel Parris would resign from the Village pulpit. When the church brethren met today at Thomas Putnam's house, they chose a committee of Putnams (John Sr. and Jr., Nathaniel, and Deacon Edward) to deal with the dissenters on behalf of the rest of the church in order to seek out "an amicable issue." Parris, for his part, informed them that he would step down as minister after his year was up in July.[2]

April 12, 1696 • Sunday
Boston

Around eight in the morning, a late snow began falling, and by noon, Samuel Sewall noticed that it had covered the ground and the houses. By five o'clock the icicles were as long as seven inches. It wouldn't melt for three days.[3]

Salem Town

While the snow fell, George Corwin died at home in Salem. (The former sheriff's body would be buried in the family tomb in his own back yard, but people later said that it was first buried in his cellar for fear Philip English would try to take revenge by stealing it. Whatever the truth of that, English continued to pursue the debt from the widow Lydia Corwin. It was presumably she who made restitution in linen and silver, items preserved as trophies by the English family for generations. When Lydia died a few years later, the estate was worth £73-8-4, its outstanding debts totaled £33-17-3, and the inventory did *not* include the disputed bob-tailed cow.[4]

April 13, 1696 • Monday
Salem Village

"In order for an amicable issue for the future," Rev. Samuel Parris wrote to Bartholomew Gedney, "upon condition that I would surcease my ministerial station here," he agreed to the proposed meeting when and where Gedney decided. "I am unwilling to hinder the good of the place, and if my remove may be beneficial, let the church be provided for, and myself be fairly dealt with in payment of all my dues [and] I shall readily gratify those who are so earnest for my giving way."[5]

April 16, 1696 • Thursday
Boston

Besides praying for relief from famine, Rev. Cotton Mather wrote a letter, signed by other local ministers as well, to the ministers in Connecticut asking them to intercede with their government to lift its embargo on corn shipments.[6]

April 20, 1696 • Monday
Salem Village

Rev. Samuel Parris and the church brethren convened at Ingersoll's ordinary to vote on Bartholomew Gedney's proposal. They selected and "fully empowered" a committee of Parris and four Putnams (now named as Nathaniel, John, Jonathan, and Benjamin) "to discourse, conclude, and agree with as many of our dissenting brethren and neighbors, who likewise shall be empowered by the rest of their party in writing under their hands" to decide the following:

1. The inhabitants would repay the "disbursements" on the ministry house and land that Parris had spent while he thought he owned it.
2. The inhabitants would pay Parris the arrears of his salary (each in proportion), either all of it or (in case of disagreement) a sum decided by a committee of four (two from each side). The four could choose a fifth in case of deadlock and decide by a majority vote.
3. Both full church members and inhabitants would see about calling a new qualified minister.
4. Once this was done, "our pastor then to attend the Providence of God in removing, or to acquit his ministerial station amongst us."

Benjamin Putnam took the church brethren's decision to Gedney in Salem, but the result was not recorded, and matters remained unsettled.[7]

April 29, 1696 • Wednesday
Salem Village

Mary Walcott, recovered from her past afflictions, married Isaac Farrar, with Rev. Samuel Parris performing the ceremony. The groom had apparently lived in the Village, but was "now of Woburn," as Parris noted in his records. (Farrar may have been a nephew of Ann Sears, jailed on a witchcraft charge in 1692.)[8]

April 30, 1696 • Thursday
Salem Town

Salem town, meanwhile, was £400 behind in salary payments to Rev. John Higginson. The senior minister pondered Salem's war-blighted businesses as well as his duty to provide for his own family, especially his deserted, distracted daughter, Ann Dolliver, once accused of witchcraft. She was out of jail and back living with her aged father, but was unlikely to recover from her oppressing melancholy.

Rev. Higginson proposed to the town that, instead of the lump sum that they owed him, Salem might promise to support his daughter, Ann Dolliver, after his own death. The town readily agreed.

(After her father's death in 1708, Ann Dolliver would board in Rehoboth—far from her own kin—with fellow witch suspects Edward and Sarah Bishop, formerly of Salem Village. Salem selectmen would send Ann's yearly maintenance to the Bishops, though by 1723, Sarah fervently wished that her boarder might be cared for elsewhere.)[9]

MAY 1696

They say that I am dead in the law.

—Elizabeth Proctor

May 2, 1696 • Saturday
Boston

Rev. Cotton Mather continued with another of his private fasts. "It being a time of unusual scarcity for bread in this place, . . . I would fast that my neighbors might be fed." The late spring had delayed the growing season, and the whole region suffered food shortages. Mather gave thanks also for the providential arrivals of supplies for his own family that surprised them just when the supplies were most needed.[1]

May 10, 1696 • Sunday
Salem Town

Twenty-year-old Elizabeth Booth (daughter of Henry Wilkins of Will's Hill, and widow of George Booth) joined the Salem town church. Appearing before the members, she confessed that she had been with child by her late husband before their marriage, but now repented, and was reconciled into the covenant. (Evidently, she did *not* mention that she had once testified as an afflicted witness against the witch suspects.) Her first child had died, but she was now eligible to present her son, young George Booth Jr., for baptism.[2]

May 19, 1696 • Tuesday
Ipswich

Samuel Sewall was worried about his wife—near to giving birth—but as Wait-Still Winthrop was ill, Sewall was obliged to serve on the Superior Court's Essex County spring session with Thomas Danforth and Elisha Cooke. The brief official record noted among other cases, Thomas Maule's appearance (to answer for the slanders in his book, *Truth Held Forth and Maintained*) and the fact that his case was bound over to the next session.

Maule, as he later recalled it, caustically informed the "High Court of Injustice" that he had the liberty of a British subject to print his book, and the right of an English merchant to sell it. When King's Attorney Anthony Checkley reminded him that slanders against persons and institutions were *not* ordinary merchandise, Maule replied that those charges weren't proven. In any case, "the priests," he said rudely, were as critical of Quakers in print.

Justice Elisha Cooke called him a "horrible liar," but the court only required a £200 bond and sureties until the next sitting.[3]

May 22, 1696 • Friday
Salem

After completing his court duties, Samuel Sewall had proceeded north to visit his parents in Newbury. (His wife, Hannah, had urged him to go.) He had returned as far as Salem, where a messenger found him shortly before noon with news that Sewall's wife had endured the difficult birth of a stillborn son. Sewall pressed onward to Boston, crossing the ferry after the bells struck five. Fortunately, Hannah was as well as could be expected at such a time.

Stung by the boy's death, Samuel wept. "The Lord pardon all my sin, and wandering, and neglect."[4]

May 27, 1696 • Wednesday
Boston

Rain dampened the festivities of Election Day, soaking the troops that escorted Lieutenant Governor William Stoughton into town. Recovered from the previous winter's illness, Thomas Danforth regained his council seat. Rev. Cotton Mather had the honor of delivering the election sermon, using the watery image in his scriptural text to great effect: "And they gathered together . . . and drew water, and poured it out before the Lord . . . and said there, 'We have sinned before the Lord.'"(I Samuel 7:6).[5]

One of the petitions presented to the General Court for consideration during the coming session was from Elizabeth Proctor, widow of John Proctor, herself convicted of witchcraft and condemned to die, but reprieved. "In that sad time of darkness before my husband was executed, it is evident somebody had contrived a will and brought it to him to sign, wherein his whole estate is disposed of." This will had passed probate, and her stepchildren "will not suffer me to have one penny of the estate, neither upon the account of my husband's contract with me before marriage nor yet upon the account of the dower which, as I humbly conceive, doth belong or ought to belong to me by law, for they say that I am dead in the law."[6]

May 30, 1696 • Saturday
Boston

Rumors had reached New England of foreign-based plots against their Protestant King William, for the Jacobite party was still determined to reinstate the deposed and exiled Catholic monarch James II. Today, an official messenger arrived in Boston by way of New York: England had foiled the latest plan to kill William and had declared a Thanksgiving at home and abroad to celebrate. (The assassination plot was only one of a series of attempts that would continue until James's grandson "Bonny Prince Charlie" was defeated in 1746.)[7]

54

JUNE 1696

Put on the whole armor of God, that ye may be able to withstand the wiles of the Devil.

—Ephesians 6:11

June 1, Monday • 1696
Boston

Rev. Michael Wigglesworth of Malden delivered the artillery sermon before Boston's mustering troops, and chose the text Ephesians 6:11: "Put on the whole armor of God, that ye may be able to withstand the wiles of the Devil." This was the same text that Rev. Deodat Lawson had used for his Salem Village lecture in March 1692.

Today, however, Wigglesworth referred to the Jacobite movement and the threat that "Popery, or something as bad as Popery," would be imposed upon them. To celebrate the discovery of the assassination plot, the artillery company fired its cannon from the Battery and the Castle.[1]

June 4, 1696 • Thursday
Boston

Rev. Cotton Mather delivered the weekly lecture with the General Court in attendance. Surely, he felt as he prayed before the assembly, God would relieve the famine still oppressing them.[2]

June 5, 1696 • Friday
Boston

In answer to Cotton Mather's prayers, "a little fleet of corn and flour" sailed into Boston some time during the night after his lecture—just when Mather's own family's pantry was nearly bare.[3]

June 10, 1696 • Wednesday
Salem Town

By now, four years had passed since the hanging of Bridget Bishop.

June 18, 1696 • Thursday
Boston

Boston and the rest of Massachusetts celebrated the official Thanksgiving in honor of King William's preservation—except for a few stubborn local "Jacobites," like the Braintree farmer who defiantly plowed his fields and was sentenced to the stocks for it.[4]

June 21, 1696 • Sunday
Salem Village

During today's service, Rev. Samuel Parris made the first of two formal announcements to his Salem Village congregation of his intended resignation.[5]

June 24 and 26, 1696 • Wednesday and Friday
Eastward

Algonquin raiders struck in Maine and killed three couples traveling home to Wells from York on June 24.

Two days later, the raiders crossed into New Hampshire, attacked locations around Portsmouth, burned some houses, and killed about a dozen people. This time, at least, rescuers saved the captives, including an old woman who survived being scalped.[6]

June 28, 1696 • Sunday
Salem Village

Rev. Samuel Parris delivered his last sermon to the Salem Village congregation, and again announced his intention to resign at month's end. (He still had not received his back pay, however.)[7]

June 30, 1696 • Tuesday
Salem Town

A committee from Salem Village returned to the county court yet again to complain "that the several committees of Salem Village for the last five years have been negligent in collecting and paying to [Rev.] Samuel Parris, their minister, his salary." The court verified that Parris's pay was to be £66 a year, and that it had not been fully collected from 1691 to 1695. The justices ordered the rates committee to make the collection in full and to pay Parris in full before the next court sitting in September, where all were to appear and to give an account of the transaction. (However, existing records for the September court would make no mention of this matter.)[8]

JULY 1696

Sleep precious dust, no stranger now to rest.

—Rev. Samuel Parris

July 7 1696, • Tuesday
Salem Village

A meeting of Salem Village inhabitants decided by "a general concurrence" that as Rev. Samuel Parris had made it clear he was no longer their minister, the Village would now find another. "Declaring ourselves also now to be at liberty from Mr. Parris," they chose search committees, and voted to pay temporary preachers twenty shillings a day.[1]

July 12 1696, • Sunday
Boston

Sabbath services all over Boston were "tumultuously interrupted," first by a house fire, and then by word from the Castle of approaching ships. D'Iberville had already captured the *Newport* off the Bay of Fundy, where it was supposed to intercept the French supply fleet. Fortunately, these vessels proved to be English, not French. Unfortunately, they brought government documents from the privy council voiding Harvard's new charter and several of Massachusetts's new laws. (These included the law against witchcraft, because it did not preserve a widow's dower rights—a clause that the legislature had not inserted, because a dower was *not* at risk under local law. Massachusetts would remain without a law against witchcraft.)[2]

July 14, 1696 • Tuesday
Salem Village

Only two weeks after her husband's resignation, Mrs. Elizabeth Parris died. Samuel would commission a fine carved slate tombstone for her from William Mumford, the Quaker stonecutter of Boston, inscribed with a short verse of his own composition:

> Sleep precious dust, no stranger now to rest,
> Thou hast thy longed wish in Abraham's breast.
> Farewell best wife, choice mother, neighbor, friend,
> We wail the less for hope of thee in the end.
>   S. P.[3]

July 19, 1696 • Sunday
Salem Town

Today marked four years since the executions of Sarah Good, Rebecca Nurse, Susanna Martin, Elizabeth How, and Sarah Wildes.

July 23, 1696 • Thursday,
Boston

Massachusetts held a fast day out of concern for the attacks at York and Portsmouth, and "to beg our daily bread and peace." But that evening, when word came that New Hampshire was in arms and that a fleet of ships was sighted off the coast, Lieutenant Governor William Stoughton returned to Boston from Dorchester and convened the council for the emergency.

Again, the ships proved to be English—the mast fleet on its yearly visit. The council, greatly relieved, dismissed.[4]

July 26, 1696 • Sunday
Cocheco, New Hampshire

But the frontiers of New England were still under attack. Several people returning from services, a sacrament Sunday in the church at Cocheco (near

Dover), perished in an ambush. The raiders killed three, wounded three, and captured three.[5]

July 27, 1696 • Monday
Boston

Lieutenant Governor William Stoughton read to his counsel a newly arrived letter from the lords of trade warning New England of a French squadron sailing for America. England promised what help it could give under the circumstances (which turned out to be none).

Later that same day, an express messenger from Colonel John Pyncheon of Springfield brought another warning. Count Frontenac and his Indian allies intended to attack Albany, or the Iroquois allies, or New England, or *all* of them, with a force of 2,000 French and 1,000 Indian allies. The Baron de St. Castine, meanwhile, would proceed southward from the Penobscot River with 400 or 500 fighting men.[6]

July 31, 1696 • Friday
Boston

The news, Samuel Sewall wrote to a colleague in England, was "nothing but rumors of war and slaughter against us by both sea and land." In addition to the attack on Dover, and the capture of the *Newport*, lightning had damaged houses and killed both people and sheep. Frost had killed most of the previous corn crop, their staple grain. A bushel of corn, which used to cost two shillings and sixpence at most, now cost up to five shillings sixpence. English wheat was *eight* shillings a bushel. The current crop of wheat and barley appeared promising despite the cool, damp summer, but most of the rye was blasted and useless. On top of it all, a "strange plague of flies" had laid their eggs in the pea crop. The hatching young bored out and flew away leaving the peas hollow.[7]

AUGUST 1696

> *The nest of all the wasps that stung us.*
>
> —Rev. Cotton Mather

August 4, 1696 • Tuesday
Pemaquid, Maine

Captain John Pyncheon's warning was accurate. A well-armed force of French and Abenaki reached Pemaquid and surrounded Fort William Henry by land and sea. The fort commander, Pasco Chubb of Andover, defied them and readied for a siege.[1]

August 5, 1696 • Wednesday
Salem Village

The Village inhabitants met to send a committee to the Boston ministers for advice in choosing a pastor, and also discussed how to collect and distribute his pay once they hired him.[2]

Pemaquid, Maine

Meanwhile, the French heavy artillery arrived at Fort William Henry on the second day of the siege. The thick fortress walls were built of stone, but the open center could not withstand bombardment from above. Pasco Chubb surrendered on condition that he and his men might leave safely. The French agreed, but their Indian allies did not and some of them attacked the retreating New Englanders. (Chubb had lured two Sagamores into the fort the previous February under a pretense of truce, then killed them in retaliation for past raids.) The victors, meanwhile, freed an imprisoned and half-dead Indian hostage, mined the fort with gunpowder, and blew it to shivers.[3]

August 10, 1696 • Monday
Boston

Today, Boston learned of the violent loss of Fort William Henry. Chubb's superiors, and many of the people, thought that his surrender was cowardly, and jailed him for a time on his return.[4]

Eastward

By now Maine farmers could hardly work their fields without ambush. Around this time, Lieutenant Governor William Stoughton dispatched three vessels Eastward, one of which was commanded by Captain John Alden. Stoughton sent Colonel (and Justice) Bartholomew Gedney by land to strengthen the garrisons with 500 men, and ordered Colonel (and Justice) John Hathorne, and also Major Benjamin Church to attack French headquarters at St. John—"the nest of all the wasps that stung us," according to Rev. Cotton Mather. When not at odds with Hathorne, Church harried the French settlers along the coast. Time, illness, wind, and dirty weather worked against the New Englanders, but d'Iberville's forces were busy securing Newfoundland, so he was unable to storm Boston as originally planned.[5]

August 12, 1696 • Wednesday
Boston

Even amid the dangers of war, the past witchcraft trials still occupied people's minds. In a conversation with Samuel Sewall today, Jacob Melyen ("upon a slight occasion," Sewall thought) "spoke to me very smartly about the Salem witchcraft." In apparent reference to Rev. George Burroughs's reputedly supernatural strength, Melyen told Sewall that "if a man should take Beacon Hill on his back, carry it away, and then bring it and set it in its place again, [I] should not make anything of that."[6]

August 13, 1696 • Thursday
Andover

After deadly raids all along southern Maine and New Hampshire, Abenaki forces reentered Massachusetts to ambush and kill two men on the road between Andover and Haverhill.[7]

August 19, 1696 • Wednesday
Salem Town

Four years ago today, the law had hanged Rev. George Burroughs, John Proctor, John Willard, George Jacobs Sr., and Martha Carrier.

57

SEPTEMBER 1696

[Samuel Willard] spake smartly at last about the Salem witchcrafts.

—Justice Samuel Sewall

September 1, 1696 • Tuesday
Salem Village

The Village inhabitants chose a committee to negotiate with "Mr. Pemerton" to be their minister. (This person was presumably Ebenezer Pemberton, a recent Harvard graduate who would decline the offer and later be a minister at Boston's Third Church—Samuel Sewall's church.) Then Rev. Samuel Parris presented a paper for them to consider, probably a request for payment as per court order, and asked for an answer within a fortnight.[1]

September 13, 1696 • Sunday
Salem Town

Rev. Cotton Mather delivered both the morning and afternoon sermons from Matthew 11:5, the gospel to the poor: "The blind receive sight, and the halt go; the lepers are cleansed, and the deaf hear; the dead are raised up, and the poor receive the Gospel."[2]

September 14, 1696 • Monday
Salem Village

The Village inhabitants met to consider Rev. Samuel Parris's paper, then chose a committee of his opponents to deal with it: Joseph Hutchinson Sr., Daniel Andrews, Joseph Herrick Sr., John Buxton, Joseph Putnam, John Tarbell, and Daniel Rea. They could negotiate with Parris or enter arbitration—a decision that ignored all prior arbitration and court decisions.[3]

September 16, 1696 • Wednesday
Boston

With several invited ministers the General Court kept a fast of its own in the Town House to pray for the men sent on the St. John expedition. Rev. Samuel Willard delivered a sermon on the text "If God be with us, who can be against us?" But just how much God sided with Massachusetts was still a matter of doubt. Willard also "spake smartly at last about the Salem witchcrafts," Samuel Sewall noted, "and that no order had been suffered to come forth by authority to ask God's pardon."[4]

September 18, 1696 • Friday
Boston

The legislature signed the "Association," as the English government now required of all officeholders. Those pledging promised loyalty to King William as lawful king, and promised to stand by him and by each other against the former king (James) and his adherents. As James's supporters included the French, this pledge was also a matter of self-defense. However, as the privy council had voided (on a technicality) the wording of the writ that convened the General Court, the legislators had "a warm discourse" on whether they could gather legally or not. Once they quieted, Lieutenant Governor William Stoughton said that he would hold the court as long as enough men showed up.[5]

September 19, 1696 • Saturday
Boston

Rev. Cotton Mather seldom stirred far from Boston, but this week he delivered sermons and lectures in Salem and Ipswich, returning to Boston on Saturday, grateful that there had been no mishaps and that a threatened storm held off until after his return.[6]

Salem Town

Today was also the fourth anniversary of Giles Corey's death by pressing.

September 22, 1696 • Tuesday
Salem Town

Four years had now passed since the last executions for witchcraft, when Martha Corey, Mary Esty, Alice Parker, Ann Pudeator, Margaret Scott, Wilmot Read, Mary Parker, and Samuel Wardwell were hanged.

September 24, 1696 • Thursday
Boston

Rev. Cotton Mather delivered the lecture, commenting on the condition of New England and of New England's churches. He also spoke out "for the safety of the College," the source of new ministers for their churches. Immediately after the sermon, the representatives voted to restore Harvard's charter (at least until England objected again).[7]

September 28, 1696 • Monday
Salem Village

The Village inhabitants met again to hear a report from the committee that they had sent "to transact with Mr. Parris relating to all the differences that are between him and our inhabitants." However, the clerk, Thomas Putnam, did not record what the committee had to say, only that its power to negotiate was continued.[8]

September 29, 1696 • Tuesday
Boston

Some men still thought that the General Court should be dissolved now that (technically) it had no legal way to convene. Lieutenant Governor William Stoughton disagreed angrily: the government could hardly be suspended completely, *especially* in time of war.[9]

OCTOBER 1696

... to consider of and agree upon what to do
about a minister.

—Salem Village inhabitants meeting

October 11, 1696 • Sunday
Salem Village

The brothers William and Aaron Way, as well as their wives, Persis and Mary, wished to be dismissed from the Village church to the church at Dorchester. (They had once lived in Dorchester, and now planned to joined a group there that was about to emigrate to South Carolina.) At their request, Rev. Samuel Parris presented their proposal to the congregation. (He was no longer their minister, but there was no other to do it.) As Parris later wrote in the church records, it "was consented to by a full or universal vote."[1]

October 12, 1696 • Monday
Salem Village

The Village inhabitants met and chose a committee to invite James Bayley, "our former minister," to preach for a month in hopes of hiring him permanently.[2]

Cambridge

Today, Lieutenant Governor William Stoughton and many of the council traveled to Cambridge to do what they could for Harvard, now that the college had lost its charter. (As it did not give visitation rights to the King, the privy council had not allowed it.) Rather than dissolve the university, Stoughton allowed it to continue as it had been (until England decided otherwise) and asked Rev. Increase Mather to continue as its president. There had already been talk of sending Mather to England to negotiate a charter directly for the college. (This idea made the legislators nervous, however, for they would not be able to alter a royal charter.)[3]

October 13, 1696 • Tuesday
Saco, Maine

Five militia men attached to the fort at Saco discovered a raiding party, then, unable to agree on a plan of escape, they ran right into an ambush and were killed.[4]

October 17, 1696 • Saturday
Salem Village

"Letters dismissive were written" for the Way families, presumably by Rev. Samuel Parris. A fact which he recorded in the church book, the last time that he wrote anything in it.[5]

October 27, 1696 • Tuesday
Salem Village

The Village inhabitants met "to receive [Rev.] Bayley's answer." James Bayley had left his Connecticut congregation and was presently a physician in Roxbury, just south of Boston. He had had no end of trouble with the Village a generation earlier and did not volunteer to repeat it now.

The Villagers still had "to consider of, and agree upon, what to do about a minister." For now, they decided to ask Mr. Emerson to come preach to them the next Sabbath. (This candidate was perhaps the schoolmaster John Emerson who had hounded Mary Tyler to confess to witchcraft.)

They decided also to keep a Day of Humiliation in November, so they could pray over the matter. They invited neighboring ministers to help: John Hale, Nicholas Noyes, Joseph Gerrish, and Jonathan Pierpont.[6]

NOVEMBER 1696

I do no more value you than I do Jack-straw.

—Thomas Maule

November 5, 1696 • Thursday
Salem Village

Evidently, Salem Village kept its Day of Humiliation, but came no closer to finding another permanent minister.[1]

November 11, 1696 • Wednesday
Salem

Justices Thomas Danforth, Elisha Cooke, and Samuel Sewall again considered Thomas Maule's "scandalous book," when the Superior Court met in Salem for Essex County. The Grand Jury indicted Maule for publishing it without a license (as England also required) and for his disrespect toward the court in May. This time, Maule had Benjamin Bullivant to represent him. Bullivant, a Boston apothecary, was an Anglican who had served under former governor Sir Edmund Andros and who remained highly critical of the current government. Today, however, he spoke for his client (in Sewall's opinion) "modestly and with respect."

Maule, however, by his own account, had a great deal to say for himself. He would respect them as representatives of the King, Maule informed the justices, but *not* as a Bishop's court, in which case, "I do no more value you than I do Jackstraw." Better to mend their own ways than to begin another persecution. He had not broken the King's law, he told the jury, for his book was all true. However, the only proof that *he* had written it, Maule continued (countering his earlier admission), was his name on the title page. And as a printed name was no more than a *specter* of a person, then the court would once again be guilty of accepting spectral evidence if it determined that he was the author solely by *that*.

The non sequitur about spectral evidence apparently convinced the jury to find the defendant not guilty. Maule gloated over the verdict but the personal slanders remained unresolved. Danforth reminded him that he still had to answer to God. In response, Maule accused the court of religious persecution.

"Take him away!" said Danforth in exasperation. "Take him away!"

(Maule soon wrote *New-England Persecutors Mauled With Their Own Weapons* to hoot at Puritanism, to gloat over the courts, and to accuse falsely the magistrates and ministers of pocketing thousands of [non-existent] pounds in fines levied on non-Puritans.)[2]

November 13, 1696 • Friday
Boston

Isaac Addington stopped by Samuel Sewall's house to tell him that Lieutenant Governor William Stoughton had "summoned" him and other notables to a dinner party in Dorchester. While they talked, Addington seemed preoccupied, then stood suddenly, saying that he was ill. He nearly fell, but Sewall caught him and "crowded him" into a chair before the justice's guest fainted completely. It looked like apoplexy, Sewall thought. Addington revived in a sweat before the doctor arrived, but had to decline Stoughton's dinner.[3]

November 17, 1696 • Tuesday
Salem Village

The Village was still without a minister. A Mr. Bradstreet had preached the previous Sabbath, and the inhabitants chose another committee to persuade him to serve a half-year trial period, "for it will be very troublesome to go after a minister every week or fortnight in winter time." (This latest candidate may have been young Simon Bradstreet, a grandson and namesake of the former governor, and a nephew of the Andover magistrate, Dudley Bradstreet, who was accused of witchcraft.)[4]

DECEMBER 1696

Great hardships were brought upon innocent persons, and (we fear) guilt incurred, which we have all cause to bewail.

—Rev. Cotton Mather

December 2, 1696 • Wednesday
Boston

Now every calamity seemed a judgment on New England. If people were not killed or captured in the border war, they were taken at sea to slavery in Algeria. If ships escaped pirates and privateers, the vessels sank in tempests. People who sickened and died ashore left survivors contemplating failed and scanty crops. And many individuals and families *still* endured the effects of the witchcraft trials. The weight of festering sin and injustice (many thought) dragged all life out of kilter. By year's end, the House of Representatives asked the local ministers for a list of shortcomings to consider in a public fast. The ministers left the job to Rev. Cotton Mather, who provided "an impartial recapitulation of the sins, whereby the divine anger has been provoked against the country."

There was much that needed improvement, he wrote, such as a growing worldliness that threatened attempts at a spiritual life, a widespread lust for material gain, and evil business practices from fraud at home to piracy abroad. "Wicked sorceries have been practiced in the land," Mather continued, referring to folk-magic, "and in the late inexplicable storms from the Invisible World thereby brought upon us, we were left, by the just hand of Heaven, unto these errors, whereby great hardships were brought upon innocent persons, and (we fear) guilt incurred, which we have all cause to bewail, with much confusion of our face before the Lord." After listing all the shortcomings, he noted that even "the successive and amazing judgments of God" had not convinced people to mend their ways, so Mather called for a day of prayer and fasting to ask God's pardon.

The House of Representatives passed the bill and ordered 500 copies to be printed, but also added a paragraph accusing the courts of blatant partiality. This allegation did not refer to the witchcraft cases, however, being the work of Nathaniel Byfield (in resentment over losing a lawsuit). The council was furious—not only at Byfield's accusation (and perhaps at Mather's call for the magistrates to enforce existing laws against immorality "equally")—but also by the fact that the lower house had initiated the bill without consulting the council first, and had then ordered it printed as if the council's approval were assured.

The council rejected the whole document.[1]

December 7, 1696 • Monday
Salem Village

Apparently, the latest ministerial candidate had agreed to a trial period, for the Village inhabitants today empowered a committee "to fetch Mr. Bradstreet" and to decide where he would board. (Rev. Samuel Parris and his diminished family were still in the parsonage, while he waited to be paid.) The meeting also decided "to give more power to the men formerly chosen to transact with Mr. Parris relating to the differences that are between him and our inhabitants about our ministry house."[2]

December 11, 1696 • Friday
Boston

Despite its irritation about the earlier fast bill, the council felt that a fast *was* necessary. It asked Samuel Sewall to compose another version, which its members considered today. This one listed the calamities that beset New England—war, crop failure, sudden death—as if some great sin were left unaccounted for. Therefore, the people should consider "whatever mistakes, on either hand, have been fallen into, either by the body of this people, or any orders of men referring to the late tragedy raised amongst us by Satan and his instruments, through the awful judgment of God."

The council approved this version and sent it to the House of Representatives, which rejected it. The two bodies argued about which one had the prerogative to propose such bills, and the *meaning* of the fast seemed swamped by resentment and pride.[3]

December 17, 1696 • Thursday
Boston

The irritable council also passed a new charter for Harvard. This one, like the rejected version, granted the right of visitation to the governor and council rather than to the distant king. (It also required the president to live at the college full-time, a maneuver against Rev. Increase Mather.)[4]

The House of Representatives, meanwhile, finally approved the disputed bill for the January fast after haggling at length over details of its wording. Both houses had acted more concerned with maintaining prerogative and pride than with righting the wrongs that the fast acknowledged, but at last, the lieutenant governor and chief justice during the witchcraft trials signed the bill into law: "I consent, Wm. Stoughton."[5]

December 18, 1696 • Friday
Boston

Reverends Increase and Cotton Mather, James Allen, and Samuel Willard sent an address to the council protesting the latest draft of Harvard's charter, principally because the crown was sure to require a royal visitation and would veto the charter if the governor and council had that post. The ministers asked that their names be withdrawn from the document.[6]

December 19, 1696 • Saturday
Boston

For now, the General Court ended its stormy session until February with a prayer, during which Nathaniel Byfield and a few others were pointedly absent. "I do not know," thought Samuel Sewall, "that ever I saw the council run upon with such a height of rage before."[7]

December 20, 1696 • Sunday
Boston

Winter clamped down in earnest with a violent snow storm. Cotton Mather changed his sermon text to Isiah 25:4 (where God is addressed as "a refuge from the storm") to expound extemporaneously on Christ as "a refuge from the storms of the wrath of God." It would grow so cold that even heavily laden sleds could cross the sea ice from Boston to Nantasket. Grain, when available, was at its most expensive in the province's history. Food of *all* kind ran short this hungriest winter since the "Starving Times" of the earliest settlements.[8]

December 21, 1696 • Monday
Boston

Samuel Sewall's wife, Hannah, and their two-year-old daughter, Sarah, were both ill again. Rev. Samuel Willard came through the deep snow to pray with the child, at her father's request, as Rev. Increase Mather had the previous week.[9]

December 22, 1696 • Tuesday
Boston

Samuel Sewall put up a note to Rev. Samuel Willard asking for public prayers on behalf of Sarah. The arrival of an angry woman, who "upbraided" him over a land dispute decision, deepened Sewall's distress. That evening, after the schoolmaster Ezekiel Cheever visited to pray for the child, Samuel and Hannah moved little Sarah into their own bedchamber.[10]

December 23, 1696 • Wednesday
Boston

Young Sarah Sewall died suddenly in her nurse's arms, while Hannah Sewall, still quite ill, was with Samuel downstairs in the new hall. "Sorrow and tears" engulfed the family. Although he had sought both medical and spiritual help, Samuel blamed himself for not being there, for neglecting *something* that might have helped save his daughter.[11]

December 24, 1696 • Thursday
Boston

Samuel Sewall felt even more a Jonah the next day when his young son Sam, practicing his Latin, read aloud a passage from Matthew 12: "Wherefore, if ye knew what this is, 'I will have mercy and not sacrifice,' ye would not have condemned the innocents." This verse, as Sewall wrote in his diary, "did awfully bring to mind the Salem tragedy." As a judge in those trials he had served inadvertently as one of Satan's instruments mentioned in his fast bill.[12]

December 25, 1696 • Friday
Boston

At noon, the Sewall family held a funeral service for Sarah at home, with each of her siblings reading a Biblical passage. Betty, who had nearly despaired over the fate of her own soul for much of this year, chose Revelation 22, where the blessed enter the Kingdom of Heaven, past the water of life and the tree of life to the throne of God. "'And they shall see His face,'" she read. "'And there shall be no night there, . . . for the Lord God giveth them light, and they shall reign forevermore.'"

Samuel said what he could "to our mutual comfort, I hope." Then he and four friends carried Sarah's small coffin past the Anglicans returning from Christmas services at King's Chapel, up the hill to the New Burying Ground, and into the brick-lined family tomb. Sewall regarded the stacked coffins holding the earthly remains of inlaws, cousins, and *six* of his own children. He placed Sarah's coffin on the foot of her maternal grandmother's box. "The Lord knows who shall be brought hither next," he said.[13]

PART VI

1697

JANUARY 1697

> *Samuel Sewall, . . . being sensible that as to the guilt contracted upon the opening of the late Commission of Oyer and Terminer at Salem . . . he is upon many accounts, more concerned than any he knows of, desires to take the blame and shame of it.*
>
> —Justice Samuel Sewall

January 1, 1697 • Friday
Boston

Samuel and Hannah Sewall, still mourning Sarah, were trumpeted awake at sunrise by New Year's revelers under their window. But as he prepared his mind for the coming fast, Judge Sewall still brooded on his dead children and prayed that the Lord would "pardon all my sins of omission and commission."[1]

January 12, 1697 • Tuesday
Boston

Robert Calef prepared for the approaching fast by writing an admonishing letter to "the ministers in and near Boston." He had assumed from their silence to his earlier letters that they agreed with his arguments. However, if the ministers attributed as many powers to the Devil as the Mathers' books did, then they must be Manichees (who believed in two creators, one good and one evil), no better than heathen Indians. To ask the afflicted *anything* was to consult a familiar spirit, *all* folk magic was devilish, and a witch was *any* anti-religious person. Calef hoped the ministers would explain *that* to their congregations during the fast. Or did they really think the Devil equal with God?[2]

January 14, 1697 • Thursday
Salem

Five years after the witch scare began, Massachusetts observed a fast to acknowledge the great wrongs done during the witchcraft trials of 1692. The fast referred also to other ills, but the trials were clearly the principal problem on most people's minds.

With no settled minister, whatever happened in Salem Village passed unrecorded. Twelve who had been jurors in 1692 signed an apology, probably read before the Salem area lecture. They asked pardon of God, of "the living sufferers," and of "all, whom we have justly offended, and do declare according to our present minds, we would none of us do such things again on such grounds for the whole world."[3]

Boston

That afternoon, Rev. Cotton Mather preached a variation of his fast bill to his North Church congregation. Besides the piracies, ungodliness, and "wicked sorceries" of folk magic, he also cited the present "scandalous contentions, and animosities" setting people against each other, as well as past "unjustifiable hardships" inflicted on "some that have conscientiously dissented from our persuasions in religion." While delivering the prayers, he felt that God would not yet leave New England desolate, but he was not comforted.[4]

Robert Calef attended the First Church's service and listened critically, while the minister defined witchcraft as a covenant with the Devil. Afterward, Calef asked him directly just where in Scripture *that* explanation occurred. There were many things, the minister answered, *not* asserted in Scripture.[5]

A few streets away at South Church, Samuel Sewall handed Rev. Samuel Willard a bill requesting prayers, and then stood before the congregation's gaze while Willard read it aloud:

"Samuel Sewall, sensible of the reiterated strokes of God upon himself and family, and being sensible that as to the guilt contracted upon the opening of the late Commission of Oyer and Terminer at Salem (to which the order for this day relates) he is, upon many accounts, more concerned than any he knows of, desires to take the blame and shame of it." Sewall, via Willard, asked the people's pardon and their prayers that God, the ultimate authority, would strengthen him against future temptations to sin, and prevent the effects of his past sins from further damaging his family or the country.[6]

(Someone reportedly asked William Stoughton why *he* did not do likewise. He replied that he had proceeded as well as he could under the circumstances. A personal apology was unnecessary, for his signing the Fast Bill into law was acknowledgment in itself.[7])

When Willard finished, Sewall bowed and sat down.

ЄPILOGUЄ

Part I: Aftermath

*As I was a chief instrument of accusing Goodwife Nurse and her two sisters,
I desire to lie in the dust, and to be humbled for it.*

—Ann Putnam Jr.

Rev. Cotton Mather spent a restless night after the Public Fast. His family was ill
and "discouraging thoughts" plagued him, he confided to his diary, "as if unavoidable marks of the Divine displeasure must overtake my family, for my not appearing with vigor enough to stop the proceedings of the judges, when the inextricable storm from the Invisible World assaulted the country." (Perhaps he
recalled his 1692 sermon series on the text Matthew 25, where the damned are
punished for what they did *not* do, when the Lord says, "Inasmuch as ye did it not
to one of the least of these, ye did it not to me.")[1]

Former constable Robert Calef, however, had no regrets for his own actions or in-
actions in 1692. He complained instead (to Rev. Benjamin Wadsworth of Boston's
First Church) that the pastor who had delivered the Fast Day sermon had not defined witchcraft according to true Scripture. Rather, his remarks could only serve
to stir the magistrates against supposed witches all over again and at the expense

of other crimes. Everyone knew Indians and other heathens worshipped Satan as a false god, Calef wrote, and *they* weren't prosecuted for it, nor did their idolatry grant them power over devils. (Rev. Wadsworth ignored the letter, and Calef turned to his next project: a book on the witchcraft trials that would include as many original documents from the accused and their kin as Maule, Brattle, and other contacts could provide.)[2]

And all the while, Salem Village ignored its obligation to pay Rev. Samuel Parris's back salary, even though he had resigned as promised. Parris, for his part, refused to move from the parsonage until the Village paid him what it owed him. Not surprisingly, none of the ministerial candidates who preached in the Village opted to stay.[3]

Indian raiders attacked Haverhill on **March 15, 1697**. (Thomas Dustin was able to save most of his children, but not his wife. Hannah Dustin—a sister of Elizabeth Emerson, executed in 1693 for infanticide—was captured. Thomas later found their newborn dead with its brains dashed out).[4]

Shortly after this calamity, a **March 23** meeting of Salem Village inhabitants decided to sue Parris from the parsonage. Parris countersued immediately for his back pay—if he left, he would never collect anything. By now, even Thomas and Nathaniel Putnam, who had once sided with Parris, were on the committees working against him.[5]

All parties appeared before the Essex County Court at Salem on **April 13, 1697**, to testify on the legality of granting Parris the parsonage. The court ruled in favor of Parris's suit, declared the Village's case unsuited, and ordered the committee to pay court costs. The Village appealed, and the matter went to arbitration. (Later that month, on **April 19**, the probate court ordered the Proctor heirs to give the widowed Elizabeth Proctor her dowry, as she was "now restored to benefit of law." How much she was able to collect is unclear.)[6]

All Massachusetts was astonished at the end of April when the kidnapped Hannah Dustin walked out of the woods alive, bringing with her two other captives and ten scalps worth a £50 bounty. The three of them had killed and scalped their captors to escape—the only prisoners who managed to do so. (Hannah had in mind her dead infant, but the dead Algonquins were *not* the same individuals who had attacked Haverhill, but rather two other men, two women, and six children.)[7]

Three arbiters—Wait-Still Winthrop, Elisha Cooke, and Samuel Sewall—considered the Salem Village troubles. Speaking for the Village, John Tarbell, Samuel Nurse,

Joseph Putnam, and Daniel Andrews addressed a complaint dated **July 21, 1697**. It explained why they could not regard Rev. Samuel Parris as "a minister of the Gospel," much less contribute to his support. By consulting the possessed—people with familiar spirits (witches)—and by believing their Devilish lies, Parris, that "instrument of our miseries," had begun the "sorest afflictions" ever to befall the Village or the country. They resented not only "his promoting such accusations, as also his partiality therein, in stifling the accusations of some, and at the same time vigilantly promoting others." They could hardly acknowledge such a man as their minister, much less hear his sermons and pay his wages.[8]

The arbiters, two of them judges of the witchcraft trials, ignored Parris's contract and prior county court decisions. On **August 30, 1697**, they ordered Parris to relinquish his deed for the ministry house and land (plus the copper in the lean-to), and ordered the Village to pay him £79-9-6. (Five years' back pay would have amounted to a more sizable figure. Either Parris's supporters had been paying him something, or the sum represented money that Parris had invested in improvements.)[9]

Robert Calef finished his book on **August 11** and titled it *More Wonders of the Invisible World*, as a jibe against Rev. Cotton Mather. Besides an account of the trials based largely on information provided by the families of the accused, Calef also included—without permission—Cotton Mather's five trial summaries from *Wonders of the Invisible World*, and Mather's as-yet-unpublished record of Margaret Rule's case. Calef's narrative took note of Samuel Sewall's apology, but only anonymously as from "one of the honorable judges." He quoted Rev. Samuel Parris's "Meditations for Peace," but made little of it. Then he added various letters and a battery of papers and petitions from Parris's opponents.[10]

His introduction blamed the outbreak on "a parcel of possessed, distracted, or lying wenches" ("vile varlets" all, guilty of "whoredoms, incest, etc."), who accused innocent neighbors by pretending to see their specters. Bloodthirsty ministers and magistrates encouraged these liars with "bigoted zeal, stirring up a blind and most bloody rage"—till they themselves were accused. All this could happen again, said Calef (disregarding the dismissal of spectral evidence, the Public Fast, and Sewall's personal apology), unless those responsible confessed their wrongs, took "the due shame to themselves," and rejected pagan and Popish methods of witch-detection. Since he himself felt called upon by God to point out such errors, he therefore addressed his book to readers "freed from the slavery of a corrupt education"—uncorrupted by Homer and Virgil, that is—and still capable of applying reason and Scripture. No Boston printer cared to collaborate with Calef, so the work remained, for the time being, in manuscript.[11]

Also on **August 31,** Winifred Benham Sr. of Wallingford, Connecticut—already tried for witchcraft in 1692—appeared before a special court at New Haven with her daughter, Winifred Jr. Both were charged with afflicting two teenaged girls and a boy. The justices ordered the suspects to appear before the Court of Assistants at Hartford in October. (They remained free on bail for the interim; the Assistants eventually declared their case *ignoramus,* but the family soon moved to New York.)[12]

Meanwhile, the land suffered from intermittent Indian raids along the frontiers as well as from a stubborn drought. If showers dampened one town, they left its neighbors dry. Water-mills stood silent above shrunken streams, and wells sank below reach. Smoke filled the air around Boston, as autumn brush fires devoured hay, fences, and timber. Already pinched by hard times, Thomas Putnam had sold off lots to his cousin Eleazer and the Topsfield men. Some time in 1697, Putnam sold his home to Samuel Braybrook, and moved his family to a small house made of recycled lumber.[13]

France, in addition, had sent a fleet to capture Newfoundland and Boston. Lieutenant Governor William Stoughton had ordered the province on alert for several weeks during the preceding summer, but fortunately the French fleet spent all its time and supplies in the north.[14]

The only maritime action in New England occurred at East Harbor, on the wrist of Cape Cod, when a French vessel landed **September 5, 1697**, and captured four sloops and a lighter. Ten men from the local Palmet tribe—led by one Hugh—repulsed the invasion (to the legislature's amazed gratitude). There was no doubt, as at Gloucester in 1692, that these were *real* soldiers and not specters.[15]

But the Abenaki, once they no longer had to wait for the canceled expedition, sent raiders as far south as Lancaster, Massachusetts.[16]

Meanwhile, Rev. Samuel Parris had sold a few adjoining acres back to Nathaniel Ingersoll, bought some rental property in Boston, and put up a bond promising to relinquish the parsonage. He wrote the quitclaim for it on **September 24**, *after* the Village had collected and paid the arbitrated sum—which it did in record time. Then, at last, he vacated the parsonage and moved away.[17]

Still without a pastor, Salem Village held a fast on **October 12, 1697**, "to seek direction" from God "about providing a minister for us," with Reverends John Hale, Nicholas Noyes, and Joseph Gerrish invited to offer prayers. (The Village also asked Hale's son Robert to be its minister, but he, too, declined, as did "Mr. Emerson" when the Villagers approached him again.)[18]

Samuel Parris, meanwhile, soon found a temporary post in Stow, where he had preached for a brief period a dozen years earlier. Since then, the Stow church had unsuccessfully sued a former minister in a contract dispute concerning ownership of the parsonage. On **November 29, 1697**, Stow offered Parris £40 a year—or less, if he would agree. He would not, but a grant from the General Court provided half the offered salary. He left after only a year, but found a stepmother for his daughters when he married Dorothy Noyes of nearby Sudbury. Possibly very distant cousins of Rev. Nicholas Noyes, she and her sisters had spent most of 1692 suing their brother for their shares of their late father's estate.)[19]

In **mid-November**, when the rains began again, Samuel Sewall journeyed to Salem for the quarterly court. He shared lodgings with Rev. John Hale of Beverly, and learned that Hale was writing about the witchcraft trials. "I fear lest he go into the other extreme," Sewall worried, since *something* had happened after all. Hale had changed his views before the trials ended, but still thought it foolish to dismiss "little sorceries" as trivia, or to suppose one knew all there was to know about whatever had occurred.[20]

"I have been from my youth," Rev. Hale wrote, "trained up in the knowledge and belief of most of those principles I here question as unsafe to be used." The common folk-magic "proofs" ought never to be meddled with. The only safe and legal proof should be two unafflicted witnesses or a corroborated confession as for other crimes. The great confusions of 1692, the genuine pain of the afflicted, and the influence of former precedents made most people overlook for too long that they acted on the Devil's lies. They overestimated *and* underestimated the powers of the Devil, who could affect victims in ways that cast suspicion on others. Because affected victims *expected* certain things to happen, their fears were terribly realized. (Hale would finish his manuscript in December, and would name it *A Modest Enquiry into the Nature of Witchcraft*. Rev. John Higginson of Salem would compose an introduction the following March, but the book would not be published until 1700—after Hale's death.)[21]

More of Rev. Cotton Mather's opinions on the subject appeared by **November** in his biography of Sir William Phips, *Pietas in Patriam*. Reading it, Rev. Increase Mather's critics bridled at Cotton's defense of his father's charter negotiations that led to Phips's government. Phips's opponents noticed that the brawls with Jahleel Brenton and Captain Richard Short were hardly mentioned. Robert Calef found the episode of the governor's horoscope a delicious irony, and turned a jaundiced eye on the passages relating to the witchcraft trials.[22]

Although some of the afflicted, Mather wrote, "were good people" who suffered real and painful tortures, he now felt that others who were "most flippant at accusing, had a far other character." As before, he suspected that masquerading devils were let in by ill-advised fortune telling, though just possibly by a more deliberate agreement with evil powers. The judges, he wrote, were "men eminent for wisdom and virtue," who tried to handle conscientiously a confusing issue with precedents from ancient Scripture and from recent English trials. However, their acceptance of spectral evidence, as reported by the afflicted, dissatisfied "many persons of great judgment, piety, and experience" from the start, who let it be known that, even if it were rare, it *was* possible for devils to impersonate the innocent. As the trials proceeded, it became clear "that the more the afflicted were harkened unto, the more the number of the accused increased." Therefore, after consulting local and New York clergy, Governor Phips ended the trials—and accusations ceased.[23]

Calef added a "Postscript," possibly written by Elisha Cooke, to his own unpublished manuscript. The new material lacerated the biography and its support of the charter, accused Increase Mather of political meddling, and blamed Cotton Mather for inciting the witchcraft persecutions.[24]

Not long after **November 22, 1697**, when a Salem Village committee asked twenty-two-year-old Joseph Green (then a Roxbury schoolmaster) to preach at the Village, New England was cautiously relieved to hear that the war with France had ended. The recently signed Peace of Ryswick obliged King Louis to acknowledge England's Protestant succession, but left the Maine/Acadia boundary disputed. Boston celebrated with a flourish of drums and trumpets on **December 10, 1697**, and with the release of French prisoners whom they no longer had to feed.[25]

Peace seemed nearly a reality in Salem Village also, where, on **December 22**, a general meeting of inhabitants voted to offer Joseph Green the post of minister, and sent a committee to Roxbury the following day. Green agreed on condition that the Villagers allow him to travel to some other church on sacrament Sabbaths to take communion (as he could not administer it himself until he was ordained); and that they honor their salary offer of £60 the first year, and £70 thereafter plus "strangers' money" (donations from out-of-town attendees who could not be taxed). However, "if once they begin to quarrel and contend; I should look upon myself to be free from any obligation to tarry with them."[26]

Having decided, Joseph Green moved north from Roxbury to Salem Village on **January 5, 1698**, during the coldest winter that anyone could remember. People walked across the frozen Charles River from Boston to Charlestown until the end of February, and snow lay deep everywhere. "Epidemical and pestilential colds" swept the area, "proved mortal to many," Rev. Cotton Mather wrote, "and grievous to most" (himself included). Boston's Sabbath assemblies thinned, and three Sundays passed in Medford with no services at all.[27]

But the winter was harder among the Indians and their captives. Prey was scarce, many Indians starved after they ate all their dogs, and a stubborn sickness consumed the weakened survivors. They had no help from France—now that the European part of the war was over—yet many of their kin remained captive in New England. Driven by frustration, desperation, and revenge, Indian raiders attacked Andover on **February 22, 1698**, at daybreak. They slaughtered twenty cattle; burned houses and barns; torched the meeting house (the fire was soon quenched); and stole the pulpit cushion. They killed former witch-suspect Rebecca Johnson's eighteen-year-old daughter, Penelope. Rev. Thomas Barnard narrowly escaped, but Dudley Bradstreet's family were all captured. With the local militia at their heels, the raiders released the Bradstreets. But when they found the home of Pasco Chubb, their old enemy from Pemaquid, they killed both him and his wife.[28]

Other roving bands hit Spruce Creek and York in Maine that spring, then Deerfield and Hatfield in Massachusetts on the Connecticut River in **mid-July, 1698**. But after Sagamore Madockawando died that fall, the other sachems proposed peace—and reminded Boston that the Treaty of Ryswick included the return of *all* prisoners, both English and Indian. John Nelson, heir of Acadia/Nova Scotia, had finally been released from his French prison, and had even helped negotiate the Ryswick Treaty. He would be back in Boston by November 30 to petition Lieutenant Governor William Stoughton for reimbursement of sums spent to ransom other captives.[29]

After months of soul-searching that hot, wet summer, Joseph Green agreed to become Salem Village's permanent minister. At his suggestion, this matter was proposed to the whole congregation—not just full members—and the majority agreed with a show of hands on **July 31, 1698**. Later, the Village subscribed nearly thirty cords of firewood for him in addition to £70 a year and use—but not ownership—of the parsonage. "If your love to me does continue and be duly manifested as hitherto it has been," Green told the people on **October 9, 1698**, "and you do all study to be quiet and maintain peace among yourselves—then I am willing to continue with you."[30]

Yet, the vote for him was not unanimous. Some still smarted over "a paper" (probably one of the pro-Parris petitions) presented to the council. Daniel Andrews, Green's distant kinsman, expected an apology for it from the church which Green amicably wrote, and, on the morning of his ordination, persuaded a church meeting to pass. John Putnam remained stubborn, but everyone else agreed, leaving a relatively peaceful setting for the ceremony. Thus, on **November 10, 1698**, Reverends Nicholas Noyes and John Hale presided—as they had almost exactly nine years earlier at Parris's ordination. They were assisted by Reverends Jonathan Pierpont of Reading, Green's former pastor Nehemiah Walter of Roxbury, and Joseph Gerrish of neighboring Wenham (whose daughter would soon marry young Rev. Green).[31]

Now, as Samuel Sewall hoped when he heard of the event, there was "likelihood of a stability of peace and settlement there." And indeed, within a few weeks, the dissatisfied brethren reconciled with the congregation and rejoined communion.[32]

Richard Coote—the Earl of Bellomont and next royal governor of Massachusetts, New York, and New Hampshire combined—did not reach Boston until **May 26, 1699**, and subsequently died in New York on **March 1701**. Lieutenant Governor William Stoughton took charge locally until his own death at age seventy on **July 7, 1701**. So the council presided until Joseph Dudley, governor at last, landed the following year on **June 11, 1702**.[33]

Robert Calef, meanwhile, had had his book published in England. Copies arrived in Boston in the **late fall of 1700**, along with an unusually early snow and a bronchial epidemic that gripped most of Rev. Cotton Mather's family and nearly killed Rev. Samuel Willard. *More Wonders of the Invisible World*, that "abominable bundle of lies," was nearly as distressing. Calef's point, that those responsible ought to admit their errors, was buried under invective and contradiction. "I am the chief butt of his malice," Cotton Mather noted.[34]

The book circulated despite some shops' refusal to carry it. The Nurse kindred and others who had provided documents for the volume would have enjoyed it. But the book must have been a thorn for Samuel Parris, now living in Watertown as a farmer, shop-keeper, and schoolmaster. Calef's remarks about "whoredoms" and "vile varlets" pretending spectral sight would have stung the once-afflicted Mercy Lewis, now Mercy Allen of Boston (who had borne a child in New Hampshire before her marriage), and Mercy Short, now Mercy Marshall (who was found guilty of adultery in 1698, and excommunicated by her pastor, Rev. Cotton Mather). Certainly, it distressed the Mathers. Calef's squibs on the dead Mather infant could only have galled the more intensely when Cotton's youngest child Samuel died on **February 7, 1701**—after two days and nights of convulsions.[35]

Several of Mather's friends rebutted Calef in *Some Few Remarks Upon a Scandalous Book*. The ministers, they repeated, had warned from the *start* that devils could impersonate the innocent. And if Calef meant to prove there were no witches, why did he quibble about the charter and the relative size of cannon balls shot from Quebec? Seven of the book committee signed the introduction, including John Barnard (whose son was cured by the motherly angel) and John Goodwin (whose children had been afflicted in 1689). But the opposition read the part containing Cotton Mather's letter and sniffed that if the Mathers didn't *write* the whole, maybe they *dictated* it.[36]

Also during the Earl of Bellomont's administration as governor, the anti-charter faction had succeeded in July 1700 in requiring that the college president live on site full time. With his church's permission, Rev. Increase Mather departed for Cambridge, but after several gloomy months of exile, he resigned on **October 17, 1701**, and hastened back to Boston. When the council asked Samuel Willard to be president, he accepted, but only if he needn't live in Cambridge. The opposition had made its point, so the council succeeded in naming Willard "*Vice*-President" and asked him to spend just one or two nights a week at the college. Both Mathers lost their frayed tempers when they heard.[37]

At the repeated request of her friends, Rev. Joseph Green broached the subject of Martha Corey to his Salem Village congregation on **December 22, 1702**. He had been obliged to preach against the continuing problem of unlawful divination the previous November. Now he asked his congregation if Goody Corey's excommunication might be reversed, to restore her name even if not her life, as it was now generally agreed that the witchcraft trials were riddled with errors. The church members thought about this proposal until **February 14, 1703**. Then the majority voted in favor of the motion—though six or seven did not. Green was generally a peacemaker, but an inhabitants' meeting on **March 11, 1703**, dealt so "unkindly" with him (perhaps as a reaction) that he resolved to avoid such meetings thereafter.[38]

The witchcraft trials were more than a decade past when the General Court began to receive petitions concerned with the 1692 trials. "Several inhabitants of Salem Village and Topsfield"—twenty-one in all, including Andover names—presented a document on **March 2, 1703**, signed by spouses and children of the condemned and by the three women who had been convicted but not executed: Abigail Faulkner Sr., Elizabeth Proctor, and Sarah Wardwell. On behalf of these three, and of the executed Rebecca Nurse, Mary Esty, Mary Parker of Andover, John Proctor, Elizabeth How, and Samuel Wardwell, they asked that "something may be publicly done to take off infamy from the names."[39]

Two more petitions followed in **June 1703**. Abigail Faulkner Sr. of Andover submitted one to remind the legislature that—although Governor Phips had reprieved her death sentence—she was still legally "a malefactor convict upon record of the most heinous crimes that mankind can be supposed to be guilty of, which besides its utter ruining and defacing my reputation, will certainly expose my self to imminent danger by new accusations."[40]

In the second petition, eleven Essex County ministers—including Joseph Green of Salem Village, John Wise of Chebago, and Thomas Barnard of Andover—asked the government to reconsider the cases, that they might order something to be "publicly done to clear the good name and reputation of some who have suffered" merely "upon complaint of some young persons under diabolical molestations."[41]

The legislature, in considering the petition of Abigail Faulkner "and sundry of Andover," read the notes of their cases and found that the only evidence against them was "weak and insufficient as to taking away the lives." Consequently, by **July 21, 1703**, the two houses agreed to acquit Abigail Faulkner and "sundry persons" of their convictions (though technically only the monarch could legally do so), and thereby restore "their just credit and reputation as if no such judgment had been had." They also ordered a bill drawn specifically to prohibit the acceptance of spectral evidence in the future.[42]

But more needed to be done, as Rev. Michael Wigglesworth of Malden wrote to Rev. Increase Mather on **July 22, 1704**. War had resumed in Europe, so the frontier was again a threat, and the very rains had ceased like a judgment. "I fear (amongst our many other provocations)," wrote Wigglesworth, "that God hath a controversy with us about what was done in the time of the witchcraft. I fear that innocent blood hath been shed, and that many have had their hands defiled therewith." He believed that the judges "did act conscientiously according to what they did apprehend then to be sufficient proof, but since that, have not the Devil's impostures appeared?" The situation needed "a public and solemn acknowledgment of it, and humiliation for it, and the more particularly and personally it is done by all that have been actors, the more pleasing it will be to God." In addition to this public repentance, "the families of such as were condemned for supposed witchcraft, have been ruined by taking away and making havoc of their estates, and leaving them with nothing for their relief." So the whole country would remain accursed until something *practical* was done for these people. It would be expensive, especially in wartime, yet it was a *necessary* expense, and could be paid in installments. Might Mather and the other Boston ministers propose the idea to the governor and council at the next session?[43]

But the government, preoccupied with Canadian attacks, would not be rushed.

While the matter hung fire and the war continued, the younger Ann Putnam asked to join the Salem Village Church. Single at age twenty-nine, she had had charge of her younger brothers and sisters since the deaths of their parents in the spring of 1699. From the usual interviews with the applicant, Rev. Green composed a relation of her conversion experience and a confession of past deeds. These he read to the congregation on **August 25, 1706**, while Ann Putnam Jr. stood silently:

In her childhood she had accused "several persons of a grievous crime, whereby their lives were taken away from them, whom now I have just grounds and good reason to believe they were innocent persons." She had believed Satan's delusions "in that sad time" and thereby "been instrumental, with others, though ignorantly and unwittingly, to bring upon myself and this land the guilt of innocent blood." She did so "not out of any anger, malice, or ill-will to any person, for I had no such thing against one of them; but what I did was ignorantly, being deluded by Satan. And particularly, as I was a chief instrument of accusing Goodwife Nurse and her two sisters, I desire to lie in the dust, and to be humbled for it." For this "so sad a calamity" she now did "earnestly beg forgiveness of God, and from all those unto whom I have given just cause of sorrow and offense, whose relations were taken away or accused."[44]

Ann acknowledged the piece and, as no one objected, was received into full communion. (Four years earlier, Betty Parris had joined one of the Watertown churches, but the text of her confession was not preserved.)[45]

But the government *still* made no amends, being briared in local and British plans against Canada, Acadia, and Newfoundland. Militias in all the colonies went on alert for months, only to find that the promised British fleet had been diverted to the war in Europe. (Another hastier British plan—plagued by desertions and tempests—ended when the British Admiral's flagship exploded off New Hampshire.)[46]

With no end to the war in sight, Philip English, George Jacobs, Jr., and several kinsmen of the other suspects presented two petitions to the government on **May 25, 1709**, asking for the restoration of the suspects' reputations and reimbursement of their estates. When Rev. Cotton Mather delivered a lecture before the General Assembly in **November 1709**, he urged further reparations, since they had all declared their disapproval of past errors in the witchcraft trials.[47]

The legislature finally acted in **May 1710** by appointing a committee of five—including Stephen Sewall, once clerk of the Court of Oyer and Terminer—to hear petitions for restitution. In **September 1710**—the same month that Port Royal surrendered again—the five convened in Salem, while the accused and bereaved flocked to them with petitions and lists of jail fees, court costs, and bail bonds—fees for every piece of paper, including pardons. Petitioners cited travel expenses, for Isaac Esty and blind James How had both visited their jailed wives twice weekly in Salem and then in Boston. Others, like Peter Green, itemized the cost of every move and charged for time spent accompanying his wife to court.[48]

Philip English submitted an inventory of £1,183-2-0 worth of confiscated items—*not* including his lost household goods, or the forfeited £4,000 bond. Edward and Sarah Bishop, now of Rehoboth, listed their prison fees and confiscated livestock, then added that their depleted estate had to support twelve children (though some of these were grown and married, and one dead even before the witch scare). Samuel Nurse estimated that his family had spent over £40 on his mother's jail fees and provisions in addition to their own trips to Salem and Boston on her behalf, but they would settle for £25—if the attainder were removed from her name. Mary Bradbury's kin figured that their grandfather had spent £20 on her case, but would accept whatever the committee offered as "we doubt not but some others might suffer more in their estates."[49]

William Good, remarried and the occasional recipient of Village charity, had been little help to his late wife in her lifetime. He now reminded the committee of Sarah's execution, their infant's death in jail, and their five-year-old's several months of imprisonment. Dorcas, "being chained in the dungeon [in the same room with pirates, prisoners of war, thieves, etc.] was so hardly used and terrified that she hath ever since been very chargeable, having little or no reason to govern herself." She was now twenty-three.[50]

Among the more mundane appropriations, made by the Massachusetts legislature in **October 1711,** was £10 to Dunstable—a poor frontier town that "had much ado to rub along"—toward the salary of its present minister, Rev. Samuel Parris, who had once again left private life for the pulpit. But the legislature's principal business was the Reversal of Attainder that, nearly twenty years after their condemnation, nullified all judgments against "George Burroughs of Wells; John Proctor, George Jacobs, John Willard, Giles Corey and Martha his wife, Rebecca Nurse and Sarah Good all of Salem aforesaid; Elizabeth How of Ipswich; Mary Esty, Sarah Wildes and Abigail Hobbs all of Topsfield; Samuel Wardwell, Mary Parker, Martha Carrier, Abigail Faulkner, Ann Foster, Rebecca Eames, Mary Post, and Mary Lacy all of Andover; Mary Bradbury of Salisbury; and Dorcas Hoar of Beverly."[51]

Their names were hereby cleared, because the original charges came from people influenced by evil spirits then, and (some of them) "of profligate and vicious" lives now. The document ended with a stipulation that "no sheriff, constable, jailer, or other officer shall be liable to any prosecution in the law for anything they then legally did in the execution of their respective offices."

Governor Joseph Dudley signed the document into law on **October 17, 1711**, along with a reparations list totaling £578-12-0. The committee distributed the money at Salem in **January** and **February 1712,** as individuals journeyed into town to collect for themselves, their family, or their neighbors. Thorndike Proctor received sums for his kin, while Deacon Benjamin Putnam came over from the Village for the £30 due William Good. Even Abigail Hobbs, so quick to confess and to accuse, was awarded £10.[52]

However, the legislature granted money only if the accused or heirs had asked for it. And the names cleared by the Reversal of Attainder were only those names specified in the petitions. Although the compensation allowed £150 for "John Proctor and wife," Elizabeth Proctor's name was omitted from the Reversal, as was Sarah Wardwell's (though her family was given £36-15-0 for "Samuel Wardwell and wife"). Elizabeth Johnson Jr. wrote to the committee in **February 1712** to remind its members that she too had been condemned, yet her name was missing from the Reversal of Attainder. Might they insert it? "Sundry," from Andover had been cleared anonymously in 1702, and the government was finished with the whole distressing matter. The name of Elizabeth Johnson Jr.—along with those of Bridget Bishop, Susanna Martin, Elizabeth Proctor, Alice Parker, Ann Pudeator, Martha Scott, Wilmot Read, and Sarah Wardwell remained unprotected.[53]

Samuel Wardwell Jr. asked if his parents' jail fees, which he had omitted before, might also be reimbursed. The committee declined.[54]

Benjamin Proctor objected that, as he was responsible in 1692 for *all* of his re-lations' debts, the sums that his half-brother Thorndike had collected for Mary, Abigail, and Joseph should be, by rights, *his*. The committee left the Proctors to ar-gue among themselves.[55]

Seven Burroughs children complained that their step-mother was compensated with the rest of them, even though she sold all of their father's goods and left them to shift for themselves when the eldest was only sixteen. The proceeds from their father's estate then passed into her next husband's hands, and "not one farthing be-stowed upon any child but her own." The committee ignored this complaint also, but the children, and then grandchildren, continued to petition as late as 1750.[56]

Philip English, *not* one of the condemned, had better luck when he was granted £200 in **November 1718**. He refused the sum as paltry, but it would pass to his estate upon his death.[57]

After the reparations committee concluded its business, the Salem church mem-bers met on **March 6, 1712**, at the home of Rev. Nicholas Noyes to review the ex-communications of Rebecca Nurse and Giles Corey. (Noyes was now the senior minister. Jonathan Corwin's accident-prone son, George—who may or may not have been thought bewitched in 1692—was the younger pastor.) With Goody Nurse's bill of attainder reversed, and spectral evidence discredited, nothing now supported the original witchcraft charge. At the urging of her son Samuel, a mem-ber of the Salem Village church, the Salem church members voted to overturn Re-becca Nurse's excommunication "that it may no longer be a reproach to her mem-ory, and an occasion of grief to her children," and to ask God's pardon for their own earlier error.[58]

Even though Giles Corey was no longer considered a wizard, they continued (overlooking that he was neither tried nor convicted), his stubborn refusal to plead, which led to his death by pressing, still seemed like the sin of suicide. "Yet the church having now testimony in his behalf, that before his death he did bitterly repent of his obstinate refusal to plead in defense of his life," the members re-versed Giles Corey's excommunication as well.[59]

Everyday life continued its rocky path as ideals and personalities collided in politics and public life, as the frontier wars staggered far into the new century, and as clashes between royal and colonial policies flared eventually into the War of Independence. Hostilities left by the witchcraft trials faded slowly as the participants aged and died. Some perished relatively young, like Rev. Joseph Green of Salem Village in **November 1715**, and the younger Ann Putnam around the same time. Rev. Nicholas Noyes was old and corpulent when a blood vessel burst in his head in **December 1718**. Eulogies praised his learning, charitable works, and pleasant conversation. Other folk, however—upon hearing that his last illness left his dead mouth full of blood—remembered Sarah Good's cry from the gallows that God would give Noyes blood to drink, and wondered if she weren't a fortune-teller after all. Rev. Samuel Parris died in Sudbury in **February 1720** in the house inherited by his second wife. His local pastor remembered Parris as "a courteous and affable gentleman" (but Sarah Cloyse's kindred in nearby Framingham probably still considered him the source of all their miseries).[60]

His resentment undiminished, Philip English outlived Noyes by nearly twenty years. If, as some later said, Noyes had apologized fully and publicly for his wrongs, then English remained unimpressed. In the **spring of 1722**, well after the minister's death, English denounced him as the murderer of John Proctor and Rebecca Nurse, then denounced Salem's church as the "Devil's church." (He had already left that congregation to found an Anglican church in Salem.) English pleaded not guilty of slander when brought before the magistrates in **August 1722**, but lost his head and insulted both church *and* justices (including Bartholomew Gedney) with "vile" and "abusive language." A night in jail for contempt of court persuaded him to apologize to the justices, but the same thing happened again in **January 1724**. In his last days, English's mind dimmed enough that his son became his guardian, yet the wealthy merchant never forgot a grudge. Persuaded on his death bed in **March 1736** to forgive Noyes and his other enemies (his descendants would say), English did so as a matter of form.[61]

Then he added, "But if I get well, I'll be damned if I forgive him!"

Part II: The Middle Way

Conviction must not be by vinegar or drollery, but by strength of argument.

—Rev. John Hale

The embarrassing confusion left by the Salem witch trials proved the greatest preventive of any future such outbreaks. Thereafter, Massachusetts courts handled only a few slander suits brought by widows (in areas distant from Salem) against gossiping neighbors. Still, people did not agree on what to make of the Salem trials.[62]

One episode that never reached court began at Littleton in **1720** when the three Blanchard sisters, aged eleven, nine, and five, began to act bewitched. They swooned, ranted, displayed wounds, were found up trees and on roofs, and reported the pursuing specter of a neighbor, Abigail Dudley. As their mother struck the space that they indicated, Elizabeth, the eldest girl, cried, "You have hit her on the bowels!" Mrs. Dudley died soon after, giving birth to her tenth child and forgiving the slurs on her name. The girls recovered, and local attention waned. Of the many who had visited them, some thought that they suffered from a physical ailment or mental distraction. Others said that they were "underwitted." The least sympathetic called them "perverse and wicked." Most believed that "they were under an evil hand, or possessed by Satan," but few thought Mrs. Dudley was at fault.

Eight years later in **1728**, after the Blanchards had moved back to their native Medford, Elizabeth was accepted for church membership there. But after hearing Rev. Ebenezer Turell deliver a sermon on lies, she approached him, on the eve of her joining, to confess that the whole witchcraft episode had been a fraud. She had meddled with fortunetelling, she said, and had wasted her time reading romantic ballads and mere fiction. She gave in to pride when people actually *listened* to the stories that she herself told, acting them out and pretending unconsciousness in order to relate invented visions. When folks speculated about witchcraft, she then acted in the ways she had heard the bewitched did act. Her sisters had joined her—all encouraged by their parents' sympathy. Elizabeth couldn't remember why they had accused Mrs. Dudley. Someone's name seemed required, but they had no grudge against her. Once they heard of her death, they fully expected her ghost to haunt them. Rev. Turell read Elizabeth's confession to the Medford church, which accepted it. Then he wrote an account of the matter as a warning against lies, pride, magic, and indulgent parents.[63]

Ten years later in **1738**—two years after Philip English's death—Judge Sewall's son Samuel Jr. chaired a legislative committee to gather further information on "the circumstances of the persons and families who suffered in the calamity" of the witch trials. Governor Jonathan Belcher likewise encouraged the General Court in **1740** to do something to help the "families as were in a manner ruined in the mistaken management of the terrible affair called witchcraft." Rev. George Burroughs's grandchildren petitioned the committee as late as **1750**, but the war with the French in Canada interrupted the inquiry, as did the later tensions that led to the War of Independence.[64]

Opinions on bewitchment paralleled the changing religious climate. The more orthodox, who emphasized an educated ministry and reasoned sermons, could not take *maleficia* seriously. The more emotional "New Light" faction, with its extemporary preaching and camp meetings, tended to accept the idea of active evil spirits—along with radical practices like women and blacks addressing its meetings. (When the Devil had apparently roared and spoken through twenty-three-year-old Martha Roberson of Boston in 1741, New Lights thought her affliction was a case of possession. Old Lights like Rev. Mather Byles and Martha's physician Dr. Samuel Mather, both grandsons of Cotton Mather, did not. In either case, witchcraft had no part in it.)[65]

Governor Thomas Hutchinson noted the Blanchard case in his *History of Massachusetts Bay* (1750) and considered it exactly the same as the earlier accusations. He also knew one of the by-then-adult Goodwin children who had been bewitched years earlier in 1688. "She had the character of a very sober virtuous woman," Hutchinson wrote, "and never made any acknowledgment of fraud." Some people still thought that the afflicted of 1692 must have had a physical ailment that made them believe they were bewitched. But Governor Hutchinson agreed with Robert Calef, and concluded that innocent people had died because of lying, self-indulgent girls, cowardly adults afraid of accusation, and credulous judges and juries—fraud from start to finish.[66]

The two views clashed again at Salem in **1811** when a young woman named Bancroft had convulsions in a house on Windmill Point. She was from "the stews of Boston"—according to one detractor—and accused a Boston woman of tormenting her. But because she prophesied during her trances, opponents referred to her as a "pretended witch."

She was afflicted at night, so evening after evening the curious flocked to her neighborhood in ever-increasing numbers, and nervously debated the possibilities "just as it would have been in 1692." A young man who visited the house found Miss Bancroft "passive and quiet" in her room surrounded by several women and men, including two ministers. One of these perceived an invisible spirit troubling her, but the mood indoors was grave and quiet. Outside, however, all was "turbulence, riot and mischief." After the crowd reached a thousand on **March 3, 1811** the selectmen and the overseers of the poor ordered the girl out of town or into the Work House. She left for Maine, the crowds dispersed, and prior opinions solidified.[67]

Repelled now by the Bancroft incident, Salem's Rev. William Bentley had already commented on the 1692 cases in a short history of Salem written in 1799. He acknowledged how widespread belief in the supernatural was, but found it hard to comprehend the "astonishing fanaticism" and "cruel superstition" of 1692. Salem then was bereft of strong leadership, but "the event did not arise in ignorance but error," he wrote. "They, who thought they saw the delusion, did not expose it. They, who were deluded, were terrified into distraction." The courts were so caught up that they admitted evidence even from children, Indians, and "tender females . . . but not one man of reputation." But by Bentley's time, people also thought that no Quaker had accused anyone, and that Rev. Burroughs performed his feats of strength at the age of eighty.[68]

Rev. Cotton Mather's *Wonders of the Invisible World* and Robert Calef's *More Wonders of the Invisible World* were never out of print for long, but, until Charles W. Upham, no one had mined the mass of seventeenth-century documents to tell the story more fully. He had written a series of *Lectures on Witchcraft* in **1831** while associate pastor at Salem's First Church (by then Unitarian). After leaving the pulpit for a strenuous career in local and Federal politics, Upham retired and expanded the lectures into his massive *Salem Witchcraft* by **1867**. He sympathized neither with the older views of Calvinism nor with the newer interest in Spiritualism. But, noting the similarities between mediums and the afflicted girls, he concluded that the latter had also held seances and acted, moreover, as one cooperating group. Upham detailed local land disputes to present greed as a motive for accusation—though none of the accusers had stood to gain so much as a handful of sod from the suspects. He reiterated the universality of belief in magic, but made it clear that he thought the girls had lied from the start, egged on by a conspiracy of ministers who had manipulated the terror to gain power.[69]

Upham's bias and inaccuracies did not go unchallenged. William Poole, then head librarian of the Boston Atheneum, noted that Upham did not support many of his conclusions with evidence, and that he overstated the ministers' involvement with the trials while disregarding their precautions on spectral evidence. "The Salem barbarities were not stopped by an abandonment of the popular theory of witchcraft, but by a reformation in the methods of conviction." Even Calef, Brattle, and other critics of the trials, wrote Poole, thought that witchcraft was possible.[70]

Upham bludgeoned Poole's criticism in a magazine article that further enlarged upon the former's conspiracy theory. He accused the Mathers of fomenting the superstition in the first place, and then of encouraging and arranging the trials. Rev. Cotton Mather's precautions only *seemed* like good advice, Upham declared, but meant exactly the *opposite* of what they said. That Cotton Mather neither revealed the names of the accused nor testified in court only proved (to Upham) that the minister really managed events from behind the scenes. Since publication of the *Lectures*, Upham's unsupported conclusion of cause and effect had already entered textbooks and public opinion. His new book became the source for the majority of subsequent writers.[71]

But many other nineteenth-century New England authors acted defensively (often with more invective than research) as if they feared that someone would confuse them with their "witch-hunting" ancestors. A growing awareness of their country's past—especially in contrast with the many other ethnic groups newly arriving in America—only helped make the less-inspiring parts of its history an even greater embarrassment. Immigrants, wearied by slums and sweat-shops, seemed ready to accept the idea of their bosses' inherited guilt, and conveniently forgot how their *own* ancestors, in their several countries, had dealt with witch suspects. "Puritan" became as much a by-word as "witch."[72]

By the end of the nineteenth century, new disciplines of psychology, sociology, and anthropology began to cast fresh light on old sorrows. That the afflicted had suffered from clinical hysteria (conversion disorder) was suggested as early as **1882** by George M. Beard. But the purpose of his book, *The Psychology of the Salem Witchcraft Trials*, was to promote the insanity defense for murder suspects, and he saved his sympathy for President James A. Garfield's assassin. Inflamed by stories of marvels, the afflicted girls, Beard felt, "became partly insane and partly entranced." But "the genuine symptoms of real disease were supplemented by malignity and crime," so that "unintentional deception was rewarded by intentional deception." It was not until Chadwick Hansen's *Witchcraft at Salem* appeared in **1969** that the bizarre and unconscious effects of clinical hysteria (as a result of genuine, if misinterpreted, fear) had much recognition.[73]

Anthropologists applied the same techniques used to study distant tribal cultures to their own Western past, and noticed that old ideas of magic actually made *better* sense in the context of their own times and places. Without accepting a literal reality of what they studied, some scholars concluded that beliefs about witchcraft had been quite useful to preserve social order: the poor would be polite to the rich for fear of accusation, and the rich would be generous to the poor for fear of magical retaliation. Others, with utter horror, viewed witch-beliefs as the projection of a society's own deepest fears and forbidden desires upon innocent scapegoats.[74]

But it was not as easy to guess why suspicions flared to become deadly at *certain* times and places and against *certain* suspects, for they did so worldwide and in widely differing cultures. In the contradictory opinions of various commentators, the Salem outbreak has been described as a society's last attempt to recapture a lost sense of holy mission by cleansing the land of evil-doers with repressive authority (that nevertheless occurred in a time of *weak* religious and political leadership); or as yet another reaction against Quakers (overlooking that some accusers *were* Quakers); or as a rural society's resistance to growing capitalist competition that split the old Medieval sense of community (except that this scenario had *already* happened); or as superstition overriding science (except when people relied *too* much on the physicians' diagnoses).*

The accusers (according to the theories) projected their own deepest guilt onto innocent scapegoats; or feared the people who expressed openly the rebellious-

---

*Kai T. Erikson, *Wayward Puritans*, 1966; Enders A. Robinson, *The Devil Discovered*, 1991; William Bentley, "A Description and History of Salem," 1799; Christine Leigh Heyrman, *Commerce and Culture*, 1984; Paul Boyer and Stephen Nissenbaum, *Salem Possessed*, 1974; Sanford J. Fox, *Science and Justice*, 1968.

ness that they themselves kept hidden; or simply lied. Men feared the women suspects because of economic envy or because of religious anxiety—though as many
women testified against other women as did men.*

More girls were "bewitched" than boys because (according to a Victorian man)
the former's refined female sensibilities were corrupted by occult practices and by
imaginative fiction, or because (according to a twentieth-century woman) they
realized subconsciously that their lives were—and always would be—more re-
stricted than their brothers'. Symptoms and seizures were the effects of fraud, en-
cephalitis, ergot-tainted rye bread, or psychosomatic fear resulting from repressed
Calvinist childhoods lit by Hell-fire and abrupt weaning—or, just possibly, by a
neighbor's actual threat of *maleficia*.†

The accused were renegades against unjust conformity; women owning more
property than usual (or beggars); feisty neighbors who argued constantly with
their accusers or who merely reminded them of some other disliked person. The
accused were spotless innocents and misunderstood herbalists. Or they were
witches in that they deliberately rebelled against Christianity (as a rebellion against
conformity or patriarchal oppression); or because they were members of a pre-
Christian religion; or because some *did* attempt *maleficia*.‡

None of the theories passed unchallenged, and none explained everything, but
scholarly debate a century after Upham no longer assumed an easy answer.

"The middle way is commonly the way of truth," Rev. John Hale had written, ". . .
but the conviction must not be by vinegar or drollery, but by strength of argument."
Nevertheless, acidic tones and outright ridicule prevailed in print from Calef to Upham and beyond. Even after scholars began to study the trials from a variety of angles, public opinion continued to condescend. Instead of recognizing a timeless
warning against jumping to conclusions that may seem reasonable at the time, later
generations too often found it easier to dismiss the unenlightened seventeenth-
century fools who were stupid enough to even consider the possibility of harmful
magic, while simultaneously never really believing the charges that they supposedly
always lied about for material gain—land, prestige, or adulterous opportunity.[75]

---

*Boyer and Nissenbaum; Lyle Koehler's *A Search for Power*, 1980; Charles W. Upham's
Salem Witchcraft, 1867; Carol F. Karlsen, *The Devil in the Shape of a Woman*, 1987; N. E. H.
Hull's *Female Felons*, 1987.

†James M. Beard, *The Psychology of the Salem Witchcraft Excitement*, 1882; Carol F.
Karlsen, *The Devil in the Shape of a Woman*, 1987; Upham; Laurie Winn Carlson's *A Fever
in Salem*, 1999; Linda R. Caporael's "Ergotism; the Satan Loosed in Salem?" 1976; Earnest
Caulfield's "Pediatric Aspects of the Salem Witchcraft Tragedy," 1943; Chadwick Hansen's
Witchcraft at Salem, 1969).

‡Koehler; Karlsen; John Demos's *Entertaining Satan*, 1982; Boyer and Nissenbaum;
Charles Sutherland Tapley, *Rebecca Nurse: Saint But Witch Victim*, 1930; Koehler; Laurie
Cabot and Tom Cowan, *Power of the Witch*, 1989; Hansen.

In general, however, the Salem witchcraft trials have been remembered not so much as an historical event, but as a stereotype and symbol. Common opinion assumed that all subsequent political woes—such as Rev. Increase Mather's and Governor William Phips's—were reactions to their parts in the witchcraft trials, and overlooked the fact that Lieutenant Governor and Chief Justice William Stoughton's career never suffered from his actions. Public opinion blames the trials on the wretched ignorance of a people repressed by an utterly joyless religion (or by *any* religion, depending on the fervor of the critic), but ignores that the steadfast accused drew strength from the same faith as their accusers. Common opinions of the accused ranges more widely—from an assumption of spotless innocence to an assumption of malevolent intent. For although the trials rightly exemplify unfair persecution, public opinion still cherishes the possibility of supernatural evil.

While scholars lamented past superstitions, the old fears and beliefs lasted longer in everyday life. Suspicious neighbors who took the law into their own hands, however, landed in court on assault charges—like the Maine farmer who beat an old woman he thought had bewitched his cattle. Mindful of 1692, New Englanders never went as far as the mob in non-Puritan Philadelphia who—in 1787, while Congress labored to draft the Constitution—hounded an old woman through the streets. The mob, convinced that that she had magically killed a child, pummeled and pelted her severely enough that she died the following day.[76]

When the young Boston lawyer John Adams visited Salem in 1766, he saw a line of locust saplings on the ledge of "Witch Hill" at the traditional site of gallows and graves. The trees, Adams mused, seemed a "memorial of that memorable victory over the 'prince of the power of the air.'" The land, no longer common, belonged to Thorndike Proctor. (A great grandson of the John Proctor hanged there, Thorndike married a great granddaughter of Judge John Hathorne.) The locusts, probably only a windbreak, but confused eventually with the hanging tree, served as a landmark for generations. Another sapling, growing near the crevice in the ledge, formed a rough ring where its trunk divided just above the root, and then grew together a few feet higher. All during the eighteenth century people passed sick babies through the gap (as their European ancestors had done for millennia through similarly divided trees and holed stones) to protect the children, by this symbolic rebirth, from rickets and evil magic.[77]

Magical precautions continued well into the nineteenth century. In Beverly beekeepers hung black mourning crepe on their hives as well as on their homes after a family death, lest the bees take offense and leave. Householders nailed a horseshoe over the door and another at each corner of the house. Gloucester folk tried not to begin any enterprise on a Friday, or to associate with thirteen of *anything*, from buttons on a dress to guests at dinner. In Marblehead, girls told their fortunes by dropping hob nails into a pot of boiling tallow under the full moon; drowned fishermen's spirits wandered home (folk said) before their bodies washed ashore; and mothers warned children, if lost, to turn their jackets inside out to prevent being pixie-led.[78]

Some people avoided discussing the trials, but even after Salem Village had become the independent town of Danvers in 1757, witches remained a serious topic of conversation for others. One nineteenth-century inhabitant, a black centenarian, told Charles W. Upham that witchcraft broke out in 1692 when the Devil stole the church record book, but ended on its retrieval. Other locals said that the Devil kept a forge at Danvers in the alder swamp below Folly Hill. Skeptics speculated that the sound, like hammers on anvils, was the call of bitterns or some other marsh birds, but neighbors called it "the Tinker," and said that "it was the Devil forging chains for some poor critter."[79]

Rev. Peter Clark, who succeeded Rev. Joseph Green in the Salem Village pulpit, was roundly ridiculed for mentioning witchcraft in a letter to an English minister, but still had to warn his congregation against "consulting witches and fortune tellers." For cunning folk still worked their charms—like old Edward Diamond of Marblehead, who lived through 1692 unaccused to continue his helpful knacks of identifying thieves and telling fortunes. His granddaughter Moll Pitcher of Lynn continued the family tradition until her death in 1813. Their reputations were always benign, but gossips were none too sure about others: the Cape Cod woman who hag-rode the thief who stole her doughnuts; the black woman in Beverly whose white neighbors were nervous enough about her reputed evil-eye to be civil; or old lady Foster of Topsfield, who was thought to have magically mired a neighbor's hay cart as late as 1830.[80]

As the nineteenth century passed, "witches" tended to be professional fortune tellers and luck sellers—or old women facing hard times alone. The squatters on Gloucester's Dog Town Common included people from both categories. Aunt Angier lived alone with her one-eyed cat on Danvers's Fox Hill. She was willing to entertain small boys (though one had stoned the eye from her cat) with ballads, while they snickered behind their hands at her voice and her red flannel cap. Children suspected town eccentrics, too, like drunken old "Ma'am Carnes" of Salem, who lived in Samuel Shattuck's former house and who sewed a shimmering cape covered with milkweed tufts.[81]

And when a room's hearth fire, reflecting in window glass, appeared to be outdoors in the dark, younger children recited:

> . . . under the tree,
> When fire outdoors burns merrily,
> There the witches are making tea.[82]

As traditional fears of *maleficia* waned, the idea of a fictitious fairy-tale witch whom no sensible adult would fear, combined awkwardly with the real events and individuals of 1692. Oliver Wendell Holmes Sr. jested about invisible hags freed from Hell to power Essex County's new electric streetcars in his poem "The Broomstick Train: or, the Return of the Witches." He prefaced it with regret for the historical tragedy, recommended his brother-in-law Upham's books, and then portrayed a different idea altogether.

> Look out! Look out boys! Clear the track!
> The Witches are here! They've all come back!
> They hanged them high,—No use! No use!
> What cares a witch for a hangman's noose?
> They buried them deep, but they wouldn't lie still,
> For cats and witches are hard to kill[83]

Memories of the actual events of 1692 mutated into folklore and family tradition. The descendants of Philip English were especially reverential. After a century they forgot that Philip had hidden in the laundry, and now said that he had announced—from prison—that God would not allow the law to touch him. When his family returned from New York (the descendants said), all of Salem rejoiced and declared a thanksgiving. Philip hosted a feast for the poor in the ruins of his mansion and asked a contrite Rev. Nicholas Noyes to dine with him twice weekly thereafter—an arrangement free of real-life grudges. A few generations later, the family said that Philip had escaped to New York on a horse shod backward to confuse trackers, and had re-entered Salem in a carriage pulled by cheering townsfolk to accept a silver cup and heartfelt apologies from Judge John Hathorne himself.[84]

Another branch of the family had a different version. Eben Hathorne, descended from Englishes *and* Hathornes, told his cousin Nathaniel Hawthorne, the novelist, that Philip forgave Judge Hathorne only on his deathbed, and then qualified it with, "But if I get well, I'll be damned if I forgive him!" All legitimate English blood had passed into Hathorne's family by marriage, said Eben, for some of Philip's children were bastards. But Eben's *own* line actually descended from Susanna English, who had so discreetly referred to "my father Philip English and wife."[85]

Susanna's daughter had once told her pastor, Rev. William Bentley, how, due to her grandfather's grudge over the confiscations, Sheriff George Corwin's body was taken from his very funeral procession. Its burial—in the deceased's own cellar— was delayed several days until the Corwin family paid its debt in linens and silver plate. Others, however, thought that Corwin's family buried his body in the cellar for fear Philip English *might* try to steal it, while Upham said that English actually seized the corpse and held it for ransom. By the twentieth century, some versions had English drag the body from Corwin's house and gallop away with it over his saddle. (All of this may stem from a misreading of the arrest warrant served to Corwin shortly before his death. For the constable attested that he had "seized the body of . . . George Corwin"—the body being a *live* one. But the corpse did remain on Corwin property, because the family burying ground was then in George's back yard.)[86]

As fading memory and speculation clouded fact, nearly anything about seventeenth-century Essex County was associated with the witchcraft trials. Victorian Salemites pointed out the Pickering house as the place where condemned witches spent the night before their executions. Because a wing from the demolished Salem Village parsonage was accursed by its past (some said), it could not be carted to its new location in 1784 until the spell was removed by removing its roof. Or so later generations told the story when few remembered that the wing was built long *after* 1692. Even Salem Village's name change to Danvers was seen as an attempt to hide a shameful past—though Lynn Village had become Reading and Charlestown Village had become Woburn without comment.[87]

When a nineteenth-century ploughman uncovered a stash of Tudor and Elizabethan coins in Danvers, at least one elderly couple thought that it was "old crooked witch money" buried by Dorcas Hoar so the law couldn't take it. This story, however, required that a convicted criminal widely considered to be dangerous would have been released to settle her personal business alone and unguarded. Similarly, because a later generation of Proctors inhabited a house at Pigeon Cove, Gloucester, people said that Elizabeth Proctor and her sons had lived at this "Witch House" during her pregnancy in 1692.[88]

Beverly's "Witch Wood" had been a hiding place for suspects in some stories. In another, Giles Corey supposedly had taken a (geographically unlikely) short cut through the notorious woods when on parole to visit kin in Gloucester. Because he thereby returned to Salem sooner than the authorities thought natural, Giles was put to death at once. But that was twentieth-century vaporing. The nineteenth century used the name "Witch Woods" because walkers often lost their way there, or thought that they glimpsed a thriving farm that no longer existed.[89]

While rationalists like Charles W. Upham theorized a web of lies, and while his country neighbors hung protective horse shoes, others found a growing interest in the paranormal. Even people with a formal education and a mainstream Protestant background began to seek benign contact with departed human spirits, to experience their presences directly, and to prove the existence of the spiritual in an increasingly materialistic society. Having lumped contemporary Spiritualists with the bewitched, Upham decided that the girls had practiced the same (to him) fraudulent techniques. But the Spiritualist Allen Putnam, who knew Upham (and whose views would have shocked his Putnam ancestors), concluded that Tituba and the girls were natural mediums temporarily controlled by disembodied spirits *mistaken* for witches. The more skeptical also discerned the parallels of behavior even when they disagreed on the accuracy of mediums in general, on the honesty of some in particular, and on the actual source of their pronouncements.[90]

In 1692 and 1693 people reported various incidents (a shower of stones, levitation, and other invisible forces) that match reports studied seriously since—sometimes for possible use in Cold War espionage by countries officially against the idea of anything non-material (the former Soviet Union and East Germany). But whether the cause of these effects is spirits, electromagnetism, an as-yet-undefined human power, or misdirection (conscious or unconscious), reports of such phenomena are an intricate part of human nature and human history. People spied Giles Corey's restless spirit in the field where he died well into the nineteenth century, and some claimed to have glimpsed Mary Bridges's ghost pacing her brother's dooryard in the twentieth.[91]

The religion of the Puritans, never static to begin with, continued to evolve, as people pondered basic spiritual concerns in constantly changing times. Three centuries after the trials, Congregationalists were among those *least* likely to accept the literal existence of the Devil—much less of witches. At the same time, after England repealed the last of its laws against "fraudulent magic" in 1951, some people publicly identified *themselves* as Witches. They defined Witches as followers of a pre-Christian nature religion—one having nothing to do with the concept of devils—that had survived secretly despite all persecution.[92]

Adherents described their ceremonies as symbolic of spiritual values and the harmonies of nature, or as means to produce a benign magic that balanced those values. Psychic power was considered a natural (even if not commonly cultivated) human ability. Not all members emphasized this interpretation. Some disagreed whether the Craft was a re-creation or an actual continuing tradition, and, if the latter, whether it included specific rites and ceremonies or only a shared spiritual attitude.[93]

Much of twentieth-century Witchcraft seemed influenced by British Egyptologist Margaret Murray's reconstruction of a nature religion that supposedly lasted long enough to face the Inquisition (*The Witch-Cult in Western Europe*, 1921). But because Murray based her conclusions on testimony obtained by torture and by the inquisitors' leading questions, most scholars have dismissed her work as an embarrassing fiction. Some practicing Witches accepted the stories at face value; others as symbolic of human nature whatever the facts.[94]

But the authority of an ancient past has strong appeal. Even Witches who have written about the anachronisms and unsubstantiated claims have also asserted the Craft's continuing history as if it were undoubted. Many have referred to those accused in 1692 as co-religionists even though there is nothing documented in New England's history to support the idea.[95]

Nevertheless, Witchcraft became a part of the late twentieth century. Its presence influenced opinion about 1692—from writers who associated the "witch" suspects with traditional pagans, to tourists who mistook Salem for a theme park. Modern Witches founded their own anti-defamation leagues to inform the public of what they actually do—which does *not*, they repeat, involve evil magic, much less devil-worship.[96]

Reoccurring fears of Satanists—or Devil-worshipers—seem rooted more in a fear of what they might do physically to their victims than in a fear of *maleficia*. Police departments and other government agencies have monitored and infiltrated, in the past, groups from terrorists to innocents, but have yet to even locate secret organized Satanists. (The California-based Church of Satan describes itself as a hedonistic group, with Satan as a symbol of unfettered human vitality.) "Ritual" crimes that make headlines appear to be the work of loners and small disorganized groups, often teenagers, who veneer their cruelties with a patchwork of occult borrowings based on an ignorance of history and comparative religion often matched by the puzzled authorities. (Before his suicide one young self-sacrifice addressed the Devil as Yahweh, a traditional name of God.)[97]

All of these varying and evolving views have influenced opinion about 1692—both generally and locally. Danvers took a serious view of a still-regretted past. When the First Church staged an "Historical Pageant" in 1922 during a week-long, townwide anniversary celebration, symbolic witch-like characters represented a dread of the unknown. In one scene, black clad Superstition and Fear menaced alarmed Villagers until repelled by Light, costumed as an angel.[98]

But Salem—most widely known from Charles W. Upham's history and from Nathaniel Hawthorne's fiction—was nicknamed "Witch City" well before the bicentennial of the trials. National events, from the Colombian Exposition onward, focused attention on local history everywhere. In Salem, where tourists preceded tourism, that meant the witchcraft trials. Although Judge Jonathan Corwin's house had been altered greatly by the additions of an eighteenth-century gambrel roof and a Victorian drug store, it attracted enough of the curious for its owner to offer tours even before 1880. This was only the beginning.[99]

Outside interest began to spur the Salem economy. Despite limited business opportunities for women, Ida Upton began a china-painting career by first offering souvenir witches on beach pebbles. Salem jeweler Daniel Low launched a thriving mail-order business by advertising a witch spoon in 1890. When he issued another design for the bicentennial in 1892, some Salem guidebooks had already reached their fourteenth edition. Unable to believe that anyone could have taken the charges of witchcraft seriously, these guides both deplored the executions and ran ads for products either decorated with witches (from spoons to beanpots) or simply named for them: "Witch Cream, a delightful toilet requisite for Sunburn, Chaps, Pimples, Wrinkles, Rough skin and for the Complexion." While many Salemites felt that the souvenir-approach trivialized the tragedy of events best forgotten if not properly mourned, more and more local entrepreneurs used "Witch City" as a synonym for Salem, from Witch City Bottling Works ("Witch City appetizer a specialty"), to Witch City Cycle ("purveyor of Wizard cycles").[100]

Tourism was strong enough by the beginning of the twentieth century to support good works. In 1908 Caroline Emmerton bought the greatly altered Turner mansion to restore it as an historic and literary attraction that would help support the House of Seven Gables Settlement Association. Even ordinary, unrestored sites drew tourists, who toiled up Gallows Hill in the 1920s, unsure of what to look for and pestered by "a lot of tormenting children wanting a cent."[101]

Tourists had better luck finding the old jail after the Massachusetts tercentenary celebrations of 1930 placed an iron marker in front of it (for that building had been rebuilt, enlarged, and converted to a private home by 1818, and greatly altered thereafter).

After five years of pestering, the curious were admitted to a lecture and exhibit, held in the cellar "dungeon," that included William Dounton's bill for keeping the witch suspects, Nathaniel Hawthorne's tea pot, and even a note from Charles Darwin (about shoreline conditions rather than witches). When workmen destroyed the "Old Witch Jail" in 1956, they discovered a hidden upstairs room against the chimney block. Three of its walls were massive vertical slabs of oak tenoned top and bottom to grooves in the frame. Experts speculated about early prison construction and salvaged a few timbers, but the rest of the evidence disappeared in dust and splinters. (Judge Jonathan Corwin's home, called the "Witch House," had been luckier in 1944 when Historic Salem Incorporated formed to prevent its demolition when the city widened the street. The house was moved slightly, restored, and returned to the city as a tourist attraction.)[102]

Entertainment, as well as historical commemoration, focused outside attention on Salem, from Arthur Miller's cautionary stage play *The Crucible* in 1953 (later televised and twice filmed), to the TV situation comedy *Bewitched* (where an ordinary mortal was married to an innately magical witch), and the more historically realistic PBS drama *Three Sovereigns for Sarah* in 1986. A few exterior shots for *Bewitched* were even filmed in Salem during the early 1970s—at a time when large sections of the historical districts were at risk from "urban renewal." This situation drew more national notice, which only increased with the bicentennial observations of the American Revolution in 1976. To answer the tourists' increasing expectations, the Salem Witch Museum opened a few years later. The first of several such enterprises, the museum portrayed its story in tableaus of costumed mannequins augmented by light and sound.[103]

The influx of bicentennial tourists and the decline of factory jobs in the region encouraged the development of tourism as a major industry. The identification of Salem as Witch City continued unabated. Throughout the twentieth century, even business concerns that did not use the name used a witch logo for products as diverse as toilet paper, potato chips, and the evening news. Despite a minority of those with mixed feelings, the town called one of its municipal street-sweepers their "Witch's Broom" and, by the last quarter of the twentieth century, had replaced the town seal (of a Chinese merchant) on its police cars with an emblem of a witch on a broomstick.[104]

Merchants augmented their usual summer street fairs and Christmas shopping with October "Haunted Happenings" that attracted thousands and had people standing in lines around the block to tour the Witch House. At the height of summer, while locals competed with tourists for parking spaces, out-of-towners besieged the Chamber of Commerce's information booth asking how to find "that witch stuff." Visitors were surprised to learn that no witches had been burned, and disappointed to hear that Judge Jonathan Corwin's house was not haunted, (though many left believing the statue of Salem's founder Roger Conant represented a witch).[105]

Tourists also found the modern Witch community. When British Witch Sibyl Leek had visited the area on a promotional tour in 1966, she told bemused reporters that there was already a coven in Salem (among other places). But the public became more aware of the city's Witches after the arrival of Laurie Cabot, who established herself by writing and lecturing on Witchcraft as a religion and as a science. The Salem Voting List began noting her profession as "Witch" in 1976. In 1977 Cabot petitioned for and received a citation from Massachusetts Governor Michael Dukakis for her work with dyslexic children that named her "Official Witch of Salem." The governor's staff who rubber-stamped the honorarium called it a "Paul Revere citation," one of many routinely processed to give its recipient the right to pasture non-existent cows on Boston Common, or to toss metaphorical tea into Boston Harbor. A spokesman for the staff was annoyed that anyone found the "joke" controversial. Salem's Witch community was soon represented on both the Salem Chamber of Commerce *and* the Council of Churches.[106]

When Governor Michael Dukakis ran for the presidency of the United States in 1988, some fundamentalist groups—lumping modern Witchcraft with Satanism, and shocked at his "abomination" of appointing an Official Witch—lampooned Dukakis in a campaign comic book, and urged him to repudiate witchcraft publicly. (This was the same year that a "rumor panic" gripped a wide area of western New York, northwest Pennsylvania, and eastern Ohio. At its culmination—a Friday the thirteenth feared to be the date for Satanic human sacrifice—many parents kept their children out of school, and police had to deal with a hundred-car convoy of vigilantes.)[107]

Nevertheless, public opinion could still refer to Salem's "witch burnings" with a straight face, or assume that the people accused in the seventeenth century were the exact counterparts of modern Witches. Preferring scapegoats to understanding, it ignored the fact that Massachusetts was only the third government in the history of witchcraft trials even to *admit* an error so it could insist "nothing" had been done.[108]

Samuel Sewall, however, has been honored in one of Albert Herter's murals of "Milestones on the Road to Freedom in Massachusetts" in the Chamber of the Massachusetts House of Representatives. Sewall's Fast Day repentance (in which Rev. Samuel Willard unaccountably wears an Anglican-like cassock) is captioned "Dawn of Tolerance"—though tolerance of precisely *what* is not explained, since the accused, as a group, were hardly different from their accusers. Consequently, the legislature was aware of the Fast Day when a descendant of Ann Pudeator petitioned in 1946 (and several times thereafter) to clear her reputation. Although the original documents, including the Reversal of Attainder that had omitted her name, were available to them, the General Court assumed that "no other action" than the Fast had been taken. Possibly influenced by the public's interest following the television broadcast of Arthur Miller's *The Crucible*, the legislature finally resolved in 1957 that, although the "shocking" witchcraft laws may have been legal in 1692, they had since been abandoned. Therefore, "no disgrace or cause for distress attaches to the said descendants." Like its predecessors, the resolve omitted several of the names, but added a clause prohibiting lawsuits based on the old proceedings. The resolve named only "Ann Pudeator and certain other persons," but it was an improvement.[109]

As the tercentennial of the trials approached in 1992, "witches" could mean fictional fairy-tale characters, neo-pagan neighbors, unfairly accused historical individuals, or a staple of tourism. Salem and Danvers (formerly Salem Village) faced the problem of dealing with the public's preconceptions. (Tourists still arrived under the impression that hundreds—even thousands—of women had been burned alive over many decades.) Rather than treat the historical events as old-fashioned embarrassments or as an occasion for gallows humor, institutions of both towns concentrated on the trials' lessons in order to emphasize the continuing need for tolerance and truth—especially in the face of public panic.[110]

Salem's tercentennial committee labored against the city's huckster reputation (as more and more downtown businesses catered to tourists rather than to inhabitants), and against the tabloid publicity of a fraud case then in the Essex Courts.

(The accused had allegedly used rituals that he called "witchcraft" to convince the "mark" to part with money.) "Witch" was so touchy a term among materialists, fundamentalists, and neo-pagans alike that the U.S. Postal Service refused to issue a stamp honoring those executed in 1692—or so it was assumed, for the U.S. Post Office gave no explanation.[111]

Some local Witches, angry that the committee did not equate them with the "witches" of 1692, distributed leaflets accusing the tercentennial committee of hate crimes and cover-ups, and then cast a reversal spell on the commemorations.[112]

Nevertheless, both Salem and Danvers successfully sponsored several restrained and appropriate commemorative events, and each town built a material monument as a public reminder to the future. Danvers, less well-known to the general public, was better able to enact its memorials on a community level, and often included descendants of the accused. (Rather than feeling shame at the kinship, most descendants relished finding a "witch" in the family tree.)[113]

One of the most fitting events of 1992 was the funeral of George Jacobs Sr. By tradition, old Jacob's body had been removed from a common pit at the gallows and buried on his farm. So it was presumably *his* bones in the lone grave opened and examined by local antiquarians in the mid-nineteenth century. The location was forgotten after the farm's abandonment. Jacob's remains were bulldozed from their resting place in the 1950s. The developer boxed the bones, which then passed into the care of various Danvers historical agencies as one of the town's odder artifacts. In August 1992, apprehensive of sensational publicity, the tercentennial committee quietly fulfilled the legal and medical requirements that surrounded even three-hundred-year-old bones, and arranged a fourth (and presumably final) interment in the Nurse Homestead burying ground, near the final resting place of Rebecca Nurse.[114]

Danvers's Tercentennial Committee persuaded the Massachusetts House of Representatives to issue in 1992 a resolution honoring "the courage and steadfastness of these condemned persons who adhered to truth when the legal, clerical, and political institutions failed them." The document named the individuals omitted from the earlier Reversal of Attainder and from the Resolve, but it only noted that the victims of 1692 were "worthy of remembrance and commemoration." Their names, however, were still technically unprotected.[115]

It took many more years of persistence on the part of Salem schoolteacher Paula Keene and Representatives J. Michael Ruane and Paul Tirone (among others) to add, on October 25, 2001, the missing names of those executed for witchcraft in 1692 to the 1957 Resolve: Bridget Bishop, Susanna Martin, Alice Parker, Margaret Scott, and Wilmot Read.[116]

Ironically, and regrettably, the fear of malefic witchcraft is still a problem in many parts of the world. Neighbors and witch-finders in Africa, India, Slovakia, the Ukraine, and elsewhere blame suspects—often women—for causing local misfortunes. In India, where vigilantes have illegally killed 483 witch-suspects in the state of Bihar during the last decade, an unprotected widow who owns land her inlaws or neighbors covet might be identified as a witch, then shunned, brutalized, driven away, or even hacked to death. Suspicious neighbors also consult soothsayers in the Slovakia/Czech border area where, in 2001, a man was charged with beating an eighty-year-old woman to death. (He said she had caused his granddaughter's epileptic seizures.)[117]

On Halloween, **October 31, 2001**, in a time when an astonished nation faced the possibility of continuing violent attacks and hidden diseases and plagues, when the appearance of long-concealed terrorists among the population sparked fearful reactions against supposed "outsiders" who had nothing to do with the threat itself, and when all certainty had vanished from everyday life, Acting Governor Jane Swift signed the act to clear the names of the people executed for witchcraft in 1692. Descendants and supporters held an ecumenical service at Salem's First Church to honor the accused in June 9, 2002 (310 years after the hangings), to proclaim, as Paula Keene said of the resolve, "the true message of tragedy and hope that this event commemorates and deserves."[118]

Even if the law could no longer hurt them, all of the individuals who had suffered very real, and painful, and unnecessary deaths in 1692 were acknowledged officially by name as *innocent*.

APPENDIXES

A desolation of names.

—Rev. Cotton Mather

Note: not all documentation has survived.

Abbreviations & Symbols

bro = brother of
d = daughter of
s = son of
ch = children
m = married to
sis = sister of
cs = cousin of
wid = widow(er) of
A = known to have been Arrested
B = released on Bail
C = Confessed to witchcraft
E = Escaped
L = Let go after questioning and/or imprisonment

N = known to have been at least Named
Q = Questioned by magistrates & jailed (unless noted)
R = sentence Reprieved
T = Tried
U = Unable to pay jail fees
W = arrest Warrant extant
! = condemned to death
* = died (while afflicted, executed, or of disease, etc.)
affl = afflicted before accused
recant = tried to recant an earlier confession

APPENDIX A

Persons Accused of Witchcraft in and around 1692

Name of Accused	Age When Accused	Residence	Profession	Relations	Results
Abbott, Arthur	50s?	Ipswich, Topsfield, Wenham border	weaver		Q L
Abbott, Nehemiah Jr.	50s?	Topsfield	weaver, "hilly faced"		Q L
Alden, Capt. John	c. 66	Boston	merchant privateer		Q E
Andrews, Daniel	49	Salem Village	brick-mason, merchant		N E
Barker, Abigail (Wheeler)		Andover		m Ebenezer Barker	Q C
Barker, Mary	13	Andover		d Lt. John Barker	Q C T
Barker, William Sr.	46	Andover	farmer		Q C T
Barker, William Jr.	14	Andover		s **William Barker Sr.**	Q C T
Bassett, Sarah (Hood)	35	Lynn		m Wm. Bassett; s-in-law = **Mary DeRich, Elizabeth Proctor**	Q
Bates, i. e. "Goody Bates"		Lynn? or Malden?			N
***Bishop, Bridget** (Playfer) (Wasselbee) (Oliver)	50s?	Salem		m Edward Bishop, "sawyer" (not to be confused with Sarah Bishop)	Q T ! * hanged 10 June 1692
Bishop, Edward	40s	Salem Village	farmer	m **Sarah Bishop**	Q E
Bishop, Sarah (Wildes)	c 40	Salem Village		m **Edward Bishop**	Q E
Black, Mary		Salem Village	Nathaniel Putnam's slave		Q

Name	Age	Boxford? or Topsfield?			N
Black (. . .), i. e. "Goody Black"					N
Bradbury, Mary (Perkins)	c 80	Salisbury	m Capt. Thomas Bradbury		Q T ! E
Bradstreet, Ann (Wood) (Price)	c 40	Andover	m **Dudley Bradstreet**		N E
Bradstreet, Col. Dudley	44	Andover	magistrate	m **Ann Bradstreet**	N E
Bradstreet, John	40	Andover	bro **Dudley Bradstreet**		N E
Bridges, Mary (Tyler) (Post) **Sr.**	48	Andover	m John Bridges, blacksmith		Q C T
Bridges, Mary Jr.	12	Andover	d John & **Mary B.**		Q C T B
Bridges, Sarah	c 20	Andover?	d john B.; step-d **Mary B.**		Q C T
Broomage, Hannah (Farnum) (Tyler)	50s?	Haverhill	m Edward Broomage		Q C
Buckley, Sarah (Smith)		Salem Village	"scragged teeth"	m Wm. Buckley; d = **Mary Witheredge**	Q T
*****Burroughs, Rev. George**	c 42	Wells, Maine	minister (not ordained), formerly of Salem Village		Q T ! * hanged 19 Aug. 1692
Busse, John	52	Boston, & Durham, N. H.	physician & minister (not ordained)	s-in-law of **Mary Bradbury**	N
Candy		Salem	slave of **Margaret Hawkes**		Q C T
Carrier, Andrew	13	Andover	s Thos. & **Martha C.**		Q C tied neck & heels

(continued)

Name of Accused	Age When Accused	Residence	Profession	Relations	Results
*Carrier, Martha (Allen)	c 50	Andover		m Thos. Carrier "alias Morgan"	Q T !* hanged 19 Aug. 1692
Carrier, Richard	18	Andover		s Thos. & **Martha C.**	Q C tied neck & heels
Carrier, Sarah	8	Andover		d Thos. & **Martha C.**	Q C B
Carrier, Thomas Jr.	10	Andover	farmer	s Thos. & **Martha C.**	E C
Carroll, Hannah (. . .)		Salem		m Nathaniel C.	W
Carter, Bethia (Pearson) **Sr.**	40?	Woburn		m Joseph C.	Q B
Carter, Bethia Jr.	21	Woburn		d **Bethia Carter Sr.**	W W
Cary, Elizabeth (Walker)	c 50	Charlestown		m Capt. Nathaniel C.	Q E
Churchill, Sarah	20	Salem	servant to **George Jacobs Sr.**		Q C affl recant
Clark, Mary (Johnson) (Davis)		Haverhill		m Edward C.; wid. Ephraim D.; sis-in-law of **Eliz. & Rebecca J.**	Q
Clenton, Rachel	63	Ipswich		divorced from Laurence C.	Q
Cloyse, Sarah (Towne) (Bridges)	54	Topsfield		m Peter C.; sis **Mary Esty & Rebecca Nurse**	Q
Cole, Sarah (Asselbee)	34	Lynn		m John C., cooper; sis-in-law **Sarah Cole** of Salem	Q T affl
Cole, Sarah (Davis?)		Salem		m Abrahan C., tailor; sis-in-law **Sarah Cole** of Lynn	Q B

Name	Age	Place	Details	Status	Notes
Coleson, Elizabeth	16	Reading	d Adam & Mary Coleson	A	eluded arrest four months
Coleson, Mary (Dustin)	42	Reading	m Adam C., school master; d **Lydia Dustin**	Q	
***Corey, Giles**	c 80	Salem	farmer; m **Martha Corey**	Q*	pressed to death 19 Sept 1692
***Corey, Martha** (. . .) (Rich)		Salem	m **Giles Corey**	Q T!*	hanged 22 Sept 1692
Dane, Rev. Francis	76	Andover	minister of Andover; d = **Abigail Faulkner**; d-in-law = **Deliverance Dane**; nieces = **Martha Carrier, Eliz. How**	N	
Dane, Deliverance (Hasseltine)	41	Andover	m Nathaniel Dane; s of **Rev. Francis D.**	Q	
Darling ?, . . . (. . .) (or **Downing**)			perhaps Mary (Bishop) (Barney) Darling; m John D. of Salem Village	N	
Day, Phebe (Wildes)	35	Gloucester	m Timothy Day; sis **Sarah Bishop**; step-d **Sarah Wildes**	A	
Denmark, Bridget?	20s	Boston, once of Maine & N. H.	perhaps **Mrs. Thatcher's** maidservant; d Patrick & Hannah D.		

(continued)

Name of Accused	Age When Accused	Residence	Profession	Relations	Results
DeRich, Mary (Bassett)	37	Salem Village		m Michael DeRich; sis = **Sarah Basset,** sis-in-law = **Elizabeth Proctor**	A
Dicer, Elizabeth (Austin)		Gloucester & Boston		m Wm. D., seaman	A
Dike, Rebecca (Dolliver)	52?	Gloucester		m Richard Dike; sis-in-law = **Ann Dolliver**	A
Dolliver, Ann (Higginson)		Gloucester & Salem		m Capt. Wm. Dolliver who deserted her, lived with f Rev. Jn. Higginson of Salem	A Q
Downing, Mehitable (Braybrook)	40	Ipswich		m Jn. D.	A
Draper, John		Andover			Q C
*****Dustin, Lydia** (. . .)	c 80	Reading	"crooked back"	wid of Josiah Dustin	Q T U died in jail 10 Mar. 1693
Dustin, Sarah	39	Reading		d **Lydia Dustin**	Q T
Eames, Daniel	28	Boxford	farmer	s **Rebecca Eames**	A Q
Eames, Rebecca (Blake)		Boxford		m Robert E.; s = **Daniel Eames**	R
*****Esty, Mary** (Towne)	58	Topsfield		m Isaac e:; sis = **Sarah Cloyse, Rebecca Nurse**	Q A L A T ! * hanged 22 Sept. 1692
Elwell, Esther (Dutch)	53	Gloucester		m Sml. E.	Q

Name	Age	Town	Occupation	Relations/Notes	Status
Emerson, Martha (Toothaker)	24	Haverhill		m Joseph E.; d **Roger & Martha Toothaker**; aunt = **Martha Carrier**	Q
Emmons, Joseph	40?	Manchester	shoe-maker?		N
English, Mary (Hollingsworth)		Salem	kept shop?	m Philip English; d **Eleanor H.**	Q E
English, Philip	41	Salem	merchant born Philippe L'Anglais in Jersey	m **Mary English**	Q E
Farrar, Thomas Sr.	c 77	Lynn	farmer		A
Farrington, Edward	30	Andover	farmer		Q C indicted in Jan. '93 but sentence "staid"
Faulkner, Abigail (Dane) **Sr.**	40	Andover		m Francis Faulkner; d **Rev. Dane**	Q C T ! R
Faulkner, Abigail Jr.	8	Andover		d Francis & **Abigail F. Sr.**	Q C B
Faulkner, Dorothy	10	Andover		d Francis & **Abigail F. Sr.**	Q C B
Flood, Capt. John	c 55	Rumney Marsh	landowner, militia capt.		W
Fosdick, Elizabeth (Thomas?) (Lisley) (Betts)	36	Malden		m John Fosdick	Q
*****Foster, Ann** (Alcock?)	70s	Andover		wid Andrew Foster; "mother of Abraham Foster" & **Mary Lacy** Sr; grm **Mary Lacy Jr.**	Q C T ! died in jail 3 Dec. 1692

(continued)

Name of Accused	Age When Accused	Residence	Profession	Relations	Results
Frost, Nicholas		Piscataqua, N. H.			N
Fry, Eunice (Potter)	50	Andover		m Deacon John Fry	Q C B
Gl[. . .], M			i.e. confessor M (Mrs.? G.?)		C
Gale, . . . (. . .)		Beverly?			N
Good, Dorcas (or **Dorothy**)	4 or 5	Salem Village		d **Sarah Good**	Q B
*****Good, Sarah** (Stoular) (Poor)	30s	Salem Village		m William G.; d = **Dorcas G.**	Q T ! * hanged 19 July 1692
Green Mary (Green)		Haverhill		m Peter G.	E (twice) B
Griggs, . . . (. . .) "Goody Griggs"	60s?			maybe Rachel (Hubbard) Griggs	if so, m physician Wm. Griggs; aunt of Elizabeth Hubbard
Hale, Sarah (Noyes)	36	Beverly		m Rev. John Hale	N
Haffield see **Clenton**					
Hardy, Thomas		Great Island, Piscataqua, N. H.	in court as drunkard		N
Hart, Elizabeth (Hutchinson?)		Lynn		m Isaac Hart	Q
Hawkes, Margaret (. . .)		Salem, "late of Barbadoes"		wid Thomas Hawkes? owned **Candy**	A
Hawkes, Sarah	21	Andover		d **Sarah Wardwell** by 1st husb., Adam Hawkes	A
Hoar, Dorcas	50s?	Beverly	told fortunes	wid Wm. H.	Q T ! C R

Name	Age	Town			Q C T ! R
Hobbs, Abigail	15	Topsfield	had been servant to **Rev. George Burroughs** in Casco Bay	d **Wm. Hobbs** & step-d of **Deliverance Hobbs**	
Hobbs, Deliverance (. . .)		Topsfield		m **William Hobbs**; step-d = **Abigail H.**	Q C
Hobbs, William	c 50	Topsfield	farmer, swept meeting house	m **Deliverance Hobbs**; f **Abigail H.**	Q B
Hollingsworth, Eleanor (Story)	58	Salem		wid Wm. H.; d = **Mary English**	N, died 1689
*__How, Elizabeth__ (Jackson)	50s?	Ipswich		m James How; sis **John Jackson**; niece of **Rev. Dane**	Q T ! * hanged 19 July 1692
How, James	c 57	Ipswich	farmer, blind	m. **Eliz. How**; nephew of **Rev. Dane**; cs = **Eliz Johnson**, & **Abigail Faulkner**	N
Howard, John	30s?	Rowley	laborer, swept meeting house		Q B
Hutchins, Frances (. . .)	60s?	Haverhill		wid John H.; son Samuel H.; Rep. to Gen. Ct. 1692	A B
Indian, Tituba (see Tituba)					
Ireson, Mary (Leach)	50s?	Lynn		m Benj. I.	Q
Jackson, John Sr.	50s?	Rowley	laborer	bro. **Eliz. How**; s = **John Jackson Jr.**	Q
Jackson, John Jr.	22	Rowley	laborer	sn **John Jackson** Sr.; aunt = **Eliz. How**	Q C

(continued)

Name of Accused	Age When Accused	Residence	Profession	Relations	Results
*Jacobs, George Sr.	c 80	Salem	farmer, (walked with two canes, perhaps no teeth)	m Mary; s = **George Jacobs Jr**; d-in-law = **Rebecca Jacobs**; grdau = **Margaret Jacobs22**	Q T ! * hanged 19 Aug. 1692
Jacobs, Margaret	17	Salem	worked for grandfather, **George J. Sr.**	dau **George Jr.** & **Rebecca J**; grf = **George J. Sr.**	Q C T affl. recant
Jacobs, Rebecca (Andrews) (Frost)	46	Salem Village	"crazy & distracted & broken in mind" 12 years	m **George J. Jr**; bro = **Daniel Andrews**; dau = **Margaret J**; f-in-law = **George J. Sr.**	Q T
Johnson, Abigail	11	Andover		d Stephen & **Elizabeth Johnson**; grdau **Rev. Dane**	Q B
Johnson, Elizabeth Sr. (Dane)	c 50?	Andover	"weak, incapatious, fearfull."	wid. Stephen J; dau **Rev. Francis Dane**; dau = **Abigail, Eliz. Jr.** sis-in-law = **Rebecca Johnson** & **Mary Clark**	Q C T
Johnson, Rebecca (Aslebee)	50	Andover	swept meeting house	wid Timothy J; sis **Sarah Cole** of Lynn; sis in law = **Eliz. Johnson Sr.** & **Eliz. Clark**	Q C

Name	Age	Place	Notes	Relationship	Code
Johnson, Rebecca Jr.	c 17	Andover		dau **Rebecca Johnson Sr.**	Q C
Johnson, Stephen	c 13	Andover		s of Stephen & **Eliz. J.**	Q C B
Lacy, Mary (Foster) **Sr.**	40	Andover		m Laurence Lacy; dau **Ann Foster**; dau = **Mary L. Jr.**	Q C
Lacy, Mary Jr.	18	Andover		dau Laurence & **Mary Lacy**; **grdau Ann Foster**	Q C T
Lawrence, . . . , (. . . .)			perhaps **Mary Lacy Sr.?** whose husb's name, Lawrence, had varied spelling		N
Lee, John		Ipswich?			N
Lilly, Jane (. . .) (Osgood)	50s	Reading / Andover		wid George Lilly; m John M.	Q B **Marston, Mary** / Q C T
***Martin, Susanna** (North)	70s	Amesbury	"a short old woman"	wid George Martin	Q T ! hanged 19 July 1692
Mather, Rev. Cotton	30	Boston	minister 2nd Church	sn Rev. Increase & **Maria** (Cotton) **M.**	N (in 1693)
Mather, Maria (Cotton)		Boston		m Rev. Increase M.; sn = **Rev. Cotton M.**	N by later gossip
Moody, Ann (. . .) (Jacobs)		Boston		m Rev. Joshua Moody	N by later gossip
Morrell, Sarah		Beverly		dau Peter & Mary M.	Q
Nurse, Rebecca (Towne)	71	Salem Village		m Francis N.; sis = **Sarah Cloyse, Mary Esty**	Q T ! * hanged 19 July 1692

(continued)

Name of Accused	Age When Accused	Residence	Profession	Relations	Results
Obinson, Mary (. . .)		Boston		m Wm. O., tanner	N
Oliver, Bridget (see **Bridget Bishop**)					
***Osborne, Sarah** (Warren?) (Prince)		Salem Village			Q* died in prison 10 May 1692
Osgood, Mary (Clement)	60s	Andover		m Capt. John Osgood	
***Parker, Alice** (. . .)		Salem		m John P., fisherman	Q T ! hanged 22 Sept. 1692
***Parker, Mary** (Ayer)		Andover	subject to catalepsy	wid Nathan Parker; d = **Sarah P.**	Q T ! * hanged 22 Sept. 1692
Parker, Sarah	14	Andover		d Nathan & **Mary P.**	A
Paine, Elizabeth (Carrington)	53	Malden		m Stephen P.	Q
Pease, Sarah (. . .)		Salem		m Robert P., weaver	W
Penney, Joan (. . .) (White) (Braybrook)		Gloucester		wid Thomas Penney; step-d = **Mehitable Downing**	A
Phips, Lady Mary (Spencer) (Hull)		Boston		m Sir William Phips, Gov. of Mass.	N
Post, Hannah	30?	Boxford		dau Richard & Mary Post (now **Mary Bridges**); sis = **Susanna & Mary Post**	Q C T

Name	Age	Residence	Note	Relationship	Status
Post, Mary	28	Rowley		dau Richard & Mary Post (now **Mary Bridges**); sis = **Hannah & Susanna Post**	Q C T ! R
Post, Susanna	26	Andover or Boxford?		dau Richard & Mary Post (now **Mary Bridges**); sis = **Hannah & Mary Post**	Q C T
Prince, Margaret (. . .)	66	Gloucester		wid Thomas Prince	Q B
Proctor, Benjamin	33	Salem		s **John** & Martha **P.**	W
Proctor, Elizabeth (Bassett)	40s?	Salem		m **John Proctor**; stepsn = **Benjamin P.**; ch = **Sarah & Wm.**; sis **Mary DeRich**; sis-in-law = **Sarah Bassett**	Q T ! R
***Proctor, John**	60	Salem	farmer	m **Elizabeth Proctor**; ch =**Benjamin, Sarah, Wm.**	Q T ! * hanged 19 Aug. 1692
Proctor, Sarah	16	Salem		d **John & Elizabeth P.**	W
Proctor, William	17	Salem		s **John & Elizabeth Proctor**	Q
***Pudeator, Ann** (. . .) (Greenslett)				wid Jacob Pudeator	Q T ! * hanged 22 Dept. 1692
Randall, Mary		Westfield or Northampton	free on bond for good behavior in 1692	d William & Mary R.	Q Dept. 1691

(continued)

Name of Accused	Age When Accused	Residence	Profession	Relations	Results
*Read, Wilmot (. . . .)		Marblehead		m Samuel Read	Q T ! * hanged 22 Sept. 1692
Rice, Sarah (Davis)		Reading		m Nicholas Rice	Q
Robinson, Dean	c 20	Andover	farmer?		N
Roe, Abigail	15	Gloucester		grsn of **Rev. Francis Dane**	
				d Hugh & **Mary Roe**	A
Roe, Mary (Prince)	34	Gloucester		m Hugh Roe; d = **Abigail Roe**	A
Roots, Susanna (. . .)		Beverly		wid Josiah Roots?	A
S . . . . (. . .) a widow addressed as "GS" (Goody S.?)					E
Salter, Henry		Andover	farmer		E
Saltonstall, Nathaniel	53	Haverhill	landowner militia officer, Oyer & Terminer judge, resigned		N
Sawdey, John	13	Andover			B
*Scott, Margaret (Stevenson)	70s?	Rowley		wid Benjamin Scott	Q T ! * hanged 22 Sept. 1692
Sears, Ann (. . .) (Farrar)		Woburn		m John Sears	A B
Sheldon, Susanna	18	Salem	servant	d Wm. & Rebecca S.	Q C affl.
Shepard, Rev. Jeremiah		Lynn	minister of Lynn		N by later gossip

Name	Age	Residence	Notes	Relation	Code
Soames, Abigail	37	Salem		d Morris & Eliz.? S.; perhaps grd of **Goody Kendall** of Cambridge hanged for witchcraft	Q
Sparkes, Martha	36	Chelmsford	in jail through 1692	m Henry S.	A 27 Oct. 1691
St[evens]?		Andover			N fled
Swift, Sarah (Clapp)	50s?	Milton		m Thomas Swift; their servant = **Mary Watkins**	N
Taylor, Mary (Harrington)		Reading		m Seabred Taylor	Q C T
Thatcher, Margaret (Webb) (Sheafe)	67	Boston		wid Rev. Thomas Thatcher; servant = **Bridget Denmark**	N
Tituba (also called **Tituba Indian**)		Salem Village	slave to Rev. Sam. Parris, she & John both "Spanish Indians"	m John Indian	Q C
Tookey, Job		Beverly	laborer, waterman		Q T
Toothaker, [Margaret?]	9	Billerica		"dau of **Roger Toothaker**," arrested with mother **Mary T.**	A
Toothaker, Mary	48	Billerica		m **Roger Toothaker**; dau = **Margaret Toothaker, Mary Emerson**; sis = **Martha Carrier**	Q C T

(continued)

Name of Accused	Age When Accused	Residence	Profession	Relations	Results
Toothaker, Roger	58	Salem (deserted family, stayed in Billerica)	folk healer, cunningman, witch-finder	m Martha T.	Q* died Boston Jail June 16, 1692, of "natural causes"
Tyler, Hannah	13?	Andover		d Hopestill & **Mary Tyler**	T
Tyler, Johanna	12	Andover		d Hopestill & **Mary Tyler**	Q C B T
Tyler, Joseph	25			s Moses & Prudence T.; stepsis = Martha Sprague	N
Tyler, Martha	16	Andover		d Hopestill & **Mary Tyler**	Q C B
Tyler, Mary (Lovett)	35	Andover		m Hopestill Tyler	Q C T
Usher, Hezekiah	53	Boston	merchant	bro = John U., Lt. Gov., N. H.	A E
Vincent, Rachel (. . .) (Cook) (Langton)		Gloucester		wid William Vincent	A
Wardwell, Mercy	19	Andover		d **Samuel & Sarah W.**	Q C T
*****Wardwell, Samuel**	49	Andover	farmer, carpenter fortune-teller	m Sarah Wardwell	Q C T ! hanged 22 Sept. 1692
Wardwell, Sarah (Hooper) (Hawkes)	42	Andover		m **Samuel Wardwell**	Q C T ! R
Warren, Mary	20	Salem	**Proctor**'s hired girl		Q C affl, recant

Name	Age	Location	Description	Relations	Status
Watkins, Mary		Milton	servant to **Swift** family, petitioned to be sold as bondservant		Q C T affl, recant, tried suicide
White, ... (. . . .), i.e., Goody White or Whits	20s?	Boston			N
White, Judah		Boston	a "Jersey maid" once at Casco Bay		N
*****Wildes, Sarah** (Averill)		Topsfield		m John W.; sn = Constable Ephraim W.; stepdaus = **Sarah Bishop** & **Phebe Day**	Q T ! * hanged 19 July 1692
Wilford, Ruth		Haverhill			A
Wilkinson, ... (. . . .)		Malden		S. Cole of Lynn saw spectre of "wife of John Wilkinson of Malden," perhaps Abigail (Gowing) W.?	N
*****Willard, John**	20s?	Salem Village or Boxford	farmer, average height, black hair	m Margaret Wilkins grd of Bray W.	flees, caught, Q T ! * hanged 19 Aug. 1692
Willard, Rev. Samuel	52	Boston	minister 3rd Church		N
Wilson, Sarah (Lord) Sr.		Andover		m Joseph W.	Q C B
Wilson, Sarah Jr.		Andover		d Joseph & **Sarah W.**	Q C B
Witheredge, Mary (Buckley)		Salem Village		wid Sylvester W; d Wm. & **Sarah Buckley**	Q T

Also:

Mrs. Thatcher's maid, Boston (see **Bridget Denmark**)

A sister of the wife of John Wilkinson, Malden, N

Nathaniel Dane's manservant, Andover, A

Sarah Davis of Newbury (arrested "betwixt Wenham and Ipswich" on June 28, 1692, by the constable who arrested Mary Bradbury the same day; petitioned with Mary Watkins to be sold as bondservant).

Others are assumed to have been witch suspects solely because they were jailed during 1692. (Court records make it clear people were jailed on other charges—burglary, etc.—though specific reasons are sometimes lost.) These include:

Chamberlain, Rebecca (Shelly?)—Billerica, m William C.; died in Cambridge jail September 26, 1692.

Cox, Mary—perhaps Mary (Mason) Cox of Salem, age 45, wife of George C.; or her daughter Mary age 20.

Durrant, John, Billerica, 50s? farmer; died in Cambridge jail October 27, 1692.

Ryer, Thomas

Connecticut Suspects

Allen, John Hartford, Secretary of Connecticut

Benham, Winifred (King?). Wallingford, m Joseph B.

Benham, Winifred Jr. Wallingford, dau Joseph & Winifred B.

Clawson, Elizabeth (Periment?). Fairfield, m Stephen C.

Crump, . . . (. . .), i.e., "Goody Crump"

Crosia, Hugh. Stratford

Disborough, Mercy (Holbridge). Campo, m Thomas D.

Harvey, Hannah. Fairfield, dau Josiah & Mary H.

Harvey, Mary (Staples). Fairfield, m Josiah H.; dau Mary Staples

Miller, . . . (. . .). Fairfield

Staples, Mary (. . .). Fairield

APPENDIX B

The Afflicted

These people were named as victims in court documents or other contemporary sources. The list does not include the "confessors," small children diagnosed by their fearful parents, or grown men who did not take legal action for their illnesses.

Name of Afflicted	Age	Residence	Relations
Babson, Eleanor (Hill)	61	Gloucester	wid James Babson
* **Ballard, Elizabeth** (Phelps)	30s	Andover	m Joseph Ballard
Bailey, Joseph	44	Newbury	
Barnam, ...		Andover?	
Bibber, Sarah (. . .) (. . .)	36	Salem	m John Bibber
Bixsbey, Hannah (Chandler)	30s	Andover	m Daniel Bixsbey; cs = **Eliz. Ballard**
Booth, Alice	14	Salem	d widow Schafflin
Booth, Elizabeth	18	Salem	d widow Schafflin
Booth, Elizabeth (Wilkins)	16	Salem	m **George Booth**; sis **Daniel** & **Rebecca Wilkins**
Booth, George	21	Salem	s widow Schafflin; m **Elizabeth** (Wilkins) **Booth**

Name of Afflicted	Age	Residence	Relations
Branch, Katherine		Fairfield, Conn.	Dnl. Westcott's French servant girl
Bragg, Henry	10	Salem	s William B.
Brown, Mary (Fellows?)	50s	Reading	wid Josiah Brown
Chandler, Phebe	12	Andover	d Wm. & Bridget C.; cs = **Sarah Phelpes**
Chibbun, Joanna (perhaps **Susanna Sheldon**?)			
Churchill, Sarah	20	Salem	d John & Sarah? C **George Jacob Sr.**'s hired girl
Cole, John	30s	Lynn	m **Sarah Cole**
Cole, Sarah (Aslebee)	34	Lynn	m **John Cole**; sis **Rebecca Johnson**
Coleman, Sarah		Rowley	
Daniel, Mary	14	Rowley	
DeRich, John	16	Salem	s **Mary DeRich**; aunts = **Sarah Bassett, Elizabeth Proctor**
Dodd, Johanna		Marblehead	d Thomas Dodd
*Farnum, Ralph Sr.	59?	Andover	
*Fitch, Mary (Stevens)	50s	Gloucester	m John Fitch
Foster, Hannah (Eames)	31	Andover	m **Ephraim Foster**; d **Rebecca Eames**
*Foster, Rose	14	Andover	d Ephraim & **Hannah Foster**; grd **Rebecca Eames**
Fuller, Elizabeth	14	Ipswich	d Joseph & Mary F.; cs **Mary F.**
Fuller, Mary	c 14	Ipswich	cs **Elizabeth F.**
Goodall, Margaret (Lazenby)?	"ancient"	Salem	wid Robert G.?
Herrick, Mary	16	Wenham	d John & Mary (Readington) H.
Hewes, Betty			
Hill, Mary	25	Salem	d Zebulon H.; niece **Elaenor Babson**
Hobbs, Deliverance	c 50	Topsfield	m **William H.**; stepm **Abigail H.**
Hubbard, Elizabeth	17	Salem Village	d Benjamin H.; niece of Rachel Griggs
Hutchinson, Jane (Phillips)	20s	Salem Village	m Benjamin H.
Indian, John		Salem Village	m **Tituba**, slave of Rev. Parris

Name of Afflicted	Age	Residence	Relations
Lewis, Mercy	17	Salem Village	d Phillip L.; Tom Putnam's maid, had worked for Rev. Burroughs
Maccarter, Rebecca (Meacham)	30s	Salem	m John M.
Marshall, Mary (Swain) (Clark)	50?	Reading	wid Thomas Clark & Edward Marshall
Martin, Abigail	16	Andover	d Samuel Martin
Parris, Elizabeth (Eldridge) **Sr.**	c 44	Salem Village	m Rev. Samuel Parris; d = **Elizabeth Parris Jr.**
Parris, Elizabeth Jr. (Betty)	9	Salem Village	d Rev. Samuel & **Elizabeth P.**
Phelpes, Sarah	9	Andover	d Samuel Phelpes; cs = **Phebe Chandler**
Pickworth, Mary	17	Salem	d John P.
Pope, Bethshua (Folger)	30s	Salem	m Joseph Pope
Putnam, Ann (Carr) **Sr.**	31	Salem Village	m Thomas P;. d = **Ann P. Jr.**
Putnam, Ann Jr.	12	Salem Village	d Thos. & **Ann Putnam**
Rea, Jemima	12	Salem Village	d Daniel Rea
Reddington, Mary (Gould)	c 71	Topsfield	
Ring, Joseph	27	Amesbury	
Sargent, Mary (Duncan)	33?	Gloucester	m William S., the J.P.
Sheldon, Susannah	18	Salem	d William S.
Short, Mercy	17	Boston	d Clement & Faith Short
Sprague, Martha	16	Andover	d Phineas & Mary Sprague; stepd Job Tyler
***Swan, Timothy**	29	Andover/Haverhill	
Thorne, Mary	c 14	Ipswich	
Towne, Rebecca		Topsfield	d William & Mary T.; aunts = Sarah Cloyce, Mary Esty, Rebecca Nurse
W. . ., Capt. . . [**Wycomb, Daniel?**]	[57?]	[Rowley?]	[d = **Frances Wycomb**]
Walcott, Mary	17	Salem Village	d Jonathan & Mary W.
Warren, Mary	20	Salem	the Proctors' hired girl
Watkins, Mary		Milton	d Thomas & Mary W.; Swifts' hired girl

Name of Afflicted	Age	Residence	Relations
Weston, Elizabeth	29?	Reading	d John Weston
Whetford, . . . (. . .) i.e. "Goody Whetford"		Salem	
Wilkins, Bray	c 81	Salem Village	grf of all **Wilkinses** below & **Eliz.** (Wilkins) **Booth**; grs-in-law = **John Willard**
*****Wilkins, Daniel**	17	Salem Village	s Henry & Rebecca W.; uncle = **John Willard**; bro **Eliz. Booth, Rebecca W.**
Wilkins, Rebecca		Salem Village	d Henry & Rebecca W.; sis **Eliz. Booth** & **Daniel W.**
Wilkins, Samuel	19	Salem Village	s Samuel W. Sr.
*****Williams, Abigail**	11	Salem Village	niece of Rev. Parris
Woodwell, Elizabeth		Salem	
Wycomb, Frances	20?	Rowley	d **Capt. Daniel Wycomb** [Capt. W.]

Also:

"Peter Tufts's Negro woman (Nannee?)		Medford	
"a girl at Pitman's"		Manchester	
Rule, Margaret (1693)	20?	Boston	d John & Emm R.

APPENDIX C

Salem Village Church Membership during the Time of Samuel Parris

Nov. 19, 1689

1. Samuel Parris
2. Nathaniel Putnam
3. John Putnam
4. Bray Wilkins
5. Joshua Rea
6. Nathaniel Ingersoll
7. Peter Cloyse
8. Thomas Putnam
9. John Putnam Jr.
10. Edward Putnam
11. Jonathan Putnam
12. Benjamin Putnam
13. Ezekiel Cheever
14. Henry Wilkins
15. Benjamin Wilkins
16. William Way
17. Peter Prescott
18. [Samuel Abbie]
19. Abraham Walcott
20. Zechariah Goodale

1. Elizabeth Parris
2. Rebecca Putnam
3. Anna Wilkins
4. Sarah Rea
5. Hannah Putnam
6. Sarah Putnam
7. Sarah Putnam
8. Deliverance Walcott
9. Persis Way
10. Mary Abbie

Jan. 9, 1689/90

Date		
Jan. 12, 1689/90		11. Sarah Cloyse
Feb. 9, 1689/90		12. Elizabeth Cutler
Feb. 16, 1689/90		13. Priscilla Wilkins
	21. Aaron Way	14. Mary Way
		15. Mary Putnam
	22. James Putnam	16. Mary Flint
Mar. 2, 1689/90	23. Samuel Nurse	17. Lydia Putnam
	24. John Tarbell	
Mar. 16, 1689/90	25. Thomas Wilkins	
	26. Samuel Sibley	
Mar. 23, 1689/90		19. Mary Nurse
		20. Hannah Holten
Mar. 30, 1690	27. George Flint	21. Elizabeth Flint
		22. Ruth Fuller
Apr. 27, 1690		23. Lydia Hutchinson
		24. Martha Corey
		25. Mary Sibley
May 25, 1690		26. Sarah Bishop
June 8, 1690		27. Abigail Cheever
Aug. 10, 1690		28. Elizabeth Gould
May 31, 1691		29. Hannah Wilkins
		30. Sarah Fuller
June 4, 1691		31. Ann Putnam
July 12, 1691		32. Abigail Walcott
		33. Elizabeth Buxton
		34. Abigail Holten
Aug. 30, 1691		35. Hannah Wilkins
July 23, 1693	28. Joseph Whipple "on 1 Nov. next"	
Sept. 17, 1693		36. Sarah Prince
Sept. 24, 1693		37. Hannah Ingersoll
Mar. 11, 1694	29. Jonathan Wilkins	
Jan. 27, 1694/95		38. Mary Wheldon
May 31, 1695	30. Thomas Fuller	
Oct. 8, 1695	Peter & Sarah Cloyse dismissed to Marlborough.	
May 31, 1696		39. Mary Hutchinson
		40. Hannah Putnam
Oct. 11, 1696	William & Persis Way, Aaron & Mary Way dismissed to Dorchester Church.	

APPENDIX D

Petitioners for the Accused

These lists name people who signed petitions on behalf of the various accused, but does not include additional people who also testified in court or who wrote favorable depositions.

Two Petitions for Rebecca Nurse

Aborn, Samuel Jr.
Andrews, Daniel
Andrews, Sarah
Bishop, Edward Sr.
Bishop, Hannah
Cloyse, Peter
Cook, Elizabeth
Cook, Isaac
Endicott, Samuel
Felton, Nathaniel Sr.
Holton, Joseph Sr.
Holten, Joseph Jr.
Hutchinson, Joseph
Hutchinson, Lydia
Leach, Sarah

Osborne, Hannah
Osborn, William
Philips, Margaret
Phillips, Tabitha
Phillips, Walter Sr.
Porter, Elizabeth
Porter, Israel
Putnam, Benjamin
Putnam, Jonathan
Putnam, Joseph
Putnam, Lydia
Putnam, Rebecca
Putnam, Sarah
Rea, Daniel
Rea, Hepzibah
Rea, Joshua
Rea, Sarah

Sibley, Samuel
Swinnerton, Esther
Swinnerton, Job

A Petition for John Proctor, and Another for John and Elizabeth Proctor

Andrews, John Sr.
Andrews, John Jr.
Andrews, Thomas (of Ip.)
Andrews, William
Burnham, John Sr.
Burnham, John Jr.
Butler, William
Choate, John
Choate, Thomas
Cogswell, John Sr.
Cogswell, John Jr.
Cogswell, Jonathan
Cogswell, William Sr.
Cogswell, William Jr.
Endicott, Hannah
Endicott, Samuel
Eveleth, Joseph
Fellows, John
Felton, John
Felton, Nathaniel Sr.
Felton, Nathaniel Jr.
Felton, Mary
Foster, Isaac
Fraile, Samuel
Gaskell, Edward
Gaskell, Provided
Gaskell, Samuel
Gidding, Samuel
Goodhue, William
Holten, James
Holten, Ruth
Locker, George
Lovkin, Thomas
Low, Thomas Sr.
Marsh, Mary
Marsh, Priscilla
Marsh, Samuel

Marsh, Zachariah
Marshall, Benjamin
Perkins, Isaac
Perkins, Nathaniel
Smith, George
Stone, Samuel
Story, William
Thomson, William
Varney, Thomas
White, James
Wise, John (Rev.)

Petition for Mary Bradbury

Allen, Benjamin Sr.
Allen (wife of Benj.)
Allen, Benjamin Jr.
Allen, James
Allen, John
Allen, Mary
Allen, Rachel
Allen, William (of Ip.)
Ambrose, Henry
Ambrose (wife of Henry)
Bill, Samuel
Bill (wife of Saml.)
Brown, Abraham
Brown (wife of Abe.)
Brown, Hannah
Brown Henry Sr.
Brown (wife of Henry Sr.)
Brown, Nathaniel
Buswell, Isaac
Buswell (wife of Isaac)
Buswell, Sarah
Buswell, William
Carr, Elizabeth
Carr, William
Clough, John
Clough (wife of John)
Clough, Thomas
Clough (wife of Thos.)
Colby, Samuel
Conner, John

Conner (wife of Jn.)

Conner, Sarah

Downer, Robert

Downer, Sarah

Eastman, Ann

Eastman, Benjamin

Eastman, Elizabeth (Sr.)

Eastman, Elizabeth (Jr.)

Eastman, John

Eastman, Nathaniel

Eastman, Roger

Eastman, Samuel

Eastman, Sarah

Eaton, Ephraim

Eaton, Joseph

Eaton, Mary

Evans, Hannah

Evans, Thomas

Fellows, Abigail

Fellows, Samuel Sr.

Fellows, Samuel Jr.

Fletcher, Joseph

Fletcher (wife of Jos.)

French, Abigail

French, John Sr.

French, Joseph

French, Mary

French, Samuel

French (wife of Sml.)

Gatchell, Elizabeth

Greley, Andrew

Greley (wife of And.)

Greley, Philip

Greley (wife of Philip)

Hacket, Sarah

Hooke, Elizabeth

Hooke, William

Long, Richard

Long (wife of Rich.)

Maxfield, Elizabeth

Maxfield, John

Moody, Daniel

Moody, Elizabeth

Morrill, Isaac

Morrill, Jacob

Morrill, Phoebe

Morrill, Susannah

Osgood, Abigail

Osgood, William

Page, Joseph

Page, Onesiphris

Page (wife of On.)

Pike, Martha

Ring, Hannah

Ring, Jarvis

Severance, Lydia

Severance, Nathaniel

Severance (wife of Nath.)

Severance, Susannah

Smith, Richard

Smith (wife of Rich.)

Stevens, Dorothy

Stevens, Hannah

Stevens, Joanna

Steven, John

Stevens, Nathaniel

Stevens (wife of Nath.)

Thomson, John

Tongue, Steven

Tongue (wife of Ste.)

True, Joseph

True (wife of Jos.)

Tucker, Benony

Tucker, Ebenezer

Tucker, Moses?

Watson, John

Watson (wife of John)

Whittier, Mary

Whittier, Nathaniel

Winsley, Ephraim

Winsley, Mary

Four Petitions for Several Accused in Andover

Abbott, George

Abbott, John Jr.

Abbott, William

Asselby, John

Ballard, William

Barker, Ebenezer

Barker, John

Barnard, Elizabeth

Barnard, Thomas (Rev.)

Barnott, Stephen

Blanchard, Samuel

Bradstreet, Ann

Bradstreet, Dudley

Bridges, John

Chandler, Bridget

Chandler, John

Chandler, Thomas Jr.

Chandler, William Sr.

Chandler, William Jr.

Dane, Francis Sr. (Rev.)

Dane, Francis Jr.

Dane, Hannah

Dane, Johnson

Dane, Nathaniel

Davis, Ephraim

Fry, James

Fry, John

Hoult, Oliver

Hoult, Samuel

Hooper, John

Hooper, Thomas

Ingalls, Henry Sr.

Ingalls, Henry Jr.

Ingalls, John

Ingalls, Samuel

Johnson, Mary

Johnson, Thomas Sr.

Marble, Joseph

Marston, John

Martin, Samuel

Osgood, Christopher

Osgood, Hooker

Peters, Andrew

Peters, Mary

Peters, Samuel

Peters, William

Poor, Daniel

Preston, John

Robinson, Joseph

Robinson, Phebe

Russell, James

Russell, Mary

Russell, Robert

Stevens, Benjamin

Stevens, Elizabeth

Stevens, Ephraim

Stevens, Joseph

Tyler, Hopestill

Wright, Elizabeth

Wright, Walter

Johnson, Thomas Jr.

APPENDIX E

Persons Known To Have Entered Complaints against Witch Suspects
(Accuser is in boldface, accused in lightface)

Babson, Ebenezer
Dicer, Elizabeth
Prince, Margaret

Ballard, Joseph
Lacy, Mary Sr.
Lacy, Mary Jr.

Bragg, Henry
Carroll, Hannah
Cole, Sarah (of Salem)

Brown, Mary
Cole, Sarah (of Lynn)

Buxton, John
Abbott, Nehemiah Jr.
Bishop, Edward
Bishop, Sarah
Black, Mary
Esty, Mary
English, Mary

Hobbs, Deliverance
Hobbs, William
Wildes, Sarah

Cheever, Ezekiel
Bishop, Bridget
Corey, Giles
Hobbs, Abigail
Warren, Mary

Dodd, Thomas
Frost, Nicholas

Foster, Ephraim
Howard, John
Jackson, John Sr.
Jackson, John Jr.

Hill, Zebulon
Penney, Joan

Holten, Joseph
Abbott, Nehemiah Jr.
Alden, John
Carrier, Martha
Flood, John
Fosdick, Elizabeth
How, Elizabeth
Proctor, William
Read, Wilmot
Rice, Sarah
Toothaker, Mary

Hutchinson, Benjamin
Cary, Elizabeth
Esty, Mary

Hutchinson, Joseph
Good, Sarah
Osborn, Sarah
Tituba

Ingersoll, Nathaniel
Andrews, Daniel
Buckley, Sarah
Coleson, Elizabeth
Carter, Bethia Jr.
DeRich, Mary
Farrar, Thomas Sr.
Hart, Elizabeth
Jacobs, George Jr.
Jacobs, Rebecca
Pease, Sarah
Proctor, Benjamin
Proctor, Elizabeth
Witheredge, Mary

Kenney, Henry
Corey, Martha

Keyser, Eliezer
Emmons, Joseph

Martin, Samuel
Barker, Mary
Barker, William Sr.
Johnson, Abigail
Johnson, Elizabeth Sr.
Marston, Mary

Preston, Thomas
Good, Sarah
Osborn, Sarah
Tituba

Putnam, Edward
Good, Dorcas
Good, Sarah
Ireson, Mary
Osborn, Sarah
Tituba

Putnam, John Jr.
Bassett, Sarah
Bishop, Bridget
Candy
Carrier, Martha
Carter, Bethia Sr.
Carter, Bethia Jr.
Corey, Giles
Dustin, Sarah
Esty, Mary
Hawkes, Margaret
Hobbs, Abigail
Proctor, Sarah
Roots, Susanna
Sears, Ann
Warren, Mary

Putnam, Jonathan
Good, Dorcas
Nurse, Rebecca

Putnam, Nathaniel
Fosdick, Elizabeth
Paine, Elizabeth

Putnam, Thomas
Abbott, Nehemiah Jr.
Andrews, Daniel
Bassett, Sarah
Bishop, Edward
Bishop, Sarah
Black, Mary
Buckley, Sarah
Burroughs, George

Putnam, Thomas *cont'd*
Candy
Cary, Elizabeth
Carter, Bethia Sr.
Carter, Bethia Jr.
Coleson, Elizabeth
Dustin, Lydia
Dustin, Sarah
Esty, Mary
English, Mary
English, Philip
Fosdick, Elizabeth
Good, Sarah
Hart, Elizabeth
Hawkes, Margaret
Hoar, Dorcas
Hobbs, Deliverance
Hobbs, William
Jacobs, George Jr.
Jacobs, Rebecca
Martin, Susanna
Morrell, Sarah
Osborn, Sarah
Proctor, Sarah
Roots, Sarah
Sears, Ann
Tituba
Wildes, Sarah
Witheredge, Mary

Rayment, Thomas
DeRich, Mary
Ireson, Mary
Proctor, Benjamin
Pease, Sarah

Swan, John
Clark, Mary

Swan, Robert
Clark, Mary

Swan, Timothy
Post, Mary

Tyler, Joseph
Howard, John
Jackson, John Sr.
Jackson, John Jr.

Tyler, Moses
Barker, Mary
Barker, William Sr.
Johnson, Elizabeth Sr.
Johnson, Abigail
Marston, Mary

Walcott, Jonathan
Abbott, [Arthur?]
Alden, John
Burroughs, George
Carrier, Martha
Dustin, Lydia
English, Philip
Flood, John
Fosdick, Elizabeth
Hoar, Dorcas
How, Elizabeth
Martin, Susanna
Morrell, Sarah
Proctor, Elizabeth
Proctor, William
Read, Wilmot
Rice, Sarah
Toothaker, Mary

Whipple, Joseph
Fosdick, Elizabeth
Paine, Elizabeth

Willard, Simon
Emmons, Joseph

ENDNOTES

Introduction

1. Cohn, 115.
2. SWP, 168–169.
3. Josselyn, 228; Winship, 27–36.
4. Samuel Willard in Miller, *Puritans*, 1:185; Hall, "Literacy," 2:102, 104; Fischer, 23–24, 112–113.
5. Cotton Mather in T. Holmes, *Cotton Mather*, 2:1058–1061; EQC 9:604–606; VanCleef, 8; Lambert, 2:423–424; Thatcher, 641.
6. I. Mather, *Angelographia*, 72, 106–10, 12–14.
7. Lawson, *Christ's Fidelity*, 2; I. Mather, *Angelographia*, 108–109, 112–116.
8. I. Mather, *Angelographia*, 118; Hale, 13, 139; I. Mather, *Remarkable*, 214–216.
9. C. Mather, *Wonders*, 38.
10. Hale, 14–16; Calef, 29.
11. Sewall, *Diary*, 9 March 1693; Job 2:l0; Urien Oakes in P. Miller, *Puritans*, 1:363.
12. K. Thomas, 89, 91, 80, 82–83.
13. Hall, *Worlds*, 103; I. Mather, "Diary," 359; Calef, 40–41.
14. Macfarlane, 126, 219, 222; C. Mather, *Memorable*, 6–7.
15. Weisman, 186; K. Thomas, 522; Demos, *Entertaining*, 177–178, 171–172, 170; SWP, 87, 122–123.
16. Hale, 148; SWP 751, 444–445, 308; SWP 752, 568.
17. Letter of Robert Pike to Jonathan Corwin in Upham, *Salem*, 2:542; EQC 8:356; K. Thomas, 437, 438; I. Mather, *Cases*, 41–42.
18. Mather-Calef, 265; C. Mather, *Magnalia* (1977), 326; Hale, 131; Cotton Mather to John Richards in "Mather Papers," 396.
19. Josselyn, 301; Calef, 48.
20. Karlsen, 48, 66–67, 72, 74, 75, 70–71; Demos, *Entertaining*, 93–94; and Koehler, 282.
21. Demos, *Entertaining*, 92; Karlsen, 48, 65–66; Gragg, *Salem*, 9.
22. Demos, *Entertaining*, 12; Weisman, 18.
23. G. Kittredge, *Witchcraft*, 219; Weideger, 123–125; Koehler, 90; Karlsen, 155–157.
24. Weideger, 237–244; Benko, 106, 128; Horace, 97–101, 245.
25. SWP, 593–594; Weisman, 184; SWP, 623–624.
26. EQC 2:159–160.
27. EQC 8:293; EQC-VT, 52–75–1, 52–77–1, 52–77–2.
28. Weisman, 24; C. Mather, *Wonders*, 78–80; Lawson, *Christ's Fidelity*, 62–65; Willard, "Brief Account" in Demos, *Remarkable Providences*, 359; Hale, 25, 79–80; S. Noyes, 293.
29. Demos, *Entertaining*, 249.

30. C. Mather, *Wonders* 27–32.

31. "The Liberties of the Massachusets Colonie in New England, 1641," in Powers, 544; *Acts*, 1: 90–91.

32. Fischer, 340, 526, 523, 710, 127.

33. SWP 566–567, 560, 101–102, 847, 822, 227, 557–558, 600–601.

34. Demos, *Entertaining*, 156–165; Karlsen, 223–227, 262, 230; Weisman, 51; EQC 9:237; Innes, 407.

35. Brattle, 179–180.

36. Hansen, *Witchcraft*.

37. Herbert, 188.

38. Ibid.; *Mosby's Medical*, 532, 902, 903 and *Harrison's Principles*, 1133–1134, 97.

39. "Return," 111; SWP 664; Calef, 185, 306 in Burr; Karlsen, 336–337 n. 19.

40. Lawson, *Brief and True*, 161; Hale, 132–135; Hansen, *Witchcraft*, 31; compare Upham, *Salem*, 2:386–387; K. Thomas, 272–273, 270 n. 4; C. Mather, *Magnalia* (1977), 326; 270, n. 4; Black, 87–88, 155–157.

41. K. Thomas, 212–252; Demos, *Entertaining*, 80–84; Hole, 129–147; Lawson, *Christ's Fidelity*, 64–65; Hale, 142; Scot, 192; Deposition in S. G. Drake, *Annals*, 287.

42. C. Mather, *Magnalia* (1977), 326; I. Mather, *Remarkable*, 269; Lawson, *Christ's Fidelity*, 62–65.

43. I. Mather, *Remarkable*, 264; SWP 103; Taylor, 542–544; SWP 450, 772–773, 561, 563, 98–99.

44. Mark 3:23.

45. Perley, *Salem*, map, 1:1.

46. Dunton, *Letters*, 255; N. Noyes, "Elegy," 239.

47. Sibley, *Harvard*, 2:239–246; S. Phillips, *Elegy*, 5.

48. Perley, "Court Houses," EIHC 47(1911): 103–105; J. D. Phillips, 314–315 and map; Boyer, *Salem Possessed*, 87.

49. Perley, "Rial Side," EIHC 55(1919): 49–74; Perley, "Center of Salem Village," EIHC 54(1918): 225–245.

50. Boyer, *Salem Possessed*, 37–39; Perley, "Groton," EIHC 51(1915): 257–270; Perley, "Endicott Lands," EIHC 51(1915):374–378; Perley, "The Plains," EIHC 54(1918): 289–316; Upham, *Salem*, map in 1; Boyer, *Salem Possessed*, 123; Greene, "Bray Wilkins"; SWP 368; S. Noyes, 627–628.

51. Petition, etc., in Boyer, *S-V Witchcraft*, 229–234; Boyer, *Salem Possessed*, 40–45; SV Records, Oct. 8, 1672, Feb. 2, 1684/5, May 10, 1686, Sept. 3, 21, 25, 1686, Oct. 1, 1686; Upham, *Salem*, 1: 238–242.

52. Hutchinson, 1: 282–289.

53. Sibley, *Harvard*, 2:291–299; SV Records Nov. 11, 1672, Dec. 26, 1672, Nov. 14, 1673, June 23, 1673, Sept. 11, 1684, Feb. 28, 1684/85, Mar. 6, 1684/85; Perley, "Center of Salem Village," 227 and map opp. 225; Fischer, 117.

54. Morgan, *Visible Saints*, 88, 34–35; Hall, *Worlds*, 15.

55. Bayley's Feb. 11, 1678/79 letter in Boyer, *S-V Witchcraft*, 242; SV Records 23 June 23, 1673, Nov. 7 and 14, 1673, Feb. 21, 1673/4; Perley, "Center of Salem Village," 233–34 and map opp. 225; Feb. 21, 1673/74 deed in Boyer, *S-V Witchcraft*, 240–241; Boyer, *Salem Possessed*, 46.

56. Bayley's Feb. 11, 1678/79 letter in Boyer, *S-V Witchcraft*, 242.

57. SV Records, Feb. 11 1679; Salem Church Records, 143; petitions and depositions in Boyer, *S-V Witchcraft*, 242–246.

58. Salem Church, *Records*, 147; Boyer, *S-V Witchcraft* for Higginson's Apr. 21, 1679, letter, 246–247, Bayley's July 31, 1679, letter, 248, Sept. 11, 1679, SV Record in petition, 249, Oct. 15, 1679, petition, 249–251.

59. Boyer, *Salem Possessed*, 49; Rutman, 195–197, 162.

60. B. K. Brown, 141–142.

61. SV Records, Apr. 6, 1680, Bayley's bills date to Oct. 25, 1681; Perley, "Center of Salem Village," 234–235; Sibley, *Harvard*, 2:295–296.

62. Russell, 140–141; Otis, 29–35.

63. Upham, *Salem*, 1:256–57; SV Records, Nov. 25, 1680; in Boyer, *Salem Possessed*, 54; Morse case papers in S. G. Drake, *Annals*, 258–296.

64. SWP 176; SV Records, Feb. 16, 1680, Jan. 6, 1691.

65. Perley, "Center of Salem Village," 231–232; for the corrected location, Trask, *"The Devil Amongst Us,"* and "Raising the Devil"; Cummings, 26, 28–29; EQC 9:47–49.

66. SV Records, Dec. 27, 1681; Watt's Apr. 11, 1682 letter in *S-V Witchcraft*, 170–171.

67. Bailey, *Andover*, 421–423; EQC 8:100; *Record of Governor and Council of Mass. Bay*, 5:325, 343–346; "Andover Town Meeting Records," Oct. 10, 1681, and Jan. 2, 1681/2; Mass. Archives 11:15; Sibley 3:174–175.

68. EQC 9: 30–32, 47–49.

69. SV Records, Feb. 22, 1683/84, Dec. 25, 1683, Dec. 18, 1684, Aug. 16, 1683; Lawson, *Christ's Fidelity*, from unpaginated introduction "To the Reader"; OED 3:202.

70. SV Records, Jan. 17, 1683/84, Feb. 22, 1683/84, Mar. 12, 1685/86, Sept. 11 & 24, 1684, Feb. 28, 1684/85, Mar. 6, 1684/85, Mar. 6, 1685/86.

71. DAB 15:356–357; Hutchinson 1:285; Murdock, 154–155.

72. Murdock, 153–154, 183, 185–186.

73. Hutchinson, 1:286, 288.

74. Hutchinson, 1:297–298; Hammond, 149; Winsor 1:377; SV Records, Dec. 10, 1686; Salem Church *Records*, 164; Winsor 2:4–5.

75. Hutchinson 1:304–308; Jeremiah Shepard in *Andros Tracts*, 1:96; Cotton Mather, "Declaration" in *Andros Tracts*, 1:13–14.

76. Sewall, *Diary*, Dec. 21, 22, 1686; Hutchinson, 1:303 note; "Charges against Andros," Hutchinson, 1:168–169.

77. SWP 164; SV Records, Dec. 16, 1686, Jan. 14, 1686/87, Feb. 16 & 28, 1686/87, and the arbiters' Feb. 14, 1686/87, letter entered after Feb. 18, 1686/87, meeting.

78. SV Records, Feb. 18, 1686/87, letter.
79. SV Records, Feb. 18, 1686/87; Mass. Archives, 128:248–249.
80. C. Mather, *Decennium*, 186–187; S. Davis, 109.
81. "Charges against Andros," in *Andros Tracts*, 1:153, 151.
82. Ibid. 1:150–156; C. Mather, *Magnalia* (1977), 316 and n. 470; C. Mather, *Diary*, 134–135.
83. SWP 164; SV Records, Mar. 16, 1686/87; Lawson, "Narrative," 527.
84. SV Records, Oct. 1, 1686, Jan. 14, 1686/87, Sept. 11, 1684, Dec. 16, 1686, Feb. 14, 1686/87, letter after Feb. 28, 1686/87, entry; SV Records Mar. 6, 1684/85, Feb. 18, 1686/7, Apr. 7, 1687.
85. Sewall, *Diary*, Aug. 24, 1687; Hutchinson, 1:303–304; Murdock, 182, 185–189; Silverman, *Cotton Mather*, 64–65.
86. SV-VR; J. Hull, 156; Moriarity; Gragg, "Barbadoes," 111–112.
87. Moriarty; Savage, 3:345–346; Gragg, "Barbadoes," 112; Roach, 2–3; Suffolk Deeds, 12:285, 17:298.
88. Hall, *Worlds*, 164–167.
89. Hurd, *Middlesex*, 1:641; Savage, 3:345–346; SV-VR; Sewall, *Diary*, Nov. 16, 1688; C. Mather, *Memorable*, Burr 103–105.
90. Hale, 23; Hansen, "Metamorphosis"; Breslaw; Twombly, 187–188, 193–194.
91. SV-VR Dec. 20, 1688; C. Mather, *Magnalia* (1855), 2:374–376; Parris' 1697 deposition for three unrecorded meetings on Nov. 15 & 25, 1688, and 10 Dec. 10, 1688, in S. G. Drake, *Delusion*, 3:198–199; Sewall, *Diary*, Aug. 16 and Nov. 16, 1688; C. Mather, *Decennium*, 187–188; Hutchinson, 1:315; C. Mather, *Decennium*, 193–194; Winsor, *Boston*, 2:12, 1:30; C. Mather, *Magnalia* (1977), 293–294.
92. Murdock, 193–196.
93. Hutchinson, 1:316–317; C. Mather, *Magnalia* (1977), 294, 465; Silverman, *Cotton Mather*, 69; "Declaration" in *Andros Tracts*, 1:11–20.
94. "Petition of the Inhabitants of Maine," *Andros Tracts*, 1:176–178; C. Mather, *Wonders*, in Burr 219–220.
95. Parris's deposition in S. G. Drake, *Delusion*, 3:198–199; Hall, *Shepherd*, 187, 193–196; Thatcher, 643–648; Thoreau, 54; Knight, 2:444.
96. Parris in S. G. Drake, *Delusion*, 3:199–200; SV Records Mar. 26, 1685.
97. Parris in S. G. Drake, *Delusion* for May 17, 1689; SV Records, Nov. 25, 1680, Feb. 16, 1680/81, Apr. 17, 1684, Sept. 24, 1684.
98. Parris in S. G. Drake, *Delusion*, 3:201; SV Records, Jan. 27, 1683/84.
99. SV Records, June 18, 1689.
100. SV Records, Oct. 10, 1689, Feb. 16 &18, 1686/87; Perley, "Beverly," 301–302; SV Records, Mar. 3, 1686/87; SWP 750; Essex Deeds, 9:71;Perley, op. cit. 231–232.
101. Parris, *Sermon*, 38; Silverman, *Cotton Mather*, 44–45.
102. Joshua 5:9; Parris, *Sermon*, 38–51; see Hall, *Worlds*, 156, 159; C. Mather, *Magnalia* (1855) 2:224.
103. Boyer, *Salem Possessed*, frontispiece for covenant.
104. SV Records, Dec. 17, 1689; Topsfield Town Records, 1:69, 74.
105. Parkman, 196–197, 225; 218–219; Hutchinson, 1:330–333.
106. SV-VR Feb. 19, 1690, Samuel Cheever birth; SV Church Records Mar. 30, 1690.
107. C. Mather, *Decennium*, 205; Barnes, "Phips," 274–278; Karraker; George.
108. Barnes, "Phips," 282–286; Murdock, 198–199.
109. Mass. Archives 35: 161–162, 172–173; C. Mather, *Magnalia*, (1977), 299; Sewall, *Diary*, March 21 & 22, 1689/90; Fraser, 290.
110. C. Mather, *Decennium*, 218, 220; Parkman, 240–243; S. Davis, 104–105.
111. Hutchinson, 1:337; *Calendar*, 13: 264.
112. SV Church Records, Dec. 23, 1689, and Jan. 12, 1689/90 in Boyer, *S-V Witchcraft*, 270; Gragg, "Samuel Parris," 231–234; SV Church Records, May 25, & 27 Apr. 27, 1690; Perley, *Salem*, 3:292; SWP 248.
113. C. Mather, *Magnalia* (1977), 300–301; C. Mather, *Decennium*, 214; Parkman, 247, 294.
114. C. Mather, *Magnalia* (1977), 195–197, 305–306, 310, 316; Parkman, 276–281, 283–291, 297.
115. Cambridge Association, 263.
116. SV Records, Oct. 24 & 28, 1690.
117. Hutchinson, 1:341 n.; EQC-VT 50–15–1; C. Mather, *Magnalia* (1977), 307–308, 315–316; Parkman, 295–298; Murdock, 229, 230–231; Hutchinson, 1:333–335; "Charges against Andros and others," in *Andros Tracts*, 1:149–173; E.R. and S.S., "The Revolution in New England Justified," in ibid. 1:73–74; Murdock, 231; C. Mather, *Magnalia* (1977), n. 474; Hutchinson 1:333–334.
118. SV Records, Jan. 6, 1690/91 (printed as 1690/2), Oct. 10, 1690.
119. SV Records, Apr. 3, 1691, cf. Nov. 4, 1686, and Mar. 16, 1686/87; Salem Town Records 3:221, 248; Perley, "Center of Salem Village," 236 and map opp. 225.
120. SV Church Records, Nov. 30, Dec. 3, 1690, Mar. 31, June 28, 1691.
121. SV Church Records, June 4, 1691; Hoyt, *Old Families*, 84–86; Boyer, *Salem Possessed*, 135; Karlsen, 209; EQC-VT 51–3–1.
122. Booth, 196–200; Hutchinson, 2:326 n.; Hammond, 157.
123. C. Mather, *Decennium*, 228–229; Hutchinson, 1:341–343.
124. EQC-VT 57–63–1 through 57–65–4; Mass. Archives, 36:220; S. Noyes, 627–628, 429–430; Karlsen, 227.
125. Mass. Archives, 37:84a, 144, letters of July 21 & Sept. 28, 1691.
126. C. Mather, *Decennium*, 229; Hammond, 157.
127. Hutchinson, 1:343–349; C. Mather, *Magnalia* (1977), 319, 320; Murdock, 240–241, 243, 403–404, 246 n. 2.

128. Hutchinson, 1:349–350, 2:11; C. Mather, *Magnalia* (1977), 318, 321; Murdock, 239–240, 251–252, 249.

129. Hampshire County Court of Common Pleas, Book 2 of the original, typescript vol. A(1664–1812):301, 306; Savage, 3:507; Mass. Archives 135:64, 40:622; SWP 740; Barrett; S. Noyes, 650; Middlesex Folio 1678–82–4; Middlesex Court Records, Pulsifer transcript 3:239, 240.

130. Mass. Archives, 81:125; SV Church Records, Oct. 8, 1691; SV Records, Oct. 16, 1691; Parris in S. G. Drake, *Delusion*, 3:198–199.

131. Hammond, 158; SV Church Records, Nov. 2, 1691.

132. SV Church Records, Nov. 10, 1691; Hammond, 158.

133. Hammond, 158; SV Church Records, Nov. 15 & 18, 1691.

134. Parris, *Sermons*, 170–178.

135. SV Records, Dec. 1, 1691.

136. Deposition in Upham, *Salem*, 1:295–296.

137. Salem *Town Records*, 3:250; Mass. Archives 81:128, 131, 132; Sewall, *Diary*, Dec. 2, 4 & 25, 1691; C. Mather in T. Holmes, *Cotton Mather*, 350.

138. EQC-VT 57–65–1; SV-VR, Nov. 12, 1691.

139. Hale, 132–135; Hansen, *Witchcraft*, 31; SWP 228; G. L. Kittredge, *Witchcraft*, 190; Simmons, 109.

Chapter 1: January 1692

1. Tully, 1692; H.B.

2. Upham, *Salem*, 2:2–6.

3. SV Records, Jan. 6, 1690/91.

4. Sewall, *Diary*, Jan. 4, 1692; Parris, *Sermons*, 178, 179, 183, 184, 185; Gragg, "Samuel Parris," 226.

5. C. Mather, *Magnalia* (1977), 322.

6. Suffolk Court Records, 1:412.

7. Tully; H.B.; Sewall, *Diary*, Jan. 12, 1692.

8. SV Records, Jan. 8, 1692.

9. Tully; H.B.; Sewall, *Diary*, Jan. 12, 1692; Salem, Records, 3:256.

10. Sewall, *Diary*, Jan. 12, 1692.

11. SWP 634.

12. Tully; H.B.; Love, 481; Hammond, 160; C. Mather, *Diary*, 1:145–6; C. Mather, *Midnight Cry*, 17.

13. Essex Deeds, 9:70–71; Perley, "Center of Salem Village," 233–4, map op. 225.

14. SWP 750, 753.

15. SWP 750–751, 753; SV Church Records Apr. 14, 1693.

16. Tully; B.H.; Calef, Burr, 342; SWP 612.

17. SWP 753–754.

18. Northall, 115.

19. Suffolk Court Files 32: 2707; W. Johnson, 14, 124; Northall, 124.

20. SWP 754; Suffolk Files 32:2707.

21. SV Records, Jan. 23, 1692, Dec. 26, 1672.

22. SWP 748, 750, 753, 754–755.

23. Sewall, *Diary*, Jan. 24, 1692.

24. Hammond, 160; C. Mather, *Decennium*, 230–231; Pike, 127; Sewall, "Letter-Book," 1:129; Parkman, 366–369.

25. Suffolk Court Records 1:413–419.

26. Hammond, 160; Sewall, *Diary*, Jan. 26, 1692; C. Mather, "Brand," in Burr, 259; Sewall, "Letter-Book," 1:129.

27. C. Mather, *Magnalia* (1977), 347–348.

28. George Burroughs's Jan. 27, 1691/92, letter, Mass. Archives 37:259; Moore, "Notes on Bibliography," 272.

29. Tully; H.B.; SV Records, Jan. 28, 1692.

30. SWP 476; Greene, "Salem Witches: George Jacobs," 68–69; SWP 477.

31. Tully; H.B.; C. Mather, *Decennium*, 231.

Chapter 2: February 1692

1. Salem, *Town Records*, 3:259; Benes, 47–50.

2. Suffolk Court Records, 1:420; S. Noyes, 137; *Court of Assistants*, 1:358–359; Karlsen 230, Koehler 111, EQC 9:237.

3. SWP 362.

4. EQC 5:124, 7:183, 8:432–433, 9:579–580; Boyer, *S-V Witchcraft*, 139–147.

5. SWP 368–369; Lawson, *Brief And True;* Burr, 159; SWP 375; EQC-VT 51–100–1, 52–94–2, 52–95–1 & 3, 52–96–2; Perley, *Salem*, 1:305–306.

6. SWP 355; Perley, "Part of Salem No. 8," 97; SV VR Dec. 10, 1691; SWP 360.

7. C. Mather, *Diary*, 1:137–138, n.

8. Sewall, *Diary*, Feb. 8, 1692; C. Mather, *Magnalia* (1977), 319–321.

9. C. Mather, "Political Fables" in *Selections*, 363–371, 365.

10. C. Mather, *Diary*, 1:144, 147 n.; Levin, *Cotton Mather*, 103–104; Newton in P. Miller, *Errand*, 228; I. Mather to John Richards in Silverman, *Cotton Mather*, 77.

11. C. Mather letter to John Richards in "Mather Papers," 390–391; Levin, *Cotton Mather*, 173–174; C. Mather in T. Holmes, 836–840.

12. Tully; H.B.; Parris, *Sermons*, 186, 190, 193.

13. SV-VR Feb. 15, 1692; E. Putnam, 1:72–73; SWP 601.

14. Essex Deeds 9:109; Perley, "Ryal Side," 63; SV Records, Jan. 1690/91, rates list.

15. Sewall, *Diary*, Feb. 19, 1692; Hutchinson, 2:50.

16. C. Mather, *Decennium*, 232–233; Mass. Archives, 70:249.

17. I. Mather, *Cases of Conscience*, 19–20.

18. Hammond 160; Tully; H.B.

19. Koehler 169; C. Mather, *Angel*, 234; Calef, Burr, 342; SWP 612.

20. Hale 23; Calef, Burr, 342 and note; SV Church Records, Mar. 27, 1692; C. Mather, *Memorable Providences*, Burr, 104; I. Mather, *Remarkable Providences;* Burr, 21–23.

21. Hale, 23–25; Calef, Burr, 342; Lawson, *Brief and True;* Burr, 162–163.

22. K. Thomas, 437–438, 543–544.

23. Hale, 24.

24. SWP 355, 609–610, 612, 756.

25. Hansen, *Witchcraft*, 79–81.

26. Hale, 24.

27. Ibid. 25.

28. SWP 373.

29. SWP 362, 752, 611–612; Sewall, *Diary*, Feb. 27, 1692; Boyer, *Salem Possessed*, 193–194; Essex Probate 308:228–229.

30. Hammond, 160; Sewall, *Diary*, Feb. 28, 1692; Ludlum, 15, 70.

31. SWP 372–373.

32. SWP 355, 745; Hammond, 160.

33. SWP 355, 609, 745; Perley, "Ryal Side," 49; Perley, "Part of Salem No. 8," 97.

34. SWP 750, 362, 750, 751, 752, 754, 752, 361, 751, 752, 751, 752, 755; Armstrong, 193–196; Campbell, 186–187

35. Calef, Burr, 343.

36. SWP 752, 362.

Chapter 3: March 1692

1. SWP 355, 356, 746, 611, 751, 372.

2. Hammond, 160; SWP 252, 357.

3. Tully; H.B.; SWP 391; Upham, *Salem* 2:26.

4. SWP 357, 358, 360–361, 746, 356–357, 358.

5. Sarah Good examination, SWP 356–357, 358–359, 360, 362.

6. Sarah Osborn examination, SWP 609–610, 610–611, 360.

7. SWP 948.

8. Tituba examination, SWP 361, 747–750, 750–753, 746, and later depositions 757; Upham, *Salem* 2:26.

9. OED

10. Trask, "*Devil,*" 11, 65; Perley, *Salem*, 2:38; Sibley, *Harvard*, 5:37–38.

11. SWP 746, 370, 955.

12. SV Records, March 1, 1692.

13. SWP 371; Tully; H.B.

14. SWP 377.

15. SWP 370.

16. SWP 370.

17. SWP 364, 372, 955.

18. SWP 746, 753–755; Hale, 26.

19. Hale, 26–27; Calef in Burr, 343.

20. SWP 372.

21. SWP 372.

22. SWP 668–669, 352–353.

23. SWP 746; Lawson, *Brief*, 148; SWP 948, 951.

24. Suffolk Court, ms. 1:421.

25. SWP 747, 955; Hale, 27.

26. SWP 668; EQC 4:207–209, 3:377, 7:135–136; SWP 797–798, 753.

27. Murdock, 254.

28. Morison, 263; Cambridge Association, 267; T. Holmes, *Cotton Mather*, 684.

29. SWP 953–954.

30. Mass. Archives 49:621; Innes, 405; Suffolk Files 32:275; EQC 8:335; Powers, 213–214; John Dounton in Powers, 212.

31. Salem *Town Records*, 3:265.

32. Tully; H.B.

33. SWP 953.

34. Calef, Burr, 352; Powers, 231.

35. Hale 25; Calef, Burr 342.

36. Calef, Burr 342.
37. J. Hull, 156; Roach, 2, 3; Lawson, *Brief*, 153, 160.
38. SWP 260–262.
39. SV Church Records, April 27, 1690; deposition in Moore, "Notes on the History," 186–187; SV Church Records, in "Baptisms At Salem Village," 235.
40. SWP 252.
41. SWP 801; Karlsen, 203–205.
42. SWP 801.
43. SWP 683–684.
44. SWP 264; Wheatland, 105; Henderson, 181, 199.
45. SWP 595, 603.
46. "Andover Town Records," March 14, 1692.
47. SWP 258, 667.
48. SWP 264–265.
49. SWP 260.
50. EQC 1:172; 6:190–1; 7:91,147; 3:77, 89; Salem Church, *Records*, 170–171.
51. Tully; H.B.; SWP 597, 670–671, 664, 683–684, 584–586.
52. SWP 216, 219; Tully; H.B.
53. Suffolk Court Records 1:421–422.
54. SWP 603–604; SV-VR, Abigail Putnam, b. 27 Oct. 1692.
55. SWP 264; SV-VR, and Perley, *Salem*, 1:385–386, Eleazer Pope, b. 4 Dec. 1692; Lawson, *Brief*, 155; Perley, *Salem* 1:246–247.
56. SWP 604.
57. SWP 247; Perley, *Salem*, 2:187; Savage, 3:10; Trask, *"Devil,"* 127.
58. Lawson, *Brief*, 148; Tully.
59. Tully; B.H.; Lawson, *Brief*, 153–154.
60. From Giles Corey's exam in Trask, *"Devil,"* 153; SWP 259–260.
61. Lawson, *Brief*, 154.
62. SWP 250, 251, 254.
63. SWP 258, 263, 597, 596; Lawson, *Brief*, 158.
64. SWP 247–248; Trask, *"Devil,"* 153.
65. Lawson, *Brief*, 155; Trask, *"Devil,"* 122; Martha Corey's examination is from Parris's notes, SWP 248–255, Lawson, *Brief*, 154–157.
66. SWP 260–602.
67. SWP 262.
68. SWP 604, 352.
69. SWP 948.
70. Tully; H.B.; SWP 604.
71. Tully; H.B.; Salem, Town Records, 3:258.
72. Perley, *Salem* 3:5, 2:161–162; SWP 593–4; see "A Platform of Church Discipline" in C. Mather, *Magnalia* (1855), 2:224.
73. SWP 355, 603, 745, 585–586; Calef, Burr, 359.
74. SWP 604; Lawson, *Brief*, 157–158.
75. Isaiah 40:1, 49:1, 50:1; SWP 600–1.
76. SWP 258, 597.
77. SWP 583, 351.
78. Sewall, *Diary*, Mar. 23, 1692; *Calendar*, 13:564; Mass. Archives 37:323, 327–327a, 328; Coleman, 215–218.
79. SWP 604, 583, 351; Lawson, *Brief*, 159.
80. Rebecca Nurse examination SWP 584–587); Lawson, *Brief*, 158–160.
81. S. Noyes, 429–430.
82. Cf. Benjamin Wadsworth in Hall, *Worlds*, 159.
83. Lawson, *Brief*, 158, 158–9; SWP 585, 604–605.
84. SWP 587, 588, 589, 590, 591.
85. Lawson, *Brief*, 159, 160.
86. Ibid., 158; Lawson, *Christ's Fidelity*, 1.
87. Lawson, *Christ's Fidelity*, 16, 23, 25, 55, 62, 66, 73–74, 25, 23, 63–5, 69, 70, 73, 76; Ephesians 6:11–18; cf. Laurence Saunders in Hall, *World*, 121.
88. SWP 683, 259–260; Trask, "*Devil*," 63.
89. SWP 683–4; Perley, "Endicott Lands," 371–372; OED.
90. SWP 599.
91. Lawson, *Brief*, 160.
92. Hansen, *Witchcraft*, 31; Hale, 133; Lawson, *Brief*, 161.
93. SV Church Records, March 25, 1692.
94. SWP 670 and 265.
95. Lawson, *Brief*, 160.
96. Cheney, 94–95; Parris, *Sermons*, 183, 194 (compare the transcription in Trask, *"Devil,"* 110–114); John 6:70.
97. Calef, Burr, 346; Lawson, *Brief*, 161; SWP 606.

98. Parris, *Sermons*, 194–198; SWP 597, 659.
99. SV Church records, March 27, 1692.
100. SWP 603.
101. SWP 670–671, 664; Trask, *"Devil,"* 123.
102. SWP 667, 674–675.
103. EQC-VT, 52–91–1 to 52–97–4, 52–75–1 to 52–77–2; Nathaniel Saltonstall in "Saltonstall Papers," 207–208; Waters, 1: 456.
104. Demos, *Entertaining*, 20–33.
105. Murdock, 254; *Calendar*, 14: 24–25, 68, 235, 26–27, 92; C. Mather, *Parentator*, 155–156; Mass. Archives 61: 309, 369a.
106. SWP 215, 219, 217; Deposition of Thomas Burnham, March 1692 # 106: Maine Historical Society, Coll. 77, box 1, Folder 19. On-line <http://etext.virginia.edu/salem/witchcraft/archives/MEHS/mehs_1.html>
107. SWP 215, 954, 950.
108. Lawson, *Brief*, 160; SWP 477.
109. SWP 597, 659.
110. Lawson, *Brief*, 160–161, 164; Calef, Burr, 345–346.

Chapter 4: April 1692

1. Lawson, *Brief*, 160–161; SWP 659; Revelation 5:9, Psalm 110:1, Psalm 149:1 in *Psalms*, 336, 235, 313.
2. SV Records, Jan. 6, 1990/91.
3. SWP 669.
4. SWP 667.
5. SWP 683–684, 798, 796, 800; Hansen, Salem, 53–54.
6. SWP 795, 798; Lawson, *Brief*, 162.
7. SWP 795, 352, 793, 802–803; OED.
8. SWP 218.
9. SWP 657; Perley, *Salem* 1:131; S. Noyes, 429–430.
10. SWP 677.
11. Cambridge Association, 267.
12. Perley, "Rial Side," 63, i.e., Edward Bishop the 2nd.
13. Middlesex Records, 146; SWP 953.
14. Lawson, *Brief*, 161, 152, and Burr's notes 148.
15. Mass. Archives 40:621.
16. SWP 677.
17. SWP 244; Perley, *Salem,* 3:22–23.
18. SWP 660, 244.
19. SWP 657–658, 662.
20. SWP 221.
21. SWP 658.
22. SWP 259; S. Noyes, 628.
23. SWP 659, presumably today.
24. C. Mather, *Diary*, 1:145–146 and notes; T. Holmes, 284.
25. C. Mather, *Midnight*, 622, 49.
26. SWP 658, 661–662; Sewall, *Diary*, Apr. 11, 1692; DAB 5:66–67.
27. Sewall, *Diary*, Apr. 11, 1692; SWP 661. Sarah Cloyce examination, SWP 658–659.
28. SWP 675.
29. Elizabeth Proctor examination, SWP 659–660, plus depositions as noted.
30. SWP 678, 683.
31. SWP 675.
32. Calef, Burr, 347.
33. SWP 221, 662–663, 663–664, 678–679, 679. Sewall, *Diary*, Apr. 11, 1692; SWP 1032; Perley, *Salem*, 2: 22–23.
34. Tully; H.B.; SWP 678, i.e., "last night"; Perley, *Salem*, 1:441–442, 3:84–85; Perley, "Part of Salem No. 14," 24–25, "Salem No. 4," 100, map 97; Tolles, 180; Council, 222; SWP 946.
35. Calef, Burr, 348; "Further Account," 171; Perley, "Endicott Lands," 371–372; Perley, "Ryal Side," 69 and map op. p. 44.
36. SWP 677–678, 258; Reading town records in Eaton, 17.
37. SWP 953; 873; Mass. Archives 40: 621–622; Trask, *"Devil,"* 154.
38. SWP 727.
39. SWP 597, 667, 241, 416.
40. SWP 601–602.
41. SWP 258, 416, 242.
42. SWP 601–602; SV Vital Records, Apr. 15, 1692.
43. SWP 239.
44. SWP 414–415, 413; S. Noyes, 29, 341; Topsfield VR, 55; Perley, "Hawthorne, No. 2," 135; SWP 413–415.
45. SWP 420.

46. SWP 239–240.
47. SWP 86.
48. SWP 87; Giles Corey examination in Trask, *"Devil,"* 152–154.
49. A 1697 petition in Boyer, *S-V Witchcraft*, 266.
50. SWP 259–260; catechism in *New-England Primer*.
51. Abigail Hobbs examination, SWP 405–409.
52. Mary Warren examination, SWP 793–794.
53. Bridget Bishop, examination, SWP 83–85 and 85–87; Some quotes, like her opening plea (83, 85), combine variants from the two versions; EQC 7:329–330; D. L. Greene, "Bridget Bishop," 129–138; "Bridget," Anderson, 207; Perley, *Salem*, 1:131.
54. SWP 89–90, 90–91, 87–88, 88–89, 109.
55. Mary Warren examination, second half, SWP 794.
56. SWP 949, 795, 796.
57. Mary Warren confession, SWP 795–796; Perley, *Salem*, 2:22–23.
58. Abigail Hobbs confession, SWP 409–410; Perley, *Salem*, 1:131.
59. Tully; H.B.; SWP 420, 421–422, 428.
60. Hale 29; SWP 164, 164–165.
61. SWP 483–484; Perley, "Northfields No. 3," 190, 187 map.
62. *Ipswich Antiquarian*, Vol. 3 No. 36 (May 1883):2–3; also Trask, *"Devil,"* 155.
63. SWP 287–288, 805–806; Perley, *Salem*, 1:450.
64. Upham, *Salem*, 2:139–140; Ezekiel 10:10.
65. Mary Warren confession, SWP 796–799.
66. SWP 171–172.
67. SWP 172, 422.
68. SWP 809.
69. Bentley, *Diary*, 2:24.
70. SWP 524, 145, 224, 423, 343, 529, 66, 523, 531, 597, 522, 67, 522; Hale, 31, 33; C. Mather, *Wonders*, 217; S. Noyes, 123.
71. SWP 49–50, 805; Hale, 34.
72. Deliverance Hobbs examination, SWP 419–422.
73. Nehemiah Abbott examination, SWP 49–50; Abbott, 3:3–25.
74. William Hobbs examination, SWP 425–428.
75. Sarah Wildes examination, SWP 806–807; EQC 1:179, 3:66.
76. W. Davis Jr., "Wildes," 129; SWP 807–808, 809.
77. SWP 661–662; Mary Esty examination SWP, 288–290.
78. W. Davis Jr., "Wildes," 143, 146–147; SWP 95; D. L. Greene, "Bridget Bishop," 132–136; EQC 9:515, 517, 518, 565, 570; SWP 95–97, 111–112; EQC-VT 50–19–1; SV Church Records, May 25, 1690.
79. Bentley, "Salem," 269; EQC 9:448–9; Bentley, *Diary*, 2:23; Trask, *"Devil,"* 156.
80. SWP 49–50.
81. Mary Black examination, SWP 113–114. Upham, *Salem* 2:136.
82. SWP 949.
83. *Ipswich Antiquarian*, 2–3, and Trask, *"Devil,"* 55; SWP 881.
84. SWP 850; Calef, Burr 361; SWP 848.
85. Deliverance Hobbs's confession SWP 423; SWP 363 for date.
86. Webster, 11–12, 37–40, i.e., 3 May New Style.
87. SWP 320; S. Noyes, 627–628; SV-VR; Perley, "Endicott Lands," 373; Perley, "Cedar Pond," 23; Perley, "Brooksby," 357.
88. Corey, "Will," 32.
89. SWP 389, 850.
90. SWP 847.
91. SWP 851.
92. Taylor, 101–107, 109–110, 112; Tomlinson, 54; Godbeer, 163–164.
93. Sewall, *Diary*, Apr. 25, 1692.
94. SWP 389–390, 320.
95. SWP 320–321.
96. Suffolk Court Records, 1:423–430.
97. Elisha Hutchinson in Mass. Archives 37:347, 364.
98. SWP 105, 320–321.
99. SWP 105.
100. SWP 851.
101. SWP 953.
102. C. Mather, *Diary*, 1:146–148, 151–152.
103. SWP 105–106; D. L. Greene, "Bridget Bishop," 133; cf. SWP 95–97.
104. SWP 106, 151, 273, 549–550, 313.
105. Testimony in Noble, "Some Documentary Fragments," 18–19.
106. SWP 376.
107. SWP 565–566.

Chapter 5: May 1692

1. SWP 495, 496–497.
2. Tully; H.B.; SWP 552, 314–315, 152, 391; C. Mather, *Wonders*, Burr, 229–230.
3. Coleman, 1:202; S. Noyes, 493; SV-VR February 1690/91; EQC-VT 51–19–1, 51–30–1, calls the defendant "Sarah" and "Mary."
4. Calef, Burr, 383; Eaton, *Reading*, 6; Middlesex Folio, 1681–96–2; Lechford, 177; SWP 935–936.
5. SWP 400–401; EQC 7:42–55, 181–183; Hurd, *Essex*, 689–690; Dorcas Hoar examination, SWP 389–391.
6. Brattle, 171.
7. SWP 392–393.
8. SWP 558–559; EQC 4:129, 3:403–404, 133; D. Greene, "Susanna Martin," 196–199; EQC 4:184–187, 4:347, 5:148, 235–236, 244, 293, 297, 299.
9. SWP 552, 549–550; Susanna Martin examination, SWP 550–552, 553–555, and a fragment in C. Mather, *Wonders*, Burr, 229–230; Lawson, "Narrative," 2:532–533.
10. I Samuel 28:3–25.
11. SWP 873, 555, 556.
12. SWP 949; Mass. Archives 40:622–623.
13. SWP 375–376.
14. SWP 170.
15. SWP 152; S. A. Drake, *New England Legends*, 201–202.
16. Allen, 78.
17. SWP 170, 597, 596; Putnam, E., 29.
18. SWP 949, 953, 873.
19. SWP 91–92.
20. Anderson, 207.
21. SWP 845.
22. SWP 166; D. Greene, "Third Wife of George Burroughs," 43–44; N. Thompson, "Hannah Fisher," 17–18; Perley, *Salem,* 3:45–46.
23. SWP 152.
24. Sewall, *Diary*, May 4, 1692; Hammond, 161; Mass. Archives 81:133; General Court, 214–215.
25. SWP 847–848; D. Greene, "Bray Wilkins," 3–5.
26. SWP 802–803; EQC-VT, 49–147–1.
27. SWP 176–177; McTeer, "Aslebees," 231–233.
28. General Court, 216–217; Council, 170.
29. SWP 314–315; Noble, 19.
30. SWP 623; Perley, "Northfields, No. 3," 190.
31. SWP 848, 845.
32. SWP 168; SV-VR.
33. Parris, *Sermons*, 199.
34. SWP 729, 277.
35. SWP 323; EQC-VT 49–122–2, 49–123–4; EQC 7:410.
36. SWP 171.
37. SWP 169; Matthew 4:1–11; Luke 4:1–13; SWP 171.
38. SWP 729, 277.
39. George Burroughs examination, SWP 153–154; N. Thompson, 19; *Salem Church Records*, 39, 42.
40. SWP 153, 171, 168–169, 171, 153, 166.
41. SWP 154, 419–420, 422, 410–412, 161–162, 176–178, 154; Perley, *Salem*, 3:171; C. Mather, *Wonders*, Burr 219–20; MFA 1:62–63.
42. SWP 729; S. Sewall, *Woburn*, 637; Farrar, 320–321.
43. SWP 277; Lechford, 177; "Middlesex Folio" 1681–96–2; SWP 936–937; Savage, 4:490.
44. SWP 729; S. Sewall, *Woburn*, 598; R. Thompson, 173, 107–108, 105; EQC 4:207–209; Mass. Archives 40:621, 623.
45. SWP 729; S. Sewall, *Woburn*, 598; Woburn VR, 1:43.
46. S. Noyes, 142, 98–99; SWP 475, 483, 211–212, 475; *Maine Records*, 328, 335; Folsom, 113–116.
47. SWP 483, 837.
48. SWP 837; Greene, "Bray Wilkins," 11; Perley, *Salem* 2:54.
49. Mass. Archives 40:621, 623; SWP 873, 475–476, 473.
50. George Jacobs Sr. first examination SWP 474–476.
51. EQC 6:292–329.
52. SWP 489.
53. SWP 211–212; Perley, *Salem* 1:131; Perley, "Part of Salem No.24," 123–124; D. Greene, "George Jacobs," 74–75; Sibley, *Harvard*, 2:239–246; Brattle, 172–173.
54. SWP 953–954.
55. SWP 838.
56. SWP 838, 841–842.
57. SWP 484, George Jacobs Sr. second examination; SWP 476–477.
58. SWP 479, 777–779.
59. SWP 623, 476, 484, 485, 489, 905–906, 802; Margaret Jacobs in Calef, Burr, 364–365.

60. SWP 484.
61. SWP 154, 559, 560–562.
62. SWP 849, 486.
63. SWP 154, MHS ms. makes it clear May 11 refers to Abigail Hobb's testimony; Calef, Burr, 364–365.
64. SWP 819.
65. SWP 410–412.
66. Mary Warren examination SWP 799–802.
67. SWP 627–628; Perley, "Part of Salem No. 23," 62–64.
68. SWP 701, Ann Pudeator examination, 702–703; Perley, *Salem* 2:122–123, 398; S. Noyes, 289; EQC 8:59–60.
69. SWP 634 (SWP tangles the two Goody Parkers); Alice Parker examination, SWP 623–624; Perley, "Part of Salem No. 21," 167.
70. Ms. and SWP 364 has "he denied not," but the sense seems to mean "she" denied not.
71. SWP 473, 873, 953; Mass. Archives 40:621–624.
72. SWP 149, 390.
73. SWP 733; Babson, *History of Gloucester*, 161–162; Perley, "Part of Salem No. 8," 98; Abigail Soames examination, SWP 733–736.
74. Swan, 158; EQC 7:420, 8:147, 237, 367, 372; Perley, "Part of Salem No. 8," 98.
75. EQC 8:237.
76. SWP 735, 623; Lawson, *Brief*, 162.
77. SWP 736.
78. SWP 736–737; M. Jacobs in Burr, 364–365.
79. C. Mather, "Brand," 259–260; S. Noyes, 631; SWP 953.
80. C. Mather, "Brand," 270, 276; C. Mather, *Memorable Providences*, 107.
81. SWP 382, 487, 493.
82. SWP 821, 848, 849.
83. Sewall, *Diary*, May 14, 1692; C. Mather, *Diary*, 1:148; Hammond, 161; Mass. Archives, 61:309; Broadbent in *Calendar*, 13:653; Silverman, *Cotton Mather*, 80; Tully; H.B.
84. C. Mather, *Diary* 1:149; Matthew 14:15.
85. SWP 145, 839.
86. SWP 191–192; Bailey, 208, 70–71; Abbott MS, "Chandler," "Allen"; Andover VR 1:100.
87. SWP 381, 999, 496–497, 820–821; Calef, Burr, 371; D. Greene, "Jacobs," 72.
88. SWP 820.
89. SWP 851.
90. SWP 839, 237.
91. SWP 191–192; "Plan of Andover"; Andover Town Records, Oct. 14, 1690.
92. Sewall, *Diary*, May 16, 1692; Hammond, 161; Council, 165–168; *Calendar*, 13:653.
93. Sewall, *Diary*, May 16, 1692.
94. SWP 821, 845–849, 849, 852; SV-VR May 16, 1692.
95. SWP 820, 821; Boyer, *Salem-Village Witchcraft*, 166; Calef, Burr, 361.
96. SWP 820–821, 493.
97. SWP 822.
98. SWP 841, 848.
99. SWP 238.
100. Council, 169–170.
101. SWP 381, 829; Mass. Archives, 135:20.
102. SWP 381, 382, Elizabeth Hart's indictment is dated May 28 in SWP 282–283, but this is clearly May 18 in the original, Suffolk Court Files #2668; Koehler, 196–197.
103. Farrar, 316–317; EQC VT 49–123–4, 49–122–2, 49–124–3; EQC 4:209, 7:410; SWP 324.
104. SWP 487; EQC 6:49, 114, 7:427, SWP 146–147, 389; "Proctor," *Register* 60:209; Sarah Buckley examination, SWP 145.
105. SWP 906–907, 149, 150.
106. "Proctor," *Register* 60: 208–209; SWP 837–838.
107. SWP 494–495; Calef, Burr, 371; D. Greene, "Jacobs," 73; SWP 495, 494; Calef, Burr, 371.
108. SWP 771–773; Hazen, 149–150; SWP 308; Hoyt, "Button Family," 348–349; Savage, 2:83; SWP 772.
109. SWP 526, John Willard examination, 826–829, 823–826.
110. D. Greene, "Bray Wilkins," 16, 111–113.
111. SWP 830–834.
112. SWP 301, 297, 805, 772, 874, 949.
113. SWP 172–173.
114. SWP 949, 954.
115. Tully; H.B.; SWP 297, 830–834; Perley, "Hawthorne: Part of Salem," 334, map opp. 333; E. Putnam, 1:56–57; SV-VR.
116. SWP 191–192.
117. SWP 95–97, 772–773, 949; D. Greene, "Bridget Bishop," 132.
118. SWP 300–301, 297–298, 296; Putnam, 1:37–38.
119. Council, 171; *Calendar*, 14:24.
120. SWP 294–295, 287–288.

121. SWP 295, 301, 298–299, 694, 298, 692, 692–623; Savage, 3:73, 4:58; *Salem Records*, 3:250; Perley, "Read Farm," 242.
122. SWP 295, 301.
123. SWP 721, 691, 77, 721, 692–693.
124. Silverman, *Cotton Mather*, 79, 82; C. Mather, "Sermon Notes," frame 50–75.
125. SWP 693.
126. Tully; H.B.; SWP 949, 77, 722.
127. SWP 290–291, 301; Lawson, "Narrative," 2:530; C. Mather, *Magnalia* (1977) 1:327–328.
128. SWP 655, 639, 655–656, 639, 874.
129. Nathaniel Cary in Calef, Burr, 350–351; Council, 172; SWP 949–950, 874; Hammond, 161.
130. SWP 692.
131. SWP 953; Mass. Archives 40:621; Council, 190–191.
132. SWP 950.
133. Sewall, *Diary*, May 24, 1692; Council, 172; Hutchinson, 2:10, 6.
134. SWP 765. SWP's "Jerson Toothaker" should be "Ireson [and] Toothaker."
135. SWP 255. "Dorothy Good."
136. Cary in Calef, Burr, 351–352; Hammond 161.
137. SWP 673–674; Putnam, 1:16–17; Perley, *Salem*, 2:22–23; Wells, 48–49.
138. Council, 170; Hammond, 161; Love, 481, 260; Hale, 26; SWP 117; Eaton, *Reading*, 95, 115; E. Putnam 1:62–63.
139. Council, 173–177.
140. Ibid, 176; D. C. Brown, "Forfeitures," 88–89.
141. Washburn, 147, 147–148, 252, 255–257; Sibley, *Harvard*, 1:194–210, 2:1–8.
142. Lawson, *Brief*, 160; DAB 13:46–47.
143. Taylor, 110–112, 63, 101; Tomlinson, 54–55; Godbeer, 163–164.
144. SWP 207.
145. SWP 207, 183; Burr, 350–351; Hammond, 161; Hazen, 149–150.
146. Mass. Archives 11:62.
147. Tomlinson, 54–55; Taylor, 43–44.
148. Tully; H.B.; SWP 433, 449–450; E. Towne, *Towne*, 21–22.
149. SWP 457, 688; Babson, *Gloucester*, 72.
150. SWP 436, 597, 436, 871.
151. SWP 314–315; Noble, 19.
152. SWP 339, 183, 92–95.
153. SWP 434–435, 450.
154. "Cambridge Association," 267.
155. SWP 435, 867.
156. Sibley, *Harvard*, 3:330–331; Brattle, 177–178; SWP 867–868; see Feb. 2, 1692.
157. SWP 315–318; EQC-VT 49–137–1.
158. Baird, 2:192; Konig, 172–174.
159. SWP 719, 539, 183; EQC 9:36.
160. Alden in Calef, Burr, 353–354; Finney-MacDougal, 5.
161. *Calendar*, 13:564; Barnes, "Phippius Maximus," 538; EQC-VT 50–5–1, 50–5–2, 50–7–1, 50–101–1, 50–102–1; *Court of Assistants*, 1:352–353; Mass. Archives, 37:120; Hutchinson, 2:68.
162. Elizabeth How examination, SWP 434–436.
163. SWP 437–438, 442–443.
164. SWP 436–437.
165. Martha Carrier examination, SWP 184–186; SWP 189, 192.
166. Cf. the Charles Osgood portrait of the Judge's novelist descendant, Nathaniel Hawthorne, in the Peabody Essex Museum, Salem, Massachusetts.
167. SWP 186–187.
168. SWP 711; Roads, 45, 31; Wilmot Read examination, SWP 713–714.
169. Alden in Calef, Burr 353–355.
170. Ibid, 354; Mass. Archives 40:623.
171. SWP 872, 665.
172. SWP 695–697, 950; John Proctor letter in Calef, Burr, 363; *Andros Tracts*, 1:153.
173. SWP 605.
174. SWP 950, 867–868.
175. C. Mather, "Mather Papers," 391–397.

Chapter 6: June 1692

1. SWP 172–173.
2. SWP 802–803.
3. SWP 211.
4. SWP 591, 835; Mass. Archives 40:621; SWP 953–954, 375; Mass. Archives 40:623 here called "Dorothy Good."
5. SWP 600–601.
6. Tomlinson 55–56.

7. SWP 839–840.

8. SWP 375, 599.

9. SWP 591, 835, 632–633, 340, 339.

10. SWP 106–107, 606–607.

11. Perley, "Court Houses," 103–104; Perley, "Part of Salem in 1700, [No. 1]," 172; Perley, "Part of Salem in 1700, [No. 14]," 29, 35, 36; Calef, Burr, 355; Brattle, 184.

12. C. Mather, *Wonders*, Burr, 223, 229; Salem Records, 3:265.

13. SWP 109, 904–905; Lawson, "Narrative," 2:535; EQC 7:329–330.

14. Anderson, "Bridget Bishop," 207; SWP 83; D. Greene, "Bridget Bishop," 137–138, 129, 138; EQC 4:90, 6:386–387.

15. C. Mather, *Wonders*; Burr, 249; EQC-VT 47–99–1 through 3, 47–100–1 and 2, 47–101–1; SWP 92–4; OED q.v.; *Essex Probate*, 3:319.

16. C. Mather, *Wonders*; Burr, 223–224; Brattle, 174–175; and Parris in Drake, *Witchcraft Delusion*, 2:142, 145; SWP 106, 702; D. Greene, "Bridget Bishop," 135.

17. SWP 87–90, 104, 94–95, 101–102; C. Mather, *Wonders*; Burr, 224–225.

18. SWP 99–101; C. Mather, *Wonders*; Burr, 226–227; Perley, "Part of Salem, No. 14," 24–25.

19. SWP 92–94; C. Mather, *Wonders*; Burr, 227–228.

20. Winsor 1:187; Perley, *Salem*, 2:268; Babson, *Gloucester*, 161–162; SWP 97–99; C. Mather, *Wonders*; Burr, 225–226.

21. Hale, 156; Perley, *Salem*, 2:271.

22. SWP 103, 101; C. Mather, *Wonders*; Burr, 225, 228.

23. C. Mather, *Wonders*; Burr, 228; Brattle, 184, 174–176.

24. SWP 108–109; Brattle, 187–188; Hammond, 162; C. Mather, *Wonders*; Burr, 223.

25. SWP 106–108.

26. Tomlinson, 55–56; Godbeer, 164–166.

27. SWP 684, 840, 595, 442–443, 605, 838.

28. SWP 340; R. Thompson, 185–186, 228 note 31.

29. R. Thompson 175–176, 237 notes 52 and 53; A. Putnam, 1:62–163; Brooks, *Medford*, 561–562; Peter Tufts will, Middlesex Probate, Cambridge, Massachusetts, docket #22994; Middlesex Folio 1673–187–1.

30. SWP 463.

31. SWP 759, 763, 853, 457; Tookey examination, SWP 759–761.

32. EQC 8:330–338.

33. Ibid., 335.

34. C. Mather, *Optanda* (i.e., on Proverbs 17:27) 1, 5, 8, 11, 5, 14, 24–25; T. Holmes, *Cotton Mather*, 2:768.

35. C. Mather, *Decennium*, 233, 229.

36. SWP 463, 464; Perley, *Salem*, 1:18, 305–306; Savage, 3:62; Mary Ireson exam, June 1692 #36: Ireson examination, BPL Ms.q.Ch.K.1.40.2.211. On-line <http://etext.virginia.edu/salem/witchcraft/archives/BPL/B20.html>

37. SWP 271; Perley, *Salem*, 1:157–158; Babson, *History of Gloucester*, 81–82; Swan, "Bedevilment," 160; EQC 9:114–115; John Higginson letter in "Higginson Letters," 198–200; John Higginson will, Essex Probate 310:64–65; John Higginson letter, 31 Aug. 1698, Higginson Family Ms.; SWP 271–272; Ann Dolliver exam, June 1692 #37: Dolliver examination, BPL Ms.Ch.K.1.40.2.194. On-line <http://etext.virginia.edu/salem/witchcraft/archives/BPL/B19.html>

38. Hammond, 162; Council, 193.

39. SWP 761–762; Perley, *Salem* 3:127.

40. S. Noyes, 123, 164; Stackpole, *New Hampshire*, 1:39, 183–184; SWP 423.

41. SWP 263; Perley, *Salem* 2:193.

42. General Court Records 4:202–203; C. Mather, *Magnalia* (1977), 323.

43. SWP 108–109; General Court Records, 225; Brattle, 184; Calef, Burr, 355; Sewall, *Diary*, March 3, 1692/93— letter before March 7, 1693 entry.

44. General Court Records, 224; C. Mather, *Optanda*, 36, 43, 48, 49, 69, 51, 56–58, 42–43, 44, 45.

45. SWP 243.

46. Tully.

47. SWP 108–109, 481; Hammond, 162; Perley, "Part of Salem No. 7," 145–149, and Perley, "Where the Salem 'Witches' Were Hanged," 1–18; Calef, Burr, 360; Tully.

48. Hall, *Worlds*, 79–81; Calef, Burr, 361; Wilson, 114–115, 126–130.

49. Hale, 156; Matthew 12:31.

50. SWP 109.

51. General Court Records 4:225.

52. C. Mather, *Decennium*, 233; Bourne, 196–198.

53. C. Mather, *Decennium*, 233–235, 239; Parkman, 378, Webster, 41–42.

54. General Court Records, 226.

55. C. Mather, *Decennium*, 236–239.

56. Ibid., 239; Webster, 42.

57. General Court Records, 226; Council, 178.

58. Tomlinson, 56.

59. General Court Records, 226–227; *Acts*, 1:27–28.

60. SWP 1040–1041, 1042–1043.

61. General Court Records, 227–228; *Acts* 1:27; D. C. Brown, "Forfeitures," 89–91; C. Mather, *Magnalia* (1977), 242–244; "The Return of Several Ministers Consulted by his Excellency, and the Honorable Council, upon the pre-

sent Witchcrafts in Salem Village," in Levin, *What Happened?*, 110–111, 234–234); I. Mather, *Cases of Conscience*, introduction.

62. SWP 773–774, 992–993; Mass. Archives 40:622.

63. Tully.

64. *Acts*, 1:41–42; General Court Records 4:229.

65. Tully; H.B.; SWP 598–599; Perley, "The Plains," 306–308.

66. SWP 957; Mass. Archives 40:622.

67. SWP 480, 159–160.

68. SWP 401–402, 995–996.

69. Parris, *Sermons*, 199.

70. SWP 146–147.

71. SWP 606; Perley, *Salem* 1:353.

72. SWP 370–371; Lawson, "Narrative" 2:530; SWP 371.

73. Tomlinson 56–57.

74. General Court Records, 231.

75. SWP 115, 198, 213, 528, 526–528; Lynch, 15; "Plan of Andover."

76. Hale, 38; SWP 198, 526–527; Pope, *Haverhill Emersons*, 19–20, 24, 31; Hazen, 149–150; EQC 9:603; Sewall, *Diary*, Oct. 16, 1691; EQC-VT 46–131–1, 47–3–1, 47–4–1, 47–104–1, 51–99–1.

77. General Court Records, 232–233; *Acts* 1:29–34.

78. SWP 413.

79. William Milborne petition in "Witchcraft Papers," *Register* 27(1873):55; Moore, "Notes on the History," 171; General Court Records, 4:233–4; "Thomas Newton," DAB 13:46–47.

80. SWP 440–442.

81. SWP 374.

82. General Court Records, 234–235; *Acts*, 1:34–35, 38–39.

83. Morison, *Harvard* 2:490; "Cambridge Association," 268; "Return," 110–111.

84. SWP 597–598.

85. Calef in Burr, 356; C. Mather, *Wonders*, in Burr, 229; EQC 5:124, 7:183, 8:432–433, 9:579–580.

86. SWP 368–369; Perley, "Part of Salem Village," 186.

87. SWP 369, 375.

88. SWP 363, 373–377.

89. Calef, Burr, 357–358.

90. SWP 757, 997.

91. SWP 606–607, 106–107, 107–108.

92. SWP 956; D. Greene, "Susanna Martin," 198–199; Anderson, *Great Migration Begins* 3: 1431–1433, 1:375–381; Perkins, *Perkins*, 1:7, 11–12, 15 & 2:6; Avery, *Averell*, 73–115; Towne, *Towne*, 21–22; S. Noyes, 104, 123; SWP 423; Hoyt, *Salisbury*, 69–70.

93. SWP 956; EQC 8:377, 387, 9:30, 601–604.

94. General Court Records, 235; *Acts*, 1:37, 27–29, 30–34, 36.

95. Taylor, 113–116; Tomlinson 56, 7–12, 56.

96. SV-VR; Boyer, *S-V Witchcraft*, 220–221; Torrey, 204.

97. SWP 571, 577; C. Mather, *Wonders*, Burr, 229; Calef, Burr, 357; Lawson, "Narrative" 2:534, 530–531 (presumably today).

98. C. Mather, *Wonders*, Burr, 230–231; SWP 569–5670; cf. Starkey, 273, on Jimsonweed.

99. SWP 569, 566–567, 577; C. Mather, *Wonders*, Burr, 232.

100. SWP 562–3; C. Mather, *Wonders*, Burr, 231–232.

101. SWP 563–564; Mather, *Wonders*, Burr, 235.

102. SWP 572, 567–568, 566–567; C. Mather, *Wonders*, Burr, 232, 239–240, 233.

103. SWP 560–561; C. Mather, *Wonders* Burr, 235.

104. SWP 558–559; C. Mather, *Wonders*, Burr, 234.

105. SWP 564–566; C. Mather, *Wonders*, Burr, 235–236; Lawson, "Narrative," 2:534.

106. SWP 571–572.

107. SWP 578; C. Mather, *Wonders*, Burr, 234–235.

108. C. Mather, *Wonders*, Burr, 236.

109. Calef, Burr, 356 but cf. SWP 80–81, 598, etc.

110. SWP 594.

111. SWP 600, 595, 593.

112. Calef, Burr, 358–359.

113. SWP 603–4, 600, 593–594; EQC-VT 57–63–1.

114. SWP 588.

115. Calef, Burr, 358–359.

116. C. Mather, *Wonders*, Burr, 237; Calef, Burr, 356; SWP 448–449.

117. SWP 440–444, 449–450.

118. SWP 438–439, 442–443, 439; C. Mather, *Wonders*, Burr, 240.

119. SWP 451–452, C. Mather, *Wonders*, Burr, 238.

120. SWP 439, 450–451; C. Mather, *Wonders*, Burr, 239, 240.

121. SWP 454–455, 445–447 453; C. Mather, *Wonders*, Burr, 239–240; SWP 684, 667, 263, 811.

122. SWP 810; B. Gould, 48–49; W. Davis Jr., "Wildes Family," 139–141; EQC 1:179, 3:66, 117, 118.
123. SWP 810.
124. SWP 808–809.
125. SWP 816–818.
126. SWP 812–816.
127. Calef, Burr, 360; Brattle and note in Burr, 186–187; Robbins, 599–600.
128. *Calendar*, 13:663; Mass. Archives 61:320; Tully.
129. *Calendar*, 13:664; Mass. Archives 48:202, 61:369.
130. SWP 843; D. Greene, "Wilkins," 9–10; SV-VR, Dec. 20, 1692; C. Mather, *Magnalia* (1855), 2:374–375.

Chapter 7: July 1692

1. John Emerson in C. Mather, *Decennium*, 243–247; Babson, *History of Gloucester*, 59–61; Babson, *Notes*, 87; Finney-MacDougal, 1–12.
2. SV Records, July 1, 1690.
3. SWP 385, 453, 194.
4. General Court Records, 237; *Acts*, 1:35–36, 29–30, 34–35, 36; Mass. Archives 48:200–201.
5. SWP 395–397, 433; Ann Pudeator examination, SWP 702–703; Perley, *Salem*, 2:122.
6. SWP 704–705.
7. SWP 116, 125–128.
8. SWP 180–181.
9. Salem Church, *Records*, 172, 127.
10. Hutchinson, 2:39–40; cf. Keyne, 237–9; SWP 592–593, 585; Dunton, *Life*, 177; Sewall, *Diary*, Dec. 14, 1717.
11. *Calendar*, 13:663–664; Thwing, 88–89.
12. Candy examination, SWP 179; Hale, 80–81.
13. Hutchinson, 2:26.
14. SWP 592–593.
15. Calef, Burr, 358–359, 388.
16. Council, 181–182.
17. Hale, 80.
18. SWP 848.
19. *Acts*, 1:35–36; C. Mather, "Brand," 269–270, 261; C. Mather, *Decennium*, 206–208; Hammond, 162; Windsor, *Boston*, 2:ix.
20. Tully; H.B.; Hammond, 162; C. Mather, *Magnalia* (1977) 279; Morison, 2:465–470; Sibley, *Harvard*, 4:119.
21. Mass. Archives 40:264; Washburn, 148; Parker, 1:55; DAB 13:246–247.
22. SWP 302.
23. Emerson in C. Mather, *Decennium*, 243, approximate date.
24. Council, 182–184; Sibley *Harvard*, 5:13–17.
25. SWP 527, 528.
26. Emerson in C. Mather, *Decennium*, 243.
27. Ibid., 243–244.
28. Ibid., 244.
29. Tully; H.B.
30. SWP 377–378; Calef, Burr, 359.
31. Sewall, *Diary*, July 13, 1692.
32. "Andover Town Records," July 13, 1692.
33. Love, 273, 481; Hammond, 162; C. Mather, *Magnalia* (1977), 346.
34. Emerson in C. Mather, *Decennium*, 244.
35. SWP 527, 523–524.
36. Emerson in C. Mather, *Decennium*, 244–245.
37. Council, 184–185; *Calendar*, 13:678, 653; Barnes, "Phippius Maximus," 538–539.
38. SWP 342; EQC 9:513–514; Pierce, 1032–1033; C. Mather, *Decennium*, 222; Stearns, 266–268; T. Holmes, *Cotton Mather*, 1030; *Court of Assistants*, 1:303–304; C. Mather, *Magnalia* (1855), 2:413–414.
39. SWP 341, 342, Ann Foster confession, SWP 342; "Plan of Andover."
40. SWP 950.
41. SWP 930.
42. SWP 342–343; Hale, 30; Pierce, 1032.
43. Hale, 30–31.
44. Emerson in C. Mather, *Decennium*, 245.
45. Tully; H.B.; Hammond, 163.
46. SWP 343 Ann Foster confession, SWP 343.
47. Council, 185–186; Emerson in C. Mather, *Decennium*, 245–246.
48. S. A. Drake, *Border Wars*, 85.
49. C. Mather, *Decennium*, 240; SWP 308; Blodgette, 371–372.
50. Tully; H.B.; SWP 308; Hazen, 149–150.
51. SWP 377–378; Hammond, 163; C. Mather, August 8, 1692, letter to John Cotton in *Diary*, 1:142; Calef, Burr, 358; K. Thomas, 506–507; Hutchinson 2:40; Sewall, *Diary*, Dec 14, 1717.

52. C. Mather, "Brand," 269.
53. SWP 513; J. Smith, 177–179.
54. Calef, Burr, 361; Wilson, 114, 127; Tapley, 68; Perley, "Part of Salem No. 7," 149; Tully; Bentley, "Description," 268.
55. SWP 516–517, 531, 521, 519.
56. SWP 529.
57. Sewall, "Letter-Book," 1:132; Brattle, 184.
58. Sewall, *Diary*, July 20, 1692; *Psalms*.
59. C. Mather, "Brand," 269.
60. SWP 707–708.
61. Council Records, 2:186–188.
62. SWP 519; Pierce, 124.
63. SWP 343 (Ann Foster's second examination), 514 (Mary Lacy Sr.'s "2d Examination"), 520–526, 531–532 (two versions of the examination where Ann Foster, Mary Lacy Sr. and Mary Lacy Jr. were questioned together); additional material in Trask, *"Devil,"* 156–157; SWP 197–198, 343.
64. SWP 514, 532; Ewell, 46–47, 167, map opp. 168.
65. "Middlesex Folio," 1674–67–4; Billerica VR, 292, 34.
66. "Andover Town Records", October 14, 1690.
67. SWP 523; James 1:12, 1 Peter 5:4.
68. SWP 197.
69. Examinations of Richard Carrier, SWP 197–198, 529–530; Richard and Andrew Carrier, 526–9; Andrew Carrier, 530; Trask, *"Devil,"* 157.
70. John Proctor in Calef, Burr, 363; "Body of Liberties," in Powers, 538; *Andros Tracts* 1:171.
71. SWP 529.
72. SWP 197–198, 529.
73. SWP 307.
74. C. Mather, August 5, 1692 letter to John Cotton in *Diary*, 1:142; SWP 119–120.
75. SWP 961; Martha Emerson examination, SWP 308–309.
76. SWP 309, 308; Job 13:15.
77. Proctor letter in Calef, Burr, 362–364.
78. Tully; "Baptisms," 236.
79. Tomlinson, 64–65.
80. Council, 190–191; Church, 2:83–84.
81. Emerson in C. Mather, *Decennium*, 246–247.
82. Gage, 172–173.
83. Suffolk Court Files, #2754, 2672; Mass. Archives 37:379, 1:428, 40:622, 624; SJC 1:38.
84. *Calendar*, 13:678; Barnes, "Phippius Maximus," 538–539; Randolph, 7:411–412.
85. Essex County, General Sessions, ms. 1:1–2; SWP 946.
86. SWP 115, 131.
87. Gage, 142.
88. Ibid., 170, 172.
89. Sewall, *Diary*, July 27, 1692; Savage 1:108; Calef, Burr, 371.
90. SWP 116–117.
91. SWP 117–118.
92. SWP 131, 887, 882–883, 924–925; Savage, 4:354.
93. SWP 924–5, 143, 961, 994–995; Trask, *"Devil,"* 157–158.
94. SWP 845.
95. SWP 961, 994–995.
96. SWP 767, 769; S. Noyes, 285–286, 541; EQC 2:226–232.
97. SWP 183 and 767–769, Mary Toothaker examination.
98. Brigham, vii-ix; Perley, "Part of Haverhill," 163; SWP 143, Hannah Bromage examination.
99. SWP 961, 994–995.
100. Cary in Calef, Burr, 352; Sibley, *Harvard*, 4:91–92; Sewall, *Diary*, July 30, 1692; Middlesex Court Records, 158.
101. SWP 845.
102. SWP 845; Parris, *Sermons*, 199.
103. SWP 188, 192.
104. Gage, 172.

Chapter 8: August 1692

1. Cambridge Association, 268; I. Mather, *Cases*, 32.
2. Hazen, 127–128.
3. Hutchinson 2:51; Church, 83; C. Mather, *Magnalia* (1977), 346; Randolph, 7:413.
4. Calef, Burr, 360; C. Mather, *Wonders*, Burr, 241; SWP 189.
5. SWP 188; C. Mather, *Wonders*, Burr, 241.
6. C. Mather, *Wonders*, Burr, 244, 241.
7. SWP 189, 190; C. Mather, *Wonders*, Burr, 241–242.
8. SWP 192; C. Mather, *Wonders*, Burr, 242–243.

 9. SWP 190–191, 193–194, 191–192; C. Mather, *Wonders*, Burr, 243–244.
10. C. Mather, *Wonders*, Burr, 244; Lawson, "Narrative," 2:530.
11. C. Mather, *Wonders*, Burr, 241.
12. SWP 963–964; Cook, 75.
13. SWP 686–687, 689–690, 664, 681–683.
14. SWP 668, 673.
15. SWP 664, 670–671, 665–666.
16. Calef, Burr, 360.
17. SWP 645, 139; Gage, 176–177; Brigham, 24.
18. SWP 956; Gage, 176.
19. SWP 189, 297, 165, 167–170, 486.
20. SWP 213.
21. Eaton, 58, 115; Wyman, 657; SWP 540, 742.
22. SWP 961, Mary Clark examination, 213–214.
23. Lawson, "Narrative," 2:530.
24. Brattle, 178; Winsor, 2:530; Usher, 7–12.
25. SWP 296, 263–264, 480–486.
26. Gage, 172.
27. Sewall, *Diary*, Aug. 4, 1692; Love, 481; C. Mather, *Diary* 1:142–143; C. Mather, *Selected Letters*, 40–41.
28. Love, 261; Hammond, 163; Silverman, *Cotton Mather*, 107; Levin, *Cotton Mather*, 202; T. Holmes, *Cotton Mather*, 1255; Cotton Mather's sermon is in C. Mather, *Wonders*, Bell edition, 34–88.
29. C. Mather, *Wonders*, Bell, 70; Sewall, *Diary*, Aug. 4, 1692.
30. C. Mather, *Wonders*, Bell, 68–69; R. Pike in Upham, *Salem* 2:539–540; Lawson, "Narrative," 2:528–532, 352; Calef, Burr, 389; SWP 853, 457.
31. C. Mather, *Diary*, 1:151–152, 142.
32. C. Mather, *Selected Letters*, 40–41, letter to John Cotton; Lawson, "Narrative," 2:535.
33. D. Greene, "Wilkins," 9–10; SWP 842–844, 850.
34. SWP 1008–1009.
35. SWP 479, 486, 482–483.
36. SWP 476.
37. Lawson, "Narrative," 2:535.
38. C. Mather, *Wonders*, Burr, 216–217.
39. C. Mather, *Wonders*, Burr, 217–218; Lawson, "Narrative," 529.
40. C. Mather, *Wonders*, Burr, 218–219; Hale 34–35.
41. C. Mather, *Wonders*, Burr, 218; SWP 153, 982–983; *Salem Church Records*, 34, 41, 42.
42. C. Mather, *Wonders*, Burr, 216, 219–220; SWP 160, 162, 154.
43. C. Mather, *Wonders*, 220, 218; EQC 9:30–32, 47–49; Anderson, *Great Migration Begins* 2:885.
44. SWP 176, 162–163, 163.
45. C. Mather, *Wonders*, Burr, 221.
46. C. Mather, *Wonders*, Burr, 221–222; Hansen, *Witchcraft*, 9–10, 76.
47. I. Mather, *Cases*, postscript.
48. Hale, 35, 31; C. Mather, *Wonders*, Burr, 220.
49. I. Mather, *Cases*, 70.
50. SWP 727; Gage, 170–175.
51. SWP 201; Savage, 1:108.
52. SWP 503, 539, 741–2; Pope and Hooper, 1–7; Tully; H.B.; Sewall, *Diary*, Aug. 16, 1692.
53. R. Pike letter in Upham, *Salem* 2:538–544, 2:449–452; SWP 503, 558–570, 573.
54. SWP 328–329.
55. SWP 201, 503, 307, 504; Brigham, 18, 24–25; Savage 3:407.
56. SWP 503, 504.
57. Abbott ms. "Dane," "Johnson," "Faulkner"; SWP 883, 328, 503, 504.
58. SWP 201, Sarah Carrier examination.
59. SWP 203, Thomas Carrier Jr. examination.
60. SWP 503, Elizabeth Johnson Jr. examination.
61. D. Bradstreet letter in "Hutchinson Papers," 126; SWP 882–883.
62. SWP 882.
63. SWP 327–328; "Plan of Andover"; Savage 1:358–359; Greven, 79–80.
64. SWP 327, 328, 201–202, Sarah Carrier examination.
65. SWP 503–505, Elizabeth Johnson Jr. examination, 183, 872.
66. SWP 327–328, Abigail Faulkner examination.
67. SWP 328–329.
68. Church, 2:87–88; Hammond, 163; Usher, 9–12; Brattle, 178.
69. C. Mather, *Decennium*, 240–241.
70. D. Greene, "George Jacobs," 69; SWP 476, 998.
71. SWP 997–998; Calef, Burr, 364; Upham, *Salem* 2:575.
72. D. C. Brown, "Forfeitures," 87–88, 96, 100, 101.
73. Ibid., 102–104, 105; Calef, Burr, 362, 361; SWP 667, 684.

74. "Examination of Daniel Emms/Eames," Daniel Eames exam, August #74 & #76: Mass Hist. Soc. Misc. Bound Ms. On-line <http://etext.virginia.edu/salem/witchcraft/archives/MassHist/H51A.html>

75. B.H.

76. "Examination of Daniel Emms/Eames," Daniel Eames exam, August #74 & #76: Mass Hist. Soc. Misc. Bound Ms. On-line <http://etext.virginia.edu/salem/witchcraft/archives/MassHist/H51A.html>

77. Abbott ms., "Robinson."

78. SWP 230.

79. SV Church records, Aug. 14, 92.

80. Gage, 174–175; SW 784–785.

81. Sewall, *Diary,* Aug. 16, 1692.

82. C. Mather, *Selected Letters*, 41–42.

83. SWP 1008.

84. SWP 459, 961; EQC VT 48–134–1; Byam, 1–5; H. Noyes, 46; EQC 1:303.

85. Calef, Burr, 364–365, and M. Jacobs letter, Calef, Burr, 365–66.

86. SWP 178, 467.

87. SWP 459, 961, 281; Hurd, *Essex*, 968; Perley, *Boxford*, 29–31.

88. Sewall, *Dairy*, Aug. 19, 1692; Brattle, 177.

89. C. Mather, *Wonders*, Bell, 85.

90. Calef, Burr, 361–362, 364.

91. Ibid., 360.

92. SWP 281; Perley, "Part of Salem No. 7," 146.

93. Calef, Burr, 361–362; Brattle, 177; SWP 1008.

94. Calef, Burr, 360–1; Brattle, 177; Levin, *Cotton Mather*, 212–215; Silverman *Cotton Mather*, 109–111.

95. Bentley, "Description," 268; Calef, Burr, 361; "A Further Account of the Tryals," 171.

96. SWP 281.

97. SWP 279–280, Rebecca Eames examination; Perley, *Boxford*, 24–31.

98. SWP 284–285.

99. D. Greene, "George Jacobs," 71; Perley, "Where the Salem 'Witches' Were Hanged"; W. P. Upham, *House of John Proctor*, 4, 8; Endicott, 53; Lincoln R. Stone, 152.

100. M. Jacobs, letter in Calef, Burr, 365–366; SWP 496–497.

101. SWP 998, 592.

102. SWP 245.

103. SWP 961, 460.

104. SWP 149–150; Perley, *Salem*, 1:249.

105. Bentley, *Diary*, 2:24–25; writ in Goodell, 47; Noble, 19–20; SWP 988; Hawthorne, 74–75, 584–585.

106. *Calendar,* 13:653; Middlesex County Court, 158; Robbins, 599–600; Brattle, 186–187.

107. Brattle, 178–179; D. C. Brown, "Forfeitures," 108.

108. Bentley, *Diary*, 2:25; SWP 988–991; Goodell, 47, 18; D. C. Brown, "Forfeitures," 103–109.

109. SWP 961.

110. Tully; H.B.; SWP 956; Gage, 176.

111. C. Mather, "Brand," 269, 260, 286.

112. SWP 956.

113. Mass. Archives 40:624; R. R. Johnson, 162.

114. Sewall, *Diary*, Aug. 25, 1692; Love, 256.

115. Brigham, 24–25, 18; Pierce, 130–131, 122, 124; Blodget, 166.

116. SWP 882, 465, 648.

117. SWP 465, 63–64; Brigham, 18, 29.

118. SWP 467, 465, 947–948.

119. Hutchinson, 1:321–322; S. A. Drake, *Border Wars*, 89–92; Coleman, 2:216; Parkman, 375–376; R. R. Johnson, 71; Webster, 180.

120. SWP 466–467.

121. SWP 647, 466–467, John Jackson Sr. examination; Blodgett, 166; EQC-VT 50–68–2, 50–68–4; EQC 6:27–29.

122. Deleted in proofs.

123. SWP 468.

124. SWP 469–470, John Jackson Jr. examination.

125. Blodget, 165; SWP 954, 950.

126. Hale 33; SWP 59, 546.

127. SWP 69.

128. Tully; H.B.; Love, 481; *Salem Church Records*, 172–173.

129. SWP 546, 59.

130. SWP 742.

131. SWP 227; Love, 256; McTeer, "Children of John Aslebee's Daughters," 80–83; Perley, *Salem*, 3:138.

132. SWP 231.

133. SWP 65.

134. SWP 59–60, 60–61, Mary Barker examination.

135. SWP 545–546, Mary Marston examination.

136. SWP 65–67, 67–68, William Barker Sr. examination.

137. SWP 499, 501, 883.
138. SWP 499, 501, 328.
139. SWP 502, 883, 503–505, 500; Holman, 1058.
140. SWP 500–502, Elizabeth Johnson Sr. examination, 883; EQC-VT 51–66–2; Mass. Archives 81:129.
141. SWP 501; EQC 3:5.
142. SWP 328–329, Abigail Faulkner second examination.
143. SWP 68–69; Hale, 33–34.
144. SWP 281–282, Rebecca Eames confession.
145. "Essex General Sessions," 1:69.
146. SV Church Records Aug. 31, 1692.
147. SWP 387, 388, 629, 630, 633; Savage, 3:407.
148. SWP 792, 387–388; Pierce, 130.
149. SWP 629, 791–792.

Chapter 9: September 1692

1. SWP 783, 781, 791, 387, 781; EQC 6:387; Pope, *Hooper*, 1–11; E. Smith, 1–2.
2. W. Johnson, 14–15, 124–125.
3. SWP 783, 388.
4. SWP 783–784, Samuel Wardwell examination, 1006.
5. SWP 387–388, Sarah Hawkes examination, 751; K. Thomas, 445.
6. SWP 781–782, Mary Wardwell examination.
7. SWP 791–792, Sarah Wardwell examination, 920–921; Andover, *Vital Records*, 2:489.
8. SWP 73–74, 75–76, William Barker Jr. examination in two similar versions, 72–73.
9. SWP 509–510, Stephen Johnson examination, 510–511.
10. SWP 388, 781–782, 76, 510, 723, 629, 630, 631; Savage, 3:407.
11. Sewall, *Diary*, Sept. 1, 1692; Steffen, "Sewall Children," 168.
12. Sewall, *Diary*, Oct. 29, 1719, May 12, 1720, Apr. 2, 1725; Roads, 39.
13. SWP 280–281; EQC 9:530, 595; Mass. Archives 135:144, 168; Byam, 1–4.
14. SWP 631–632, Mary Parker examination, 629; Abbott ms., "Parker" and "Ayer."
15. Brattle, 177; C. Mather, *Brand*, 259–260, 269; C. Mather, *Diary* 1:147–148.
16. C. Mather, *Selected Letters*, 43–44, 45–46; C. Mather, *Diary*, 1:151–152; C. Mather, *Wonders* (Bell), 20–21,22, 24–25; T. Holmes, *Cotton Mather*, 1247; Levin, "Did the Mathers Disagree," 34–36.
17. Randolph, 7:409, 419, 420–427; Barnes, "Phippius Maximus," 535, 538; Mass. Archives 61:465.
18. SWP 651; Trask, *"Devil,"* 160; Babson, *History of Gloucester*, 82–83, 153; Finney-MacDougal, 1–5.
19. SWP 65; Trask, *"Devil,"* 160.
20. SWP 723, 741, 742, 539, 540.
21. Noble, 15; SWP 237, 273.
22. Council Records, 2:192–193.
23. "Cambridge Association," 268; Morison, 491–492; Silverman, *Cotton Mather*, 224.
24. SWP 539, 540, 741, 345, 651, 311; D. Greene, "Wilkins," 105–106; Savage, 3:73; Essex Co. General Sessions, 1:13.
25. EQC 7:238; SWP 651; S. Noyes, 197.
26. Babson, *History of Gloucester*, 129, 82–83; EQC 2:36–38, 4:441, 7:116; SWP 651–652; Trask, *"Devil,"* 160.
27. SWP 741, 540, 539.
28. SWP 741–742, Mary Taylor examination.
29. SWP 933–934.
30. SWP 539–540, Jane Lilly examination.
31. SWP 542–543.
32. SWP 540, Mary Coleson examination; Eaton, 58, 115; Wyman, 657.
33. SWP 957.
34. SWP 311.
35. SWP 345; S. Noyes, 222, 248.
36. SWP 66, 68, 703–704, 257–258, 293–294.
37. SWP 245, 490, 269; Calef, Burr, 366; Mass Archives 40:623.
38. SWP 616; Holman, 1058; *Records of Governor and Company*, 5:325, 343–346.
39. SWP 703–704, 257–258, 292; Calef, Burr, 366.
40. SWP 397–399; EQC 7:42–55, 181–183.
41. SWP 400, 401.
42. SWP 393–394.
43. SWP 394.
44. Lawson, "Narrative," 2:534; Sewall, *Diary,* Sept. 21, 1692; K. Thomas, 464.
45. SWP 626–627.
46. *Acts*, 1:29–30.
47. Randolph, 7:419.
48. SWP 706, 121, 119–120.

49. SWP 624–625, 623.
50. SWP 634, 626, 628.
51. SWP 632–633.
52. SWP 97–99, 635–636, 97.
53. SWP 292.
54. SWP 292, 302.
55. SWP 634.
56. SWP 507–508, Rebecca Johnson examination; Andover Town Records, July 13, 1692; Bailey, 412; McTeer, "Aslebees of Andover," 233–234, and "Children of John Aselbee's Daughters," 12–14; W. Johnson, 14, 124; SWP 507; Abbott Ms., "Haggett."
57. SWP 508.
58. SWP 723, Henry Salter examination; R. Thompson, 118, 225; EQC 5:230.
59. SWP 724.
60. SWP 917–919, 931–932, 616; I. Mather, "Recantation," 223–224; Brigham, 24–26; Savage 2:454–455; Farnham, 4; SWP 503–504; Trask, "Devil," 159.
61. I. Mather, "Recantations," 222; Bailey, 137; Abbott ms. "Osgood," "Fry"; SWP 618–620, 971–972, 855–856, 1009; Perley, Salem 3:239.
62. SWP 971–972.
63. SWP 882; Calef, Burr, 376.
64. I. Mather, "Recantations," 223; Brigham, 24–26.
65. SWP 615–616.
66. I. Mather, "Recantations," 223–224; Sibley, Harvard, 2:471–474.
67. SWP 615–617, Mary Osgood examination; I. Mather, "Recantations," 222.
68. SWP 725–726.
69. Trask, "Devil," 159.
70. SWP 57, 915–916, 971–972; I. Mather, "Recantations," 222–224.
71. SWP 262, 121–122, 293.
72. SWP 227, 172–173. Tucker; 141–146; Clement, 10–14.
73. Calef, Burr, 366; SWP 242, 257–258; D. C. Brown, "Case of Giles Corey," 287.
74. SWP 260–261.
75. SWP 302–303, undated petition; N. E. H. Hull, 8, 115; Haskins, 51, 90–91.
76. SWP 222–223; E. E. Towne, 21–22.
77. SWP 302, 301–302, 303, 106–107, 296; Calef, Burr, 368.
78. SWP 702–703.
79. SWP 705–706, 802.
80. EQC 4:214, 410, 5:377, 6:193, 316, 7:239, 8:59–60, 232, 422–423.
81. SWP 707, 708–709, 703.
82. SWP 122–123, 123–124.
83. SWP 124–125, 126, 127.
84. SWP 126.
85. SWP 119–120.
86. SWP 238.
87. Calef, Burr, 366; SV Church Records, Sept. 11, 1692.
88. SWP 417, 344.
89. SWP 235.
90. SWP 232–233.
91. SWP 641; Swan, 168; Finney-MacDougal, 3, 5; Calef, Burr, 353.
92. SWP 709–710; EQC 9:110.
93. SWP 303–304.
94. Sewall, Diary, Sept. 21, 1692; SWP 403–404; Calef, Burr, 371; SWP 995–996.
95. SWP 981; S. Perley, "Groton," 368.
96. SWP 641; Parris, Sermons, 199–206.
97. SV Church Records, Sept. 11, 1692.
98. Tully; H.B.; SWP 245.
99. Council, 193–194.
100. Calef, Burr, 366; Mass. Archives 40:623.
101. SWP 341, 524–525, 201; EQC 9:513–514.
102. SWP 513, 514, 515.
103. SWP 784, 741–742, 403–404.
104. SWP 786.
105. SWP 641.
106. Calef, Burr, 355, 178; Upham, Salem, 2:246; Shaw, 6.
107. Mass. Archives 135:101; SWP 238, 957.
108. SWP 714.
109. SWP 715–717.
110. Roads, 31.
111. SWP 786, 787, 788.

112. SWP 787; Pierce, 131–132; SWP 787–788; Abbott ms., "Ballard."
113. SV Church Records, Sept. 14, 1692; Parris, *Sermons*, 205.
114. Tomlinson, 56–57.
115. Tully; H.B.
116. SWP 546, 510, 782.
117. SWP 145, 149–150, 858.
118. SWP 160–161; different wording in Levin, *What Happened*, 80; C. Mather, *Wonders*, Burr, 220.
119. Gage, 173, 174–175.
120. Gage, 171–172; Blodget, 329–330; EQC 2:53, 1:387.
121. Gage, 174, 175; SWP 727–728.
122. SWP 279–280, 284–285.
123. Sewall, *Diary*, Sept. 19, 1692.
124. SWP 235.
125. SWP 228.
126. SWP 775, 986, 616, 159, 503; I. Mather, "Recantations," 224; Calef, Burr, 372; Brattle, 180.
127. Council, 194; Mass. Archives 61:331–332; Tully.
128. SWP 335, 775.
129. SWP 335, 775.
130. SWP 67, 633; Gage, 173.
131. Sewall, *Diary*, Sept. 19, 1692; Calef, Burr, 366; Salem Church, *Records*, 219; SWP 257; Calef, Burr, 366.
132. Tomlinson, 57–59.
133. SWP 328, 280, 284, 342–343, 514; Brattle 185.
134. SWP 413–415, 405–409, 410–412.
135. Calef, Burr, 366.
136. SWP 388.
137. SWP 698–699, William Proctor examination, 698–699; Savage 3:424–425.
138. Hammond, 163; Mass. Archives 61:331–332; Randolph, 7:413.
139. SWP 420, 409, 410.
140. Mass. Archives 61:331–332.
141. Church, 92.
142. Salem Church, *Records*, 173; S. G. Drake, *Delusion*, 3:172–173.
143. Thomas Putnam letter in C. Mather, *Wonders*, Burr, 250; Sewall, *Diary*, Sept. 20, 1692.
144. EQC 6:190–191; T. Putnam in C. Mather, *Wonders*, Burr, 250.
145. Tully; H.B.; Sewall *Diary*, Sept. 19, 1692; Calef, Burr, 367; Perley, "Part of Salem No. 15," 71.
146. Sewall, *Diary*, Sept 20, 1692; Milton, 397; footnote by George E. McCracken to Nelson, 145–146.
147. Wells, 187; Perley, "The Woods," 190–191; SWP 985–986.
148. SWP 985–986.
149. Thomas Putnam in Burr, 250.
150. SWP 641–642.
151. Sewall, *Diary*, Sept. 19 and 20, 1692.
152. T. Holmes, 1256–1258; C. Mather to Stephen Sewall in "Letters of C. Mather," 107–108.
153. SWP 642, 952.
154. Karlsen, 95–98; EQC 1:250; Penney, 23–24.
155. Penney, will of Thomas Penney, 22.
156. Trask, *"Devil,"* 164.
157. SWP 952.
158. SWP 403–404.
159. Sewall, *Diary*, Sept. 21, 1692.
160. SWP 229, 225.
161. Burr, 369.
162. Calef, Burr, 367–368.
163. Ibid., 369; C. Mather, *Wonders*, Burr, 249.
164. Sewall, *Diary*, Sept. 22, 1692; C. Mather, in "Letters," 107–108.
165. C. Mather, *Wonders* (Bell) 5; Brattle, 184.
166. Tully; H.B.; Windsor, 2:495–496; Sewall, *Diary*, Sept. 21 and 22, 1692.
167. Sewall, *Diary*, Sept. 22, 1692.
168. Ibid.
169. Mass. Archives 3:473–474; Hutchinson, 1:322; *New York Documents* 9:544, 555.
170. S. G. Drake, *Annals*, 200; SWP 880–881; Swan, 174; Karlsen 95–98; EQC 5:311; EQC-VT 47–57–1 and 3.
171. SWP 636–637; Essex Probate 9:595.
172. Mass. Archives 3:473–434, 475.
173. Ibid.
174. SWP 228, 232–233, 934–935.
175. SWP 228.
176. Tully; H.B.; Essex General Sessions, 1:4–8; SWP 473–474.
177. Gage, 176.
178. Bailey, 220–221, 140; SWP 1006; Pope, Hooper, 4–5; Smith, 26–27; McTeer, "Asselbees of Andover," 233–235.

179. Essex deeds ms., 9:70–71.
180. Randolph, 5:80–81, 7:421.
181. Randolph, 7:411–413; Hammond, 163.
182. Sewall, *Diary*, Sept. 29, 1692; Hammond, 164; Tully; H.B.; Mass. Archives 61:331–332; Hutchinson, 2:46; Calef (1700), 154; Burr, 201.
183. R. R. Johnson, 73–75, 143.
184. SWP 232–233.

Chapter 10: October 1692

1 Brattle, 179–180; Sewall, *Diary*, Aug. 6, 1695; Suffolk Court Records 1:192.
2. Calef, Burr, 372.
3. Calef, Burr, 372; I. Mather, *Cases*, 49–50.
4. Calef, Burr, 372–373.
5. Calef, Burr, 373; Swan, 169–171; SWP 880–881; Walter G. Davis, *Ancestry of Nicholas Davis*, 223–226; Babson, *History of Gloucester*, 143–145, 79–80; Davis, "Wildes," 273.
6. C. Mather, *History of Wonders*, Burr, 247; Lawson, "Narrative," 2:532; Calef, Burr, 370.
7. SWP 225–227; S. Noyes, 416; Sewall, *Diary*, Oct. 1, 1692.
8. Cambridge Association, 268.
9. I. Mather, *Cases*, 1–4, 14, 21–24, 8–10, 28, 33, 42, 49, 51, 52–53, 66, 67.
10. Cambridge Association, 268.
11. Samuel Willard, Introduction to *Cases*, 2, cf. Sewall, *Diary*, Oct. 11, 1692.
12. Ibid.; SWP 442–443.
13. Penney, 23–24.
14. Sarah Cole of Lynn examination, SWP 227–228; Hale, 132–133.
15. SWP 229, 957, 231–232.
16. SWP 231–232.
17. Joseph Dudley letter in "Letter From Phips," 348–349, 353–358; Burr, 195 (note); *Calendar*, 13:699; "Witchcraft in New York," 274.
18. SWP 335–336.
19. SWP 533–534.
20. SWP 511–512.
21. Brattle, 180–181 (ie. before Brattle's Oct. 8, letter), 189, 374–375 (also SWP 971–972).
22. Calef, Burr, 370; C. Mather, *Wonders*, Burr, 247–248; SWP 65, 979–980.
23. Sewall, *Diary*, Oct. 7, 1692.
24. Hammond, 164; Burr, 167–168; Brattle, 169–190.
25. Hammond, 164; Tully; H.B.
26. Hammond, 164; Tully; H.B.; T. Holmes, *Cotton Mather*, 1249.
27. Hammond, 164; Sewall, *Diary*, Oct. 10, 1692.
28. "Letter of Phips," 354–358.
29. "Witchcraft in New York," 274–276.
30. Sewall, *Diary*, Oct. 11, 1692; Burr, 250–251.
31. Hammond, 169; General Court, 238.
32. SWP 875–876.
33. Phips to Blathwayt, Burr, 196–198 and SWP 861–863.
34. Phips to Nottingham, *Calendar*, 13:721.
35. Burr, 206–7; T. Holmes, *Cotton Mather*, 1266.
36. Burr, 206–207; Phips in Burr, 197; T. Holmes, *Cotton Mather*, 1259, and C. Mather, Oct. 20, 1692 letter to John Cotton, 551–552, in Ibid., quoted by courtesy of the Trustees of the Boston Public Library; C. Mather, "The Author's Defence," in *Wonders*, 5–6, 12, in Bell edition, 211–212 (Burr); C. Mather, *Diary*, 1:153; Gragg, *Crisis*, 192.
37. C. Mather, *Wonders*, Bell, 12–15, 20–21, 15–19, 20–27.
38. C. Mathers, *Wonders*, Burr, 215–244, 244, 248–249, 220, and Bell, 135–139, 140–159.
39. T. Holmes, *Cotton Mather*, 1249; Levin, "Did the Mathers Disagree?"; C. Mather, *Wonders*, Burr, 211, 236, 244; C. Mather in T. Holmes, *Cotton Mather*, 551.
40. C. Mather, *Wonders*, Burr, 212–213.
41. C. Mather to John Cotton, Oct. 20, 1692 in T. Holmes, *Cotton Mather*, 551–2; C. Mather, *Diary*, 1:153; I. Mather, *Cases*, [73], cf. Cambridge Association, 268.
42. *Acts*, 1:40–1; General Court, 239; D. C. Brown, "Forfeitures," 109–110.
43. *Acts*, 1:41–2; General Court, 239; Council, 194–5.
44. SWP 136–137.
45. SWP 665–666.
46. General Court, 240; Sewall, *Diary*, Oct. 15, 1692; Brattle, 184; SWP 740.
47. "SV Baptisms," 636.
48. Hansen, *Witchcraft*, 202–203; Tomlinson, 59–60.
49. *Acts*, 1:68–9; SWP 876–878.
50. General Court, 241; Webster, 43.

51. I. Mather, "Recantation," 221–225; SWP 971–972; Brattle, Burr, 189; I. Mather, *Cases*, 70; Brattle, 173, 180, 189; SWP 284.
52. SWP 284, 533–534.
53. SWP 383–834, 720.
54. Sewall, *Letter Book*, 1:133.
55. C. Mather to John Cotton, in T. Holmes, *Cotton Mather*, 551–552, quoted by courtesy of the Trustees of the Boston Public Library.
56. Willard, *Some Miscellany Observations*; 3–7,10–12, 15; Moore, "Notes on the Bibliography," 248–249; Brattle, Burr, 169.
57. Sewall, *Diary*, Oct. 21, 1692.
58. *Acts*, 1:46–8, 48–9, 58–9; General Court, 242.
59. Council, 196.
60. Parris, *Sermons*, 206–215.
61. SV Baptisms, 236; SV-VR #36, born 26 Sept. 1692.
62. Sewall, *Diary*, Oct. 23, 1692.
63. General Court, 242; Middlesex Court Records, 158.
64. *Acts*, 1:42–43, 59–60; General Court, 243; Council, 196–197; *Calendar*, 14:24.
65. Hutchinson, 1:321–2; Parkman, 376–7; Hammond, 164; Charlevoix, 1:226–8; Webster, 180.
66. General Court, 243–244; Council, 197–8; Sewall, *Diary*, Oct. 26, 1692; Moore, "Notes on the History," 172; Love, 264; S. Noyes, 104.
67. General Court, 244; Sewall, *Diary*, Oct. 27, 1692.
68. SV-VR.
69. SWP 1009, Sarah Wilson Jr. confession, 335.
70. R. Tomlinson, 60; Hansen, *Witchcraft*, 203–4.
71. General Court, 244–5; Sewall, *Diary*, Oct. 28, 1692.
72. Sewall, *Diary*, Oct. 28, 29, 1692; Tully; H.B.
73. Sewall, *Diary*, Oct. 29, 1692; *Calendar*, 14:24, 68.
74. *Calendar*, 14: 24, 67–68.
75. Taylor, 43–44, 77–78; Tomlinson 60; Hansen 203.
76. General Court, 245–6; *Acts*, 55–56; Moore, "Notes on the History," 168; Powers, 544–545.
77. Sewall, *Diary*, Oct. 29, 1692.
78. "SV Baptisms," 236; SV-VR; SWP 839, 851.
79. Hammond, 164; Charlevoix, 1:226–8.
80. Parkman 377; Charlevoix 1:226; Coleman, 2:217–218; R. R. Johnson, 75–77; Webster, 43–44.
81. Tully; H.B.; General Court, 246.
82. SWP 360–361; Upham, *Salem* 2:457.

Chapter 11: November 1692

1. Middlesex Court Records, 158.
2. *Acts*, 43–5, 51–5, 69–70; General Court, 247; Council, 199.
3. SWP 740, undated; Upham, *Salem*, 2:354 and Mass. Archives 135:64 for date; Barrett, "Barrett," 257–64; S. Noyes, 650; Middlesex Folio 1678–82–4; Middlesex Court Records, Pulsifer transcript, 3:239, 240.
4. Hale, 63–64; Sibley, *Harvard*, 2:320–323.
5. General Court, 247; Council, 199–200, 176; Wilbour, 23–24.
6. *Acts*, 61; Sewall, *Diary*, Nov. 4, 1692.
7. SWP 306; Calef, Burr, 373; Babson, *History of Gloucester*, 164–169, 93–94, 71.
8. *Acts*, 62–63.
9. General Court, 248; Council, 200–201.
10. Tully; H.B.; Sewall, *Diary*, Nov. 5, 1692.
11. SWP 305; Swan, 171–173.
12. Burr, 369; Savage, 2:330.
13. Sewall, *Diary*, Nov. 6, 1692.
14. SWP 636–637.
15. General Court, 249; Council, 201.
16. Tully; Cambridge Association, 268.
17. Calef, Burr, 373; Babson, *History of Gloucester*, 71–72.
18. SWP 306, 800–1; Calef, Burr, 373; Elizabeth Hubbard vs. Abigail Row, etc., November 1692 #18: Mass. Hist. Soc. Misc. Bound Ms. On-line <http://etext.virginia.edu/salem/witchcraft/archives/MassHist/H49A.html>
19. *Acts*, 49–51, 60–61; General Court, 249–250; Sewall, *Diary*, Nov. 16, 1691.
20. SWP 665.
21. *Acts*, 99–100.
22. *Acts*, 56–57, 57–58.
23. General Court, 251.
24. General Court, 252; Burr, 369.
25. Burr, 369.

26. Brattle, 184; Richard Trask introduction to Hale, viii; Hale, 35; Tully; Burr, 369; Calef, Burr, 369, mistakenly dated Oct.

27. Hale, 11.

28. General Court, 252; Sewall, *Diary*, Nov. 15, 1692; *Calendar,* 14:63–64.

29. C. H. Abbott ms. "Ballard"; Perley, *Salem*, 1:353; Savage 3:512; SWP 606.

30. Taylor, 118–119; Tomlinson 64.

31. *Acts*, 64–65, 100; General Court, 253.

32. Tully; General Court, 253–254.

33. SWP 496–497; D. Greene, "George Jacobs," 72.

34. *Acts*, 63–64, 76–78; General Court, 254.

35. Council, 203–204.

36. Sewall, *Diary* Nov. 19, 1692.

37. Barnes, "Phippius Maximus," 538–539; Mass. Archives 61:465.

38. *Calendar*, 14:25, 67, 67–68.

39. Sewall, *Diary*, Nov. 20, 1692.

40. C. Mather, "Brand," Burr, 259–264, 266–267; C. Mather, *Decennium*, 207–208.

41. Sewall, *Diary*, Nov. 22, 1692.

42. C. Mather, "Brand," Burr, 260–261, 265–266.

43. General Court, 255; *Acts*, 70–71; Mass. Archives, 100:406.

44. *Acts*, 72–76, 78–79, 84–88.

45. Mass. Archives, 100:407–408.

46. Sewall, *Diary*, Nov. 25, 1692.

47. *Acts*, 71; General Court, 256; Council, 204.

48. General Court, 257; Mass. Archives, 40:275.

49. General Court, 257.

50. C. Mather, "Brand," Burr, 260–261, note 4; Mark 9:28–29.

51. Mass. Archives 40:623; *Acts*, 79–84, 88–90; General Court, 258.

Chapter 12: December 1692

1. General Court, 258.

2. C. Mather, "Brand," 260–261 and note 1, 261.

3. Mass. Archives 40:623; General Court, 258–259.

4. General Court, 259; Mass. Archives 40:623; SWP 730; Farrar, 320–321.

5. SWP 333–334.

6. C. Mather, "Brand," 261 and note 1, 265.

7. SV-VR; Perley, *Salem* 1:305–306.

8. Calef, Burr, 383–384; Mass. Archives 40:625; SCJ 1:52; Teele, 124–125.

9. SWP 284–285.

10. General Court, 259; Council, 204–205.

11. Sewall, *Diary*, Dec. 6, 1692; Tully; H.B.

12. SWP 739.

13. SWP 878–879.

14. *Acts*, 100; General Court, 260; Sewall, *Diary*, Dec. 6, 7, 1692; Council, 206–208; Brattle, 184; SWP 665; Mass. Archives 40:623.

15. SV Records Dec.7, 1692.

16. SWP 205–206, 541–542; S. Sewall, *Woburn*, 598; Eaton, 95.

17. SWP 879–880; Mass. Archives 135:66; Perley, *Salem* 3:200; EQC-VT 55–54–2; SWP 947.

18. General Court, 260–261; Council, 208–209.

19. Sewall, *Diary*, Dec. 8, 1692.

20. Council, 209–210; General Court, 261; *Acts*, 78–84, 88–90, 84–88.

21. SWP 992; Tully; H.B.

22. SWP 353, 994; Lawson, *Brief*, 159; Mass. Archives 40:623.

23. *Acts*, 28–29.

24. Parris, *Sermons*, 215.

25. *Acts*, 90.

26. General Court, 262.

27. SWP 954.

28. Tully; H.B.; General Court, 262.

29. SV Records Dec. 13, 92.

30. SWP 880–881, 950; Swan, "Bedevilment," 174; SWP 652–653.

31. Mass. Archives 40:626

32. SWP 430–431; Mass. Archives 40:622.

33. *Acts*, 90–91; SWP 885–886; General Court, 263.

34. *Acts*, 55–56.

35. Moore, "Notes on the History of Witchcraft," 168–170; D. C. Brown, "Forfeitures," 110; Hole, 199.
36. *Acts*, 95–99.
37. C. Mather to John Richards, Dec. 14, 1692, "Mather Papers," 397–401; C. Mather, Diary 1:163–164.
38. SWP 652–653, 880; S. Noyes 192.
39. *Acts*, 91–95, 29–30.
40. Hammond, 164.
41. SWP 379–380, 994–995, 880–881, 956.
42. *Acts*, 91–95, 90, 95–99, 90–91; General Court, 263–264; Phips, Burr, 196–198, 200–201.
43. Council, 210–211.
44. Sewall, *Diary*, Dec. 22, 1692; Noble, 20.
45. C. Mather, "Brand," 265–266, 262, 271–275.
46. Lawson, "Narrative," 2:531–532.
47. C. Mather, "Brand," 276, 264–267.
48. C. Mather, "Brand," 262–277; C. Mather letter in *Magnalia* (1855) 2:551; C. Mather in G. L. Kittredge, "C. Mather's Scientific Communications," 32; Revelation 12:9, 20:2; March 18, 1692/93 letter, John Allen to I. Mather in Hutchinson 2:45.
49. Tully; H.B.
50. SWP 347–348, 620–621.
51. Council, 211–112; Love, 482; Sewall, *Diary*, Oct. 26, 1692.
52. SWP 460–461.
53. Sewall, *Diary*, Dec. 22, 1692.
54. Sewall, *Diary*, Dec. 22, 1692; Council, 212.
55. SWP 887; 897–898.
56. Sewall, *Diary*, Dec. 23, 1692.
57. Beverly, VR, 1:161.
58. Burr, 207; T. Holmes, *Cotton Mather*, 1238, 1260 note 1.
59. Tully; H.B.; C. Mather, "Brand," 274.
60. SV Church Records, Dec. 26, 1692.
61. Ibid.
62. Essex General Sessions 1:10–12; Babson, *History of Gloucester*, 148–151, 150–1; SWP 651.
63. SV Church Records, Dec. 26, 1692.
64. Sewall, *Diary*, Dec. 27, 1692.
65. Council, 213.
66. Burr, 207; T. Holmes, *Cotton Mather*, 1260 note 1.
67. SWP 887; Savage 1:433; E. Putnam, 55–56.
68. Love, 264, 482.
69. C. Mather, *Diary*, 1:161; C. Mather, "Brand," 277.
70. Andover Town Records, Dec. 30, 1692; SWP 1000.
71. SWP 897, 901, 894, 890, 893, 529–530, 317–318; Savage 4:316–317, 1:147.
72. Essex General Sessions 1:13; Greene, "Wilkins," 106.
73. C. Mather, "Brand," 277.
74. SWP 896, 899, 898, 892; Babson, *History of Gloucester*, 164–167.
75. SWP 274–275, 957.
76. SWP 54–55.
77. C. Mather, "Brand," 277–278.

Chapter 13: January 1693

1. Tully.
2. SV Records, Jan. 6, 1690.
3. SWP 889, 895, 147; Perley, *Salem* 1:306.
4. SWP 881–883; Holman, 1013–1015, 1058; SWP 882.
5. SWP 903–904, 887; Tully; SCJ, 1.
6. SWP 904; SCJ, 1; Sibley, *Harvard*, 1:470–471.
7. Calef, Burr, 382; OED.
8. Mass. Archives 135:101, 40:623–624; SWP 959.
9. *Calendar* 14:25; Mass. Archives 61:541.
10. *Calendar*, 14:67–68, 25, 68, 64, 67; Mass. Archives 61:350, 351, 351a, 352, 463.
11. SCJ 1:1; SWP 904–911.
12. SWP 904–905, 908, 494–495, 910–911, 494, 382–383.
13. SWP 905–906, 489; M. Jacobs' letter in Burr, 364–365; Poole's notes, 29–30; EQC-VT 55–54–1, 2, 3.
14. SWP 906–907, 908–909.
15. SWP 723, 504–505, 540–541, 742, 909–910, 763, 763–764, 910–911; Brigham, 29; SCJ 1:6.
16. SWP 911–912, 913–914, 914–915, 915–917; SCJ 1:7.
17. SWP 467, 469, 648, 508, 698.
18. SWP 709, 917–919; SCJ 1:12.

19. Andover VR 2:432; Farnham, 4.
20. EQC-VT 54–1 through 54–36–2; Suffolk Files 2770.
21. SWP 919.
22. SWP 136, 309, 701, 211, 211–212; I. Mather, "Recantations," 224.
23. SWP 919–920; Calef, Burr, 382.
24. SWP 920–921, 921–922, 1005–1006.
25. SWP 233, 231, 114.
26. SWP 923–924.
27. Tully; SWP 319
28. Tully; SWP 317–318, 893, 319.
29. SWP 924–925, 925–926, 927–928, 928–929, 929–930; Noble, 24.
30. SWP 132.
31. SWP 348–349.
32. SWP 954, 467.
33. SV Church Records, Jan. 12, 1693.
34. SWP 71, 897, 337, 778–779, 910–911, 855–856.
35. SWP 533–534.
36. SWP 1001, 236.
37. SWP 223, 981, 403–404; SV Church Records, April 30, 1693.
38. SCJ 1:29; Calef, Burr, 382; Phips, Burr, 201; SWP 904–932; Noble, 23–24.
39. Phips, Burr, 201, approx. date.
40. Parris, *Sermons*, 215–223.
41. SV Church Records, Jan. 15, 1693.
42. Moore, "Notes on the Bibliography," 260.
43. *Calendar*, 14:9–10, 1–2, 13:719–720; Totten.
44. *Calendar*, 13:119–120 and 14:9–10, 28, 21–22, 193, 195, 11, 5; Barnes, "Phippius Maximus," 542–543.
45. Essex General Sessions, 1:15–16; Tully; EQC-VT 54–3 to 54–36–2.
46. Essex General Sessions, 1:16–17.
47. Ibid., 19; Parris letter in Rosenthal, 206.
48. Essex General Sessions 1:17–19; *Acts*, 1:56–57.
49. SV Church Records, Jan. 17, 1693.
50. Council, 217; *Calendar*, 14:10.
51. *Calendar*, 14:68, 67–68; Mass. Archives, 40:624, 61:355, 356.
52. Sewall, *Diary*, Jan. 22, 1693.
53. Tully.
54. SV Church Records, Jan. 25 (sic.?), 1693.
55. "SV Baptisms," 236; SV VR.
56. *Calendar*, 14:5–6; Hansen, *Witchcraft*, 206–207.
57. *Calendar*, 14:11–12.
58. Sewall, *Diary*, Jan. 27 & 28, 1693.
59. Perley, *Salem*, 2:22–23; SWP 795; EQC-VT 56–60–1.
60. SWP 958.
61. Tully; Sewall, *Diary*, Jan. 29, 1693.
62. Council, 218.
63. "Further Account," 171.
64. Phips, Burr, 201.
65. SWP 932, 769, 744; Noble, 24.
66. SCJ 1:31; SWP 958; Mass. Archives 135:101.
67. "Further Account," 171.

Chapter 14: February 1693

1. Tully; Calef, Burr, 382–383; SWP 932; SCJ 1:32; "Further Account," 172; Phips, Burr, 201.
2. "Further Account," 172; SCJ 1:36; SWP 542–354.
3. SWP 932–933, 933–934, 934–935.
4. SWP 935–936; SCJ 1:35; Calef, Burr, 383; "Further Account," 172.
5. SWP 936–937.
6. Calef, Burr, 383.
7. Council, 219.
8. Andover VR 2:555 has Feb. 1 or 2, his gravestone 2.
9. SWP 542–543.
10. SV Records Feb. 3, 1693.
11. Moore, "Notes on the Bibliography," 260; Evelyn, 5:130.
12. SV Church Records, Feb. 5, 8, 1693; Matthew 19:15–17; C. Mather, *Magnalia* (1855), 2:258–259; Greene, "Wilkins," 16, 111–112.
13. Tully; SV Church Records for Feb. 5 & 7 1693.

14. Tully; SV Church Records, Feb. 7, 1693 (after Feb. 16, 1693); Hale 132–133; Hansen, *Witchcraft*, 30–31.
15. General Court, 264–265.
16. SV Church Records, Feb. 8, 1693.
17. General Court, 265–266.
18. Tully; C. Mather, "Brand," 278.
19. General Court, 266; SWP 958.
20. C. Mather, *Diary*, 1:160.
21. C. Mather, "Brand," Burr 278–279.
22. General Court, 267; SV Records, Feb. 14, 1693; *Acts*, 1:62–63.
23. General Court, 268.
24. *Calendar,* 14:24–25, 20, 26–27.
25. General Court, 268–269; C. Mather, *Parentator*, 149–51; *Calendar,* 14:63–64; Morison, 2:499.
26. Council, 220–222.
27. SV Church Records, Feb. 16, 1693.
28. General Court, 269; *Acts* 1:101–103, 104–105.
29. Sewall, *Diary*, March 3, 1693 letter.
30. *Acts*, 1:103–104; General Court, 269–270; Council, 233–234.
31. Council, 224–225; *Calendar,* 14:28–30.
32. Council, 225.
33. Ibid.; *Calendar* 14:225.
34. Phips in Burr, 198–202; Mass. Archives 61:542; *Calendar,* 14:28, 29, letters of Feb. 20 and 21 1693.
35. Hammond, 164–165.
36. C. Mather, "Brand," 285, 278–279, 283–284.
37. EQC-VT 57–64–3, 57–65–3.
38. D. Greene, "Jacobs," 69; George Jacobs, Will, Essex Probate docket #14712.
39. Love, 273, 482; Council, 219.
40. Council, 226–227.
41. SCJ 1:55; Suffolk Files #2770.
42. Pierce, 130–131.
43. Mass. Archives 61:368, 372.

Chapter 15: March 1693

1. *Calendar,* 14:91, 74, 80; Mass. Archives 61:371, 376, 372, 541, 347–349.
2. SWP 958, 1005, 995–996; Phips in Rosenthal, 219–220.
3. General Court, 271.
4. Sewall, *Diary*, March 3, 1693 letter.
5. General Court, 271–272; Council, 228–229.
6. Parris, *Sermons*, 223–232.
7. *Calendar,* 14:58; Mass. Archives 61:372, 451.
8. Cambridge Association, 268–269.
9. Mass. Archives 61: 372, 506–507, 510–511.
10. General Court, 272.
11. Phips in Rosenthal, 219–210; SWP 988.
12. General Court, 272–273.
13. Sewall, *Diary*, March 3, 1693.
14. C. Mather, "Brand," 280; Cheney, 134; Acts 16:25–26.
15. General Court, 273–274; Sewall, *Diary*, March 9, 1693.
16. SWP 958.
17. General Court, 274; Wilbour, 25.
18. Mass. Archives 61:372, 541.
19. General Court, 274; Sewall, *Diary*, March 11, 1693.
20. General Court, 275–276; *Calendar,* 14:172–173, 169, 310.
21. Sewall, *Diary*, March 13, 1693; Boston, *Report* 7:212–213.
22. Suffolk Files #2770.
23. C. Mather, "Brand," 284.
24. C. Mather, *Diary*, 1:164.
25. C. Mather, "Brand," 280–283.
26. C. Mather, "Brand," 285.
27. General Court, 276; *Calendar,* 14:54.
28. C. Mather, "Brand," 285–286.
29. General Court, 277; Sewall, *Diary*, March 17, 1693.
30. J. Allen in Hutchinson, 2:45.
31. Andover VR, 1:142.
32. *Calendar,* 14:56.
33. Sewall, *Diary*, March 22, 1693.

34. Council, 229–230.
35. SWP 958.
36. SV Church Records Mar. 27, 1693, Nov. 13, 1693, letter entered with Feb. 7, 1695.
37. SCJ 1:55; Suffolk Files #2770; Essex General Sessions 1:28–30; *Acts* 1:103.
38. SV Church Records Mar. 28, 1693; Parris, Nov. 13, 1693, letter with February 1695 Church Records.
39. C. Mather, *Diary* 1:163–164; name corrected in Silverman, *Cotton Mather,* 123, 440.
40. Mass. Archives 61:541, 542–543; *Calendar,* 14:74, 77, 376, 512.
41. Mass. Archives 61:376, 487, 512, 510, 541; *Calendar,* 14:74, 77.
42. Council, 230–232; C. Mather, *Diary* 1:163–164.
43. C. Mather, *Diary,* 1:163–164.

Chapter 16: April 1693

1. C. Mather, *Angel,* 272; C. Mather, *Diary,* 1:163.
2. C. Mather, *Diary,* 1:163–164; Job 2:10.
3. Parris, *Sermons,* 232–241.
4. C. Mather, *Diary,* 1:163–164; C. Mather, "Brand," 286.
5. SV Church Records, April 14, 1693, and "Sundry Objections" with Feb. 7, 1695.
6. SV Church Records, April 20, 1693.
7. SV Church Records, April 21, 1693.
8. SCJ 1:36, 38.
9. SCJ 1:51, 50.
10. SCJ 1:52.
11. SCJ 1:52.
12. Phips in Rosenthal, 219–210.
13. SV Church Records, April 30, 1693.

Chapter 17: May 1693

1. Parris, *Sermons,* 241–245.
2. Hammond, 165.
3. SWP 938–939; Suffolk Files #2763.
4. SCJ 1:53–60; Suffolk Files #2760; SWP 699, 60, 73, 939–940, 940–941, 348–349, 941–942, 132, 942–943, 59–60, 943–944.
5. Tomlinson, 60–63; Godbeer, 169–170.
6. SWP 333–334, 967–968; Phips, Burr, 201; *Calendar,* 14:5–6, 156.
7. "Andover Town Records," July 13, 1692, and Dec. 20, 1698.
8. SWP 1032
9. SWP 945–946.
10. Calef, Burr, 343.
11. Clinton and Jacobus, 51; Suffolk Files #3227.
12. SWP 981; Savage, 1:230.
13. SWP 981, 989–991; Savage, 1:230; Bentley, Diary, 2:25; Noble, 19–20.
14. SWP 1022.
15. SWP 994.
16. SV Church Records, May 18, 1693, Nov. 13, 1693.
17. Hammond, 165.
18. Murdock, 331–333.
19. Sewall, *Diary,* May 31, 1693.

Chapter 18: June 1693

1. Murdock, 333; Hutchinson 2:53; Sewall, *Diary,* June 1, 1693.
2. Parris, *Sermons,* 245–251.
3. EQC-VT 55–54–1 & 2, 55–102–1; D. Greene, "Jacobs," 69–71; Perley, *Salem,* 3:85.
4. Sewall, *Diary,* June 8, 1693; C. Mather, *Diary,* 1:164–165; Ulrich, 97–201.
5. *Calendar,* 14:viii-x, 204; Sewall, *Diary,* June 8, 1693; Barnes, "Phippius Maximus," 541–545.
6. Hammond, 165; *Calendar,* 14:217.
7. C. Mather, *Diary,* 1:167.
8. Sewall, *Diary,* June 26, 1693; Hutchinson, 2:54; C. Mather, *Diary,* 1:167.
9. Sewall, *Diary,* June 12, 1693.
10. General Court, 286–287.
11. Cambridge Association, 269–270.
12. Sewall, *Diary,* June 23, 1693.

13. Sewall, *Diary*, June 26, 1693.
14. D. Greene, "Jacobs," 71–72.
15. Ibid., 68–70.
16. EQC-VT 55–54–1 & 2, 55–102–1.
17. Council, 243; C. Mather, *Diary,* 1:166–167.
18. Murdock, 348.

Chapter 19: July 1693

1. Parris, *Sermons*, 251–256.
2. Hammond, 165; Sewall, *Diary*, July 5, 1693.
3. Hammond, 165; C. Mather, *Diary,* 1:166; Love, 519–520.
4. Mass. Archives 11:76–77; SV Church Records, Nov. 13, 1693, letter after Feb. 7, 1695.
5. SV Church Records, Nov. 13, 1693.
6. Cambridge Association, 269–270; C. Mather, *Magnalia* (1855), 2:250.
7. Sewall, *Diary*, June 11, 1693.
8. General Court, 297; Mass. Archives 30:330a; *Calendar,* 14:157, 176–177.
9. Maine Historical Society ms., Fogg Coll. 420, vol. 18; Watkins. July 1693, #9: Maine Hist. Soc. Fogg Coll. 420, vol. 18. On-line <http://etext.virginia.edu/salem/witchcraft/archives/MEHS/mehs_2.html>
10. Hutchinson, 2:56–57; SCJ 1:49; Randolph, 7:421; Barnes, "Phippius Maximus," 536–537; *Calendar,* 14:398; Mass. Archives 61:451.
11. Sewall, *Diary*, July 24, 1693.
12. Sewall, *Diary*, July 26, 1693.
13. Council, 239; Sewall, *Diary*, July 27, 1693.
14. *Calendar,* 14:13, 56, 165, 133, 169; Hammond, 165.
15. Phips, Burr, 201; *Calendar,* 14:50, 156–157.

Chapter 20: August 1693

1. Hammond, 165; *Calendar,* 14:217.
2. Sewall, *Diary*, Aug. 4, 7, 1693; *Calendar,* 14:137–138.
3. Hammond, 165; C. Mather, *Decennium*, 248–251; Parkman, 381; Sewall, *Diary*, Aug. 4, 1693; Calef (1700), 25.
4. Parris, *Sermons*, 256–263.
5. Sewall, *Diary*, Aug. 6, 7, 1693.
6. Sewall, *Diary*, Aug. 7, 1693.
7. Sewall, *Diary*, Aug. 9, 1693.
8. Cambridge Association, 270; C. Mather, *Magnalia* (1855), 2:250–251.
9. C. Mather, *Decennium*, 248–251; C. Mather, *Magnalia* (1977), 338–339; Sewall, *Diary*, Aug. 19, 1693.
10. Mass. Archives 105:25; Suffolk Court of Common Pleas, Record Book (1692–1698), 63.
11. Sewall, *Diary*, Aug. 19, 1693; C. Mather, *Magnalia* (1977), 339–340.

Chapter 21: September 1693

1. Parris, Sermons, 263–272.
2. Barnard, 92.
3. C. Mather, *Wonders*, Burr, 248; C. Mather, *Diary,* 1:86–87, 162–163, 167, 168; I. Mather, *Angelographia*, 40–47; Silverman, "Note on the Date of Cotton Mather's Visitation by an Angel," 82–86; Levin, "When Did Cotton Mather See the Angel?" 271–275.
4. C. Mather, *Diary,* 1:171–173; Perley, *Salem* 1:68, 3:298.
5. C. Mather, "Another Brand," Burr, 310–311; S. Noyes, 600; Thwing database.
6. C. Mather, *Diary,* 1:171–172.
7. C. Mather, "Another Brand," Burr, 310–311.
8. SV Church Records, Sept. 11, 1693.
9. C. Mather, "Another Brand," 310–311; C. Mather, *Diary,* 1:172–173.
10. C. Mather, "Another Brand," 310–316, 320, 322, 337–338; C. Mather, *Diary,* 1:172–173; T. Holmes, *Surreptious Printing*, 3, 5–6, 11.
11. Calef, Burr, 324–327.
12. C. Mather, "Another Brand," 333–336.
13. Sewall, *Diary*, Sept. 13, 1693.
14. Sewall, *Diary*, Sept. 15, 1693.
15. C. Mather, "Another Brand," 321; Calef, Burr, 327–328.
16. Calef, Burr, 327–328.
17. Calef, Burr, 324–327, 327–328.
18. C. Mather in Calef, Burr, 335.

19. C. Mather, *Diary* 1:172–173.
20. Sewall, *Diary*, Sept. 25, 1693; *Mayo*, 101, 110.
21. Sewall, *Diary*, Sept. 27, 1693; *Mayo*, 110.
22. Calef, Burr, 328–329.

Chapter 22: October 1693

1. Parris, *Sermons*, 272–281.
2. C. Mather, *Diary,* 1:173–174.
3. Ibid., I74.
4. Ibid.
5. Ibid.; Sewall, *Diary*, Oct. 7, 1693.
6. C. Mather, *Diary,* 1:174–175.
7. C. Mather, "Another Brand," 316–317.
8. SV Church Records, Oct. 13, 1693.
9. Ibid., Oct. 14, 1693.
10. Ibid., Oct. 15, 1693.
11. Ibid., Oct. 19, 1693.
12. Ibid., Oct. 22, 1693.
13. C. Mather, "Another Brand," 318.
14. SV Church Records, Oct. 23, 1693.

Chapter 23: November 1693

1. Parris, *Sermons*, 281–288
2. SV Church Records, Nov. 5, 1693.
3. Temple, 28, 506, 483.
4. SV Church Records, Nov. 13, 1693.
5. Sewall, *Diary*, Nov. 24, 1693; Calef, Burr, 329–332.
6. Hutchinson, 2:58–59; Barnes, "Phippius Maximus," 545; *Calendar,* 13:678, 14:169, 171.
7. Hutchinson, 2:59; Sewall, *Diary*, Nov. 25, 1693.
8. SV Church Records, Nov. 26, 1693.
9. Sewall, *Diary*, Nov. 28, 1693; *Calendar,* 14:294.

Chapter 24: December 1693

1. Parris, *Sermons*, 288–293.
2. General Court, 316–317.
3. Calef, Burr, 329; C. Mather, "Another Brand," 318.
4. General Court, 321, 325.
5. Essex Genearl Sessions 1:45; Perley, "Part of Beverly, No. 3," 302.
6. C. Mather, *Diary,* 1:178–179; Levin, *Cotton Mather*, 247.

Chapter 25: January 1694

1. Parris, *Sermons*, 293–298.
2. Calef, Burr, 324–333.
3. C. Mather in Burr, 333–338.
4. C. Mather, *Diary,* 1:179.
5. Sewall, *Diary*, Jan. 17, 1694.
6. Calef, Burr, 328–341.
7. *Calendar,* 14:233.
8. Sewall, *Diary*, Jan. 19, 1694.

Chapter 26: February 1694

1. Parris, *Sermons*, 298–303.
2. Calef (1700), 26–27.
3. Sewall, *Diary*, Feb. 24, 1694.

Chapter 27: March 1694

1. Parris, *Sermons*, 303–308; SWP 585.
2. SV Church Records, Mar. 4, 1694; D. Greene, "Bray Wilkins," 11.
3. In Calef (1700), 39–40; Cambridge Association, 271.
4. Gill, 36; Calef (1700), 66–77.
5. Calef (1700), 72–83.
6. SV Church Records, Mar. 9, 2, 1694; D. Greene "Wilkins," 7–8, 102, 103, 105.
7. Essex Court of Common Pleas 17:17.
8. Ibid., 17:19.

Chapter 28: April 1694

1. Parris, *Sermons*, 308–313.
2. Sewall, *Diary*, Apr. 2, 1694; Hammond, 165–166.
3. Sewall, *Diary*, Apr. 2, 1694; Hammond, 166.
4. Sewall, *Diary*, Apr. 6, 1694; Hammond, 166.
5. C. Mather, *Diary*, 1:180–181.
6. Hammond, 166.
7. Calef (1700), 27–30, 31; C. Mather, *Diary*, 1:163–164.
8. Perley, *Salem*, 3:70; LeBeau, 6; Essex Court of Common Pleas 7:61.
9. General Court, 333; SV Town Records, Apr. 28, 30, 1694.

Chapter 29: May 1694

1. Parris, *Sermons*, 313–323.
2. Cambridge Association, 271.
3. Upham, *Salem*, 2:478.
4. Hammond, 166; C. Mather, *Decennium*, 252.
5. Sewall, *Diary*, May 30, 1694; *Calendar*, 14:294–295.

Chapter 30: June 1694

1. Parris, *Sermons*, 323.
2. Hammond, 166; *Calendar,* 14:294–295.
3. EQC-VT 57–63–1 through 57–65–4.
4. SV Church Records before June 17, 1694 entry.
5. H. Mather, 109.
6. C. Mather, *Diary,* 1:181.
7. SV Church Records, June 17, 1694.
8. Ibid., June 21, 1694.
9. General Court, 356.
10. Essex General Sessions, 1:69.
11. EQC-VT 57–63–1 through 57–65–4; Essex Court of Common Pleas, 7:20.
12. SV Church Records, June 24, 1694; SV Town Records, June 24, 1694.

Chapter 31: July 1694

1. SV Town Records, July 3, 1694.
2. Sewall, *Diary*, July 4, 5, 1694; Hammond, 167; *Calendar,* 14:246, 250, 306; C. Mather, *Magnalia* (1977), 350.
3. *Calendar,* 14:246, 250, 306.
4. *Calendar,* 14:306.
5. SV Church Records, July 8, 5, 1694.
6. *Calendar,* 14:309, 310, 354–355; C. Mather, *Decennium*, 252.
7. SV Church Records, July 13, 1694.
8. C. Mather, *Decennium*, 252.
9. Sewall, *Diary*, July 18, 1694; Hammond, 166–167; J. Pike, 128; C. Mather, *Decennium*, 252–253.
10. *Calendar,* 14:312.
11. Hammond, 167.
12. *Calendar,* 14:349; Hutchinson, 2:62.
13. C. Mather, *Decennium*, 253.
14. In Calef (1700), 83–87.
15. Sewall, *Diary*, July 27, 1694; Hammond, 167; J. Pike, 128.
16. Sewall, July 27, 1694.
17. Ibid.

Chapter 32: August 1694

1. *Calendar,* 14:316, 354–355; Hammond, 167.
2. Hammond, 167.
3. Sewall, *Diary,* Aug. 6, 1694.
4. Hammond, 168.
5. Calef (1700), 87–90.
6. Ibid., 39–40.
7. C. Mather, *Decennium,* 254.
8. Ibid.
9. Sewall, *Diary,* Aug. 31, 1694.

Chapter 33: September 1694

1. Cambridge Association, 272.
2. "Savage Papers," 685–686; Silverman, *Cotton Mather,* 135–136, 441.
3. C. Mather, "Mather-Calef," 266–267.
4. C. Mather, *Decennium,* 254–255.
5. Parkman, 386.
6. SV Town Records, Sept. 15, 1694.
7. SV Church Records, Sept. 20, 29, 1694.
8. Ibid., Sept. 29, 1694.
9. SV Church records, Sept. 29, 1694.

Chapter 34: October 1694

1. Parris, *Sermons,* 323.
2. General Court, 369.
3. Sewall, *Diary,* Oct. 28, 1694.
4. Calendar 14:390; General Court, 375.

Chapter 35: November 1694

1. Sewall, *Diary,* Nov. 1, 1694.
2. SV Church Records, Oct. 29 and Nov. 2, 1694.
3. Sewall, *Diary,* Nov. 3, 1694.
4. SV Church Records, Nov. 4, 1694.
5. Sewall, *Diary,* Nov. 7, 1694.
6. Ibid., Nov. 9, 1694.
7. SV Church Records, Nov. 11, 1694.
8. Sewall, *Diary,* Nov. 15, 1694; *Calendar,* 14:397.
9. Sewall, *Diary,* Nov. 17, 1694; Winsor, 2:viii–ix.
10. SV Church Records, Nov. 18, 1694.
11. C. Mather, *Decennium,* 255; Mass. Archives 8:36–38, 40.
12. Mass. Archives 40:313, 30:437; C. Mather, *Decennium,* 256; C. Mather, *Magnalia* (1977), 340.
13. Sewall, *Diary,* Nov. 21, 1694.
14. SV Church Records, Nov. 26, 1694.
15. SV Town Records, Nov. 30, 1694.
16. SV Church Records, Nov. 30, 1694.

Chapter 36: December 1694

1. SV Church Records Dec. 2, 1694.
2. Sewall, *Diary,* Dec. 4, 1694.
3. SV Church Records, Dec. 6, 1694.
4. Ibid.
5. Sewall, *Diary,* Dec. 25, 1694.

Chapter 37: January 1695

1. Boyer, *S-V Witchcraft,* 218, 220.
2. Ibid., 220, 206–212.

3. Ibid., 220.
4. Ibid., 220.
5. Ibid., 221; SV-VR June 29, 1692; SWP 172–173; Torrey, 204.
6. Boyer, *S-V Witchcraft*, 221; Sewall, *Diary,* Jan. 16, 1695.
7. Boyer, *S-V Witchcraft*, 221.
8. SV Church Records, Jan. 21, 1695.
9. Boyer, *S-V Witchcraft*, 221.
10. SV Church Records, Jan. 27, 1695.
11. Boyer, *S-V Witchcraft*, 219, 218, 214, 221–222.
12. Ibid., 221–222.
13. Ibid., 219.
14. Ibid., 221–222, 213–214.
15. SWP 360–361; Upham, *Salem,* 2:457.
16. SV Church Records, Jan. 27, 31, 1695.

Chapter 38: February 1695

1. SV Church Records, Feb. 7, 1695.
2. Boyer, *S-V Witchcraft*, 219–220.
3. Sewall, Diary, Feb. 9, 12, 1695; SV Church Records, Feb. 12, 1695.
4. Sewall, *Diary,* Feb. 9, 12, 1695; *Calendar,* 13:653; Bentley, *Diary,* 2:24.
5. C. Mather, *Magnalia* (1977), 350–352; *Calendar,* 14:234; Barnes, "Phippius Maximus," 548–551; Hutchinson, 2:63–66.
6. C. Mather, *Magnalia* (1977), 352–353; Hutchinson, 2:63–66.
7. Sewall, *Diary,* Feb. 9, 1695; Burr, 306 note 1; Silverman, *Cotton Mather,* 133; Calef (1700), 30; C. Mather, "Mather-Calef," 244–245.
8. Weisman, 33; Silverman, *Mather,* 122; C. Mather, "Mather-Calef," 243, 258, 257, 244–245, 249, 250.
9. C. Mather, "Mather-Calef," 250, 253, 264–266.
10. Boyer, *S-V Witchcraft*, 259–260.

Chapter 39: March 1695

1. Calef (1700), 30–33; Gill, 35.
2. SV Church Records, March 1, 1695.
3. Boyer, *S-V Witchcraft*, 217.
4. Sewall, *Diary*, March 16, 17, 1695; SV-VR, March 17, 1695.
5. Sewall, *Diary*, March 17, 18, 6, 15, 1695.
6. Calef (1700), 33–37.
7. SV Town Records, March 21, 1695.
8. Sewall, *Diary*, March 29, 1695.
9. SV Church Records, March 31, 1695.

Chapter 40: April 1695

1. SV Church Records, March 1, Apr. 3, 4, 1695.
2. Ibid., Apr. 4, 1695 and Nov. 20, 1694.
3. Sewall, *Diary*, Apr. 5, 1695.
4. Ibid., Apr. 9, 29, 1695.
5. Ibid., Apr. 29, 1695.

Chapter 41: May 1695

1. Perley, *Salem,* 3:334–335, 200; SWP 879–880.
2. Sewall, *Diary*, May 5, 1695.
3. Ibid., May 6, 1695; Cambridge Association, 273; SV Church Records between Apr. 4 and June 2, 1695 (in Boyer, *S-V Witchcraft*, 260–262).
4. SV Church Records between Apr. 4 and June 2, 1695 (in Boyer, *S-V Witchcraft*, 308–309).
5. Boyer, *S-V Witchcraft*, 215.
6. Sewall, *Diary*, May 8, 1695.
7. C. Mather, Magnalia (1977), 346–347; Barnes, "Phippius Maximus," 551.
8. C. Mather, *Decennium*, 259.
9. Boyer, *S-V Witchcraft*, 214.
10. Sewall, *Diary*, May 13, 25, 1695, and Nov. 21, 1694.

11. Ibid., May 29, 1695.
12. SV Church Records between Apr. 4 and June 2, 1695 (in Boyer, *S-V Witchcraft*, 262–263).

Chapter 42: June 1695

1. SV Church Records, June 2, 3, 1695.
2. Boyer, *S-V Witchcraft*, 215–216.
3. Murdock, 346.
4. Boyer, *S-V Witchcraft*, 216–217.
5. Ibid., 217–222; Perley, *Salem*, 3:85.
6. Sewall, *Diary*, June 22, 1695.
7. Essex Court of Common Pleas, 7:41; Essex Court of General Sessions, series 4, 2:14.

Chapter 43: July 1695

1. Parris, *Sermons*, 323.
2. Sewall, *Diary*, July 26, 1695.

Chapter 44: August 1695

1. Cambridge Association, 273; C. Mather, *Magnalia* (1855), 2:258–259; SV Church Records, Apr. 3, 1695.
2. Murdock, 346.
3. SWP 767–768; C. Mather, *Decennium*, 260; J. Pike, 129; Hazen, 130–131.
4. Sewall, *Diary*, Aug. 6, 1695; Thwing database.
5. Sewall, *Diary*, Aug. 8, 1695.
6. Ibid.
7. C. Mather, *Diary,* 1:181.
8. Sewall, *Diary*, Aug. 13, 1695.

Chapter 45: September 1695

1. Calef (1700), 38–42.
2. Gill, 35.
3. Calef (1700), 42–48.
4. Gill, 34–35.
5. Sewall, *Diary*, Sept. 17, 1695; C. Mather, *Decennium*, 260.
6. Essex Court of Common Pleas, ser. 5, 7:43 verso, 46 verso.

Chapter 46: October 1695

1. SV Church Records, Oct. 5, 1695.
2. C. Mather, *Decennium*, 260; Sewall, *Diary*, Oct. 7, 1695.
3. SV Church Records, Oct. 8, 9, 10, 1695.
4. Love, 274.

Chapter 47: November 1695

1. SV-VR Nov. 22, 1695.

Chapter 48: December 1695

1. Maule, *Truth*; Jones, 13.
2. Maule, *Truth*, 176, 47, 164–165; Chamberlain, 69; Hale, 155–157.
3. Maule, *Truth*, 155, 165, 192, 182.
4. Ibid., 164–165, 65–76, 39, 218.
5. Sewall, *Diary*, Dec. 14, 1695.
6. SV Town Records, Dec. 13, 1695.
7. Sewall, *Diary*, Dec. 14, 1695.
8. Jones, 18.
9. Jones, 18–19; Sewall, *Diary*, Dec. 19, 1695.

Chapter 49: January 1696

1. Sewall, *Diary*, Jan. 6, 1696.
2. Ibid., Jan. 13, 1696.
3. SV-VR Jan. 31, 1696; Roach, 15.

Chapter 50: February 1696

1. C. Mather, *Diary,* 1:183.
2. Ibid., 1:185–186.
3. Sewall, *Diary*, Feb. 22, May 3, Aug. 24, Nov. 25, 1696.
4. Ibid., Feb. 26, 1696.
5. Ibid., Feb. 26, 1696.
6. Curwen, 214; C. Mather, *Diary,* 1:190.
7. C. Mather, *Diary,* 1:185–186.
8. Ibid.

Chapter 51: March 1696

1. SV Town Records, March 24, 1696.
2. C. Mather, *Diary,* 1:190.
3. Essex General Sessions, 2:41–42.

Chapter 52: April 1696

1. C. Mather, *Diary,* 1:190–191.
2. SV Church Records, Apr. 9, 13, 1696.
3. Sewall, *Diary*, Apr. 12, 1696.
4. Curwen, 214; Perley, "Part of Salem, No. 2," 68–69; Bentley, *Diary,* 2:26; Essex Probate Records 307:238–240.
5. SV Church Records, Apr. 13, 1696.
6. C. Mather, *Diary,* 1:191.
7. SV Church Records, Apr. 20, 1696.
8. SV-VR; Woburn VR 3:92; Farrar, 319.
9. Salem Town Records, Apr. 30, 1696; Sarah Bishop to Thomas Barton in Higginson Papers.

Chapter 53: May 1696

1. C. Mather, *Diary,* 1:192–193.
2. Salem Church, *Records*, 175–176, 43.
3. Sewall, *Diary*, May 18, 1696; Jones, 19–20; Maule, *New England Persecutors*, 56.
4. Sewall, *Diary*, May 18, 1696, & p. 1076 in Thomas ed.
5. Ibid., May 27, 1696; C. Mather, *Diary*, 1:195.
6. SWP 963–964.
7. Sewall, Diary, May 30, 1696.

Chapter 54: June 1696

1. Sewall, *Diary*, June 1, 1696; Lawson, *Christ's Fidelity*.
2. C. Mather, *Diary,* 1:196.
3. Ibid.
4. Love, 483; Sewall, *Diary*, June 20, 1696.
5. SV Town Records, July 7, 1696.
6. C. Mather, *Decennium*, 261; J. Pike, 130.
7. SV Town Records, July 7, 1696.
8. Essex General Sessions, 2:57–58.

Chapter 55: July 1696

1. SV Town Records, June 25, July 7, 1696.
2. Sewall, *Diary*, July 12, 1696; C. Mather, *Decennium*, 262; *Acts* 1:38–39, 90–91.
3. Elizabeth Parris gravestone, Wadsworth Cemetery, Danvers, Massachusetts; Forbes, 28–34.
4. Love, 274–275, 483, 275; Sewall, *Diary*, July 23, 1696.

5. C. Mather, *Decennium*, 262; J. Pike, 130.
6. Sewall, *Diary*, July 27, 1696.
7. Sewall, *Letter Book*, 1:165–166.

Chapter 56: August 1696

1. Sewall, *Diary*, Aug. 4, 1696.
2. SV Town Records, Aug. 1, 5, 1696.
3. Sewall, *Diary*, Aug. 5, 1696; Hutchinson 2:69–70; C. Mather, *Decennium*, 262.
4. Sewall, *Diary*, Aug. 10, 1696; Hutchinson, 2:69–70.
5. Hutchinson 2:71–76; C. Mather, *Decennium*, 262–263; C. Mather, *Diary* 1:209; Sewall, *Letter Book* 1:165.
6. Sewall, *Diary*, Aug. 12, 1696.
7. J. Pike, 130.

Chapter 57: September 1696

1. SV Town Records, Aug. 28, Sept. 1, 11, 14, 1696; Sibley, 4:107–113.
2. C. Mather, *Diary,* 1:204.
3. SV Town Records, Sept. 11, 14, 1696.
4. Sewall, *Diary*, Sept. 16, 1696; Love, 265, 483.
5. Sewall, *Diary*, Sept. 18, July 27, 1696.
6. C. Mather, *Diary,* 1:204–205.
7. Ibid., 205.
8. SV Town Records Sept. 26, 28, 1696.
9. Sewall, *Diary*, Sept. 29, 1696.

Chapter 58: October 1696

1. SV Church Records, Oct. 11, 1696; D. Greene, "Bray Wilkins," 4–5.
2. SV Town Records, Oct. 10, 12, 1696.
3. Sewall, *Diary*, Oct. 10, 1696, and page 357, note, in Thomas ed.; Murdock, 348; Morison, 2:512.
4. C. Mather, *Decennium*, 263.
5. SV Church Records, Oct. 11, 1696.
6. SV Town Records, Oct. 23, 27, 1696; Savage 2:117–118; I. Mather, "Recantation," 223.

Chapter 59: November 1696

1. SV Town Records, Oct. 27, 1696.
2. Sewall, *Diary*, Nov. 11, 1696; Jones, 21–22; Maule, *New England Persecutors*, 58–62.
3. Sewall, *Diary*, Nov. 13, 1696.
4. SV Town Records, Nov. 13, 17, 1696; Savage, 1:236; Burr, 372.

Chapter 60: December 1696

1. Sewall, *Diary*, Dec. 2, 1696; C. Mather, *Diary,* 1:211; Love, 266–268, 268–269.
2. SV Town Records, Dec. 3, 7, 1696.
3. Sewall, *Diary*, Dec. 2, 1696 and p. 361–362, notes, Thomas, ed.
4. Ibid., Dec. 18, 1696 and p. 362, notes, Thomas, ed.
5. Ibid., Dec. 19, 1696 and p. 362, notes, Thomas, ed.
6. Ibid., Dec. 18, 19, 1696.
7. Ibid., Dec. 19, 1696.
8. Ibid., Dec. 21, 1696; C. Mather, *Diary,* 1:212; Hutchinson, 2:76.
9. Sewall, *Diary*, Dec. 21, 1696.
10. Ibid., Dec. 22, 23, 1696.
11. Ibid., Dec. 23, 1696.
12. Ibid., Dec. 24, 1696.
13. Ibid., Dec. 25, 1696.

Chapter 61: January 1697

1. Sewall, *Diary*, Jan. 1, 1697.
2. Calef (1700), 48–52.

3. Calef in Burr, 387–388.
4. C. Mather, *Diary,* 1:214–216.
5. Calef (1700), 53.
6. Sewall, *Diary*, Jan. 14, 1697.
7. Hutchinson, 2:46.

Epilogue

1. C. Mather, *Diary,* 1:216, 150.
2. Calef (1700), 52–53; T. Holmes, *Surreptitious*, 9.
3. Boyer, *S-V Witchcraft*, 264–265; SV Town Records, March 2, 23, 1697.
4. J. Pike, 131; C. Mather, *Decennium*, 263–264.
5. Boyer, *S-V Witchcraft*, 264.
6. Boyer, *S-V Witchcraft*, 264–267; Essex Court of Common Pleas 8:73v; Essex Probate, #22851.
7. J. Pike, 131; C. Mather, *Decennium*, 265–266.
8. Boyer, *S-V Witchcraft*, 265–267.
9. Ibid.; Essex Deeds 14:245v.
10. Calef, Burr, 307, 386–387.
11. Ibid., 298, 206, 305, 296.
12. Tomlinson, 65; Karlsen, 44.
13. Sewall, *Diary,* Oct. 16, 20, Nov. 12, 1697; Sewall, *Phaenomena*, 38; C. Mather, *Decennium*, 266–267; J. Pike, 131; Perley, "Hawthorne," 342–343.
14. C. Mather, *Decennium*, 267–268.
15. J. Pike, 132; Mass. Archives 30:438; H. C. Kittredge, *Cape Cod*, 160–161.
16. C. Mather, *Decennium*, 269–270.
17. Essex Deeds 14:245v, 175, 428.
18. SV Town Records, Oct. 5, 15, 1697.
19. Clark 1:691–692; Sibley, "Parris," 63–64; Middlesex Probate, #16076.
20. Sewall, *Diary*, Nov. 12, 16, 19, 1697.
21. Hale, 10, 162, 167, 12, 7.
22. C. Mather, *Diary,* 1:245; C. Mather, *Magnalia* (1977), 347–348.
23. C. Mather, Magnalia (1977), 332, 326, 329, 331–332.
24. Calef (1700), 145–155; T. Holmes, *Surreptitious*, 11.
25. SV Town Records, Nov. 22, 1697; J. Green, "Commonplace Book," 244–245; Sewall, *Diary*, Dec. 10, 1697; Hutchinson, 2:82–83.
26. SV Town Records, Dec. 1, 20, 1697; Green, "Commonplace," 244–245.
27. Green, "Commonplace," 245; Sewall, *Diary*, Jan. 7, Feb. 20, 21, 1698; C. Mather, *Diary*, 1:247.
28. C. Mather, *Decennium*, 278; Sewall, *Diary*, Feb. 24, 1698; McTeer, "Children of Aslebee's Daughters," 15.
29. C. Mather, *Decennium*, 270; Hutchinson, 2: 78–80; DAB 7:417–418; Mass. Archives 70:389.
30. J. Pike, 132; Green, "Commonplace," 245–246; SV Town Records, Sept. 23, 1698.
31. Green, "Commonplace," 247–248, 250; SV Church Records, Nov. 10, 1698.
32. Sewall, *Diary*, Nov. 10, 1698.
33. Hutchinson 2:86, 90, 94; Murdock, 350–351; Sewall, *Diary*, June 11, July 7, 1701.
34. Sewall, *Diary*, Sept. 29, Oct. 9, Nov. 12, 1700; C. Mather, *Diary* 1:370–372.
35. Gill, 9, 58; Bond, 1:391; Roach, 16–18; S. Noyes, 429–430; Calef, Burr, 306; C. Mather, *Diary*, 1:261 note, 382–383.
36. Gill, 8, 4; C. Mather, *Diary,* 1:373.
37. Murdock, 356–358; Sewall, *Diary*, Oct. 18, 20, 24, 1701.
38. SV Church Records, Dec. 1702, Feb. 14, 1703, added at end of 1707; J. Green, "Diary," Nov. 8, Dec. 27, 1702, March 11, 1703.
39. SWP 966–967.
40. SWP 967–968.
41. SWP 969–970.
42. SWP 970.
43. Wigglesworth in D. P. Corey, *Malden*, 337–338.
44. Savage 3:497; Upham, *Salem*, 2:510.
45. Bond, 1:391.
46. Hutchinson, 2:125, 131, 132, 142–145.
47. SWP 972–974; C. Mather, *Diary,* 2:19, 32; T. Holmes, *C. Mather Bibliography*, 1070.
48. Hutchinson, 2:134–135; SWP 991–992, 991–992, 987, 995.
49. SWP 989–991, 979–980, 1003–1004, 980–981; Perley, *Salem,* 2:180–181.
50. SWP 1019–1020; SV-VR Jan. 18, 1696.
51. Mass. Archives 11:193–194, 382, 353, 571–571a; SWP 1015–1017.
52. SWP 1017–1018, 1019, 1025.
53. SWP 970.
54. SWP 1025.

55. SWP 1032.
56. SWP 1040–1043.
57. SWP 1045–1046; LeBeau, 7–8.
58. Salem Church, *Records*, 218–219.
59. Ibid., 219.
60. J. Green, "Diary," 330 note; Perley, *Salem*, 2:109–110; Salem Church, *Records*, 253; S. Phillips, "Elegy"; Calef, Burr, 308; Hutchinson, 2:40; Loring, 71; Boyer, *S-V Witchcraft*, 145; Roach, 21.
61. Essex General Sessions 4:76–78; Mass. Archives 11:413–414; Essex Probate, #9082; LeBeau, 8; Bentley, "Description," 267, Hawthorne, 75.
62. Allen; "Witchcraft at Hingham."
63. Turell; Littleton VR, 93, 710.
64. Upham, *Salem*, 2:481–482.
65. Minkema.
66. Hutchinson, 2:16–17
67. Bentley, *Diary*, 4:9–10; B. Browne, 304.
68. Bentley, "Description," 265–268.
69. Upham, *Salem*, 1:2–6, 61–92, 4–5, 362–371.
70. Poole, *Cotton Mather.*
71. Upham, "Salem Witchcraft and Cotton Mather; Hansen, *Witchcraft*, xii.
72. Savage, 2:277.
73. Beard, 15, 49.
74. MacFarlane, 248; Cohn, 115.
75. Hale, 11.
76. Koehler, 444; Morgan, "The Witch and We the People."
77. Perley, "Part of Salem No. 7," 148; Bentley, "Description," 268, and *Diary*, 1:250; "Report of the Committee," 286; Perley, "Where the Salem 'Witches' Were Hanged," 11, 18; Streeter, 10–11; G. L. Kittredge, *Witchcraft*, 148.
78. King, 195–196, 198–199; Roads, 36, 41.
79. Mudge, 61–62; Upham, *Salem* 2:520; Fowler, 119.
80. Upham, *Salem* 2:513; Sibley, *Harvard*, 5:616–623; S. A. Drake, *New England Legends*, 137–144; G. L. Kittredge, *Witchcraft*, 219, 528; King, 196; Towne, "Topsfield," 28.
81. Dorson, 169; Fowler, 124–127; King, 156–160.
82. Whittier, 352.
83. O. W. Holmes, 301–304.
84. Bentley, *Diary*, 1:23–26; Noble, 19; English ms., 20, 21.
85. Hawthorne, 74–75; Noble, 20.
86. Bentley, *Diary* 2:26; Perley, "Part of Salem No. 2," 69; Upham, *Salem*, 2:470; Alderman, 155; Goodell, *Further Notes*, 47.
87. King, 89; Trask, "Raising the Devil," 198; Mudge, 62; Hawthorne, 278; Alderman, 175–176; Hurd, *Middlesex*, 860, 879.
88. Fowler, 123–124; Leonard, 20; Swan, 177.
89. Harrison and Woodward, 70; King, 203–204.
90. Upham, *Salem*, 2:1–2; A. Putnam, 232, 256, 264, 440–442; Wendell, 129–147; Quincy, 439–451.
91. Bayless, 165–166; Rogo, 36–37; Auerbach, 50–52, 200–202, 345–346; SWP 225, 264–265; Calef, Burr, 337–338; Ebon; Upham, *Salem* 2:339–340; Myers, 171.
92. Lyons, xiv.
93. Adler, 303; 184–187; Bourne, 150; Cabot, 2; Luhrmann, 45.
94. Cohn, 110, 115–116, 98–123; Butler, 111–118.
95. Luhrmann, 242–243, 245; Adler, 184–187, 303.
96. Cabot; SEN, Oct. 19, 1991, "Witch Video."
97. Victor, 24, 27–32, 289, 108–117; Lyons, 109–110; Safran.
98. Hartigan, 91.
99. Ives; Hill and Nevins; Tolles, 181–182.
100. Gillespie, 4; Meek, 145–146; Stutzenberger, 200–201, 193; Ives, 9; Gillespie, 6; Hill and Nevins, 111, inside back cover.
101. Emmerton, 29–30; Arvedson, 45.
102. Lutts; A. Goodell, "Witch Jail," ms.; Tolles, 123, 182.
103. Miller, *Timebends*, 336; Ehrenfeld, 67, 68.
104. Pillsbury and Koruth, SEN May 9, 1987, "Salem Scenes."
105. Ehrenfeld, 67; Lanza, "Tourism," SEN June 9, 1987; "Salem: a Hainting Success," SEN June 11, 1987; Korieth, "Tourism's Answer Man," SEN June 11, 1987; "Identity Problem," SEN June 18, 1987.
106. Dodson, 109–110, 193; "White Magic Anyone?" *Globe*, April 24, 1966; Salem, *List of Polls 1976*; "Gov. Dukakis Unwittingly Gives 'Witch' Her Wish," SEN Apr. 28, 1977.
107. W. Scott; "Names and Faces," *Globe*, Aug. 7, 1988; "Convention Notebook," *Globe* Aug. 14, 1988; Victor, 27–32.
108. Hansen, *Witchcraft*, 224–225.
109. *Acts in 1957*, 1047–1048; SWP, 1017.
110. Stevens, "Tourists Talk," *North Shore Weekly*, Aug. 9, 1992.
111. Dabilis, "Salem Bothered," SEN, Mar. 1, 1992.

ENDNOTES TO THE EPILOGUE

112. Ouellette, "Witching Year," *North Shore Sunday*, May 6, 1990; "Witch Accuses Committee," SEN Sept. 13, 1991; "Salem's Plan Offends Witches," *Globe*, Sept. 18, 1991.

113. Salem press kit; "In Salem Village in 1692," exhibit at the Danvers Historical Society, 1992; Salem Village Tercentennary Committee of Danvers, "Witchcraft in Salem Village," and "Dedication of the Salem Village Witchcraft Victim's memorial."

114. Endicott, 52; R. Stone, 52; Fearer, "Burial of George Jacobs, Sr." *Danvers Herald*, Aug. 6, 1992.

115. Salem Village Tercentenary Committee of Danvers, "A Commemorative Evening of Reconciliation."

116. E-mail communication from Paula Keene, Oct. 26, 2001; Chapter 122 of the Acts of 2001; "New Law Exonerates," *Globe*, Nov. 1, 2001.

117. Kremmer, "In India," *Globe*, Aug. 6, 2000; "Vigilante," *Boston Metro*, Jan. 8, 2002; Whitmore, "Killing Shows Slovak Belief," *Globe*, Sept. 2, 2001.

118. *Globe*, Nov. 1, 2001; E-mail communications from Paula Keene, July 14, 2001, Nov. 18, 2001.

BIBLIOGRAPHY

An asterisk (•) denotes a work of particular significance and value.

AAS—American Antiquarian Society
Council—"Council Records, 1686–1687, 1692–1698"
Court of Assistants—Mass. Bay, Record of the Court
CSM—Colonial Society of Massachusetts
DAB—*Dictionary of American Biography*
DHS—Danvers Historical Society
EIHC—*Essex Institute Historical Collections*
EQC—Essex County, Record of the Quarterly Courts
EQC-VT—Essex County, "Verbatim Transcription"
General Court—"General Court Records."
Mass. Archives—"Massachusetts Archives" manuscript scrapbooks
MFA—Museum of Fine Arts, *New England Begins*
NEQ—*New England Quarterly*
OED—*Oxford English Dictionary*
Register—*New England Historic Genealogical Society Register*
SEN—*Salem Evening News*
SV—Salem Village
SV-VR—Salem Village Vital Records
SWP—Boyer, *Salem Witchcraft Papers*
TAG—*The American Genealogist*
VR—Vital Records

Manuscripts

American Antiquarian Society, Worcester, Massachusetts.
Mather Papers. Mather, Cotton. "Sermon Notes." Microfilm.

Andover Historical Society, Underhill Research Library, Andover, Massachusetts
Abbott, Charlotte Helen. "Early Records of the Families of Andover." Typescripts.

Boston Public Library, Rare Books Department, Boston Massachusetts.
Willard, Simon. Notes of the 6 June 1692 examination of Ann Dolliver. Ms.Ch.K.1.40.2.194. On-line <http://etext. virginia.edu/salem/witchcraft/archives/BPL/B19.html>
Willard, Simon. Notes of the 6 June 1692 examination of Mary Ireson. Ms.q.Ch.K.1.40.2.211. On-line <http://etext. virginia.edu/salem/witchcraft/archives/BPL/B20.html>

Connecticut Historical Society, Hartford, Connecticut.
Parris, Samuel. "Sermon Notebook."

Danvers Archival Center, Danvers, Massachusetts.
"A Book of Record of the Severall Publique Transactions of the Inhabitants of Salem Village Vulgarly Called the Farms" (includes vital records).

Essex County Probate Court, Salem, Massachusetts.
Essex County Deeds.

Maine Historical Society, Portland, Maine.
Burnham, Thomas. Versus Rachel Clinton. Coll. 77, box 1, Folder 19. On-line <http://etext.virginia.edu/salem/witchcraft/archives/MEHS/mehs_1.html>
Watkins, Mary. Release from jail. Fogg Coll. 420, vol. 18. On-line <http://etext.virginia.edu/salem/witchcraft/archives/MEHS/mehs_2.html>

Massachusetts Archives, Dorchester, Massachusetts.
"Andover Town Records." Vol. 1670–1716. L. D. S. microfilm #878781.
"Council Records, 2(1686–1687, 1692–1698)," on microfilm.
Essex County Wills.
"General Court Records (Record of Governor and Council)," vol. 6. (April 18, 1689 to December 10, 1698 on one microfilm reel.)
"Massachusetts Archives" scrapbook volumes, all on microfilm:
    11 (Ecclesiastical) 1679–1739.
    30 (Indian) 1639–1705.
    35 (Inter-charter) 1689–1690.
    36 (Inter-charter) 1690–1691.
    37 (Inter-charter) 1691–1692.
    40 (Judicial) 1683–1724.
    48 (Legislature) 1643–1732.
    61 (Maritime) 1671–1694.
    70 (Military) 1680–1703.
    81 (Minutes of Council) 1689–1732.
    100 (Pecuniary) 1629–1694.
    105 (Petitions) 1643–1775.
    128 (Usurpation) 1688.
    135 (Witchcraft) 1656–1750.
"Middlesex County Court Records." Transcribed in 1851 under Commissioner of the County, David Pulsifer. Vol.1 (1649–1663), original vol. 2 burned, 3(1671–1686), 4(1681–1686).
"Middlesex County Court Records, 1689–1699."
"Middlesex Folio." Microfilm.
Middlesex County Wills.
"Photostatic Copy of Records of County Court, Suffolk, 1680–1692." 2 vol. photostat copy of 1 vol. original.
"Suffolk County Court of Common Pleas Record Book, 1692–1698."
Suffolk County Deeds.
"Suffolk Court Files." Bound scrapbooks of documents, numbered by docket.
"Superior Court of Judicature" 1(1692–1695). 1892 transcript.

Massachusetts Historical Society, Boston, Massachusetts.
Miscellaneous Bound Manuscripts.
    Examination of Daniel Emms/Eames, 13 August 1692. On-line <http://etext.virginia.edu/salem/witchcraft/archives/MassHist/H51A.html>
    Hubbard, Elizabeth. Versus Abigail Row, Esther Elwell, Rebecca Diks, November 8, 1692. On-line <http://etext.virginia.edu/salem/witchcraft/archives/MassHist/H49A.html>
    Warren, Mary. Versus Daniel Ames, January 1693. On-line <http://etext.virginia.edu/salem/witchcraft/archives/MassHist/H53A.html>
    Thwing, Annie Haven. "The Thwing Index: Inhabitants and Estates of the Town of Boston, 1630–1800."

New England Historic and Genealogical Society Library, Boston, Massachusetts.
"Court of Common Pleas and General Sessions [Hampshire County, Massachusetts.]" Book 2 of the original in Typescripts Vol. A. (1664–1812) on L. D. S. Microfilm #905340, Roll 72–16.

Peabody Essex Museum, James Duncan Phillips Library, Salem, Massachusetts.
"Court of Common Pleas, series 5, Salem, Waste Book," vol. 7 (1692–1695), vol. 8 (1695–1698).
"Court of General Sessions of the Peace," Series 4: vol. 1 (1692–1695), 2(1695–1696), 3(1696–1718/19), 4(1718/19–1727).
English, [Katherine Dana], "Facts About the Life of Philip English of Salem Collected by Mrs. Philip English." Typescript, 1943.
Goodell, Abner, "The Story of the Old Witch Jail. May 11, 1956." Typescript.

Higginson Family Papers.
  Bishop, Sarah. 1723 letter to Thomas Barton.
  Higginson, John. 31 Aug. 1698 letter to "My Beloved Son."
Lutts, Carlton G. "Salem Witchcraft Original Timbered Jail Cell Discovered." Typescript, 1956.
Parris, Samuel, "Sermons." microfilm copy of manuscript book in the Connecticut Historical Society, Hartford, Conn.
"Salem Town Records, 1694–1697, 1701–1702." Transcript.
"Verbatim Transcription of the Records of the Quarterly Courts of Essex County Massachusetts." Typescript volumes
  compiled by the WPA under Clerk of Courts, Archie N. Frost.

Published Sources:
Books, Magazines, Journals

Abbott, Lemuel Abijah. *Descendants of George Abbott of Rowley.* 2 vols. self-published, 1906.
Acts and Resolves Passed by the General Court of Massachusetts in the Year 1957. Boston: Commonwealth of Mass-
  achusetts, 1957.
The Acts And Resolves, Public and Private, of the Province of the Massachusetts Bay. vol. 1 Boston: Commonwealth
  of Massachusetts, 1869.
Adams, James Truslow. *The Founding of New England.* Boston: Atlantic Monthly Press, 1921.
Adler, Margot. *Drawing Down the Moon: Witches, Druids, Goddess-Worshipers, and Other Pagans in America
  Today.* Boston: Beacon Press, 1979.
Alderman, Clifford Lindsey. *The Devil's Shadow: the Story of Witchcraft Trials in Massachusetts.* New York: Wash-
  ington Square Press, 1970 (paper).
Allen, Neal W. Jr. "A Maine Witch." *Old-Time New England* 61(1971):75–81.
Anderson, Robert Charles. "Bridget (Playfer) (Wasselbe) (Oliver) Bishop: Her Origin and First Husband." *TAG*
  64(1989):207.
*Anderson, Robert Charles. *The Great Migration Begins: Immigrants to New England, 1620–1633.*
  3 vols. Boston: New England Historic Genealogical Society, 1995.
Andover, Town of, *Vital Records of Andover, Massachusetts to the End of the Year 1849.* 2 vols. Topsfield: Topsfield
  Historical Society, 1912.
The Andros Tracts. 3 vols. Edited by W. H. Whitmore. Boston: The Prince Society, 1868; New York: Burt Franklin,
  [1971].
Armstrong, Edward A. *The Folklore of Birds.* London: Collins, 1958.
Arvedson, George. *Salem With a Guide.* Salem:1926.
Auerbach, Loyd. *ESP, Hauntings And Poltergeists: A Parapsychologist's Handbook.* New York: Warner Books, 1986.
Avery, Clara A. *The Averell—Averill—Avery Family.* 2 vols., n. p., [1914?].
Babson, John J. *History of the Town of Gloucester, Cape Ann, Including the Town of Rockport.* Gloucester: Proctor
  Brothers, 1860; Gloucester: Peter Smith, 1972.
Babson, John J. *Notes And Additions to the History of Gloucester—Second Series.* Salem: The Salem Press, 1891.
Bailey, Sarah Loring. *Historical Sketches of Andover.* Boston: Houghton, Mifflin and Company, 1880.
Bailyn, Bernard. *The New England Merchants in the Seventeenth Century.* New York: Harper & Row, paper edition
  of Harvard University Press original, 1955.
Baird, Charles W. *History of the Huguenot Emigration to America.* 2 vols. New York: Charles W. Baird, 1885; Balti-
  more: Regional Publishing Company, 1966.
"Baptisms At The Church In Salem Village, Now North Parish, Danvers." EIHC 15(1878):235–237.
Barker, Ellen Fry. *Fry Genealogy.* New York:1920.
Barnard, John. "Autobiography of Rev. John Barnard." In Demos, *Remarkable Providences.*
Barnes, Viola F. "Phippius Maximus." NEQ 1(1928):532–553.
Barnes, Viola F. "The Rise of William Phips." NEQ 1(1928):271–394.
Barrett, Joseph Hartwell. "Thomas Barrett of Braintree, William Barrett of Cambridge, and Their Early Descendants."
  Register 42(1888):257–264.
Bayless, Raymond. *The Enigma of the Poltergeist.* West Nyack, N. Y.: Parker Publishing Company, Inc., 1967.
Beard, George M. *The Psychology of the Salem Witchcraft Excitement of 1692.* New York: G. P. Putnam's Sons, 1882.
Benes, Peter, and Philip D. Zimmerman. *New England Meeting House and Church:1630-1850.* Boston: Boston Uni-
  versity and the Currier Gallery of Art, 1979.
Benko, Stephen. *Pagan Rome and the Early Christians.* Bloomington: Indiana University Press, 1984.
Bentley, William, "A Description and History of Salem." MHS *Collections*, first series, 6(1799):212–288.
Bentley, William. *The Diary of William Bentley, D. D. Pastor of the East Church Salem, Massachusetts.* 4 vols. Salem:
  Essex Institute, 1907; Gloucester: Peter Smith, 1962.
Beverly, Town of. *Vital Records of Beverly, Massachusetts to the End of the Year 1849.* 2 vols. Topsfield: Topsfield
  Historical Society, 1906.
Billerica, Town of. *Vital Records of Billerica, Massachusetts to the Year 1850.* Boston: New England Historic
  Genealogical Society, 1908.
Black, Henry Campbell. *Black's Law Dictionary*, rev. 4th ed. St. Paul, Minn.: West Publishing Co., 1968.
Black, Robert C. *The Younger John Winthrop.* New York: Columbia University Press, 1966.
Blodgette, George Brainard, and Amos Everett Jewett. *Early Settlers of Rowley, Massachusetts.* Rowley:1933.

Bond, Henry. *Genealogies of the Families and Descendants of the Early Settlers of Watertown, Massachusetts*. 2nd. ed. Boston: New England Historic Genealogical Society, 1860.

Boston, City of. *A Report of the Record Commissioners of the City of Boston, Containing the Boston Records from 1660 to 1701*. [vol. 7]. Boston: The City of Boston, 1881.

Bourne, Lois, *Witch Amongst Us*. New York: St. Martin's Press, 1985.

Boyer, Paul, and Stephen Nissenbaum. *Salem Possessed: The Social Origins of Witchcraft*. Cambridge: Harvard University Press, 1974.

*Boyer, Paul, and Stephen Nissenbaum, eds. *Salem-Village Witchcraft: A Documentary Record of Local Conflict in Colonial New England*. Belmont, Cal.: Wadsworth Publishing Company, 1972: Boston: Northeastern University Press.

*Boyer, Paul, and Stephen Nissenbaum, eds. *The Salem Witchcraft Papers: Verbatim Transcripts of the Legal Documents of the Salem Witchcraft Outbreak of 1692*. 3 vols. New York: DaCapo Press, 1977.

*Brattle, Thomas. "Letter of Thomas Brattle, F. R. R., 1692." In Burr.

Breslaw, Elaine G. "The Salem Witch from Barbados: In Search of Tituba's Roots." EIHC 128(1992):217–238.

Brigham, Williard Tyler. *The Tyler Genealogy: the Descendants of Job Tyler of Andover, Massachusetts, 1619–1700*. 2 vols. Plainfield, N.J., and Tylerville, Conn., 1912.

Brooks, Charles. *History of the Town of Medford, Middlesex County, Massachusetts*. Revised and enlarged by James M. Usher. Boston: Rand, Avery & Co., 1886.

Brown, B. Katherine. "The Controversy Over the Franchise in Puritan Massachusetts, 1654 to 1674." In Vaughan.

Brown, David C. "The Case of Giles Corey." EIHC 121(1985):282–299.

Brown, David C. "The Forfeitures at Salem, 1692." *William & Mary Quarterly*, 3rd ser. 50(1993):85–111.

Browne, Benjamin F. "Youthful Recollections of Salem, Part 1." *EIHC* 49(1913):193, 289.

*Burr, George Lincoln, ed. *Narratives of the Witchcraft Cases 1648–1706*. New York: Charles Scribner's Sons, 1914; New York: Barnes & Noble, 1946.

Butler, Jon, "Witches, Healing and Historians' Crazes." *Journal of Social History* 18(1983):111–118.

Byam, Edwin Colby, and Jack Randolph Hutchins. *Descendants of John Hutchins of Newbury and Haverhill, Massachusetts*. Rockville, Maryland, 1975.

Cabot, Laurie, and Tom Cowan. *Power of the Witch*. New York: Delacorte Press, 1989.

*Calef, Robert. *More Wonders of the Invisible World*. London: Nathaniel Hiller and Joseph Collier, 1700; facsimile reproduction. Bainbridge, N.Y.: York Mail-Print, 1972. Also selections in Burr.

Calendar of State Papers, Colonial Series, America and the West Indies. Edited by J. W. Fortiscue. Vol. 13(1689–1692) and 14(Jan. 1693–14 May 1696). London: His Majesty's Stationery Office, 1901 and 1903.

Cambridge Association, "Records of the Cambridge Association." MHS *Proceedings* 17(1879–80):262–281.

Campbell, Bruce. *The Oxford Book of Birds*. London: Oxford University Press, 1964.

Caporael, Linda R. "Ergotism: the Satan Loosed in Salem?" *Science* 192(1976):21–6.

Carlson, Laurie Winn. *A Fever in Salem: a New Interpretation of the New England Witch Trials*. Chicago: Ivan R. Dee, 1999.

Caulfield, Earnest. "Pediatric Aspects of the Salem Witchcraft Tragedy." *American Journal of Diseases of Children* 65(1943):788–802.

C[hamberlain], R[ichard], *Lithobolia: or, the Stone-Throwing Devil*. London:1698. In Burr.

Charlevoix, Pierre Francis Xavier de. *History and General Description of New France*. 6 vols. John Gilmary Shea, trans. New York: F. P. Harper, 1900.

Cheney, C. R. *Handbook of Dates for Students of English History*. London: Offices of the Royal Historical Society, 1945.

Church, Benjamin. *The History of the Eastern Expeditions*. Edited by Henry Martin Dexter. Boston: J. K. Wiggin And Wm. Parsons Lunt, 1867 (the second half of *Entertaining Papers Relating to King Philip's War*, 1716).

Churchill, Winston. *History of the English Speaking People*. Edited by Mortimer Wheeler, Hugh Trevor-Roper and A. J. P. Taylor. 12 vols. London: BPC Publishing Ltd., 1969, 1971.

Clark, George F. "Stow." In Hurd's *Middlesex*.

[Clement, William?]. *The Darling Family in America*. New York: William M. Clement, 1913.

Clinton, E. J., and Donald Lines Jacobus. "The Clinton Family of Connecticut." *Register* 69(1915):50–63.

Cohn, Norman. *Europe's Inner Demons: an Enquiry Inspired by the Great Witch-Hunt*. New York: Basic Books, 1975.

Coleman, Emma Lewis. *New England Captives Carried to Canada*. 2 vols. Portland, Maine: Southworth Press, 1925.

Cook, Goerge Allen. *John Wise: Early American Democrat*. New York: King's Crown Press, Columbia University, 1952.

Cooke, Albert B. "Damaging the Mathers: London receives the News from Salem." NEQ 65(1992) 302–308.

Corey, Deloraine Pendre. *The History of Malden, Massachusetts, 1633–1785*. Maiden:1899.

Corey, Giles, "Giles Corey's Will." *Register* 10(1856):32.

Cousins, Norman. *Anatomy of an Illness as Perceived by the Patient*. New York: W. W. Norton & Co. Inc., 1979.

Crosby's Salem, Peabody, Danvers and Marblehead Directory, 1930. Wollaston, Mass.: Crosby Publishing Co., 1930.

Cummings, Abbott Lowell. *The Framed Houses of Massachusetts Bay, 1625–1725*. Cambridge: Harvard University Press, 1979.

Curwen, John H. *A History of the Ancient House of Curwen*. Kendal (U. K.): Titus Wilson And Son, 1928.

Davis, Sylvanus. "The Declaration of Sylvanus Davis." MHS *Collections*, 3rd series, 1(1875):101–112.

Davis, Walter Jr. "The Wildes Family of Essex County, Massachusetts." EIHC 42(1906):129–141.

Davis, Walter Goodwin. *The Ancestry of Nicholas Davis, 1753–1832*. Portland, Maine: The Anthoensen Press, 1956.

Demos, John Putnam. *Entertaining Satan: Witchcraft and the Culture of Early New England*. New York: Oxford University Press, 1982, paperback, ed.

Demos, John Putnam, ed. *Remarkable Providences 1600–1760*. New York: George Braziller, 1972.

Derry, T. K., and M. G. Blakeway, *The Making of Britain 2: Life and Work Between the Renaissance and the Industrial Revolution*. London: John Murray, 1969.

Dictionary of American Biography. Dumas Malone, ed. New York: Charles Scribner's Sons, 1946.

Dodson, James. "It's Still Easy to Meet a Witch in Salem." *Yankee*, October 1986, 106–115, 188–193.

Dorson, Richard M. *Jonathan Draws the Longbow*. Cambridge: Harvard University Press, 1946.

Drake, Samuel Adams. *A Book of New England Legends and Folk Lore*. Revised edition. Rutland, Vt.: Charles E. Tuttle Company, 1971, reprint of 1906 edition.

Drake, Samuel Adams. *The Border Wars of New England*. New York: Charles Scribner's Sons, 1897.

Drake, Samuel G. *Annals of Witchcraft in New England*. 1869. Reprint. New York: Arno Press, 1977.

Drake, Samuel G. *The Witchcraft Delusion in New England*. 3 vols. New York: Burt Franklin; Reprint of No. VII Woodward's Historical Series, 1866.

Dunton, John. *Letters from New-England*. W. H. Whitmore, ed. Boston: Prince Society, 1867.

Dunton, John. *Life and Errors of John Dunton*. New York: Garland Publishing, 1974, facsimile edition of 1705 original.

Eaton, Lilley. *Genealogical History of the Town of Reading, Mass*. Boston: Alfred Mudge & Son, Printers, 1874.

Ebon, Martin. *Psychic Warfare: Threat or Illusion?* New York: McGraw Hill Book Company, 1983.

Eckstorm, Fannie Hardy. *Old John Neptune And Other Maine Indian Shamans*. Portland, Maine: The Southworth-Anthoensen Press, 1945.

Ehrenfeld, Tom, and John Engstrom. "Selling Satan." *Boston Globe Magazine*, 26 October 1986, 18–19, 54–5, 59–62, 66–71.

Emerson, Everett. *Puritanism in America 1620–1750*. Boston: Twayne Publishers, 1977.

Emmerton, Caroline O. *The Chronicle of Three Old Houses*. Salem: The House of Seven Gables Settlement Association, 1935, 1985.

Endicott, C. M. "Minutes for a Genealogy of George Jacobs, Senior, of Salem Village." EIHC 1(1859):52–5.

Erikson, Kai T. *Wayward Puritans: a Study in the Sociology of Deviance*. New York: John Wiley & Sons, 1966.

*Essex, County of. *The Probate Records of Essex County, Massachusetts*. 3 vols. Salem: The Essex Institute, 1917–1920.

*Essex, County of. *Records of the Quarterly Courts of Essex County, Massachusetts*. George Francis Dow, ed. 9 vols. Salem: The Essex Institute, 1911–1975.

Essex Institute. *Visitor's Guide to Salem*. Revised edition. Salem: The Essex Institute, 1953.

Evelyn, John. *The Diary of John Evelyn*. Edited by E. S. DeBeer. 6 vols. Oxford: The Clarendon Press, 1955.

Ewell, John Louis. *The Story of Byfield: A New England Parish*. Boston: George E. Littlefield, 1904.

Farnham, Russell C. *The New England Descendants of the Immigrant Ralph Farnum*. 2 vols. Portsmouth, N. H.: Peter E. Randall, 1999.

[Farrar?, Timothy?]. "Memoir of the Farrar Family." *Register* 6(1852):315–328.

Finney-MacDougal, Catherine. *The Babson Genealogy, 1637–1977*. Watertown: Eaton Press, 1978.

*Fischer, David Hackett. *Albion's Seed: Four British Folkways in America*. New York: Oxford University Press, 1988.

Folsom, George. *History of Saco and Biddeford*. Saco: 1830; Bowie, Maryland: Heritage Books, 1984.

Forbes, Harriette. *Gravestones of Early New England and the Men Who Made Them 1655–1800*. Boston: Houghton Mifflin Co., 1927; New York: DaCapo Press, 1967.

Fowler, Samuel P. "Hawthorne in Danvers." Danvers Historical Society, *Historical Collections* 12(1924):118–127.

Fox, Sanford J. *Science and Justice: The Massachusetts Witchcraft Trials*. Baltimore: The Johns Hopkins University Press, 1968.

Fraser, Antonia. *The Weaker Vessel: Women in Seventeenth Century England*. New York: Alfred A. Knopf, 1984.

"A Further Account of the Tryals of the New-England Witches." Anonymous letter (John Dunton?) included with some editions of Cotton Mather's *Wonders of the Invisible World*.

Gage, Thomas. *The History of Rowley*. Boston: Ferdinand Andrews, 1840.

George, Robert H. "The Treasure Trove of Phips." NEQ 6(1933):294–318.

Gill, Obadiah et al. *Some Few Remarks Upon a Scandalous Book*. Boston: I. Green, 1701. Evans microcard 975.

Gillespie, C. B. *Illustrated History of Salem And Environs*. Salem: The Salem Evening News, 1897.

Godbeer, Richard. *The Devil's Dominion: Magic and Religion in Early New England*. New York: Cambridge University Press, 1992.

Goodell, Abner Cheney Jr. *Further Notes on the History of Witchcraft in Massachusetts*. Cambridge: John Wilson And Son, University Press, 1884.

Gould, Benjamin Apthorp. *The Family of Zaccheus Gould of Topsfield*. Lynn, Mass.: Thos. P. Nichols, 1895.

Gould, Philip. "New England Witch-Hunting and the Politics of Reason in the Early Republic." NEQ 68(1993):58–82.

Gragg, Larry D. "The Barbadoes Connection: John Parris and the Early New England Trade with the West Indies." *Register* 140(1986):99–113.

Gragg, Larry D. *The Salem Witch Crisis*. Westport, Conn.: Preager, 1992.

*Gragg, Larry D. "Samuel Parris: Portrait of a Puritan Clergyman." EIHC 119(1983):209–237.

Green, Joseph. "The Commonplace Book of Joseph Green 1675–1715." Edited by Samuel E. Morison. CSM *Transactions* 34(1937–1942):191–233.

*Green, Joseph. "Diary of Rev. Joseph Green of Salem Village." Parts 1–2 edited by George Francis Dow, EIHC 8(1866):215–224, 10(1869):79–104, part 3 edited by Samuel P. Fowler 36(1900):323–330.

Greene, David L. "Bray Wilkins of Salem Village Ma., and His Children." Parts 1–2 TAG 60(1984):1–18, 101–113.

*Greene, David L. "Salem Witches I: Bridget Bishop." TAG 57(1981):129–138.

*Greene, David L. "Salem Witches II: George Jacobs." TAG 58(1982):65–76.

*Greene, David L. "Salem Witches III: Susanna Martin." Parts 1–2. TAG 58(1982):193–204, 59(1983):11–22.

Greene, David L. "The Third Wife of George Burroughs." TAG 56(1980):43–45.

Greven, Philip J. Jr. *Four Generations: Population, Land, and Family in Colonial Andover, Massachusetts*. Ithaca, N. Y.: Cornell University Press, 1970.

*Gura, Philip F. *A Glimpse of Sion's Glory: Puritan Radicalism in New England, 1620–1660*. Middleton, Conn.: Wesleyan University Press, 1984.

H. B. [Benjamin Harris?]. *Boston Almanac for the Year of Our Lord God 1692*. Boston: Benjamin Harris and John Allen, 1692. (Evans microcard 595).

*Hale, John, *A Modest Enquiry into the Nature of Witchcraft*. Boston: Benjamin Eliot, 1702. Facsimile reprint, Bainbridge, N.Y.: York Mail-Print, 1973.

Hall, David D. *The Faithful Shepard: A History of the New England Ministry in the Seventeenth Century*. New York: W. W. Norton & Company, Inc., 1972.

Hall, David D. "Literacy, Religion and the Plain Style." in MFA.

Hall, David D. "Witchcraft and the Limits of Interpretation." NEQ 58(1985):253–281.

*Hall, David D. *Worlds of Wonder, Days of Judgement: Popular Religious Belief in Early New England*. New York: Alfred A. Knopf, 1989.

Hammond, Laurence, "Diary of Laurence Hammond." MHS *Proceedings* 2nd ser. 7(1891–1892):144–172.

Hansen, Chadwick. "Andover Witchcraft and the Causes of the Salem Witchcraft Trials." in *The Occult in America: New Historical Perspectives*. Edited by Howard Kerr and Charles L. Crow. Urbana: University of Illinois Press, 1983.

Hansen, Chadwick, "The Metamorphosis of Tituba, or, Why American Intellectuals Can't Tell an Indian Witch from a Negro." NEQ 47(1974):3–12.

*Hansen, Chadwick. *Witchcraft at Salem*. New York: George Braziller, 1969.

Harrison's Principles of Internal Medicine. 11th ed. Edited by Eugene Brunwald et al. New York: McGraw Hill, Co., 1987.

Harrison, Nancy Jo T., and Jean L. Woodward, eds. *Along the Coast of Essex County*. Boston: Junior League of Boston, 1970.

Hartigan, Lillian R., Albert Virgil House, et al., "Historical Pagent," in *250th Anniversary of the First Church of Danvers Congregational*. Danvers: First Church of Danvers, 1922.

Haskins, George L. "Lay Judges: Magistrates and Justices in Early Massachusetts." In *Law in Colonial Massachusetts, 1630–1800*. Edited by Daniel R. Coquillette. Boston: Colonial Society, Massachusetts, 1984.

Hastings, James. *Dictionary of the Bible*. Revised and ed. by Frederick C. Grant and H. H. Rowley. New York: Charles Scribner's Sons, 1963.

Hawthorne, Nathaniel. *The American Notebooks*. Edited by Claude M. Simpson. Ohio State University Press, 1932, 1960, 1972. vol. 8 of *The Centenary Edition of the Works of Nathaniel Hawthorne*.

Hazen, Henry A. *History of Billerica, Massachusetts*. Boston: A. Williams And Co., 1883.

Henderson, Jean W. *Woodburn, Coffin and Allied Nantucket Families*. Silver City, Nevada:1995.

Herbet, Wray. "An Epidemic in the Works." *Science News* 122(1982):188–190.

Heyrman, Christine Leigh. *Commerce and Culture: The Maritime Communities of Colonial Massachusetts, 1690–1750*. New York: W. W. Norton & Company, 1984.

"Higginson Letters." MHS *Collections*, 3rd. ser. 7(1838):196–222.

Hill, Benjamin D., and Winfield S. Nevins, *An Illustrated Guide to the North Shore of Massachusetts Bay*. 14th ed. Salem: North Shore Publishing Co., 1892.

*Hill, Frances. *The Salem Witch Trial Reader*. New York: DaCapo Press, 2000.

Hole, Christina. *Witchcraft in England*. London: B. T. Batsford Ltd.; New York, Charles Scribner's Sons, 1947.

Holman, Mary Lovering. *Ancestry of Charles Stinson Pillsbury and John Sargent Pillsbury*. 2 vols. Concord, N.H.:1938.

Holmes, Oliver Wendell. *The Complete Poetical Works of Oliver Wendell Holmes*. Boston: Houghton, Mifflin And Co., 1895.

Holmes, Thomas James. *Cotton Mather: A Bibliography of His Works*. 3 vols. Newton, Mass.: Crofton Publishing Corporation, 1974. Reprint of Cambridge: Harvard University Press, 1940.

Holmes, Thomas James. *The Surreptitious Printing of One of Cotton Mather's Manuscripts*. Cambridge: Harvard University Press, 1925.

Horace [Quintus Horatius Flaccus]. *Horace: Stories, Epistles and Ars Poetica*. H. Rushton Fairclough, trans. Cambridge: Harvard University Press, 1926.

Hoyt, David W. "The Button Family of Haverhill." EIHC 46(1910):348–349.

Hoyt, David W. *The Old Families of Salisbury and Amesbury, Massachusetts*. Somersworth, N.H.: New England History Press, 1981. Reprint of 1897–1919 originals.

Hull, John. "The Journal of John Hull." AAS *Transactions*. 3(1857):126–316.

Hull, N. E. H. *Female Felons: Women and Serious Crime in Colonial Massachusetts*. Urbana: University of Illinois Press, 1987.

Hurd, D. Hamilton, ed. *History of Essex County, Massachusetts*. 2 vols. Philadelphia: J.W. Lewis & Co., 1888.

Hurd, D. Hamilton, ed. *History of Middlesex County, Massachusetts*. 3 vols. Philadelphia: J. W. Lewis & Co., 1890.

"Hutchinson Papers." MHS *Collections*, 3rd ser. 1(1825):1–152.

Hutchinson, Thomas. *The History of the Colony and Province of Massachusetts-Bay*. 3 vols. Edited by Lawrence Shaw Mayo. Cambridge: Harvard University Press, 1936.

Innes, Stephen. *Labor in a New Land: Economy and Society in Seventeenth-Century Springfield*. Princeton, N. J.: Princeton University Press, 1983.

Ipswich Antiquarian Papers. 36(May 1883):2–3.

[Ives, Henry P.?], *Visitor's Guide to Salem*. [Salem]: Henry P. Ives, [1880].

Johnson, Richard R. *John Nelson Merchant Adventurer*. New York: Oxford University Press, 1991.

Johnson, William W. *Johnson Genealogy: Records of the Descent of John Johnson of Ipswich and Andover, Massachusetts 1635–1892*. North Greenfield, Wisconsin:1892.

Jones, Matt Bushnell. "Thomas Maule, the Salem Quaker, and Free Speech in Massachusetts Bay, with Bibliographical Notes." EIHC 72(1936):1–42.

Josselyn, John. "An Account of Two Voyages to New-England." MHS *Collections*, 3rd ser. 3(1833):211–354.

Karlsen, Carol F. *The Devil in the Shape of a Woman: Witchcraft in Colonial New England*. New York: W. W. Norton & Company, 1987.

Karraker, Cyrus H. "The Treasure Expedition of Captain William Phipps to the Bahama Banks." NEQ 5(1932):731–752.

Keyne, Robert. "Proceedings of Excommunication Against Mistress Ann Hibbins of Boston." In Demos, *Remarkable Providences*.

King, Caroline Howard. *When I Lived in Salem, 1822–1866*. Brattleboro, N. H.: Stephen Daye Press, 1937.

Kittredge, George Lyman. "Cotton Mather's Scientific Communications to the Royal Society." AAS *Proceedings* 26(1916):18–57.

Kittredge, George Lyman. *Witchcraft in Old and New England*. Cambridge: Harvard University Press, 1929; New York: Atheneum, 1972.

Kittredge, Henry C. *Cape Cod: Its People and Their History*. Boston: Houghton Mifflin Company, 1930.

Knight, Sarah Kemble. *The Journal of Madame Knight*. In Miller, *The Puritans*.

Koehler, Lyle. *A Search for Power: The "Weaker Sex" in Seventeenth-Century New England*. Urbana: University of Illinois Press, 1980.

Konig, David T. "A New Look at the Essex 'French': Ethnic Frictions and Community Tensions in Seventeenth-Century Essex County, Massachusetts." EIHC 110(1974):167–180.

Lambert, Barbara. "Social Music, Musicians, and Their Musical Instruments In and Around Colonial Boston." In *Music in Colonial Massachusetts*.

*Lawson, Deodat. *A Brief and True Narrative Of Some Remarkable Passages Relating to Sundry Persons Afflicted by Witchcraft*. Boston: Benjamin Harris, 1692. In Burr, *Narratives*.

Lawson, Deodat. *Christ's Fidelity the Only Shield Against Satan's Malignity*. Boston: B. Harris, 1692. Evans microcard 643.

Lawson, Deodat. "Narrative." From the 1704 edition of *Christ's Fidelity*, in Upham, *Salem Witchcraft*, 2:527–537.

LeBeau, Bryan F. "Philip English and the Witchcraft Hysteria." *Historical Journal of Massachusetts* 15(1987):1-20.

Lechford, Thomas. *Notebook Kept by Thomas Lechford, Esq., Lawyer*. Edited by Samuel Jennison, Alfred D. Foster, and Edward Everett Hale Jr. Cambridge: John Wilson And Son, 1885.

Leonard, Henry C. *Pigeon Cove And Vicinity*. Boston: F. A. Searle, 1873.

"Letter from Sir William Phips and Other Papers Relating to Witchcraft, Including Questions to Ministers and Their Answers." Abner C. Goodall, Jr. trans. MHS *Proceedings*, 2nd series, 1(1884–1885):339–354.

"Letters of Cotton Mather, Samuel Sewall, John Callender, Adam Winthrop, and Others." *Register* 24(1870):107–123.

*Levin, David. *Cotton Mather: The Young Life of the Lord's Remembrancer, 1663–1703*. Cambridge: Harvard University Press, 1978.

Levin, David. "Did the Mathers Disagree About the Salem Witchcraft Trials?" AAS *Proceedings* 95(1985):19–37.

Levin, David. "When Did Cotton Mather See the Angel?" *Early American Literature* 15(winter 1980–1981):271–275.

Levin, David, ed. *What Happened in Salem?* 2nd edition. New York: Harcourt, Brace & World, 1960.

Littleton, town of, *Records of Littleton, Massachusetts*. Littleton: Town of Littleton, 1900.

Loring, Israel. *The Journal of the Rev. Israel Loring (1682–1772) of Sudbury*. Louise Parkman Thomas, ed. Columbus, Ohio:1983.

Love, William DeLoss Jr. *The Fast and Thanksgiving Days of New-England*. Boston: Houghton, Mifflin And Company, 1895.

Ludlum, David. *The Country Journal New England Weather Book*. Boston: Houghton, Mifflin, Co., 1976.

Luhrmann, T. M. *Persuasions of the Witch's Craft: Ritual Magic in Contemporary England*. Cambridge: Harvard University Press, 1989.

Lynch, Shawn. *"Our Sinne of Ignorance": Andover, 1692*. Andover and North Andover Historical Societies, 1995.

Lyons, Arthur. *Satan Wants You: The Cult of Devil Worship in America*. New York: The Mysterious Press, 1988.

Macfarlane, Alan. *Witchcraft in Tudor and Stuart England: A Regional and Comparative Study*. New York: Harper & Row Publishers, 1970.

*Mappen, Marc, ed. *Witches and Historians: Interpretations of Salem*. Huntington, N.Y.: Robert E. Kneger Publishing Company, 1980.

Maine. *Province and Court Records of Maine*. 6 vols. Portland: Maine Historical Society, 1928–1975.

Massachusetts Bay. *Records of the Court of Assistants of the Colony of Massachusetts Bay, 1630–1692*. 3 vols. Parts 1–2 edited by John Noble, part 3 by John F. Cronin. Boston: County of Suffolk, 1901, 1904, 1928.

"The Mather Papers." MHS *Collections*, ser. 4. 8(1868).

Mather, Cotton. *The Angel of Bethesda*. Edited by Gordon W. Jones. Barre, Mass.: American Antiquarian Society and Barre Publishers, 1972.

*Mather, Cotton. "A Brand Pluck'd Out of the Burning." Included in Calef, *More Wonders*, see Burr.

*Mather, Cotton. *Decennium Luctuosum*. Boston: Samuel Phillips, 1699. Included in *Narratives of the Indian Wars, 1675–1699*. Edited by Charles H. Lincoln. New York: Charles Scribner's Sons, 1913; New York: Barnes & Noble, 1941.

*Mather, Cotton. *Diary of Cotton Mather*. Edited by Worthington Chauncy Ford. MHS Collections, 7th ser. 7(1911), 8(1912) numbered as vols. 1–2. Reprint New York: Frederick Ungar.

Mather, Cotton. *Magnalia Christi Americana*. London: Thomas Parkhurst, 1702; 2 vol. edition. Hartford: Silas Andrus And Son, 1855. Another edition (of Books I and II only) edited by Kenneth B. Murdock and Elizabeth W. Miller. Cambridge: Harvard University Press, 1977.

Mather, Cotton. *Memorable Providences Relating to Witchcrafts and Possessions.* Boston: R.P., 1689. Evans microcard 486. Selections in Burr.

Mather, Cotton. *A Midnight Cry.* Boston: Samuel Phillips, 1692. Evans microcard 622.

Mather, Cotton. *Optanda: Good Men Described and Good Things Propounded.* Boston: Benjamin Harris, 1692. Evans microcard 623.

Mather, Cotton. *Parentator.* Boston: Nathaniel Belknap, 1724. Evans microcard 2557.

Mather, Cotton. *Selected Letters of Cotton Mather.* Edited by Kenneth Silverman. Baton Rouge: Lousiana State University Press, 1971.

*Mather, Cotton. *Selections from Cotton Mather.* Edited by Kenneth B. Murdock. New York: Harcourt, Brace and Company, 1926; New York: Hafner Publishing Co. (paper).

*Mather, Cotton. *The Wonders of the Invisible World.* Boston: Sam. Phillips, 1693 (actually 1692). Reprint re-titled *Cotton Mather on Witchcraft.* New York: Bell Publishing Co., n.d. Also selections in Burr.

*Mather, Cotton, and Robert Calef. "Mather-Calef Paper on Witchcraft." Edited by [W. C.] Ford. MHS *Proceedings* 47(1913–14):240–268.

Mather, Horace. *Lineage of Rev. Richard Mather.* Hartford: Cape, Lockwood & Brainard, 1890.

Mather, Increase. *Angelographia.* Boston: Samuel Phillips, 1696. Evans microcard 756.

*Mather, Increase. *Cases of Conscience Concerning Evil Spirits.* Boston: Benjamin Harris, 1693 (actually 1692). Evans microcard 658.

Mather, Increase. "Diary of Increase Mather." MHS *Proceedings,* 2nd ser. 13(1899–1900):338–374.

Mather, Increase. *An Essay for the Recording of Illustrious Providences.* Boston:1684; facsimile reprint New York: Garland Publishing, 1977. Selections under its short title *Remarkable Providences* in Burr.

*Mather, Increase. "Recantation of Confessors of Witchcraft." MHS *Collections,* 2nd ser. 3(1815):221–225.

Mayo, Lawrence Shaw. *The Winthrop Family in America.* Boston: Massachusetts Historical Society, 1948.

Maule, Thomas [Tho. Philathes pseud.]. *New-England Persecutors Mauled With Their Own Weapons.* New York: William Bradford, 1697. Evans microcard 801.

Maule Thomas. *Truth Held Forth and Maintained.* New York: William Bradford, 1695. Evans microcard 730.

McTeer, Frances Davis, and Frederick C. Warner, "The Aselbees of Andover, Mass." TAG 40(1964):231–237.

McTeer, Frances Davis, and Frederick C. Warner, "Children of John Aslebee's Daughters, Browne—Johnson—Frye—Cole." TAG 41(1965):8–16, 77–83.

Meek, Henry, compiler. *The Naumkeag Directory for Salem, Beverly, Danvers, Marblehead, Peabody, Essex And Manchester.* Editions for 1890–1891 and 1895–1896. Salem: Salem Observer Office, 1890, 1895.

Miller, Arthur. *The Crucible.* New York: Bantam Books, 1952.

Miller, Arthur. *Timebends: a Life.* New York: Grove Press, 1987.

Miller, Perry. *Errand into the Wilderness.* Cambridge: Harvard University Press, 1956; New York: Harper & Row, 1956, paper.

Miller, Perry. *The New England Mind: From Colony to Province.* Cambridge: Harvard University Press, 1953.

*Miller, Perry, and Thomas H. Johnson, eds. *The Puritans.* Revised 2 vol. ed. New York: Harper Torchbooks, Harper & Row, 1963.

Milton, John. *The Poetical Works of John Milton.* London: J. M. Dent & Sons, 1909.

Minkema, Kenneth P. "'The Devil Will Roar in Me Anon': The Possession of Martha Roberson." In *Spellbound: Women and Witchcraft in America,* edited by Elizabeth Reis. Wilmington, Delaware: S. R. Books, 1998.

Moore, George H. "Notes on the Bibliography of Witchcraft in Massachusetts." AAS *Proceedings,* new series 5(1888): 249–272.

Moore, George H. "Notes on the History of Witchcraft in Massachusetts." AAS *Proceedings,* new series 2(1882): 162–181.

Morgan, Edmund S. *The Puritan Family: Religion and Domestic Relations in Seventeenth-Century New England.* Revised ed. New York: Harper & Row, 1966.

Morgan, Edmund S. *Visible Saints: the History of a Puritan Idea.* Ithaca: Cornell University Press, 1963.

Morgan, Edmund S. "The Witch and We, the People." *American Heritage,* Aug.-Sept. 1983:6–11.

Moriarty, G. Andrews. "Genealogical Notes on Rev. Samuel Parris of Salem Village." EIHC 49(1913):354–355.

Morison, Samuel Eliot. *Harvard College in the Seventeenth Century.* 2 vols. Cambridge: Harvard University Press, 1936.

Mosby's Medical & Nursing Directory. Edited by Lawrence Urdang and Helen Harding Swallow. St. Louis: The C. V. Mosby Company, 1983.

Mudge, August. "Some Account of an Interview with Miss Sarah Cross of Reading." DHS, *Collections* 20(1932):61–62.

*Murdock, Kenneth B. *Increase Mather, the Foremost American Puritan.* Cambridge: Harvard University Press, 1925.

*Museum of Fine Arts, Boston. *New England Begins: The Seventeenth Century.* 3 vols. Boston: Museum of Fine Arts, 1982.

Music in Colonial Massachusetts 1630–1820. vol. 1, "Music in Public Places." Boston: The Colonial Society of Massachusetts, 1980.

Myers, Arthur. *The Ghostly Register.* Chicago: Contemporary Books, 1986.

Nelson, Glade Ian. "Mary (Burrough) (Homer) (Hall) Tiffany." TAG 48(1972):145–6.

The New-England Primer. Facsimile. Boston: Ginn & Company, n. d.

New Testament Octapla: Eight English Versions of the New Testament in the Tyndale—King James Tradition. Luther A. Weigle, ed. New York: Thomas A. Nelson, n. d.

New York Documents Relative to the Colonial History of the State of New York. Edited by E. B. O'Callaghan. Albany: Weed, Parsons and Company, 1855.

*Noble, John, ed. "Some Documentary Fragments Touching the Witchcraft Episode of 1692." CSM *Transactions* 10(1904–1906):12–25.

Northall, G. F. *English Folk-Rhymes*. London: Kegan Paul, Trench, Trubner & Co., Ltd., 1892; facsimile by Detroit: Singing Tree Press, 1968.

Noyes, Henry E., and Harriette E. Noyes. *Genealogical Record of Some of the Noyes Descendants of James, Nicholas and Peter Noyes*. 2 vols. Boston:1904.

Noyes, Nicholas. "An Elegy Upon the Death of the Rev. Mr. John Higginson." *Register* 7:237–240.

*Noyes, Sybil, Libby, Thornton Charles, and Walter Goodwin Davis. *Genealogical Dictionary of Maine and New Hampshire*. 5 vols. Baltimore: Genealogical Publishing Co., 1972.

Old-Time New England. Special Province House Issue. 62(1971 1972).

Otis, James. *The Story of Old Falmouth*. New York: Thomas Y. Crowell, 1901.

Oxenbridge, Susanna. Will in "Genealogical Gleanings in England." *Register* 44(1890):87–88.

Oxford University. *A New English Dictionary on Historical Principles*. 12 vols. Oxford: Clarendon Press, 1888–1928.

Paige, Lucius R. *History of Cambridge, Massachusetts*. Boston: H. O. Houghton And Company, 1877.

Parker, Herbert. *Courts and Lawyers of New England*. 4 vols. New York: The American Historical Society, 1931.

Parkhurst, Winifred Chadwick, and Barbara Carolyn Perley. *Updated Dwellings of Boxford*. Boxford:1977.

Parkman, Francis. *Count Frontenac and New France Under Louis XIV*. Boston: Little, Brown And Company, 1927.

*Parris, Samuel. *The Sermon Notebook of Samuel Parris, 1689–1694*. Edited by James F. Cooper and Kenneth P. Minkema. Boston: The Colonial Society of Massachusetts, 1993.

Partridge, John. *Monthly Observations and Predictions*. Boston: Benjamin Harris, 1692. Evans microcard 627.

"Pedigree of Dane." *Register* 8(1854):148.

Penney, J. W. *A Genealogical Record of the Descendants of Thomas Penney of New Gloucester, Maine*. Portland, Maine: Thurston Print, 1897.

Perkins, George A. *The Family of John Perkins of Ipswich, Massachusetts*. 3 vols. Salem:1889.

Perley, M. V. B. "James Howe of Ipswich and Some of His Descendants." EIHC 54(1918):33–38.

Perley, Sidney. "Beverly in 1700. No. 3." EIHC 55(1919):273–303.

Perley, Sidney. "Brooksby, Salem in 1700." EIHC 50(1914):357–365.

Perley, Sidney. "Cedar Pond Region, Salem in 1700." EIHC 51(1915):23–40.

Perley, Sidney. "Center of Salem Village in 1700." EIHC 54(1918):225–245.

Perley, Sidney. "The Court Houses of Salem." EIHC 48(1911):101–123.

Perley, Sidney. *The Dwellings of Boxford*. Salem: Essex Institute, 1893.

Perley, Sidney. "Endicott Lands: Part of Salem in 1700." EIHC 51(1915):361–382.

Perley, Sidney. "Groton: Part of Salem in 1700." EIHC 51(1915):257–270.

Perley, Sidney. "Hathorne: Part of Salem Village in 1700 [No. 1]." EIHC 53(1917):332–344.

Perley, Sidney. "Hathorne: Part of Salem Village in 1700 [No. 2]." EIHC 54(1918):115–145.

Perley, Sidney. *The History of Boxford, Essex County, Massachusetts*. Boxford:1880.

*Perley, Sidney. *The History of Salem, Massachusetts*. 3 vols. Haverhill: Record Publishing Company, 1928.

Perley, Sidney. "Northfields, Salem in 1700. No. 3." EIHC 49(1913):186–192.

Perley, Sidney. "Part of Haverhill in 1700." *Essex Antiquarian* 3(1899):161–168.

Perley, Sidney. "Part of Salem in 1700." Parts 1, 2, 7, 8, 14, 19, 21, 23. *Essex Antiquarian* 2(1898):167–174, 3(1899):65–71, 5(1901):145–149, 6(1902):97–10l, 8(1904):20–37, 9(1905):72–86 and 162–171, 10(1906):60–74, 114–130.

Perley, Sidney. "Part of Salem Village in 1700." EIHC 52(1916):177–191.

Perley, Sidney. "The Plains: Part of Salem in 1700." EIHC 54(1918):289–316.

Perley, Sidney. "The Read Farm, Salem in 1700." EIHC 50(1914):241–244.

Perley, Sidney. "Ryal Side: Part of Salem in 1700." EIHC 55(1919):49–74.

Perley, Sidney. "Where the Salem 'Witches' Were Hanged." EIHC 57(1921):1–18.

Perley, Sidney. "The Woods, Salem in 1700." EIHC 51(1915):177–196.

Phillips, James Duncan. *Salem in the Seventeenth Century*. Boston: Houghton Mifflin Company, 1933.

Phillips, Samuel. *An Elegy Upon the Deaths of Those Excellent and Learned Divines, The Reverend Nicholas Noyes, A. M. And the Reverend George Curwen, A. M.* [1717?].

Pierce, Frederick Clifton. *Foster Genealogy*. Chicago:1899.

Pike, John. "Journal of the Rev. John Pike." MHS *Proceedings*, 1st. ser. 14(1875–1876):117–152.

Poole, William Frederick. *Cotton Mather and Salem Witchcraft*. Boston: University Press, 1869. Offprint from April 1869 *North American Review*.

Poole, William Frederick. "Notes to Thomas Hutchinson, 'The Witchcraft Delusion of 1692.'" *Register* 24(1870): 381–414.

Pope, Charles Henry. *The Haverhill Emersons: Part First*. Boston: Murray And Emery Company, 1913.

Pope, Charles Henry, and ThomasHooper. *Hooper Genealogy*. Boston: Charles Henry Pope, 1908.

Powers, Edwin. *Crime and Punishment in Early Massachusetts, 1620–1692: a Documentary History*. Boston: Beacon Press, 1966.

"Proctor." *Register* 60(1906):208–209.

The Psalms, Hymns and Spiritual Songs of the Old and New Testament. Cambridge: Samuel Green, 1651 (aka *Bay Psalm Book*.) Evans microcard 33.

Putnam, Allen. *Witchcraft of New England Explained by Modern Spiritualism*. Boston: Colby And Rich, Publishers, 1880.

Putnam, Eben. *A History of the Putnam Family in England and America*. 2 vols. Salem: The Salem Press Publishing And Printing Co, 1891, 1907.

Quincy, Josiah P. "Cotton Mather and the Supernatural in New England History." MHS *Proceedings*, 2nd ser. 20(1906–7):439–453.

Randolph, Edward. *Edward Randolph, Including His Letters and Official Papers from the New England, Middle, and Southern Colonies in America, and the West Indies. 1678–1700.* 7 vols. Edited by Thomas Scrope Goodrich. Boston: The Prince Society, 1909; New York: Burt Franklin, 1967.

Reilly, Elizabeth Carroll. *A Dictionary of Colonial American Printers' Ornaments and Illustrations.* Worcester: American Antiquarian Society, 1975.

"Report of the Committee on the Authenticity of the First Meeting House in Salem." EIHC 39(1903):209–293.

"The Return of Several Ministers." in Levin, *What Happened in Salem?*

Rice, Charles B. "Historical Address." In *Proceedings at the Celebration of the Two Hundredth Anniversary of the First Parish at Salem Village, Now Danvers, October 8, 1872.* Boston: Congregational Publishing Society, 1874.

Roach, Marilynne K. "That child, Betty Parris": Elizabeth (Parris) Barron and the People in Her Life." EIHC 124(1988):1–27.

Roads, Samuel Jr. *The History and Traditions of Marblehead.* Boston: Houghton, Osgood And Company, 1880.

Robbins, Stephen L. "Samuel Willard and the Spectre of God's Wrathful Lion." NEQ 40(1987):596–603.

Robinson, Enders. *The Devil Discovered: Salem Witchcraft, 1692.* New York: Hippocrene Books, 1991.

Rogo, D. Scott. *The Poltergeist Experience.* New York: Penguin Books, 1979.

Rosenthal, Barnard. *Salem Story: Reading the Witch Trials of 1692.* New York: Cambridge University Press, 1993.

Russell, George Ely. "Nathaniel Burrough of Maryland, Massachusetts, and England." TAG 60(1984):140–142.

Rutman, Darret B. *Winthrop's Boston: Portrait of a Puritan Town, 1630–1649.* New York: W. W. Norton & Company, 1965.

Safran, Claire. "The Devil Made Me Do It." *Woman's Day* 22 Nov. 1988:146–147, 150, 152–153.

Salem, City of. *List of Polls 1976.* Salem: Board of Registrars, 1976.

Salem, First Church of. *The Record of the First Church in Salem, Massachusetts, 1629–1736.* Edited by Richard D. Pierce. Salem: Essex Institute, 1974.

Salem, Town of. *Town Records of Salem.* 3 vols. Salem: The Essex Institute, 1868, 1913, 1934.

Salem Village. "A Book of Record of the Several Publique Transactions of the Inhabitants of Salem Village, Vulgarly Called the Farms." DHS *Historical Collections* 13(1925):91–122, 14(1926):65–99, 16(1928):60–80.

"Saltonstall Papers." MHS *Collections* 8(1972).

Sargent, Emma Worcester. *Eps Sargent of Gloucester and His Descendants.* Boston: Houghton Mifflin Company, 1923.

"Savage Papers." MHS *Proceedings* 44(1910–11):685–686.

Savage, James. *A Genealogical Dictionary of the First Settlers of New England.* 4 vols. Reprint. Baltimore: Genealogical Publishing Company, 1965.

Scot, Reginald. *The Discoverie of Witchcraft.* New York: Dover Publications, 1972 (1584 original).

Scott, Walter. "Walter Scott's Personality Parade." *Parade Magazine.* 28 Aug. 1988:2.

Sewall, Samuel. "Commonplace Book." In vol. 2 of *Diary* (MHS ed.).

*Sewall, Samuel. *The Diary of Samuel Sewall 1674–1729.* MHS *Collections* 5th ser. 5(1878), 6(1879), 7(1882), numbered as vols. 1–3. Also a 2 vol. edition edited by M. Halsey Thomas. New York: Farrar, Straus And Giroux, 1973.

Sewall, Samuel. *The History of Woburn, Middlesex County, Mass.* Boston: Wiggin And Lunt, Publishers, 1868.

Sewall, Samuel. "Letter-Book of Samuel Sewall." MHS *Collections*, 6th ser. 1(1886) and 2(1888).

Sewall, Samuel. *Phaenomena Quaedam Apocalyptica.* Boston: Bartholomew Green and John Allen, 1697. Evans microcard 813.

Shaw, Herbert Kinney. *Families of the Pilgrims: John Alden.* Boston: Massachusetts Society of Mayflower Descendants.

Sibley, John Langdon. *Biographical Sketches of Graduates of Harvard University, in Cambridge Massachusetts.* Cambridge: Charles William Sever, 1873, 1881, 1885, etc.; New York: Johnson Reprint Corporation, 1967.

Sibley, John Langdon. "Rev. Samuel Parris." *Register* 12(1858):63–64.

Silverman, Kenneth. *The Life and Times of Cotton Mather.* New York: Harper & Row, Publisher, 1984.

Silverman, Kenneth. "A Note on the Date of Cotton Mather's Visitation by an Angel." *Early American Literature* 15(1980):82–86.

Simmons, William S. *Spirit of the New England Tribes: Indian History and Folklore, 1620–1984.* Hanover, N. H.: University Press of New England, 1986.

Smith, Ethel Farrington. *Adam Hawkes of Saugus, Mass. 1605–1612.* Baltimore: Gateway Press, 1980.

Smith, Joseph H. ed. *Colonial Justice in Western Massachusetts (1639–1702): The Pyncheon Record.* Cambridge: Harvard University Press, 1961.

Spanos, Nicholas P., and Jack Gottleib. "Ergotism and the Salem Witch Trials." *Science* 194(1976):1390–1394.

Stackpole, Everett S. *History of New Hampshire.* 4 vols. New York: The American Historical Society, [1916?].

Starkey, Marion L. *The Devil in Massachusetts: a Modern Enquiry into the Salem Witch Trials.* New York: Alfred A. Knopf, 1949; New York: Anchor Books, Doubleday & Co. (paper).

Stearns, Ezra Scolley. "Simon Stone the Soldier at Exeter." *Register* 66 (1912):266–268.

Steffen, Charles G. "The Sewall Children in New England." *Register* 131(1972):163–172.

Stiles, David. "Middleton." In Hurd, *Essex.*

Stone, Laurence. "The Disenchantment of the World." *The New York Review of Books,* 12 Dec. 1971, 17–25.

Stone, Lincoln R. "An Account of the Trial of George Jacobs for Witchcraft." EIHC 2(1860):49–52.

Stow, Town of. "Rev. Samuel Parris." (Town record excerpts) *Register* 12(1858):63–64.

Streeter, Gilbert L. *Salem Before the Revolution.* Salem: Aylward, Huntress & Dennis, 1896; offprint from EIHC 32(1896).

Stutzenberger, Albert. *American Historical Spoons: the American Story in Spoons.* Springdale Springs: Bookmaster, 1953.

Swan, Marshall W. S. "The Bedevilment of Cape Ann." EIHC 117(1981):153–177.

Tapley, Charles Sutherland. *Rebecca Nurse: Saint But Witch Victim.* Boston: Marshall Jones Company, 1930: Danvers, Danvers Alarm List Company, 1979.

Taylor, John M. *The Witchcraft Delusion in Colonial Connecticut 1647–1697.* The Grafton Press:1908; Williamstown, Mass.: Corner House Publishers, 1984.

Teele, A. K., ed. *The History of Milton, Mass. 1640 to 1887.* Milton:1887.

Temple, J[osiah] H. *History of Framingham, Massachusetts, Early Known as Danforth's Farms 1640–1800.* Framingham: Town of Framingham, 1887.

Thatcher, Peter. "Thatcher's Journal." In Teele.

Thomas, Keith. *Religion and the Decline of Magic.* New York: Charles Scribner's Sons, 1971.

Thompson, Neil D. "Hannah Fisher, First Wife of the Rev. George Burroughs." *Register* 155(2001):17–19.

Thompson, Roger. *Sex in Middlesex: Popular Mores in a Massachusetts County, 1649–1699.* Amherst: University of Massachusetts Press, 1986.

Thoreau, Henry David. *Cape Cod.* Edited by Dudley C. Lunt. New York: W. W. Norton & Co., 1951.

Thwing, Annie Haven. *The Crooked & Narrow Streets of the Town of Boston, 1630–1822.* 2nd rev. ed. Boston: Charles E. Lauriat Co., 1925.

Tolles, Bryant F., and Carolyn K. Tolles. *Architecture in Salem: an Illustrated Guide.* Salem: Essex Institute and Historic Salem, Inc., 1983.

Tomlinson, R. G. *Witchcraft Trials of Connecticut.* Hartford: Connecticut Research, 1978.

Topsfield, Town of. *Town Records of Topsfield, Massachusetts.* 2 vols. Topsfield: Topsfield Historical Society, 1917, 1920.

Torrey, Clarence Almond. *New England Marriages prior to 1700.* Edited by Elizabeth P. Bentley. Baltimore, Maryland: Genealogical Publishing Co., 1985.

Totten, John Reynolds. "Anneke Jans-Bogardus (1599–1663)." *New York Genealogical and Biographical Record* 57(1926):119–142.

Towne, Alice Peterson and Clark, Marietta. "Topsfield in the Witchcraft Delusion." *The Historical Collections of the Topsfield Historical Society* 13(1908):23–38.

Towne, Edwin Eugene. *The Descendants of William Towne.* Newtonville, Mass.:1901.

Trask, Richard. *"The Devil Amongst Us": A History of the Salem Village Parsonage.* Danvers: Danvers Historical Society, 1971.

*Trask, Richard. *"The Devil Hath Been Raised": A Documentary History of the Salem Village Witchcraft Outbreak of March, 1692.* Danvers, Mass.: Yeoman Press, 1997. Revised and enlarged edition of book originally published for the Danvers Historical Society by Phoenix Publishing of West Kennebunk, Maine, 1992.

Trask, Richard. "Raising the Devil." *Yankee.* May 1972:74–77, 190–201.

Tucker, Eleanor. "The Gowing Family of Lynn, Massachusetts." *Essex Genealogist,* Feb. 1988, 39–42, and Aug. 1988, 141–146.

Tully, John. *An Almanac for the Year of Our Lord MDCXCII.* Cambridge: Samuel Philips, 1692. Evans microcard 630.

Tully, John. *An Almanac for the Year of Our Lord MDCXCIII.* Boston: Benjamin Harris, 1693. Evans microcard 682.

Turrell, Ebenezer. "Detection of Witchcraft." MHS *Collections,* 2nd ser. 10(1833):6–22.

Twombly, Robert C., and Robert H. Moore. "Black Puritan: the Negro in Seventeenth-Century Massachusetts." In Vaughan.

*Ulrich, Laurel Thatcher. *Good Wives: Image and Reality in the Lives of Women in Northern New England 1650–1750.* New York: Alfred A. Knopf, 1982.

*Upham, Charles W. *Salem Witchcraft.* 2 vols. Reprint of 1867 orig., Williamstown, Mass.: Corner House Publishers, 1971.

Upham, Charles W. "Salem Witchcraft and Cotton Mather. A Reply." Morrisania, N.Y.:1869. Offprint from Sept. 1869 *The Historical Magazine.*

Upham, William P. *House of John Proctor, Witchcraft Martyr.* Peabody, Mass.:1916.

Usher, Edward Preston. *A Memorial Sketch of Roland Greene Usher 1823–1895.* Privately printed, 1895.

VanCleef, Joy, and Kate VanWinkle Keller. "Selected American Country Dances and Their English Sources." *In Music in Colonial Massachusetts.*

Vaughan, Alden T., and Francis J. Bremer. *Puritan New England: Essays on Religion, Society, and Culture.* New York: St. Martin's Press, 1977.

Victor, Jeffrey S. *Satanic Panic: the Creation of a Contemporary Legend.* Chicago: Open Court, 1993.

Washburn, Emory. *Sketches of the Judicial History of Massachusetts from 1630 to the Revolution in 1775.* Boston: Charles C. Little and James Brown, 1890.

Waters, Thomas Frank. *Ipswich in the Massachusetts Bay Colony.* 2 vols. Ipswich: Ipswich Historical Society, 1905.

Watkins, Walter K. "Mary Watkins." *Register* 44(1890):168–170.

Webster, John Clarence. *Acadia at the End of the Seventeenth Century: Letters, Journals And Memoirs of Joseph Robineau DeVillebon.* St. John, N. B.: The New Brunswick Museum, 1934.

Weideger, Paula, ed. *History's Mistress: a New Interpretation of a Nineteenth-Century Ethnographic Classic.* Harmondsworth, U.K.: Penguin Books Ltd., 1986. Selections from *Das Weib* by Hermann H. Ploss and Maximilian Bartels.

*Weisman, Richard. *Witchcraft, Magic and Religion in Seventeenth Century Massachusetts.* Amhurst: University of Massachusetts Press, 1984.

Wells, John A. *The Peabody Story.* Salem: Essex Institute, 1972.

Wendell, Barrett. "Were the Salem Witches Guiltless?" EIHC 29(1892):129–147.

Wheatland, Henry. "Notice of Some Descendants of Joseph Pope of Salem." EIHC 8(1866):104–118.

Whittier, John Greenleaf. *The Poetical Works of John Greenleaf Whittier.* Boston: James R. Osgood and Company, 1878.

Wilbour, Benjamin Franklin, and Carlton C. Brownell. *Notes on Little Compton.* Little Compton, R.I.: Little Compton Historical Society, 1970.

*Willard, Samuel. "A Brief Account of a Strange and Unusual Providence of God Befallen to Elizabeth Knapp of Groton." In Demos, *Remarkable Providences.*

*[Willard, Samuel] under pseud. P. E. and J. A. *Some Miscellany Observations on Our Present Debates Respecting Witchcrafts, in a Dialogue Between S. & B.* Philadelphia: William Bradford, 1692. (Actually Boston). Evans micro-card 631.

Wilson, Keith D. *Cause of Death: a Writer's Guide to Death, Murder and Forensic Medecine.* Cincinatti: Writer's Digest Books, 1992.

Winship, Michael P. "Encountering Providence in the Seventeenth Century: the Experiences of a Yeoman and a Minister." EIHC 126(1990):27–36.

Winsor, Justin, ed. *The Memorial History of Boston, Including Suffolk County, Massachusetts, 1630–1880.* 4 vols. Boston: Ticknor and Co., 1881.

"Witchcraft at Hingham." *Register* 5(1851):263.

"Witchcraft in New York." *Collections of the New York Historical Society* 2(1869):273–276.

"Witchcraft Papers." *Register* 27(1873):55.

WPA (Federal Writers' Project of the Works Progress Administration for the State of Massachusetts). *The WPA Guide to Massachusetts.* (Original title *Massachusetts: A Guide to its People and Places*). Boston: Houghton Mifflin Co., 1937; New York: Pantheon Books, 1983.

Wyman, Thomas Bellows. *The Genealogies and Estates of Charlestown, Massachusetts, 1629–1818.* Boston: David Clapp and Son, 1879; Somersworth, N.H.: New England History Press, 1982.

Newspapers
Boston Globe, Boston, Mass.

Apr. 24, 1966, "White Magic Anyone? Witch Here Seeking a Blasted Heath."
July 25, 1987, Dablis, Andrew J., "To Some in Salem, Witch Image is a Hex."
Aug. 7, 1988, "Names & Faces: Bewitches and Bemused."
Aug. 14, 1988, "Convention Notebook: Dukakis Comic Not Funny, Group Says."
Sept. 18, 1991, English, Bella, "Salem's Plan Offends Witches."
Mar. 1, 1992, Dablis, Andy, "Salem Bothered, Bewildered by Witchcraft Case."
August 6, 2001. Kremmer, Janaki Bahadur. "In India Villages, Cries of 'Witch.'"
Sept. 2, 2001. Whitmore, Brian. "Killing Shows Slovak Belief in Mystics."
Nov. 1. 2001. "New Law Exonerates Five Executed as Salem Witches."

Boston Metro, Boston, Mass.

Jan. 8, 2002. "Vigilante Faces Murder Charge in 'Witch' Death."

Danvers Herald, Danvers, Mass.

Aug. 6, 1992, Fearer, Myrna, "The Burial of George Jacobs Sr., 300 Years Later."

North Shore Sunday, Ipswich, Mass.

May 6, 1990, Oulette, John. "The Witching Year."
Dec. 22, 1991, "Spell of Trouble."
Apr. 26, 1992, "Which City is Witch City?"
Aug. 9, 1992, Stevens, Alexander. "The Tourists Talk," 17–18.

Salem Evening News, Salem, Mass.

Apr. 28, 1977, "Gov. Dukakis Unwittingly Gives 'Witch' Her Wish."
May 1, 1987, Pillsbury, Mark,"Witch Rap Burns Gauthier."
May 9, 1987, Pillsbury, Mark and Karyn Koruth, , "Salem Scenes."
June 9, 1987, Lanza, Michael, "Tourism: Both a Boon and a Headache."
June 11, 1987, Korieth, Karyn, "Tourism's Answer Man."
October 30, 1989, "Salem: A Haunting Success."
June 18, 1987, "An Identity Problem / Roger Conant's Statue Mistaken for a Witch."
Sept. 13, 1991, "Witch Accuses Committee of Bigotry."
Sept. 19, 1991, "Witch Video."

Ephemera

Salem Village Witchcraft Tercentennial Committee of Danvers. "A Commemorative Evening of Reconciliation," Sept. 20, 1992, program.
Salem Village Witchcraft Tercentennial Committee of Danvers. "Dedication of the Salem Village Witchcraft Victims' Memorial." 9 May 1992 program.
Salem Village Witchcraft Tercentennial Committee of Danvers. "Witchcraft in Salem Village Now Danvers, Masstts."
Salem Witch Trials Tercentenary, Memorial Dedication Press Kit, Aug. 5, 1992.

Online

*University of Virginia. *Salem Witchraft* website at: http://etext.lib.virginia.edu/salem/witchcraft

Maps

Roach, Marilynne K. *A Map of Salem Village and Vicinity in 1692*. Watertown, Mass.:1985, 1990.
Rockwell, Forbes, Carl R. Smith, Gratia Mahony, James S. Batchelder. *Plan of Andover in the Province of Massachusettts Bay, 1692*. Andover and North Andover Historical Societies, 1992.

INDEX

Page numbers in italics indicate illustrations.

ACKNOWLEDGMENTS

When I first journeyed to Salem, I found more historical remains than I'd expected, but also tourist presentations that did not match what I had already read about the subject. Brooding over the discrepancies as I crossed Salem Common, I realized that I might at least attempt to write my *own* version about what happened. At that point, a sea bird called from overhead, and looking up, I saw a common tern hovering between me and the mid-day sun until the brightness around those wings was too much to look at. I've never seen a tern in Salem since. In the euphoria of the moment, I took that one as a sign, and decided to at least *try* to write a history of the trials. That was on May 29, 1975. The project took longer than expected.

During the course of my researching this book, institutions have moved, merged, or re-fashioned themselves. Some reference volumes have disappeared from library shelves—disaccessioned, stolen, or consigned to the limbo of off-site storage. On the other hand, obscure manuscripts—some newly re-discovered—have become more available either in print, as microfilm, or on line.

Dozens of individuals and institutions have aided and abetted the project with their help and by their collections of books and artifacts. For those who also granted permission to quote from material in their collections, published and un-published (as specified in the notes and bibliography), I wish to thank:

The Boston Public Library, Boston, especially the Rare Book Department and the Trustees; the Colonial Society of Massachusetts, Boston; the Connecticut Historical Society, Hartford; the Prudential Board of the First Church, Danvers; the Maine Historical Society, Portland; the Massachusetts Archives, Dorchester; the

Massachusetts Historical Society, Boston; the Peabody Essex Museum, Salem, especially its James Duncan Phillips Library under the auspices of Eugenia Fountain, William LaMoy, Katherine Richardson, Barbara Ward, and Jane Ward; and thanks to Richard Trask in his aspect of publisher at Yeoman Press, Danvers, for permission to quote from his collection *The Devil Hath Been Raised.*

I also owe thanks to: the American Antiquarian Society, Worcester; the Andover Historical Society's Underhill Research Library; Elizabeth C. Bouvier, Archivist of the Supreme Judicial Court of Massachusetts, Boston, for help with a very obscure question; the Danvers Alarm List Company, the eighteenth century re-enactment organization which—with the Nurse Homestead Association—has done so much to preserve Rebecca Nurse's farm; the Danvers Archival Center, Danvers, and its knowledgeable and ever-helpful Archivist Richard Trask; the New England Historic and Genealogical Society, Boston, whose reference library helped sort out the book's huge cast of characters.

I owe thanks also to the public libraries of Salem, Cambridge, Concord, Newton, Waltham, and Watertown—my home base. Without the public libraries, the whole subject would have remained a closed book.

Thank you to Jane Langdon, Georgess McHargue, Marcia Sewall, and the rest of the Twelves for their personal encouragement and professional advice. I owe particular thanks to Alison D'Amario, education director of the Salem Witch Museum, Salem, for her faith in this project, and for putting me in touch with Michael Dorr— the editor who had faith in this book. Thank you, Michael, for your expertise, enthusiasm, and perseverance with this long project. And I have nothing but gratitude for my family's good wishes over the years, most particularly my mother, Priscilla Roach, who has heard me hold forth on every aspect of the witchcraft cases more times than one would think mortal patience could bear.

Marilynne K. Roach
Watertown, Massachusetts
June 2002

ABOUT THE AUTHOR

Marilynne K. Roach is the author and illustrator of the children's book *In the Days of the Salem Witchcraft Trials* and was a frequent contributor to the *Boston Globe*. She lives in Watertown, Massachusetts.

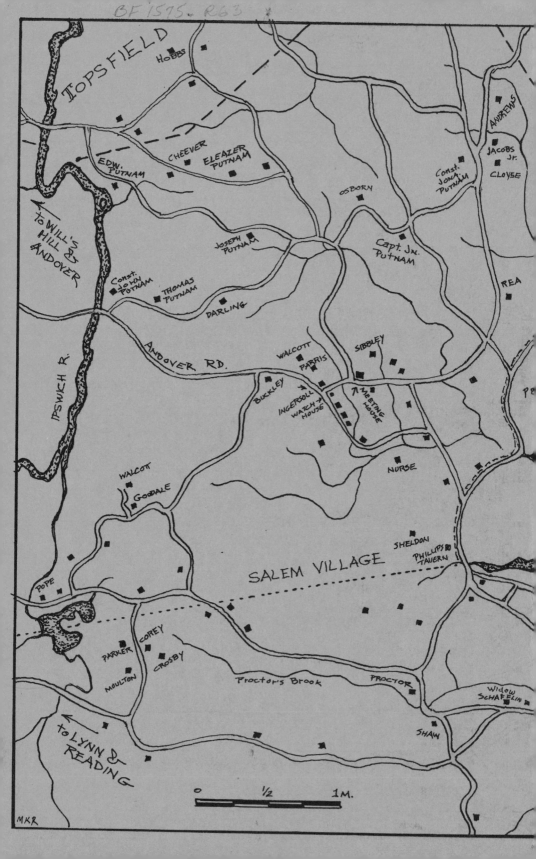